T0184061

Lecture Notes in Computer Science 11584

More information about this series at http://www.springer.com/series/7409

Aaron Marcus · Wentao Wang (Eds.)

Design, User Experience, and Usability

User Experience in Advanced Technological Environments

8th International Conference, DUXU 2019
Held as Part of the 21st HCI International Conference, HCII 2019
Orlando, FL, USA, July 26–31, 2019
Proceedings, Part II

Editors
Aaron Marcus
Aaron Marcus and Associates
Berkeley, CA, USA

Wentao Wang
Zuoyebang, K12 education
Beijing, China

ISSN 0302-9743 ISSN 1611-3349 (electronic)
Lecture Notes in Computer Science
ISBN 978-3-030-23540-6 ISBN 978-3-030-23541-3 (eBook)
https://doi.org/10.1007/978-3-030-23541-3

LNCS Sublibrary: SL3 – Information Systems and Applications, incl. Internet/Web, and HCI

This Springer imprint is published by the registered company Springer Nature Switzerland AG
The registered company address is: Gewerbestrasse 11, 6330 Cham, Switzerland

Foreword

The 21st International Conference on Human-Computer Interaction, HCI International 2019, was held in Orlando, FL, USA, during July 26–31, 2019. The event incorporated the 18 thematic areas and affiliated conferences listed on the following page.

A total of 5,029 individuals from academia, research institutes, industry, and governmental agencies from 73 countries submitted contributions, and 1,274 papers and 209 posters were included in the pre-conference proceedings. These contributions address the latest research and development efforts and highlight the human aspects of design and use of computing systems. The contributions thoroughly cover the entire field of human-computer interaction, addressing major advances in knowledge and effective use of computers in a variety of application areas. The volumes constituting the full set of the pre-conference proceedings are listed in the following pages.

This year the HCI International (HCII) conference introduced the new option of "late-breaking work." This applies both for papers and posters and the corresponding volume(s) of the proceedings will be published just after the conference. Full papers will be included in the *HCII 2019 Late-Breaking Work Papers Proceedings* volume of the proceedings to be published in the Springer LNCS series, while poster extended abstracts will be included as short papers in the HCII 2019 *Late-Breaking Work Poster Extended Abstracts* volume to be published in the Springer CCIS series.

I would like to thank the program board chairs and the members of the program boards of all thematic areas and affiliated conferences for their contribution to the highest scientific quality and the overall success of the HCI International 2019 conference.

This conference would not have been possible without the continuous and unwavering support and advice of the founder, Conference General Chair Emeritus and Conference Scientific Advisor Prof. Gavriel Salvendy. For his outstanding efforts, I would like to express my appreciation to the communications chair and editor of *HCI International News,* Dr. Abbas Moallem.

July 2019 Constantine Stephanidis

HCI International 2019 Thematic Areas and Affiliated Conferences

Thematic areas:

- HCI 2019: Human-Computer Interaction
- HIMI 2019: Human Interface and the Management of Information

Affiliated conferences:

- EPCE 2019: 16th International Conference on Engineering Psychology and Cognitive Ergonomics
- UAHCI 2019: 13th International Conference on Universal Access in Human-Computer Interaction
- VAMR 2019: 11th International Conference on Virtual, Augmented and Mixed Reality
- CCD 2019: 11th International Conference on Cross-Cultural Design
- SCSM 2019: 11th International Conference on Social Computing and Social Media
- AC 2019: 13th International Conference on Augmented Cognition
- DHM 2019: 10th International Conference on Digital Human Modeling and Applications in Health, Safety, Ergonomics and Risk Management
- DUXU 2019: 8th International Conference on Design, User Experience, and Usability
- DAPI 2019: 7th International Conference on Distributed, Ambient and Pervasive Interactions
- HCIBGO 2019: 6th International Conference on HCI in Business, Government and Organizations
- LCT 2019: 6th International Conference on Learning and Collaboration Technologies
- ITAP 2019: 5th International Conference on Human Aspects of IT for the Aged Population
- HCI-CPT 2019: First International Conference on HCI for Cybersecurity, Privacy and Trust
- HCI-Games 2019: First International Conference on HCI in Games
- MobiTAS 2019: First International Conference on HCI in Mobility, Transport, and Automotive Systems
- AIS 2019: First International Conference on Adaptive Instructional Systems

Pre-conference Proceedings Volumes Full List

1. LNCS 11566, Human-Computer Interaction: Perspectives on Design (Part I), edited by Masaaki Kurosu
2. LNCS 11567, Human-Computer Interaction: Recognition and Interaction Technologies (Part II), edited by Masaaki Kurosu
3. LNCS 11568, Human-Computer Interaction: Design Practice in Contemporary Societies (Part III), edited by Masaaki Kurosu
4. LNCS 11569, Human Interface and the Management of Information: Visual Information and Knowledge Management (Part I), edited by Sakae Yamamoto and Hirohiko Mori
5. LNCS 11570, Human Interface and the Management of Information: Information in Intelligent Systems (Part II), edited by Sakae Yamamoto and Hirohiko Mori
6. LNAI 11571, Engineering Psychology and Cognitive Ergonomics, edited by Don Harris
7. LNCS 11572, Universal Access in Human-Computer Interaction: Theory, Methods and Tools (Part I), edited by Margherita Antona and Constantine Stephanidis
8. LNCS 11573, Universal Access in Human-Computer Interaction: Multimodality and Assistive Environments (Part II), edited by Margherita Antona and Constantine Stephanidis
9. LNCS 11574, Virtual, Augmented and Mixed Reality: Multimodal Interaction (Part I), edited by Jessie Y. C. Chen and Gino Fragomeni
10. LNCS 11575, Virtual, Augmented and Mixed Reality: Applications and Case Studies (Part II), edited by Jessie Y. C. Chen and Gino Fragomeni
11. LNCS 11576, Cross-Cultural Design: Methods, Tools and User Experience (Part I), edited by P. L. Patrick Rau
12. LNCS 11577, Cross-Cultural Design: Culture and Society (Part II), edited by P. L. Patrick Rau
13. LNCS 11578, Social Computing and Social Media: Design, Human Behavior and Analytics (Part I), edited by Gabriele Meiselwitz
14. LNCS 11579, Social Computing and Social Media: Communication and Social Communities (Part II), edited by Gabriele Meiselwitz
15. LNAI 11580, Augmented Cognition, edited by Dylan D. Schmorrow and Cali M. Fidopiastis
16. LNCS 11581, Digital Human Modeling and Applications in Health, Safety, Ergonomics and Risk Management: Human Body and Motion (Part I), edited by Vincent G. Duffy

17. LNCS 11582, Digital Human Modeling and Applications in Health, Safety, Ergonomics and Risk Management: Healthcare Applications (Part II), edited by Vincent G. Duffy
18. LNCS 11583, Design, User Experience, and Usability: Design Philosophy and Theory (Part I), edited by Aaron Marcus and Wentao Wang
19. LNCS 11584, Design, User Experience, and Usability: User Experience in Advanced Technological Environments (Part II), edited by Aaron Marcus and Wentao Wang
20. LNCS 11585, Design, User Experience, and Usability: Application Domains (Part III), edited by Aaron Marcus and Wentao Wang
21. LNCS 11586, Design, User Experience, and Usability: Practice and Case Studies (Part IV), edited by Aaron Marcus and Wentao Wang
22. LNCS 11587, Distributed, Ambient and Pervasive Interactions, edited by Norbert Streitz and Shin'ichi Konomi
23. LNCS 11588, HCI in Business, Government and Organizations: eCommerce and Consumer Behavior (Part I), edited by Fiona Fui-Hoon Nah and Keng Siau
24. LNCS 11589, HCI in Business, Government and Organizations: Information Systems and Analytics (Part II), edited by Fiona Fui-Hoon Nah and Keng Siau
25. LNCS 11590, Learning and Collaboration Technologies: Designing Learning Experiences (Part I), edited by Panayiotis Zaphiris and Andri Ioannou
26. LNCS 11591, Learning and Collaboration Technologies: Ubiquitous and Virtual Environments for Learning and Collaboration (Part II), edited by Panayiotis Zaphiris and Andri Ioannou
27. LNCS 11592, Human Aspects of IT for the Aged Population: Design for the Elderly and Technology Acceptance (Part I), edited by Jia Zhou and Gavriel Salvendy
28. LNCS 11593, Human Aspects of IT for the Aged Population: Social Media, Games and Assistive Environments (Part II), edited by Jia Zhou and Gavriel Salvendy
29. LNCS 11594, HCI for Cybersecurity, Privacy and Trust, edited by Abbas Moallem
30. LNCS 11595, HCI in Games, edited by Xiaowen Fang
31. LNCS 11596, HCI in Mobility, Transport, and Automotive Systems, edited by Heidi Krömker
32. LNCS 11597, Adaptive Instructional Systems, edited by Robert Sottilare and Jessica Schwarz
33. CCIS 1032, HCI International 2019 - Posters (Part I), edited by Constantine Stephanidis

34. CCIS 1033, HCI International 2019 - Posters (Part II), edited by Constantine Stephanidis
35. CCIS 1034, HCI International 2019 - Posters (Part III), edited by Constantine Stephanidis

http://2019.hci.international/proceedings

8th International Conference on Design, User Experience, and Usability (DUXU 2019)

Program Board Chair(s): **Aaron Marcus, *USA*, and Wentao Wang, *P.R. China***

- Sisira Adikari, Australia
- Claire Ancient, UK
- Jan Brejcha, Czech Republic
- Silvia De los Rios, Spain
- Marc Fabri, UK
- Josh Halstead, USA
- Wei Liu, P.R. China
- Yang Meng, P.R. China
- Judith Moldenhauer, USA
- Jingyan Qin, P.R. China
- Francisco Rebelo, Portugal
- Christine Riedmann-Streitz, Germany
- Elizabeth Rosenzweig, USA
- Patricia Search, USA
- Marcelo Soares, P.R. China
- Carla G. Spinillo, Brazil

The full list with the Program Board Chairs and the members of the Program Boards of all thematic areas and affiliated conferences is available online at:

http://www.hci.international/board-members-2019.php

HCI International 2020

The 22nd International Conference on Human-Computer Interaction, HCI International 2020, will be held jointly with the affiliated conferences in Copenhagen, Denmark, at the Bella Center Copenhagen, July 19–24, 2020. It will cover a broad spectrum of themes related to HCI, including theoretical issues, methods, tools, processes, and case studies in HCI design, as well as novel interaction techniques, interfaces, and applications. The proceedings will be published by Springer. More information will be available on the conference website: http://2020.hci.international/.

General Chair
Prof. Constantine Stephanidis
University of Crete and ICS-FORTH
Heraklion, Crete, Greece
E-mail: general_chair@hcii2020.org

http://2020.hci.international/

Contents – Part II

DUXU and Robots

DUXU for AI and AI for DUXU

Dialogue, Narrative, Storytelling

Visual DUXU

Interacting with Intelligent Digital Twins

Alexie Dingli and Foaad Haddod(✉)

University of Malta, Msida 2080, Malta
{alexiei.dingli,foaad.haddod.15}@um.edu.mt

Abstract. This paper details the Human Computer Interaction (HCI) components of an Intelligent Digital Twin (IDT) system for a semiconductor manufacturing company using gamming visual effects, 3D Computer Aided Design (CAD) and sound effects. The designed digital twin (DT) system will allow users to detect any irregularities (such as equipment failures and defects) in the manufacturing processes, in a timely manner and test some changes without an actual touching of the physical components. The project aims to design an IDT system that enhances the user's interaction by visualizing big data in such a way which can be easily understood and processed. Thus, allowing the user to intervene and control the entire production processes from the virtual console. The designed IDT system will enhance the UX of the system through the use of new interaction methodologies. The user will have full control of the data flow which is flowing from a data lake through for example, a gazing, a gesturing and a voice recognition interface which will provide contextual information based upon the user's viewpoint. The current phase of the project investigates the use of Cave VR technology to improve the immersion and the interaction between the user and the virtual system. We seek to develop a virtual environment that makes the users feel they are naturally interacting in a visually-immersed environment irrespective of where they are located. By enhancing the interaction of the user with these new technologies, we will provide a better UX that would create an efficient system which reduces the overall costs of managing the plant and concretely realize the aspirations of Industry 4.0.

Keywords: Human Computer Interaction · Intelligent Digital Twin · User experience · Semiconductor manufacturing · Interaction

1 Introduction

Driven by the trend of Internet of Things (IoT), industrial big data, and Industry 4.0, the concept of smart manufacturing will continue to grow, and new technologies and methods will emerge in the manufacturing intelligent systems domain. One of intelligent technologies that have been recently introduced into industry is known as 'digital twin'. This proposed project is linked with a semi-conductor manufacturing facility. The semiconductor manufacturing settings generally include a big number of operations and process. This is accompanied by the installation of data collection sensors located in the entire manufacturing facilities and machines. As a result, valuable data, that includes different measurements and different parameters readings, can be logged.

A. Marcus and W. Wang (Eds.): HCII 2019, LNCS 11584, pp. 3–15, 2019.
https://doi.org/10.1007/978-3-030-23541-3_1

Considering the massive volumes of the acquired data, it is becoming more challenging to keep using the traditional data analyses and visualisation tools.

Digital Twin (DT) is based on the concept of cypher-physical simulations (Lin et al. 2018). The main idea of a DT technology contains a combination of physical production process, virtual designed of complex assets, and data flow from both the physical and the virtual systems (Tao et al. 2018). Thus, as a result, there is a need to achieve a high level of convergence and synchronization. Semiconductor manufacturing process generates a massive amount of data. Such data can be effectively invested and analysed to determine some hidden insights. DT promises to visualize, control, and use all of the collected data and create smooth interaction between users and the manufacturing processes. Thus, DT will make the production processes designs more visualized (Tao et al. 2018). It can be used to collect haptic feedback from users to improve the user experience while using the systems. Thus, a unique real-time synchronized communication can be achieved between users and designed digital replica of any physical manufacturing process (El Saddik 2018).

In this project, we seek to design an Intelligent DT (IDT) system within a semiconductor manufacturing to be able to provide a nearly natural interaction to allow users controlling and monitoring the entire factory, in real-time. Thus, it will make the company ready for effective decision-making purposes. The designed interaction of the developed IDT system will consist of the following key stages; (1) design of an advanced virtual environment using a gaming engine. (2) use voice recognition interaction to interact with a virtual assistant in order to discuss real-time scenarios and help take better decisions. (3) use leap motion and Virtual Reality controllers to interact with virtual products and help improve their design without interrupting the physical system. Figure 1 shows the main designed key interaction stages of the IDT system.

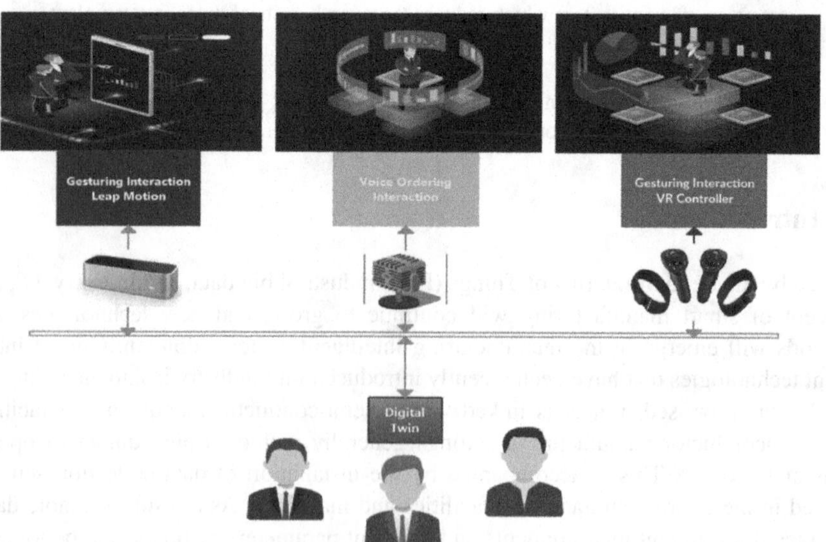

Fig. 1. Interaction key stages of the IDT system (Source: Self)

This paper is structured as follows. Section 1, Introduction the topic of the paper. Section 2 provided literature review about the concept of DT technology in the semiconductor industry, the concept of human computer interaction in VR and DT and the concept of user experience in VR and DT systems. Section 3 includes background information about four main themes directly related to the project namely; smart manufacturing, the concept of digital twin technology, DT within the semiconductor industry, human computer interaction, and user experience. Section 4, designing an IDT system as a case study in the semiconductor manufacturing process. Finally, Sect. 5 concludes by reporting the progress of the project and highlights the future plans of the second and the third phases of the project.

2 Literature Review

2.1 Smart Manufacturing

Smart manufacturing (SM) is a concept which refers to the use of smart technologies within manufacturing facilities. It is seen as a newer version of what has been known as intelligent manufacturing (IM), reflecting the magnitude and impact of smart technologies such the Internet of Things, Cloud Computing, Cyber-Physical Systems and Big Data on Industry 4.0 (Yao et al. 2017). Smart manufacturing refers to using advanced data analytics to complement physical science for improving system performance and decision making (Wang et al. 2018). Smart manufacturing system include two main elements; (1) data management and (2) data analysis and these provide real-time actionable information that can be used to optimize and build system intelligence into manufacturing operations (Kuhn and Ahrens 2017). With the advances in big data and DT, smart manufacturing is becoming the focus of global manufacturing transformation and upgrading (Qi and Tao 2018).

2.2 The Concept of Digital Twin Technology

The term 'digital twin' is not new and it was firstly introduced by Dr. Michael Grieves, in 2003, in his Executive Course on Product Management Lifecycle (PML) at the University of Michigan in the United States (Grieves 2014). What is new; however, is the recent interest in the DT concept and applications that is fueled by the emergence of the digitization of manufacturing, cyber-physical systems, and the need to gather large amounts of data and process (big data) (Schleich et al. 2017). Moreover, the concept of Industry 4.0 has also further impacted the visibility of using more DT applications within different sectors. DT consists of three main parts: (1) physical product to be 'virtually twinned'; (2) virtual product mimicking the physical product/twin; and (3) connected data that ties the physical and virtual products (twins) together (Tao et al. 2018). Thus, the main objective of the DT is to design, test, manufacture and use the virtual version of the physical product, process, operation, or system (Grieves and Vickers 2017).

Since its introduction, the concept of DT and its definition have been presented in several ways. For example, Boschert and Rosen (2016, p. 59) state that "the vision of the DT itself refers to a comprehensive physical and functional description of a component, product or system, which includes more or less all the information which could be useful in all—the current and subsequent—lifecycle phases". It is also defined as the creation of the virtual models for physical objects in the digital way to simulate their behaviors (Qi and Tao 2018). The DT is a hierarchical system of mathematical models, computational methods and software services, which provides near real-time synchronization between the state of the real-world process or system and its virtual copy (Borodulin et al. 2017). Furthermore, DT is able to consistently provide all subsystems with the latest state of all the required information, methods and algorithms (Brenner and Hummel 2017). In a factory, DT is about creating and maintaining a digital representation of the real world of the factory and supporting its management and reconfiguration by the means of optimization and simulation tools, which are fed with real and updated factory data (Kuts et al. 2017).

This paper provides information about the use of DT technologies within a manufacturing plant. Based on these definitions, the DT can be summarized in three main characteristics; (1) Real-time reflection; (2) Interaction and convergence; and (3) Self-evolution (Tao et al. 2018). Real-time reflection is a key feature of any DT system. The included communication middleware within the DT system should offer real-time interworking environments that provides accurate reflection of a virtual model about physical asset and time synchronization between each simulator (Yun et al. 2017). DT systems allow real-time monitoring of the status and progress of the physical 'twins' through real-time data collection, data integrations, and analysis (Tao and Qi 2017). On the other hand, the DT characteristic of interaction and convergence includes three main aspects; (a) interaction and convergence in the physical space; (b) interaction and convergence between historical data and real-time data; and (c) interaction and convergence physical space and virtual space (the twins) (Tao et al. 2018). Finally, the 'self-evolution' characteristic of DT refers to the ability to continuously update, in a real-time, the acquired data so that the virtual models of the DT system can be continuously improved by comparing the physical and virtual twin design and configurations (Tao et al. 2018; Tuegel et al. 2011).

2.3 Digital Twin and Semiconductor Industry

The digitalization of manufacturing fuels the application of sophisticated virtual product models, which are referred to as DTs and this applies throughout all stages of product realization (Schleich et al. 2017). Since the concept of DT was proposed, it has been applied in many industrial fields and has demonstrated its great potential. DT, with the characteristics of ultra-high synchronization and fidelity, convergence between physical and virtual product, etc. has high potential application in product design, product manufacturing, and product service (Tao et al. 2017). Industry 4.0 is one of the most prevalent subjects in production engineering and intelligent DT technology acts as an important element of this fourth industrial revolution. An intelligent DT for a production process enables a coupling of the production system with its digital equivalent as a base for an optimization with a minimized delay between the time of data acquisition and the creation of the DT (Uhlemann et al. 2017). Semiconductor manufacturing processes are considered as "the most capital-intensive and fully automated manufacturing systems" and usually there are a massive number of similar equipment and tools employed in one processing line (Khakifirooz et al. 2018). Thus, it is crucial to design an intelligent DT system that manages the ingested Big Data of those manufacturing processes and leverages the interconnectivity of the machines in order to reach the goal of intelligent, resilient and self-adaptable machines (Lee et al. 2015). Based on that, DT interacts with these physical entities in the semiconductor factory together with their functions (Balta et al. 2018).

2.4 Human Computer Interaction in DT Systems

Interaction in virtual environments is different from the interaction with traditional computer-generated virtual interfaces. In the DT system there are several technologies that can be used to design accurate and nearly realistic environments for example; Virtual reality, Augmented Reality or 3D CAD simulations. In some use cases, users of such designed environments need to rotate, roll, twist and turn. Thus, this requires access to 6D elements (up, down, front, back, left, and right) in the developed systems. (Dix 2009). Human interaction has some factors that might affect how a human's emotion and personality affect human-technology interaction (Szalma 2014). Since computers have been invented, they have become a key element in our lives and the method users interact with computers have been improved and become such an important matter. Most of the current used interactions techniques are built on some PC standard interactions tools and methods, for example, VR technology enables some new interaction technologies that use PC's tools such as a mouse to provide some physical and natural interactions (Vélaz et al. 2014). In addition, VR has enabled some other recent interaction including gesturing, gazing, and voice interactions. Using such interactions will enhance the user's experience when the try DT experience. The ability to design a high level of visualization and allow users to use their hands and move freely to interact with the 6D environment can provide "attractive and natural alternative to these cumbersome interface devices for human-computer interaction" (Rautaray and Agrawal 2015, p. 2). Furthermore, using eye-gazing can provide more effective interaction. In VR, the technique of eye tracking and movement has been used to calculate the user's intention. Such interaction can be implemented to "focus depth implementation in a standard VR headset" (Pai et al. 2016, p. 171). In another recent project, it has been used to record users voice orders in real time to interact with VR environments (Kefi et al. 2018). Voice-recognition ordering can be used to interact with some objects in computer-generated 6D environments where users pronouncing some keywords representing instructions for different functions such as: pick, drop, next, and play. In this designed IDT system, voice interaction plays a crucial role and it has provided a very positive influence on the users' experience and interaction.

2.5 User Experience

Virtual Reality (VR) technology always gave high importance to user experience (Ux) when developing interactive applications (Rebelo et al. 2012). (Olsson et al. 2013) stated the UX is related to the interaction between users and products. There are several aspects rather than the usability of products that UX assessed, such as; efficiency, effectiveness, and satisfactory interaction. It can provide more emotional relationships between the user and the designed applications (Desmet et al. 2007). Thus, UX can be defined as "a holistic concept describing the subjective experience resulting from the interaction with a technological product or service. Both instrumental (e.g. utility, usability, and other pragmatic elements) and non-instrumental (e.g. pleasure, appeal, aesthetics, and other hedonic elements)" (Olsson and Salo 2011, p. 76). Most of the human responses such as beliefs, perceptions, emotions, psychological responses, and preferences can be included in UX and can be measured and accomplished during or after using any designed system (Ritsos et al. 2011).

In virtual environments, UX was always one of the crucial elements that needed to be considered. Thus, there was a necessity to design very advanced virtual environments and applications to make users feel influenced and immersed to interact easily with the designed environmental elements. In this project, UX involves the interaction between users and the designed virtual environment application with a focus on the interaction effects between the users and the digital replica of the physical semiconductor plant.

3 Interaction Approach for IDT in Semiconductor Factory System

DT has brought a lot of potential promises to overcome monitoring and visualization challenges. It made it easier to detect and predict such hidden challenges more than ever. This project contains three main levels; Top Management level, Middle Management level and Executive level. This paper focuses on the human interaction of the Top Management level. The designed DT aims to help the company's CEOs to better understand their production lines. Thus, they become closer to the physical production plants without being personally at any production lines when they need to make any critical decisions. Since there is the need to develop a smooth interaction between the CEOs and the designed DT system, the following elements were added including 3D equipment, tools models, virtual assistant model and interactive 3D dashboard.

3.1 The Manufacturing Plant Environment

In order to achieve a high level of immersion in the IDT system, a number of natural effects were used. There is a need to improve the level of visualization in order to provide more details about all the production line's elements. The semiconductor manufacturing plant is made of a large number of equipment, different production processes, different manufacturing levels, sections and a variety of other devices. A 3D computer aided design (CAD) design for the equipment was developed using Adobe SkeckUP, where a number of parts and component were designed to represent most of the manufacturing processes. The main reason to use CAD was to make sure to end up with 3D models that are made based on a variety of accurate and detailed components. Such methodology can be very helpful to design complex assets and help the DT systems to provide more information about those assets. Figure 2 shows a screen shoot for the designed DT of the manufacturing plant environment in use in our test system.

Fig. 2. A screen shot of the virtual wire bonding production line (Source: Self).

In addition, this approach will allow users to interact directly with the different components and better understand their behaviour. Gaze detection together with VR controllers will help users focus on any part of the machines and visualise the require statistics when they are needed. Users will be able to walk and pick those virtual parts using a leap motion device a computer hardware sensor that supports hand and finger motions as input. Such interaction can be enhanced with voice recognition in order to elicit further explanations when interacting with the developed virtual assistant. Figure 3 shows a diagram that explains one of our scenarios whereby we can see the interaction between the users and the virtual 3D equipment.

3.2 The Virtual Assistant

From the early stages of development on this project, a decision was made to give a greater attention to the level of interaction between users and the designed system. In recent years, a good number of new interaction techniques have been developed. One of these recent methods was used to provide a user-friendly interface that allows users to interact smoothly with the digital replica of a very complex semiconductor manufacturing process. The system is built on a live stream of data that was gathered in a real-time manner from the manufacturing line. As a matter of fact, semiconductor manufacturing provides a massive amount of data about all the different manufacturing processes, materials, and operators. After evaluating monitoring system of an international semiconductor manufacturing company that we conduct research with, we have realized that is very difficult to control the fast flow of data through interactive dashboards. It has always been a challenge to determine which parameters should be given priority in order to make fast and accurate decisions. In addition, using traditional interaction techniques such as; mouse, keyboard, and touch devices, can cause delay and damage when dealing with emergency situations that require instant attention.

An Artificial Intelligence virtual agent was designed to take care of all the users' required information. Users can interact directly via speech orders to ingest information about the manufacturing processes through the virtual DT system. In addition, and to

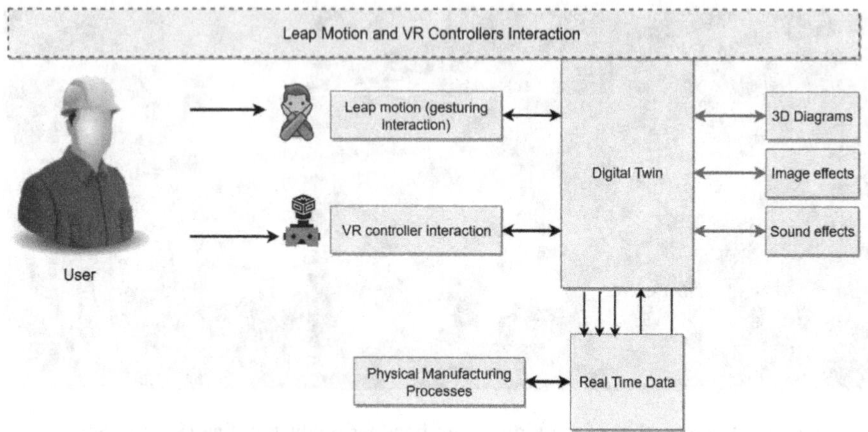

Fig. 3. The gesturing interaction diagram (Source: Self).

add more realistic interactions through the digital replica, user's movement capability was added to allow users to move from equipment to another while they are investigating unforeseen failures that might occur in the manufactory process. Natural language processing using machine intelligence was used to translate users' voice commands into written words. IBM Watson Speech-to-Text API[1] with unity IBM-Watson-SDK was used to read voice commands which are used to invoke other functions such as; "move to the failure source" or "show statistics that are counted form the collected data in real-time". Figure 4 illustrates the applied voice interaction.

This interaction has a number of advantages; for instance, the used hardware, can use this easy-to-use service that uses machine intelligence to apply language grammar and generate very accurate transcription. Also, the API supports 7 different languages which can make it easy to gather the feedback from the virtual assistant and translate it into different languages. This feature will make it easy to distribute the designed model over different plants and can be used by different users without the need to make major changes in the language packages used. In addition, the approach used does not require expensive microphone hardware since it correct the voice and grammar mistakes to make sure the virtual assistance gets accurate and correct orders. Another IBM Watson API was used, the Text-To-Speech API. This toolkit was used to invoke different functions based on the user's original voice order and to provide the requested information in very speedy way thus avoiding issues of. Figure 5 shows the methodology for the virtual assistant response.

3.3 3D Statistics Visualization

To achieve this, all the decision makers need to have enough information to make accurate decisions. During this project, a new approach was designed to make the

[1] https://www.ibm.com/watson/services/speech-to-text/.

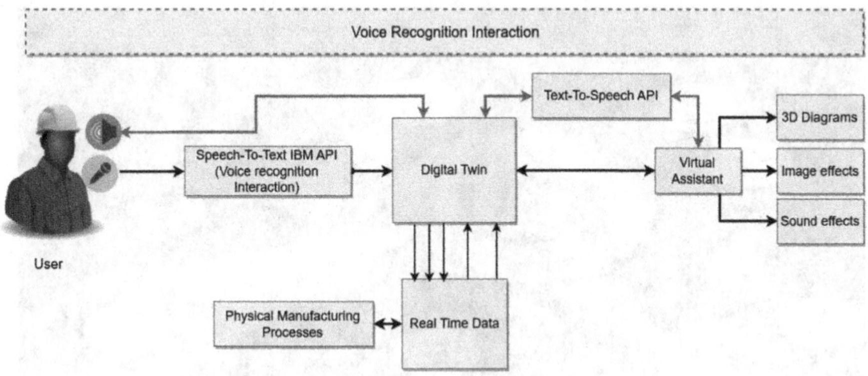

Fig. 4. Voice interaction diagram (Source: Self).

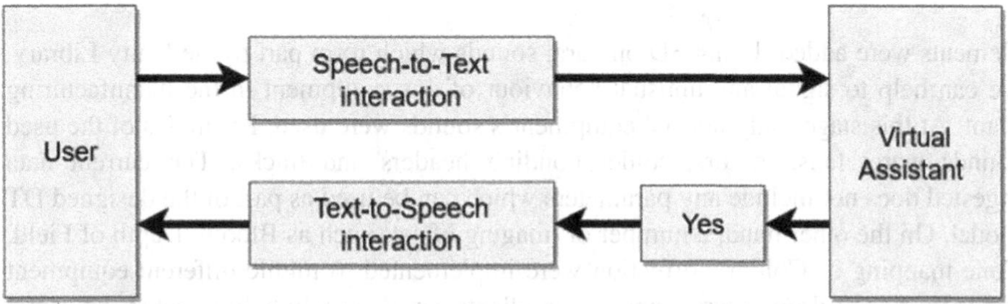

Fig. 5. Voice recognition interaction with the virtual assistant (Source: Self)

user's interaction easier by visualising all of the collected statistics pertaining to the manufacturing process in real-time. Both 3D and 2D diagrams were added to the DT system to be available whenever they are needed. Two main interaction tools are used including VR Controllers and the leap motion to help users select, remove, pause and refresh all the designed systems. The DT environment includes a virtual section for data analysis. As it can be seen in Fig. 6, this section contains a number of screens that can be interacted with. In the Cave VR experience, the gestures captured through the leap motion are used to interact with the 3D diagrams. Apart from the VR controllers and leap motion tools, the developed virtual assistant can help users to answer any questions when they are need. Even though the project is still under development, the initial feedback from the top managers was very positive.

3.4 Image and Sound Effects

Since some of the DT virtual equipment are mechanical components, there was a need to implement different techniques in order to improve the user's interaction when there is a sudden or predicted failure. In order to boost user immersion, a number of sound

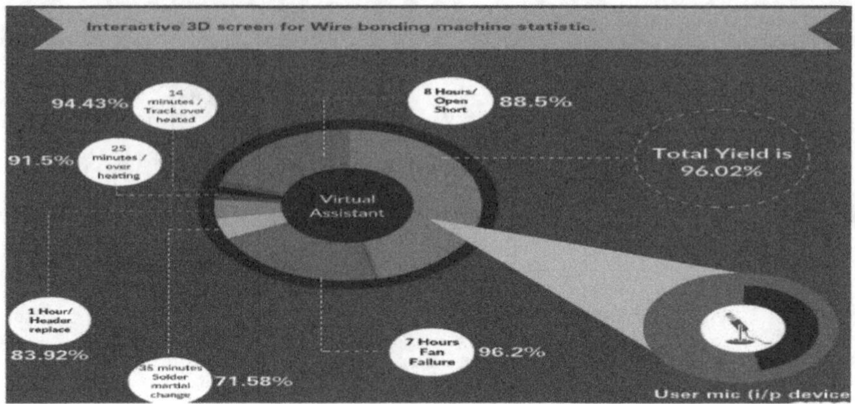

Fig. 6. A screen shot of the designed virtual dashboard (Source: Self)

elements were added. Using 3D binaural sounds which form part of the Unity Library, we can help to signal any unusual behaviour of any equipment in the manufacturing plant. At this stage, only normal equipment's sounds were used. Examples of the used sounds were; fans, motors, solder bonding headers and tracks. The current data ingested does not include any parameters which can be used as part of the designed DT model. On the other hand, a number of imaging effects such as Bloom, Depth of Field, Tone mapping or Colour Correction were implemented to mimic different equipment status in case of drop-down events. Such effects can definitely help to catch the users' attention in order to respond to failure events. Figure 7 shows an over heat scenario that was visualized using image effects. Using 3D binaural sounds, users can respond to sound sources and grab their attention so that they only focus on the source that has problems.

Fig. 7. Visualized over-heating scenario in the designed DT system (Source: Self)

4 Results and Future Work

4.1 Results

The use of DT in manufacturing has a promising future. After a number of months working on developing this project, there were a number of key achievements that have been accomplished. A crucial key element that has added more value to the developed system was the user interaction experience. By implementing a number of different human interaction techniques, the system has become more user-friendly and interactive and thus helped users to make faster reactions. The designed virtual assistant has successfully improved the interaction between the users and the designed DT system. There is also the possibility to enhance it further by providing more answers and suggest more explanations to the users. Virtual assistant makes the user experience even easier and helps users to interact with the whole system thus reducing the dependency on the virtual hardware and the visualized statistics.

In the coming years, it is expected that an enriched big data environment incorporating smart manufacturing ideas such as intelligent DT will further enable advanced analytics. As a result, visual computing will become a new and exciting field of research linked to the challenges of the next industrial revolution. Thus, it is crucial to design an intelligent DT system that manages Big Data and leverages the interconnectivity of machines in order to reach the goal of intelligent, resilient and self-adaptable machines besides the high capability of improving the user experience and interaction within the DT system. There were obviously a number of which provided useful insights into the applicability of improving user interaction and UX using the intelligent DT technology within the manufacturing industry. Such insights will be beneficial to future human-computer interaction approaches within DT technology. Realistic features can be added, smoother interaction can be implemented, and big achievements can be obtained as a result of combining these advances.

4.2 Future Work

The project is at the implementation and development for the first phase. Based on the promising results that the project has gained so far, more attention will be given to the Conversational Virtual Agent via different forms of interaction with agents, including chat, voice and 3D interaction. In addition, the leap motion interaction will be developed in the future to help users interact with a virtual laboratory (VL). In this VL, the engineers will be able to interact with virtual products and test different scenarios virtually. It will help engineers to test virtual products using real-time data and historical information from the previous scenarios in the DT system. Thus, there will be no need to interrupt any physical production processes to test new improvements. Based on the initial feedback and results obtained so far from this project's work, we will be implementing more interaction techniques such as; auto gazing to pick up and select equipment for the big data system. The VR technology will be used to design a DT system that can be displayed using a head mounted display. This AR aims to provide a window over the DT on handy tablets in order to allow engineers to work freely through production lines, simulate, discuss and suggest future procedures in real time.

5 Conclusion

Digital twin technology is capable of integrating various technologies in one robust system. This includes the capability of implementing and improving users' interaction techniques within DT systems. Such interactions can reflect on the user's experience while trying the designed DT. This project aimed to design a realistic DT system to immerse users in digital replica of physical assets in an attempt to make decision makers become closer to their manufacturing processes. This project had a number of key achievements and integrated virtual reality interactions together with leap motion interaction to help users better understand the manufacturing process and smoothly interacting with all the digital twin's assets. The initial results have shown a great potential in the proposed interaction techniques and managed to design a user-friendly experience through the use of the designed DT system.

References

Balta, E.C., Tilbury, D.M., Barton, K.: A centralized framework for system-level control and management of additive manufacturing fleets. In: 2018 IEEE 14th International Conference on Automation Science and Engineering (CASE), pp. 1071–1078. IEEE, August 2018

Borodulin, K., Radchenko, G., Shestakov, A., Sokolinsky, L., Tchernykh, A., Prodan, R.: Towards digital twins cloud platform: microservices and computational workflows to rule a smart factory. In: Proceedings of the 10th International Conference on Utility and Cloud Computing, pp. 209–210. ACM, December 2017

Boschert, S., Rosen, R.: Digital twin—the simulation aspect. In: Hehenberger, P., Bradley, D. (eds.) Mechatronic Futures, pp. 59–74. Springer, Cham (2016). https://doi.org/10.1007/978-3-319-32156-1_5

Brenner, B., Hummel, V.: Digital twin as enabler for an innovative digital shopfloor management system in the ESB Logistics Learning Factory at Reutlingen-University. Procedia Manuf. **9**, 198–205 (2017)

Desmet, P.M., Porcelijn, R., Van Dijk, M.B.: Emotional design; application of a research-based design approach. Knowl. Technol. Policy **20**(3), 141–155 (2007)

Dix, A.: Human-computer interaction. In: Liu, L., Özsu, M.T. (eds.) Encyclopedia of Database Systems, pp. 1327–1331. Springer, Boston (2009). https://doi.org/10.1007/978-0-387-39940-9_192

El Saddik, A.: Digital twins: the convergence of multimedia technologies. IEEE MultiMed. **25**(2), 87–92 (2018)

Grieves, M.: Digital twin: manufacturing excellence through virtual factory replication. White paper (2014)

Grieves, M., Vickers, J.: Digital twin: mitigating unpredictable, undesirable emergent behavior in complex systems. In: Kahlen, F.-J., Flumerfelt, S., Alves, A. (eds.) Transdisciplinary Perspectives on Complex Systems, pp. 85–113. Springer, Cham (2017). https://doi.org/10.1007/978-3-319-38756-7_4

Kefi, M., Hoang, T.N., Richard, P., Verhulst, E.: An evaluation of multimodal interaction techniques for 3D layout constraint solver in a desktop-based virtual environment. Virtual Reality **22**, 1–13 (2018)

Khakifirooz, M., Chien, C.F., Chen, Y.J.: Bayesian inference for mining semiconductor manufacturing big data for yield enhancement and smart production to empower industry 4.0. Appl. Soft Comput. **68**, 990–999 (2018)

Kuhn, D., Ahrens, J.: Smart manufacturing for continuous, high-technology glass production. In: 77th Conference on Glass Problems: A Collection of Papers Presented at the 77th Conference on Glass Problems, Greater Columbus Convention Center, Columbus, OH, 7–9 November 2016, vol. 612, p. 45. Wiley, May 2017

Kuts, V., Modoni, G.E., Terkaj, W., Tähemaa, T., Sacco, M., Otto, T.: Exploiting factory telemetry to support virtual reality simulation in robotics cell. In: De Paolis, L.T., Bourdot, P., Mongelli, A. (eds.) AVR 2017. LNCS, vol. 10324, pp. 212–221. Springer, Cham (2017). https://doi.org/10.1007/978-3-319-60922-5_16

Lin, W.D., Low, Y.H., Chong, Y.T., Teo, C.L.: Integrated cyber physical simulation modelling environment for manufacturing 4.0. In: 2018 IEEE International Conference on Industrial Engineering and Engineering Management (IEEM), pp. 1861–1865, December 2018

Olsson, T., Lagerstam, E., Kärkkäinen, T., Väänänen-Vainio-Mattila, K.: Expected user experience of mobile augmented reality services: a user study in the context of shopping centres. Pers. Ubiquit. Comput. **17**(2), 287–304 (2013)

Pai, Y.S., Outram, B., Vontin, N., Kunze, K.: Transparent reality: using eye gaze focus depth as interaction modality. In: Proceedings of the 29th Annual Symposium on User Interface Software and Technology, pp. 171–172. ACM, October 2016

Qi, Q., Tao, F.: Digital twin and big data towards smart manufacturing and industry 4.0: 360 degree comparison. IEEE Access **6**, 3585–3593 (2018)

Wang, J., Ma, Y., Zhang, L., Gao, R.X., Wu, D.: Deep learning for smart manufacturing: methods and applications. J. Manuf. Syst. **48**, 144–156 (2018)

Rautaray, S.S., Agrawal, A.: Vision based hand gesture recognition for human computer interaction: a survey. Artif. Intell. Rev. **43**(1), 1–54 (2015)

Rebelo, F., Noriega, P., Duarte, E., Soares, M.: Using virtual reality to assess user experience. Hum. Factors **54**(6), 964–982 (2012)

Ritsos, P.D., Ritsos, D.P., Gougoulis, A.S.: Standards for augmented reality: a user experience perspective. In: International AR Standards Meeting, pp. 1–9, February 2011

Schleich, B., Anwer, N., Mathieu, L., Wartzack, S.: Shaping the digital twin for design and production engineering. CIRP Ann. **66**(1), 141–144 (2017)

Szalma, J.L.: On the application of motivation theory to human factors/ergonomics: motivational design principles for human–technology interaction. Hum. Factors **56**(8), 1453–1471 (2014)

Tao, F., Qi, Q.: New IT driven service-oriented smart manufacturing: framework and characteristics. IEEE Trans. Syst. Man Cybern.: Syst. (2017)

Tao, F., et al.: Digital twin-driven product design framework. Int. J. Prod. Res. 1–19 (2018)

Tao, F., Cheng, J., Qi, Q., Zhang, M., Zhang, H., Sui, F.: Digital twin-driven product design, manufacturing and service with big data. Int. J. Adv. Manuf. Technol. **94**(9–12), 3563–3576 (2018)

Tao, F., Cheng, J., Qi, Q., Zhang, M., Zhang, H., Sui, F.: Digital twin-driven product design, manufacturing and service with big data. Int. J. Adv. Manuf. Technol. **94**, 1–14 (2017)

Tuegel, E.J., Ingraffea, A.R., Eason, T.G., Spottswood, S.M.: Reengineering aircraft structural life prediction using a digital twin. Int. J. Aerosp. Eng. **2011** (2011)

Vélaz, Y., Arce, J.R., Gutiérrez, T., Lozano-Rodero, A., Suescun, A.: The influence of interaction technology on the learning of assembly tasks using virtual reality. J. Comput. Inf. Sci. Eng. **14** (4), 041007 (2014)

Yao, X., Zhou, J., Zhang, J., Boër, C.R.: From intelligent manufacturing to smart manufacturing for Industry 4.0 driven by next generation artificial intelligence and further on. In: 2017 5th International Conference on Enterprise Systems (ES), pp. 311–318. IEEE, September 2017

Yun, S., Park, J.H. and Kim, W.T.: Data-centric middleware based digital twin platform for dependable cyber-physical systems. In: 2017 Ninth International Conference on Ubiquitous and Future Networks (ICUFN), pp. 922–926. IEEE, July 2017

Making Packaging Waste Sorting More Intuitive in Fast Food Restaurant

Yu-Chen Hsieh[1](✉), Yi-Jui Chen[1], and Wang-Chin Tsai[2]

[1] Department of Industrial Design, National Yunlin University of Science and Technology, Douliu, Yunlin, Taiwan
Chester.3d@gmail.com

[2] Department of Creative Design, National Yunlin University of Science and Technology, Douliu, Yunlin, Taiwan
forwangwang@gmail.com

Abstract. Consumers are accustomed to classifying garbage in front of recycling stations after finishing their meal at fast food restaurants. However, due to a lack of knowledge about the recyclability of the garbage items, and confusion caused by the weak design of the instruction system provided, many users are not able to complete the sorting task quickly or correctly. The low success rate of the customer's garbage sorting subsequently results in employees having to spend more time and energy in the following rectifying work, which leads to extra and unnecessary costs for the corporation. Therefore, our researchers have attempted to explore the recycling process from a more cognitive perspective, and proposed a new concept for the sorting task, which is more intuitive and less confusing.

Our research was designed into two stages. The first stage is to summarize the criteria of intuitive design with literature reviews, and make adjustments to the current recycling instruction system. The second stage is to conduct simulation experiments to verify the efficiency and correct rate of the new instruction system. Our research is anticipated to verify that an instruction system based on intuitive theory is more efficient, and less confusing to users. The research results will not only be a benefit to the fast food industry, but also to the other recycling instruction systems used in our daily lives.

Keywords: Intuitive · Garbage sorting · Recycling process · Sorting · Cognitive

1 Introduction

1.1 Research Background

It is now commonplace for fast food restaurant patrons to sort the packaging waste from their meal to dispose of into recyclables and trash. More often than not, however, these consumers may experience confusion during sorting sometimes to the point of simply chucking the entirety of their waste into one sorting bin, diminishing the efficacy of waste sorting as restaurant workers will need to commit extra effort into re-sorting the waste, which generates extra cost for businesses. Those responsible for

A. Marcus and W. Wang (Eds.): HCII 2019, LNCS 11584, pp. 16–31, 2019.
https://doi.org/10.1007/978-3-030-23541-3_2

coming up with the recycling programs for businesses may believe that adequate instruction has already been provided for the consumer to follow in waste sorting; after all, labels and text instructions are on waste bins as well as symbols and icons on the food packaging enough for the average consumer to figure out what goes where. But is that really the case? Our researchers are intrigued at this everyday occurrence and have taken action to investigate the cause of waste sorting confusion for consumers and whether there is a way to design waste to be more in line with the consumer's cognitive process so that waste sorting efficacy and accuracy can be increased.

1.2 Observation on Current Systems

Our researchers used McDonald's, currently the largest fast food hamburger restaurant chain in Taiwan, as their target of observation. The recycling system of MacDonald's Taiwan (McD's) labels its food packaging into recyclables and non-recyclables so that the restaurant patrons may sort their waste into the proper waste bin according to the labels (Table 1). In order to investigate the problems and potential aspects of confusion consumers may have when faced with a system for recycling, the researchers have come up with a questionnaire of 6 questions and with it surveyed 40 adult consumers, half of each gender, when they had just finished their meals and completed the disposal of their waste. The results of the survey are as illustrated in Table 1.

Table 1. Symbols on McD's food packaging and corresponding recycling symbols

	Corresponding Symbols on McD's Food Packaging	Corresponding Symbols at Recycling Station
Recycable waste		資源回收垃圾 RECYCLABLE WASTE
General Waste		一般垃圾 GENERAL WASTE

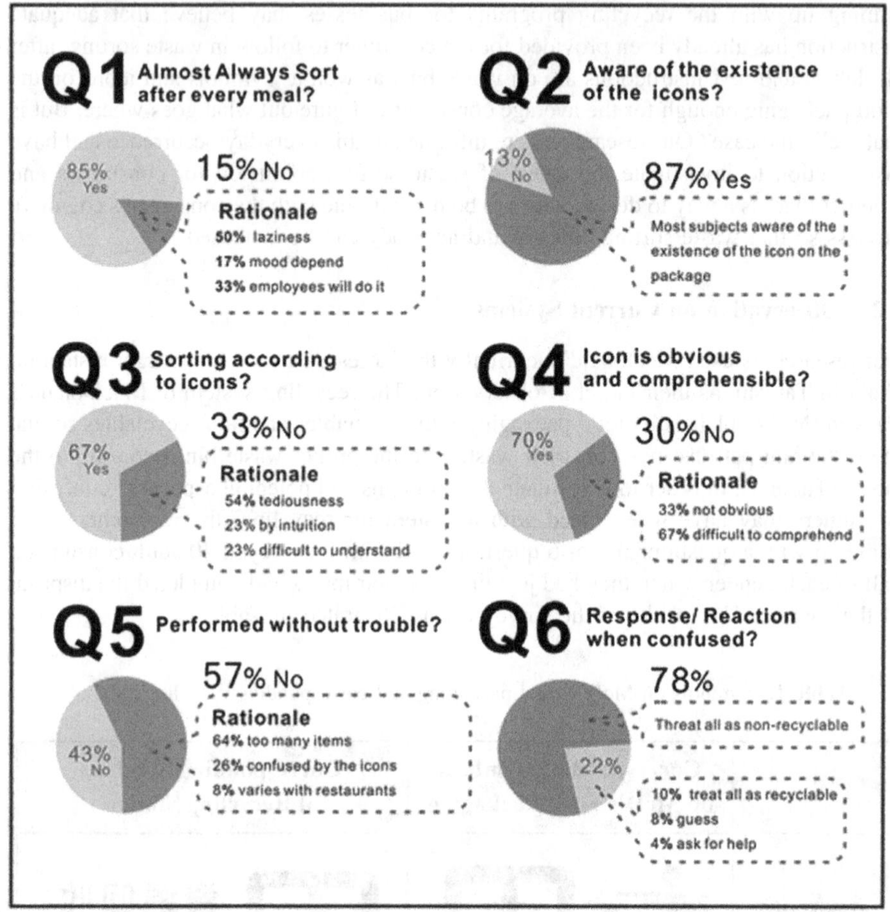

Fig. 1. Results of questionnaire on the use of fast food restaurant's recycling system

From the results of the surveys (Fig. 1), some interesting phenomenon can be seen:

- Although labels are present, users still feel sorting according to labels to be tedious (question 3).
- Many may feel confused seeing the labels to be unclear or too complex (question 4).
- Even with labels, many hesitate over sorting, especially for too many items and confused by the icons (question 5).
- Primary reason for confusion was due to uncertainty or over-variety of waste types (question 5).

From this rudimentary survey that was able ascertain that difficulty with categorizing waste and the labeling are problems associated with sorting, from which the following questions emerge:

1. Why is it that, under labeled instructions, consumers still experience tediousness with sorting according to labels and attempts to categorize through their own cognitive process?
2. Why is it that users are still confused with waste which have been categorized through available labels, and feel that there are too many varieties to sort?
3. What is the problem with the task of waste sorting? Can improving the concept of sorting and the labeling alleviate the problems found above?

2 Reference Discussions

When discussing fast food waste sorting, the current system hopes to achieve one goal: Identify recyclable waste and ordinary waste. This seemingly simple task actually involve complicated identification processes and decision making. Given that fast food recycling systems expect customers to find the labels and sort according to the labels, the customers may in fact find it overly tedious to look for the labels and sometimes one was not even found. Furthermore, even if a label is found, the customer still has to refer to previous knowledge and experience to make the right decision, which is where confusion occurs. For example, something that the customer believes is recyclable is actually considered general waste, such as PLA transparent plastic lids (made from corn starch resin, a biodegradable organic material). A more common occurrence of problem is when the consumer doesn't see the label and is unable to determine the recyclability of certain waste items. What follows is to sort in confusion, or to abandon sorting altogether. In order to gain insight into the questions raised above, this research will focus on the areas below for reference discussion: (1) Knowledge and behavior; (2) Intuition and functional level; (3) Intuitive design; (4) Theories on sorting and symbol recognition.

2.1 Knowledge and Behavior

In one of their research, Spool [23] mentioned that 'Product design' is a process that has to bridge the 'knowledge gap', the gap between Target Knowledge, or the intended amount of knowledge a user should have to operate a product, and Current Knowledge, which is what users currently have in order to recognize the interface provided. When the two levels of knowledge touch or overlap, Instinctive Operation is achieved.

Norman [18] explained the relationship between precise behavior and imprecise behavior through an experiment on the recognition of coins. In the experiment, he provides several similar pictures of American pennies, and only one of them is the correct coin design. Although less than half of all college students tested were able to correctly identify the picture, in truth, it does not affect the usage of the pennies, since all they have to do is to separate them from nickels, dimes, and quarters without having to register the subtleties of the design. Even though the experiment involved American coins, the same principle applies to other domains. We often forget that the design of a product has to minimize the amount of knowledge a user is required to operate it, as most of the time, all the product needs to do is get the job done, ideally without very much user input. For example, when finding a location, all that most people require are certain key landmarks without the details of the streets and alleyways and distances. We often neglect that we are equipped with basic navigational functions and rapid problem solving capabilities; Giving someone too much details in direction would only generate confusion.

Furthermore, Norman believes that behavior is the result of guidance by both outside information and innate knowledge, and people don't have to be aware of precise knowledge of every detail of all knowledge as long as the information is suffice to handle everyday situations. Norman gives four reasons for this: (1) knowledge is present both inside the mind and outside; (2) Highly accurate knowledge is often unnecessary; (3) The world is already full of natural limitations that guide behavior; (4) Cultural limitations as well as social customs often reduce the number of behavioral choices. Taken together, knowledge of the task at hand, and environmental and social limitations, work together to equalize the amount of available knowledge and operational knowledge, which produces correct judgment. On the other hand, when the two knowledge levels have a wide gap, it creates usability issues. Before we ask the user to correctly identify trash, have we examined the level of knowledge and experience required of the task is complete and rudimentary?

2.2 Intuition and Functional Level

From a psychological perspective, Intuition is an ability that accesses knowledge without logic or rationalization. Jung [10] describes it as an irrational function where the process is mostly without conscious thought. In the discussion of user behavior, it is considered an intuitive non-conscious process, as in, it does not enter the thinking process but instead is a result that emerges unconsciously from past knowledge or experience [1, 7]. UI expert Blacker and his research team defines Intuition as the following after discussion with various scholars: Intuition is a type of cognitive processing that utilizes knowledge gained through prior experience (stored experiential knowledge). It is a process that is often fast and is non-conscious, or at least not recallable or verbalizable [2–4].

Raskin [20] also attempted to define Intuition through the example of a computer mouse. Even something as simple as a computer mouse to the modern person could confuse either a Starship engineer from the future [StarTrek VI scene with Chief Engineer Montgomery Scott] or a Literature teacher from 20 years before the invention of personal computers because no such product existed during their time so therefore no past experience could be referenced. Raskin therefore defines Intuition as a behavior modified by familiarity or that which uses readily transferred or existing skills.

In the SRK task model proposed by Rasmussen [21], human function is categorized into three types: (1) Skill based; (2) Rule based, and (3) Knowledge Based. When people are executing a task, they draw from these types interchangeably depending on the situation. Of the three, skill based is function that is based on instinctive reaction and the vast pool of past experience; it is the type that is able to complete a task without thinking it through and therefore accomplished a task the quickest. Furthermore, Newell [17] ordered the reaction time of four different bands of task processing from longest to shortest: (1) social band; (2) rational band; (3) cognitive band; (4) biological band. The reaction time of task processing in the biological band is the shortest, measurable in milliseconds, and the reaction time in the social band is the longest, sometimes from days to months. Once task processing enters the rational band, the required time is measured in 102 s, which still exceeds actions that is measured in minutes. Therefore, Newell suggests that design should be applied to shorten the task processing time in the cognitive band. For example, the cognitive process that connects symbol and functional meaning should belong to the biological band of task processing, and in order to achieve intuitive reaction, the thought process involved for the user should be minimized in order to achieve the task with the easiest of task processing.

2.3 Designing for Intuition

Blacker et al. [3] investigated the relationship between Intuitive design and operational experience through an experiment involving television remote control. They discovered that the ease of operation increased along with experience and concluded that as operating knowledge of the product increased, task processing time relatively decreased. It therefore stands that an intuitively operable product must decrease the likelihood of users employing cognition, and requires no prior instructions for the user to perceive how a product is used. This allows those with less experience to operate a product with the same ease as someone with experience. Complex cognitive thinking consumes a great amount of mental energy, and the more a user is required to think and make decision, the more of that mental energy is consumed, making users unwilling to continue its operation, resulting in a phenomenon known as ego depletion, which is deeply unpleasing to the user and creates a negative experience of use [11, 19]. Active Japanese Designer, Fukasawa Naoto, has also suggested the concept of "Without Thought" design, where a behavioral trend is identified through studying people's unconscious behavior, and applied to the product design. He believes that a great number of products on sale today that is designed to work by stimulating the senses but overstimulation interrupts the unconscious cognitive activity, so the design that best expression of intuitive design is something that works in harmony with the human unconsciously [16]. Blackler et al. [4] proposes three points in designing a product that is intuitively usable:

1. Location of product features: should be easily visible without too much effort from the user
2. Types of features (structure, shape, color, labels): the design of the interface should relate to its function
3. Functions of the features and how it is operated: method of operation should be associated to similar experience in order to make operation more intuitive

If we wish to allow the user to effortlessly operate the product non-cognitively or without thought, we must be mindful of the influence of past experience, since past experience may not necessarily have a positive influence on the current operation [5, 12].

If users now face so much confusion over the process of waste sorting, we can conjecture that past experience is in conflict with the sorting task at hand. How to employ a more intuitive design allowing users to efficaciously complete the sorting task without much cognitive input is a great research challenge.

2.4 Sorting Theory and Symbol Recognition

In theories concerning cognition, the primary purpose of sorting involves the conjecture of features without form, especially for novel stimuli. For example, in a zoological situation we may sort animals into "Tigers" or "Zebras" to indicate whether they are threatening or not. The act of sorting connects the stimulus we experience to what we have previously learned or to information we find relevant. We can therefore interpret the act of sorting as a inference on formless properties. The process of learning to perform sorting is one of great importance, as it relies heavily on all of our cognitive abilities to properly organize, absorb information, and develop new concepts that surpass previous understandings. In addition, sorting often simultaneously involve multiple dimensions or different forms of abstract thinking, which makes learning to sort a great challenge [13]. As apparent from the above definition and discussion on sorting, it is a skill more difficult than it seems. It was thought that the restaurant customers would perform sorting happily and quickly while the inherent difficulty of the task of sorting, as well as the difference of understanding for each individual of the recyclability of each item (or possessed knowledge thereof), were both neglected. This can potentially generate feelings of conflict as well as confusion, since individuals, children and adult alike, would in default perform the most basic kind of sorting, which is sorting through the most fundamental visual properties such as color, orientation, shape, etc [15, 22]. Furthermore, Johansen and Palmeri [9] in their sorting experiments discovered that when learning to sort, people will tend to perform rule-based sorting during the beginning before transitioning to exemplar-based sorting after repetition.

In this research, the factors that influence a user's sorting efficacy, other than the knowledge required for making judgment on relevant items, also include the clarity of symbol, which concerns its color and shape. In design-related issues, the general consensus is that color of the symbol is a stronger emotional trigger than the outline of the symbol [14, 24]. In addition, experiments by Fullera and Carrascoa [6] revealed that when identifying colors, the closer the images are to a primary color, the easier they are to identify, and that designers can utilize the saturation and contrast of a color to increase the efficiency of identification. In terms of the shape, although humans are not as acute as they are with color, just in terms of shapes humans are better with circles than other shapes [8] and during recognition will pay attention to circular items first. Hence, the circle is a more preferred shape when making labels, as they produce a better identification result. In summary, people respond to color as a stimulus quicker than the shape, and so in designing labels the use of color is particularly important. In addition, the design for the label can benefit from adapting a circular contour, and the use of a highly vivid primary color, all of which increase attractiveness and identifiability.

2.5 Reference Summary

Based on the above literature, our researchers have devised directions for tackling the issue of recycling process improvement:

- Reducing the level of thinking needed from within the rational band to the cognitive band, since reducing the level of thinking is how a system achieves intuitive use for the user.
- Imprecise knowledge can nonetheless be guided to achieve the correct behavior, and how to avoid having users of different knowledge and experience background to perform complex judgment of waste categorization, how guidance can be redesigned may be the key to this challenge.
- Rethinking about the past experiences of the user can prevent conflicts between that experience and the sorting design of fast food restaurants.
- Simplification of symbol instructions by introducing ways to make pairing and recognition simper and easier.

The researchers employed a new guidance model that changes the question of "Is this piece of waste recyclable (rational band) into something like "which bin should this piece with this symbol go into?" (cognitive band) in an attempt to apply an adjustment in the decision making process to simplify and raise the accuracy of the waste sorting process. To this end, an interesting experiment will be conducted to test a sorting method that is designed to bypass reasoning and trigger action simply through the matching of pictures to see if this is what it takes to increase sorting efficacy and decrease waste sorting confusion.

3 Research Method

Our researchers used McDonald's hamburger chain restaurant as the object of observation, and believe its waste sorting system has the following problems:

- The symbols are overcomplicated, as it displays body movement, abstract symbols, and both English and Chinese instructions (Fig. 1)
- Even with symbols as guidance the user will nevertheless ponder the properties of the item being sorted, which will lead to conflict with known knowledge of what is and is not recyclable material.
- The level of thinking that this system asks the user to employ still belongs to rationalization, which means the user is required to think about the properties of a waste item which does not produce quick reactions.

Based on the problems discovered, our researchers attempted to shift the thought process of the sorting activity by using a novel conceptual design to minimize the chances of the user thinking about the properties of the waste items, which in turn should also reduce the conflict that may arise between the user's knowledge case and the instructions given on the waste items. The goal will be to simplify the thinking process during sorting, to remove the user from thinking about whether or not an item is recyclable, and focus on matching symbols to the correct sorting bin.

3.1 Experiment Group Design

Our researchers have come up with 3 systems of labels designed to simplify the thinking process. The designs only employ color and circular symbols which are simple triggers of reaction and attention.

Table 2. Label contents of the four testing groups

Testing Groups			Label Contents		
			Packaging	Waste Station	Methods
Reference Label System	A	Recycable		資源回收 垃圾 RECYCLABLE WASTE	Combinational guidance: symbol, and text instructions
		Non-recycable		一般垃圾 GENERAL WASTE	
Experimental Label Systems	B1	Recycable			Color-guided
		Non-recycable			
	B2	Recycable			Symbol-guided
		Non-recycable			
	B3	Recycable			Color-and-Symbol -guided
		Non-recycable			

The three groups are B1: matching colors, B2: matching symbols, and B3, colored symbols. The three systems are designed to bypass the concept of recyclability so that the user will only focus on matching colors and symbols, thus taking away the rational thinking required to judge the recyclability of an item. The original system is labeled 'A', and 'B2', 'B2', and 'B3' makes 4 label systems in total (Table 2).

3.2 Simulated Packaging and Equipment

McDonald's does provide additional receptacles for leftover food and ice, which does not create any sorting issues. Therefore, our researchers focused on those food packagings that do get confused. The researchers picked out five items that are often found in a McDonald's meal: 1. Hamburger packaging; 2. French Fries packaging; 3. Drink cups; 4. Drink lids; and 5. Straws. The only item that is recyclable is the cup, while all other items, due to their being coated in oil and the lid being bio-degradable, all belong to normal (non-recycled) waste. To simplify the experiment, the designs and patterns on the packaging have been removed, and their base color is decidedly white. In these five waste items, other than the drink straw which is unsuitable for printing, all the other items in each group follow the current McDonald's practice of printing labels onto the packaging at the exact same size and place. Furthermore, the recycling stations are made in the same dimensions as the ones that McD's currently uses, but they are simplified to having only two openings, each with their corresponding image of recyclables or general waste. The recycling stations also have white base color (Fig. 2).

Fig. 2. One example of the simulated packagings and recycling station.

3.3 Subjects and Procedure

The experiment consists of four groups of 30 participants. The participants consists of college and post-graduate students, half of both gender. The experiment was conducted in a well-lit laboratory. For the sorting activity, the operating time, accuracy, and the participant's subjective feedback are recorded. The procedure of the experiment is as follows:

1. Before the experiment, the images on the recycling stations are covered up with a black non-see-through cloth. The participants are asked to hold their trays containing randomly assigned mock food packaging while standing in front of the recycling station.
2. The participants then are informed of the objective of the experiment. They are told that this is an experiment for the observation of the fast food restaurant sorting process. They are asked to sort the food packaging items on their trays according to the labels found. They are not to raise questions or ask for assistance once the experiment commences.

3. The experiment is timed. The time starts when the black cloth is removed revealing the waste sorting image and ends when the participant has completed sorting and pout the tray on top of the recycling station, completing the experiment.
4. The researchers record sorting period time, sorting accuracy, and have the participants fill out a questionnaire that asks the participants for their subjective feedback. The questionnaire is designed to understand if the participants felt the sorting system was easy to use, easy to comprehend, quick decision making, and comfort to use, each evaluation with a score from 1 to 5.

4 Results

4.1 Sorting Time and Error Times

From the sorting time data it is obvious that the three B groups required significantly less time than the control group, requiring less than half the time it took the control group (Fig. 3).

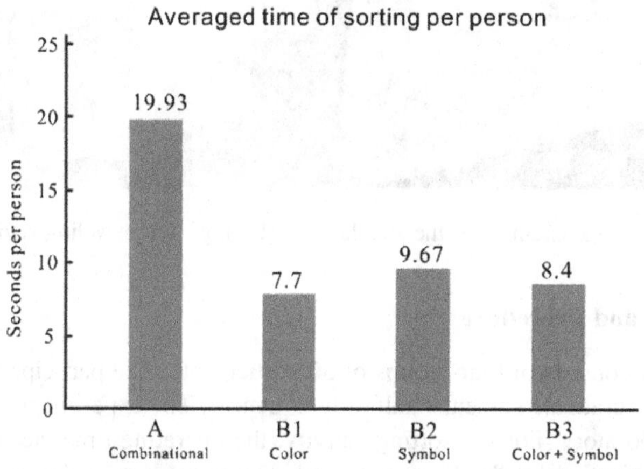

Fig. 3. Averaged sorting time of four testing groups

In terms of accuracy, the A control group with 30 people accumulated a total of 37 mistakes, while the B1 group had 1 mistake, and B2 and B3 group had 3 mistakes each (Fig. 4). In other words, each participant in A control group makes an average of 1.23 mistakes and those in the B1 group makes an average of 0.03 mistakes. And those in B2 and B3 groups made an average of 0.1 mistakes. All the B groups performed vastly more accurately than group A.

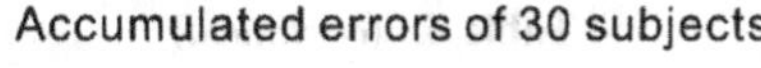

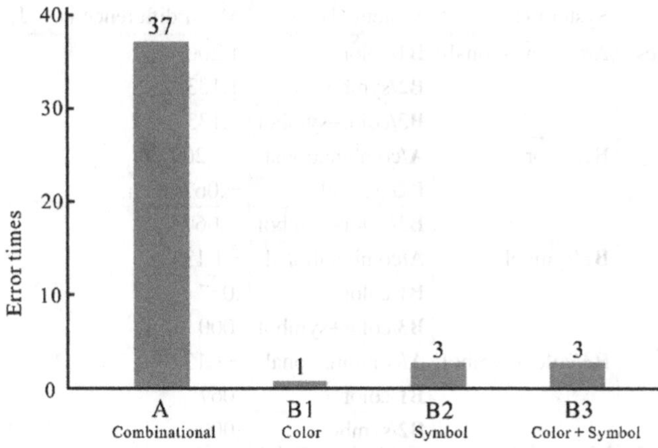

Fig. 4. Accumulated error numbers of four testing groups

ANOVA values were calculated for figures from the four groups, and the results were significant (Table 3). Turkey post hoc tests were conducted to compare the four sets of figures, and the results show that the three new designs were significantly different to the control in terms of sorting time, accuracy, and mistakes made. However, there were no significant differences between the three new designs. Statistical figures are as Table 4.

Table 3. ANOVA test for four guiding systems

	F value	Sig.
Sorting time	50.786	.000*
Error times	34.540	.000*

*The mean difference is significant at 0.05 level.

Table 4. Post hoc test by Tukey for comparing sorting time and error times

	System (I)	System (J)	Mean difference (I − J)	Sig.
Sorting time	**A**/combinational	**B1**/color	12.233*	.000
		B2/symbol	10.267*	.000
		B3/color+symbol	11.533*	.000
	B1/color	**A**/combinational	−12.233*	.000
		B2/symbol	−1.967	.313
		B3/color+symbol	−.700	.927
	B2/symbol	**A**/combinational	−10.267*	.000
		B1/color	1.967	.313
		B3/color+symbol	1.267	.682
	B3/color+symbol	**A**/combinational	−11.533*	.000
		B1/color	.700	.927
		B2/symbol	−1.267	.682

(continued)

Table 4. (*continued*)

	System (I)	System (J)	Mean difference (I − J)	Sig.
Error times	A/combinational	**B1**/color	1.200*	.000
		B2/symbol	1.133*	.000
		B3/color+symbol	1.133*	.000
	B1/color	**A**/combinational	−1.200*	.000
		B2/symbol	−.067	.964
		B3/color+symbol	−.067	.964
	B2/symbol	A/combinational	−1.133*	.000
		B1/color	.067	.964
		B3/color+symbol	.000	1.000
	B3/color+symbol	**A**/combinational	−1.133*	.000
		B1/color	.067	.964
		B2/symbol	.000	1.000

Note: *The mean difference is significant at 0.05 level.

4.2 Evaluation of Subjective Feedback

Once the participants have completed the sorting task, the researchers gave them four criteria on subjective experience (ease of use, ease of comprehension, quick decision making, and comfort of use) for evaluation with a score of 1 to 5. The average score for the four criteria are distributed as indicated on Fig. 5. It is apparent that the four criteria of the three B groups scored significantly better than those of the A control group, and B1 with color guided method has the best performance in all criteria.

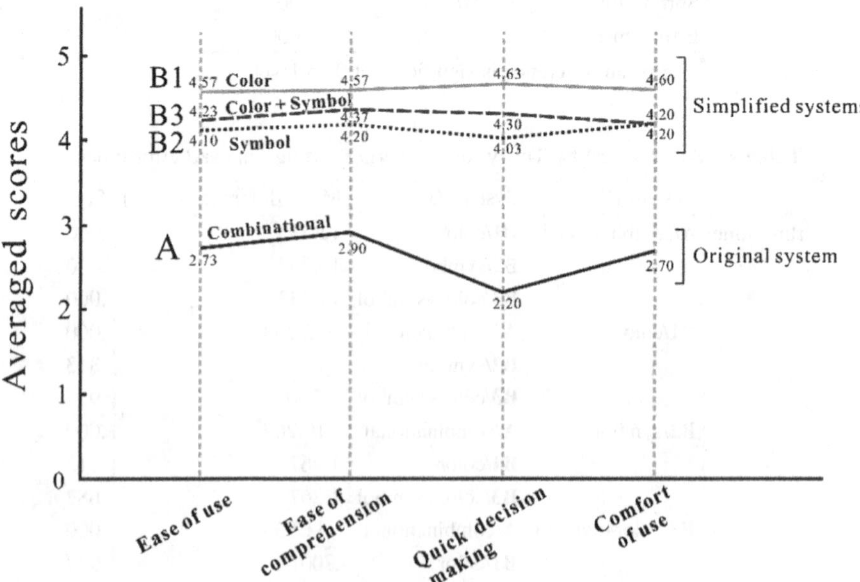

Fig. 5. Averaged score of the subjective evaluation for all testing groups.

5 Discussions

Our experiments show that all 3 designs are superior to the current system that McD's uses in terms of both time saved and increase in accuracy. The subjective feedback parameters such as easy of use and quick decision making are also better than the original recycling system. There are no significant differences of parameters between the three new designs, most likely since the objective of all of them was to reduce the amount of reading of the object the user has to conduct. When the information received and the decision making needed are both simplified, operational efficiency can be dramatically improved as well as the operation itself greatly simplified. The initial results from the experiment confirmed that the simplification of the thinking process can reduce user confusion, making an activity like sorting more efficient as well as more accurate.

In the experiment, the same instructions were given to the four participant groups, which is to simply sort the items according to the labels. However, since the meanings contained in the labels had a fundamental change, the results were drastically different. The original labels permeate our lives and when users see the type of instructions given will habitually activate the thinking process. Yet the user's knowledge base of what constitutes recyclable or non-recyclable waste and the correct knowledge required to sort the way they asked to conduct can be quite different. This means that the user is unable to trust the labels and instructions provided, and this generates confusion.

On the other hand, the original waste sorting system intended to pass on various messages, such as the action of waste disposal, the properties of recycling, and even the nuances of a bilingual text-based instructions. Yet what was not realized is that the majority when sorting waste tend to want to complete the task quickly, and there are increasingly fewer individuals who would take the time out to read the sorting instructions in detail instead of completing the task quickly by applying intuition or experience. The overwhelming amount of information provided had unintentionally confused the users, and this is apparent in the subjective evaluation data. It is worth bringing up that many of the participants of the three new design groups, once they're done with the surveys, would ask the researchers out of curiosity what the meaning of the images provided were. This suggests that while the participants were conducting a sorting task that required them to think less, they are not applying knowledge regarding the recyclability of items to the actions, and are instead completing the task almost without any thinking, which did allow them to complete the sorting task with high accuracy. This confirms that allowing users to sort using intuition and imprecise knowledge is actually a method that achieves high accuracy.

6 Conclusion and Suggestions

From what seems like a simple experiment with a symbol matching activity, this research has demonstrated that the simplification of the thinking process can transform what was once a rational "categorization" task into a simple "matching" task, which has the advantage of greatly enhancing sorting efficiency and task affinity. This confirms that, to achieve a given task accurately, the user doesn't necessarily need the concrete knowledge. Our research provides those who work in recycling related fields a way of redesigning a sorting system to make it more simple. On the other hand due to the limitations in manpower and funding, the study was not able to fully explore all of the details or conduct an investigation on a larger scale. The following are future research suggestions for those who are interested in this topic:

1. The task of waste sorting to achieve recycling involves more than the efficacy of sorting. Reaching a balance between simplifying the task of sorting and allowing the user to be educated on the knowledge related to sorting is what will achieve a waste sorting system design that is the most ideal.
2. This research removed elements of an assortment of color and images design elements on food packaging. The mock items simulating waste food packaging were all white, which means that the participants found the images right away. These items in the real world are usually abundant in colorful and image-filled design elements, which potentially make the task of locating a recycling related image more difficult. Future research can be conducted to investigate where, how, and what size to place recycling related images taking these design elements into account.
3. This research purposefully used images that are extreme abstract for the experiment, and yet in reality the ubiquity of conventional recycling symbols should also be considered. How these symbols can be incorporated into a novel sorting process may provide a challenge in practice.

References

1. Bastick, A.: Intuition: How We Think and Act. Wiley, Chichester (1982)
2. Blackler, A.L., Popovic, V., Mahar, D.P.: The nature of intuitive use of products: an experimental approach. Des. Stud. **24**(6), 491–506 (2003)
3. Blackler, A.L., Popovic, V., Mahar, D.P.: Investigating users' intuitive interaction with complex artifacts. Appl. Ergon. **41**, 72–92 (2010)
4. Blackler, A.L., Popovic, V., Mahar, D.P., Gudur, R.R.: Facilitating intuitive interaction with complex artifacts. Design Research Society (DRS), Chulalongkorn University, Bangkok, Thailand, 1–4 July 2012 (2012)
5. Eysenck, H.J.: Genius: The Natural History of Creativity. Cambridge University Press, Cambridge (1995)
6. Fullera, S., Carrascoa, M.: Exogenous attention and color perception: performance and appearance of saturation and hue. Vis. Res. **46**(23), 4032–4047 (2006)
7. Gelman, R. Au, T.K.F.: Perceptual and Cognitive Development (Handbook of Perception and Cognition). Academic Press, Richmond (1996). ISBN 10: 0122796608
8. Hsu, T.F.: Graphical symbols: the effects of information loads on recognition performance, Doctoral Dissertation. National Taiwan University of Science and Technology, 63 (2010, unpublished)
9. Johansen, M.K., Palmeri, T.J.: Are there representational shifts during category learning. Cogn. Psychol. **45**, 482–553 (2002)
10. Jung, C.G.: Psychological Types, Collected Works of C.G. Jung, vol. 6. Princeton University Press, Princeton (1971). ISBN 0-691-01813-8

11. Kahneman, D.: Thinking Fast and Slow. Penguin Group, UK (2012)
12. Klein, G.: Sources of Power: How People Make Decisions. MIT Press, Cambridge (1998)
13. Lamberts, K., Goldstone, R.J.: Handbook of Cognition, pp. 183–184. SAGE (2005)
14. Lin, Y.C., Guan, S.S.: A study on the relationship between color and form of product. Ind. Des. **28**(2), 148–153 (2000)
15. Markman, E.M. Callanan, M.A.: An analysis of hierarchical classification. In: Sternberg, R. J. (ed.) Advances in the Psychology of Human Intelligence, vol. 2, pp. 325–365 (1984)
16. Moggridge, B.: Naoto Fukasawa. Phaidon Press, US (2014)
17. Newell, A.: Unified Theories of Cognition. Harvard University Press, Cambridge (1990)
18. Norman, D.A.: The Design of Everyday. Perseus Books Group (2013)
19. Otgaar, H., Alberts, H., Cuppens, L.: Ego depletion results in an increase in spontaneous false memories. Conscious. Cogn. **21**(4), 1673–1680 (2012)
20. Raskin, J.: Intuitive equals familiar. Commun. ACM **37**(9), 17 (1994)
21. Rasmussen, J.: Deciding and doing: decision making in natural contexts. In: Klein, G., Orasanu, J., Calderwood, R., Zsambok, C.E. (eds.) Decision Making in Action: Models and Methods, Ablex, Norwood, pp. 159–171 (1993)
22. Rosch, E., Mervis, C.B., Gray, W.D., Johnson, D.M., Boyes-Braem, P.: Basic objects in natural categories. Cogn. Psychol. **8**, 382–439 (1976)
23. Spool, J.: What makes a design seem intuitive? User Interface Engineering (UIE), 10 January 2005. http://uie.com/articles/design_intuitive/
24. Zhu, J.Y.: Color Science and Match Colors. China Youth Publishing Group (2004). ISBN 957202731X

The Research on Quantificational Method of Chromatic-Light Emotion in Automotive Interior Lighting

Jiaying Lu(✉) and Jiong Fu

Institute of Design Trend, Design School,
Shanghai Jiao Tong University, Shanghai, China
lujiaying@sjtu.edu.cn

Abstract. With the development of new lighting technologies, automotive interior ambient light extends from basic Illumination function to comfort and personalization function. However, the application of ambient lamp light lacks theoretical support and scientific quantitative basis, and has great blindness and randomness. How to use the emotion and preference aroused by chromatic-light scientifically is the key to solve the above problems. In the experiment, 12 chromatic-light stimuli were output with chroma and hue as variables. The emotions aroused by light were quantitatively studied by experimental psychological methods. By factor analysis, we obtained three monochrome affective factors: activity, evaluation and adaptability. In the correlation analysis of the influence of chromatic-light attributes on emotion, it was found that the chroma had the greatest influence on chromatic-light emotion, followed by the hue of chromatic-light. By analyzing the preference of chromatic-light, we find that yellow light is preferred.

Keywords: Automobile interior · Chromatic-light emotion · Chromatic-light preference · Quantitative research

1 Introduction

As the gaps of automobiles quality are becoming smaller and smaller, automobile interior decoration has become a key factor affecting consumers 'car purchase decision. As a part of interior decoration, interior lighting has attracted more and more attention. Functional ambient lighting system can meet the sensory needs of passengers in different environments. Car lights play a role in not only basic interior and exterior lighting but also customer experience and personalized areas.

The use of ambient lamp can convey the perception of physical space within the composition, Background design language, heighten the atmosphere in the car, improve the driving experience and the grade of the car, and play an important role in brand recognition, feature creation, style determination and many other aspects. Chromatic-light raises peoples' general concern, because it can bring people abundant emotion and emotional experience. With the development and application of new

A. Marcus and W. Wang (Eds.): HCII 2019, LNCS 11584, pp. 32–43, 2019.
https://doi.org/10.1007/978-3-030-23541-3_3

lighting technology, it provides a broader space for the creation of automobile interior atmosphere. However, due to the lack of basic research on the emotional recognition of chromatic-light, there is a great blindness and randomness in the design of automotive interior ambient light.

At present, the design of interior ambient lights of automobiles mainly relies on the experience and preferences of designer (such as lighting supervisors and lighting designers). Users usually choose their preferred ambient lights from the given lighting conditions. For example, the brand-new Mercedes-Benz E-Class car provides 64 different color ambient lights for owners to choose. However, this experiential feeling cannot be expressed in a scientific or quantitative way, not to say be used for reference by others. Furthermore, customers' inappropriate use of color and brightness will result in lighting effect which is contrary to the original intention of the design.

Then the fundamental reason for the above problems is the lack of a theoretical support and quantitative reference basis to guide the design of ambient light based on chromatic-light emotional perception. Literature studies mainly focus on two aspects: lighting emotional perception and color emotional perception.

Many studies have confirmed that light affects circadian rhythms, moods, preferences and cognition. In 2008, Vogels developed a method called Atmosphere Metrics, which quantifies the environmental atmosphere experienced by human observers through semantic differences [1–4]. She carried out a series of experiments, using factor analysis and other data analysis methods to compare the experimental results. The experimental results show that atmospheric perception can be defined in at least two aspects: comfort and liveliness. By changing the illumination condition variables and accumulating more data in different experimental environments, two other dimensions were found: tension and separation.

Russell and Pratt try to describe the concept of "emotional quality attributable to the environment" [5]. They developed a two-dimensional bipolar space, which can be described by two orthogonal dimensions: pleasant - unpleasant and exciting - sleepy or exciting - gloomy and painful, tense - relaxed.

However, most of the experiments defining lighting atmosphere perception use traditional lighting technology, which is different from automotive interior ambient lights. The ability of LED to adjust spectrum makes this research pay attention to the theory of color application at the same time. Since Spearman C. founded factor analysis method and Osgood C. E. established semantics difference analysis method, the research of color emotion has become more scientific and systematic. The single-color emotion research mainly focuses on extracting a few potential factors by SD method and factor analysis method to generalize the emotional scale of color [6–12], [13–15]. Although the scale of color emotions used by various researchers is different in quantity and content, some similar color emotional factors, such as warmth, activity and evaluation, have been founded.

However, from previous studies, it is not difficult to find that all the studies are only aimed at the small angle of object color observation and evaluation experiments. And these research results have only been expanded in fashion, fabric printing and dyeing, fashion color and other fields. It is unknown whether the quantitative research results of color emotion can be applied to the observation conditions of light color in automobile interior atmosphere.

With the above in mind, this study uses factor analysis method and semantic difference analysis method to study interior atmosphere perception under monochrome illumination of automotive interior atmosphere lamp, quantitatively measures and parameterizes the color emotion aroused by it through experimental psychology method, finds out the cognitive regularity characteristics of people's color light through statistical analysis, and obtains the basic emotional scale of chromatic-light perception.

2 Method

2.1 Experimental Setup

Commercial white LEDs and a Telelumen® multi-LED system was used in the present study as test light sources. The latter is a lighting system comprising 16 narrow-band LEDs, which is capable of constructing a spectral power distribution (SPD) of many light sources.

The material atmosphere of automobile interior was simulated by automobile central control plastic parts (length 0.7 m, width 0.3 m), automobile interior leather samples (length 0.4 m, width 0.4 m) and automobile interior fabric samples (length 0.4 m, width 0.4 m). In this study, the material atmosphere of automobile interior was used as the observation object under ambient lighting environment. Material samples are provided by automotive interior suppliers, and the area ratio of different materials in the samples is the same as the proportion of practical one. The observer sat one meter away from the experimental device for observation and evaluation, as shown in Fig. 1.

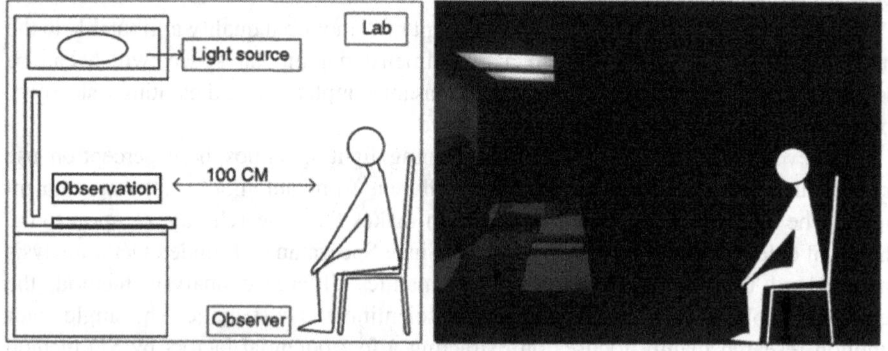

Fig. 1. Environment for visual assessment.

2.2 Lighting Parameters

With hue and Chroma as variables, there are 12 conditions in the whole experiment. Table 1 lists the experimental parameters of chromatic-light properties used under each condition. Because in the design of automobile interior ambient lamp, the brightness can be adjusted by users themselves, and the brightness range is small, only 0–25 cd/m^2. So, in this experiment, only chroma and hue are variables, and the brightness is kept at about 25 cd/m^2.

Table 1. Specifications of the twelve experimental conditions.

Conditions	Symbols	L*	C*	h*	a*	b*
1	C71C	25.5	71	205.72	−3.85	−70.90
2	C60C	24.4	60	205.72	−3.26	−59.91
3	C100 M	25.1	100	337.3	−40.89	−91.26
4	C60 M	25.1	60	337.3	−24.53	−54.76
5	C100Y	25.3	100	103.67	65.56	75.51
6	C60Y	25.6	60	103.67	39.33	45.31
7	C100R	25.1	100	36.26	13.13	−99.13
8	C60R	24.0	60	36.26	7.88	−59.48
9	C100G	24.8	100	148.75	−45.79	−88.90
10	C60G	24.8	60	148.75	−27.48	−53.34
11	C100B	25.2	100	305.72	−55.24	−83.36
12	C60B	24.8	60	305.72	−33.15	−50.01

2.3 Observers

In the experiment, 26 observers including 13 males and 13 females. Their ages ranged from 20 to 25 years with a mean of 23.2 years. They were all Chinese students at the Shanghai Jiao Tong University. All of them had normal color vision according to the Ishihara test.

2.4 Questionnaire

We designed a questionnaire, referring to the problems used in the study of lighting atmosphere perception and color emotion, to study the interior atmosphere perception under monochrome illumination of automobile interior atmosphere lamp. Ten native Chinese (university staff or students) with normal eyesight participated in the study. Participants were asked to choose perceptual terms describing the experimental environment. It is common in Chinese words that one word can have multiple meanings. To make sure that the meaning of the scale was precise, word pairs are used in this study.

The questionnaire uses a total of 52 word pairs (bipolar scale). As shown in Appendix 1, the translation from English to Chinese may not be accurate. However, by using word pairs instead of single words, we can make sure that each Chinese term has a clear definition. In addition, the questionnaire asked the subjects to describe subjectively each monochrome light condition with three aspects: brightness (high, medium, low), chroma (high, medium, low), such as "this is a purple light with medium brightness and low chroma".

2.5 Procedure

The observer entered the laboratory and participated under independent lighting condition (D65 luminance: 25 cd/m^2, LED). This is a neutral condition, different from any experimental condition. A 30-s neutral condition occurs during the transition between two continuous conditions to eliminate the visual effects of the previous monochrome light. After each experimental condition appeared, the observer responded to the questionnaire after 30 s of adaptation. Each observer was randomly assigned a total of 13 conditions (12 different monochrome light conditions plus repetition condition D65).

In the experiment, for each experimental condition, the observer used 52 emotional scales to describe the presented color stimulus with five levels of semantic difference, and then evaluated the next color stimulus in turn. The experimenters asked questions orally and each observer answered them orally. This was done to reduce the workload for each observer and to avoid the visual adaptation caused by white paper used to record data.

3 Results and Discussions

3.1 Gender Differences in Perception

Statistical analysis of the experimental data was carried out to investigate the difference of perception of monochrome light atmosphere between male and female observers. Variance analysis showed that there were significant gender differences in conditions C100M (P = 0.000), C100Y (P = 0.001), C60Y (P = 0.000), C100B (P = 0.000), C60B (P = 0.000).

Combining with the subjective description of monochrome light, we found that men are more sensitive to brightness than women. Therefore, under the condition of C100 M, men generally believe that the monochrome light has high brightness and more stimulation. In the monochrome light descriptions of yellow and purple phases, we find that men tend to perceive warm red and yellow phases, and their descriptions of yellow and purple phases are generally accurate. Women are prone to feel the cold blue-green color. Most women think that yellow light is biased towards green light and purple light is biased towards blue-white light.

3.2 Factor Analysis

In order to improve the feasibility of future wider color gamut monochrome experiments, we used dimensionality reduction factor to simplify the emotional scale. We used Principal component analysis to extract factors from 52 affective scales, and used the maximum variance method of vertical orthogonal rotation to perform factor rotation. Seven common factors were obtained. The affective scale of the same common factor is clustered by Pearson product difference correlation analysis, and the affective scale is finally reduced to 26 pairs. According to Osgood's Semantic Difference Method, these 26 pairs of emotional scales are divided into three groups according to their semantics, as shown in Table 2.

Table 2. 26 emotion scales in the experiment.

Factors	Emotion scales
Activity	Cool-warm, cheerful-detached, feminine-masculine, lovely-sharp, rational-emotional, dynamic-static, calm-angry, relaxed-nervous, keen-dull
Potentiality	Comfortable-uncomfortable, inviting-isolated, pleasant-unpleasant, peaceful-defiant, active-inactive, inspiring-dejected, bright-dim, shallow-deep, dedicated-abstracted
Evaluation	Simple-luxurious, elegant-rugged, deluxe-low, stable-disturbed, beautiful-ugly, advanced-backward, like-dislike, traditional-modern

26 pairs of subjective evaluation experimental data of emotional scale were analyzed. KMO is the KMO value of Kaiser-Meyer-Olkin sampling suitability measurement statistic. The larger the KMO value, the more common factors between variables, the more suitable for factor analysis. The KMO value here is 0.914 and KMO > 0.9, which is suitable for factor analysis.

Table 3 lists the factor loads of each scale. Five main factors were extracted from the principal component analysis, accounting for 70.423% of variance. They were labeled as factors 1 to 5, with differences of 33.585%, 20.619%, 8.027%, 4.216% and 3.976%, respectively. For each factor, eigenvalues are calculated to indicate the importance of the factor. The factors with more than one eigenvalue are all listed in Table 3, although some variances are small (the variance of factor 4–5 is less than 7%).

Table 3. Factor loadings of atmosphere dimensions using 26 scales.

Scales	Total variance				
	Factors 1	Factors 2	Factors 3	Factors 4	Factors 5
Stable-disturbed	**0.808**	−0.276	0.086	0.043	0.078
Peaceful-defiant	**0.798**	−0.262	−0.091	0.104	−0.038
Relaxed-tense	**0.792**	0.265	0.095	0.196	0.046
Comfortable-uncomfortable	**0.788**	−0.076	0.096	0.300	−0.002
Pleasant-unpleasant	**0.762**	0.260	0.302	0.145	−0.050
Like-dislike	**0.704**	−0.024	0.234	0.326	0.194
Inviting-isolated	**0.680**	0.420	−0.082	0.190	−0.103
Beautiful-ugly	**0.677**	0.112	0.407	0.275	0.203
Elegant-rugged	**0.624**	−0.019	0.416	0.129	0.031
Calm-angry	**0.529**	−0.495	0.254	−0.075	0.135
Cool-warm	−0.034	**−0.891**	0.126	−0.073	0.013
Feminine-masculine	−0.013	**0.853**	−0.056	−0.094	−0.218
Cheerful-detached	0.141	**0.834**	0.084	0.091	−0.013
Lovely–sharp	0.314	**0.793**	−0.052	−0.146	−0.100
Rational-emotional	0.205	**−0.781**	0.114	0.209	0.164
Dynamic-static	−0.181	**0.664**	0.046	0.331	0.025

(*continued*)

Table 3. (*continued*)

Scales	Total variance				
	Factors 1	Factors 2	Factors 3	Factors 4	Factors 5
Simple-luxurious	0.466	**−0.541**	−0.343	0.239	−0.135
Advanced-backward	0.391	−0.029	**0.692**	0.239	0.140
Traditional-modern	0.273	−0.008	**−0.664**	−0.095	0.330
Deluxe-low	0.485	−0.054	**0.657**	0.086	0.189
Keen-dull	0.333	−0.316	**0.587**	0.421	−0.109
Bright-dim	0.273	0.023	0.213	**0.814**	−0.015
Active-inactive	0.435	0.347	0.156	**0.590**	−0.046
Inspiring-dejected	0.314	−0.107	0.448	**0.477**	−0.019
Dedicated-abstracted	0.394	−0.277	0.135	**0.459**	0.267
Shallow-deep	−0.038	0.267	0.037	−0.006	**−0.858**
% of Variance	33.585%	20.619%	8.027%	4.216%	3.976%
Cumulative%	33.585%	54.204%	62.231%	66.447%	70.423%

Considering the low variance explanations of factors 4 and 5, only factor 1–3 are considered as important perceptual dimensions. These will be used for the following analysis. It can be seen from Table 3 that the high load of Factor 1 is related to the sense of stability, relaxation, comfort and aesthetics. For factor 2, cool - warm, feminine - masculine, enthusiasm - indifferent, lovely - sharp, rational - emotional, dynamic - static, simple - luxurious, these emotional scales have a high factor load. For factor 3, advanced - backward, traditional - modern, advanced - low, keen - dull, these emotional scales have a high factor load. The three factors are adaptability factor, vitality factor and evaluation factor.

3.3 The Influence of Chromatic-Light Parameters

Pearson product difference correlation analysis of color attributes (luminosity value L*, chroma value C* and chroma angle H*) with emotional scales and emotional factors of color light will reveal the full impact of lighting conditions on scales. However, a complete design (2 (brightness) 2 (CCT) 6 (hue) will require at least 24 monochrome conditions. In this study, only chroma and hue were taken as variables, including all 52 groups of emotional scales. All 12 conditions had the same illumination (about 25 cd/m^2), two chromas (high and low) and six hues (RGBCMY). Therefore, the influence of lightness value L* on emotional scales was very limited.

Table 4 lists the scales significantly affected by the parameters, with significant effects ($p < 0.05$) and almost significant effects ($0.05 < P5 < 0.1$) marked in bold. The results show that the chroma values of chromatic-light are not significantly correlated with the six emotional scales of “cold-warm”, “feminized-masculinized”, “warm-indifferent”, "lovely-sharp", "dynamic-static", "simple-luxurious". They are all significantly correlated with other emotional scales, especially with evaluation and adaptability factors. It can be seen that the chroma of chromatic-light has an important influence on the evaluation of the overall atmosphere of automobile interior.

The hue of chromatic-light mainly affects the emotional scale of the evaluation factors. It is worth noting that many chromatic-light emotions are affected by the comprehensive properties of chromatic-light, such as the emotional scale of the evaluation factors and the "graceful-rough" of the adaptability factors. In order to create the emotional atmosphere of the above-mentioned chromatic-light, both hue and chroma of the chromatic-light should be taken into account. The "beautiful-ugly" emotional scale is affected by three attributes at the same time, that is, people's evaluation of the beautiful chromatic-light is also affected by hue, chroma, and luminosity.

Table 4. Correlation analysis of chromatic-light emotions and parameters.

Factor	Scales	Chromatic-light parameters		
		L*	C*	H*
Adaptability	Stable-disturbed	0.063	0.241**	-0.038
	Peaceful-defiant	0.083	0.213**	0.010
	Relaxed-tense	0.024	0.165**	0.001
	Comfortable-uncomfortable	0.070	0.242**	−0.053
	Pleasant-unpleasant	0.055	0.157**	−0.038
	Like-dislike	0.032	0.267**	−0.054
	Inviting–isolated	0.064	0.077	0.048
	Beautiful-ugly	0.096*	0.297**	−0.129**
	Elegant-rugged	0.050	0.218**	−0.147**
	Calm-angry	0.076	0.253**	−0.098*
Activity	Cool-warm	0.040	−0.040	0.166**
	Feminine–masculine	0.106*	−0.051	−0.039
	Cheerful-detached	0.012	−0.041	0.063
	Lovely–sharp	0.044	0.059	0.026
	Rational-emotional	0.031	0.144**	−0.038
	Dynamic–static	−0.019	−0.006	−0.023
	Simple–luxurious	−0.083	0.029	0.072
Evaluation	Advanced–backward	0.021	0.171**	−0.190**
	Traditional-modern	0.068	−0.078	0.119*
	Deluxe–low	0.045	0.249**	−0.173**
	Keen–dull	0.015	0.145**	−0.132**

Note: * Relevance reached $P < 0.05$ significant level (double tail test); ** Relevance reached $P < 0.01$ significant level (double tail test).

To sum up, the chroma of chromatic-light is an important factor affecting the emotional expression of chromatic-light in automobile interior atmosphere, followed by the hue of chromatic-light. In this experiment, the brightness of chromatic-light is not a variable, and its influence will be further discussed in future experiments as a variable.

3.4 Analysis of Chromatic-Light Preference

We used Pearson product difference correlation coefficient r to analyze the correlation between chromatic-light preference and other 25 chromatic-light emotions. The results in Table 5 show that there is a high correlation between chromatic-light preference and chromatic-light emotion "comfort-discomfort", "beauty-ugliness". The correlation coefficients are all above 0.7. In addition, it has a high correlation with the chromatic-light emotions such as "happy-unhappy", "relaxed-tense", "positive-negative",

Table 5. The relationship between chromatic-light preference and other scales.

Scales	Beautiful-	Cool-	Bright-	Pleasant-	Relaxed-
/	.837**	.125**	.358**	.528**	.536**
Scales	Active-	Inspiring-	Keen-	Dedicated-	Peaceful-
/	.616**	.411**	.323**	.414**	.583**
Scales	Comfortable-	Calm-	Stable-	Inviting-	Cheerful-
/	.706**	.449**	.568**	.427**	.179**
Scales	Feminine-	Lovely-	Rational-	Deluxe-	Elegant-
/	.095*	.239**	.166**	.628**	.590**
Scales	Advanced-	Traditional -	Dynamic-	Simple -	Shallow-
/	.333**	−0.012	.180**	0.061	-0.054

"peaceful-provocative", "stable-restless", "high-level-low", "elegant-rough". However, there is little or no correlation between "feminization-masculinization", "tradition-modernity", "simplicity-luxury", "superficiality-depth" and chromatic-light preference.

That is to say, when a color light environment can arouse people's feeling of comfortable, beautiful, happy, relaxed, positive, peaceful, elegant and other emotion, then the chromatic-light environment is adorable, on the contrary, if the chromatic-light arouses the above negative emotional feelings, then the chromatic-light is not adorable.

Linear regression was used to analyze the relationship between monochrome light preference and affective factors in different hues. The results showed that high-chroma red light could evoke strong positive feelings of vigorous emotional factors. Low-chroma red light can evoke positive feelings of some evaluative emotional factors, such as "high-low". High-chroma yellow light evokes a better sense of adaptability and intimacy, while low-chroma yellow light does not produce significant emotional response. High-chroma green light makes people respond strongly to adaptive emotional feelings and is prone to evoke provocative and uncomfortable feelings. Low-chroma blue light is more likely to evoke positive dynamic emotional feelings and adaptive emotional feelings, and is considered to be static and elegant chromatic-light. Purple light can cause positive evaluative emotional feelings, in addition, low-chroma purple light can arouse adaptive feelings.

To sum up, the hue and chroma of chromatic-light have a great influence on active emotional feelings. Warm chromatic-light causes positive active emotion, while cold chromatic-light causes negative active emotion. The evaluative emotional feeling of chromatic-light is mainly affected by the hue of chromatic-light. The evaluative emotional feeling aroused by yellow and green chromatic-light is weak, while the evaluative emotional feeling aroused by purple chromatic-light is stronger. As for the adaptive emotional feeling, it is mainly affected by the chroma of chromatic-light. Thus, in the actual design of automobile interior ambient lamp, when a chromatic-light source is selected to create atmosphere, the desired atmosphere can be achieved as long as the chroma and hue of chromatic-light are controlled.

4 Conclusion

The purpose of this study is to study the perception of interior atmosphere under monochrome light of automobile interior atmosphere lamp, reveal the differences between different genders, and finally find out the influence of color parameters on interior atmosphere perception.

By quantifying 12 monochrome light stimuli, visual evaluation experiments were carried out on 52 chromatic-light emotional scales. Through principal component analysis and correlation analysis clustering, 26 emotional scales were finally obtained for experimental analysis. Through factor analysis, three affective factors were obtained: activity, evaluation, adaptability.

In addition, the relationship between chroma, hue and chromatic-light emotion is also analyzed. The results show that the chroma of the chromatic-light has the greatest influence on the chromatic-light emotion in this study, followed by the hue of the chromatic-light. In this study, the subjects' favorite pure color is yellow light, and the least favorite pure color is green light.

In the design of automotive interior ambient lamp, the brightness can usually be adjusted by the user himself, and the range of brightness is small, so it is not a variable in this study, we will do further exploration in future experiments. In addition, in visual evaluation, due to the limitation of sample size, the conclusion of chromatic-light preference differences caused by regional and age differences cannot be well supported. In future research, the capacity of different samples should be increased, and we will study the chromatic-light preference differences in depth.

Appendix 1

No	Scales in English	Scales in Chinese	No	Scales in English	Scales in Chinese
1	**uninhibited**-inhibited	自由的-拘束的	27	bright-dim	明亮的-昏暗的
2	**exciting**-sag	振奋的-萎靡的	28	keen-dull	敏锐的-迟钝的
3	**pleasant**-unpleasant	愉快的-不快的	29	dedicated-abstracted	令人专注的-无关紧要的
4	elegant-rugged	优雅的-粗犷的	30	arousing-**lethargic**	令人清醒的-昏昏欲睡的
5	close-**terrifying**	向往的-恐惧的	31	rational-emotional	理性的-感性的
6	advanced–backward	先进的-落后的	32	**cool-warm**	凉爽的-温暖的
7	like-dislike	喜欢-不喜欢	33	confident-hesitating	可信赖的-犹豫的
8	artistic-**business-like**	文艺感的-商业感的	34	lovely-sharp	可爱的-锐利的
9	spiritual-vulgar	脱俗的-俗气的	35	optimistic-sad	开朗的-忧郁的
10	natural-artificial	天然的-人工的	36	open	开放的-私密的
11	comfortable-**uncomfortable**	舒适的-不适的	37	energetic-tired	精力充沛的-疲乏的
12	delightful-**oppressive**	舒畅的-压抑的	38	active-inactive	积极的-消极的
13	soft-hard	柔软的-坚实的	39	classical-fashion	古典的-时尚的
14	inviting–isolated	容易接近的-有距离感的	40	deluxe–low	高级的-低级的
15	cheerful-**detached**	热情的-冷漠的	41	noble-tawdry	高贵的-卑俗的
16	busy-deserted	热闹的-冷清的	42	shallow-deep	浮浅的-深沉的
17	fresh-corrupt	清爽的-浑浊的	43	**relaxed-tense**	放松的-紧张的
18	light-colorful	清淡的-浓艳的	44	urban-countryside	都市的-田园的
19	ethereal-heavy	轻的-重的	45	dynamic–static	动态的-静态的
20	strong-weak	强劲的-无力的	46	traditional-modern	传统的-现代的
21	forward-retreat	前进-后退	47	steady-impetuous	沉稳的-浮躁的
22	simple–**luxurious**	朴素的-豪华的	48	calm-angry	冷静的-愤怒的
23	peaceful-defiant	平和的-挑衅的	49	sweet-bitter	甜美的-苦涩的
24	beautiful-ugly	美丽的-丑陋的	50	suitable-unsuitable to automotive interior	适合-不适合（汽车内饰）
25	expand-shrink	膨胀-收缩	51	nimble-clumsy	敏捷的-笨拙的
26	feminine–masculine	女性化的-男性化的	52	stable-disturbed	安定的-不安的

Note: The bold terms marked with an asterisk were used by Vogels.

References

1. Vogels, I.: Atmosphere metrics: development of a tool to quantify experienced atmosphere. In: Westerink, J.M.D.M., Ouwerkerk, M., Overbeek, T.J.M., Pasveer, W.F., de Ruyter, B. (eds.) Probing Experience: From Assessment of User Emotions and Behaviour to Development of Products, pp. 25–41. Springer, Dordrecht (2008). https://doi.org/10.1007/978-1-4020-6593-4_3
2. Vogels, I.: Atmosphere metrics: a tool to quantify perceived atmosphere. In: International Symposium Creating an Atmosphere, Grenoble, France (2008)
3. Vogels, I., Sekulovski, D., Clout, R., Moors, R.A.: Quantitative study on the impact of light on the atmosphere of an environment. In: Yener, A.K., Ozturk, L.D. (eds.) 11th European Lighting Congress on Lux Europa 2009. Turkish National Committee on Illumination, Istanbul, pp. 385–392 (2009)
4. Vogels, I., de Vries, M., van Erp, T.: Effect of coloured light on atmosphere perception. Interim Meeting of the International Colour Association: Colour-Effects and Affects, Stockholm, Sweden. Paper No. 060 (2008)
5. Russell, J.A., Pratt, G.A.: Description of the affective quality attributed to environments. J. Pers. Soc. Psychol. **1980**(38), 311–322 (1980)
6. Eysenck, H.J.: A critical and experimental study of colour preferences. Am. J. Psychol. **54** (3), 385–394 (1941)
7. Guilford, J.P., Smith, P.C.: A system of color-preferences. Am. J. Psychol. **72**(4), 487–502 (1959)
8. Wright, B., Rainwater, L.: The meanings of color. J. Gen. Psychol. **67**(1), 89–99 (1962)
9. Kobayashi, S.: The aim and method of the color image scale. Color Res. Appl. **6**(2), 93–107 (1981)
10. Sato, T.: Quantitative evaluation and categoring of human emotion induced by color. Adv. Color Sci. Technol. **2000**(3), 53–59 (2000)
11. Sato, T., Kajiwara, K., Xin, J.H., et al.: Numerical expression of color emotion and its application. In: 9th Congress of the International Colour Association. International Society for Optics and Photonics, vol. 4421, pp. 409–413 (2002)
12. Ou L C, Luo M R, Woodcock A, et al. A study of colour emotion and colour preference. Part I: Colour emotions for single colours[J]. Color Research & Application, 2004, 29(3): 232-240 (2004)

An Evaluation Method of the Influence of Icon Shape Complexity on Visual Search Based on Eye Tracking

Zijing Luo[1], Chengqi Xue[1(✉)], Yafeng Niu[1,2], Xinyue Wang[1], Bingzheng Shi[3], Lingcun Qiu[3], and Yi Xie[2]

[1] School of Mechanical Engineering, Southeast University, Nanjing 211189, China
ipd_xcq@seu.edu.cn

[2] Science and Technology on Electro-Optic Control Laboratory, Luoyang 471023, China

[3] Shanghai Academy of Spaceflight Technology, Shanghai 201109, China

Abstract. In order to evaluate the icon shape complexity from the aspects of human visual cognition, the present paper summarizes two factors of icon shape affecting visual cognition, and establishes a new formula which can quantify the complexity of two-dimensional icon shape. The outcome of test applying the formula indicates the method has ability to quantify the shape complexity of different icons. Meanwhile, the paper studies the influence of different levels of shape complexity of icon on visual search through eye tracking experiments. The results of the eye tracking experiment show that the level of icon shape complexity should be in a reasonable interval which measured by the formula provided in this paper. Because of the ability to quantify the complexity of the icon,the method can improve the design and the application of icon according to visual cognition.

Keywords: Icon shape complexity · Visual search · Eye tracking · Visual cognition

1 Introduction

With the increasing amount of information carried by the interface, the icon as a general visual information expression form an important part of the human-computer interface, such as a navigation marker in the navigation bar, an abstract representation of an object in the map interface and a function in in the software tool command column. However, due to the lack of systematic evaluation indicators, the icon design is likely to cause over abstract and complicated, which increases the visual search load of users. Therefore, it is necessary to make an objective assessment of the shape complexity of the icon and study its influence on the user's visual search.

Recently, visual complexity research has attracted the attention of scholars in the computer field. Shape analysis containing polygon, image and other actual object is one of important application in this filed. But few people research on quantitative calculation

A. Marcus and W. Wang (Eds.): HCII 2019, LNCS 11584, pp. 44–55, 2019.
https://doi.org/10.1007/978-3-030-23541-3_4

of icon shape complexity, and verify it with behavioral experiments, for the main challenges followed:

(a) Most icons' shapes include plenty of contours which is more complex than a single closed polygon, so there is no standard measurable about visual cognition variable for the calculation like analyzing polygons.
(b) Although many scholars have explained and measured the complexity of icons, few combined the visual cognition of the complexity of icons with the measure of the complexity of icons.

2 Background

The cognitive study on the shape complexity of two-dimensional icons belongs to visual complexity research in the field of cognitive science. Many different fields of scholars have studied the visual complexity of graphics from the aspects of visual cognition and cognitive computing.

Feldman et al. [1] suggested segments of negative curvature (i.e., concave segments) literally carry greater information than do corresponding regions of positive curvature (i.e., convex segments), and calculated the information volume of the closed contour based on the information entropy theory. Lim and Leek [2] believed that the curvature information calculation proposed by Feldman et al. is not suitable for the calculation of smooth curve contours and correct them.

But generally straight lines and curved lines exit in two-dimensional icon outlines, it is difficult to calculate the global information amount by using the curvature. In order to measure the complexity of icon or two-dimensional graphics, some researchers have applied different ways to quantify these objects.

Chen et al. [3] introduced three parameters of global distance entropy, local angle entropy and random traces to calculate the complexity of two-dimensional graphics. Dai et al. [4] selected the local angle entropy, global distance entropy, equivalent circle and adjacent distance to establish the icon complexity regression model which was used to estimate the complexity of the icon. However, they did not consider about the factor that the number of icon outlines has a significant impact on icon complexity.

In the aspect of visual cognition of graphics or icons, the visual complexity of two-dimensional icons is closely related to the way people visually recognize shapes [5]. The brain internally characterizes the shape of two-dimensional graphics by methods like principal component analysis. Meanwhile, the semantic system affects the processing of contour shapes [6].

McDougall et al. [7] defined the more the number or type of elements inside the icon, the higher the complexity of the icon for the complexity of the physical appearance of the icon. And proposed that reducing icon complexity should therefore become a priority in interface design, especially involve a strong search component.

Bertamini and Wagemans [8] concluded the convex contour is the main component of the two-dimensional contour, and the concave contour is the boundary point of each part of the two-dimensional contour, which consumes more attention and contains more information. The complexity of contours needs to be considered suitably as a factor when calculating icon shape complexity.

Wang et al. [9] explored the effect of the thickness and color of the icon on the user's visual search, and found that the efficiency of searching concerning with the location and color, but they did not consider the relationship of shape complexity of icon.

However, few studies apply visual cognitive conclusions to compute icon complexity. This paper proposes an icon complexity calculation which combine the theory of visual cognition and complexity calculation of two-dimensional graphics.

3 Measure of Icon Shape Complexity

3.1 Icon Shape Complexity Definition

According to the research of visual cognition of two-dimensional graphics, we define the complexity of two-dimensional icon which consists of two aspects. The first one is the number of polygon contours of the icon shape, the greater the number of contours, the higher the visual complexity; the second one is the features of the icon's contour, including the angle and the concavity.

It is obviously that human is more acceptable to certain angles, such as 90° and 180° or 0°. As shown in Fig. 1(a), obviously, the two polygons with the same number of angles but not the value of angles have different complexity, and the left one is simpler based on general cognition. So different angles with different amount of information result to different levels of complexity on visual cognition.

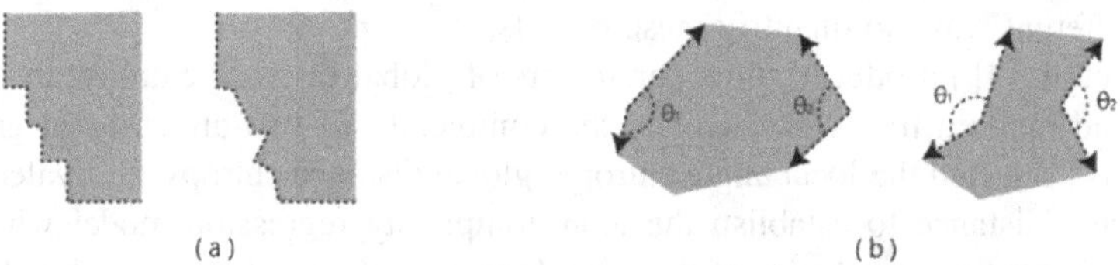

Fig. 1. (a) Two polygons with the same number of angles but not the value of angles. (b) Two polygons with same angle value of adjacent edges but not same concavity.

As for concavity, we believe that the concave contour is a boundary point of different shapes in visual cognition, and the amount of information of it will be larger than the convex contour. The psychological validity of this informational analysis is supported by a host of empirical findings demonstrating the asymmetric way in which the visual system treats regions of positive and negative curvature [1]. For example, as shown in the picture Fig. 1(b), two polygons with same angle value of adjacent edges but not same concavity do not share same complexity towards human visual cognition, and the right one generally is more complicated.

3.2 Calculation Model of Icon Shape Complexity

Based on the Shannon entropy theory [10], we use local rotation angle entropy [1] formula to calculate the entropy value of each contour of icon and cumulative summation. As shown in the following formula, suppose α is a collection of all possible events, $p(\alpha)$ is a collection the probability of occurrence of an event α, then the Shannon entropy of α is defined as

$$H(\alpha) = -p(\alpha)log[p(\alpha)] \tag{1}$$

In order to get local rotation angle entropy, we use the basic algorithm for detecting contours in OpenCV, which is the computer vision library, to detect contours and find icon outline feature points, then filter the feature point set to obtain a simplified icon outline feature point set. The following figure shows an example that the contours of the car icon after optimization which has five-layer outline drawn in different colors. The difference between this algorithm and other detection contour algorithms is that it is sensitive to the angle of the contour. When the contour is a horizontal or vertical line, the algorithm only remains the first and last two endpoints, therefore, it can more accurately detect the contour feature points of the polygon, and it is very useful for the calculation of the angle entropy value. Finally, we use the coordinate values of these contour points to calculate the rotation angle (Fig. 2).

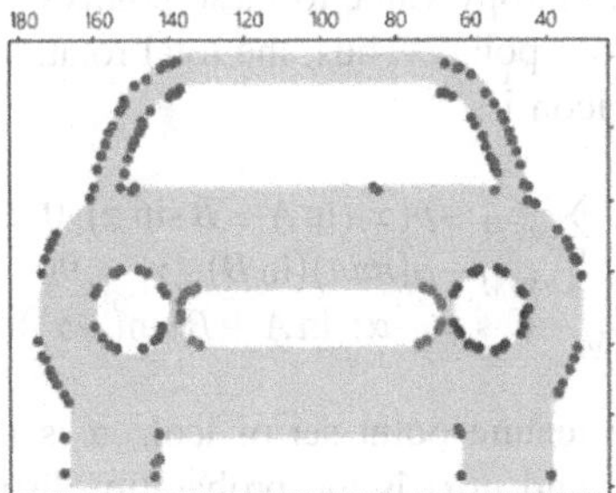

Fig. 2. The size of the car icon used for contour detection is 300 × 300 pixels, and the color of the five feature points represents five contours which are detected by the algorithm. (Color figure online)

Each contour point has a corresponding α, and set the rotation angle α obey the probability distribution function as shown in formula 1, which is similar to the Von Mises probability distribution [1].

$$p(\alpha) = Aexp(B \sin \alpha) \tag{2}$$

Where B is a centralized measure, the larger B is, the more concentrated the distribution is near the position measurement center; A is a constant term (depending on B); the α value corresponding to counterclockwise rotation is positive, which means this point is a convex outline point. On the contrary, the α value corresponding to clockwise rotation is negative, which means this point is a concave outline point. As shown in Fig. 3, the closer α is to 90°, the larger $p(\alpha)$. Conversely, the closer to 0°, the smaller the value.

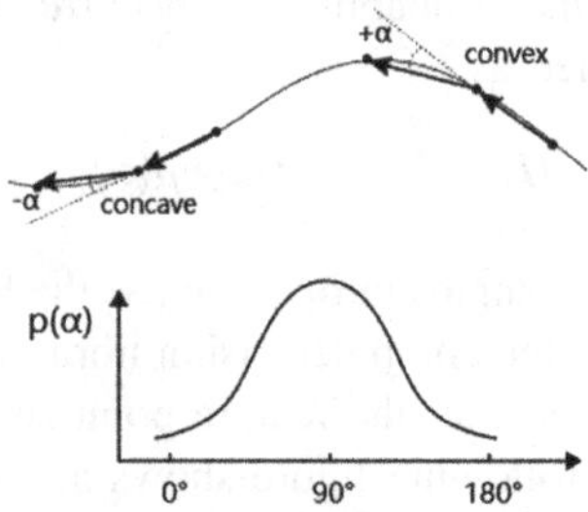

Fig. 3. The contour points with different concavities and convexities corresponding to negative and positive angles and the probability distribution of the rotation angle α.

Therefore, the Shannon entropy corresponding to the rotation angle is $H(\alpha) = p(\alpha)log[Aexp(B\sin\alpha)]$ Obviously, the probability distribution of the rotation angle of each point in the icon outline is independent. To get closer to the complexity definition in Sect. 3.1, we calculate the entropy values of the 90° and 0-degree rotation angles respectively, assign a lower entropy value to these points and assign a higher entropy weight of the concave contour points. Thus, the total rotation angle entropy of one of outline feature point set of icon is

$$h(\alpha) = \begin{cases} \sum_{\alpha \in M} -p(\alpha)(\ln A + B\sin\alpha), 0 < \alpha < 90 \\ \sum_{\alpha \in M} -p(min)(\ln B), |\alpha| = 90, |\alpha| = 0 \\ \sum_{\alpha \in M} -C * p(-\alpha)(\ln A + B\sin(-\alpha)), -90 < \alpha < 0 \end{cases} \quad (3)$$

Where *M* is one of outline feature point set of icon, α is the angle of rotation of a contour feature point in *M*, and $p(\alpha)$ is the probability distribution in formula 2, let *A = 1, B =* −*1,* therefore $p(min) = 1$. C is the enhancement coefficient of the concave outline points. Generally, icons often contain multiple outlines, thus the final icon shape complexity is

$$H'(\alpha_{ij}) = \sum_{i}^{n} \sum_{j}^{m} h(\alpha_{ij})/1000 \quad (4)$$

Where *m* is one of outline feature point set of icon which is same as *M* of formula 3, *n* is outline feature point set of icon and $m \in n$. The higher the value of the H′, the higher the shape complexity.

In order to verify the validity of the formula, we selected randomly 70 two-dimensional icons as test samples, some of which are shown in the Fig. 4, and then used the formula to calculate the complexity of the sample icons. We recruited 25 testers to score the complexity of the icon using the dual comparison method, and then sort the icons by the scores of each icon. The orders of icon shape complexity calculated by the formula is consistent with the orders of the questionnaire scores, which indicates the formula is an effective method to quantify the shape complexity of icon.

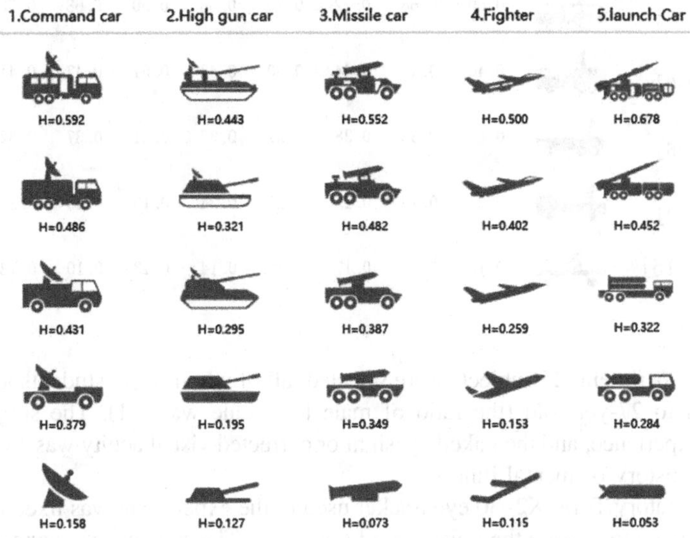

Fig. 4. The results of calculated shape complexity of icon samples.

4 Experimental Design

4.1 Experimental Purpose

In this paper, the experiment was designed to explore which level of shape complexity icon is best in visual search. Therefore, the eye tracking technology [11] is applied to the experiment to analyze the visual search behavior by eye movement path, the distribution of fixation points, the gaze time, reaction time and correct rate. These experimental results are important bases for analyzing the visual search performance of different icon shape complexity interfaces and the impact on visual search [12].

4.2 Method and Materials

Based on the calculation of icon shape complexity formula above, as shown in the Table 1, we divide the shape complexity of 45 icons (300 × 300 px) into five levels (H_1 = [0.6,0.75], H_2 = [0.45,0.6], H_3 = [0.3,0.45], H_4 = [0.15,0.3], H_5 = [0,0.15]) and there is an icon sample corresponding to the complexity level in the each row of table. In order to eliminate the impact of semantics on the visual perception of icons, the same level of complexity icons own same semantics [13]. As shown in the Fig. 5, 9 numbered icons of the same complexity level are placed in a 3 × 3 matrix by random array algorithm, and subjects needs to search target icon in it. The searching process would be recorded by the eye tracker device.

Table 1. The five levels of 40 icons shape complexity

Level/array	Icon sample	0	1	2	3	4	5	6	7	8
H_1= [0. 6, 0. 75]		0. 60	0. 68	0. 72	0. 70	0. 68	0. 60	0. 68	0. 70	0. 66
H_2= [0. 45, 0. 6]		0. 46	0. 48	0. 44	0. 50	0. 47	0. 51	0. 47	0. 41	0. 42
H_3= [0. 3, 0. 45]		0. 42	0. 38	0. 38	0. 37	0. 37	0. 41	0. 37	0. 32	0. 38
H_4= [0. 15, 0. 3]		0. 21	0. 19	0. 22	0. 24	0. 24	0. 19	0. 19	0. 20	0. 19
H_5= [0, 0. 15]		0. 12	0. 18	0. 17	0. 12	0. 14	0. 13	0. 10	0. 12	0. 13

In this experiment, 25 subjects were selected, all of whom were students aged from 23-year-old to 27-year-old (the ratio of male to female was 1:1). The subjects had computer experience, and the naked eyesight or corrected visual acuity was 1.0. Above, there is no history of mental illness.

The laboratory Tobii X2–30 eye tracker used in the experiment was fixed under the computer screen to capture the trajectory of both eyes. The subjects were experimented in a natural sitting position; there was no noise and low illumination (40 W fluorescent) during the experiment. Adjust the eye tracker according to the sitting posture of the subject. The eye of the subject is as flat as possible with the center of the screen. During the test, the distance from the eye to the screen is about 65–70 cm; the pixel of the computer display is 1028 × 1024, and the refresh rate is 75 Hz.

4.3 Experiment Procedure

Each experiment starts with one subject. After the subject sat in front of the screen in the laboratory, we need to adjust the distance between the eye movement equipment and the subject. Before the beginning of the formal, the eye movement equipment is calibrated and the participants complete a set of exercises. After one minute of rest, the formal experiment begins.

The target icon memory page displays a single icon in 2000 ms, then the search page displays the 3 × 3 array icons which have same complexity level like the target icon. In addition, the target icon is one of the 9 icons randomly placed in the array. There are five complexity levels of icons in the experiment. Subject need to remember the target icon first displayed, and automatically enter the search page. The subject searches for the target icon in 9 icons with the system timing. After finding the target icon, the subject presses the space bar to complete the search task, and the timing stops. If the subject did not find the target, click the right mouse button. If the participant does not click the space bar, the screen will continue to display this page and the system will continue to time. After a test is completed, the screen displays the next target icon until all visual search tasks are finished and five sets of target icons in different complexity levels appear in random order. As shown in Fig. 6, the total experiment process for one subject average cost 20 min.

Fig. 5. The 3 X 3 matrix of icons which share same level of complexity

4.4 Experimental Result

The experimental results include behavioral data and eye movement data. The behavioral data contains reaction time and response accuracy, as shown in Table 2. The eye movement data mainly involves the AOI gaze time, the hot zone map and the number of eye hop paths. We use SPSS to do the analysis of variance, and use Tobi Studio to analyze eye movement data. The abnormal data caused by the factors are deleted, and the number of deletions is less than 2%. The following Table gives the behavioral data.

Table 2.

Shape complexity level	Average reaction time/s	Standard deviation of reaction	Response accuracy/ %	Standard deviation of response accuracy
H_1 = [0.6,0.75]	2.656	0.304	48%	0.044
H_2 = [0.45,0.6]	2.522	0.394	50%	0.187
H_3 = [0.3,0.45]	1.550	0.923	66%	0.219
H_4 = [0.15,0.3]	1.309	0.439	72%	0.148
H_5 = [0.0,0.15]	1.582	0.185	46%	0.240

We perform ANOVA on the response time and accuracy, and the factor is the shape complexity level of the icon. For the correct rate, From the table, the complexity of H_4 has the highest correct rate, but the accuracy rate of H_1 and H_5 rank in the last two. The results of the variance analysis of repeated measurements show that the complexity has obvious significant effect on the search performance, $F = 2.103$, $p = 0.048$, then further post-testing on complexity, the results indicate the complexity of H_4 is significantly different from the complexity of H_1, H_2 and H_5, the average $p = 0.040$. There is no obvious difference between the complexity of H_4 and H_3. About the response time,

Subjects spent the least amount of time on the complexity of H_4, and slightly higher than the complexity of H_3, however, the complexity of H_1 and H_2 are time consuming for subjects. The results of ANOVA show that the complexity has enormous impact on the response time, $F = 7.185$, $p = 0.001$. Multiple comparison results indicate the complexity of H_4 and H_5 have significant difference with the complexity of H_1 and H_2, because the value of p between them less than 0.05. Obviously, the complexity of H_4 has the highest search performance than the others. It can be concluded that when the shape complexity of the icon shape is reduced, the time of the visual search becomes shorter, but when it is as low as a certain degree, the correct rate of the search is significantly lowered.

We have selected representative experimental materials representing different complexity levels to analyze AOI gazing time, number of gazes, overall hot zone map and visual search path when analyzing eye movement data.

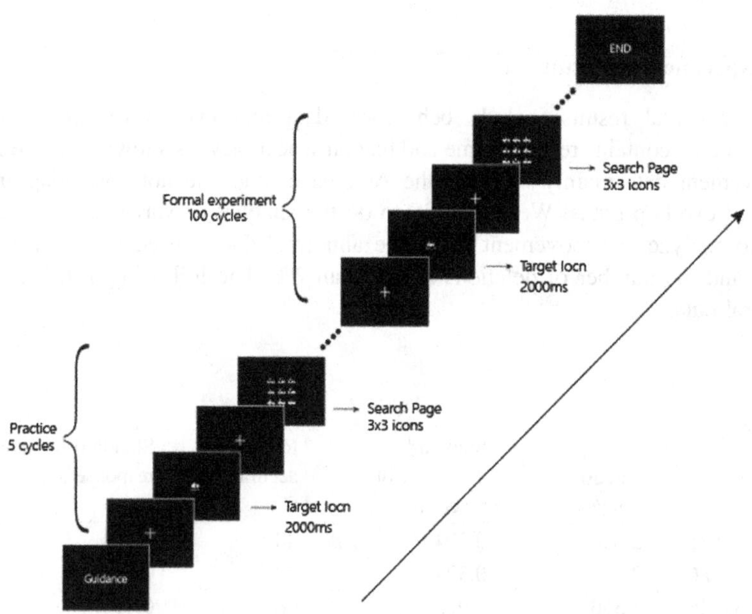

Fig. 6. Icon visual search experiment process example

At each level of complexity, we select the corresponding search page and plot the area of interest to analyze the average time of the first gaze. As shown in Fig. 7, it reflects the difficulty of extracting information which means the longer the duration, the more difficult it is to get information from the display area. According to the chart above we can conclude that it is hard to extract the information from the search page as a result of the complexity of H1 is too complicated and the complexity of H5 is too abstract.

As shown in Fig. 8, the number of eye movements of the target icon of H_1 is more than the target icon of H_5, which means subjects could take less time to remember the features of icon's shape when learning the target icon with low complexity levels. From

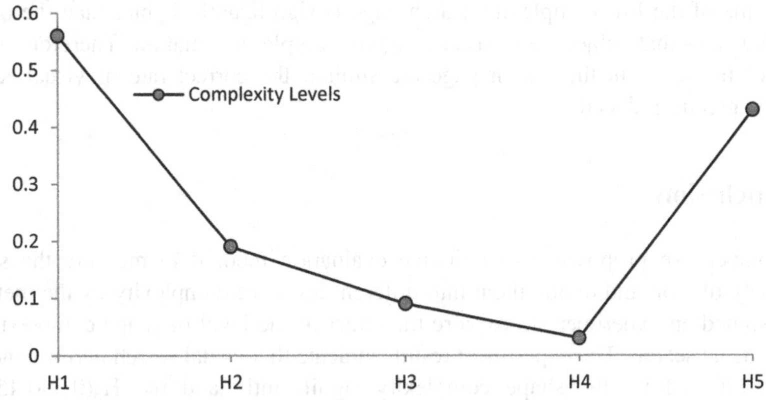

Fig. 7. Time to first fixation mean of entire search page

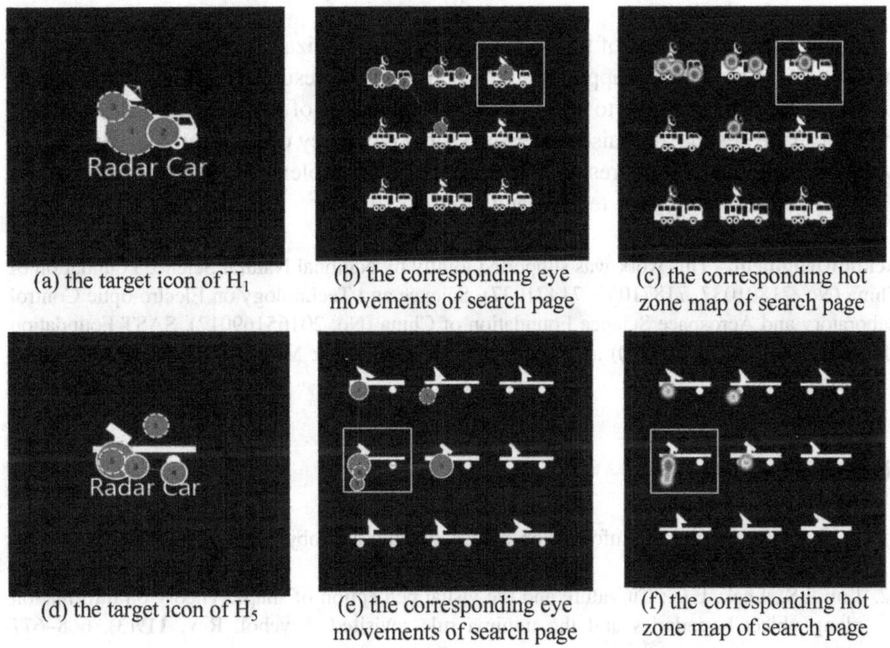

(a) the target icon of H_1 (b) the corresponding eye movements of search page (c) the corresponding hot zone map of search page

(d) the target icon of H_5 (e) the corresponding eye movements of search page (f) the corresponding hot zone map of search page

Fig. 8. The eye movements and hot zone maps of target pages and search pages recorded by Tobi Studio

the eye movement trajectory in Fig. 8(b) and (e), we can find the subject mainly performs visual search through remembering the shape feature, that is, the subjects' search strategy [14] is basically the same. However, when searching for a simple shape, the subject's gaze time will be shorter during the search, for example, as shown in the hot zone map of Fig. 8(c) and (f) below, the depth of color representing the length of gazing time of the low-complexity search page is significantly lighter than the others which indicates that subjects are easier to ignore simple information. Therefore, if the shapes of the icons in the search page are similar, the correct rate of visual search would be greatly reduced.

5 Conclusion

In this paper, we proposed a quantitative evaluation method to measure the shape complexity of icon and divide them into different levels of complexity by the method, then designed an experiment to explore the effect of the level of shape complexity of icon on visual search. The experiment results indicate that visual search performance of icons is affected by the shape complexity significantly and the H_3(0.3–0.45) or H_4(0.15–0.3) shape complexity show the highest performance. Furthermore, based on the eye tracking technology, we analyzed the eye movement feature of subjects. These data reveal that it is more difficult to extract information from icons with too high or too low shape complexity.

The evaluation method of this paper provides a quantization scheme for icon shape analysis and classification application. In addition, the results of visual search experiment can help the designer to optimize the visual search of the interface icon, improve the icon shape design, and raise the visual search efficiency of the interface icon. Future work research mainly explores the influence of icon complexity of other dimensions on visual cognition, like color, texture and style.

Acknowledgment. This work was supported jointly by National Natural Science Foundation of China (No. 71801037, 71871056, 71471037), Science and Technology on Electro-optic Control Laboratory and Aerospace Science Foundation of China (No. 20165169017), SAST Foundation of China (SAST No. 2016010) and Equipment Pre-research & Ministry of education of China Joint fund.

References

1. Feldman, J., Singh, M.: Information along contours and object boundaries. Psychol. Rev. **112**(1), 243–252 (2005)
2. Lim, I.S., Leek, E.C.: Curvature and the visual perception of shape: Theory on information along object boundaries and the minima rule revisited. Psychol. Rev. **119**(3), 668–677 (2012)
3. Chen, Y., Sundaram, H.: Estimating complexity of 2D shapes. In: IEEE Workshop on Multimedia Signal Processing. IEEE (2005)
4. Lingchen, D., Jiajing, Z., Ren, P., Jian, W., Jinhui, Y.: Calculation measure of icon shape complexity. J. Comput.-Aided Des. Comput. Graph. **29**(10), 16–20 (2017)
5. Haushofer, J., Baker, C.I., Livingstone, M.S.: Privileged coding of convex shapes in human object-selective cortex. J. Neurophysiol. **100**(2), 7–53 (2008)
6. Boucart, M., Humphreys, G.W.: Global shape cannot be attended without object identification. J. Exp. Psychology. Hum. Percept. Perform. **18**(3), 785–806 (1992)

7. Dougall, S.J.P., De Bruijn, O., Curry, M.B.: Exploring the effects of icon characteristics on user performance: the role of icon concreteness, complexity, and distinctiveness. J. Exp. Psychol. Appl. **6**(4), 291–306 (2000)
8. Bertamini, M., Wagemans, J.: Processing convexity and concavity along a 2-D contour: figure–ground, structural shape, and attention. Psychon. Bull. Rev. **20**(2), 191–207 (2013)
9. Haiyan, W., Yamei, H., Mo, C., Chengqi, X.: Analysis of cognitive model in icon search behavior based on ACT-R model. J. Comput.-Aided Des. Comput. Graph. **28**(10), 1740–1749 (2016)
10. Shannon, C.E.: A mathematical theory of communication. Bell Syst. Tech. J. **27** (1948)
11. Kuo, F.Y., Hsu, C.W., Day, R.F.: An exploratory study of cognitive effort involved in decision under Framing-an application of the eye-tracking technology. Decis. Support Syst. **48**(1), 81–91 (2010)
12. Huang, K.C., Chiu, T.L.: Visual search performance on an LCD monitor: effects of color combination of figure and icon background, shape of icon, and line width of icon border. Percept. Mot. Skills **104**(2), 562–574 (2007)
13. Zhang, J., et al.: Study on the effects of semantic memory on icon complexity in cognitive domain. In: Harris, D. (ed.) EPCE 2016. LNCS (LNAI), vol. 9736, pp. 147–157. Springer, Cham (2016). https://doi.org/10.1007/978-3-319-40030-3_16
14. Everett, S.P., Byrne, M.D.: Unintended effects: varying icon spacing changes users' visual search strategy. In: Sigchi Conference on Human Factors in Computing Systems. ACM (2004)

Three-Dimensional Representation in Visual Communication of Science

Marco Neves[1(✉)] and Pedro Gonçalves[2]

[1] CIAUD – Research Center for Architecture, Urban Planning and Design Lisbon School of Architecture, University of Lisbon, Lisbon, Portugal
mneves@fa.ulisboa.pt

[2] Lisbon School of Architecture, University of Lisbon, Lisbon, Portugal
pedro.gox@gmail.com

Abstract. Technology has been used to communicate complex information and brought opportunities for science development and science communication. Three-dimensional representation systems allow design to use image and video in innovative ways and enable organization of more suitable content for effective understanding. This paper addresses the use of three-dimensional representation systems to disseminate complex concepts related to science. We reviewed its course from scientific illustration of natural species, to the use of detailed infographics as direct communication in newspapers. We also undertook visual experiments to demonstrate the use of such three-dimensional representation systems in science communication, and proceeded with an evaluation from experts. This research allowed us to find connections between visual communication and complex concepts coming from science. Three-dimensional representation systems have features which generate benefits for science communication and understanding.

Keywords: Science communication · Three-dimensional representation systems · Theoretical photorealism · Visual communication

1 Introduction

Throughout history, design has found ways to produce content suited for audiences with whom it communicates. This study sought to understand the evolution of three-dimensional representation systems in visual communication, gathering examples related to cinema and image production, as well as audiovisual media, with its focus directed towards visual communication of science. Based on the need to explore through images, a universe as vast as that of science, the study pursued to find examples and to understand the role of three-dimensional representation systems in visual communication of scientific areas, nowadays and throughout recent history. A small experiment was carried out and an evaluation was made to assess the relevance of three-dimensional representation systems in scientific communication, with positive results.

A. Marcus and W. Wang (Eds.): HCII 2019, LNCS 11584, pp. 56–65, 2019.
https://doi.org/10.1007/978-3-030-23541-3_5

2 Theoretical Framework

2.1 Big Data

Our days are filled with technological advances which enables production of large amounts of information. According to Gadepally and Zachary [1], sources of information are also derived from social behavior on the internet and social networks. They depend on our present context to become a more visible flow. An explicit problem arising from technological ambition, according to Chavez [2] is the unbearable amount of information produced which has to be stored and archived in an accessible way for later use. The problem of information production and its consequent management is called 'big data'. This problem triggers other concerns related to communication in general. Based on the excessive volume of knowledge from most diverse areas, population stands exposed to a dense variety of information which is sometimes not authentic or beneficial. Chavez [2] suggests we live in a period where data grows further critical and where several times it goes unnoticed. The design action on problems of large amounts of information for a broad public is called information design. This area of design finds ways to act and present society with means to organize its communication. It has been growing and attending the 'big data' problem.

2.2 Visual Communication of Science

Science communication can be defined as the transmission of complex concepts of rigorous detail, derived from analytical study, to the public through accessible language. By consequence it should encourage an easy understanding. For communication to be effective, different communication agents, such as journalists, researchers, politicians, but also design professionals need to filter contents generated by everyone in the scientific community. These several agents also need to define key points, transmitted afterwards to the public through written, scientific papers, or magazine articles, posters or conferences; or by images as infographics and scientific illustrations [3].

The concept of scientific illustration is closely linked in its origin to detailed design of animal species, associated with biology. Since the beginning of scientific exploration, scientists have felt the need to represent, through illustrations, natural phenomena related to their fields of study, such as, botany or geology [4]. Scientific illustrations have assumed ever since, the importance of a scientific document, as they complement written descriptions and visually document information regarding the object of study. Such illustrations were like proofs of the discoveries [4], they became essential to knowledge in a time where photography still did not exist as a way of register reality. For that reason, these drawings served the purpose of recording in an analytical and impartial way, the object of study [5].

Before the 1970s, NASA visual communication artists worked in conjunction with Disney and other entities such as Chesley Bonestell, designer and illustrator, to engage readers in exploring themes as space. Images can function by themselves, by presenting something that attracts attention and creates interest or curiosity. For this reason, innovative representation systems are used in visual communication of science. The use of three-dimensional images for exploration of a concept has been gaining a presence in visual communication of science for the advantages these systems present.

2.3 Reach for Realism

The use of digital technologies for imaging has been a trend, as reported by Trivedi [6]. The digitization of the world and creative ideas have been codified in increasingly complete digital software. However, since the beginning of the 21st century, an initiative has taken place to introduce three-dimensional representation of objects as a way of visual communication. One of the main characteristics associated with these technologies is the close representation of our observed reality. This sense of realism as obtained by three-dimensional generated images known today is the result of advances in technology. According to Wong [7], software has experienced accelerated evolution, accompanied by exploration of computers and their capabilities.

The relationship between three-dimensional representation systems and science communication depends on the ability to represent a method in a realistic, precise and objective manner. It is necessary three-dimensional systems can guarantee this requirement with rigor, for this connection to be established. Nowadays, technical capacity is able to produce photo realistic quality content, as there was certainly a need to overcome past problems in representation.

Lack of realism in representing objects occurs directly linked to the problem posed by Masahiro Mori, which he defined as 'uncanny valley.' Mori [8] presents the concept of robotics and the construction of mechanical models of human figures. Mori describes construction of robots with human attributes runs the risk of causing repulsion when contacting real users. Like Wong [7], Mori [8] mentions that the human being is very incisive to find details and characteristics, both of form and behavior, of other individuals. For this reason, details which are not genuine are assumed to be non-real or simulated. Like human behavior, the concept of 'uncanny valley,' introduced by Mori, also applies to other transpositions, mechanical or artificial, in the real world.

To illustrate the problem, Mori elaborated a graphic, which we adapted in Fig. 1. It is possible to identify that the basis of proximity between humans and machines, considered by the author, are industrial robots (A).

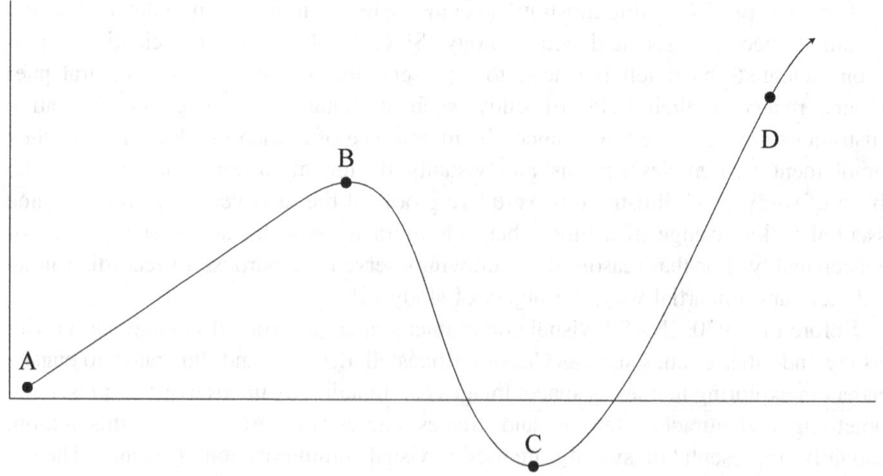

Fig. 1. Index of realism, adapted from Masahiro Mori.

They do not have any direct relationships with humans as their function completely dictates their construction, behavior, and appearance. At a second level we can find stylized and unrealistic robots or representations such as dolls and toys (B). There are anatomical relationships recognized but exaggerated, such as the ASIMO robot, and placed outside real understanding. Finally, there is a peak where human/machine relationship is lost, which is interaction with another human individual (D). However before this, is where 'uncanny valley' appears. The relationship between mechanisms and their objectives is very close but very distant concerning similarity between themselves and their users. The perception of reality and its transformation into something material has been the subject of a change on the part of artists.

According to Scott [9], engineers and visual artists will constantly have the will to achieve a replica of human characteristics. Taking a specific case, it is possible to verify that robot Sophia presents a set of factors associated with the human figure, the relationship between its mechanisms and its objectives are very close, but very distant in terms of similarity between it and its users (C).

The same objective is sought in the field of visual communication. Conceptual artists who produce visual elements for films also encounter the problem of transposing real-world details into digital environment. As Scott [9] points out, the connection between general public and cinema easily denounces a weaknesses which digital representation still presents. Nowadays, many effects are invisible, and software produces photographic quality images. However, reaching this level required creative and technological decisions.

2.4 Evolution of Three-Dimensional Representation Systems

Three-dimensional representation systems owes part of their growth to cinema. An example of the importance of using three-dimensional representation systems is observable in the 1993 film 'Jurassic Park'. Under the direction of Steven Spielberg, animatronics were first used to represent dinosaurs. However, it was necessary to produce more complex movements which required a rethinking of how to provide them. Three-dimensional representation systems were used to create a product that could not be made otherwise. Throughout the history of modern cinema, over the last two decades, three-dimensional representation systems have gained more visibility and importance as a way of creating illusions and providing innovative experiences to the public.

In 2009, another milestone was reached in the use of digital animation in three dimensions with the film 'Avatar' under the guidance of its director James Cameron. In the film an essential improvement was introduced to blend real actors with digital elements. In this way, it became possible for the director to instantly understand the relationship between his actors and their future interactions, when the film was delivered to the digital effects team. According to Wong [7], approximately 70% of the film was produced thanks to introduction of real-time rendering in digitally recorded scenes. Afterwards, actors interacted with each other as characters, while the camera captured digital environments around them, and from a real-time channel, the director could have a low-quality simulation of how the scene would be, before of it being rendered. The effect, called real-time rendering, has been increasingly used in film, advertising, and video games.

In 'Avatar,' James Cameron used yet another innovative method called 'motion capture' that allows real actors to play animated characters. This effect is created through a point triangulation system drawn on the face and clothes of actors, are recorded by a series of cameras and localization sensors which map their movements. All movement data is applied in a three-dimensional system, and a simulation of character gesture is generated in conjunction with real-time rendering system.

The detail achieved by advances and decisions made throughout history has allowed a spectrum of uses of three-dimensional systems to be expanded and exploited in other areas: from advertising and graphic design to science communication.

2.5 Representation of Scientific Concepts

It is worth introducing a critical concept to establish the link between three-dimensional representation systems and science communication. Alan Warburton [10] presents the idea of 'theoretical photorealism', which is based on image composition to simulate, predict or represent concepts that do not have photographic records. According to Warburton, there are elements beyond the reach of human vision, and whose presence is confirmed, which can be represented according to this theory. Planets and celestial bodies, cells and microscopic features can be represented, but also atmospheric effects such as the presence of wind or temperature. The need to present images about these phenomena is a matter of science communication. The importance of three-dimensional representation of images related to science has been evident in the last decade since digital systems have had their growth and evolution.

Between Design and Science. In the science fiction film 'Interstellar' (2014), directed by Christopher Nolan, a black hole, called Gargantua, which assumes the central dramatic tension of the film is represented. Nolan, known for using practical effects in his movies, conducted the recording in real-world spaces, using different locations to represent different moments of the film. However, due to the lack of real images of this space phenomenon, Nolan used three-dimensional rendering technologies to generate black hole images.

As in previous cases, the lack of capacity to respond to a creative need was the driving force for advances in digital technology. Huls [11] states that the way we visually represent scientific concepts tells a lot about how we think of them at the moment they are represented.

From a scientific point of view, this is an initiative to represent phenomena still to be explored visually and hence generate material for dissemination of its respective area. The scientific community, according to Wong [7], has features which are not accurate enough to present compelling visual conclusions. All communication in the film, whether dialogues or astronauts suits, were thought to convey confidence to the viewer, to give the impression everything being transmitted was a representation of the real world [12]. In this way, the presence of any effect would have to be as real as the rest of the film. Special effects studio Double Negative was in charge of space plans and black hole views. Mathematical knowledge of astrophysicist Kip Thorn was used, which was committed to build scientific facts, which in turn, led to special effects being made.

This case demonstrates the importance of using special effects as a way of producing realities, but also how three-dimensional representation systems assume significance in science communication to the public. Collins [13] refers to the effects of 'Interstellar' as the bridge between art and science.

In the same way, Warburton [10] points out the development of three-dimensional computation and that the 'Interstellar' case is part of his 'theoretical photorealism' category. It describes mathematical theories with tested and validated fundamentals may be subject to visual interpretation by digital artists. According to Warburton, representation of the black hole as presented in the film exposes a phenomenon scientifically proven, but never observed or captured by a conclusive image. The interpretation of the concept is presented as a visual simulation, not as a real proof.

3 Experiment and Evaluation

A small three-dimensional system for visualizing scientific communication was developed. This experiment used the presented concepts and consisted of creating images of planets, produced according to Warburton 'theoretical photorealism' and based on an applied study of 'procedural textures'. Composition of complex materials for application in a spherical model allows the design of various profiles and representation of planets, specifically controlling their factors and relations.

According to Hurt [14], the method to generate representations related to astronomy, namely planets, is based on association and knowledge collected during research done in this scientific area. Taking into account the requirements to represent planet Earth, we have considered mandatory aspects to be present in the model, namely oceans and continents, rivers, poles, mountains and valleys, as well as simple effects such as clouds and atmosphere. The system allows users to change any value to produce a completely different result, depending on communication needs.

For this study, we developed 24 images, to test the use of three-dimensional representation with visual communication of science. Figures 2 and 3 are examples of this procedure.

In essence, the obtained results from image creation should demonstrate benefits when compared to current production process. In other words, it intends to make clear that the use of functions found in three-dimensional representation environments are beneficial.

After creating such images, we conducted an evaluation on the relationship between three-dimensional systems and science communication carried out by visual means. Based on literature review and on the development of this images, it was important to evaluate this relation by a group of specialists. This evaluation was done through questionnaires and placed our images for representation of planets, elaborated using procedural textures, before the understanding of these specialists. As evaluators of this development, we invited experts from two areas, who collaborate. We selected 5 researchers working in astronomy and in science, in broad terms and design

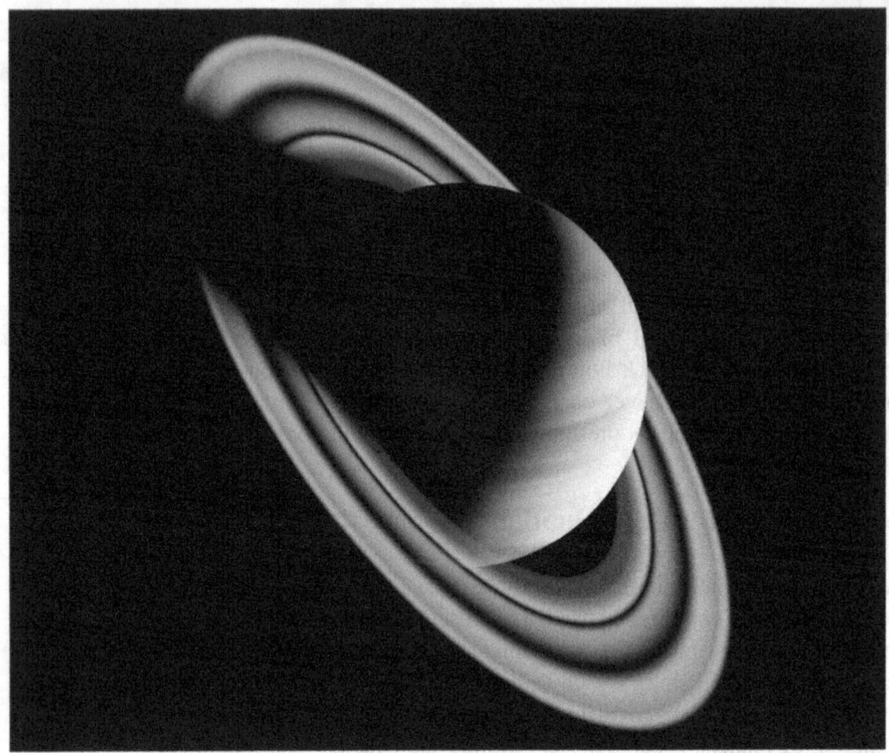

Fig. 2. Render of a planet according to planet Saturn reference.

professionals who regularly work with three-dimensional representation systems. All collaborated to evaluate the system as a technical resource for creating quality results for visual communication. The expert's assessment followed a two-part script: an introduction to the research subject, followed by an explanation of the research problem and design solution; and in a second moment, evaluation of developed visual elements. We intended to evaluate the system in specific situations, where communication of scientific concepts depends on visual rigor. We also tried to observe, for all images, the most relevant limitations. The results of the questionnaires helped establish an understanding of the two areas together, commenting on a beneficial procedure for both. For design, the existence of an automated model, capable of obtaining a result with high detail, implies acceleration of production processes. The change of one or more variables, using three-dimensional representation systems, is beneficial because the generated model can be observed from multiple angles and perspectives. For science, it is essential to produce images that accompany scientific proof or speculation. Collaboration with design, in constitution of more incisive communication, is the main idea extracted from this evaluation.

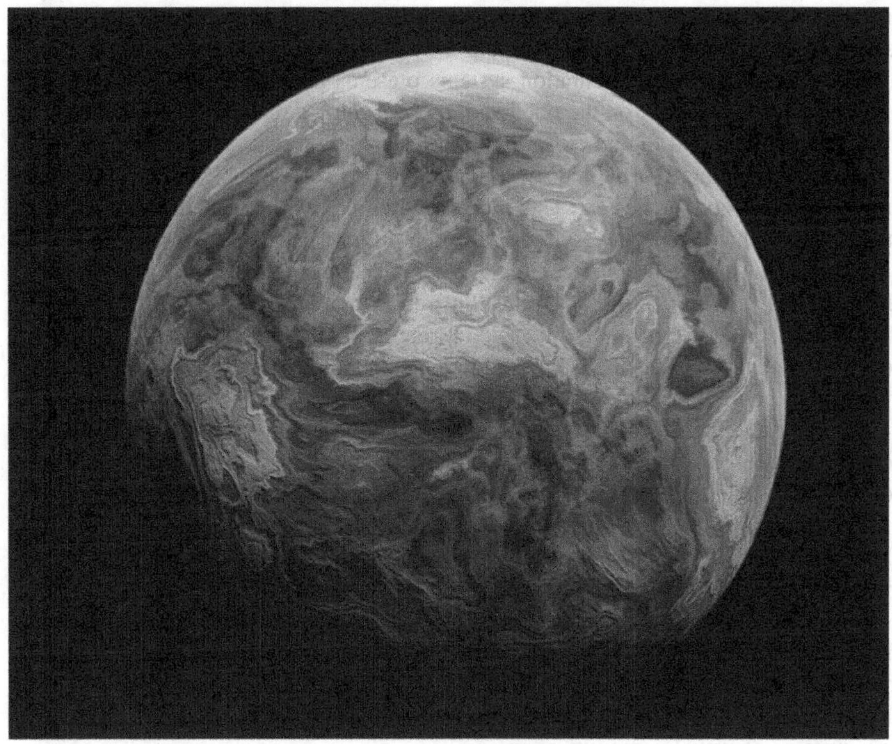

Fig. 3. Render of a planet according to planet Earth reference.

4 Conclusion

Based on obtained results during research, and gathered knowledge, it is essential to recognize, that three-dimensional representation systems are prevailing tools for visual communication and understanding of concepts related to science. In this context, accelerated evolution of technology, means of information and the amount of data generated consequently, dictates communication is transformed and adapted to reach different audiences.

Since its growth and use in cinema, as a means of reproducing available realities and drawing on the interest of general public, the notion of 'uncanny valley' and breaking barriers between digital and photographic production, three-dimensional representation systems have gained increasing presence in visual communication. In the same way, we can verify its continuous use in design, assuming the importance of images in advertising. In another phase, cinema assumed responsibility of exploiting three-dimensional representation systems capacities and presented, in the last century, more and more realistic results. According to creative needs, more innovative production processes were also adapted to reduce the difficulty between understanding real and digital content, while also including benefits in production stages. Functionalities with motion capture and real-time rendering arise with the goal of integrating procedures designed to solve a problem, culminating in an increasingly realistic and fearless result, raising the bar for possible following advances.

Three-dimensional representation systems presents an instrument for visual communication on two levels: on the one hand, by producing a realistic result of a creative idea, bringing real and digital closer. On the other hand, for design, the use of three-dimensional systems is benefited by a community to solve problems and find innovative methods and processes. The process combines with creativity and a visual environment which creates everything from real to unreal.

Science thus uses design to simulate complex concepts that are the result of technological progress. From scientific illustration, through infographic composition until the extensive use of three-dimensional representation systems, it is important to conclude that the means of visual communication production are as current as the information being transmitted by them.

One key to relate science to visual design is, in the light of research, the so-called concept of theoretical photo-realism introduced by Warburton [10]. It establishes the advantage of using a visual medium to generate realistic images, with the need to present public with evidence of an innovative, supposed or invisible concept. Combination between both areas results in something that, as evaluated, has advantages in visual result and in production process.

An interesting phenomenon observed during research is the fact that most referenced authors are published their articles in the last decade. The community regarding three-dimensional representation in general and its applications in design and science have increasingly found motivations, supports, and means to explore details that define new systems of visual communication.

Acknowledgements. The authors would like to thank the funding support by the Foundation for Science and Technology of the Ministry of Science, Technology and Higher Education of Portugal under the project UID/EAT/04008/2013 (CIAUD).

References

1. Gadepally, V., Zachary, J.: Using 3D Printing to Visualize Social Media Big Data. MIT, Lincoln Laboratory, Massachusetts (2014)
2. Chavez, D.: Is 3D visualization the next step for big data? (2012). https://www.wired.com/insights/2012/11/3d-visualization-big-data/. Accessed 09 Sept 2018
3. Boon, S.: What is this 'science communication' you speak of? (2014). http://www.cdnsciencepub.com/blog/what-is-this-science-communication-you-speak-of.aspx. Accessed 23 Sept 2018
4. Modzy, M.: The art and details of scientific illustration (2017). https://nhmu.utah.edu/blog/2017/01/29/art-and-details-scientific-illustration. Accessed 08 Sept 2018
5. Meier, A.: When art was the scientist's eye: 400 years of natural history illustrations (2013). https://hyperallergic.com/97027/when-art-was-the-scientists-eye-400-years-of-natural-history-illustrations/. Accessed 08 Sept 2018
6. Trivedi, G.: The importance of 3D animation and visualization in construction and manufacturing (2013). http://www.truecadd.com/news/the-importance-of-3d-animation-and-visualization-in-construction-and-manufacturing. Accessed 13 Sept 2018

7. Wong, F.: Why CG sucks (Except it doesn't) (2012). https://www.youtube.com/watch?v=bL6hp8BKB24. Accessed 08 Sept 2018
8. Mori, M.: The uncanny valley: the original essay by Masahiro Mori (2012). https://spectrum.ieee.org/automaton/robotics/humanoids/the-uncanny-valley. Accessed 08 Sept 2018
9. Scott, G.: 5 lifelike robots that take you straight into the uncanny valley (2017). https://www.inverse.com/article/36745-5-lifelike-robots-that-take-you-straight-into-the-uncanny-valley. Accessed 08 Sept 2018
10. Warburton, A.: Goodbye uncanny valley (2017). https://vimeo.com/channels/staffpicks/237568588. Accessed 08 Sept 2018
11. Huls, R.: NASA images aren't always real, this is how space artists create them. https://www.youtube.com/watch?v=xc1V9d8jrr8. Accessed 07 Sept 2018
12. Nolan, C., Thomas, E.: Foreword, in Thorne, K.: The Science of Interstellar. W. W. Norton & Company, New York (2014)
13. Collins, D.: The Visual Effects of Interstellar: Bridging Art and Science (2015). https://www.siggraph.org/discover/news/visual-effects-interstellar-bridging-art-and-science. Accessed 08 Oct 2018
14. Hurt, R.: The NASA Illustrator Who Hides Sci-Fi Easter Eggs in Official Images of Space | WIRED Lab (2016). https://www.youtube.com/watch?v=F4v8rytVy50&t=19s. Accessed 08 Sept 2018

Mobile Web Design: The Effect of Education on the Influence of Classical and Expressive Aesthetics on Perceived Credibility

Kiemute Oyibo(✉), Ifeoma Adaji(✉), and Julita Vassileva(✉)

University of Saskatchewan, Saskatoon, Canada
{kiemute.oyibo, ifeoma.adaji}@usask.ca,
jiv@cs.usask.ca

Abstract. Research has shown that the *perceived credibility* of mobile web design can be largely determined by the two dimensions of *visual aesthetics*: *classical* and *expressive*. However, there is limited research on how users' education moderates the relationships between both dimensions of *visual aesthetics* and *perceived credibility*. To bridge this gap, we conducted an empirical study among 526 subjects to investigate how education moderates the influence of *classical* and *expressive aesthetics* on the *perceived credibility* of mobile website. Specifically, we focused on four visual designs of a mobile website homepage, in which products and/or services are laid out. Our results show that, irrespective of the level of education of users and the visual design of the mobile website, the perception of both dimensions of *visual aesthetics* has a significant impact on *perceived credibility*, with *classical aesthetics* having a stronger impact than *expressive aesthetics* overall. Moreover, we found that the effect of *classical aesthetics* on *perceived credibility* is stronger for higher education users than for lower education users, while the effect of *expressive aesthetics* on *perceived credibility* is stronger for lower education users than for higher education users. Our findings suggests that *classical aesthetics*(perceived visual clarity) is more likely to influence higher education users than lower education users to perceive a mobile website as *credible*, while *expressive aesthetics* (perceived visual enrichment) is more likely to influence lower education users than higher education users to perceive a mobile website as *credible*. Web designers of e-commerce mobile websites can leverage these findings to enhance the *perceived credibility* of their websites by the respective user groups.

Keywords: Mobile website · Classical aesthetics · Expressive aesthetics · Credibility · Education

1 Introduction

Credibility is an important factor in the design of websites and users' decisions to use them as their source of information, online products and services. Research [1] shows that users use *perceived credibility* to determine whether they should stay on a website or move to another. More importantly, users employ visual cues, such as aesthetic attributes, to determine the *credibility* of websites. Prior research [2, 3] has shown that

A. Marcus and W. Wang (Eds.): HCII 2019, LNCS 11584, pp. 66–79, 2019.
https://doi.org/10.1007/978-3-030-23541-3_6

visual aesthetics—composed of two basic dimensions (*classical aesthetics* and *expressive aesthetics*)—has the ability to predict the *perceived credibility* of mobile websites. *Classical aesthetics* has to do with the traditional notion of *aesthetics*, which borders on user interface (UI) simplicity, clarity and pleasantness. On the other hand, *expressive aesthetics* has to do with the expressive/creative power of the designer, particularly his/her ability to go beyond de facto standards and conventions. It borders on UI complexity, sophistication and enrichment [4]. Prior research [2, 3, 5] shows that both dimensions are strongly related and individually influence the *perceived credibility* of mobile websites. However, there is a limited understanding of how demographic factors, such as education, moderate the interrelationships between both dimensions of *visual aesthetics* and *perceived credibility*. Prior research [2, 3] mostly focused on the moderating effect of demographic factors such as age and gender. To bridge this gap, we conducted an empirical study among 526 subjects from a mixed population to investigate how education moderates the relationship between *classical* and *expressive aesthetics* and their individual influence on the *perceived credibility* of mobile website design. We based our investigation on four different aesthetic mobile website (homepage) designs: (1) multicolor list-based website, (2) minimalist list-based website, (3) moderate-color list-based website, and (4) moderate-color grid-based website. We used multiple website designs to examine how the moderating effect of education with respect to the three interrelationships is replicable or generalizes across different visual designs to confirm our findings.

Our results show that, irrespective of the level of education of users, both dimensions of *visual aesthetics* have a significant influence on *perceived credibility*, with *classical aesthetics* having a stronger influence than *expressive aesthetics* does. This finding is replicated across at least three of the website designs. Moreover, we found that the influence of *classical aesthetics* on *perceived credibility* is stronger for higher education users than for lower education users, while the influence of *expressive aesthetics* on *perceived credibility* is stronger for lower education users than for higher education users. In a nutshell, our findings suggest, irrespective of the level of education of users, both dimensions of *visual aesthetics* are important factors users consider in the judgment of the *perceived credibility* of a mobile website. More specifically, the perception of *classical aesthetics* (pleasantness, clarity and simplicity) is more likely to influence higher education users than lower education users in the judgment of the *perceived credibility* of a mobile website. On the other hand, the perception of *expressive aesthetics* (sophistication, enrichment and complexity) is more likely to influence lower education users than higher education users in the judgment of the *perceived credibility* of a mobile website. E-commerce and other domain-specific website designers can leverage these findings to enhance their website designs and their *perceived credibility* by the respective user groups.

The paper is organized as follows. Section 2 provides a background on the main web design concepts and constructs used in the paper; Sect. 3 presents the related work; Sect. 4 presents the research method; Sect. 5 presents the results; and Sect. 6 discusses the results, while Sect. 7 dwells on the conclusion of the paper.

2 Background

In this section, we provide an overview of the mobile web design concepts and constructs investigated in this paper (Table 1).

Table 1. Overview of mobile web design concepts and constructs

Concept	Definition
Web design	Web design refers to the visual design of a website, including the aesthetic design and presentation of graphical/textual elements in a way that is visually and emotionally appealing and easy to use.
Visual aesthetics	*Visual aesthetics* refers to the visual appeal of a website to the eyes and emotions [6]. Basically, it is composed of two key dimensions: *classical aesthetics* and *expressive aesthetics* [4].
Classical aesthetics	*Classical aesthetics* is one of the two key dimensions of *visual aesthetics*. It characterizes the traditional notion of beauty, which is described by terms such as "well-organized," "symmetrical," "clean," "clear," etc. [4]. It is closely associated with *perceived usability* [4, 5].
Expressive aesthetics	*Expressive aesthetics* is the second dimension of *visual aesthetics*. It characterizes the creativity and originality of the designer, including his/her ability to go beyond design conventions to create stimulating and engaging web designs. Thus, it is described by terms such as "creative," "fascinating," "sophisticated," etc. [4]. It is closely associated with *perceived persuasiveness* [7].
Perceived credibility	*Perceived credibility* refers to the believability of a website by its users. According to [8], users judge the *perceived credibility* of a website based on two key dimensions: the *perceived trustworthiness* of the website and the *perceived expertise* of the designer.

3 Related Work

A substantial amount of research has been done with respect to web design in the mobile and desktop domains. We review a cross-section of the related studies. Fogg et al. [9] carried out a large-sample study to investigate the design attributes that will most likely influence the *credibility judgment* of websites. They found that *design look* (a construct related to *visual aesthetics*) has the strongest influence on the *perceived credibility* of websites, followed by *information design/structure*. Similarly, Robins and Holmes [1] investigated the relationship between the *perceived aesthetics* and *perceived credibility* of a website. They found that websites with high-aesthetic treatment are more likely to be judged *credible* than websites with low-aesthetic treatment. In the mobile domain, Oyibo et al. [10, 11] investigated the interplay of *perceived aesthetics*, *perceived usability* and *perceived credibility*. The authors found that, irrespective of gender [10] and culture [11], *perceived aesthetics* has a stronger influence than *perceived usability* on the *judgment of credibility*. At a finer-grain level, Oyibo et al. [2, 3] investigated the interplay of the two dimensions of *visual aesthetics* (*classical aesthetics* and *expressive aesthetics*) [4] and the *perceived credibility* of mobile websites. With regard to tourism-based websites [2], they found that, irrespective of age and gender, *classical aesthetics* has a stronger influence on *perceived credibility* than *expressive aesthetics* does. Similarly, with regard to health-based websites [3], they found that, irrespective of gender, *classical aesthetics* has a stronger influence on *perceived credibility* than *expressive aesthetics* does. Specifically, in the health domain, the influence of *expressive aesthetics* on *perceived credibility* turned out to be non-significant. Moreover, different studies, such as [2, 3], found that there is a strong relationship between both dimensions of *aesthetics*.

However, to the best of our knowledge, as evident in our review, there are no studies that have investigated the moderating effect of education on the interrelationships among *classical aesthetics*, *expressive aesthetics* and *perceived credibility* in web design. Our study aims to bridge this gap by focusing on the mobile domain which, given the portability and ubiquity of smartphones, has been growing in leaps and bounds over the years [12].

4 Method

This section focuses on the research objective and design, research hypotheses, measurement instruments and the demographic information of participants.

4.1 Research Objective and Design

This study aims to investigate the moderating effect of education on the interrelationships that exist among *classical aesthetics, expressive aesthetics* and *perceived credibility*. Specifically, we set out to answer the following research questions (RQs) in the context of mobile web design:

RQ1. Are the interrelationships among *classical aesthetics, expressive aesthetics* and *perceived credibility* moderated by the education of the users?
RQ2. Is the moderation of the interrelationships by education replicable across different levels of visual design?

To answer the above research questions, we designed four versions of a mobile website (hypothetically named "G-Ranch") in the tourism domain.[1] Figure 1 shows all four versions, which are related by the visual design and/or layout. The first version (WA) is a multicolor design based on the list layout; the second version (WB) is a minimalist design based on the list layout; the third version (WC) is a moderate-color design based on the list layout; and the fourth version (WD) is a moderate-color design based on the grid layout. All four web designs were systematically arrived at based on a UI transformation framework we called "Artifact-Action Framework," the detail of

[1] The four web designs (homepages) are adapted from actual websites on the market in 2014: m.wakanow.com, mobile.united.com, mobile.utah.com and tourismwinnipeg.com. They are basically used to search for tourism-based services such as places, hotels, etc. At the time of writing this paper, most of them had been redesigned by their owners [12].

which is explained in [12]. For example, we came about the WB design by transforming the WA design (making it gray and adding icons). Similarly, we came about the WC design by transforming the WB design (making it unicolor—blue color scheme).

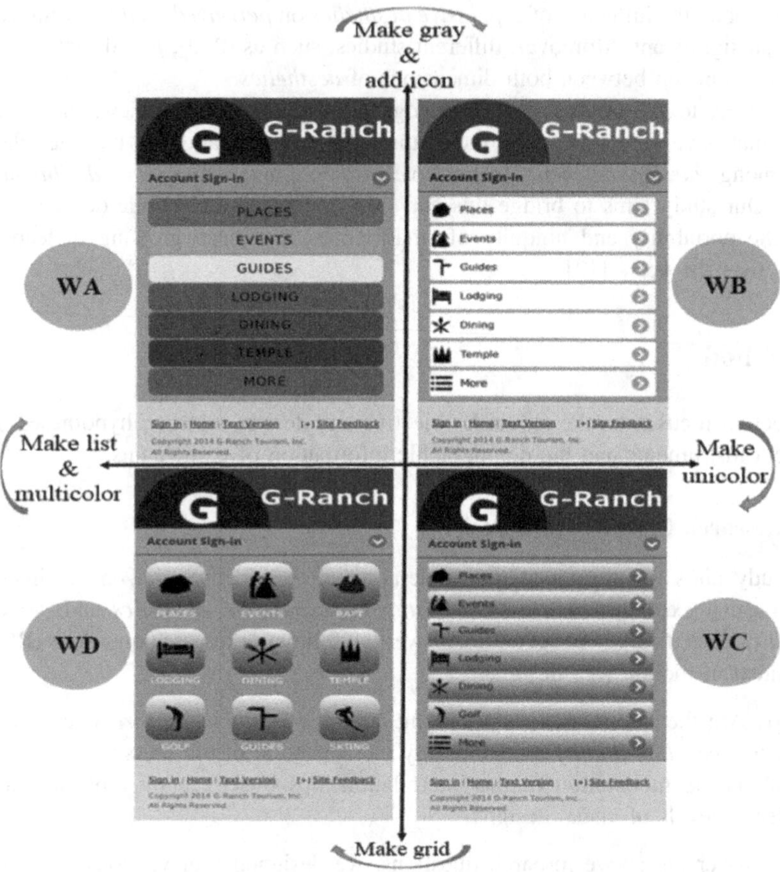

Fig. 1. Systematically designed mobile websites [12] (Color figure online)

4.2 Research Hypotheses

Figure 2 shows a diagrammatic representation of our hypotheses. These hypotheses are based on the existing literature and Lightner's [13] finding, in particular. Specifically, Lightner [13] found that the sensory impact of e-commerce sites became less important with increase in the education level of respondents. Sensory impact refers to how the aesthetic attributes of a site (e.g., stylistic use of visual elements such as color) influence users' buying behavior and/or preferences for the examined website. Thus, given that *expressive aesthetics* is more visually stimulating, arousing and user-involving [4] than *classical aesthetics*, we hypothesize that the former will be more important to lower education users than higher education users, while the latter will be more important to higher education users than lower education users in the judgment of *web credibility*.

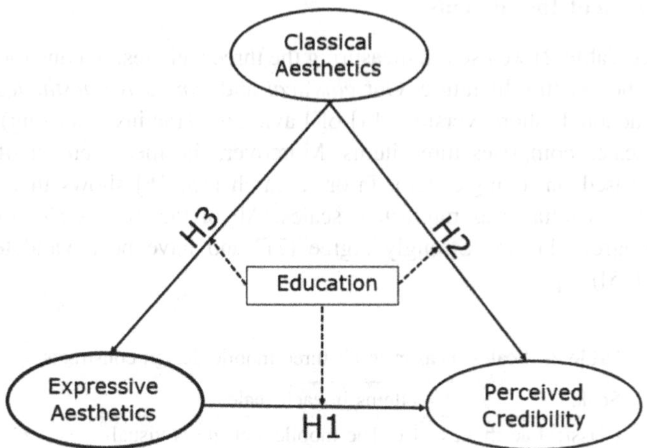

Fig. 2. Hypothesized path model

With regard to the different web designs shown in Fig. 1, our hypotheses are formally stated as follows:

H1a: The perception of *expressive aesthetics* will have a stronger effect on *perceived credibility* for lower education users than higher education users for web design WA.
H1b: The perception of *expressive aesthetics* will have a stronger effect on *perceived credibility* for lower education users than higher education users for web design WB.
H1c: The perception of *expressive aesthetics* will have a stronger effect on *perceived credibility* for lower education users than higher education users for web design WC.
H1d: The perception of *expressive aesthetics* will have a stronger effect on *perceived credibility* for lower education users than higher education users for web design WD.
H2a: The perception of *classical aesthetics* will have a stronger effect on *perceived credibility* for higher education users than lower education users for web design WA.
H2b: The perception of *classical aesthetics* will have a stronger effect on *perceived credibility* for higher education users than lower education users for web design WB.
H2c: The perception of *classical aesthetics* will have a stronger effect on *perceived credibility* for higher education users than lower education users for web design WC.
H2d: The perception of *classical aesthetics* will have a stronger effect on *perceived credibility* for higher education users than lower education users for web design WD.

With respect to H3, given the paucity of research on the moderating effect of education in mobile web design, we used an exploratory approach to determine which of the respective relationships between *classical* and *expressive aesthetics*—those for the lower education group or those for the higher education group—is stronger.

4.3 Measurement Instruments

The scales (see Table 2) we used in measuring the three web design constructs in Fig. 2 are based on the existing literature. Our *classical* and *expressive aesthetics* scales are based on the adapted (short) version [14] of Lavie and Tractinsky's (long) scales [4]. Each of the scales comprises three items. Moreover, the measurement of *perceived credibility* is based on a single item. Prior research [15, 16] shows that single-item scales could be as reliable as multi-item scales. All of the three scales ranged from "Strongly Disagree (1)" to "Strongly Agree (7)" and have been validated in prior studies (e.g., [15]).

Table 2. Scales measuring all three mobile design constructs

Scale	Items in each scale
Classical aesthetics	1. The mobile website is visual 2. The mobile website is clean 3. The mobile website is pleasant
Expressive aesthetics	1. The mobile website is fascinating 2. The mobile website is sophisticated 3. The mobile website is creative
Perceived credibility	The mobile website is credible

The study adopted a within-subject design, meaning that each participant answered the presented questions on all four web designs: (1) multicolor list-based design (WA), (2) minimalist list-based design (WB), (3) moderate-color list-based design (WC), and (4) moderate-color grid-based design (WD). In the online survey, we presented the four designs to participants in this order: WC, WA, WB and WD. Prior to presenting each of the four website designs and the items in Table 2 to participants, we provided the opening statement to set the tone for the study: "*Assume you were looking for a website on travels and tourism on your mobile phone, and you happened to open this webpage by clicking on one of the links returned by a search engine.*" Afterwards, below the image of each website design, we presented participants with the question: "*Please rate the website [label of website] on the following criteria based on your first impression.*" All of the six items in the *classical aesthetics* and *expressive aesthetics* scales were randomized as a block of questions. Finally, we presented participants with the question on *perceived credibility*: "*Based on your first impression of the mobile webpage [label of website], please rate its credibility level.*" In addition, we asked participants to provide demographic information such as gender, age, education level, etc.

4.4 Participants

The study was submitted to and approved by the Behavioral Research Ethics Board of our university, after which the questionnaire was posted on social media (Facebook), our university website and emailed to potential participants to partake anonymously. A total of 526 participants from Canada, Nigeria, Ghana, Brazil, China and others—after cleaning—took part in the study. Participants were given a chance to win a gift card of CAD $50. Table 3 shows the breakdown of the demographic information of participants based on country of origin.

Table 3. Participants' demographics (adapted from [10])

Variable	Group	NG	GH	BR	CH	CA	OTH	ALL	PER
Gender	Male	115	37	34	46	25	25	282	53.6%
	Female	40	13	16	63	71	31	234	44.5%
	Unidentified	1	0	0	6	2	1	10	1.9%
Age	18–24	118	6	16	51	55	18	264	50.2%
	25–34	32	40	21	59	31	31	214	40.7%
	>34	2	3	13	5	12	6	41	7.8%
	Unidentified	4	1	0	0	0	2	7	1.3%
Years on Internet	<10	116	12	8	82	13	9	230	43.7%
	>=10	50	38	42	33	85	48	296	56.3%
Education	Technical/Trade	8	0	1	12	4	1	26	4.9%
	High School	108	2	8	9	40	10	177	33.7%
	Bachelor	21	36	13	67	42	13	192	36.5%
	Postgraduate	11	9	28	25	11	31	115	21.9%
	Unidentified	8	3	0	2	1	2	16	3.0%
	Subtotal	156	50	50	115	98	57	526	100%
	National %	**29.7**	**9.5**	**9.5**	**21.9**	**18.6**	**10.8**	**100%**	

NG = Nigeria, GH = Ghana, Br = Brazil, CH = China, CA = Canada, OTH = Other countries, PER = %
Technical/Trade and High School = Lower education group (38.6%)
Bachelor and Postgraduate = Higher education group (58.4%)

5 Results

In this section, we present the results of our structural equation model (SEM) analysis, including the assessment of the measurement models, analysis of the structural models and the multigroup analyses based on education level.

5.1 Evaluation of Measurement Models

Our SEM models [17] was built using the Partial Least Square Path Modeling (PLSPM) package ("plspm" [18]) in the R programming language. Prior to analyzing the structural models, we evaluated the respective measurement models for the four website designs to ensure the required preconditions for structural analysis were meant. The results of the evaluations are now presented.

Indicator Reliability. This criterion was met, as all of the indicators in the respective measurement models for the four website designs had an outer loading on their constructs that was greater than 0.7 [17].

Internal Consistency. This criterion, for each construct, was measured using the composite reliability metric (Dillon-Goldstein rho), which was greater than 0.7 [17].

Convergent Validity. The Average Variance Extracted (AVE) was used to assess the convergent validity of each construct in the respective measurement models. Our results showed that the AVE for each construct exceeded the threshold value of 0.5 [17].

Discriminant Validity. This criterion was evaluated using the crossloading of each construct on the other constructs. With respect to each construct, we found no indicator that loaded higher on any other construct than the one it was meant to measure [17].

5.2 Analysis of Structural Models

Figure 3 shows the structural models of the interrelationships among all three web design constructs (*classical aesthetics*, *expressive aesthetics* and *perceived credibility*) for the two user groups and for all four web designs.

For brevity and easy comparison of model parameters, we have combined all eight models for the lower and higher education groups in one overall model. In general, the models are characterized by three parameters: goodness of fit (GOF), coefficient of determination (R^2) and path coefficient (β). The GOF for each model indicates the predictive power of the model, i.e., how well the model fits its data [18]. The R^2-value for each model represents the amount of variance of a given endogenous construct explained by its exogenous constructs. Finally, the β-value indicates the strength of the relationship between two constructs in the respective models. Overall, the GOF values for our models range from 62% to 74% (which is deemed acceptable), while the R^2 values range from 48% (moderate) to 75% (high) [18]. Moreover, except for the relationship between *expressive aesthetics* and *perceived credibility* for web design WC, all of the interrelationships are significant. Specifically, the relationship between *classical aesthetics* and *expressive aesthetics* is the strongest (ranging from 0.75 to 0.86, $p < 0.0001$), followed by the relationship between *classical aesthetics* and *perceived credibility* (ranging from 0.33 to 0.68, $p < 0.0001$) and the relationship between *expressive aesthetics* and *perceived credibility* (ranging from 0.15 to 0.39, $p < 0.01$).

Moreover, our multigroup analyses showed that there are significant differences ($p < 0.05$) between the two user groups with respect to the three interrelationships. First, the relationship between *classical aesthetics* and *perceived credibility* is stronger for the higher education group than the lower education group. This finding is

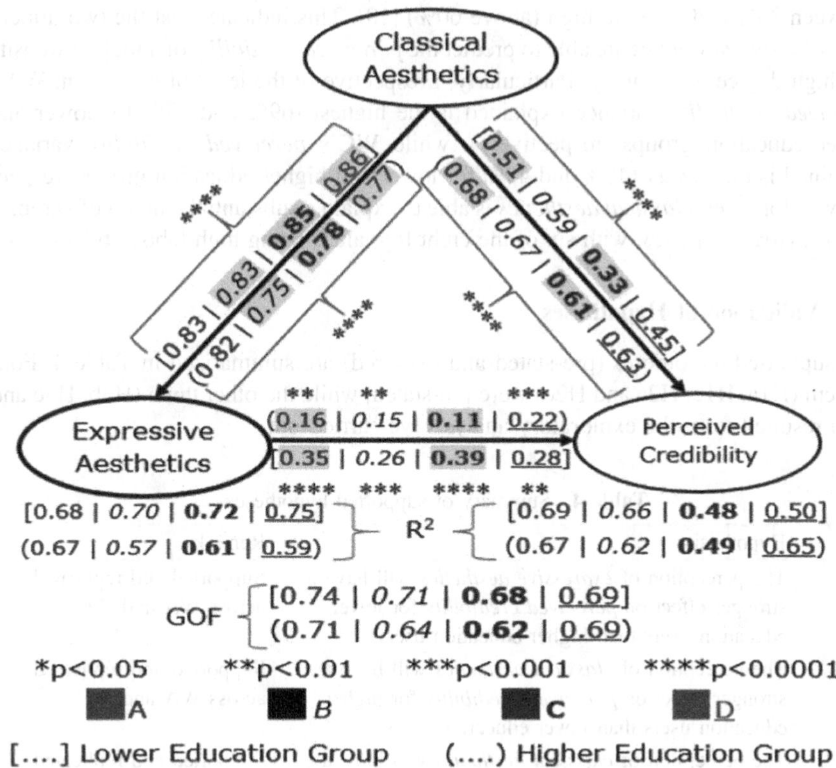

Fig. 3. Subgroup models (highlighted coefficients indicate multigroup differences, p < 0.05)

replicable across at least two of the website designs (WA and WC) as evident in the highlighted β-values. Second, the relationship *between expressive aesthetics* and *perceived credibility* is stronger for the lower education group than the higher education group. Similarly, this finding is replicable across at least two of the website designs (WA and WC) as evident in the highlighted β-values. Finally, the relationship *between classical* and *expressive aesthetics* is stronger for the lower education group than the higher education group. This finding is replicable across three of the web designs (WB, WC and WD) as evident in the highlighted β-values. We discuss these significant group differences in Sect. 6.

6 Discussion

The results of our SEM analysis (see Fig. 3) reveal that, in mobile web design, the three interrelationships among *classical aesthetics*, *expressive aesthetics* and *perceived credibility* are significant (p < 0.01), regardless of the education level of the users and the aesthetic attributes of the web design. Moreover, the variance of *perceived credibility* explained by the two dimensions of visual aesthetics ranges from moderate (between 30% and 60%) to high (above 60%) [18]. This indicates that the two dimensions of *visual aesthetics* are able to predict the *perceived credibility* of a mobile website to a high degree of accuracy. Particularly, irrespective of the level of education, WA's *perceived credibility* variance explained is the highest (69% and 67% for lower and higher education groups, respectively), while WC's *perceived credibility* variance explained is the lowest (48% and 49% for lower and higher education groups, respectively). Moreover, *classical aesthetics* is able to explain a substantial amount of variance of *expressive aesthetics*, with six of the eight R^2-values being high (above 60%).

6.1 Validation of Hypotheses

Our supported hypotheses (pre-stated and explored) are summarized in Table 4. Four of them (H1a, H1c, H2a and H2c) were pre-stated, while the other three (H3b, H3c and H3d) resulted from the exploratory analysis we carried out.

Table 4. Summary of supported hypotheses

No.	Hypothesis	Remark
H1a H1c	The perception of *expressive aesthetics* will have a stronger effect on *perceived credibility* for lower education users than higher education users.	Supported and replicated across WA and WC
H2a H2c	The perception of *classical aesthetics* will have a stronger effect on *perceived credibility* for higher education users than lower education users.	Supported and replicated across WA and WC
H3b* H3c* H3d*	The perception of *classical aesthetics* will have a stronger effect on *expressive aesthetics* for lower education users than higher education users.	Supported and replicated across WB, WC and WD

*Hypothesis that was not pre-stated but found to be true by the SEM analysis

The validation of H1a and H1c in the first set of hypotheses indicates that users with lower education are more likely than users with higher education to use perceived *expressive aesthetics* as a basis for judging the *perceived credibility* of mobile websites. This finding is replicated across two of the web designs: multicolor website (WA) and moderate-color website (WC). This means that, regardless of the actual visual design, lower education users are more likely than higher education users to use perceived expressive or complex features (*fascinating*, *creative*, *sophisticated*, etc.) to judge the two websites in question as *credible*. This finding is in line with Lightner's [13], who found that the visual impact of e-commerce sites (which employed stylistic use of visual elements such as color) on users' buying behavior and/or preferences became less important as the education level of respondents increased. Thus, based on our finding and Lightner's [13], we conclude that visually stimulating and arousing websites are more likely to be perceived as *credible* by lower education users than higher education users. Moreover, this finding suggests that visually stimulating and arousing websites, which mostly employ expressive features, are more likely to be judged as *credible* by lower education users than higher education users. This finding is evident in Oyibo et al.'s [12] prior study, in which they found that a higher percentage of Nigerian respondents (with lower education level) ranked the WA design (which, due to its colorfulness, is most aesthetically expressive – from the designer's perspective) as more *credible* compared to the Canadian respondents (with higher education level). On the flipside, a higher percentage of Canadian respondents (with higher education level) ranked the WA design as least credible compared to the Nigerian respondents (with lower education level). However, due to the possible influence of culture, our current finding among a mixed population needs further investigation, especially among a homogeneous population, in which the two education groups belong to the same culture.

On the other hand, the validation of H2a and H2c in the second set of hypotheses indicates that users with higher education are more likely than users with lower education to use perceived *classical aesthetics* as a basis for judging the *perceived credibility* of websites. Again, this finding is replicated across two of the web designs (WA and WC), both of which have different color schemes. This means that, regardless of the actual visual design, higher education users are more likely than lower education users to use perceived classical or simple features of a website (*clean*, *pleasant*, *orderly*, etc.) to judge a website as *credible*. Moreover, this finding suggests that less visually stimulating and arousing websites, which only employ basic features, are more likely to be judged as *credible* by higher education users than lower education users. This finding is evident in a prior study by Oyibo et al. [12], in which the authors found that a higher percentage of Canadian respondents (with higher education level) ranked the WB web design (the least aesthetically expressive – from the designer's perspective) as more *credible* compared to the Nigerian respondents (with lower education level). On the flipside, a higher percentage of Nigerian respondents (with lower education level) ranked the WB design as least *credible* compared to the Canadian respondents (with higher education level). Again, just like in the previous case, due to the possible influence of culture, this current finding among a mixed population needs further investigation among a homogeneous population, in which the two education groups belong to the same culture.

Further, it is interesting to note that, for the other two web designs (WB and WD), the relationship between *expressive aesthetics* and *perceived credibility* is stronger for the lower education users than for the higher education users, except that the numerical differences between the respective path coefficients are not statistically significant at $p < 0.05$. For example, with respect to WB, the path coefficient for the relationship in question is ($\beta = 0.26$, $p < 0.001$) for the lower education group and ($\beta = 0.15$, $p < 0.01$) for the higher education group. However, the numerical difference did not translate into statistical significance. Similarly, for both web designs (WB and WD), the relationship between *classical aesthetics* and *perceived credibility* is stronger for the higher education users than the lower education users, except that the numerical differences between the respective path coefficients are not statistically significant at $p < 0.05$. For example, with respect to WB, the path coefficient for the relationship in question is ($\beta = 0.67$, $p < 0.0001$) for the higher education group and ($\beta = 0.59$, $p < 0.0001$) for the lower education group. However, the numerical difference did not translate into statistical significant. Despite the non-significant statistical differences between the respective path coefficients for the two education groups with respect to WB and WD (discussed above), the numerical differences between them tend to confirm the validation of H1 and H2 across the WA and WC web designs.

Finally, using exploratory analysis, we found that the influence of *classical aesthetics* on *expressive aesthetics* is stronger for the lower education group than the higher education group, which is replicated across WB, WC and WD. This finding is an indication that *perceived expressive aesthetics* partially mediates the influence of *classical aesthetics* on *perceived credibility*. This partial mediation, our mediation analysis showed, is stronger for the lower education group than for the higher education group.

In a nutshell, the overall significance of our findings is that, in the judgment of *perceived credibility* of mobile websites, *expressive aesthetics* (perceived fascination, creativity and sophistication) is more relevant to lower education users than to higher education users, while *classical aesthetics* (perceived pleasantness, clarity and simplicity) is more relevant to higher education users than to lower education users. Web designers can leverage these findings to tailor e-commerce websites to the respective user groups in order to enhance the *perceived credibility* of their websites.

6.2 Limitations and Future Work

Our study has a number of limitations. We focus here on three of the main limitations. The first and foremost limitation is that our study is based on users' perception of the presented websites. This may threaten the generalizability of our findings to the experimental context in which users have to actually interact with the four web designs. The second limitation of our study is that its findings are in the context of mobile web design, which may not generalize to the desktop domain. The third limitation of our study is that our findings are in the context of a mixed (heterogeneous) population, in which important demographic variables such as age, gender and culture are not controlled for in the analysis of the structural models. To address the above limitations, in future work, we recommend further studies be carried out in an experimental setting, in the desktop domain and among a homogeneous population, in which one or more of the aforementioned demographic variables are controlled for, to verify the generalizability of our findings.

7 Conclusion

We presented a model of the moderating effect of education on the interrelationships among *classical aesthetics*, *expressive aesthetics* and *perceived credibility* in mobile web design. We found that lower education users are more likely to use *expressive* (aesthetic) features (perceived creativity and sophistication of the web design) to judge the *perceived credibility* of mobile websites than higher education users. On the other hand, we found that higher education users are more likely to use *classical* (aesthetic) features (perceived cleanness, pleasantness and simplicity of the web design), which are strongly related to *perceived usability* [5], to judge the *perceived credibility* of mobile websites than lower education users. Moreover, we found that the relationship between *classical aesthetics* and *expressive aesthetics* is stronger for lower education users than higher education users. These findings provide interesting insights into how the level of education of mobile website users can moderate the interrelationships among the two dimensions of *visual aesthetics* and the *perceived credibility* of mobile websites. Designers can leverage these insights in the development of e-commerce websites optimized for the respective user groups based on their level of education.

References

1. Robins, D., Holmes, J.: Aesthetics and credibility in web site design. Inf. Process. Manag. **44**, 386–399 (2008). https://doi.org/10.1016/j.ipm.2007.02.003
2. Oyibo, K., Adaji, I., Orji, R., Vassileva, J.: What drives the perceived credibility of mobile websites: classical or expressive aesthetics? In: Kurosu, M. (ed.) HCI 2018. LNCS, vol. 10902, pp. 576–594. Springer, Cham (2018). https://doi.org/10.1007/978-3-319-91244-8_45
3. Oyibo, K., Ifeoma, A., Vassileva, J.: What drives the perceived credibility of health apps: classical or expressive aesthetics. In: HealthRecSys Workshop, Vancouver, Canada (2018)
4. Lavie, T., Tractinsky, N.: Assessing dimensions of perceived visual aesthetics of web sites. Int. J. Hum. Comput. Stud. **60**, 269–298 (2004)
5. Oyibo, K., Vassileva, J.: What drives perceived usability in mobile web design: classical or expressive aesthetics? In: Marcus, A., Wang, W. (eds.) DUXU 2017. LNCS, vol. 10288, pp. 445–462. Springer, Cham (2017). https://doi.org/10.1007/978-3-319-58634-2_33
6. Oyibo, K., Adaji, I., Vassileva, J.: The effect of age and information design on the perception of visual aesthetic. In: British Human Computer Interaction Workshop, Belfast, UK (2018)
7. Oyibo, K., Ifeoma, A., Olabenjo, B., Orji, R., Vassileva, J.: The interplay between classical aesthetics, expressive aesthetics and persuasiveness in behavior modeling. In: 32nd Human-Computer Interaction Conference, Belfast, Northern Ireland (2018)
8. Fogg, B.J.: Persuasive Technology: Using Computers to Change What We Think and Do. Morgan Kaufmann, San Francisco (2003)
9. Fogg, B.J., Soohoo, C., Danielson, D.R., Marable, L., Stanford, J., Tauber, E.R.: How do users evaluate the credibility of Web sites?: a study with over 2,500 participants. In: Proceedings of the 2003 Conference on Designing for User Experiences, pp. 1–15 (2003)
10. Oyibo, K., Vassileva, J.: The interplay of aesthetics, usability and credibility in mobile website design and the moderation effect of gender. SBC J. Interact. Syst. **8**, 4–19 (2017)
11. Oyibo, K., Vassileva, J.: The interplay of aesthetics, usability and credibility in mobile websites and the moderation by culture. In: Proceedings of the 15th Brazilian Symposium on Human Factors in Computer Systems - IHC 2016, pp. 1–10 (2016)
12. Oyibo, K., Ali, Y.S., Vassileva, J.: An empirical analysis of the perception of mobile website interfaces and the influence of culture. In: Proceedings of Personalized Persuasive Technology Workshop, Salzburg, Austria, pp. 44–56 (2016)
13. Lightner, N.J.: What users want in e-commerce design: effects of age, education and income. Ergonomics **46**, 153–168 (2003). https://doi.org/10.1080/00140130210000035280
14. van Schaik, P., Ling, J.: The role of context in perceptions of the aesthetics of web pages over time. Int. J. Hum. Comput. Stud. **67**, 79–89 (2009)
15. Setterstrom, S.: Assessing credibility and aesthetic perception across different exposure times on a health care information website (2010)
16. Bergkvist, L., Rossiter, J.R.: The predictive validity of multiple-item versus single-item measures of the same constructs. J. Mark. Res. **44**, 175–184 (2007). https://doi.org/10.1509/jmkr.44.2.175
17. Hair, J.F., Hult, G.T.M., Ringle, C.M., Sarstedt, M.: A Primer on Partial Least Squares Structural Equation Modeling (PLS-SEM). Sage Publications, Washington, D.C. (2014)
18. Sanchez, G.: PLS Path Modeling with R. Trowchez Editions, Berkeley (2013)

Water Cartography

João Paulo Ramos Piron[1(✉)] and Luisa Paraguai[2(✉)]

[1] Pontifical Catholic University of Campinas, Campinas, Brazil
joaopaulopiron@gmail.com
[2] Master Program in Language, Media and Art (LIMIAR), Pontifical Catholic University of Campinas, Campinas, Brazil
luisa.donati@puc-campinas.edu.br

Abstract. The text presents cartography as methodological exercise and path writing, which operationalize infographic concepts and techniques in the production of narrative. It is about the environmental condition of the Tietê River, based on data from the SOS Mata Atlântica Foundation's "Observando o Tietê" [Observing the Tietê River] project, which depends on the direct participation of the local community in the collection and monitoring processes. The description of the infograph articulates choices, organizes ideas, and materializes data, designing behaviors. It proposes the river as protagonist and lived place, understanding that visual representations mediate man and his social and political phenomena. Finally, we are interested in articulating the sense of smell as a differential operator of the proposed narrative, seeking to evoke a perceptual experience - an encounter with/between objects and spaces in the production of tacit knowledge. And, the use of Mário de Andrade's poem is justified, as a sensitive dialogue between memory and time-space lived.

Keywords: Art and design · Data visualization and narratives · Cartography and method

1 Introduction: Cartography as Method and Narrative

This text is concerned with mapping as a procedural action that structures descriptions of a certain space. The narrative and methodological dimensions to create and manipulate representations, aiming at reading, reflection, understanding and communication of information are prioritized. In this sense, we will be composing cartography and infography, as a design exercise in the field of Digital Design, which sought to impact and reflect society's behavior on the urgency of preserving Brazilian rivers. To this end, the projected infograph was exhibited at the Tietê River Memorial Museum in the city of Salto, São Paulo, receiving school visits during the period from November 2017 to January 2018, and today it is in the headquarters of the SOS Mata Atlântica Project in city of Itu, São Paulo.

Cartography is an exercise in reporting, which records worldviews, everyday actions, processes of meaning, and participates in the designing behaviours of citizens and readers. By knowing the place where one lives, being able to circulate in public spaces and participating in community life, potentiates subjective exercises, defines territories, and contextualizes experiences.

A. Marcus and W. Wang (Eds.): HCII 2019, LNCS 11584, pp. 80–93, 2019.
https://doi.org/10.1007/978-3-030-23541-3_7

An embodied experience that "makes possible both the finiteness of my perception and its opening out upon the complete world as a horizon of every perception" (Merleau-Ponty 1999: 408). This phenomenological dimension, which "is part of the qualitative character of many of our experiences ... because they are experiences of individual particular objects" (Montague 2011: 121). Thus, they constitute cultural processes of signification, for "we move from direct and intimate experiences to those involving more and more symbolic and conceptual apprehensions" (Tuan 2011: 136). From the detection of information as environmental sensorial stimuli to the cognitive processes of signification, we are culturally and socially modelled, to a certain extent, in the actions of recoding, association and understanding.

The polysemic nature of the infograph responds to our initial intention to organize the information sensorially, because from the view the other senses can provide data of the surroundings, that take us in such a way "to produce not only a figure, but a pulsating world of life "(Ibid.: 18) (Tuan 2011). Smell, in particular, arouses emotions intensely and rapidly, because olfactory signals penetrate directly into the limbic system of the brain, the nucleus of emotions and memory, traversing far fewer synapses than signals emanating from other senses. Above all, the smell and the other non-visual senses are deeply connected to the experience of pleasure.

Thus, in this text we are interested in articulating the sense of smell as a differential operator of the proposed narrative, seeking to evoke a perceptual experience - an encounter with/between objects, memories and spaces in the production of tacit knowledge. A production of dynamically and collectively shaped meanings always in process. Smells are evocative, situating us in a particular time and space, can order spatialities and constitute the notion of place, when singularly activated by passers-by. For Tuan (2011) and de Certeau (2008: 201) space is being updated by practices, conventions and modes of use, and transforming into place - "an instantaneous configuration of positions."

If cartography as a science works with territories and their representations, in a similar way we also take it as a method, since we operate with the doing of research in process. For Deleuze and Guattari (1995: 22) cartography is based on the principles of the concept of "rhizome", as map "is open, connectable in all its dimensions, detachable, reversible, constantly susceptible to changes". With this methodological perspective, the objectives are subordinated to the research process itself, which happens as a subjective action of intervention. For this reason, the cartographic proposal suggests a reversal of the traditional conception of method (metá-hódos) for hódos-metá because it prioritizes the course itself. The method emphasizes the constant dialogue between researcher and object of study, subject and context, understanding that from these encounters there may be movements that modify both one and the other. It is a subject-dependent, flow-seeking method that organizes sensitivities and actions, shaped by their sensorimotor skills and intellectual abilities (de Oliveira and Paraíso 2012).

2 The "Observando o Tietê" [Observing the Tietê River] Project: Water Collection Routes

The visualization project seeks to validate the commitment and engagement of those involved in the "Observando o Tietê" [Observing the Tietê River] project, based on the collection of water samples [i] Piray River [ii] and Tietê River. As affirmed by Passos et al. (2015: 57), "the aim of cartography is precisely to draw the network of forces to which the object or phenomenon in question is connected, dealing with its modulations and its permanent movement." The chemical kit describes the procedures for the measurement of water parameters, chemical data such as phosphate, potassium, pH, turbidity and oxygen, providing instructions on how to handle the collection of these data. The tubes containing the water and its specific reagents are positioned on top of cardboards for visual comparison, based on a palette of colours corresponding to a chemical state (Fig. 1). Comparing is a way of qualifying and signifying the reading processes, as states Andrade (2008: 41): "comparisons and differentiations facilitate the comprehension of information." On that account we opted for the use of pieces of cardboard as operational element for the reading of the infograph that will be projected, with a view to evoking experiences and creating links, "in a dynamic wherein knowing and doing present themselves as simultaneous and inseparable actions." (Passos et al. 2015: 102).

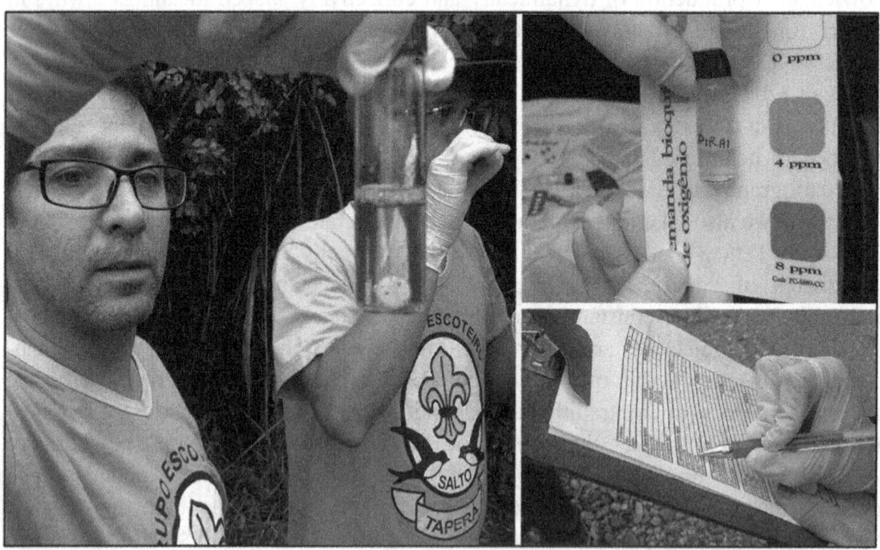

Fig. 1. Process for measuring water parameters, using the cards for comparison of each chemical component by color. (Used with permission.)

In this sense, during the collection of the water samples, the scouts spoke about their own experiences as observers and the relevance of sharing the exercise of preservation of the environment with the next generations. The affective bonds are exercised on a monthly basis through the monitoring of the waters, considering the future of our natural resources and their eminent scarcity. Attentive to the plan of events, we were gradually awakened to the connexions, and bonds were born inside of us.

The foam that is formed on the margins of the Tietê River evidences the accumulation of detergents and cleaning products in general (Fig. 2). Hence, the results on sewage management in urban areas through which the river crosses present themselves as fundamental information in the infograph, as "the reports are examples of how writing, anchored in experience and performatizing the events and occurrences, can contribute to the production of data during a research" (Passos et al. 2015: 73).

Fig. 2. Process of collecting the Tietê river water (Used with permission.)

The importance of giving visibility to these individuals who work for change, for the desire to transform society through personal and collective actions becomes evident from this experience with the observers. In the end, we were all completely involved with the project, "at this point, it is no longer a researching subject in the process of delimiting their object. Subject and object are fused together and emerge from an affective plane" (Passos et al. 2015: 74). Accompanying the sampling process and becoming aware of the movements that govern the genesis of the "Observando o Tietê" project has altered our perception about the courses of action that need to be taken in the next stages of the intervention-research, "a knowledge process that is not limited to describing or classifying the formal contours of the objects of the world, but above all deals with tracing the very movement that animates them, in other words, their constant production process (Passos et al. 2015: 92).

The classifications, hierarchizations, dichotomies, forms and figures, all of which are so familiar in our everyday lives, must disappear, even if for brief moments, in order for the bodies to expose themselves in their most intensive state of variation, in other words, that is, as pure qualities that have not yet been reduced to categories of representation (Passos et al. 2015: 100).

The collection experience was essential to mobilize the principles that guide data visualization, and thus to begin with we sought representations of the Tietê River, based on the understanding that "representations are 'models', which are essential to guide creative actions" (Passos et al. 2015: 37).

3 Data Visualization: Hierarchies and Information

The first visual representation of the cartography of the Tietê River was the Spanish map drawn by Don Luis de CéspedesXeria, governor of Paraguay, in 1628 (Fig. 3). In this map there is no concern for documenting the river in a realistic manner. Rather, it focuses on marking the crossing points and paths, and showing its tributaries. It is interesting to note and understand the historical construction, no matter whether "through multiple, even if conflicting, visions of the same entity." (Passos et al. 2015: 29).

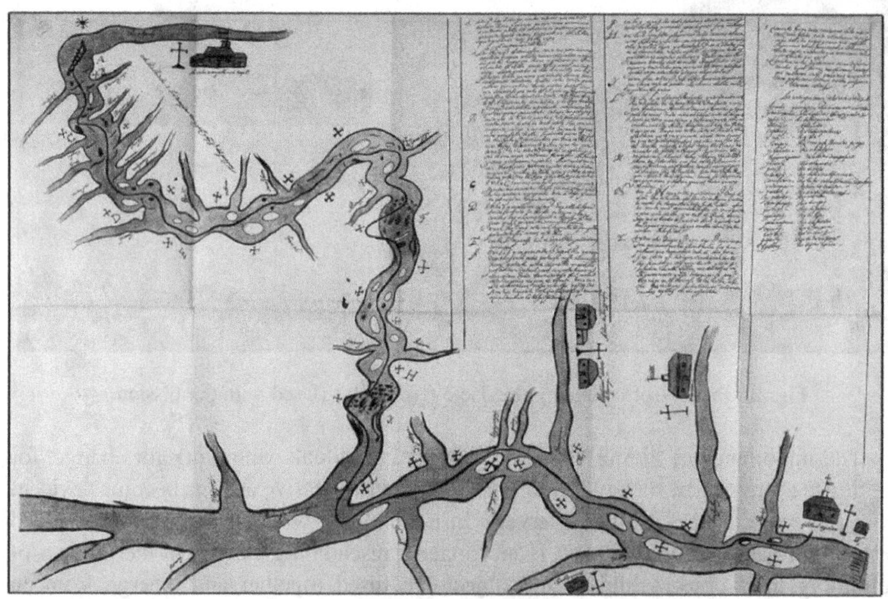

Fig. 3. The map (1628) is from the Don Luis de Cespedes Xeria's letter. The copy is from 1917 (http://historiasalto.blogspot.com/2015/06/tiete-um-rio-repleto-de-historias.html).

The Tietê River is part of the history of the state of São Paulo, as points out Nóbrega (1978, p. 30): "(…) during a certain period in time, the TietêRiver can be identified with the very life - soul and body, tradition and progress, glory and misery – of São Paulo." Nóbrega (1978) Therefore, it is important to assign *tags* to the Tietê River as an entity per se, a living being which, "flows across us and transforms the future at each passing moment, like a past in movement," as affirm Passos et al. (2015: 60).

Another representation of the River can be found in the poetry of Mário de Andrade, "Meditaçãosobre o Rio Tietê" [Meditation on the Tietê River], from 1945, where the poet presents a critical view about man's relationship with nature, in a conversation between him and the river permeated with questions about his experiences, poetically exposing the state of the waters and the evils of life in the city. In this way, life of/in the Tietê River can be understood as a living entity, comprising many layers, from the organelles to the molecules that compose water. More complex systems are formed in a cumulative sense, acting and functioning as interdependent connections among objects (Vassão 2010). Regarding the "Observando o Tietê" project as a multiplicity of articulations of the biological and chemical aspects of water, our intention was to establish a visual semantic relation with microscopic cellular representations, organelles and molecules, for the production of the infograph. Thus, once these articulations were presented a semantic panel was developed (Fig. 4), which is fundamental for visually organizing the representations by means of tags: water, *living organisms, molecules, cells, life* and *DNA*. Bürdek (2006) affirms that images clarify doubts about the meaning of words, and the semantic panels become an ideation tool in the project-oriented development.

It is increasingly necessary to employ visualization methods in the development and configuration of products. Verbal descriptions of targets, concepts and solutions are no longer sufficient, particularly in the development of design, which is incorporated within the global aspects (Bürdek 2006: 265).

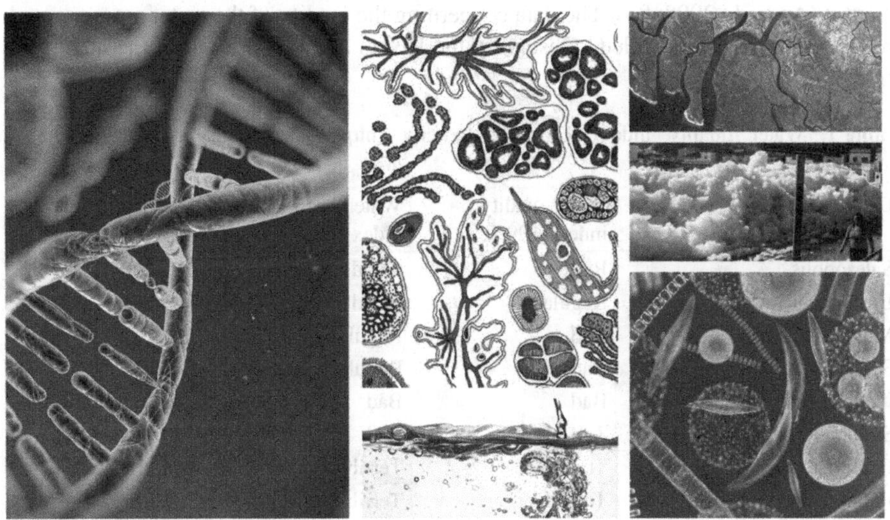

Fig. 4. Semantic panel (Used with permission.)

3.1 Infograph: Method and Development

The Andrade (2008: 82–87) method encompasses the stages "Focus or Edit, Defining the Target Audience, Collection of Information, Analysis of Information, Hierarchization of Information, Exchange of Elements, Provision of Parameters, Aim of

Approach and Checklist." Below we describe some of these stages in more detail, though it is worth noting that they do not occur in a linear manner, even if they have been set forth sequentially here. At the "Focus or Edit" stage, according to Andrade (2008: 71), "highlight the distinctive characteristics of the information contained in the design product (…) thereby rendering the information more specific and comprehensive." In this way, we present results pertaining to the quality of the water and to the respective sewage sludge management in the largest cities through which the River flows, proposing an articulation between the elements and a reflection about the impact of the action of man on the natural cycles of water and the courses of rivers, using a metaphor that flirts with the poem presented in the introduction. Kanno (2013: 72) corroborates by stating that "what determines the correct infograph process is the way the theme is approached. Within each entry, the infograph will take on the specific mission of explaining or visually illustrating an aspect."

In the "Defining the Target Audience" stage, we delimited a group of readers who were over fourteen years of age as per the contents of the curriculum to which youngsters are exposed in our education system, which include topics on biology, chemistry, geography and notions of 'sustainable development' and 'sustainability'. It is also interesting to note that the infograph was presented at the Memorial do Rio Tietê (Tietê River Memorial) museum, which has monthly school visits.

In the "Collection of Information" stage, we began to research databases with a view to "bringing together a maximum of information relating to the subject covered in the selected segment of the infograph. To discuss a given topic, one must first lean about it (Andrade 2008: 83). The data concerning the quality of the water are presented in the Technical Report titled "Observing the Rivers 2017: A portrait of the quality of

Table 1. Water quality index according to city (https://www.sosma.org.br/quem-somos/publicacoes/).

City	Water quality index (1993)	Water quality index (2017)	Distance from spring
Salesópolis	Regular	Good	17 km
Biritiba Mirim	Regular	Good	34 km
Mogi das Cruzes	Bad	Regular	61 km
Suzano	Bad	Regular	88 km
Itaquaquecetuba	Bad	Bad	102 km
São Paulo	Terrible	Bad	139 km
Osasco	Terrible	Terrible	164 km
Pirapora do Bom Jesus	Terrible	Terrible	203 km
Cabreúva	Terrible	Terrible	260 km
Itu	Terrible	Regular	272 km
Salto	Terrible	Regular	283 km
Porto Feliz	Terrible	Regular	331 km
Tietê	Terrible	Regular	385 km
Barra Bonita	Terrible	Regular	576 km

the water and the evolution of the impact indicators of the Tietê Project", compiled by the NGO SOS Mata Atlântica (Table 1) and Companhia Ambiental do Estado de São Paulo (CETESB) [Environmental Company of the State of São Paulo] (Table 2). First established in 1986, the SOS Mata Atlântica Foundation is a non-governmental organization that is active in the conservation of the country's most threatened forests and associated coastal and marine environments. The Foundation seeks to ensure sustainable development and quality of life for human beings. And CETESB, since 1968, has been the State Government agency responsible for the control, supervision, monitoring and licensing of pollution-generating activities, with the fundamental concern of preserving and recovering the quality of water, air and soil.

Table 2. Amount of sewage collected and treated according to city (http://www.cetesb.sp.gov.br/aguas-interiores/publicacoes-e-relatorios/).

City	Amount of sewage collected	Amount of sewage treated
Salesópolis	77%	98%
Biritiba Mirim	56%	99%
Mogi das Cruzes	93%	53%
Suzano	89%	70%
Itaquaquecetuba	62%	14%
São Paulo	88%	75%
Osasco	70%	43%
Pirapora do Bom Jesus	45%	46%
Cabreúva	67%	100%
Itu	98%	74%
Salto	92%	96%
Porto Feliz	99%	100%
Tietê	97%	38%
Barra Bonita	100%	28%

In the "Analysis of Information" stage, we opted for using the map, seeing that the data from the "Observando o Tietê" project locate/situate their results based on the cities along the river's natural course. Initially the map would present the Tietê River's course from the left to the right, following the Western reading path, without showing a genuine geographical representation of the area. Thus we opted for visualizing the river's course as a traceable path that encounters urban life – in the form of cities - along its path. According to Andrade (Andrade 2008: 84), "quite often, part of the information collected at a previous stage is not actually fundamental for the reader's comprehension at all."

In the stage of "Hierarchization of Information", the information is hierarchized in three levels. The First Level shows the cities in different scales, organized along the course of the Tietê River, presenting data on the distance from its source; the Second Level provides data concerning the quality of the water samples collected by SOS Mata Atlântica; the Third Level presents data related to sewage and the course of river the,

Table 3. Cities x Sewage collected.

City	< 70%	70% - 90%	> 90%
Salesópolis			
Biritiba Mirim			
Mogi das Cruzes			
Suzano			
Itaquaquecetuba			
São Paulo			
Osasco			
Pirapora do Bom Jesus			
Cabreúva			
Itu			
Salto			
Porto Feliz			
Tietê			
Barra Bonita			

underpinning the main narrative. During this stage, we also organized data concerning the sewage system, in order to create categories between the numbers, and in turn reducing the amount of information (Tables 3 and 4).

In the "Exchange of Elements" stage, we analyzed the semantic panel once again, in order to extract from it the visual elements needed for composing the visual metaphor of the infograph. Thus emerged the idea of presenting the cities as cells, or, more precisely, single-cell organisms positioned along the course of the river, bearing in mind that the reader would be able to visualize the organization and the colors of the organelles, and therefore clearly understand the information about the quality of the water and management of the sewage. In Data Humanism – A Visual Manifesto, Lupi (2017) defends the use of analog data drawing as a tool for comprehending visuality, and thus we began to explore the forms of the semantic panel, producing a number of sketches in the search for an effective manner of visualizing the information.

In the "Provision of Parameters" stage, the readers can compare elements to comprehend the visual compositions. Tufte (1997: 79–80) states that human thought is based on estimated quantities that are best understood when related through

Table 4. Cities x Sewage treated.

City	< 25%	25% - 50%	50% - 75%	> 75%
Salesópolis				■
Biritiba Mirim				■
Mogi das Cruzes			■	
Suzano			■	
Itaquaquecetuba	■			
São Paulo			■	
Osasco		■		
Pirapora do Bom Jesus		■		
Cabreúva				■
Itu			■	
Salto				■
Porto Feliz				■
Tietê		■		
Barra Bonita		■		

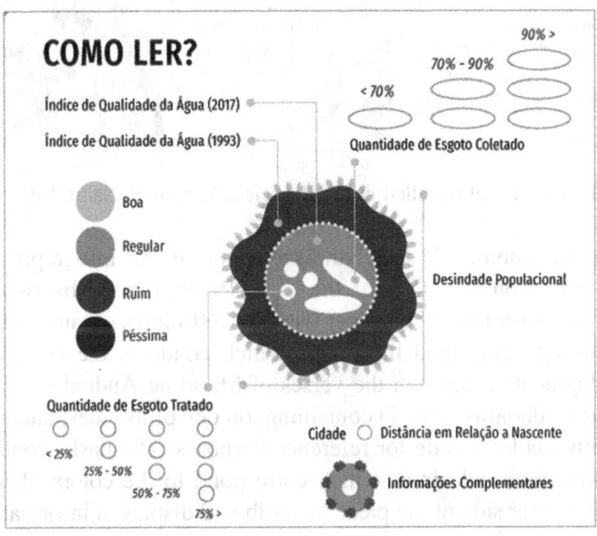

Fig. 5. Parameters: scalable forms and colors.

comparative parameters - namely light/dark, high/low, large/small – which the author calls “Parallelism”. Therefore the use of different colors (light/dark) in each of the cell structures (Fig. 5) allows the reader to create a comparative analysis between the quality of the river before and after the “Observando o Tietê” project, and its interventions for depollution. And the use of scalable forms (large/small) to visualize the population density also generates a parallelism that assists in the reading process. Whether we are evaluating changes over space or time, plotting out variables, the essential point is to make intelligent and appropriate comparisons.

Another important concept for the visual composition is “Multiples in Space and Time” (Tufte 1997: 105), where multiple frames are viewed as essential for narrating a process that involves the same objects. In this way, by organizing multiple cells throughout the Tietê river’s course, a proposed path is suggested to the reader, providing parameters for comparisons that reveal repetitions of and changes in patterns (Fig. 6).

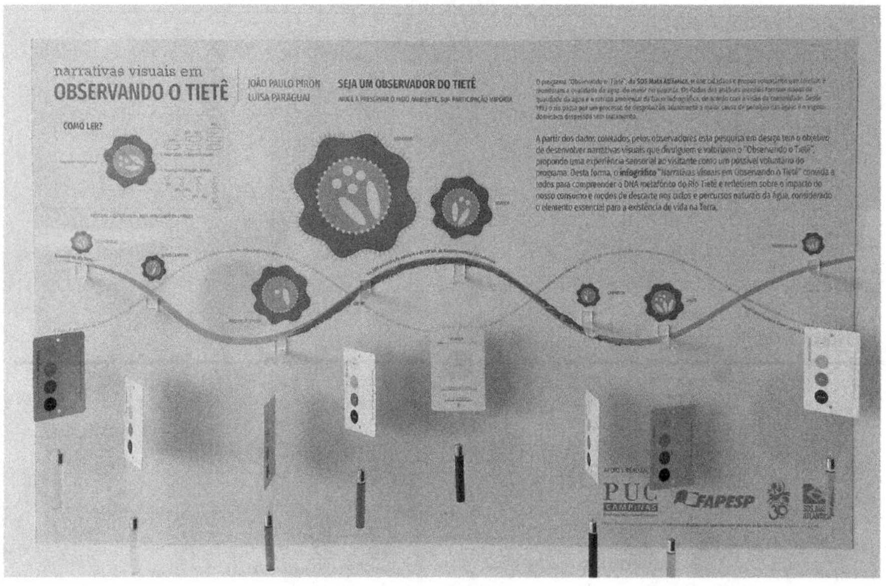

Fig. 6. Panel installed at the Rio Tietê Memorial, Salto, SP.

In the “Aim of Approach” stage, the metaphor of the infograph addresses the presentation of a metaphoric DNA of the Tietê River, formed by two perspectives (Fig. 6): the tracks, the course of the river with the cells/cities organized throughout its existence as a living being, and the poem, which conducts the narrative about the environmental degradation through the verses of Mário de Andrade.

We produced cardboards (Fig. 7) containing, on one of its sides, data relating to the water quality with a color palette for reference purposes. The flasks contain a colorful mixture made with food colorings, which correspond to the colors of the aforementioned palette. The other side of the piece of cardboard displayed information regarding the distance of the town or city vis-à-vis the Tietê River's source, as well as circles inside of which a sample of the smell of the cleaning products discharged in the domestic sewage was applied.

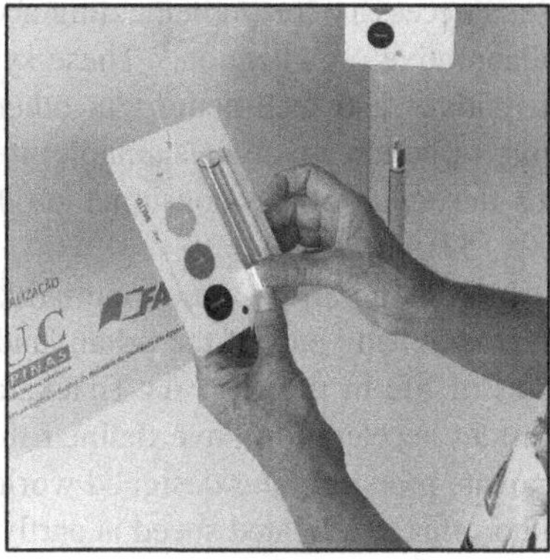

Fig. 7. Cardboard and its color palette for comparisons.

4 Final Considerations

The main objective of the "Observando o Tietê" project is to organize volunteers from a particular locality to monitor the river from a new perspective, based on the knowledge of its chemical aspects and with an awareness of its importance for the natural cycles and natural courses. The message is clear: all of us should be observers in order to achieve some form of significant change, according to Manzini (2008: 53): "The quality of a particular context is the result of the care and safe-keeping provided by all the people who reside in it." Bearing in mind these aspects of the project, we quote the author:

In fact, these are cases that, in their quest for concrete solutions, ultimately reinforce the social fabric, generating new and more sustainable ideas of well-being, and putting them into practice. More specifically, such ideas attach great value to our 'common assets', to an attentive and respectful attitude, to collaborative action, to new forms of community and to new concepts of 'locality' (Manzini 2008: 64).

Therefore, within the social, political and historical context, the designer must take on the role of evoking the network of threads, formulating proposals for rehabilitating the warps of the social-cultural fabric, and designing actions, services and products that add value to and reinforce it. Bertolotti et al. (2016) write about the role of the designer:

[…] designers can be cast as mediators, playing a dual role in the contemporary mediascape: as story listeners, they collect stories from the audience and their repertoires and, as storytellers, they organise these stories into experiences (Bertolotti et al. 2016: 73).

The proposal set forth by the infograph was to value the "Observando o Tietê" project and its observers, positing the content produced as a means to potentiate changes in behaviour. The proposal of the SOS Mata Atlântica project must be disseminated but we must bear in mind that the project does not end with the infograph, seeing that this is a projected action. In contemporaneity, the designer must systematically reflect on and ponder the project, which, in the words of Manzini (2008: 84), is an "enabling solution, a system of products, services, communication and whatever else is necessary for implementing accessibility, effectiveness and the replicability of a collaborative organization." These systems must be capable of generating sustainable alternatives and well-being, "in other words, in order for any idea focused on well-being to be effectively sustainable, it must (re)discover the quality of the context, and thus the value of the consumer products and of slow, contemplative time (Manzini 2008: 57).

In thinking about a metropolis like São Paulo, in which the pollution of the Tietê River is already part of the urban landscape and passes unnoticed by the brisk, hurried gazes of life in the city. As Thackara (2005: 29) writes: "for generations, speed and constant acceleration have defined the way we communicate, eat, travel around, and innovate products. Our designed world reinforces the value we place on speed". For the author, this accelerated speed is partly the cause for our predicament, as we continue to consume our natural resources at an ever-increasing rate, and on the verge of collapse. Thus, it is necessary to discover/rediscover local discontinuities and raise visibility, so as to create experiences and potentialize affects.

5 Notes

[i] (https://www.sosma.org.br/projeto/observando-os-rios/) The "Observing the Rivers" Project is carried out in the upper and middle Tietê river basins and sub-basins of the Sorocaba, Piracicaba, Capivari and Jundiaí rivers. It brings together communities and mobilizes them around the water quality of rivers, streams from the localities where they live. The initiative is open to the population, who can participate in the monthly monitoring, using a kit developed by the SOS Mata Atlântica Project, a Brazilian environmental Non-Governmental Organization (http://www.sosma.org.br/en/). This kit makes it possible to evaluate the rivers from a total of 16 parameters, which include levels of oxygen, phosphorus, PH, odor, visual aspects, among others, and classifies water quality in five scoring levels, according to legislation: bad (from 14 to 20 points), bad (from 21 to 26 points), regular (from 27 to 35 points), good (from 36 to 40 points) and great (over 40 points).

[ii] The data collection was carried out with the scouts Orlando Jr. De Freitas, Andréia Lourenço and Thiago Noronha Dinardi, from the Taperá Scout Group, who participate in the rivers monitoring project.

[iii] The Piray River is situated in a more remote area of the municipality, though its importance lies in the fact that it is a tributary of the Jundiaí River, which in turn flows into the Tietê River. The fluvial junctions and hierarchies in a hydrographic basin reinforce the metaphor of 'fabric', where supporting warps and networks of threads represent structural arrangements.

References

Merleau-Ponty, M.: Fenomenologia da Percepção. Martins Fontes, São Paulo (1999)
Montague, M.: The phenomenology of particularity. In: Bayne, T., Montague, M. (eds.) Cognitive Phenomenology. Oxford University Press, Oxford (2011)
Tuan, Y.-F.: Space and Place. The Perspective of Experience. Seventh Printing. University of Minnesota Press, Minneapolis (2011)
de Certeau, M.: A invenção do cotidiano: 1. Artes de fazer. Editora Vozes, Petrópolis (2008)
Deleuze, G., Guattari, F.: Mil Platôs, Capitalismo e Esquizofrenia, vol. 1. Editora 34, Rio de Janeiro (1995)
de Oliveira, T.R.M., Paraíso, M.A.: Mapas, dança, desenhos: a cartografia como método de pesquisa em educação. In: Pro-Posições, vol. 23, no. 3(69), pp. 159–178, set/dez (2012)
Passos, E., Kastrup, V., da Escossia, L.: Pistas do método da cartografia: Pesquisa-intervenção e produção de subjetividade. Sulina, Porto Alegre (2015)
Andrade, R.C.: Sistematização de um método para a produção de infográficos com base no estudo de caso do jornal Folha de São Paulo. Trabalho de Conclusão de Curso (Graduação em Design Gráfico). Centro de Educação Comunicação e Artes, Universidade Estadual de Londrina, Londrina (2008)
Nóbrega, M.: História do rio Tietê. Governo do Estado, São Paulo (1978)
Vassão, C.A.: Metadesign: ferramentas, estratégias e ética para a complexidade. Edgard Blücher, São Paulo (2010)
Bürdek, B.E.: História, teoria e prática do design de produtos. Edgard Blücher, São Paulo (2006)
Kanno, M.: Infografe: Como e porque usar infográficos para criar visualizações e comunicar de forma imediata e eficiente. Infolide, São Paulo (2013)
Lupi, G.: Data humanism: the revolutionary future of data visualization (2017). Printmag. http://www.printmag.com/information-design/data-humanism-future-of-data-visualization/. Accessed 27 Feb 2019
Tufte, E.R.: Visual Explanations. Graphic Press, Connecticut (1997)
Manzini, E.: Design para a inovação social e sustentabilidade. Comunidades criativas, organizações colaborativas e novas redes projetuais. E-papers, Rio de Janeiro (2008)
Bertolotti, E., Daam, H., Piredda, F., Tassinari, V. (eds.): The Pearl Diver, the Designer as Storyteller, vol. 1. Dipartimento di Design, Politecnico di Milano, Milano (2016)
Thackara, J.: In the Bubble. Designing in a Complex World. The MIT Press, Cambridge (2005)

Search-Efficacy of Modern Icons Varying in Appeal and Visual Complexity

Mick Smythwood[1(✉)], Siné McDougall[2], and Mirsad Hadzikadic[1]

[1] University of North Carolina at Charlotte, Charlotte, NC 28223, USA
{ksmythwo,mirsad}@uncc.edu

[2] Bournemouth University, Bournemouth, Fern Barrow, Poole BH12 5BB, UK
smcdougall@bournemouth.ac.uk

Abstract. Users' levels of satisfaction increase when their interactions are swift and they experience the interface as easy to use. Given that most interactions start with searching for the icon for the application you wish to use, characteristics affecting the efficacy of icon search are important. This study mimicked icon search on mobile devices in order to examine which characteristics were most important in determining speed of search and ease of interaction. Given what is known of visual search processing, it was not surprising that visual complexity was the primary determinant of search speed. The visual aesthetic appeal of the icons, often thought to be so important, had no significant effect on search time for icons. The reasons for this are discussed in the commentary on the role of visual complexity and aesthetic appeal when used in mobile application icon design.

Keywords: Icon design · Visual search · Evaluation · Complexity · Appeal

1 Introduction

Interface designers commonly use icons in menu design (Schröder and Ziefle 2006). Incorporating icons in a menu improves menu selection (Bailly et al. 2014) not least because icons are easier to search for and find in an interface than words (McDougall et al. 1999). Icons have the potential to communicate meaning effectively across language boundaries and support a universal mode of communication (Rogers 1989; Böcker 1996). Moreover, icons are typically small and therefore provide a good amount of information per pixel. However, because icons are small, they can be restricted in their ability to communicate complex meaning effectively. In addition, icons convey information semasiographically, in a nonverbal manner without a clear set of rules as would be the case for written language. This creates inherent ambiguity which must be resolved by designers and users alike (Carr 1986).

Well-designed icons can offer a user-friendly experience by simply being easier to search for. When it is easy to search for and find the icon you wish to use, ease of processing increases. When icons are designs using visual characteristics that contribute to their ease of use this, in turn, increases user satisfaction (Reber et al. 1998; Schwarz and Winkielman 2004; Alter and Oppenheimer 2009). Reducing the speed of processing in locating icons might seem a minimal advantage to overall usability.

A. Marcus and W. Wang (Eds.): HCII 2019, LNCS 11584, pp. 94–104, 2019.
https://doi.org/10.1007/978-3-030-23541-3_8

However, users notice performance costs as small as 150 ms (Gray and Boehm-Davis 2000). Since icon search is a task users perform repeatedly, time advantages can quickly add up. These timesavings positively affect user experience (McDougall and Reppa 2013).

This study focuses on the perceptual fluency of icon search, which refers to the ease of processing of an icon, as opposed to conceptual fluency, which involves elements of meaning. We propose that because the use of icons is proliferating on visual interfaces, visual search for icons, which is primarily perceptual, is an increasingly important component of icon and interface use. Interfaces, particularly those used for mobile phones, consist of application icons as a key entry point to functionality. Since a key part of what users have to do when using icons is to locate them amidst others in order to access the functions they represent, this experiment focuses on icon search performance. This search component has received relatively little research attention to date.

Because the functions and applications behind mobile application icons are themselves increasingly more complex, the icons similarly have increasing levels of visual complexity. Mobile gaming applications are a perfect example of this trend. Additionally, as the number of mobile applications increases, the design of the icons representing them increases in complexity as well. As the design space narrows with every new icon, icon designers naturally create more complex icons than they did before. It follows then that an understanding of how an icon's visual complexity interacts with other icon characteristics in affecting performance stands to benefit the mobile application icon designer.

2 Background

This study mimicked an icon search task on mobile devices in order to examine which characteristics were most important in determining speed of search and ease of interaction. Figure 1 in the Materials section illustrates the search task employed in measuring icon search time. First, the target icon was shown along with a next button. After the user clicked on the next button, a 9-icon matrix was displayed. The time from when the user clicked the next button to when they clicked on the target icon in the matrix was recorded as the target icon's search time. The distractor icons were of a heterogeneous mixture, according to the icon characteristics being tested.

Previous research using this search task found that an icon's visual complexity, measured using previously obtained subjective ratings and complexity metrics of an icon's complexity, affected search time significantly (McDougall et al. 1999). Users found simpler icons faster than complex ones. Other icon characteristics such as concreteness, familiarity, and aesthetic appeal had an impact on icon search (McDougall et al. 1999; McDougall and Reppa 2008; Reppa et al. 2008; Reppa and McDougall 2015).

Importantly, very little previous research has examined the effect of icon appeal on visual search (Reppa et al. 2008; Reppa and McDougall 2015). Given the importance of creating appealing as well as functional displays on mobile phones, the effect of appeal was also considered in this experiment. The little research published to date found that the aesthetic appeal of an icon interacts with its complexity in affecting search time: visual search for complex icons was easier when icons were appealing (Reppa and McDougall 2015).

This is important because of the increasing emphasis on creating appealing interfaces to enhance user experience. This area of work therefore investigates the relationships between key icon characteristics, which may facilitate ease of use by promoting perceptual fluency, i.e. visual complexity and/or aesthetic appeal.

A key aim of this experiment was to examine whether or not visual complexity and appeal had an effect on search for icons likely to appear on today's mobile devices. There has been limited research to date examining the effects of icon characteristics on visual search (McDougall et al. 2000, 2006; Reppa et al. 2008; Reppa and McDougall 2015). This work suggested that key determinants of visual search was icon complexity (simpler icons were found faster) and that this may interact with the visual appeal of the icons. However, the icon sets used in previous research were from a wide range of interfaces and were not representative of icons currently used in mobile computing. In order to make the icon sets used in the experiment more representative of current icon use, a set of icons from recent corpora was combined with icons representing mobile applications in current use (Prada et al. 2015; Smythwood and Hadzikadic 2019).

3 Hypotheses

Participants were asked to search for icons in displays. Based on the limited previous research to date, it was hypothesized that simpler icons would be located in displays more quickly than more complex icons (McDougall et al. 2000). Search was also expected to be particularly fast when icons were both simple and visually appealing (i.e. visual appeal would enhance search times creating an interaction between icon complexity and visual appeal; Reppa and McDougall 2015). Finally, it was expected that search performance would improve familiarity with icons over blocks of learning trials (McDougall et al. 2000; Reppa and McDougall 2015).

4 Method

4.1 Participants

Twenty-three students from the undergraduate research pool at the University of North Carolina at Charlotte participated in the visual search experiment. The students were from a mix of different majors taking courses to fill required electives. Each participant received research credit for completing the experiment.

Of the 23 total participants, 10 were male and 13 were female. The average age of participants was 24 years old. All student participants had normal or corrected-to-normal vision.

4.2 Materials

The trend toward increasing levels of complexity is reflected in the different icon stimulus sets used in experimentation to date. Figure 1 contains sample icons from each of the three different sets. Two are from existing icon corpora with ratings of icon characteristics designed to facilitate icon control and the third is a set of mobile application icons obtained from Google Play and Apple Store (McDougall et al. 1999; Prada et al. 2015). Icons from the first corpus have been used in icon studies over the past several years (McDougall et al. 1999), whereas those from the second have been created more recently for use in experimentation (Prada et al. 2015). The present research utilized icons from all three icon sets. By including icon sets of different types, the aim was to strengthen the validity and potential generalizability of our findings.

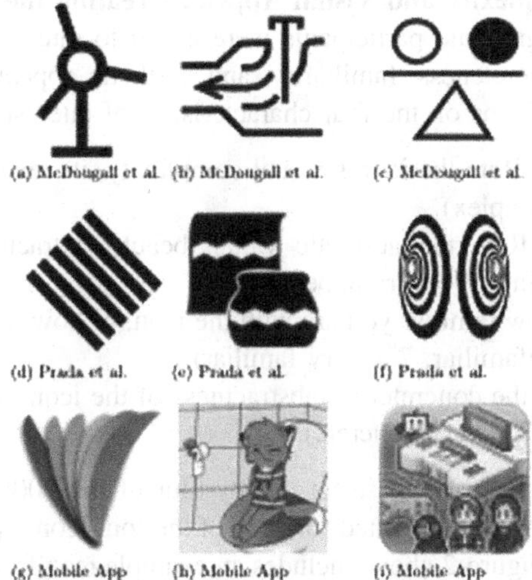

Fig. 1. Icons from each stimulus set used to construct the set used in this study.

The complexity and visual appeal of the icons was varied orthogonally creating four sets of six icons (see Fig. 2).

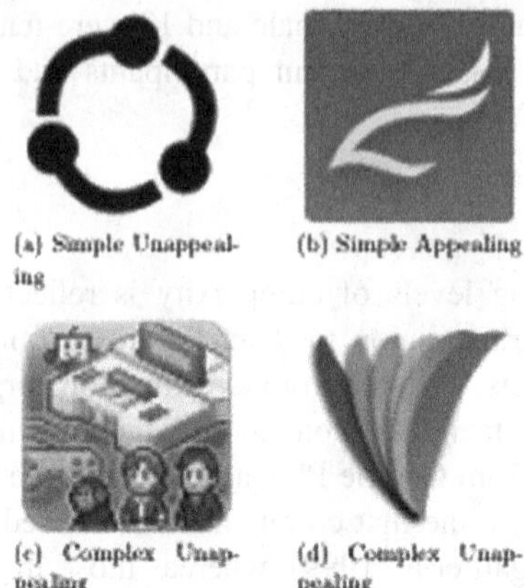

(a) Simple Unappealing (b) Simple Appealing

(c) Complex Unappealing (d) Complex Unappealing

Fig. 2. Examples of each of the four types of icons created by varying icon complexity and visual appeal orthogonally.

Measuring Icon Complexity and Visual Appeal; Creating the Test Icon Set
Fifty university undergraduate participants were asked to rate a set of 200 icons on visual complexity, concreteness, familiarity, and aesthetic appeal on a scale of 1–7. Instructions for rating icons on the four characteristics of interest were as follows:

> Visual Complexity: Rate the icon's visual complexity, its level of detail (1 = very simple, 7 = very complex)
> Aesthetic Appeal: Rate the aesthetic value, beauty, attractiveness of the icon (1 = very unappealing, 7 = very appealing)
> Familiarity: Rate how familiar you are with the icon, or how often you have seen it before (1 = very unfamiliar, 7 = very familiar)
> Concreteness: Rate the concreteness/abstractness of the icon, how realistic it looks (1 = very abstract, 7 = very concrete).

The ratings were then used to select twenty-four of the 200 icons for use in the search experiment. Icons were selected for each of the four icon types using the ratings obtained (see Fig. 2). Figure 2 above includes an example icon from each Complexity-Appeal group. As can be seen from Table 1, it was possible to vary icon complexity and appeal while holding familiarity and concreteness relatively constant. Table 1 provides the ANOVA across icon characteristics. Table 1 includes mean ratings for each Complexity-Appeal group across all four icon characteristic ratings collected.

Table 1. Mean and standard deviations for each icon characteristic across the stimulus set. F-values from ANOVA and Newman-Keuls analysis of the four icon type groups.

Icon Design Char.	Type of icon								F(3, 23)	Newman-Keuls
	CA		CU		SA		SU			
	M	SD	M	SD	M	SD	M	SD		
Appeal	3.94	0.23	3.24	0.18	3.72	0.23	3.06	0.21	*21.8	CA, SA > CU, SU
Complexity	4.39	0.40	4.07	0.34	3.16	0.56	2.97	0.31	*16.4	CA, CU > SA, SU
Concreteness	3.58	0.95	3.49	0.73	2.89	0.54	2.76	0.24	2.31	CA, CU, SA, SU
Familiarity	2.43	0.51	2.41	0.48	2.35	0.59	1.97	0.38	1.13	CA, CU, SA, SU

Note: CA = complex and appealing, CU = complex and unappealing, SA = simple and appealing, SU = simple and unappealing.
* $p < 0.05$

4.3 Procedure

The participants were told they would be presented with an icon for 2 s before they would be expected to click a "Next" button to continue to a 3 × 3 matrix of icons. See Fig. 3 for an example trial. They were instructed to click on the target icon as quickly as possible once they clicked the "Next" button. Their first choice was the only icon selection they would be allowed to make; after which they could continue to the next trial by clicking another "Next" button.

There were series of 24 search task trials, with each icon being shown once in each block of trials as the search target. Icons appearing as distractors were controlled so that a mix of two of each of the four types of icons appeared as background distractors equally often in each block of trials. There were six blocks of trials for each participant. Participants were given short breaks between blocks of trials.

Fig. 3. Icon search task.

4.4 Design

A 2 × 2 × 6 design was employed with icon complexity (Complex/Simple), icon appeal (Appealing/Unappealing) and blocks of trials (Blocks 1–6) as within-subjects factors. All factors were repeated measures taken from the same participants. Response time was used to measure ease of visual search.

We ran blocks of trials with short breaks between. The effect of learning icons over time was mimicked by presenting participants with blocks of search trials. We conducted the experiments in the controlled environment of a lab. Running multiple blocks enabled examination of learning effects over time and the lab environment facilitated accurate measurement. It allowed us to answer the question of whether the same predictive "rules" apply when users have learned the icon set they are searching for.

5 Results

Errors accounted for 1.5% of all trials. There were no differences in error rates between any of the conditions (*p* values < .05). We used an alpha level of .05 for all statistical tests and partial eta-squared as a measure of effect size. Bonferroni corrections were used throughout. Figure 4 illustrates the mean response times for each type of icon presented across six blocks of learning trials.

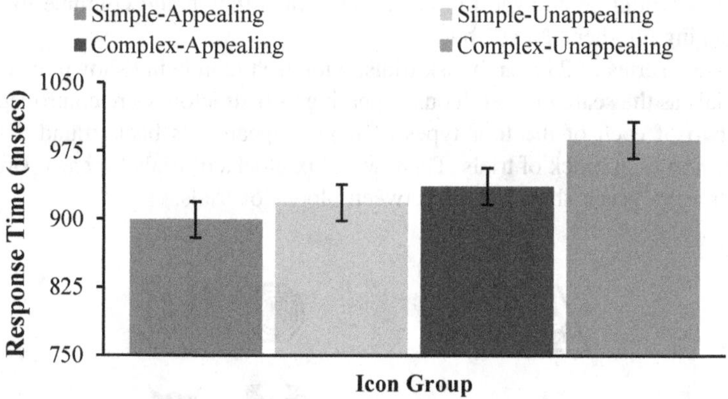

Fig. 4. Mean response time in milliseconds for Complexity-Appeal groups

By-items analysis of variance was carried out to examine the effects of icon complexity (complex vs simple) and visual appeal (appealing vs unappealing) on search response times. The analysis of variance revealed that icon complexity significantly affected search times, F(1, 20) = 4.55, p = .045, eta-squared = .185, with search times for complex icons being longer than for simple (means for simple and complex here). However, there was no main effect of icon appeal on visual search, F(1, 20) = 1.98, p = .175, eta-squared = .090. Neither was there a joint interaction between complexity and appeal on icon search time, F(1, 20) = .421, p = .524, eta-squared = .021.

Tests of within-subjects effects on complexity, appeal, and block revealed a significant effect of learning on search time across blocks, F(4, 100) = 5.13, p = .000, eta-squared = .204. Tests of within-subjects contrasts revealed a difference in search time between Blocks 1 and 2 (F(1, 20) = 4.75, p = .041, eta-squared = .100) and between Blocks 5 and 6 (F(1, 20) = 5.15, p = .034, eta-squared = .205). There were no other significant effects.

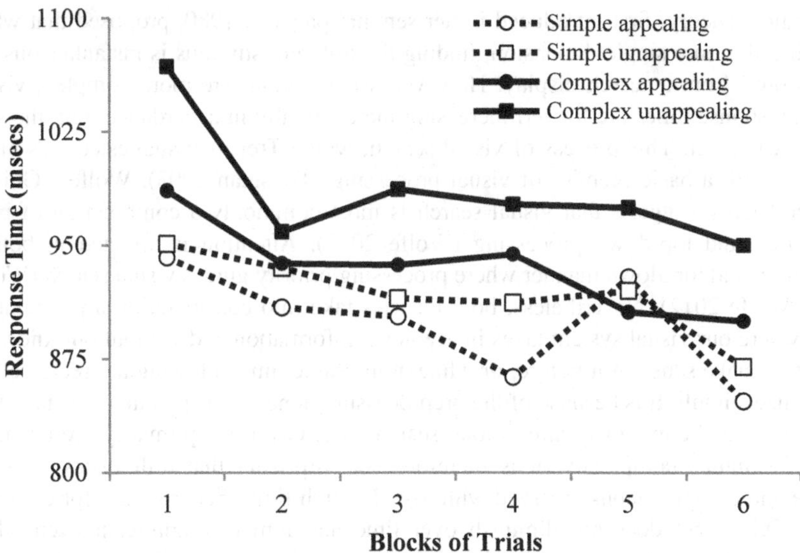

Fig. 5. Response times for each type of icon presented in the search task across blocks of trials

6 Discussion

The results from our study revealed the role of visual complexity in icon search was significant. In concert with previous findings, we found that simple icons were found faster than complex ones (McDougall et al. 2000). Also previously, icon appeal and visual complexity exhibited a joint effect on search performance (Reppa et al. 2008; Reppa and McDougall 2015). Those findings suggested that when the icon was complex, appeal provided a significant time advantage (Reppa et al. 2008).

A key aim of the present experiment was to examine whether or not visual complexity and appeal had an effect on search for icons likely to appear on today's mobile devices. There has been only limited research to date examining the effects of icon characteristics on visual search (McDougall et al. 2000, 2006; Reppa et al. 2008; Reppa and McDougall 2015). The previous work that has been done was performed with icon sets that were not representative of icons currently used in mobile computing. In order to make the icon sets used in the experiment more diverse and representative of current icon use, a set of icons from previously existing corpora was combined with icons representing mobile applications currently used.

Was the role of these characteristics the same as for other previous icon sets in a visual search task? Findings were mixed.

6.1 Visual Complexity

As previously, it took longer for participants to find complex icons than simple icons (Reppa et al. 2008; McDougall et al. 2000). The importance of complexity in visual search has been well documented (Treisman 2003; Wolfe 2012). Treisman's Feature Integration Theory, first introduced in her seminal paper in 1980, proposed that when stimuli differ on a single dimension, finding the different stimulus is instantaneous - it "pops out" from a search display. However, when stimuli are more complex, visual search response times are longer, increasing incrementally in accordance with the size of the search set. This process of visual search, which Treisman suggested was hard-wired, is still a basic premise of visual processing (Treisman 2003). Wolfe's Guided Search Theory suggests that visual search is most commonly a combination of both bottom-up and top-down processing (Wolfe 2012). Attention is directed in both a bottom-up and top-down manner where processing priority guides visual search (Wolfe 1994; Wolfe 2012). Nevertheless, both theories take into consideration a preattentive stage where our visual system takes in low-level information and without our knowing begins to make sense of it before, or while at the same time, allowing a directed effort to localize stimuli. It is because of the preprocessing done in this preattentive stage that an icon's visual complexity affects total search time. Given the primarily pre-attentive role of stimulus complexity, it is therefore not surprising that differences between simple and complex icons emerged with visual search times being longer for complex icons. This effect does not diminish over time and remains significant even when participants have learned the visual search task and become familiar with the icons across a series of blocks of trials. See Fig. 5. This was consistent with current findings (McDougall et al. 1999).

6.2 Aesthetic Appeal

Icon appeal did not appear to affect search times. Importantly, in contrast to earlier findings reported (McDougall and Reppa 2008), this experiment showed that visual complexity did not act together with icon appeal to enhance visual searching of interfaces. These earlier findings suggest that when the task was difficult, such as when the icon was complex, appealing icons were found more quickly in visual search than unappealing icons (McDougall and Reppa 2008). The findings from the present study therefore suggest that aesthetic appeal does not bias perceptual systems by giving priority to attractive stimuli, unlike detecting faces in a crowd where happy or appealing faces are found first (Becker et al. 2011).

Since the icon characteristics used in devising the search experiment were balanced across complexity and appeal while concreteness and familiarity were controlled, the results offer an "objective" look at top predictors of search performance. Recent efforts to examine the combined effects of 3 icon characteristics yielded confounding results given the existence of confounding variables (Smythwood and Hadzikadic 2019), while previous, relevant work suffered from the confounding variable of familiarity when testing for complexity-appeal search time differences (Reppa and McDougall 2015).

Our results were dependent on the range of visual complexity and the range of appeal among our icon types in the stimulus set. By including icons from existing mobile applications, we were able to include a broad variety of icons varying significantly in visual complexity as well as appeal. The variety of icons presented may mean that visual appeal becomes a less distinctive icon characteristic which does not 'stand out' visually in a way that is likely to aid visual search and suggests that the effects of appeal may depend on the contextual effects of the search set. In practical terms, when icon sets are diverse in nature, visual appeal may be less important in determining how quickly users can locate icons.

7 Conclusions

7.1 Implications for Interface Design

Icons designed with particular design characteristics in mind facilitate the visual processing involved in icon menu search. Given the ubiquity of icon menu interfaces in modern mobile computing, advantages in visual processing easily compound to provide smooth and fluent user experiences. This research has shown that the duration of visual search for icons is likely to be least when:

- icons are simple rather than complex
- icon appeal may not affect search times for icons on a display however, other research has shown that it may affect users' attitudes towards the display (Reppa and McDougall 2015).

7.2 Lesson Learned

To provide ecological validity to the results of experiments that use design artifacts as stimuli, it is good to incorporate real-world stimuli that are currently in use. As a design space expands, previous research must be revisited in order to extend the discussion. By incorporating more current and varied stimuli with existing corpora, we were able to provide a more comprehensive picture of the effects of visual complexity and appeal on the search of icons.

References

Alter, A.L., Oppenheimer, D.M.: Uniting the tribes of fluency to form a metacognitive nation. Pers. Soc. Psychol. Rev. **13**(3), 219–235 (2009)

Bailly, G., Oulasvirta, A., Brumby, D.P., Howes, A.: Model of visual search and selection time in linear menus. In: Proceedings of the SIGCHI Conference on Human Factors in Computing Systems, pp. 3865–3874 (2014)

Becker, D.V., Anderson, U.S., Mortensen, C.R., Neufeld, S.L., Neel, R.: The face in the crowd effect unconfounded: happy faces, not angry faces, are more efficiently detected in single and multiple target visual search tasks. J. Exp. Psychol. Gen. **140**(4), 637 (2011)

Böcker, M.: A multiple index approach for the evaluation of pictograms and icons. Comput. Stand. Interfaces **18**(2), 107–115 (1996)

Carr, W.: Theories of theory and practice. J. Philos. Educ. **20**(2), 177–186 (1986)

Gray, W.D., Boehm-Davis, D.A.: Milliseconds matter: an introduction to micro-strategies and to their use in describing and predicting interactive behavior. J. Exp. Psychol. Appl. **6**(4), 322–335 (2000)

McDougall, S.J.P., Curry, M.B., Bruijn, O.: Measuring icon and icon characteristics: norms for concreteness, complexity, meaningfulness, familiarity and semantic distance for 239 icons. Behav. Res. Methods Comput. Instrum. **31**, 487–519 (1999)

McDougall, S.J.P., de Bruijn, O., Curry, M.B.: Exploring the effects of icon characteristics on user performance: the role of icon concreteness, complexity and distinctiveness. J. Exp. Psychol. Appl. **6**, 291–306 (2000)

McDougall, S., Reppa, I.: Why do I like it? The relationships between icon characteristics, user performance and aesthetic appeal. Proc. Hum. Factors Ergon. Soc. Ann. Meet. **52**(18), 1257–1261 (2008)

McDougall, S., Reppa, I.: Ease of icon processing can predict icon appeal. In: Kurosu, M. (ed.) HCI 2013. LNCS, vol. 8004, pp. 575–584. Springer, Heidelberg (2013). https://doi.org/10.1007/978-3-642-39232-0_62

McDougall, S., Tyrer, V., Folkard, S.: Searching for signs, symbols, and icons: effects of time of day, visual complexity, and grouping. J. Exp. Psychol. Appl. **12**(2), 118–128 (2006)

Prada, M., Rodrigues, D., Silva, R.R., Garrido, M.V.: Lisbon Symbol Database (LSD): subjective norms for 600 symbols. Behav. Res. Methods **48**(4), 1370–1382 (2015)

Reber, R., Winkielman, P., Schwarz, N.: Effects of perceptual fluency on affective judgments. Psychol. Sci. **9**(1), 45–48 (1998)

Reppa, I., McDougall, S.: When the going gets tough the beautiful get going: aesthetic appeal facilitates task performance. Psychon. Bull. Rev. **22**(5), 1243–1254 (2015)

Reppa, I., Playfoot, D., McDougall, S.: Visual aesthetic appeal speeds processing of complex but not simple icons. Proc. Hum. Factors Ergon. Soc. Ann. Meet. **52**(18), 1155–1159 (2008)

Rogers, Y.: Icon design for the user interface. Int. Rev. Ergon. **2**, 129–154 (1989)

Schröder, S., Ziefle, M.: Icon design on small screens: effects of miniaturization on speed and accuracy in visual search. Proc. Hum. Factors Ergon. Soc. Ann. Meet. **50**(5), 656–660 (2006)

Schwarz, N., Winkielman, P.: Processing fluency and aesthetic pleasure: is beauty in the perceiver's processing experience? Pers. Soc. Psychol. Rev. **8**(4), 364–382 (2004)

Smythwood, M., Hadzikadic, M.: The effects of icon characteristics on search time. In: Ahram, T., Falcão, C. (eds.) AHFE 2018. AISC, vol. 794, pp. 57–67. Springer, Cham (2019). https://doi.org/10.1007/978-3-319-94947-5_6

Treisman, A.: What shall we do with the preattentive processing stage: use it or lose it? J. Vis. **3**(9), 572 (2003)

Wolfe, J.M.: Guided Search 2.0: a revised model of visual search. Psychon. Bull. Rev. **1**(2), 202–238 (1994)

Wolfe, J.M.: Guided Search 4.0: current progress with a model of visual search. In: Gray, W. (ed.) Integrated Models of Cognitive Systems, pp. 99–120. Oxford University Press, New York (2012)

Examining the Influence of Visual Stimuli and Personal Characteristics on Users' Willingness-to-Wait Time and Waiting Patterns

Jingyi Zhou[1] and Pengyi Zhang[2(✉)]

[1] School of Psychological and Cognitive Sciences, Peking University, Beijing, China
1500013707@pku.edu.cn

[2] Department of Information Management, Peking University, Beijing, China
pengyi@pku.edu.cn

Abstract. Waiting is inevitable in many interaction scenarios. Prior research suggests that waiting experience is associated with factors at both individual and contextual levels. This paper reports an experiment study examining the influence of visual stimuli and personal characteristics on users' waiting behavior. Our results show that higher delayed gratification (individual) is associated with longer waiting duration and shorter strategy formation time. As for features of visual stimuli (contextual), rotating-bright loading icons lengthen time perception and discourage people from waiting. These results provide design implications such as personalized waiting duration and ways to create better waiting experience.

Keywords: Waiting · Delayed gratification · Loading icon · Time perception

1 Introduction

In many interaction scenarios, users have to wait before a preferred outcome occurs. For example, they may have to wait for a loading page when surfing the Internet, or they may need to keep a healthy but less-tasteful diet before any weight-loss. Their waiting behaviors are less understood. It is of great importance to understand what keeps users wait and what makes them give up, in order to effectively adjust waiting behavior in the right direction. Since waiting behaviors are determined by both individual-level dispositions (e.g. personal characteristics like delayed gratification [1]) and contextual inducements (e.g. environmental stimuli: the speed of countdown [2] & loading icon [3]) [4], this paper addresses the research questions from two aspects:

RQ1: How does personal characteristics, e.g. capacity of delayed gratification, influence users' waiting behavior?
RQ2: How does characteristics of the visual stimuli, e.g. movement status and level of illumination, influence users' waiting behavior?

A. Marcus and W. Wang (Eds.): HCII 2019, LNCS 11584, pp. 105–117, 2019.
https://doi.org/10.1007/978-3-030-23541-3_9

Waiting is a common phenomenon in everyday human-computer interaction (HCI) scenarios. The experience of waiting is an important part of perceived satisfaction of the service or software. Although the increased speed of Internet reduces the discomfort of waiting, in many situations, waiting is still inevitable and very likely unbearable to users. Therefore, providing a pleasant experience in users' waiting scenarios is an important topic for HCI.

Prior research has mostly focused on the effect of contextual-level factors on waiting [5–7], and we know little about how individual characteristics influence users' waiting behavior. In fact, the individual-level factors and contextual-level factors always coexist and interact with each other in real-life situations. Hence, in this study, we modify one paradigm to test the impacts of these factors in the same scenario, which enables us to examine the different influences induced by different factors. We also use a real-life waiting task to make the experiment more relatable to the users. Our study reveals how these two factors affect waiting (more specifically willingness-to-wait time and waiting patterns) and provides practical implications to interaction design.

The rest of paper is organized as follows: First we introduce related work which leads to our hypothesis; then we describe our experiment design in the methodology section. We then present our findings, followed by conclusion and implications for design.

2 Related Research and Hypotheses Development

2.1 Waiting in Human-Computer Interaction

Previous research has paid close attention to the limits of how long people wait in different scenarios, and discovered ways to increase waiting time. For example, Nah found that the maximum waiting time is 2 s for a regular tasks [8]. While Nielson's research indicated that the waiting limits varied from 0.1–10 s which depended on the context (task) and attention [9], Galletta and others demonstrated that, after waiting 4 s, people's performance level dropped significantly. They also showed that 8 s was the watershed of attitude change [10]. Ceaparu and others found that when people watched mobile videos, waiting and preference were two main factors influencing user experience [11].

Some research focuses on the different forms of waiting stimuli on waiting durations. Passive, progressive and interactive screens are three most common types of loading screen in user interface [5]. They have different usage scenarios in which they serve different purposes. The passive loading screen, which is a cycle that rotates at a set speed, is usually used when the waiting time is less than the progressive and interactive screens [6]. However, there is no standard for how fast the passive loading icon should rotate in order to create the best possible experience for the user. Other research explores certain features of waiting stimuli on waiting durations. For example, research shows that users' perception of time can be influenced by progressive function and loading duration of the loading symbol [7]. Furthermore Kim and colleagues tested several different types of loading symbols in their study and indeed found that a waiting symbol designed according to tested guidelines reduced the users perceived waiting time.

2.2 Individual Level: Delayed Gratification

In most cases, waiting is a process of delayed gratification, which means people wait to pursue valuable long-run rewards instead of small short-run ones [12]. For a long time, researchers believe that waiting duration is determined by a relatively stable personal characteristic: capacity of delayed gratification (future-oriented self-control) [13, 14]. The most famous experiment about waiting and delayed gratification is the marshmallow experiment conducted by Mischel [15]. Research following this work suggests that delayed gratification was a relatively stable personal characteristic which could predict performance of adults based on their childhood behavior [16]. Research shows that people with higher capacity of delayed gratification are more patient and less impulsive [17]. The neural mechanism of delayed gratification also proves its stability [18].

Delayed gratification is made up of two parts: (1) delay choice (the choice phase that selects between an immediate reward and a delayed one); (2) delay maintenance (the waiting phase that the participant keeps the choice of delayed gratification while the immediate reward is still available) [19]. Similarly, waiting behavior consists of a choice phase and a the maintenance phase. The length of maintenance phase reflects the willingness of participants to wait for the reward. People wait longer for larger preferred rewards have higher capacity of delayed gratification. Thus, our first hypothesis is:

H1: Higher capacity of delayed gratification is associated with longer willingness-to-wait time (WTW).

2.3 Contextual Level: Visual Stimuli

Recent psychology research has recognized the influence of environment on waiting behavior [14]. Taking the interaction with complex environment into account, waiting behaviors are regarded as a value-based decision-making process [17]. In other words, users' waiting-or-not decision is a calculated cost-benefit analysis. People learn about the environment from repeated interaction and adjust their waiting behavior after calculating their benefits and costs [12]. The most obvious cost of waiting is the consumption of time. Waiting for a reward is at the cost of time to get other potential rewards. The new interpretation of waiting offers the possibility to change or cultivate people's waiting behavior through the distortion of subjective time perception. Söderström and his colleagues conducted an exploratory study and found that different speeds on loading screens led to the changes of participants' time perception. Specifically, the more quickly loading screen rotated, the faster the participants' felt time passed by [3].

Time perception is influenced by many factors. Research has found that the movement status and level of illumination have great impact on time perception [20]. For movement, research found that moving or flickering visual stimuli are typically judged longer than static ones using temporal reproduction method [21, 22]. Kanai and other psychologists further revealed that the temporal frequency of a visual stimulus was the only factor that could distort time perception [23]. Serving as the "clock" of perceived duration, faster temporal frequency of stimuli (e.g. rotating more times in a second) can speed up people's inner clock and thus elongate the subjective time perception, making them less willing to wait. Higher intensity illumination also increases subjective time duration [24]. Goldstone and colleagues found that when judging the duration of red lights, participants always chose the bright stimuli as the longer duration, comparing to standard light dim.

Therefore, our hypotheses on visual stimuli are:

H2a: The waiting time with rotating stimuli is shorter than static ones.
H2b: The waiting time with brighter stimuli is shorter than darker ones.

In conclusion, delayed gratification—seen as a stable personal characteristic—may shift the waiting duration or shape waiting patterns in a general level. When it comes to the opinion of value-based decision, waiting is changed through trial-by-trial accumulation. Hence, it is also important to analyze the effect of delayed gratification and features of visual stimuli in different levels.

3 Methods

3.1 Tasks and Participants

We design our experiment under McGuire and Kable's delayed gratification paradigm [12]. 24 participants were asked to perform a series of task trials to harvest monetary rewards (virtual coins) in 20 min, and receive rewards based on the coins collected. The process of one trial is shown in Fig. 1(a).

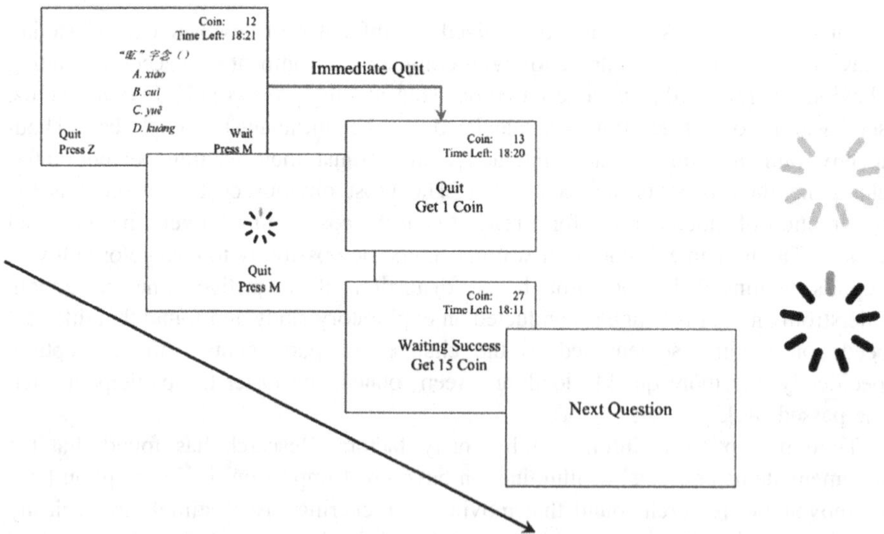

Fig. 1. (a) Left: Process of one trial (the waiting stimuli vary in different trials); (b) Right: Sample stimuli of different illuminations (Bright vs. Dark).

In each trial, participants encountered rare Chinese character recognition questions that they could not answer. They were faced with two options: quitting immediately to receive 1 coin at the cost of 1 s (the immediate reward choice), or waiting for the search result to get 15 coins at the cost of a random length of time (the delayed reward choice). The predefined waiting time followed a truncated generalized Pareto distribution, which was considered as the default distribution of an unknown environment (see Fig. 2) [12]. While waiting, they could change their minds and quit at any time and receive 1 coin. In the process of waiting, 4 different visual stimuli (moving/rotating vs. statics and bright vs. dark) and blank screen (baseline) were randomly shown on the display (see Fig. 1(b)). The temporal frequency of rotating stimuli was 6 Hz. For illuminance, the average gray value of bright stimuli was 251 (0–255, 0 was black while 255 was white); for darker was 233.1.

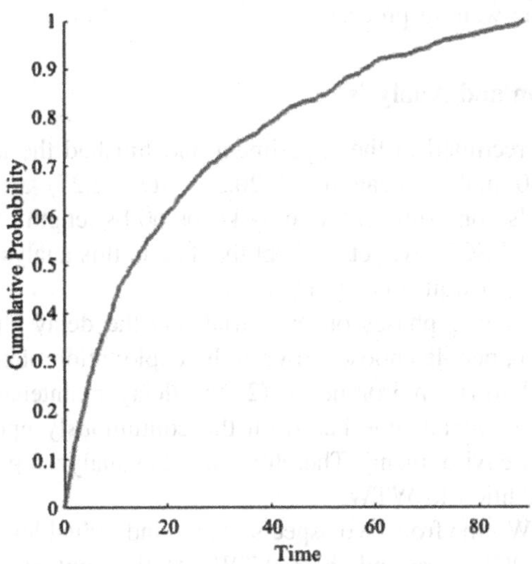

Fig. 2. Cumulative Probability of truncated generalized Pareto distribution ($k = 2, \sigma = 20, \theta = 0$, truncated at 90 s)

Participants were instructed the rules of the waiting game by the experimenter before performing and also informed that the stimuli were randomly displayed on the screen. They were also given a same 20-s task as practice to ensure their correct understanding of the rules. Head support was used to ensure that participants kept looking at the center of the screen in the process. After the task, they completed translated delayed gratification inventory (DGI) [25] and were given a short post-session interview about their waiting strategy during the whole task for the reference of further data analysis. DGI had good reliability and validity.

The predefined waiting time followed a truncated generalized Pareto distribution ($k = 2$, $\sigma = 20$, $\theta = 0$,, truncated at 90 s), whose quartile upper boundaries were 4.31, 12.81, 30.56, 89.78. Instead of randomly sampled on each trial, waiting time was sampled from each quartile in random sequence before a quartile is repeated to reduce the within-condition variability at the cost of slight sequential structure of waiting time.

3.2 Experimental Design

We used a within subject design with 2 (movement) × 2 (illumination) experimental conditions and a control condition. These 5 conditions were randomly distributed to each choose-to-wait trials.

To ensure enough trials in each conditions, the experimental duration was set to 20 valid minutes, which only included the time that quitting costs and waiting consumes. The feedback and skip screens did not count in the consumed time. The question screen did not count in the consumed time, which allowed participants to think and have short breaks during the long task.

Time left to complete and total coin were shown on the upper right screen all the time except during the waiting process.

3.3 Data Collection and Analysis

24 Participants were recruited in the experiment and finished the task. Data from 23 valid participants (10 males, mean age = 20.35, SD = 2.27) are used for further analysis. There was also one subject that only keeps 600-s length of record due to the mistakenly hitting the 'ESC' key, yet we kept the data in this analysis since it does not change his willingness-to-wait time (WTW).

There were two waiting phases on each trial: (1) the delay choice phase (when deciding to wait or not, people choose between the exploitation of certain strategy and exploration of an unknown environment); (2) the delay maintenance phase (people adapt their willingness-to-wait time based on the continuously updating information with the interaction of environment). Therefore, we also analyzed participants' general waiting patterns in addition to WTW.

We analyzed WTW time from two aspects. At the individual level, we analyzed the correlation between DGI score and their WTW. At the contextual level, we tested whether different features of loading icon distort the time perception and thus lead to the difference of WTW. Therefore, we used 2 × 2 repeated measure ANOVA to measure the differences between illuminance and rotation speed.

As for waiting patterns, we analyzed the changes of waiting behavior as time elapsed. Regarding waiting as a continuous process allowed us to see how people emerge their waiting habits.

4 Results

4.1 Capacity of Delayed Gratification and Waiting Time

Finding 1: Higher capability of delayed gratification is related to longer waiting time. We examined the relation between the capacity of delayed gratification and participants' WTW. The former variable was measured by Delayed Gratification

Inventory [25]. As for the latter, we used the overall wait-and-quit trials that deleting outliers as average WTW, since these trials revealed participants' real WTW time on a certain trial.

We used quartiles method to remove outliers of each data in Matlab R2016b since the data did't follow normal distribution. The quartiles method eliminated data points that were more than 1.5 interquartile ranges (IQRs) below the first quartile (Q1) or above the third quartile (Q3), which was widely applied to abnormal distribution. The elimination of outliers was repeated till no more outlier.

Using SPSS 23.0, results showed that DGI score was positively related to average WTW in a marginally significate level (Spearman coefficient: $r = 0.392$, $p = 0.079 < .01$, 2-tailed).

4.2 Features of Visual Stimuli and Waiting Time

We extracted all wait-and-quit trials as valid ones to analyze whether people's WTW are influenced due to the distortion of time perception under different stimulus displays. In the preprocessing period, we also used quartile method to eliminate outliers. Then, we calculated the means of each condition for every participants as their WTW under different conditions.

Influences of Movement and Illumination on WTW. Finding 2a: Two features of stimulus, movement and illumination, influence people's waiting time: moving stimulus and brighter stimulus are related to shorter waiting duration.

To figure out whether stimuli in different movement and illumination status have a distinctive impact on people's WTW, we conducted a 2 × 2 repeated measure ANOVA to analyze the difference in SPSS 23.0. The descriptive statistics in each condition are shown in Table 1.

Table 1. Descriptive statistics of each condition ($M \pm SE$, $N = 23$)

	Bright	Dark	Blank
Rotating	5.734 (0.614)	6.120 (0.639)	6.692 (0.784)
Static	6.391 (0.608)	7.112 (0.817)	

The results showed that there was no significant interaction between movement and illumination ($F(1,22) = .267$, $p = .611 > .05$). And the main effect of movement and illumination were both significant (For movement: $F(1,22) = 8.261$, $p = .009 < .05$; For illumination: $F(1,22) = 5.665$, $p = .026 < .05$), confirming that the movement and illumination of the stimulus bias people's WTW. Specifically, the quicker the stimulus rotated and the brighter the stimulus displayed, the shorter participants were willing to wait (See Fig. 3).

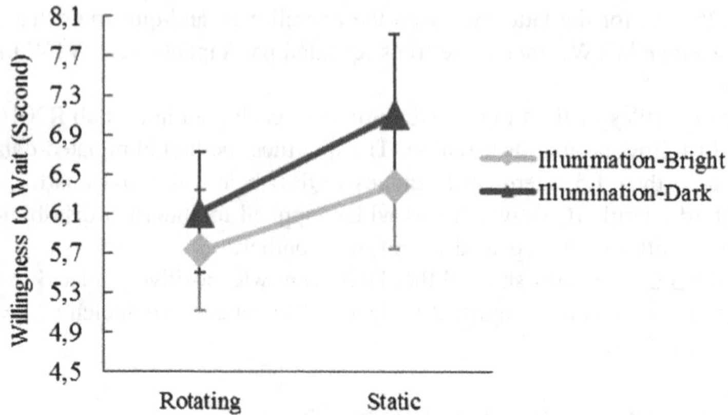

Fig. 3. Willingness to wait under different movement and illumination conditions ($M \pm SE$)

Comparison of Experimental and Control Conditions on WTW. Finding 2b: Compared with blank screen, users are less willing to wait when faced with fast-moving bright stimulus, and more willing to wait under static and dark stimulus (see Fig. 4).

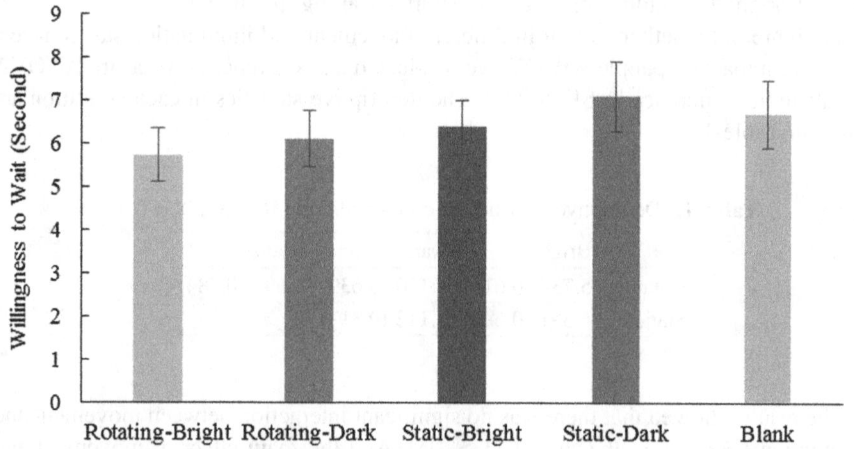

Fig. 4. Willingness to Wait under different stimulus displays ($M \pm SE$).

Since stimulus do influence waiting time in a different way, it is meaningful to know whether people distinctively wait longer or shorter when waiting under such stimuli than a blank screen.

Hence, we separately compared each experimental condition with control one by using 1 × 5 repeated measure ANOVA. Results showed the main effect of experimental condition was significant ($F(4,88) = 3.481$, $p = .011 < .05$). Specially, that the rotating-brighter stimulus made WTW marginally shorter than blank screen ($p = .077 < .1$), and much more shorter than static loading icons (Rotating-Bright v.s. Static-Bright: $p = .039 < .05$; Rotating-Bright v.s. Static-Dark: $p = .014 < .05$) (see Fig. 4).

4.3 Waiting Patterns Analysis

General Waiting Patterns. Besides exploring specific behavior on each trials, we wanted to see people's waiting behavior in a bigger picture. Specifically, we were curious about if there were different patterns of waiting policy as time elapsed, which were both affected by people's innate waiting strategy and the interaction with environment.

Using Matlab R2016b to draw scatter diagrams of waiting time on each trial as time elapsed, we could directly see 3 distinctive patterns of waiting policy (Fig. 5 presents representative patterns of all participants).

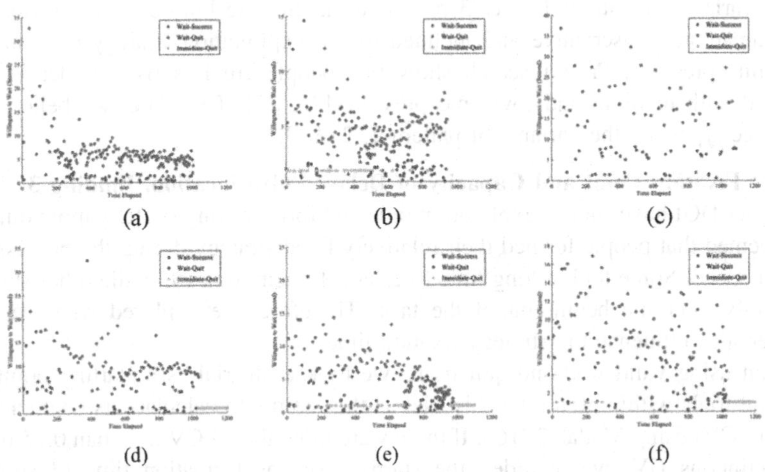

Fig. 5. (a) Pattern 1: Exploration; (b) Pattern 2: Hybrid; (c) Pattern 3: No strategy; (d), (e), (f) Variants of a, b, c. (Blue points: Wait-success trials; Red: Wait-quit trials; Yellow: Immediate-quit trials) (Color figure online)

Pattern 1. Exploration: The distinctive features of exploration waiting pattern are (1) participants seldom take the immediate quitting as their choice, which means they are more willing to explore and interact with the unknown environment; (2) participants can calibrate their waiting duration as time elapsed and settle the waiting limit to maximize their benefits of waiting. The exemplary pattern is demonstrated in Fig. 4(a).

Pattern 2. Hybrid. The significant feature of such pattern is repeated switches between waiting and immediate quitting (see in Fig. 4(b)). Some of them can adapt their waiting limit after the periodic exploration of waiting.

Pattern 3. No strategy. Not all data has an obvious pattern of waiting strategy. Some scatter diagrams show that the participants do not establish a waiting limit during the task, and thus we conclude them as no strategy (see in Fig. 4(c)).

Variants of Pattern 1 and 2 and No Strategy. Some data shown a drastic change by the end of the task: some people just quitted what they had done before and chose to quit immediately instead (see Fig. 4(d), (e), (f)). Such phenomenon occur in all patterns yet the beginning point varies.

The difference between pattern 1 and 2 is the different ratio of explorations to exploitations. Exploitation refers to the action of skipping to obtain 1 coin, which is the obvious and fixed strategy in this experiment. On the other hand, exploration means the actions to interact with environment with more uncertainty. People with pattern 1 are more willing to deal with uncertainty while people with pattern 2 are relatively more conservative that they stick to exploitation strategy for most of time and still distribute some to make exploration. These are two common patterns viewed in this experiment.

The variants of pattern 1, 2 & 3 reveals an interesting but common phenomena: people are more conservative and inclined to use exploitation strategy continuously under time pressure. Prior research show that people are less risky under high as compared with medium and low time pressure [26, 27]. Therefore, we believe that these three types are the variants of pattern 1, 2, & 3.

Strategy Fixation Point and Capacity of Delayed Gratification. Finding 3: Users with higher DGI have shorter exploration time and form waiting strategy more quickly.

It seemed that people formed their relatively fixed strategy during the process in a different speed. Some took a long time to establish their strategy, while other stuck to one shortly after the beginning of the task. Therefore, we explored what personal characteristics influence the strategy fixation time.

Again using valid wait-and-quit trials, we took each trial as a starting point and extract all trials within 50 s after this trial as the sample to calculate its coefficient of variation (CV) using Matlab 2016b. If there were more than 4 CV less than 0.15 of any five continuous CV, we regarded the starting trial as formation time of strategy. Using SPSS 23.0, results showed that DGI score was negatively related to the formation time in a significate level (Spearman coefficient: $r = -0.667$, $p = 0.018 < .05$, 2-tailed).

5 Conclusion and Discussion

5.1 Summary and Interpretation of Findings

Inspired by two interpretations of waiting behavior, we examine the effect of delayed gratification and two features of visual stimuli (movement vs. illumination) on people's waiting-times and patterns.

Results confirm the effects of visual stimuli and capacity of delayed gratification on users' willingness-to-wait time. People with higher DGI score indeed voluntarily wait longer. Two features of visual stimuli, the bright and fast-rotating, also show the tendency to shorten our willingness-to-wait time. By examining the effect of different features of visual stimuli, our study suggests time perception may be an effective mediating variable that can change people's waiting behavior.

The influences of the capacity of delayed gratification on waiting behavior are two-fold: (1) Good capacity of delayed gratification enhance waiting duration, helping to explore in depth; (2) yet users with high DGI tend to stick to quickly established strategy which prevent them from exploring more about the variation of complex environment in width.

5.2 Limitations and Future Work

There are some limitations of the experiment. First of all, different contrast of visual stimuli may have impact on time perception. One study do show that a reduction of apparent duration of a visual stimulus when an intermediate contrast test interval was briefly preceded by a high contrast context as compared to when preceded by a low contrast context [28]. The scale of time suppression of contrast happens in milliseconds, which may have slight influence even if contrast be the confound factors of this experiment. Secondly, visual stimuli with different illumination and moving speed may serve as the progressive information of waiting. For example, loading screens and indicators in the interface give the user an increased perceived performance for the software [29]. Besides, Jang and colleagues confirmed that the changing status of lightness exert informative effect on users' intuitive perception [30]. Stimuli used in this experiment are often put on the loading page to indicate the progress. Therefore, we cannot eliminate the effect that different types of stimuli have on informative status. However, the repeated scenario decreases the informative effect of visual stimuli because participants gradually realize that there are no information signaling the status of waiting process.

Our study, along with prior study conducted by Söderström and his colleagues [3], suggests the possibility of distortion of time perception in waiting. Future work may also consider improving waiting durations by changing the presentation mode of elapsed time in the screen.

5.3 Design Implications

The understanding of waiting behavior exert great impact not only on users, but also on designers across industry. Therefore, designers may have a relatively valid indicator of users' waiting preference and personalize waiting offer for different users based on their capacity of delayed gratification from their profiles and behavioral data.

Through a short inventory of delayed gratification, systems may predict users' willingness-to-wait time more accurately and roughly draw a general waiting pattern in a repeated waiting scenario.

In some situations when waiting is inevitable for user, designers may want to keep users waiting. For instance, the poor internet connections, the overloading of servers.

Under this circumstance, a more user-friendly waiting icons can be designed to shorten users' subjective time perception and help them wait for what they want in a more efficient way. For example, the loading icon may change its rotating speed according to the situation of internet connection to prevent unnecessary waiting. Or when users exercise in front of electrical devices, a better design that indicates waiting process may help them persist longer and thus beneficial for them.

While under other circumstances, advertisers or designers wish people to wait. Therefore, the design has to fool our perception which, is an extremely delicate operation. Our study provides the evidence of the temporal frequency (rotating speed) and illumination as effective tools to lie to users, which can be combined with informative widgets such as progress bar.

Acknowledgements. This research is supported by the "Provost's Undergraduate Research Fellowship" of Peking University and by NSFC Grant #71603012.

References

1. Rung, J.M., Young, M.E.: Learning to wait for more likely or just more: greater tolerance to delays of reward with increasingly longer delays. J. Exp. Anal. Behav. **103**(1), 108–124 (2015)
2. Ghafurian, M., Reitter, D.: Impatience induced by waiting: an effect moderated by the speed of countdowns. In: Proceedings of the 2016 ACM Conference on Designing Interactive Systems. ACM (2016)
3. Söderström, U., Bååth, M., Mejtoft, T.: The Users' Time Perception: the effect of various animation speeds on loading screens. In: Proceedings of the 36th European Conference on Cognitive Ergonomics. ACM (2018)
4. Hefer, B., Karabenick, S.A.: Inherent association between academic delay of gratification, future time perspective, and self-regulated learning. Educ. Psychol. Rev. **16**(1), 35–57 (2004)
5. Nah, F.-H.F.: A study on tolerable waiting time: how long are web users willing to wait? Behav. Inf. Technol. **23**(3), 153–163 (2004)
6. Nielson Norman Group website page. https://www.nngroup.com/articles/website-response-times/. Accessed 29 Jan 2018
7. Galletta, D.F., Henry, R., McCoy, S., Polak, P.: Web site delays: how tolerant are users? J. Assoc. Inf. Syst. **5**(1), 1–28 (2004)
8. Ceaparu, I., Lazar, J., Bessiere, K., Robinson, J., Shneiderman, B.: Determining causes and severity of end-user frustration. Int. J. Hum.-Comput. Interact. **17**(3), 333–356 (2004)
9. Hohenstein, J., Khan, H., Canfield, K., Tung, S., Cano, R.P.: Shorter wait times: the effects of various loading screens on perceived performance. In: Proceedings of the 2016 CHI Conference Extended Abstracts on Human Factors in Computing Systems. ACM (2016)
10. Nielson Norman Group website page. https://www.nngroup.com/articles/progress-indicators/. Accessed 29 Jan 2018
11. Kim, W., Xiong, S., Liang, Z.: Effect of loading symbol of online video on perception of waiting time. Int. J. Hum.-Comput. Interact. **33**(12), 1001–1009 (2017)
12. Mcguire, J.T., Kable, J.W.: Decision makers calibrate behavioral persistence on the basis of time-interval experience. Cognition **124**(2), 216–226 (2012)

13. Mischel, W., Cantor, N., Feldman, S.: Principles of self-regulation: the nature of willpower and self-control. In: Higgins, E.T., Kruglanski, A.W. (eds.) Social Psychology: Handbook of Basic Principles, pp. 329–360. Guilford Press, New York (1996)
14. Mcguire, J.T., Kable, J.W.: Rational temporal predictions can underlie apparent failures to delay gratification. Psychol. Rev. **120**(2), 395–410 (2013)
15. Mischel, W., Ebbesen, E.B.: Attention in delay of gratification. J. Pers. Soc. Psychol. **16**(2), 329–337 (1970)
16. Mischel, W., Shoda, Y., Rodriguez, M.: Delay of gratification in children. Science **244** (4907), 933–938 (1989)
17. Wulfert, E., Block, J.A., Santa, A.E., Rodriguez, M.L., Colsman, M.: Delay of gratification: impulsive choices and problem behaviors in early and late adolescence. J. Pers. **70**(4), 533–552 (2010)
18. Casey, B.J., et al.: Behavioral and neural correlates of delay of gratification 40 years later. Proc. Natl. Acad. Sci. U.S.A. **108**(36), 14998–15003 (2011)
19. Toner, I.J., Smith, R.A.: Age and overt verbalization in delay-maintenance behavior in children. J. Exp. Child Psychol. **24**(1), 123–128 (1977)
20. Matthews, W.J., Meck, W.H.: Temporal cognition: connecting subjective time to perception, attention, and memory. Psychol. Bull. **142**(8), 865–907 (2016)
21. Lhamon, W.T., Goldstone, S.: Movement and the judged duration of visual targets. Bull. Psychon. Soc. **5**(1), 53–54 (1975)
22. Brown, S.W.: Time, change, and motion: the effects of stimulus movement on temporal perception. Atten. Percept. Psychophys. **57**(1), 105–116 (1995)
23. Kanai, R., Paffen, C.L., Hogendoorn, H., Verstraten, F.A.: Time dilation in dynamic visual display. J. Vis. **6**(12), 8 (2006)
24. Goldstone, S., Lhamon, W.T., Sechzer, J.A.: Light intensity and judged duration. Bull. Psychon. Soc. **12**(1), 83–84 (1978)
25. Hoerger, M., Quirk, S.W., Weed, N.C.: Development and validation of the Delaying Gratification Inventory. Psychol. Assess. **23**(3), 725–738 (2011)
26. Zur, H.B., Breznitz, S.: The effect of time pressure on risky choice behavior. Acta Physiol. (Oxf) **47**(2), 89–104 (1981)
27. Edland, A., Svenson, O.: Judgment and decision making under time pressure: studies and findings. In: Svenson, O., Maule, A.J. (eds.) Time Pressure and Stress in Human Judgment and Decision Making, pp. 27–40. Springer, Boston (1993). https://doi.org/10.1007/978-1-4757-6846-6_2
28. Bruno, A., Johnston, A.: Contrast gain shapes visual time. Front. Psychol. **1**(6), 170 (2010)
29. Bouch, A., Kuchinsky, A., Bhatti, N.: Quality is in the eye of the beholder: meeting users' requirements for Internet quality of service. In: Proceedings of the SIGCHI Conference on Human Factors in Computing Systems. ACM (2000)
30. Jang, J., Suk, H.: Disappearing icons: informative effect through changing color attributes of app icons. In: 2014 IEEE International Conference on Consumer Electronics (ICCE). IEEE (2014)

DUXU for Novel Interaction Techniques and Devices

User-Centered Gestures for Mobile Phones: Exploring a Method to Evaluate User Gestures for UX Designers

Ariane Beauchesne[1(✉)], Sylvain Sénécal[1], Marc Fredette[1], Shang Lin Chen[1], Bertrand Demolin[1], Marie-Laure Di Fabio[2], and Pierre-Majorique Léger[1]

[1] HEC Montréal, Montréal, Canada
ariane.beauchesne@hec.ca
[2] Desjardins Group, Montréal, Canada

Abstract. The objective of this paper is to explore how users react to certain gestures (e.g., swipe, scroll, or tap) for certain use cases. More specifically, the goal is to explore and suggest guidelines to user experience (UX) designers when choosing gestures for specific use cases on a smartphone application. Building on the Task-technology fit theory, we are specifically interested in the degree of alignment between gestures and each mobile use case. We hypothesize that some gestures are better aligned with certain use cases because they require less cognitive effort than others. In other words, certain gestures are likely to become so natural for users that they do not have to consciously invest effort to accomplish these gestures. Likewise, we hypothesize that the emotional valence of gestures will be affected by the use case. To attain this objective, a lab-experiment was conducted with 20 participants, where cognitive load and emotional valence were measured. Results suggest that the combination of gestures and use cases have an impact on the user cognitive load and valence. These findings contribute to human-computer interaction (HCI) research by providing insights to help user experience (UX) designers select appropriate gestures.

Keywords: Mobile applications design · Usability methods and tools · Guidelines · User experience · Cognitive load

1 Introduction

One of the most important aspects in designing, creating, and developing applications and interfaces, is creating something that feels natural for the user [1]. To do so, design teams need to understand their users: how they feel, what they need, and what they think [2]. Therefore, it seems only logical that with user-centered designs, products should feel natural in the hands of users. They should be able to use these products to attain their goals effectively, with efficiency and satisfaction [3, 4]. While using a mobile application, the interaction is an important factor for achieving usability and for creating something intuitive for the user. Mobile operating systems and applications each use their own set of guidelines when designing different gestures, making it hard

A. Marcus and W. Wang (Eds.): HCII 2019, LNCS 11584, pp. 121–133, 2019.
https://doi.org/10.1007/978-3-030-23541-3_10

for users to know what gestures to use. In addition, different types of content can be presented in many ways (called use cases): tutorial, choices, text, etc., making it even harder for users to know how to interact with different applications or interfaces.

To reduce the impact of all these different options, choosing appropriate gestures for different types of use cases can simplify the experience for users. External consistency between different platforms is essential to provide a constant experience to users through their daily use of technology [5].

The literature on product development phases shows the importance of including testing and prototyping at the beginning of that process [6]. Research shows that those tests need to include the input from users from the very beginning to save time, money, and to better understand user preferences and points of view [7, 8]. While research in user-centered design is becoming more present in today's design processes, there appears to be a gap in the literature concerning the type of gestures that are more appropriate for different use cases in mobile applications. Understanding the impact of gestures on the success and ease of use of applications is even more important now, because user interface design does contribute to the success and the acceptance of applications [9]. In addition, theories such as the Task-technology theory suggest that the alignment of tasks, technologies, and users have a real impact on the usability and the performance of a product [10].

Therefore, the objective of this paper is to explore how users react to gestures for certain use cases on mobile applications. To attain this objective, a laboratory experiment with implicit measurements using psychophysiological tools such as facial emotions and eye-tracking was performed. Prototypes of different gesture/use case combinations in the online banking context were presented to participants to investigate how gestures affect the user's experience. Based on these results, we present insights to UX designers to help them explore and choose appropriate gestures for specific use cases for smartphones.

2 Theoretical Background and Hypothesis Development

2.1 Task-Technology Fit Theory

Goodhue and Thompson [10] define the task-technology fit as "the degree to which a technology assists an individual in performing his or her portfolio of tasks" (p. 216). The theory is based on three levels of inputs: task characteristics, technology characteristics and individual characteristics. When interacting together, these factors influence the fit between task and technology and determine its usability and performance (see Fig. 1) [11]. This theory has been a central point in management information system (MIS) literature. However, recent literature is now showing that small variations in how the information is presented in haptic interfaces can have an impact on the experience of users [12]. Building on the task-technology fit theory, we are specifically interested in the degree of alignment between gestures and each mobile use case.

2.2 Use Case

Use cases are defined in literature as a way in which a user interact with a system [13]. Here the term is transposed to define it as a way that a user can use the information in the application. In other words, information can be presented in different ways on a mobile phone, here called use cases. Moreover, in mobile applications, two formats have emerged to present the information when it does not fit on one page: horizontal or vertical. The use cases can then be presented with these two formats. Little research has tested the effect of the orientation format for mobile phones on users. A study comparing horizontal and vertical tab switching when web browsing showed that horizontal formats (swiping) provide faster and less frustrating results compared to vertical formats (scrolling) [14]. While another study comparing shopping swipe-based interfaces (horizontal) and scroll-based interfaces (vertical) shows that the horizontal interfaces lead to greater cognitive absorption and playfulness [15]. With the same idea, a research solely based on a computer found that adding horizontal swiping affected positively the intentions to use the website [16].

2.3 Gestures

A gesture is an interaction technique that can be defined as "a way of using a physical input/output device to perform a generic task in a human-computer dialogue" [12] (p. 112). Touch gestures are now becoming the norm in mobile phones and applications. They first emerged when touch screens became available and users needed to apply these gestures to navigate the content. They were also used to solve the problem of information not fitting on one page, which caused users to have to apply additional gestures to get to the rest of the information [17]. Research shows that haptic interfaces have a real impact on users' level of engagement [15]. Gestures need to be effective to decrease users' cognitive load while using an application [14].

At first, mobile gestures were mostly tapping and vertical scrolling (see Table 1) [16]. Now horizontal swiping is becoming part of the basic gestures family. According to the literature, including horizontal gestures can increase perceived enjoyment and user engagement [18]. Lateral gestures such as swiping also suggest an increase in cognitive absorption, reuse intentions, and task performance [15].

For this study, gestures found in popular utilitarian and hedonic applications have been selected according to basic gestures used for most touch commands (see Table 1. Basic gestures for touch commands).

Furthermore visual indicators such as arrows or scrolling bars and feedback like nudging can be included in designs to facilitate the comprehension of gestures and thus, create applications that are more usable [19, 20].

Table 1. Basic gestures for touch commands

Swipe	Lateral scrolling	Vertical scrolling	Tap

Quickly brush surface with fingertip in one direction or the other	Move fingertip over surface without losing contact	Move fingertip over surface without losing contact	Briefly touch surface with fingertip

2.4 Psychophysiological Measures in User Experience

Evaluating user experience when it includes gestures can be a difficult task because its evaluation is not mainly based on performance. Gestures can, for example, be evaluated on the ease of use, the playfulness and the reuse intentions [15]. For this reason, we chose to not only focus on explicit measures (e.g., self-reported) but also on implicit ones. Implicit measures are able to offer researchers results of the user experience not only after but also during the experience. While explicit non-continuous measures have been much used throughout the past decades in UX studies and are a great way to measure UX [21], recent research is now showing that psychophysiological measures can provide real time insightful data [22–25].

Dirican and Göktürkb define a psychophysiological measure as a "measure [that provides] an unobtrusive and implicit way to determine the user's affective or cognitive state on the basis of mind-body relations" [23] (p. 1362). While there are some limitations with psychophysiological measures, there are also many advantages [23, 26]. Among others, implicit measures can eliminate the bias of users giving their retroaction on the task. These measures are objective, unobtrusive, and continuous [24, 27, 28].

In this study, using real-time measures was important, because many tasks were performed (20 tasks) and the goal is to recognize gestures that feel natural, are easy and not frustrating for the user. For this reason, we decided to use the following measures: pupil diameter for measuring mental workload and facial emotion to measure emotional valence.

Pupil Diameter. According to Adam [29] and Harrison [30], the user's cognitive load is an aspect that researchers in HCI and UX tend to neglect. Cognitive load can be defined "as a multidimensional construct representing the cognitive demands associated with performing a specific task" [31] (p. 2). It plays a key role in evaluating user experience. Research has established the correlation between pupil diameter and cognitive load [32–35].

However, pupil dilation can be affected by the light conditions because of the reflex of the pupil [36] so measuring outdoors might bias the collected data [29]. To prevent such bias, this experiment was run in an indoor lab setting.

The pupil can vary in sizes from .2 mm to .8 mm. Users with low cognitive load have a non-dilated pupil, while users with higher cognitive load have a dilated pupil [36]. The more difficult a task is, the higher the cognitive load [37]. This measure may provide a reliable index to find a relationship between task difficulty and the size of the pupil [36].

Using the Task-technology fit theory, we are interested to explore the degree of alignment between gestures and use cases. This alignment should bring out better and worse combinations of gestures and use cases. Thus, we posit the following hypothesis:

H1: The alignment between the type of gesture and the use case influences cognitive demand.

Emotional Valence. Studies on facial expressions and emotions have interested many researchers in, among others, psychological and physiological fields. These studies use physiological measures to identify a range of emotions like sadness or anger [38]. Now UX research is also becoming interested in evaluating emotions to further understand users [39]. Emotional valence is one of the dimensions of emotions, it ranges between a pleasant emotion and an unpleasant one [40]. Assessing this dimension is important when trying to measure user experience on a task that should feel natural. To measure emotional valence, facial recognition analysis tools are used to detect facial muscle movements in order to infer emotions [41].

Again based on the Task-technology fit theory, we then posit the following hypothesis:

H2: The alignment between the type of gesture and the use case influences emotional valence.

3 Research Method

3.1 Context

This study used mobile utilitarian applications. In other words, the prototypes were tested during use cases that users could come across everyday. Prototypes were developed based on banking applications. From checking their account to reading articles on retirement savings, online banking is now part of the customers' everyday life. In 2018, around 70% of Americans accessed their bank accounts via a mobile device [42]. Over the past years, banks began to understand the importance of designing and creating an experience which would fulfil the needs of users. Testing and shedding light on the most natural gestures could greatly improve those everyday interactions with the online banking system. Furthermore, simple banking interactions like the ones used in this test are common not only in banking applications, but also in many others. Choosing simple daily tasks would also ensure a faster task completion for the user.

3.2 Participants

To test our hypotheses, an experiment was conducted. Twenty participants between the age of 20 and 46 were recruited for this study (Mage = 28.7, SD = 8.70; 11 women). Every participant received a monetary compensation. Half of the participants were recruited via our school panel while the other half were recruited through an external firm. The second group was recruited externally to ensure a broader age distribution. Participants were pre-screened for glasses, laser eye surgery, astigmatism, epilepsy, neurological and psychiatric diagnoses. This project was approved by the Ethics Committee of our institution.

3.3 Design and Procedure

The experimental design of this study is based on two main within-subject factors: use cases and gestures. Five utilitarian use cases were explored: filling out a form (C1), discovering a tutorial (C2), browsing an application menu (C3), reading a text (C4), and using a dashboard (C5) (see Table 2). For each use case, four mobile gestures were tested. These gestures represent common gestures used in a utilitarian context: swiping (SW), lateral scrolling (LS), vertical scrolling (VS), and tapping (TA) (Table 1). During a one-hour test, participants first performed a baseline task to measure their cognitive and emotional reactions in their normal and calm state. Participants watched a standardized relaxing video to achieve the desired state [43]. After, participants performed 20 use cases (each use case with each gesture) on an iPhone 6 Plus in a counterbalanced way. Each use case was performed on a prototype and began with an entry page detailing which type of use case participants were going to perform; then the participants performed the use cases, and closed the application when they were done.

The high-fidelity prototypes necessary to represent the use cases and the gestures were developed on Atomic© and were inspired by use cases found in the banking sector. For the use cases C1, C2, C3 and C4, the content was distributed on three distinct pages, while for the C5, the content was distributed on two pages. Also, C5 was presented in an hybrid design, where only one section of the page was moving when using a gesture. The rest of the page was static. Gestures were signaled with visual indicators to give a hint to the users on which gestures should be used. The same indicators were used for every use case (see Table 3).

Table 2. 20 prototypes were created on Atomic©. Here is an example of each use cases

Filling out a form (C1)[a]	Discovering a tutorial (C2)[b]	Browsing an application menu (C3)[c]	Reading a text (C4)[d]	Using a dashboard (C5)[e]
 Étape 1 / 3 Oui Non Oui Non	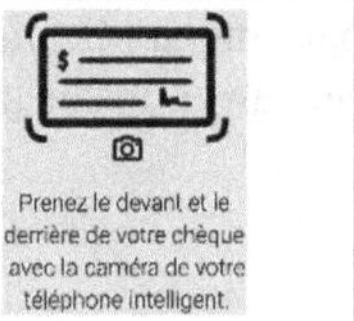 Prenez le devant et le derrière de votre chèque avec la caméra de votre téléphone intelligent.		 4 stratégies d'épargne pour réaliser tous vos projets	 Comptes et Cartes de Crédit

Translation of texts in the images
[a]C1: Step 1/3; 1. Property information; 2. Do you work with a realtor ?; 3. Are you moving to another city?
[b]C2: Take a picture of the front and the back of your check with the camera of your smartphone.
[c]C3 (first three applications only): Career; Car; My retirement.
[d]C4: 4 savings strategies to carry out all your projects. Good savings strategies are actions that will allow you to raise the amounts needed to carry out your projects in the short, medium or long term. Here are some tips to help you build the best strategy for your needs.
[e]C5: Accounts and credit cards; Checking account; Savings account #1; Savings account #2; Credit card; Your car insurance; Your home insurance.

Table 3. Visual indicators used for each gesture

Gestures' names	Visual indicators
Swiping (SW)	
Lateral Scrolling (LS)	
Vertical Scrolling (VS)	
Tapping (TA)	< >

3.4 Experimental Setup and Apparatus

The experiment took place in a laboratory, with controlled lighting, humidity, and temperature. The room was set up so the participant was sitting in front of the phone that was held by a support. Some complementary information was shown on an iPad also held by a support. The participant used the mouse to complete the questionnaire between each use case (see Fig. 1. Experimental set-up Fig. 1). The research assistants were sitting in an adjacent room behind a one-way mirror. To communicate with the participant, a microphone was used. Three types of measures were used to capture the cognitive reaction and emotion to a given gesture. A webcam was used to record the image of the participant with Media Recorder (Noldus, Wageningen, Netherlands). The videos were then processed

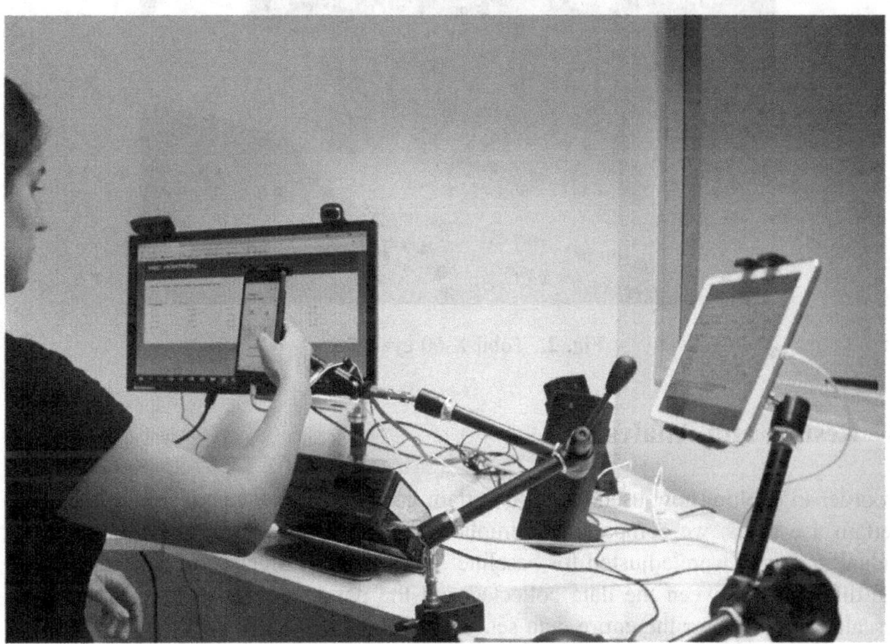

Fig. 1. Experimental set-up

through FaceReader, an automatic facial analysis tool (Noldus, Wageningen, Netherlands) to provide us with emotional valence. Finally Tobii X-60 eye-tracker (see Fig. 2) was used to capture the participants' pupil size and was set under the phone. All of the measures and data were synchronised with Observer XT (Noldus, Wageningen, Netherlands) with the guidelines provided by Léger et al. [44].

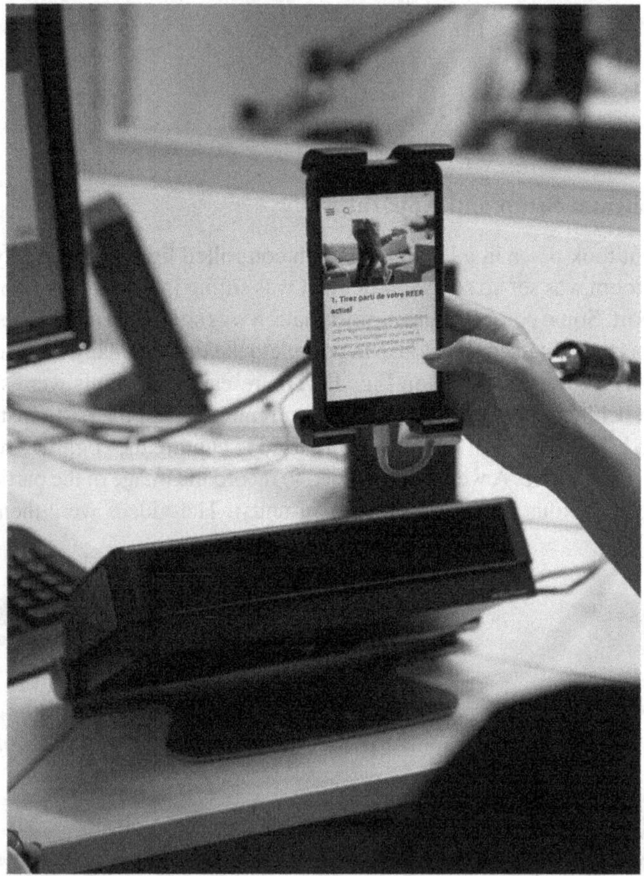

Fig. 2. Tobii X-60 eye-tracker

4 Results and Analysis

In order to explore how users react to certain gestures (e.g., swipe, scroll, or tap) for certain use cases, we compared the implicit behavioral measures. The implicit individual measures were adjusted for baseline. The adjusted values were calculated from the difference between the data collected and the participants' baseline. It was then rescaled to (–1,1) for the entire data set.

Table 4 shows the mean of the implicit measures for each combination use cases/gestures.

Table 4. Participants' mean cognitive load and valence

Gesture	Use cases	Cognitive load	Valence
Swiping (SW)	C1	–.10745	–.32227
	C2	–.14379	–.25108
	C3	–.10488	–.24626
	C4	–.1798	–.25284
	C5	–.08656	–.21009
Lateral Scrolling (LS)	C1	–.11869	–.28062
	C2	–.07469	–.26977
	C3	–.07756	–.21539
	C4	–.16407	–.24679
	C5	–.12229	–.21297
Vertical Scrolling (VS)	C1	–.09224	–.28401
	C2	–.08292	–.25817
	C3	–.07823	–.27056
	C4	–.15975	–.2372
	C5	–.07606	–.25596
Tapping (TA)	C1	–.07909	–.26513
	C2	–.12661	–.23434
	C3	–.08842	–.23459
	C4	–.17081	–.19289
	C5	–.10731	–.3286

H1 suggests that the alignment between the type of gestures and the use case influences cognitive demand. An ANOVA with a two-tailed level of significance adjusted for multiple tests comparison with the Holm-Bonferroni method was used to test if there is a significant difference between at least two means of a gestures' cognitive load for a specific use case (see Table 5). In other words, the ANOVA tests if there is, for example, a significant difference between at least two means between C1, C2, C3, C4, and C5 for the cognitive load of the swipe gesture. For all four gestures, results suggest that the participants' cognitive load is different for at least two use cases (SW, LS, VS, TA: $p < .0001$). This indicates that H1 is supported and that gestures' cognitive demand depends on the use case.

In order to test H2, which suggests that the alignment between the type of gesture and the use case influences emotional valence, the same statistical test was conducted. Results presented in Table 5 suggest again that for all four gestures users' emotional valence is significantly different for at least two use cases (SW, LS, TA: $p < .0001$; VS: $p = .0009$). Therefore, results show that H2 is supported, suggesting that the gestures' emotional valence is influenced by the use case.

Table 5. P-values of ANOVA's statistical tests

	Hypothesis	Gestures	p-value[a]
At least two values are significantly different for each use cases' cognitive load	H1	Swiping (SW)	<.0001
		Lateral Scrolling (LS)	<.0001
		Vertical Scrolling (VS)	<.0001
		Tapping (TA)	<.0001
At least two values are significantly different for each use cases' emotional valence	H2	Swiping (SW)	<.0001
		Lateral Scrolling (LS)	<.0001
		Vertical Scrolling (VS)	.0009
		Tapping (TA)	<.0001

[a]Two-tailed level of significance.

5 Discussion and Concluding Comments

This paper is an exploratory attempt to determine if gestures and use cases for mobile applications have an impact on the experience of users. Our results show that gestures emotional valence and cognitive load depend on the use case (H1 & H2). These results suggest that the combination of gestures and use cases have an impact on the user experience. Understanding the best fit between gestures and use case could significantly impact the users' experience when using mobile applications on a smartphone.

This study contributes to user experience, human computer interaction, and interface design literature in many ways. First, this study explores a subject that has not been investigated so far. The importance of choosing and designing gestures can sometimes be neglected while results clearly show that they can have an impact on user interaction with a mobile applications. Second, our research shows a way to use psychophysiological measures to evaluate gestures during an experiment. Overall, knowledge of testing and choosing adequate gestures could help designers and product owners lower the cognitive load of their users and increase their emotional valence, therefore creating a more positive experience overall.

Because this research is exploratory, some limitations needs to be acknowledged. Regarding technical limitations, there were inactivated functionalities on the prototypes. For example, a menu icon was added to the design to provide a more realistic interface and some of these icons were inactivated and would not open a menu. It is possible that some participants tried to use them. Also, this study was performed on five use cases in a utilitarian context; further research should address other specific use cases. Furthermore, the same gestures were performed more than once during the test. This may have affected the cognitive load because of learnability. However, to minimize these effects, the tasks were performed in a counterbalanced way. Finally, the age of the participants was between 20 and 46 years old. Further research could be done on older population to see if their reactions differ.

References

1. Wigdor, D., Wixon, D.: Brave NUI World. Elsevier Science Designing Natural User Interfaces for Touch and Gesture. Elsevier, Saint-Louis (2011)
2. Ferreira, B., Silva, W., Oliveira, E., Conte, T.: Designing Personas with Empathy Map, pp. 501–505 (2015). https://doi.org/10.18293/seke2015-152
3. Garrett, J.J.: The Elements of User Experience User-Centered Design for the Web and Beyond (2010)
4. International Standard: Systems and Software Engineering - System and Software Quality Requirements and Evaluation (SQuaRE) - Common Industry Format (CIF) for Usability - Evaluation Report (2016)
5. Scapin, D.L., Bastien, J.M.C.: Ergonomic criteria for evaluating the ergonomic quality of interactive systems. Behav. Inf. Technol. **16**, 220–231 (1997). https://doi.org/10.1080/014492997119806
6. Walker, M., Takayama, L., Landay, J.A.: High-fidelity or low-fidelity, paper or computer? choosing attributes when testing web prototypes. In: Proceedings of the Human Factors and Ergonomics Society Annual Meeting, vol. 46, pp. 661–665 (2002). https://doi.org/10.1177/154193120204600513
7. Snyder, C.: Paper Prototyping: the Fast and Easy Way to Design and Refine User Interfaces. Elveiser, San Francisco (2003)
8. Svanaes, D., Seland, G.: Putting the users center stage: role playing and low-fi prototyping enable end users to design mobile systems. In: Proceedings of SIGCHI Conference on Human Factors Computing Systems, vol. 6, pp. 479–486 (2004). https://doi.org/10.1145/985692.985753
9. Bano, M., Zowghi, D.: A systematic review on the relationship between user involvement and system success. Inf. Softw. Technol. **58**, 148–169 (2015). https://doi.org/10.1016/j.infsof.2014.06.011
10. Goodhue, D.L., Thompson, R.L.: Task-technology fit and individual performance. MIS Q. **19**, 213 (1995). https://doi.org/10.2307/249689
11. Lin, T.C., Huang, C.C.: Understanding knowledge management system usage antecedents: an integration of social cognitive theory and task technology fit. Inf. Manag. **45**, 410–417 (2008). https://doi.org/10.1016/j.im.2008.06.004
12. Sundar, S.S., Bellur, S., Oh, J., Xu, Q., Jia, H.: User experience of on-screen interaction techniques: an experimental investigation of clicking, sliding, zooming, hovering, dragging, and flipping. Hum. Comput. Interact. **29**, 109–152 (2014). https://doi.org/10.1080/07370024.2013.789347
13. Cockburn, A.: Structuring use cases with goals. Hum. Technol. **84121**, 1–13 (1995)
14. Warr, A., Chi, E.H.: Swipe vs. scroll: web page switching on mobile browsers. In: Proceedings of SIGCHI Conference on Human Factors Computing System - CHI 2013, vol. 2171 (2013). https://doi.org/10.1145/2470654.2481298
15. Choi, B.C.F., Kirshner, S.N., Wu, Y.: Swiping vs. scrolling in mobile shopping applications. In: Nah, F.F.-H.F.-H., Tan, C.-H. (eds.) HCIBGO 2016. LNCS, vol. 9751, pp. 177–188. Springer, Cham (2016). https://doi.org/10.1007/978-3-319-39396-4_16
16. Villamor, C., Willi, D., Wroblewski, L.: Touch Gesture Reference Guide. Touch Gesture Ref. Guid. pp. 1–7 (2011)
17. Wobbrock, J.O., Forlizzi, J., Hudson, S.E., Myers, B.A.: WebThumb : Interaction Techniques for Small-Screen Browsers, vol. 4, pp. 205–208 (2002). https://doi.org/10.1145/571985.572014

18. Dou, X., Sundar, S.S.: Power of the swipe: why mobile websites should add horizontal swiping to tapping, clicking, and scrolling interaction techniques. Int. J. Hum. Comput. Interact. **32**, 352–362 (2016). https://doi.org/10.1080/10447318.2016.1147902
19. Leung, R., MacLean, K., Bertelsen, M.B., Saubhasik, M.: Evaluation of haptically augmented touchscreen GUI elements under cognitive load. In: Proceedings of the Ninth International Conference on Multimodal Interfaces - ICMI 2007, p. 374. ACM Press, New York (2007)
20. Ruspini, D.C., Kolarov, K., Khatib, O.: The haptic display of complex graphical environments. In: Proceedings of 24th Annual Conference on Computer Graphics and Interactive Techniques- SIGGRAPH 1997, pp. 345–352 (1997). https://doi.org/10.1145/258734.258878
21. Bargas-Avila, J., Hornbæk, K.: Old wine in new bottles or novel challenges? a critical analysis of empirical studies of user experience. In: Proceedings of SIGCHI Conference on Human Factors in Computing Systems, pp. 2689–2698 (2011). https://doi.org/10.1145/1978942.1979336
22. De Guinea, A.O., Titah, R., Léger, P.-M.: Explicit and implicit antecedents of users' behavioral beliefs in information systems: a neuropsychological investigation. J. Manag. Inf. Syst. **30**, 179–210 (2014). https://doi.org/10.2753/MIS0742-1222300407
23. Dirican, A.C., Göktürk, M.: Psychophysiological measures of human cognitive states applied in Human Computer Interaction. Procedia Comput. Sci. **3**, 1361–1367 (2011). https://doi.org/10.1016/j.procs.2011.01.016
24. Mandryk, R.L., Inkpen, K.M., Calvert, T.W.: Using psychophysiological techniques to measure user experience with entertainment technologies. Behav. Inf. Technol. **25**, 141–158 (2006). https://doi.org/10.1080/01449290500331156
25. Lourties, S., Léger, P., Sénécal, S., Fredette, M., Chen, S.L.: Testing the convergent validity of continuous self-perceived measurement systems: an exploratory study **10923**, 132–144 (2018). https://doi.org/10.1007/978-3-319-91716-0
26. Allanson, J., Fairclough, S.H.: A research agenda for physiological computing. Interact. Comput. **16**, 857–878 (2004). https://doi.org/10.1016/j.intcom.2004.08.001
27. Wilson, G.M., Sasse, M.A.: Do users always know what's good for them? utilising physiological responses to assess media quality. In: McDonald, S., Waern, Y., Cockton, G. (eds.) People and Computers XIV—Usability or Else!, pp. 327–339. Springer, London (2006). https://doi.org/10.1007/978-1-4471-0515-2_22
28. Vicente, K.J., Thornton, D.C., Moray, N.: Spectral analysis of sinus arrhythmia: a measure of mental effort. Hum. Factors 171–182 (1987). https://doi.org/10.1177/001872088702900205
29. Adams, R.: Decision and stress: cognition and e-accessibility in the information workplace. Univers. Access Inf. Soc. **5**, 363–379 (2007). https://doi.org/10.1007/s10209-006-0061-9
30. Harrison, R., Flood, D., Duce, D.: Usability of mobile applications: literature review and rationale for a new usability model. J. Interact. Sci. 1–16 (2013). https://doi.org/10.1186/2194-0827-1-1
31. Xie, H., et al.: The more total cognitive load is reduced by cues, the better retention and transfer of multimedia learning: a meta-analysis and two meta-regression analyses. PLoS ONE **12** (2017). https://doi.org/10.1371/journal.pone.0183884
32. Ahlstrom, U., Friedman-Berg, F.J.: Using eye movement activity as a correlate of cognitive workload. Int. J. Ind. Ergon. **36**, 623–636 (2006). https://doi.org/10.1016/j.ergon.2006.04.002
33. Van Orden, K.F., Limbert, W., Makeig, S., Jung, T.-P.: Eye activity correlates of workload during a visuospatial memory task. Hum. Factors J. Hum. Factors Ergon. Soc. **43**, 111–121 (2001). https://doi.org/10.1518/001872001775992570

34. Chen, F., et al.: Real-time cognitive load measurement: data streaming approach. Robust Multimodal Cognitive Load Measurement. HIS, pp. 229–234. Springer, Cham (2016). https://doi.org/10.1007/978-3-319-31700-7_15
35. Ganglbauer, E., Schrammel, J., Deutsch, S., Tscheligi, M.: Applying psychophysiological methods for measuring user experience: possibilities, challenges and feasibility. In: Human-Computer Interact. INTERACT 2011 LNCS, vol. 6949, pp. 714–715 (2009). https://doi.org/10.1007/978-3-642-23768-3
36. Kramer, A.F.: Physiological metrics of mental workload: a review of recent progress. Mult. Task Perform. 279–328 (1991). https://doi.org/10.1080/00140139.2014.956151
37. Beatty, J.: Task-evoked pupillary responses, processing load, and the structure of processing resources. Psychol. Bull. **91**, 276–292 (1982). https://doi.org/10.1037/0033-2909.91.2.276
38. Ekman, P.: Facial expression and emotion. Am. Psychol. **48**, 384–392 (1993). https://doi.org/10.1037/0003-066X.48.4.384
39. Staiano, J., Menéndez, M., Battocchi, A., De Angeli, A., Sebe, N.: UX_Mate: from facial expressions to UX evaluation. In: Proceedings of Designing Interactive Systems Conference-DIS 2012, p. 741 (2012). https://doi.org/10.1145/2317956.2318068
40. Lane, R.D., Chua, P.M.-L., Dolan, R.J.: Common effects of emotional valence, arousal and attention on neural activation during visual processing of pictures. Neuropsychologia **37**, 989–997 (1999). https://doi.org/10.1016/S0028-3932(99)00017-2
41. Bartlett, M.S., Littlewort, G., Lainscsek, C., Fasel, I., Movellan, J.: Machine learning methods for fully automatic recognition of facial expressions and facial actions. In: 2004 IEEE International Conference on Systems, Man and Cybernetics, vol. 1, pp. 592–597 (2004). https://doi.org/10.1109/icsmc.2004.1398364
42. EMarketer: How Often Do US Internet Users Access Their Bank Accounts via Mobile Device? (2018)
43. Piferi, R.L., Kline, K.A., Younger, J., Lawler, K.A.: An alternative approach for achieving cardiovascular baseline: Viewing an aquatic video. Int. J. Psychophysiol. **37**, 207–217 (2000). https://doi.org/10.1016/S0167-8760(00)00102-1
44. Léger, P.-M., et al.: Precision is in the Eye of the Beholder: Application of Eye Fixation-Related Potentials to Information Systems Research. J. Assoc. Inf. Syst. **15**, 651–678 (2014). https://doi.org/10.17705/1jais.00376

Affective Haptics Research and Interaction Design

Yang Jiao, Yingqing Xu(✉), and Xiaobo Lu

Academy of Arts and Design, Tsinghua University, Beijing 100084, China
jymars@live.cn, {yqxu, luxb}@tsinghua.edu.cn

Abstract. Emotion is a salient property of the sense of touch. From a design perspective, the present study explores the affective haptics and human affective response, device analysis and interaction design. Firstly, the affective evaluation method - the Valence-Arousal Space - is analyzed in terms of haptic physiology, and the subjective and objective affective detection methods are illustrated, as well as the connection of human haptic valence and haptic stimulus by physiology research. Secondly, a series of affective haptic devices are analyzed according to human affective responses. Lastly, some affective haptics design guidelines and principles are introduced from a design perspective with the help of affective haptics research results.

Keywords: Sense of touch · Emotion · Affective haptic device · Haptic interaction design

1 Introduction

Touch brings instinct and abundant emotions to people. Different emotions by touch like shaking hands among friends, embracing from lover and mother's caressing convey different meanings of pleasure. Emotions by touch, however, could also arise unpleasant feelings: the pain of being hurt, pricking and burning sensation resulted of overcooling or overheating [1]. Touch is featured with abundant emotions which can largely affect users' emotion and experience.

There has been a long history for the research on haptics and haptic interactions. Since 1970s, four types of tactile receptors was found [2] and there were related researches on tactile psychophysics [3]. A set theories of function relation describing external physical stimuli and haptic psychological intensity has been established and consolidated. In terms of emotion, Russell et al. proposed "a circumplex model of affect" [4] in 1980s, and it innovated quantitative research on emotions. Picard et al. introduced the concept of "affective computing" [5] in 1997. It combined the emotion and human-computer interaction, striving for the intellectualization and harmonization of human-computer interaction.

Nowadays, it is yet still a huge challenge for haptics-based interaction as well as related user experience research. Currently, operations and feedbacks on haptic interactions are still relatively limited, such as the contact of touch screen: tow, tapping, force touch, and the haptic vibration or force feedback. Most of the haptic interactions reply on glass and other display screen or touch tablet made of smooth material, which

A. Marcus and W. Wang (Eds.): HCII 2019, LNCS 11584, pp. 134–143, 2019.
https://doi.org/10.1007/978-3-030-23541-3_11

lacks of richer touch information. In the process of interaction, the whole industry basically shows "vision as the main channel, touch and audition as assist" interaction mode and does not refer to the emotions that touch brings. The feeling of immersion need be enhanced.

Aimed at affective haptics interaction and design, firstly, from the human (user) perspective, this paper discusses the research methods of human emotional physiology and the feedback scheme of haptics signals. Secondly, from inside-out, this paper analyzes current affective haptics based on human emotional feedback characteristic, including a variety of affective haptic device and haptic signals that express a more abundant emotional belongings to increase user affective experience. Last but not least, based on previous human and device analysis, we explore the emotional experience design, and expect that haptic interaction and immersive experience can be enhanced.

2 Human Emotional Feedback on Haptic Signals

2.1 Emotion Evaluation Methods

People has complicated emotional activities. Generally speaking, there are two ways to evaluate emotions in terms of affective research: classification evaluation and dimension evaluation. Hevner [6] posed 67 types of emotions that can be described and divides them into 8 categories in 1935. This method, however, lacks of effective connection for different categories. Therefore, in the field of affective haptics, dimension evaluation is often used. Russell introduced "A Circumplex Modal of Affect" [4] in 1980, which put all human emotions into two dimensional plane rectangular coordinate system by "valance" and "arousal". As Fig. 1 shows:

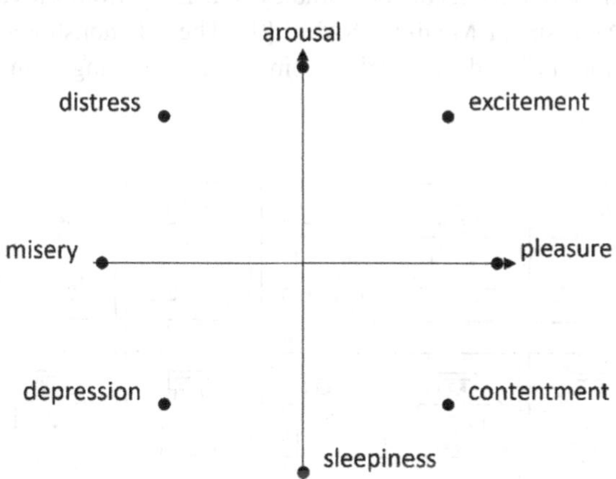

Fig. 1. A circumplex modal of affect [4], redraw by authors

In this emotional model, X-axis stands for valence and Y-axis stands for arousal. both dimensions are linear. If the value is bigger, it will be farther away from the center point and reach deeper emotion. In contrast, if it is closer to the center point, it will be emotionally lower. The zero-point stands for human normal status. The four points between two coordinate axes in the Fig. 1 (Excitement, Contentment, Depression and Destress) are the common effect of valence-arousal. More detailed 15 emotions mapping see [7]. Thus, human emotion can reflect on a point in the valence-arousal space.

Circumplex model of affect is a concise, direct and effective emotional evaluation method. Compared to diversified classification of emotions, this model uses orthogonality of valence-arousal to establish emotional space. Besides, in terms of this model, some researchers have been trying to extent more dimensions apart from valence and arousal, including the dimension of "dominance" [8]. The experiment, however, showed that the dominance degree shows a certain correlation with the other dimensions, which is not supposed to be a third independent dimension. Therefore, most current emotional evaluation is mainly using valence-arousal method. Based on this evaluation method, any external signals can affect people and map the emotional state to a point in valence-arousal plane so as to establish a connection of physical signals and human emotional feedback.

2.2 Emotion Evaluation Methods

Based on the previous emotion evaluation methods and the circumplex model of affect, the other important question is how to accurately measure human emotion and correlate it to the valence-arousal space. Normally, there are subjective and objective methods in terms of human affective measure. Subjective method means subject gives subjective opinions after trying out external signals. In fact, most affective haptics experiments follow the idea: subjects feel a certain type of haptic signal (such as vibration, friction) and give a score in the valence-arousal space subjectively to establish the connection of haptics signals and emotional feedback. Bradley and Lang from university of Florida introduced "Self-Assessment Manikin, SAM" [9]. They demonstrated a gradual process of "pleasure-misery" and "arousal-sleepiness" by showing manikin images. As Fig. 2 shows:

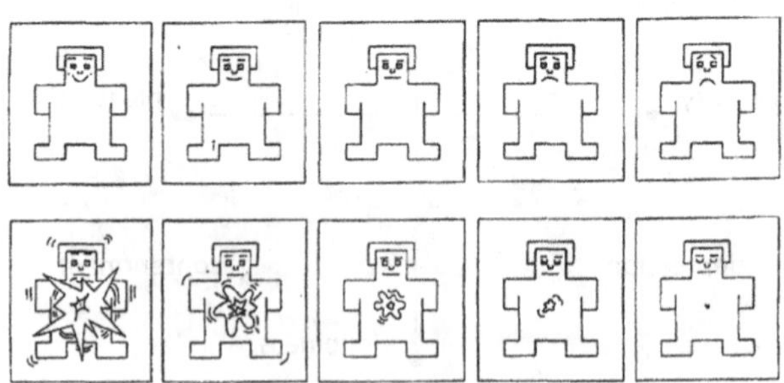

Fig. 2. Self-assessment manikin [9]

This self-evaluation model uses 5 manikins in each dimension to show different status at different degrees. It also inserts four middle status between two adjacent manikins so that each dimension has 9 status to be selected. The experiment shows that this model is effective and there is a better balance of discrimination and complexity in terms of emotion experiment, which can be employed in a wide range of applications, not only for affective haptics. but also for visual image and voice emotion experiments. [10, 11].

The subjective method can directly reflect subjects' emotions and the experiment is relatively simple. In this type of psychology and affect experiments, however, subjects cannot be accurate enough to feel their own thinking and emotion in some situations. Or for some reasons, they try to give objective answers after thinking and modifying. these are some problems that subjective method may exist.

Compared to subjective measure method, the objective method tries to get a more accurate and objective emotional response by objective observation and some equipment. The observation and identification of facial expression, voice, body language can speculate human emotional status, while galvanic skin response, heart rate and the unmyelinated afferents can precisely inspect human emotion status from the perspective of biology and neurology.

In terms of the arousal dimension, there is a significant correlation between the extracted value of galvanic skin response and heart rate and the arousal dimension of emotion, which means stronger emotion, larger signal value and vice versa. By doing so, we can measure arousal emotional state objectively. In terms of the valence dimension, the neuroscience found out from an experiment in recent years that a movement of stroking in the human hairy skin was usually linked to pleasant touch sensation. Meanwhile, low-threshold unmyelinated mechanoreceptors (C-tactile) responded most vigorously [12]. It can be inferred that C-tactile afferents show positive correlation with pleasant sensation.

Furthermore, C-Tactile experiment discussed the relations between caressing speed and the degree of pleasant sensation. As Fig. 3a shows, the swing device made reciprocating movement at specific speed. The soft brush on the tail stroke the dorsal of forearm to create stroking motion.

In terms of the relation of C-Tactile and quantitative pleasure, the average release frequency and functional relations between pleasure sensation and stroking speed are showed as Fig. 3b and c. Two curves show similarities and are presented as inverted "U". The middle part of the curve shows stronger pleasant sensation. While the speed is too slow or too fast, the sense of pleasure will decrease. Therefore, the experiment shows that when the stroking speed of haptic signal received on the hairy skin is between 110 cm/s and the pressure force is low, the pleasant sensation feels strongest [12].

The research above reveals the scheme of human haptic feedback, which can be the foundation for design theory and design instruction of affective haptic device and haptic interaction design.

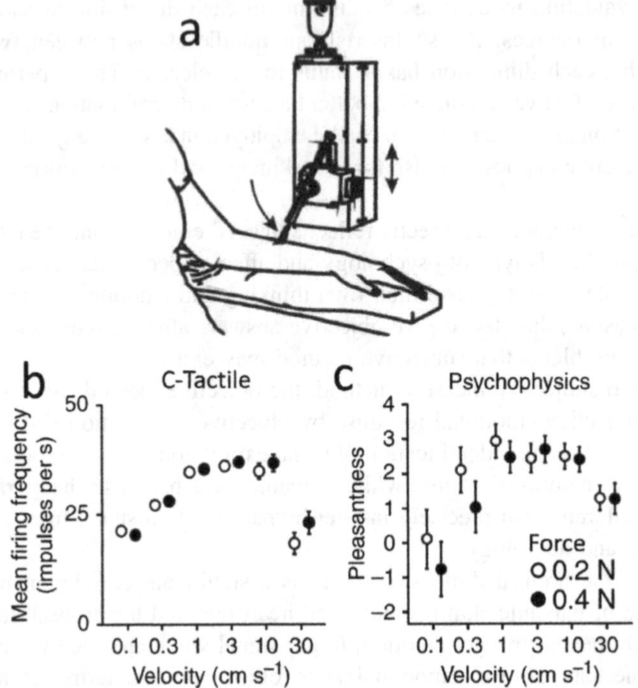

Fig. 3. C-tactile experiment and analysis of speed-valence relations [12]

3 Affective Haptic Device Analysis

According to human haptic emotion feedback scheme, based on the current hardware and technology conditions, some haptic devices have been developed in order to explore the connection of haptics and emotion as well as provide hardware basis for haptic interaction design.

3.1 Tactor and Related Device

Tactor, or vibration motor, has been usually used as haptic feedback related applications in human-computer interaction. Lots of smart or wearable devices, including mobile phone, smart watch and smart wristband put tiny tactor inside. When it gets touch with skin, human haptic receptors will receive vibrotactile signals in order to remind or recall user's attention. Normally, some parameters of the tactor can be adjusted, including vibrotactile amplitude, duration, frequency and envelope frequency. For one single tactor, Yoo [13] explored the relation between these four tactor parameters and human affective sensation. In this experiment, a tactor was attached behind a cellphone making different combinations of these four parameters. Participants were asked to held the phone and use the valence-arousal space with bipolar Likert scale to log the affective response. In terms of the arousal, vibrotactile amplitude and duration showed positive correlation with arousal. Increasing vibration frequency, under some situations, would strengthen arousal. Envelope frequency showed no obvious connection with arousal. In the respect of valence, vibrotactile amplitude and duration as well as envelope frequency showed negative correlation with valence. Increasing vibration frequency, in some situation, could increase valence [13].

To step further, under one tactor condition, increasing arousal (such as vibrotactile amplitude and duration) will greatly decrease valence, reflecting that participants tend not to receive relatively strong reminding signals. When the vibration frequency increases from 60 Hz to 200 Hz, the valence and arousal of emotion will increase. It is decided by the characteristics of human haptic receptors. Human skin is most sensitive when the vibration frequency is between 200–300 Hz [14] and during this scope, people feel more comfortable [13]. So, the above conclusion can guide haptics interaction design: in terms of haptic signal design, the vibration frequency between 200–300 Hz is often used. A more appropriate intensity of the haptic signal should be at the point of just awakening and avoid over-strong.

Currently the combination of multiple tactors is a popular research field. There are some haptic illusions in haptics conception due to not only the peripheral physiology, but human central nervous mechanisms as well, For example, a row of tactors are attached on the skin and follows a specific vibration duration and interval. Then the subject will integrate these discrete vibrations into a continuous apparent motion [15].

According to this haptic characteristics, van Erp and Huisman made use of apparent motion to imitate consecutive haptic signals [16] and explored what types of parameters of the tactors can generate relatively pleasant sensation. As Fig. 4a shows, four tactors were arranged in a row and distributed around the forearm. Tactors vibrated in one direction to imitate continuous moving sensation. In the low arousal scenario, when the equivalent speed of movement was 10 cm/s, the pleasant sensation felt strongest, as Fig. 4b shows. This result matches the conclusion of Sect. 2.2, which confirms the best pleasant sensation happens at 1–10 cm/s speed.

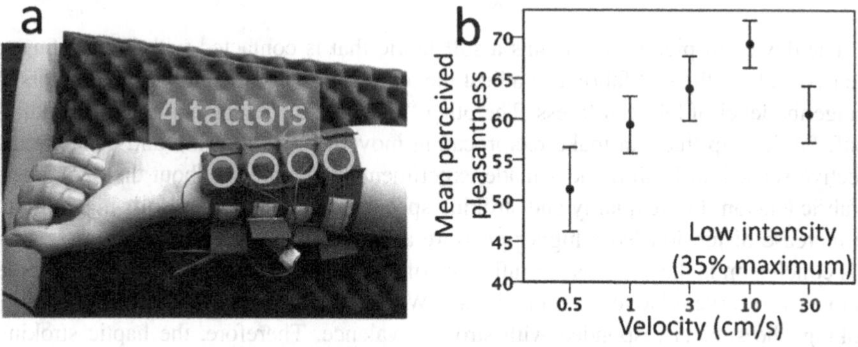

Fig. 4. Experimental setup and analysis of velocity-perceived pleasantness relations [16]

This research conclusion is very important for haptic signal design. Compared to single tactor scenario, the matrix configuration of multiple tactors can convey more abundant signals (such as vibration position, moving directions, frequency etc.). Meanwhile, designers need take haptic emotional factors into consideration. It would remarkably increase the experience of haptic interaction if the user receives pleasant sensation of haptic feedback or interaction.

3.2 Tactile Display

Tactile display has a wide range of concept. Any device that can generate haptic signals and "display" them to uses belongs to tactile display. Strictly speaking, the tactor is included, but this section put more emphasis on the system-based device. In this field, Biamchi et al. explores a fabric-based softness display [17] (shown in Fig. 5) and a novel fabric-based tactile display [18] (shown in Fig. 6).

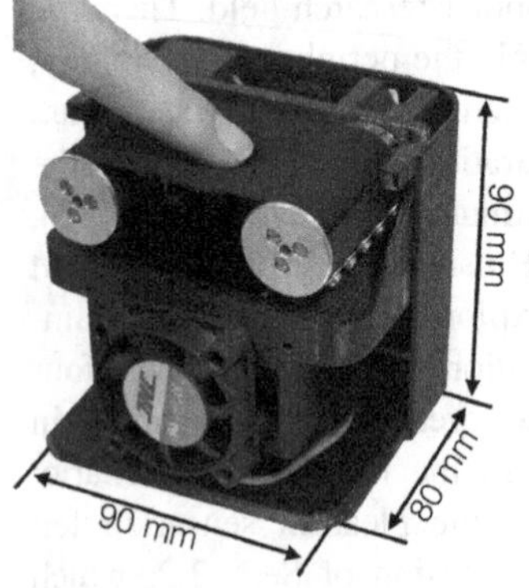

Fig. 5. A fabric-based softness display [17]

Fig. 6. Fabric-based tactile display [18]

The device in picture 5 contains a soft fabric that is contacted with human finger. The two ends of the soft fabric can adjust the tension in real-time though two motors to change the level of fabric softness. The other "caress-like" device in picture 6 contains a soft fabric strip that can make reciprocating movement on the skin and generate the affective sensation. Both devices made experiments and analysis about the parameters of fabric tension, fabric quality and stroking speed. They shared the results in common: the increase of tension led a higher pressure and the subject valence would decrease. This conclusion is the same as the influence of tactor's amplitude, which is that people tend not to receive relatively strong signals. When both devices made a relatively slow stroking, the subject responded with stronger valence. Therefore, the haptic stroking speed (110 cm/s) is not only suitable for the large area of skin surface movement but also for the relative movement of a certain place in the skin.

3.3 Affective Haptics of Touch Materials

In the field of tangible interaction, it is very important to choose a propriate type of material. Different materials and surface texture will lead to different effect, especially user emotional status. Drewing [19] explored the emotional connection of touching 47 different types of materials. In this experiment, 47 materials are put in different jars respectively. Users cannot see, but can only touch it by hand to guess what it is, describe it by adjectives and respond the emotional feedback by valence-arousal space. After analyzing these adjectives and related emotional responses, it was found that the adjectives to describe object has certain correlation with emotion. In terms of valence, the material roughness and valence had relatively weak negative correlation, which meant that if an object was rougher, the valence would be lower. While for the dimension of arousal, there was no related adjectives found.

There are abundant natural materials. In the haptic interaction process, single material information shows limited influence to people emotion. In the haptic interaction design, we need to combine material and a series of interaction activities as well as scenarios so as to benefit user's emotional state, and better serve any possible interaction purpose.

4 Affective Haptic Interaction Design

In Sect. 2, the human emotional and physiological research provide the important fundamental support on affective haptic interaction design. In Sect. 3, the review on affective haptic device reveals the usability of current affective haptics in different perspectives, such as single tactor, haptic display or haptic emotional feedback of natural materials. Based on emotions in human-computer interaction and the state of the art of affective haptics, this chapter is to discuss haptic interaction design principles and instructions from design point of view.

4.1 Follow the Foundation of Haptic Physiological Characteristics

Compared with the sense of vision and audition, the physiological characteristic of the sense of touch decides a relatively low information capacity in terms of information transfer rate during haptic interactions. Therefore, in terms of interaction design, we need to put haptic related operation and feedback to a reasonable place, and any haptic interaction activities should be based on haptic physiological characteristics.

In terms of haptic signal design for the function of reminding and awakening, we need to consider user's environment and interaction scenario. It would be a good suggestion that the intensity of haptic vibration could be self-adjusted based on the "golden" line where the user's real time attention threshold is, not only meeting the functional requirement of interaction, but hitting the pleasant sensation as well. Currently, some haptic devices such as force feedback chair, joystick and wearables can introduce haptic caress or stroking sensation of pleasure, as illustrated in previous section. Considering the haptic semantic information including vibration position and direction that haptic signals provide, we would match the appropriate vibrotactile intensity as well as stroking speed to increase pleasant sensation from both the information transfer and emotion perspectives.

4.2 Increase the Haptic Immersive Experience

One of the characteristics of haptic feeling and interaction is ambient and immersive experience. When a user is touching an object, feeling the zero-distance of himself with this device, he or she will enhance this immersive experience. So, affective haptic factors under the enhanced immersive condition will be magnified and deeply influence user's emotion and interaction experience. From the other perspective, "user experience" emphasizes the user subjective feeling during interaction, while this subjective feeling largely reflects user's emotional state. Thus, the design of emotion is significant to increase haptic interaction experience.

4.3 Multimodal Interaction by the Sense of Vision, Audition and Touch

As mentioned before, the sense of touch has relatively low information capacity. In terms of our daily human-computer interactions, from the perspective of author, the proportion of the channel of vision, audition and touch is roughly 7:2:1. Therefore, the interaction research of haptics is not haptic-only, but the interaction of multimodal. For example, in the scenario of virtual reality (VR), users can put wearable device to have immersive experience and users' fingers and body can also feel haptic signals corresponded with the scenario. Although there might be different information in terms of various channels, user' emotion state is consistent and on top of each single modal. Therefore, designers need to combine haptic emotion with the emotions of vision and audition, offer a holistic design solution and avoid emotional incongruity of each channel to create a unified and coordinated emotional experience.

5 Concluding Remarks

This paper explores the affective haptics and interaction design. By the literature review of human emotional feedback on haptic signal and affective haptic devices, the haptic interaction design principles and instructions are explored. In conclusion, haptic interaction design cannot be separated with the research and application of emotion. Based on the physiological characteristics of human haptics and emotional feedback, designers need to involve haptic signals that satisfy the user's emotional needs into the multimodal interaction scenario. Meanwhile, designers also need to refer to the state of the art of affective haptic devices, focus to the detailed interaction scenarios and real needs of the users to offer better affective experience.

Acknowledgments. The authors thank Prof. Hong Tan for her kindly instructions. This work was supported by the National Key Research and Development Plan under Grant No. 2016YFB1001402, and National Natural Science Foundation of China under Grant No. 61402250, 61232013.

References

1. Goldstein, E.B., Brockmole, J.: Sensation and Perception. Cengage Learning, Boston (2016)
2. Jones, L.A., Lederman, S.J.: Human Hand Function. Oxford University Press, New York (2006)
3. Fechner, G.T.: Elements of psychophysics. In: Dennis, W. (ed.) Readings in the History of Psychology, 1860, pp. 206–213. Appleton-Century-Crofts, New York (1948)
4. Russell, J.A.: A circumplex model of affect. J. Pers. Soc. Psychol. **39**(6), 1161 (1980)
5. Picard, R.W.: Affective Computing. MIT Press, Cambridge (1995)
6. Hevner, K.: Experimental studies of the elements of expression in music. Am. J. Psychol. **48**(2), 246–268 (1936)
7. Posner, J., Russell, J.A., Peterson, B.S.: The circumplex model of affect: an integrative approach to affective neuroscience, cognitive development, and psychopathology. Dev. Psychopathol. **17**(3), 715–734 (2005)
8. Demaree, H.A., Everhart, D.E., Youngstrom, E.A., Harrison, D.W.: Brain lateralization of emotional processing: historical roots and a future incorporating "dominance". Behav. Cogn. Neurosci. Rev. **4**(1), 3–20 (2005)
9. Bradley, M.M., Lang, P.J.: Measuring emotion: the self-assessment manikin and the semantic differential. J. Behav. Ther. Exp. Psychiatry **25**(1), 49–59 (1994)
10. Lang, P.J.: International affective picture system (IAPS): affective ratings of pictures and instruction manual. Technical report (2005)
11. Bradley, M.M., Lang, P.J.: The International Affective Digitized Sounds (IADS-2): affective ratings of sounds and instruction manual. Technical report B-3, University of Florida, Gainesville, FL (2007)
12. Löken, L.S., Wessberg, J., McGlone, F., Olausson, H.: Coding of pleasant touch by unmyelinated afferents in humans. Nat. Neurosci. **12**(5), 547 (2009)
13. Yoo, Y., Yoo, T., Kong, J., Choi, S.: Emotional responses of tactile icons: effects of amplitude, frequency, duration, and envelope. In: 2015 IEEE World Haptics Conference (WHC), pp. 235–240. IEEE (2015)
14. Summers, I.R.: Tactile Aids for the Hearing Impaired. Whurr Publishers, London (1992)
15. Israr, A., Poupyrev, I.: Tactile brush: drawing on skin with a tactile grid display. In: Proceedings of the SIGCHI Conference on Human Factors in Computing Systems, pp. 2019–2028. ACM (2011)
16. Huisman, G., Frederiks, A.D., van Erp, Jan B.F., Heylen, Dirk K.J.: Simulating affective touch: using a vibrotactile array to generate pleasant stroking sensations. In: Bello, F., Kajimoto, H., Visell, Y. (eds.) EuroHaptics 2016. LNCS, vol. 9775, pp. 240–250. Springer, Cham (2016). https://doi.org/10.1007/978-3-319-42324-1_24
17. Bianchi, M., Serio, A.: Design and characterization of a fabric-based softness display. IEEE Trans. Haptics **8**(2), 152–163 (2015)
18. Bianchi, M. et al.: Design and preliminary affective characterization of a novel fabric-based tactile display. In: 2014 IEEE Haptics Symposium (HAPTICS), pp. 591–596. IEEE (2014)
19. Drewing, K., Weyel, C., Celebi, H., Kaya, D.: Feeling and feelings: affective and perceptual dimensions of touched materials and their connection. In: 2017 IEEE World Haptics Conference (WHC), pp. 25–30. IEEE (2017)

Exploration of Ideal Interaction Scheme on Smart TV: Based on User Experience Research of Far-Field Speech and Mid-air Gesture Interaction

Xuan Li(✉), Daisong Guan, Jingya Zhang, Xingtong Liu, Siqi Li, and Hui Tong

Baidu AI Interaction Design Lab, Beijing, China
lixuan03@baidu.com

Abstract. TV, as an important entertainment appliance in family, its interaction is typical of other screen-equipped devices. Far-field speech and mid-air gesture are the new trends in smart TV interaction. Previous studies have explored the characteristics of far-field speech and mid-air gesture interactions in TV used scenes, but rarely studied the user experience in the interaction process for the two interactive modes and directly compared them. What is the ideal interactive mode for TV in the future when these two can be realized? We know very little about this. Therefore, in Study 1, we quantitatively compared the user experience of far-field speech and mid-air gesture through experiment. The results showed that there were no significant differences between the two interactive modes, and implicated their advantages and disadvantages for different operations. And then, in study 2, we explored the user preference for interaction in different operations. The results showed that there were certain regularities about the participants' preference for the two interaction channel in different situations. Based on the results mentioned above, we finally proposed the design principles of multichannel interaction fusion for different operations.

Keywords: Ideal interaction for smart TV · Mid-air gesture · Far-field speech · User experience study · Multichannel

1 Introduction

With the advent of the AI era, the development of technology has made the machine more powerful in audio-visual capabilities, and brings a variety of human-computer interactive modes, such as speech interaction, gesture interaction, and eye movement interaction. These kinds of interactions are gradually realized in various scenes of everyday life. The home scene as one of the most important scenes of human life is being discussed and studied continuously. The focus of this research is how to properly use new AI interactive modes to create an ideal interaction scheme for home scene.

Smart TV is important to meet the entertainment requirement of the whole family, especially in China. It is the indispensable appliance and the center of entertainment for each Chinese family. From the point of users, the usage of TV has the characteristics of

A. Marcus and W. Wang (Eds.): HCII 2019, LNCS 11584, pp. 144–162, 2019.
https://doi.org/10.1007/978-3-030-23541-3_12

high frequency, long time and relatively diverse operation compared to other home appliances such as refrigerator, washing machine, and air conditioner. Due to these characteristics, the user's interaction with TV can embody the user interaction characteristics with other screen-equipped. Therefore, the conclusions and design suggestions for TV interaction in this research are also valuable for other screen-equipped devices.

Even though the main interactive mode for TV is remote control and the alternatives, such as the mobile phone, iPad, TVs with near-field or far-field speech interaction function are gradually dominating the market. The characteristics of speech interaction include clear direction, good at searching, and function selection. Far-field speech interaction allows users to talk directly to the appliance without any other device. The researchers have high hopes for far-field speech interaction and think it as the most natural interactive mode [1]. This study focused on the far-field speech interaction, and the speech mentioned in our experiments all referred to far-field speech.

The speech interaction products are already in the market, meanwhile, a large number of researchers have been paying attention to gestures as a new type of interaction which is to be realized [2]. Our hands are good at continuous operation and can express rich spatial information [3, 4]. Amid numerous gestures interactive modes, the mid-air gestures, which is also known as free-hand gestures, is an interactive mode for remotely controlling TV with the advantage of natural and direct [5]. The gestures mentioned in our experiments all referred to mid-air gestures.

Based on the development of market and research, we found that, the far-field speech and mid-air gestures are the trends of the TV interaction in the future. Previous studies have already separately discussed the topics related to the implementation, user experience, and design elements of these two kinds of interactive modes. On this basis, we considered that it is important to compare the two modes directly. Because it will help us to answer what is the ideal interaction for TV when the technologies and designs which needed by the two interactive modes are mature.

Therefore, in study 1, we did experiment to compare the user experience of far-field speech and mid-air gesture interaction. For a new interactive mode, we believed the "better" means (1) easy to learn, (2) better using experience, (3) greater willingness to use. So we quantitatively compared these two new interactive modes from these three aspects. Based on the results that none of them has obvious advantage, in study 2, we explored the applicability of gestures and speech channels, and propose the multi-channel scheme.

2 Related Work

We build our work upon the prior works including comparative study of gesture and speech interaction experience, evaluation of experience for gesture and speech interaction in home scenes, and research methods for interactions in the future.

2.1 Comparative Study of Gesture and Speech Interaction Experience

In previous studies, the direct comparison of the two interactive modes including gestures and speech was focused on the vehicle scene, to solve the problem of attention distribution during driving.

Reissner [6] reviewed the advantages and disadvantages of in-car gesture and speech interactions, and considered that the combination of gestures and speech can increase both the usability of complex driver information system and driving safety. Gesture interaction is more suitable for small commands, like "next menu point" or "mute audio". And the strength of speech is compact transmission of complex instructions. In an empirical research, Angelini et al. [7] compared the gesture, speech and touch interactions on the in-vehicle infotainment system, the results showed that there was no significant difference in usability, mental workload, learnability and emotional response between the three ways. They proposed multi-modal in discussion, as a direction for follow-up research. Bastian et al. [8] directly explored multi-modal interaction. Firstly, they defined the applicability of speech and touch gestures by reviewing previous studies, in which, speech interaction applied to select objects and functions, and touch gestures applied to complete fine-grained operations. Then, in study 1, user-defined gesture and speech instruction were obtained through a formal study. In study 2, the researcher compared traditional interaction and multimodal interaction through experiments. The results showed that compare with traditional interaction, multimodal interaction has lower SUS score and lower perceived task load.

Based on the above studies, the comparison results of gesture and speech interactions in the vehicle scene mostly point to the fusion of the two modes. Although the vehicle and home scene has one same characteristic, private, the essential issue of the two scenes is quite different. The most important issue of interaction experience in vehicle scene is whether the user can rationally allocate their cognitive resources. In home scene, it is more important to enable the user to get a more comfortable experience. As a result, the conclusions of the research on gestures and speech in vehicle scene and home scene might be different.

Although in home scene, there is no empirical research to directly compare the gestures and speech mode, or integrate them together, some researchers have explored gestures and speech separately in one study. Morris [9] obtained gesture and speech interaction schemes separately by using elicitation study. But they did not make a comparison for gestures and speech. They just explained their subjective judgments that the gestures and speech have their own advantage and disadvantage. Perales et al. [10] asked participants to evaluate the efficiency and ease of use of traditional remote control, interactive remote control, gestures and voice. The results showed that the traditional remote control was the system chosen by excellence, and there was no difference between gestures and voice. However, the results of this study were not based on the comparison of user experience for various interactions under the same conditions, which means there may be some deviations.

2.2 The User Experience Evaluation of Gestures or Speech Interaction in the Home Scene

We found that there are few comparative studies on gestures and speech in home scenes. Therefore, we reviewed the previous studies about the user experience evaluation of gestures or speech interaction in home scene.

Panger [11] studied the interaction experience for mid-air gestures based on Microsoft Kinect in kitchen. The results showed that participants evaluated the gestures interactive mode as helpful. Bobeth et al. [12] found that, when participants were using iTV applications (Photo Browser, Nutrition Tracker), comparing with touchscreen and remote control, they gave the lowest score to the user experience for gesture. After conducted further analysis, the researcher suggested that the UI design affected the results. The rather linear interactions with the Photo Browser could be achieved comfortably with the remote control. For the two-level dialog-navigation of the Nutrition Tracker, direct manipulations by touch the screen seemed to be more comfortable. The results indicated that both the UI design and the content of application have influence on the user experience of different interaction mode.

Brush et al. [13] studied the user experience of manipulating speech interaction systems in the public areas of home. Through the exploratory field research in 6 families, the researchers found that although users got enthusiasm for speech interaction, there were many technical challenges in practice that make the process of speech interaction not smooth. The results of research conducted by Cheng Ying [14] showed that, from a qualitative point of view, people have gradually accepting TV with speech interaction function, and hold positive attitude about the efficiency of speech interaction.

By reviewing the previous studies, we found that there are some researches on the experience evaluation of gesture and speech interactions in the home scene. According to previous studies, experience evaluation on the gesture interaction is positive based on quantitative analysis, while evaluation about speech interaction are mostly qualitative. Therefore, it is impossible to directly compare the pros and cons of gestures and speech according to existing research.

2.3 Interactive Research Methods

This study focused on gesture and speech interaction which have not been fully realized for now. Therefore, we reviewed the research methods that had been applied to the research with interactive prototypes, but without interactive devices. The methods for research with prototypes include videos, live demonstration, a Wizard-of-Oz phone prototype with vibrotactile feedback, and a shaped prototype without feedback, high-fidelity prototypes, and so on. Among them, the high-fidelity prototype could simulate the interaction experience better than others, but the production process is complex, and it needs to base on the mature technology. The Wizard of Oz technique is a method in which participants are led to believe they are interacting with a working prototype of a system, but in reality, a researcher is acting as a proxy for the system from behind the scene, which allows the user to experience a proposed product or interface before costly prototypes are built [15].

Rico et al. [16] used the four methods mentioned above to explore users' social acceptability for new interaction method: videos, live demonstration, a Wizard-of-Oz phone prototype with vibrotactile feedback, and a shaped prototype Without feedback. The results of the study indicated that the benefits of Wizard-of-Oz include the ability to provide a hands-on experience that provides feed-back to the participants and thus guarantee of consistent performance for each participant. In previous research of the gestures generation has also adopted the method of the Wizard of Oz to let the user experience the gesture interaction which has not been technically realized. It is also applicable to the research of speech interaction interfaces [17].

3 Study 1. Comparative Study of Speech and Gesture Interaction on Smart TV

3.1 Methods

Participants. We recruited 40 participants and randomly assigned them to the gesture interaction group and the speech interaction group. After excluding two persons due to their data is invalid, the speech group had 18 participants. The gestures group's sample consisted of 20 participants. The ratio of gender and age in the two groups of participants is shown in the Table 1. The occupation of participants was diverse. None of the participants had the experience in speech or gesture interaction.

Table 1. The ratio of gender and age for the participants in gestures and speech group.

	Gender		Age		
	Male	Female	14–17	18–45	45–55
Gestures	45.0%	55.0%	20.0%	60.0%	20.0%
Speech	50.0%	50.0%	22.2%	55.6%	22.2%

Procedure. This study was conducted in a simulated home scene. We asked the participants to sit in sofa in front of the TV when they were doing the experiment, and took video to record their behavior. Firstly, the experimenter explained the procedure to the participants and informed the purpose of the recording (recording the participants' behavior) before the experiment beginning. After the participants signed informed consent, the experimenter collected the basic information of the participants. Then participants came to the two main parts: learning section and experience section (see Fig. 1). When the experiment ended, the participants need to evaluate their feeling.

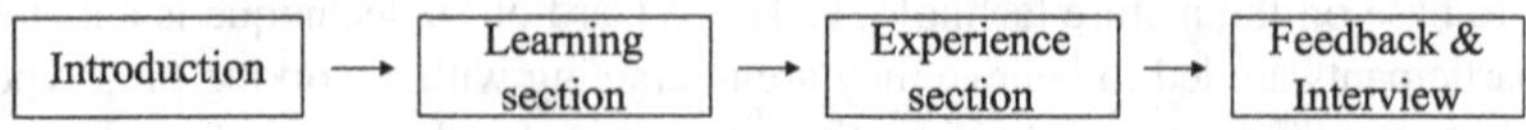

Fig. 1. Research flow chart.

Learning Section. The participants learned about the gestures and speech commands corresponding to 16 TV operations and tested through a Windows program. Firstly, the participants learned commands for all operations through 16 trials in the first round, and then be tested to make sure they could accurately recall the standard command of each operation. The operations were presented randomly in both learning and testing parts. If the participants could not recall accurately, they would continue to learn and be tested until all the gesture or speech commands can be accurately recalled during the test session. The program automatically recorded the participants' learning and test data. The recorder collected the specific answers given by the participants in each test.

Experience Section. After the learning section ended, the experience section would start. In this part, the participants were asked to manipulate the TV sitting in a sofa two metres in front of the TV by the gesture or speech command they learned corresponding to the instruction given by the experimenter. The participants were told to keep the volume of speech and the range of gestures as communicating with a person at the place of the TV. The experimenter gave feedback to participants by using the Wizard of Oz. In the Wizard of Oz, a hidden experimenter observed the gestures or speech presented by participant, and gave the corresponding feedback via using remote control to manipulate the TV. In order to keep the process running smoothly, the experimenter would provide the corresponding feedback, as long as the participants gave the gestures or speech commands similar to the standard commands. If the participants could not remember the correct commands, the experimenter would help the participants completing the instruction.

Before the formal experiment starting, three exercise tasks would be given to the participants, in which they could get familiar with the TV interface and the task format. The participants also need to read the task script to avoid misunderstanding the meaning. After the participants understand every operation task on the script, the formal experiment which including 33 tasks would start.

Feedback Section. After completing the operation task, the participants evaluated their interactive experience and willingness to use the gestures or speech interaction via a questionnaire including 0–10 grade, and accepted a brief interview.

Equipment and Materials

Experimental Equipment. The computer (Thinkpad X240) with Windows system was used in the learning section. The Changhong Q5 K TV (screen size: 55 inches; resolution: 4 K (3840 * 2160); screen ratio: 16:9) was used in exercising and experience section.

Learning Materials. The standard gestures commands were from the design library of Baidu based on an elicitation study, including 12 gesture commands to conduct 16 operations on smart TV. The standard speech commands were chosen from the DuerOS which is an intelligent speech operation system provided by Baidu. In order to avoid the description of the TV operation task remaindering the participants of the speech commands, the TV operation task was standardized and interpreted by video. When presenting the results, we used the abbreviation of the TV operation description for ease to present. The description of 16 TV operations and their abbreviation are presented in Table 2 with the corresponding the description of standard gestures and speech commands.

Table 2. The 16 television operations, abbreviation, standard gestures and speech commands.

No.	Operations	Abbreviation	Standard gesture commands	Standard speech commands
1	Turn on the device	Power-on	Clap hands	Power-on
2	Turn off the device	Power-off	Put hands across chest	Power-off
3	Mobilize operation system	Arouse	Clap hands	Xiaodu Xiaodu
4	Slide to content on top/bottom	Slide up	Move/fan hand down	Slide up/down(keep continuous sliding by repeat)
5	Slide to content on right/left	Slide left	Move/fan hand from left to right	Slide right/left n(keep continuous sliding by repeat)
6	Select an objective	Select	Point and click	Select
7	Expand content to entire screen	Full screen	Move thumb and index finger from closed to open	Full screen
8	Go back to previous step	Return	Hanging touch left top of screen	Return
9	Go back to home page	Homepage	Hanging long press left top of screen	Return to home page
10	Play last/next episode	Episode	Move/fan hand from right to left	Last/next episode
11	Speed forward to previous/following content	Speed	Clench fist and move from left to right	Speed forward/rewind
12	Stop the current playing	Pause	Click	Pause
13	Let paused content play	Play	Click	Play
14	Turn off device sound	Mute	Put index finger in front of mouth	Mute
15	Turn on device sound	Cancel mute	Put index finger in front of mouth	Cancel mute
16	Turn up/down volume	Volume	Slide palm vertical upward	Volume up/down

Formal Experience Script. In the experience section, the experimenter set a script with 33 tasks covered all 16 operations listed in Table 2. In order to conformity with TV operation habits, some operations appeared more than once in the script. Specifically, the "Select" occurred in 8 tasks("Select channel" 2 times, such as select TV series, variety show; "select TV sub channel" 2 times, such as select funny, martial arts and so on; "select specific TV program or film" 3 times; "select all teleplays" 1 time); "Arouse" occurred in 4 tasks; "Episode", "Slide up", "Slide left" occurred in 2 tasks (each direction once separately), and "Speed" occurred in 3 tasks (including speed forward to specific time, rewind a little, speed forward a little), the "Volume" occurred in 3 tasks (including adjusted to a specific value).

Experience Feedback Questionnaire. It contains 2 questions, measuring the satisfaction of interaction and the willingness to use gestures or speech command. The participants evaluated their feeling in a scale including 0–10 grade. And the higher score is the better.

Experimental Design. The experiment was a between-subject design. The independent variable was the interactive mode. The two levels of the independent variable were gesture interaction and speech interaction. The dependent variables were the learning difficulty, the satisfaction of interaction and the willingness to use of the gestures or speech interaction.

Data Calculation and Analysis. Considering that technology identification has fault tolerance which means it responds to the commands given by participants which were not precisely the same, but similar to the standard commands, we set up some fault tolerance criteria to recalculate the learning data. The criterion for speech was based on the range of speech that DuerOS can recognize. If DuerOS could recognize the speech command, then it was correct, vice versa. The criterion for gesture interaction was based on the opinion of the technician. It did not distinguish the number of fingers participants used in gestures command, the absolute positioning of the gestures' initial position, the amplitude of movement and the change. If the participant's gesture was the same as the standard gestures, or there was a difference but within the above range, it was correct, otherwise it was wrong. Based on these criteria, we recalculated the program recorded data.

We calculated the "learning rounds" and the "correct rate in first round" which collated in the learning section, as the indexes of learning difficulty. The overall learning rounds was the average rounds that the participants took to master 16 TV operations. The learning rounds for single operation was calculated by the average learning rounds the participant took to master a specific operation. The overall correct rate in first round was the average rate of correct operations for 16 TV operations after the first learning rounds. The correct rate in first round of single operation was the average correct rate of specific operation in the first time learning. The less the learning rounds and the higher the first success rate, then the interactive mode is easier to learn.

The satisfaction and willingness to use was the average of the scores given by participants during experience section.

In order to get the results of descriptive statistics and inferential statistics for the data, we used SPSS 20.0 as the data analysis tool. The independent sample t test and the independent sample nonparametric test were applied in this study.

3.2 Results

Comparison of Learning

Comparison of the Overall Learning Difficulty Between Gestures and Speech. Compared with gestures, the learning rounds of speech was less, and the correct rate in first round was higher (see Fig. 2). Furthermore, we used the independent sample t-test to compare the overall learning difficulty of gestures and speech. The results showed that both of the learning rounds ($t = 0.263$, $p = 0.794$) and the correct rate in first round ($t = -0.349$, $p = 0.729$) did not reach the significant level. Therefore, overall, there was no difference in the difficulty of learning between gestures and speech.

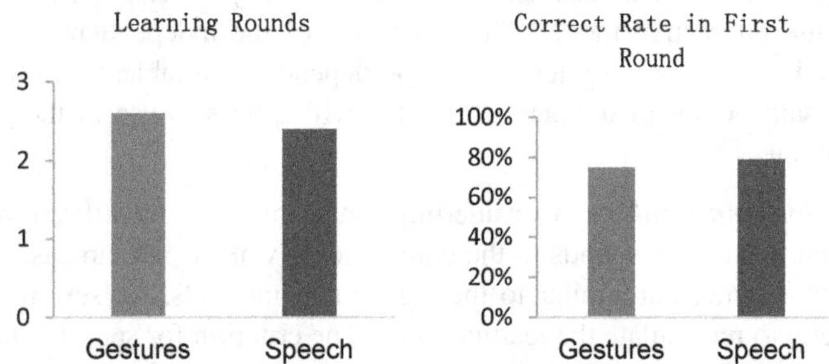

Fig. 2. The average learning rounds and correct rate in first round speech and gestures.

Comparison of Learning Difficulty for each Operation. In the learning rounds, speech is less than gestures (see Fig. 3). We used the independent sample t-test as a further analysis to compare the learning rounds for gestures and speech. The results showed that, compared with the speech commands, the learning rounds for "Power-on", "Return", "Pause", and "Play" was significantly lower than the gestures ("Power-on":

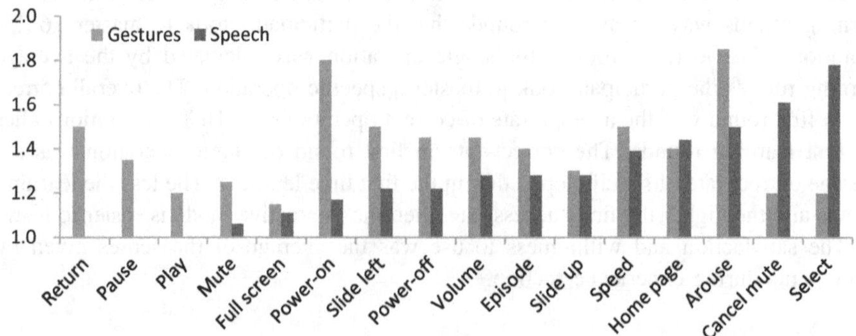

Fig. 3. The average learning rounds of speech and gesture commands for each operation.

t = 2.403, p = 0.022; "Return": t = 2.118, p = 0.041; "Pause": t = 2.526, p = 0.016; "Play": t = 2.065, p = 0.046). But for "cancel mute", the result was opposite (t = −2.466, p = 0.019). There were no significant differences in other instructions.

In the correct rate in first round, for most instruction, speech was higher than gestures (see Fig. 4). We used the independent sample nonparametric test as a further analysis to compare the correct rate in first round in gestures and speech. The results showed that, the correct rate in first round of learning "Power-on", "Return", "Pause", and "Play" was significantly lower than the gestures commands ("Power-on": z = −2.414, p = 0.016; "Return": z = −2.246, p = 0.0251; "Pause": z = −2.499, p = 0.025; "Play": z = −1.979, z = 0.048). But for "Mute cancel", the result was opposite (z = −2.239, z = 0.025). There were no significant differences in other instructions.

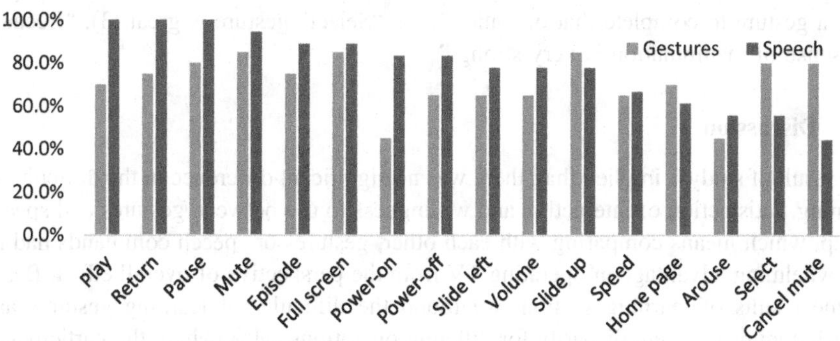

Fig. 4. The average correct rate in first round of speech and gestures for each operation.

Comparison of Interaction Satisfaction and Willingness to use Speech and Gestures

Quantitative Results. The satisfaction and willingness to use gestures was higher than speech (see Fig. 5). We used independent sample t-test as a further analysis, there was no significant difference in the score of satisfaction (t = 1.346, p = 0.187) and willingness (t = 0.811, p = 0.423) to use between speech and gestures. This means, there was no significant difference between the experience of using a gesture to operate a TV and using speech commands to operate TV.

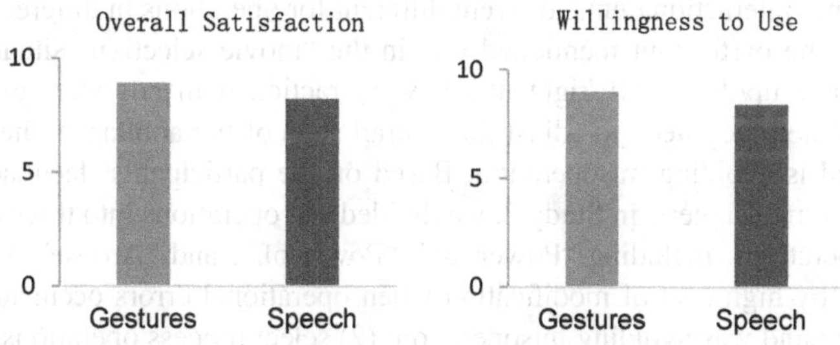

Fig. 5. The score of interaction satisfaction and willingness to use speech and gestures.

Subjective Feedback. After finished the experiment, we communicated with the participants about the feeling of using gestures or speech to operate the TV, and found that most participants hold a positive attitude. It was worth noting that some participants agreed on the applicability of using gestures or speech to certain specific instructions. The participants in speech group thought "Slide up", "Slide left" (3), "Speed" (3) were not suit for using speech commands. "People do these operations to search episode without aim, which usually happen repeatedly. It is too tired to say the speech commands over and over again". "Mute" is suitable for speech commands (5), "because it just includes two Chinese characters, which is simple and convenient to say." For the gesture group participants, many participants gave poor evaluations about the "Volume" gesture (5). "The movement range of this gesture is wide. It needs to raise arms slowly. It's too tired." The "Power-off" gesture is not preferred (4). Some participants thought that "It needs a certain feeling when turn off TV, it feels a bit too casual to just give a gesture to complete that operation"; the "Select" gesture is great (3), "Because the sense of manipulation is very strong."

3.3 Discussion

The result of study 1 implied that, there was no significant difference in the difficulty of learning, satisfaction of interaction and willingness to use between gestures and speech group, which means comparing with each other, gestures or speech commands had no overwhelming advantage in operating TV from the perspective of overall effect. Based on the results of learning section, we found the difficulty of learning gestures and speech commands were disparity for different operations. Meanwhile, the participants' subject feedback also quantitatively described that, each of the gestures and speech commands have its own advantage and disadvantage for different operations to some extent.

Based on the above results, we supposed that each of the gestures and speech commands had its own advantage and disadvantage. What should an ideal TV interaction look like? In order to answer this question, in Study 2, we quantitatively analyzed the pros and cons of gestures and speech for completing different operations, and explored the multichannel scheme based on this. According to technology acceptance model [18], "whether the user uses it" is the ultimate indicator of user acceptance. Therefore, in Study 2, we adopted the participants' preference for gestures and speech for each operation as an indicator.

Meanwhile, from the subjective feedback obtained from the study 1, we found that the participants' interaction demands were different for operations in different situation. For example, the participant mentioned that in the "movie selection" situation, when sliding the page up/down, left/right, the key interaction demands were efficient and convenient. When they need to adjust the overall state of the appliance, the key interactive demand is avoiding misoperation. Based on the participants' feedback and the suggestions from designers, in Study 2, we divided TV operations into three categories: (1) global operations, including "Power-on", "Power-off", and "Arouse", which were characterized by high cost of modification when operational errors occurring, and the interactive demand was avoiding misoperation; (2) select process operations, including "Select", "Slide up", "Return", "Homepage", "Full screen", which characterized by high frequency and repeated, and the interactive demand was efficient; (3) media control operations, including "Volume", "Speed", "Episode", "Pause" and "Play", the characteristics were that when operating, the status and the scene were diverse, and the interactive demand was flexible. In study 2, based on the categories of operation, we analyzed the participants' preference and interaction demands for gestures and speech in different operations.

4 Study 2. Preference Between Speech and Gesture Interaction on Smart TV

4.1 Method

Participants. We recruited 22 participants taking part in study 2. The participants were paid for the study. The occupations of participants were diverse. None of the participants had the experience in speech or gesture interaction.54.5% of the participants is male. The ratio of the participants who aged 14–17, 18–45, and 45–55 were 18.2%, 63.6%, and 18.2%.

Procedure, Equipment and Materials. Study 2 includes two sections which was similar with study 1. In the learning section, the difference from study 1 was that participants needed to learn both gestures and speech commands for each operation, and then be tested randomly to ensure they could master all the gestures and speech commands for every operation.

After finished the learning section, participants entered to the experience section. They could choose using gestures or speech by their own will to complete the task given by the experimenter. Meanwhile, the channel chose by the participants was recorded by the experimenter. And television feedback was still achieved through the Wizard of Oz. After completing the operation task, the participants gave a brief interview.

Experimental equipment and materials were same as Study 1.

Experimental Design. The experiment was a within-subject design. The independent variable was the television operation which including 16 levels. The dependent variable was the channel chose by participants which including gestures and speech.

Data Analysis. The script contained 16 operations, in which 7 operations occurred repeatedly, and 9 operations only occurred once. When conducted the data analysis, firstly we analyzed the consistency of interaction channel which chose by participant for the same operation in different tasks, and then analyze the participants' preference for gestures and speech for each operation based on the consistency.

Consistency. It referred to the rate of which participants chose the same interaction channel for the same operation in different tasks. If the participant chose the same interaction channel for the same operation in different tasks, it is consistent; in the contrary, it is inconsistent. According to the definition, we calculated the consistency for each operation. For example, in all 22 participants, 21 of them are consistent for "Speed", the consistency for "Speed" is 95.5%.

Preference. It referred to the choice of participant between the two interaction channel (gesture or speech) when completing an operation, which including 3 categories: (1) the proportion of using gestures; (2) the proportion of using speech; (3) the proportion of using both gestures and speech. If participant chose an inconsistent interaction channel for same operation in different tasks, then the data should be excluded.

We used SPSS 20.0 as the data analysis tool. The k related sample nonparametric test and the independent sample nonparametric test were applied in this study.

4.2 Results

Consistency of Participants' Preference for Same Operation in Different Tasks. Results show that besides "Select", consistency for the other 6 operations was above 80%(Shown in Table 3), which meant more than 80% participants chose the same interaction mode for the same operation in different tasks. However, the consistency for "Select" was relatively low, which was 54.5%.

We used related sample nonparametric test as further analysis to see whether there is significant difference in participants' preference for the same operation in different tasks. The results showed that there were differences for "Select" (chi-square = 16.349, p = 0.022), and no significant difference among the other 6 operations, which indicated that, excepted from "select", the participants' preferences were consistent in other operations.

Table 3. The proportion of consistency and inconsistency for same operation in different tasks.

	Arouse	Speed	Episode	Volume	Slide up	Slide left	Select
Consistent	84.2%	95.5%	90.5%	81.8%	84.2%	90.9%	54.5%
Inconsistent	15.8%	4.5%	9.5%	18.2%	15.8%	9.1%	45.5%

Participants' Preference for Speech and Gestures in each Operation. Overall, the participant tended to select a single channel between the gestures or speech to complete the operation (see Fig. 6). Only in 7 operations, the participant used gesture and speech interaction together at the same time, and the proportion was relatively low. The proportion for "Wake-up" was the highest, which was 6.3%.

For the case of using a single interaction channel, we used k related sample nonparametric test to analyze the difference in the proportion of gestures and speech for each operation (due to there was few data of participant using gesture and speech interaction together, we treated it as missing value. the data of "Select" was not included in the statistical analysis, due to the same reason). The results showed that there was a significant difference between the proportion of gestures and speech for each operation (chi-square = 36.248, p = 0.003), which means there was a significant difference between participants' preference of gestures and speech for each operation.

For global operations, the proportion of participants who using gestures for "Power-off" was high. On the other hand, the proportion of participants who used speech for "Arouse" and "Power-on" was high. We conducted one-sample non-parametric test, the results showed that the proportion of participants who chose to use speech for "Wake-up" was significantly higher than the gesture (z = 2.582, p = 0.007), and there was no significant difference between "Power-on" and "Power-off".

For the selection process operations, the proportion of the participants who using gestures for "Slide up", "Slide left", "Full screen", and "Select" was high. On the other hand, the proportion of participants who used speech for "Return" and "Homepage" was high. We conducted one-sample non-parametric test, the results showed that the proportion of participants who chose to use gestures for "Slide up" and "Slide left" was significantly higher than speech ("Slide up": z = 2.750, p = 0.004; "Slide left": z = 3.801, p = 0.000), and there was no significant difference in other instructions.

For the media control operations, the proportion of the participants who using gestures for "Speed forward/rewind" and "Pause" was high. And the proportion of participants who used speech for the other 7 instructions was high. We conducted one-sample non-parametric test, the results show that the proportion of participants who chose to use gestures for "Speed" was significantly higher than speech(z = 2.460, p = 0.012). While the proportion of participants who chose to use speech for "Speed to xx", "Episode", "Volume" and "Volume to xx" were significantly higher than gestures("Speed to xx": z = 2.619,p = 0.007; "Episode": z = −3.212,p = 0.001; "Volume": z = 2.345,p = 0.017; "Volume to xx": z = 2.593,p = 0.008). There was no significant difference in other instructions.

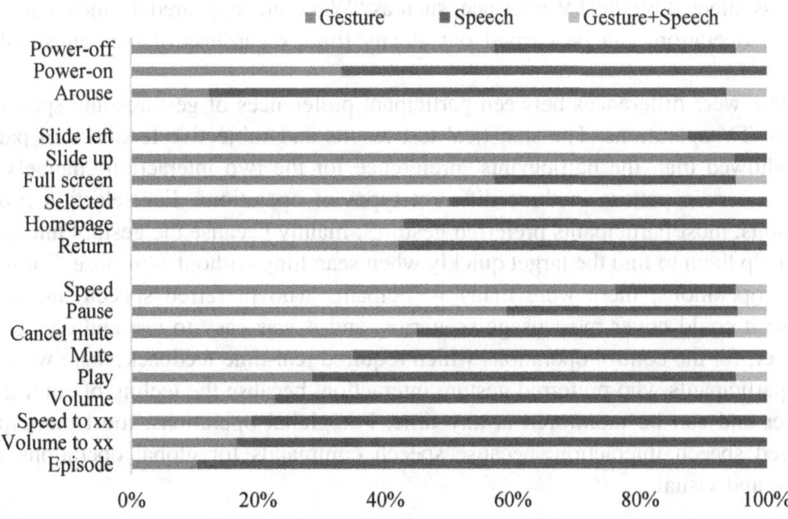

Fig. 6. The proportion of participants using speech or gestures for each operation.

Subjective Feedback. After completed the experience experiment, we interviewed the participant to figure out why they chose to use gestures or speech channels for each operation. Reasons for using gestures include: (1) Use gestures to perform "Slide up", "Slide left", "Speed", "I can get feedback from the TV interface while I'm operating, so that I can find what I want immediately when it shown in the screen, which is in keeping with my operating habits for purposeless browsing; (2) "Select", "Pause", "Play" gestures are "useful, and very efficient". The reasons for using speech include: (1) "Power-on" "Power-off", "Pause", "Play" which speech command consist of two Chinese characters are "easy to say, and very convenient." (2) The operations with specific purpose like "Speed to xx" and "Volume to xx", "could be finished in one step with speech commands"; (3) Speech command of "Arouse" ("Xiaodu Xiaodu") can associate to Baidu, "When you need to use it, you can recall it".

We also learnt about the participants' views on providing multichannel interaction at the same time. We found the participants' attitude relatively positive through their feedback. They thought that "you can choose independently for different operations and operate at any time. It feels more efficient and convenient than single channel"; "It is good to have multiple choices. If you forget one, you can use another"; "You can also switch between the two channels according to the scene. For example, when you just arrived home, you can turn on the TV directly with speech. If you are eating, then you can control it by gestures. "Participants also wanted to keep the use of remote control while having a new way of interacting, because "I'm worried about it is difficult for the elderly and children to learn to use it, and they may be unwilling to use it."

4.3 Discussion

Most operations had higher consistency in different tasks, while the consistency of the "Select" was lower. This may be because the "Select" appeared 8 times in the experiment. The interface of the TV was different in each task, and the "Select" itself was strongly correlated to the interface. Other operations that occurred multiple times were less affected by the TV interface, such as "Wake-up" appeared 4 times, but it was a global operation, can be carried out at any time, regardless of the impact of the interface.

There were differences between participant preferences of gestures and speech for different TV operations. The statistical test results and subjective feedback of participants showed that, the participants' preference for the two interaction channels presented a certain pattern in three different types of operations. For selection process operations, most participants preferred gestures, mainly because the gesture interaction could help them to find the target quickly when searching without a purpose. For media control operations, there were many participants who preferred speech interaction, because it could cover most usage scenarios, and it was easy to use and convenient. However, for the control operations which required real-time feedback, there were also some participants who preferred gesture interaction, because the feeling of control was stronger and can be monitored at any time. For global operations, most participants preferred speech interaction, because speech commands for global operations were concise and visual.

Based on the above results, we considered that the ideal interaction should be multichannel fusion. Considering the characteristics of various operations and the channel preference of users, we proposed the multichannel interaction design:

- The selection process operations require high efficiency, because it's high operating frequency, for which most users preferred gesture interaction. Therefore, in order to efficiently satisfy users' demands, we recommend strengthening the guidance of gesture interaction when designing the TV interface for selecting process operations.
- The global operations have low operating frequency and high error cost, so it is important to prevent misoperation. Although the users showed preference for the operation of "Arouse", for the overall user experience, we recommend guiding the user to use the gesture and speech together for global operations.
- In the case of media control operations, there are diverse conditions in both people's states and operation targets, that should be considered. For example, in many conditions, people are doing other things when they want to modify the volume and speed. In addition, there are both precise and fuzzy targets when modify the volume and speed. And in our results, we found the users' preferences are also different for various operations. For these reasons, we recommend to present both gesture and speech interaction guide when design the interface, for users to choose.

5 Overall Discussion

5.1 Comparison of User Experience for Speech and Gesture Interaction

In Study 1, there was no difference in learning difficulty, interaction satisfaction, and willingness to use in far field gestures and speech. The result was consistent with the qualitative results of Angelini's study [7], which was conducted in the vehicle scene. And the qualitative results also showed that the gestures and speech had advantages and disadvantages for different operations. Why there was no significant difference? We inferred that the reasons as follows: (1) the difference in different operations offset the overall difference; (2) gestures and speech are new interaction ways for participants, there may be a ceiling effect in the evaluation.

5.2 Multichannel Input Fusion

Most researchers agreed that multichannel fusion can increase the effectiveness and efficiency of interactions, and it can improve user satisfaction in a more natural and direct way [19]. But it also requires higher performance device, which means more cost. When the user experience of single channel is good enough, there is no need to choose multiple channels. In this research, the results showed that there was no difference in participant experience between gestures and speech. Both groups of participants expressed that gestures and speech were not applicable to certain operations. Therefore, in Study 2, based on participant's preference for gestures and speech for each operation and the characteristics of operation, we proposed multichannel input fusion scheme to compensate for the limitations of single channel. There were already many researchers which have done a lot of work in the field of multichannel input fusion. In some of these researches, the classification was based on the categories of task which were similar to our research. There were also some researchers divided the channel into main channel and auxiliary channel. For example, in Xiao-long's study [20] which was a multichannel human-computer interaction system research, gesture interaction was used to complete continuous tasks, and speech interaction was used to complete discrete tasks. The results showed that the efficiency of interaction method was about 17.5% higher than the traditional control methods. The continuous tasks in this study included zooming out, zooming in and so on, all of which with fuzzy demand. In our study, in the continuous task with fuzzy demand, the participants showed preference for gestures. But continuous operations may have clear demands, such as volume up to 14. Due to there are two types of continuous operations, the suggestion for design may different.

In addition, due to the suggestions for multi-channel fusion which was given in this study, has considered the characteristics of the operations. And these operation features are applicable on other screen-equipped devices. When the user selecting content, whether on TV or on projector, the interactive experience that they pursued should be efficient. So to a certain extent, the multi-channel fusion scheme derived in this study can also be extended to other screen-equipped devices (especially to large-screen devices).

5.3 Inconsistency in Results on Learning Difficulty and Preference

We found that the difference in gestures and speech learning for each operation in Study 1 was inconsistent with the participants' preference channel for each operation in Study 2. According to the technology acceptance theory, the preference was influenced by the user's evaluation given to the usefulness and ease of use. And the learning difficulty was not the only factor that affected the user's perceived usefulness and ease of use. There were many other factors, such as operational efficiency, dominance of device, and the control variable in this study, the accuracy of feedback. Moreover, from the user's perceived usefulness and ease of use to the final preferences, the whole process was also affected by some random factors, such as the presence or absence of bystanders. It was strange to adopt a new form of interaction mode around other people which was mentioned by users in their feedback. But whether the gesture or the speech interaction makes the user feel that they are relatively "not so weird"? And when the roles of others are different, whether this choice will be different or not? Researchers haven't paid enough attention to these issues which mentioned above. Morris [9] has took multiple users (relationships: couples, friends, family members) as a group in an elicitation study of gesture and speech interaction, but did not answer the questions which are mentioned above that deserves more attention in the follow-up research.

5.4 Future Directions

In the future, we will continue to pay attention to the following aspects: (1) verifying the design suggestions of multichannel fusion including both gestures and speech given by this study; (2) diversifying scene. This study only considered one of the scenes of user watching TV, sitting in the sofa in front of the TV. In future study, the scene should be extended to other scenes in different distance away from TV and with different accompanying behaviors; (3) the design of the interactive interface for multichannel fusion. This study focused on multichannel input, but how does the interface guide the user for multichannel interaction? How to feedback? The questions mentioned above are noteworthy.

5.5 Conclusion

There was no difference in learning difficulty, interaction satisfaction, and willingness to participants for gesture and speech interactions. But the gesture and speech interactions had their own advantages and disadvantages for each instruction.

The participants had different preferences for gestures and speech to different operations, and the applicability of gestures and speech for different operations has been discussed.

Based on the characteristics of each operation and the participants' preference for the interaction method, we proposed a multichannel input fusion scheme. We discussed the direction of gestures and speech improvement and further research for multichannel fusion.

References

1. Cong-Xian, Z.: Research on speech emotion recognition based on deep learning. A thesis submitted to Southeast University (2016)
2. Zaiţi, I.A., Ştefan-Gheorghe, P., Radu-Daniel, V.: On free-hand TV control: experimental results on user-elicited gestures with Leap Motion. Pers. Ubiquit. Comput. **19**(5–6), 821–838 (2015)
3. Connolly, K.J.: Psychobiology of the Hand. Cambridge University Press, Cambridge (1998)
4. Kopp, S.: The spatial specificity of iconic gestures. In: Proceedings of the 7th International Conference of the German Cognitive Science Society, pp. 112–117 (2005)
5. Shin, Y.K., Choe, J.H.: Remote control interaction for individual environment of smart TV. In: IEEE International Symposium on Personal IEEE Xplore (2011)
6. Reissner, U.: Gestures and speech in cars. In: Electronic Proceedings of Joint Advanced Student School (2007)
7. Angelini, L., Baumgartner, J., Carrino, F., Carrino, S., Caon, M., et al.: Comparing gesture, speech and touch interaction modalities for in-vehicle infotainment systems. In: Actes de la 28ième conférence francophone sur l'Interaction Homme-Machine, October 2016, Fribourg, Switzerland, pp. 188–196 (2016)
8. Pfleging, B., Schneegass, S., Schmidt, A.: Multimodal interaction in the car: combining speech and gestures on the steering wheel. In: International Conference on Automotive User Interfaces & Interactive Vehicular Applications. ACM (2012)
9. Morris, M.R.: Web on the wall: insights from a multimodal interaction elicitation study. In: ACM International Conference on Interactive Tabletops & Surfaces. ACM (2012)
10. Ramis, S., Perales, F.J., Manresa-Yee, C., Bibiloni, A.: Usability study of gestures to control a smart-tv. In: Third Iberoamerican Conference (2014)

11. Panger, G.: Kinect in the kitchen: testing depth camera interactions in practical home environments. In: Chi 12 Extended Abstracts on Human Factors in Computing Systems. ACM (2012)
12. Bobeth, J., Schrammel, J., Deutsch, S., Klein, M., Drobics, M., Hochleitner, C., et al.: Tablet, gestures, remote control?: influence of age on performance and user experience with iTV applications. In: Proceedings of the 2014 ACM International Conference on Interactive Experiences for TV and Online Video - TVX 2014, pp. 139–146 (2014)
13. Brush, A.J., Johns, P., Inkpen, K., Meyers, B.: Speech@home: an exploratory study. In: ACM Conference on Computer-Human Interaction (2011)
14. Ying, C., Wei, Z., Bo, H.: User experience research on voice function of smart TV. Design **22** (2017)
15. Martin, B., Hanington, B.: Universal Methods of Design. Rockport Publishers, Beverly (2012)
16. Rico, J., Brewster, S.: Gesture and voice prototyping for early evaluations of social acceptability in multimodal interfaces. In: International Conference on Multimodal Interfaces. DBLP (2010)
17. Klemmer, S.R., Sinha, A.K., Chen J., Landay, J.A., Aboobaker, N., Wang, A.: Suede: a wizard of Oz prototyping tool for speech user interfaces. In: ACM Symposium on User Interface Software & Technology (2000)
18. Peng, B.: An overview of the researches on technology acceptance model. Res. Libr. Sci. **1**, 2–6 (2012)
19. Jaimes, A., Sebe, N.: Multimodal Human-Computer Interaction: A Survey, Computational Vision and Image Understanding, pp. 116–134. Elsevier Science Inc., New York (2007)
20. Xiao-long, S., Hong-ni, G., Feng, H.: Multimodal interaction technology in the holographic display and control interfaces. Packag. Eng. **4**, 120–124 (2016)

How the Cognitive Styles Affect the Immersive Experience: A Study of Video-Watching Experience in VR

Wei Li[1(✉)], Xiaobo Lu[1], YiShen Zhang[2], and Huiya Zhao[2]

[1] Tsinghua University, Beijing 100084, China
stephen82226@foxmail.com, Luxiaobo23@foxmail.com
[2] iQIYI, Inc., No. 2 Haidian North 1st Street, Beijing 100080, China
zhangys08@mails.tsinghua.edu.cn,
zhaohuiya56@gmail.com

Abstract. In VR, the analog cinema experience is a common design method for video-watching function. However, will this approach increase user experience? We conducted 2 phases of experiments. First, from user interview, we found that the users' evaluation of the viewing experience in VR is polarization. Second, studies were carried out with 24 users to find what caused the big difference. Through experiments, we found that different cognitive styles affect the immersive experience of users in VR cinema video-watching, and the Spatial Presence has a more significant impact on the Sense of Being There than the other factors, thus, affecting immersion. Our findings suggest that the design of virtual scenes should consider the different cognitive styles of users, and our research provide insights into future research on user experience of video-watching in VR.

Keywords: Virtual reality · Cognitive styles · Video-watching · Immersion · Sense of Being There

1 Introduction

With the development of virtual reality technology and expansion of market, virtual reality devices are becoming everyday consumer items, and have provide a new approach to video-watching following the mobile devices, PC equipment, and cinema. Currently, the form of VR video-watching is mainly to imitate the environment and experience of cinema in reality, allowing users to watch movies in a virtual cinema without much input. The commercialization of VR cinema is mainly depending on the demand for video content and user experience that VR cinema could provide [1]. In terms of visual and auditory experience, the main reason that people go to cinema to watch movie is the shocking and immersive experience brought by the huge screen and the other facilities of cinema, which the other devices like mobile devices cannot offer. VR cinema achieve a virtual visual experience by putting the screen close to the human eye, building an "infinity" size of screen that is not constrained by the physical environment. As long as the screen is clear enough, the visual experience could surpass IMAX movies in cinema. Comparing to watching movies in cinema, people could use

A. Marcus and W. Wang (Eds.): HCII 2019, LNCS 11584, pp. 163–177, 2019.
https://doi.org/10.1007/978-3-030-23541-3_13

VR in more life scenes, such as at home, in car, or in other public place. VR expand the user scenarios for people who are looking for a movie experience at any time and place.

VR video can be divided into three categories according to user perspectives: cinematic effect video, panoramic video and panoramic interactive video. Cinematic effect video can be transcoded from traditional video such as film and television content. Panoramic video refers to the video that is recorded by the professional panoramic camera and then processed by the computer for post-processing. The video that can realize the three-dimensional (3D) space that can display the 360° panoramic image for the audience. Panoramic interactive video is a true virtual reality video of both immersion and interactivity. However, because of the high production cost and the immature technology, the panoramic videos are few and short. The average duration is about 3 min. The panoramic video cannot meet the need of users both in quantity and quality. Thus, the cinematic effect video with low production cost has become the main consumer content in VR video-viewing function [2].

Our experiments were based on a VR headset, and the experimental video are cinematic effect video and panoramic video. The VR headset we used is iQUT, a one-machine VR headset launched in China market and which main feature is video-watching. It can provide users virtual scenes as film theater and has rich video contents online. We hope to explore whether the experience in VR video-watching can reach the excellent immersive experience of cinema, and to further discover user needs so as to refine the user experience of video-watching in VR.

Our research is divided into two sections, the face to face interview and the user testing. We first conducted an in-depth interview with users who have VR machine. We found that users who purchase VR devices pay more attention to the viewing experience, and have a higher frequency of movie viewing in the cinema. When they pursue large-screen experience, IMAX will be preferred. For them, online viewing of movies is the main purpose to use VR devices. However, users' evaluation to the experience of VR video watching is polarization. Some users feel that they are immersed in the scene and feel like watching movie at cinema, while some users think that the VR cinema effect is far from reality. Moreover, these two types of people have different tolerances for the equipment errors and show different preferences to the device. Therefore, we hope to study what factors affect attitudes and experiences of users besides video content and performance of hardware. At present, there is few researches on the evaluation of video-watching experience in VR. Our research mainly focused on the Sense of Being There (Presence) of users to evaluate the immersion of VR video-viewing experience. In the second section of our research, we invited 24 users, half of which had experienced VR while the others had no experience with VR. First, we measure the user's cognitive style to divide users into two groups by their different cognitive style. Then we measured the two user groups' Sense of Being There by the IPQ scale (Igroup Presence Questionnaire) [3] to find whether the user's cognitive style had an impact on the immersion of VR video-viewing experience. Finally, we analyzed the user immersive experience and product usability satisfaction data, explored the relationship between VR product satisfaction and user experience, and identified the most important subjective sensory indicators that affect the product experience. Compared with Experienced Realism and Involvement, Spatial Presence most affects user immersion.

From our study, we conclude that the user's cognitive style could affect the user's immersion in VR video-viewing. There is a significant difference between users of the field- independence and the field-dependence in the Sense of Being There and Experienced Realism. This difference suggests that to construct the scenes of VR video-viewing, even the various other scenes in VR, it is necessary to consider different cognitive styles of users, for the experience differences caused by different cognitive styles.

2 Literature Review

2.1 The Evaluation of Immersion and Presence

Immersion is the objective degree to which a VR system and application projects stimuli onto the sensory receptors of users in a way that is extensive, matching, surrounding, vivid, interactive, and plot informing [4]. Presence, is a sense of "being there" inside a space. In Jason's opinion, immersion is technical while the presence is internal psychological. Presence is a function of both the user and immersion; however, presence is limited by immersion; the greater immersion a system/application provides, the greater potential for a user to feel present in that virtual world [5].

From the perspective of user perception, to assess the immersion of the VR video-watching experience, it can be reflected in the user's sense of presence using the product. Schubert, Friedmann and Regenbrecht established the IPQ scale (Igroup Presence Questionnaire) to evaluate the "Sense of Being There". The IPQ has three subscales and one additional general item not belonging to a subscale. The three subscales emerged from principal component analyses and can be regarded as fairly independent factors. They are:

1. Spatial Presence - the sense of being physically present in the VE.
2. Involvement - measuring the attention devoted to the VE and the involvement experienced.
3. Experienced Realism - measuring the subjective experience of realism in the VE.

The additional general item assesses the general "Sense of Being There" and has high loadings on all three factors [6].

2.2 The Evaluation of Cognitive Style

The evaluation methods of user experience of hardware products are mainly qualitative, quantitative methods, and the combination of the two is the most widely used. Mahlke believes that the user experience should include cognitive and emotional factors. Cognitive factors include technical and non-technical factors of human-computer interaction: technical factors such as system usefulness and ease of use; non-technical factors such as enjoyment and visual aesthetics. Emotional factors include direct and indirect emotional responses; they also include more complex emotional outcomes produced by cognitive processes [12, 13]. In terms of emotions, the user's satisfaction with the product's experience directly affects the user's attitude and willingness to the product. Kuniavsky Mike believes that it is difficult to accurately portray the user experience because it changes dynamically as the environment changes or interacts. Therefore, different experts and scholars have different definitions of user experience factors because of their different knowledge structures and cognitive abilities. But in general, they are mostly elaborated from the perspective of design and application [14]. John Brooke's System Usability Scale (SUS) is widely used in usability evaluation because of its simple and intuitive problems and small samples [15].

2.3 The Evaluation of Product Usability

The evaluation methods of user experience of hardware products are mainly qualitative, quantitative methods, and the combination of the two is the most widely used. Mahlke believes that the user experience should include cognitive and emotional factors. Cognitive factors include technical and non-technical factors of human-computer interaction: technical factors such as system usefulness and ease of use; non-technical factors such as enjoyment and visual aesthetics. Emotional factors include direct and indirect emotional responses; they also include more complex emotional outcomes produced by cognitive processes [12, 13]. In terms of emotions, the user's satisfaction with the product's experience directly affects the user's attitude and willingness to the product. Kuniavsky believes that it is difficult to accurately portray the user experience because it changes dynamically as the environment changes or interacts. Therefore, different experts and scholars have different definitions of user experience factors because of their different knowledge structures and cognitive abilities. But in general, they are mostly elaborated from the perspective of design and application [14]. John Brooke's System Usability Scale (SUS) is widely used in usability evaluation because of its simple and intuitive problems and small samples [15].

2.4 VR One-Machine Headsets with Video-Watching Function in China Market

At present, from sales data of China's biggest e-commerce platforms Tmall (https://www.tmall.com/) and JD (https://www.jd.com/), the mainstream of the middle and high-end brands VR One-machine headsets are Pico Neo, HTC Vive Focus, Xiao mi and iQUT. More consumers choose to buy high-end brand products, no longer blindly pursue low prices, and the user requirements for the quality of experience have increased. The high-end brand VR One-machine often provides users with a better experience at a relatively moderate price, becoming the most cost-effective choice for consumers. At the end of 2017, HTC Vive Focus and Pico Neo VR all-in-one machines were released and sold. In May 2018, Oculus Go was launched overseas, followed by its domestic version of Xiaomi VR machine on June 1. Various prices and brand VR continue to enter the Chinese market, providing consumers with more choices [16, 17]. All of the four mainstream one-machine Headsets have the basic functions of watching videos and playing games. Among them, iQUT has a 4K screen which could provide a clearer visual experience than the others. The default video-playing environment of iQUT is the giant screen, and provide other three modes: the universe starry sky, the home theater, and the normal cinema. It is convenient to directly watch videos online.

HTC Focus comes with a VIVE Video player that has two scenes, cinema and nature. The default is cinema mode, which is a relatively empty lobby with a sense of technology. The player is only used to play local files. Xiaomi's video center defaults to the cinema environment and the scene cannot be replaced. The viewing position is similar to iQUT, and can also access videos online. Both iQUT and Xiaomi have their own web players. On the video playing interface, in addition to the basic functions of Xiaomi, iQUT also has voice command functions, including play, pause, fast forward and backward, volume addition and subtraction, etc. Because of the specific market orientation and the significant advantages in video-watching functions, we choose iQUT as the experimental equipment for VR video-watching study.

3 Research Design

We designed a mixed research methodology to answer our research questions, including interviews and scale tests for users. We conducted 2 phases of research. First, by the semi-structured deep interview, we discovered the expectations and reasons for users to pursue the VR devices, and their general and video-viewing experience after pursuing. In the second phase of the study, we mainly use scales to measure and analyze the user's viewing experience indicators, comparing the Sense of Being There of users with different cognitive styles, to evaluate the immersive experience of VR video-viewing.

3.1 Study 1: Interviews of VR Users

To recruit participants for our study, we used an online questionnaire to find the potential participants, then invited who meet the criteria to come to join the research at our laboratory. We conducted 1 to 1 interview until we reached data saturation after the 10th interview. The participants consisted of three women and seven men between 19 and 40 years old, with a median age of 29. All of them have at least one VR device, and they all locate in Beijing, China. During the interview sessions, we asked the participants about their feelings of using VR and the experience of VR video-viewing, the selection criteria of VR device for video viewing and the purpose of their purchase, moreover, the consumption in VR. Then we asked them to wear iQUT and observed their behavior and operation.

From the interview section, we found that:

1. Pursuing a better viewing experience and the curiosity about new technology are the main buying motive of VR hardware.
2. The initial factors affecting user purchases are the hardware indicators such as device clarity and sound effects, and equipment convenience, content richness, and social reputation can also influence user's decision.
3. When using the same hardware, individual user experience is significantly different, which is mainly caused by non-video viewing experience such as comfort (equipment wearing and sitting posture) and physical cause (Motion sickness, dry eyes).

In general, the interview indicated that the differences of individual experience are obvious, and the attitude of watching movies is seriously divided. Through previous interviews, we wanted to explore in the following study: whether the viewing scene has an impact on the user's differentiated experience? How the different cognitive styles of the user affect the user experience? How to improve the immersion of viewing experience to satisfy users' satisfaction with VR products.

3.2 The Quantitative Study Towards Cognitive Style

Through interviews, we found that different users have great differences in the perceptions of virtual theater scenes and experiences in VR. Some users think that video watching in VR HMD has the feeling of watching movies in the cinema, but other users think that only the scenes are designed similar to cinema. Why do the same scenes make such a big difference? We tried to find answers from people's cognitive styles. We invited 24 users and divided them into two groups by conducting an Embedded Figure Test (EFT). After completing tasks such as watching movies in VR, participants were asked to fill the IPQ scale and the SUS scale.

3.3 Participants

Participants were randomly selected from the movie watching crowd, who watch movie at least once a week, to avoid research results that are affected by whether the users like watching movie or not. According to the mainstream age distribution of movie watching population (data was from iQIYI video data system), the participants were chosen from the age of 20 to 40, and the average age was 26. In order to exclude the experimental results from the user experience of using the device, we limited the user experience of using VR: 8 one-machine VR headset users, 8 VR HMD (works with PC or console) and VR glasses (like Google Cardboard) users, and 8 people who had no experience of VR. First, every participant needed to complete Embedded Figures Test (revised by Beijing normal university's psychology department, the internal reliability of the test is 0.90, and rod box test score is 0.49). According to the revised evaluation method (Qingmao Meng, etc., 1988), the user is divided into the field independent and the field-dependent by their scores, including 13 field-independent and 11 field-dependent Participants.

3.4 Research Material

In our study, the experimental equipment we used is iQUT, designed and produced by iQIYI, and it is a Headset that doesn't need a console or PC to work with. iQUT has launched in China market and already have a certain number of users. In terms of operation, the device uses a 3 DOF remote control and can be operated by using a head control in some specific scenes. In terms of screen, the model has a 4K resolution screen. In terms of video-viewing, the device builds a virtual cinema effect, visually close to the cinema. The user is "sitting" in the cinema auditorium and can take a 360° view of the cinema scene. The brightness of the surrounding environment in the cinema scene can be adjusted by the users (see Fig. 1).

Fig. 1. The cinematic effect of giant screen mode in iQUT, visually close to the cinema in reality. The user is "sitting" in the cinema auditorium and can take a 360° view of the environment.

In terms of content, users can watch movies, animations, and TV dramas online. Except the panoramic interactive video customized for VR, most of the video content is also available on the mobile device, PC, TV, etc. This provides convenience for us to compare the viewing experience between VR and other devices with the same video contents. Finally, we chose the 2D video Later Us and panoramic video Fishing Village as the experimental content. In the test, we connected iQUT to the computer through a screen capture software to observe the view and operation of the users in the VR device (see Fig. 2).

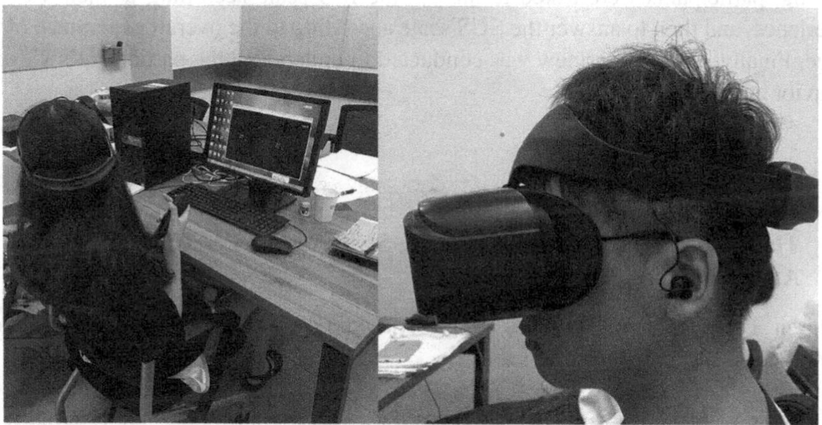

Fig. 2. Participants were wearing iQUT and their view and operation in the virtual scene could be observed by the staff from a PC which was connected to iQUT

3.5 Evaluation Tool

The Igroup Presence Questionnaire (IPQ) scale, compiled by Schubert, Friedmann, and Regenbrecht (2006), is used to assess students' Sense of Presence when using immersive virtual reality scenes. The scale is 7 points likert scale, having a total of 14 items in four dimensions. The internal consistency reliability of IPQ scale of is 0.87. Through the measurement, we can understand the immersive experience of VR device in Spatial Presence, Involvement, Experienced Realism and Presence.

SUS scale is used to evaluate the usability of the product: The questions in the scale were adjusted for the VR device. A number of empirical studies have shown that SUS works better. Tullis et al. have shown that when the sample size is limited, SUS can achieve the fastest results, and a large sample of studies (Bangor 2008) shows that the reliability coefficient of SUS is 0.91. The scale can understand the user's assessment of VR device availability, ensures device availability levels, eliminates the impact of device operations on the user's viewing experience, and understands whether the immersive experience affects user impact on product availability satisfaction.

3.6 Experimental Procedure

In this study, participants were divided into two groups according to the Embedded Figure Test results. After entering the conference room, the staff explained the purpose and procedure of the experiment and help participants to adjust the wearing of the VR equipment to ensure their comfort. After the VR device is activated and the viewing of picture is clear, participants were asked to learn the tutorial of VR, to familiarize the operation of the handle, the head control and the voice control. Then, participants were asked to find the 8K panoramic video Fishing Village and watch it. After the viewing, the user was asked to find the Later Us in the future theater, and to watch the movie for 5 min. During their watching, staff were observing their facial expression. After the viewing, participants were asked to answer the IPQ scale according to their viewing experience, and then to answer the SUS scale according to the overall experience of the usage. Finally, a brief interview was conducted to understand the participant's viewing behavior and emotion.

4 Findings

4.1 The Influence of Different Cognitive Styles on the Presence of Users After Watching Movies

Children The scores of the sense of presence after viewing the video by different cognitive styles can be seen in Table 1.

Table 1. Independent group t-test between field-dependent and field-independent.

	Field-dependent		Field-independent		T-test
	M	SD	M	SD	
Spatial Presence	3.06	0.62	3.02	1.10	ns
Presence	3.08	1.32	4.73	1.27	3.10**
Involvement	3.40	0.98	3.09	0.79	ns
Experienced Realism	2.63	0.52	4.00	0.47	2.68*

*p < .05, **p < .01, ns. = not significant

Note: M = Mean. SD = Standard Deviation.

There is a significant difference between the field-independents and the field-dependents in Presence and Experienced Realism scores after watching movies in VR. The field-independent users (M = 3.08, SD = 1.32) experience worse than field-dependent users (M = 4.73, SD = 1.27) in terms of Presence ($t = 3.10$, $p < 0.01$). Field-independent users (M = 2.63, SD = 0.52) experience worse than field-dependent users (M = 4.00, SD = 0.47) in terms of Experienced Realism ($t = 2.68$, $p < 0.05$). It shows that in the VR cinema viewing mode of iQUT, the stronger the field-independent feature, the worse the sense of Presence and Experienced Realism, and the lower the experience scores. This means the user's preferred cognitive style has an impact on the user's immersive experience. For field-dependent users, virtual reality scenes are more likely to give users an immersive experience, while field-independent users are less affected by the virtual environment. This result is consistent with the user cognitive processing theory. Previous studies on field-dependent cognitive styles have shown that individuals with different cognitive styles tend to use different strategies in the information processing process, and field-independents prefer analysis strategies, while field-dependents prefer the overall strategy. Field-dependent style users tend to rely on the external environment to make judgments, that is, rely on the original field structure, and are not good at providing new structures. The external reference is similar to the real scene, and the dependent user processes it based on this overall information, resulting in a more intense experienced realism and presence [11].

There is no significant difference between the field-independent and the field-dependent in Spatial Presence and Involvement scores after watching movie.

Between field-independent users (M = 3.06, SD = 0.62) and field-dependent users (M = 3.02, SD = 1.10), there is no difference in Spatial Presence. Field-independent users (M = 3.40, SD = 0.98) and field-dependent users (M = 3.09, SD = 0.79) have no difference in involvement (Table 1). This result might be affected by the experimental material used in the study, because the test viewing content did not involve panoramic interactive video, users didn't need interaction during the viewing process, and there was no interactive experience operation. Therefore, the viewing process didn't involve the user's exploration of the virtual space, resulting in no significant difference in involvement. This deserves more attention in the choice of content in the future test.

4.2 The Relationship Between Immersion and Usability

According to the correlation analysis by scores of different dimensions of the immersion scale and SUS scores in Table 2.

Table 2. Pearson correlations of the SUS scale and IPQ scale

		Spatial Presence	Experienced Realism	Presence	Spatial Presence
SUS scale	Pearson correlation	0.38	−0.06	0.057	0.48*
	Sig. (2-tailed)	0.07	0.80	0.793	0.017
	N	24	24	24	24

*Correlation is significant at the 0.05 level

There was a significant positive correlation between the Spatial Presence and the satisfaction of the products ($r = 0.48$, $p < 0.05$). This is reflected by the SUS scale score. It shows that the better the Spatial Presence is, the higher the satisfaction of the product. That is to say, user experience satisfaction is highly affected by the subjective experience of Spatial Presence.

5 Discussion

VR viewing allows users to experience high-quality viewing experience without leaving their homes, which is currently not available on the other mobile devices. The cost of building an IMAX auditorium in the real world is huge, and it takes time to popularize the viewing effect of the giant screen. We believe that the development space of VR video-viewing is huge, and enhancing the product viewing experience is of great significance to the application of VR devices. Our research attempted to understand the reasons for users' cognitive differences in the virtual theater scenarios, and the expectations of users for VR interactions. Our findings provide insights into future research on recognition and experience design of VR.

5.1 The Impact of High Fidelity Virtual Scene on Field-Independent Users

The construction virtual scene based on objective reality has a positive effect on the field-dependent users, but for the field-independent users, it might affect the user's cognitive judgment. Field-independent users tend to use analytical processing strategies, and they are good at analyzing organized fields. Because the VR cinema scene provides a true benchmark for the virtual environments - Cinema, and when the experience of virtual environment and the reality have details of the difference (such as the seat height, the theater audience, etc.), it weakens the user's realism experience. The more high-fidelity visual effects, the other dimensions of the user experience must also achieve the same high fidelity, in order to meet the expectations of the body which is enhanced by the visual effect. Therefore, in the subsequent research, non-high-fidelity style design, such as low poly style, can be provided to the experiment to see if this kind of scenes can enhance the viewing experience of field-independent users.

5.2 The EFT Methods and Cognitive Style

In our study, we divided users into field-independent and field-dependent types, this is a dichotomy study method. In the measurement of cognitive style, we categorized the research methods used in previous articles on field independent/field-dependent cognitive style research. In 75 articles, there are 35 articles in quantitative research, accounting for 46.6% of the total number of articles, and only 2 articles in qualitative research and mixed research, accounting for only 5.4% of the total. In the study of cognitive style, quantitative research has been widely applied; qualitative research and mixed research methods have gradually gained attention in recent years, but they are not used much. There are 21 articles using the measurement tools for the Embedded

Figures Test (EFT) [18] compiled by the Department of Psychology, Beijing Normal University in December 1981. These show that it is feasible to divide the cognitive style into field-independence and field-dependence.

Individual differences in cognitive style are empirically reflected in brain science. The differences in cognitive styles are different in brain science, the consistency of the overall strategy, the volatility of brain regions, and the distribution of left and right brain processing. In the process of face cognition, on the initial stage of face recognition, field-dependents are faster than field-independents in the starting face recognition processing [19].

Cognitive style individual outcomes are normally distributed, but may change with age, and the same person may have two or more cognitive styles. Brown pointed out that it is unreasonable to regard the lack of field independence as the existence of field dependence, because they do not have complementary relationships. People may have strong field-independent style and strong field-dependent style at the same time, but they will show different types of cognitive styles in different occasions [20]. Skehan pointed out that the opposite of field independence or field-dependence may be non-field-independent or non-field-dependent. Field-independence and field-dependence can be represented by two independent continuums, each of which represents field-independent and non-field- independent, field-dependent and non-field-dependent [21]. In EFT, the division of field- independence and field-dependence is mainly based on the level of scores, people are either field-independent or field-dependent. In fact, a person may have two or more cognitive styles at the same time, but in a certain situation, they will only show a style that matches this occasion. Therefore, dividing people into field-independent and field-dependent types cannot meet the need of people's flexible transformation style.

5.3 The Video Content Used for Testing Did not Fully Demonstrate the Characteristics of VR

The 3D movie we can access is not satisfactory because of the serious picture delay and the poor 3D effect, while the 2D content playing experience is smooth and clear, and is closer to the cinema viewing effect, so the video content used in our test is mainly 2D videos. However, the 2D videos cannot highlight the absolute advantage of VR video-viewing, which is the effect that other mobile devices can't provide, such as 3D stereo effect, panoramic effect, and interactivity. The VR products have three characteristics of immersion, imagination and interactivity. VR products are characterized by immersion, imagination and interactivity. Immersion is what makes the user feel that they are part of the virtual world created by the computer system, allowing the user to become a participant from the observer, immersing in it and participating in the activities of the virtual world. Interactivity is the natural degree to which a user can manipulate an object within a simulated environment and get feedback from the environment. Imagination is imaginative and illusory, and its content varies according to the subject. The 2D video content lacks immersion and interactivity, and the virtual cinema scenes might also limit the user's imagination. These may have an impact on our assessment of user satisfaction and immersion in the video-watching experience. Moreover, with the improvement of VR devices hardware and the richness of VR panoramic interactive video, we may wonder whether different cognitive styles have the same impact on the panoramic interactive video, if the user with different cognitive style will experience the difference in polarization or not. If not, what is the reason to eliminate this experience gap. Although we did not answer these questions at this time, this work might open the way for the further studies in this area.

5.4 The Limitations of Technology and Interaction of the Experimental Device

According to the result of our study, user experience satisfaction is highly affected by the subjective experience of Spatial Presence. We think this is partly due to the user's dissatisfaction with the operation in virtual world when using the product. Through interviews and observations, we found that the users spontaneously attempted to fast forward the movie by shaking the remote control instead of the traditional click and slide operation. This indicated that as immersed in the virtual environment, people would take a more natural way of interaction by human instinct. The sense of Spatial Presence is mainly the user's judgment that he is real in the virtual space of VR, so he will try to operate the things in the virtual space directly with the action in reality. In terms of input and interactive devices, the current mainstream interaction methods are handle buttons and sliding operations, and are still in the exploration stage for more complicated gesture recognition and motion capture. In the video-viewing function design of VR, it is necessary to further optimize the natural interaction according to the user behavior to enhance the user's sense of Spatial Presence, so as to facilitate the immersion of VR.

5.5 The Potential Social Needs of Users in Video-Viewing

Through interviews, we found that the cinema has natural sociability, and it is a social place for many users. Sometimes, going to the movies together is a social act, even greater than the cinema's superior viewing experience. People who watch movie together have a common topic, which can continue to discuss and communicate at or after watching, while VR is only a medium of video playing. From the user's point of view, the virtual cinema in the VR world looks just like the offline cinema, and the viewing mode and experience are very similar. When users wear the VR device, going to the virtual cinema, they naturally think about everything related to the offline cinema, including the social behavior, but the VR devices are currently unable to meet their communication needs. This also affects the user's evaluation of the VR viewing experience. Moreover, the cinema can't fully meet the users' communication needs. The quiet viewing environment constrains the form of communication between the audiences. People can only make a modest laughter or exclamation when the movie plays to the key picture, but no more than that. It is believed that the functions of interaction and socialization in the follow-up VR cinema will certainly make up for the pain points of the limited communication in the offline cinema and become the core advantage of VR movie theater, bringing more vivid and interesting viewing experience to users.

5.6 Future Work

Based on a large number of experimental studies and evidence from observations, Witkin et al. proposed a theoretical model of interpreting field-dependent and field-independent cognitive styles—a psychological differentiation model, in which the differentiation of individuals is in various fields of psychological activity, and field-dependence, and field-independence are the result of individual differentiation in the field of structured cognitive function [22]. Differentiation theory believes that in cognitive activities, it is reflected in the difference between field-dependence and field-independence and manifested as one side of brain function in neurophysiology. According to this theory, it is predicted that field-dependence and field-independence are related to the degree of functional differentiation of the two hemispheres [23]. In this study, we mainly measured the user's immersion and product usability satisfaction by scales, and only investigated two aspects of the user experience. In the future work can look at other aspects of behavior on user's behavior data and user physiological indicators. Therefore, the future work can more fully understand the impact of scene and cognitive style preferences on the VR viewing experience through other methods such as user behavior data and user physiological indicators. For example, whether different cognitive style individuals have differentiation in brain function during movie viewing, and Will this differentiation be affected by different VR content types.

In the interview, we learned that the high immersive viewing experience will allow users to have a stronger emotional response and have a deeper memory of the content. Future work can also look at the emotions and memory of user in VR video-viewing and analyze their impact on user experience. Whether a stronger emotional experience will have an impact on product satisfaction, and how the presentation of VR content will positively contribute to user memory. Our work is among the early work of VR video-viewing research, and we hope that our findings act as a springboard for future VR video-viewing research.

6 Conclusion

Video-viewing in VR devices has been vigorously developed in recent years and is becoming more and more popular among users, and major VR hardware manufacturers are deploying the VR device market in China. At present, VR-related research mainly focuses on the nature, characteristics, principles, application prospects and commercial value of virtual reality, research on VR viewing experience is very rare. We hope our study will take the first step in the video-viewing experience in VR and provide insight for future study. We use a combination of qualitative and quantitative methods to investigate the gap between user's viewing experience in VR virtual cinema, explore what causes this gap, and how to optimize the user experience through design. We assumed that the user experience difference may be affected by the user's cognitive style preference and used the Embedded Figure Test to measure the user's cognitive style. Then we asked the users to watch the video contents we prepared for the experiment. After watching, we asked the users to complete the IPQ scale according to the viewing experience, and to answer the SUS scale according to the product experience. The staff observed the user's operational behavior and emotional feedback during the whole process of viewing and using the VR device.

Our study found that under the VR cinema viewing mode which is built according to the actual cinema, the stronger the field-independent feature, the worse the sense of Presence and Experienced Realism, and the lower the experience score. This means the user's preferred cognitive style has an impact on the user's immersive experience. For field-dependent users, virtual reality scenes are more likely to give users an immersive experience, while field-independent users are less affected by the virtual environment. Moreover, the Spatial Presence has a more significant impact on the user experience, the better the Spatial Presence is, the higher the satisfaction of the product. Our findings suggest that the design of virtual scenes should consider the different cognitive styles of users and provide insights into future research.

Acknowledgments. This research is supported by the project of Design Theory and Applied Research about Cultural Creative Products of Virtual Reality.

References

1. Yang, H.: Virtual reality: commercial applications and impact. Chapter 8. Tsinghua University Press, Beijing (2017)
2. Yue, X.: Virtual reality: beyond the real future. 2016 China VR Industry Forecast Research Report. Internet Weekly (7), pp. 34–36 (2016)
3. Krijn, M., Emmelkamp, P.M., Biemond, R., de Ligny, C.D.W., Schuemie, M.J., Van der Mast, C.A.: Treatment of acrophobia in virtual reality: the role of immersion and presence. Behav. Res. Ther. **42**(2), 229–239 (2004)
4. Slater, M., Wilbur, S.: A framework for immersive virtual environments: speculation on the role of presence in virtual environments. Presence Teleoperators Virtual Environ. **6**(6), 603–616 (1997)
5. Jason, J.: The VR Book: Human-Centered Design for Virtual Reality, 1st edn. Morgan & Claypool, San Rafael (2015). Chapter 4: Immersion, presence, and reality trade-offs, pp. 46–47
6. Van Baren, J., IJsselsteijn, W: Measuring presence: a guide to current measurement approaches. Deliverable of the OmniPres project IST-2001-39237 (2004)
7. Friederici, A.D., Levelt, W.J.: Resolving perceptual conflicts: the cognitive mechanism of spatial orientation. Aerospace Medical Association, Washington, D.C. (1987)
8. Wo, J., Li, W., Zhou, S.: Progress in the study of cognitive style theory. Psychol. Behav. Res. **2**(4), 597–602 (2004)
9. Cuneo, F., Antonietti, J.P., Mohr, C.: Unkept promises of cognitive styles: a new look at old measurements. PLoS ONE **13**(8), e0203115 (2018)
10. Witkin, H.A.: Cognition: theory, research, promise. In: Scheerer, C. (ed.) Harper and Row, New York (1964)
11. Li, S.: Brain mechanism research on information processing process of field-dependent individuals. Ph.D. dissertation, Shandong Normal University, Jinan, China (2006)
12. Mahlke, S.: Factors influencing the experience of website usage. In: CHI 2002 Extended Abstracts on Human Factors in Computing Systems, Minneapolis, MN, pp. 846–847 (2002)

13. Mahlke, S.: Studying affect and emotions as important parts of the user experience. In: Workshop on the Role of Emotion in Human-Computer Interaction, HCI Conference, Portland (2005)
14. Kuniavsky, M.: Observing the User Experience: A Practitioner's Guide to User Research. Elsevier, Amsterdam (2003)
15. Zhang, G.: Research on P2P network lending platform based on user experience. Master's thesis, Ocean University of China, Qingdao (2013)
16. 7tin. March VR big data in 2018. http://www.7tin.cn/news/109733.html. Accessed 16 Sept 2018
17. Yivian, X.: Pico VR machine sold 618, ordinary users favor 1500 ~ 2000 price. https://yivian.com/news/47065.html. Accessed 16 Sept 2018
18. Lan, T., Li, L.: Domestic field independent/field dependent cognitive style research and thinking. Examination Wkly. 25–26 (2011)
19. Peng, X., Guo, Y.: Research on event-related potential of personality. J. Nanjing Normal Univ. Soc. Sci. Ed. 103–109 (2006). ISSN 1001-4608
20. Bahar, M.: The effect of instructional methods on the performance of the students having different cognitive styles. Hacettepe Üniversitesi Eğitim Fakültesi Dergisi **24**(24), 26–32 (2003)
21. Wu, H.: The effects of field independent/field dependent cognitive styles on incidental vocabulary acquisition under reading task. Theory Pract. Lang. Stud. **8**(7), 813–822 (2018). ISSN 1799-2591
22. Hongjia, Z., Ling, W., Min, Z.: The relations among creative cognitive style, creative personality, and creative thinking. Stud. Psychol. Behav. **16**(1), 51–57 (2018)
23. Qi, D., Wenda, Q.: A new understanding of the side function of language function in brain functional imaging research. J. Beijing Normal Univ. Soc. Sci. Ed. **4**, 60–67 (2003)

Device Transition: Understanding Usability Issues in Shifting a Device During a Task

Ngoc Thi Nguyen(✉) and Hyowon Lee

Singapore University of Technology and Design, 8 Somapah Road, Singapore 487372, Singapore
thingoc_nguyen@mymail.sutd.edu.sg, hlee@sutd.edu.sg

Abstract. Solutions for enhancing user experience in engaging multiple devices for a task largely imply a tight coupling between device combinations and their supporting user interface (UI) and interaction, thus usability issues may arise when end-users create own combinations of devices not foreseen by designers or developers. We propose the three design principles that foster spontaneous shifts in device engagement: *partnership discoverability*, *role election* and *UI-interaction election*. These principles are examined and realized through shifting cues existed in pre-transition, transition and post-transition phases of the transition pathway. Designed as independent user interfaces, shifting cues give hints to users about available nearby devices and guide the shifts in device engagement. Revisiting the design principles and know-how–so far accumulated based on the single device interaction–will be an important step towards realizing a usable interaction design that considers the increasingly common situations of using and shifting around among multiple devices while conducting a task.

Keywords: Multi-device interaction · Device composite shift · Shifting cues · Transition pathway · Spontaneous device shift

1 Introduction

For a long time, designing interactive systems and devices has mainly concerned itself with identifying target users, activities to be supported by interacting with the each type of device, appropriate interfaces and ways of interacting with the devices [1]. With usability for single use of device ensured, cross-device interaction approaches largely focus on maintaining the consistent interfaces and content synchronization [2, 3]. While these established design guidelines and practices are applicable to the shift from one device to another, they tend to limit the issues within the interactivity of 1-to-1 device. When two or more devices are used together, again, the usability aspect of user interaction with devices is constrained within that particular combination of devices [4–7].

Usability issues caused by the above self-contained usability practices start to surface when the users spontaneously change the use of devices in the manner that moves away from intended context for which the devices, systems or services are designed and built for. They escalate along with the appearances of new interactive devices, the diversity of user activities that potentially benefit from employing multiple

A. Marcus and W. Wang (Eds.): HCII 2019, LNCS 11584, pp. 178–191, 2019.
https://doi.org/10.1007/978-3-030-23541-3_14

devices, especially when the users create their own combinations of device usage which may not be foreseen by designers or developers. Furthermore, would existing UI design principles, guidelines and practices–which had mostly evolved assuming a single device use–still hold true when extended to different combinations of devices? If not, in what ways could existing body of knowledge/know-how be revised or complemented in view of this?

This work aims to take the multi-device shifting as a lens to re-visit the usability factors to evaluate the effectiveness of such interactivity and user experiences. Specifically, we explore how device transition could support spontaneous shifts in device engagement such that the level of usability is maintained or improved throughout the task. We discuss how transition-support design principles should be treated as a holistic view of pre-transition, transition and post-transition phases. These 3 phases form a *transition pathway* which allows easy communications among user-device, device-device and user-user through its informative transition interface. *Shifting cues*–the main component of the informative transition interface–are introduced and described with respect to each phase in the transition pathway. We conclude the paper with the description of our prototype that is guided by the proposed transition-support design concept.

2 Related Work

Studies on multi-device interaction have proposed various ways to utilize multiple devices to improve the usability of single device alone. This section reviews and discusses the current landscape of usability issues for the shifts in device engagement during a task.

2.1 Device Substitution (Sequential Interaction)

There are a variety of reasons for which a user decides to continue a task on a device other than the one where it has been started: re-accessing content from different devices [4], unavailability of applications/devices (e.g. required applications are not supported, device runs out of battery), user's preferences on device usage (e.g. different devices for different usage), or the transformation in the characteristics or nature of the task [8].

In the context of within-task device switching, interface consistency and content continuity between the states before and after the substitution of device have been identified as essential factors for a coherent experience [2]. The former can be achieved by synchronizing data and its structures across devices (e.g. Google cloud services) while the latter can be ensured by migrating the state of user activity from one device to another [3]. Usability factors such as how the user is informed about the "continuity" capability, what steps would be required to achieve it, or which device would be optimal for the task in the user's context are under-explored. For example, after switching from a phone to a tablet, a user may not know that the pages browsed on the phone can be re-visited easily on the tablet (e.g. via the history menu item under the settings of Google Chrome) if the same credential is used to sign in on both devices. The user is left with the transition hurdles: learning the basic requirements, applying the required setup steps and deciding which device to use to suit the context of the task and the user. In addition, in situations when the pending task is to be resumed on a device belonging to a different user–thus may have different ways of interaction with device–would the interface of the first device still be desired to maintain its consistency?

2.2 Device Adding (Intermittent/Simultaneous Interaction)

Adding devices to assist the operation of a single device is prevalent both in research community and the practices of general public today. The added devices can be used intermittently for utilizing resources offered by other devices. For example, in avoiding the need of switching between apps on the same device, people sometimes consult a digital language dictionary app running on a phone while reading an article written in a foreign language on a tablet.

A great number of research has focused in leveraging parallelly two or more devices for a single task such as placing multiple mobile devices next to one another on the same surface to form a larger display for co-viewing of shared content (e.g. Pass-them-around [9], JuxtaPinch [10]) or for moving an object beyond its screen boundary (e.g. Pinch [11, 12]). When combination of device screens could not be placed on the same plane, the smaller screen devices were often used as sub-displays and/or extended input devices to the larger screen devices. Examples of such device combinations include phone-large display (PocketPIN [13], PresiShare [14]), smartwatch-phone (Duet [15], TakeOut [16]), and smartwatch-large display [17, 18]). Again, the user must know and remember how to initiate/disconnect ad-hoc communication (e.g. bumping 2 devices against each other [12], performing pinching gesture across the displays of the 2 devices [9–11], scanning visual marker [13, 14]), what kind of input commands can be used for the joint interactions (e.g. using knuckle-touch to move icons on the home screen, the same knuckle-touch is also used for selecting multiple items of a list in an email management app [15]). At usability level, it requires either the users or the systems to remember and adapt to the interaction strategy when using different device combinations.

2.3 Device Removal (Sequential/Simultaneous Interaction)

Reasons for removing device(s) from a pre-setup ecosystem of devices include unavailability of device(s) (e.g. running out of batteries, device is used for other task, lending device to a family member) or changes in user context making it no longer favorable for such device combination (e.g. leaving home for work). Transition between the states before and after device removal seems to be a neglected topic, resulting in unexpected disruption when such withdrawal of device happens. For example, lifting up a device would abruptly break the joint display [10, 11], stopping the use of phone as TV remote control when it is used for answering phone calls.

As reported, changes in device engagement in the above solutions lack the device-to-device transition support, thus imposing this burden on manually learning, discovering and combining devices on the user in a "self-service" style. In the next section, we explore the usability factors that foster transition between devices or device combinations.

3 Device Transition

As can be easily assumed, engaging and coordinating different devices would require a suitable UI and interaction strategy that supports the user's intended task/activity. Usability aspect has been studied exhaustively for single use of device that is mostly used today, but not for those interactive devices that might enter the market in the near future. Likewise, many studies have focus on creating appropriate UIs and interaction strategies for various but expected and planned device ecologies, but not for a spontaneous combination of heterogeneous devices. It is impractical to design for every possible combination of devices that end-users may think of, so how would we achieve a sustainable design that can be reused, easy to disassemble to components to be recomposed for new interactive device or device combinations?

With usability mostly ensured within the known device or device ecology boundary in which each device takes up its own role in the overall interaction, basic design components can be formed from there. In our preliminary study [19], we refer the packing of device/device combination and such appropriate UI and interactivity together as *device composite*. The simplest form of a device composite is a single device that comes with its established UI supporting possible user interactions (Device Solitude). More complex forms of device composites involve two or more devices, each composite corresponding to a different generalized scenario of device engagement (Exclusive Input-Output, Shared Input, Shared Output, Shared Input-Output and Device Companion). In the context of shifting between device composites, interaction does not just happen between the user and the device but implies the coordination in device-to-device communication and user-to-user collaboration when such device engagement takes place. With the categories of device composites as the basis, in this paper we further abstract the situations of shifting from one device composite to another and structure the usability issues that need to be addressed in those situations.

3.1 Transition Usability

Usability has traditionally been characterized by learnability, efficiency, effectiveness, memorability, reliability in use, and user satisfaction [20, 21] and still widely used in evaluating the level of usability of user-interfaces today. When examining the shift from one device composite to another, we asked ourselves: what could be added or modified to the our understanding of usability in the form of design principles, heuristics and wealth of guidelines available today, in order to maintain or to improve usability when there are shifts in device engagement during a task?

We sought the answer for the above question through our preliminary study [19]–which we briefly describe here. 18 students and researchers (9 males)–age range from 21 to 55–who use multiple devices for their daily tasks/activities volunteered in the study. Participants brought a friend or came alone; in the latter case, one of the investigators acted as the participant's friend. They were presented a situation when shifting from one device composite to another could be easily carried out to support the goal of the tasks. The tasks were designed to challenge participants with the typing of varied-length search queries on the small screen of the smartwatch. At any time, participants were able to (but not required to) temporarily borrow the friend's smartphone and shift their input between the smartwatch and the smartphone, or coordinate with the friend in interacting with the system. We encouraged participants to think aloud during the session.

After completing all tasks, participants were asked to fill out a questionnaire which consisted of open-ended questions about the experiences they had during the session. Participants were asked to rate on five-point Likert scales how easy/difficult they considered it was to initiate the device transition and subsequent shift between them. We encouraged participants to give short explanations for their rating.

Findings from the preliminary study show that participants' decisions on within-task device changes were mainly driven by the ease of transition and the low transition cost–the cost incurring before, during and after transition. Other factors include the usability of an interface modality for a given action, the complexity of the task and the expectation of potentially faster, easier task completion. The 5 design considerations drawn out from the user study (determining ideal UI and interactivity, support for changes, smart shifting cues, situational feedback and informative environment for spontaneous device shift) emphasize the 2 key objectives in device composite transition: *minimizing* the resources expended in discovering and handling potential shift in device engagement, and *maximizing* awareness of potential collaborative interactions. The reported results and findings further led to the construction of the following design principles that stimulate the opportunistic joining or leaving of device involved in a user's goal.

Partnership Discoverability. This principle calls for design that lets devices within proximity to learn about each other's capabilities, the possibility and impact of potential collaboration. Learning the existences of devices surrounding a user's device can be achieved by using spatial sensing of devices (e.g. [22]) or through location-based services. Current ad hoc networks (e.g. Bluetooth, Wi-Fi Direct) supporting device discovery can be augmented with additional information about the potential impacts of collaboration and the friendliness of device-to-device social relationship [23] (e.g. 6.4 inch screen, loud speakers for music, Swype keyboard ~30-35 wpm, SocioCon-Friends[1]).

Nearby devices can be emphasized or be made easier to choose using the user interface technique known as *proximate selection* [24]. Device candidates can be recommended by applying criteria to suggest the best suited device or a group of devices that could be connected within the space a user can interact with. The criteria could be based on the information about the nearest distance to a user's device, the device-to-device social relationship or the highest percentage of matching between the goals and the capabilities to be provided by the shift-to device. The main issue that this principle tries to capture is that with these available technical solutions to support the discovery of connectable devices, what type of information and in what ways the discoverability should be informed to the end-user who faces the device shifting situation.

[1] SocioCon-Friends is one of the 5 types of device-to-device social relationships identified in [23].

Role Election. This principle calls for design that allows a device to nominate itself or other device for a suitable role (input device/output device/input-output device) in the combined use of devices or when the context of use changes. The common 1-way practice we often see is when connecting a device to auxiliary device(s), the latter would take over the intended modality, for example a projector will automatically act as the output device when it is connected to a laptop. This principle tries to capture the usability implications of such role election needed to be conveyed to the end-users in a suitable way. Role election would likely be followed by the UI-interaction election–to be discussed below.

UI-Interaction Election. This principle calls for design that enables a pair/ecosystem of devices to vote for the most suitable UI and interaction strategy for the context of use. Adaptation in UIs-interaction techniques may be needed when there is a mismatch in input or visual output space due to differences in device form factors, or when replacing a device that is part of a special UI-interaction technique applied system (e.g. [13, 17, 25]). Pushing suitable UI when there are changes of number of devices engaged for the task has been demonstrated in [9–11] when a shared photo was displayed across two phones placing next to each other. Lifting up either phone resulted in the photo snapped back to the hosted device. As another example, a user was presented 4 choices of media consumption on the phone when moving away from a TV: continue, continue with downscaled content, buffer the content for later use, and disconnect [26]. This principle tries to capture the aspect of device-shifting situations where the user can choose the most optimal way of UI to continue the task depending on the actual context of use.

Figure 1 presents the bi-directional shifts between device composites. In the graph, device composites are ordered according to the minimum number of devices within the respective device combination (number of devices increases from left to right). Shifting from a device composite towards the right/left side of the graph involves adding/removing one or more devices respectively. Shifting towards the top/bottom direction mainly involves the changes in device roles.

Recall that each device composite corresponds to a different generalized scenario of device engagement, thus a new interactive device will be classified as Device Solitude[2] while any spontaneous combination of devices would be classified into the device composite that best characterizes its inter-device interaction. Characteristics of changes in device engagement will call for the application of appropriate design principles. Pretend that after opening a lesson slide on a phone (Device Solitude), a lecturer receives a notification of an available nearby interactive wall display situated just around a corner. He and his students walk towards it. The lecturer casts the lesson on the wall display and uses his phone as a laser pointer (Exclusive Input-Output) while explaining the concept to his students. His students can also turn their smartwatches or phones into laser pointers to join in the discussion (Shared Output). This fictional scenario contains 2 levels of shifts: between device composites and within a device composite. The first shift from Device Solitude to Exclusive Input-Output involves

[2] Device Solitude refers to the use of a single device that comes with its established UI supporting user interactions. For other device composites, see [19].

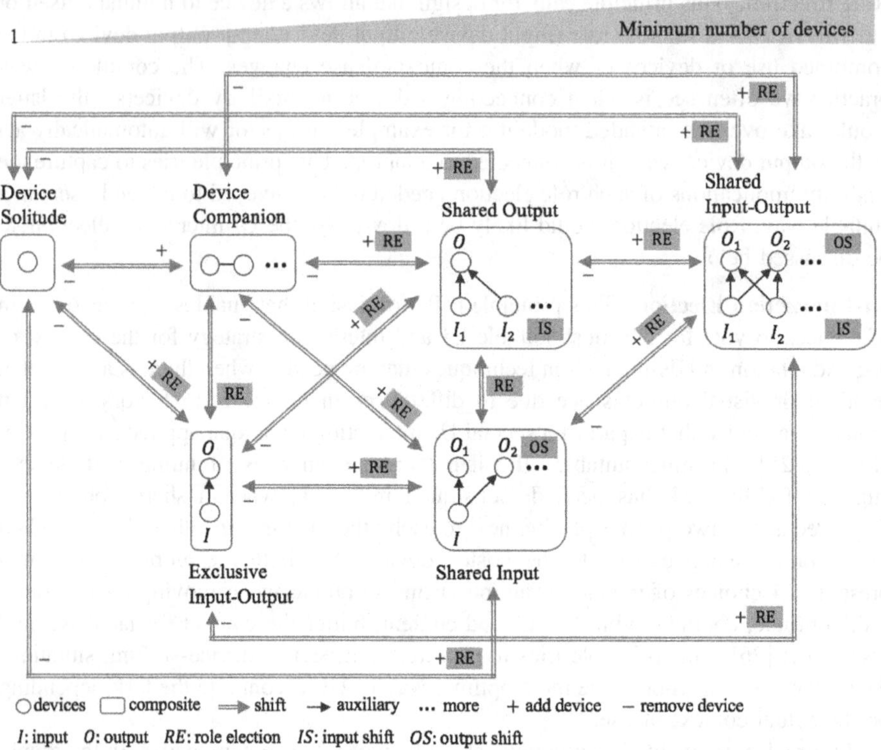

Fig. 1. Bi-directional shifts between device composites involve either the addition (+) or removal (−) of device(s), followed by Role Election (RE) in some cases. Input Shift (IS) and/or Output Shift (OS) take place within the device composites having shared input and/or output device(s).

adding a new device (wall display) and a nomination of the phone becoming an input device. This role election triggers the election for UI-interaction strategy that is suitable for the interactivity. The second shift from Exclusive Input-Output to Shared Output happens when more devices joining the interaction session. Role election takes place, followed by internal Input Shift (shift within a device composite) when the lecturer authorizes his students devices to become auxiliary input devices to the wall display. The Input Shift and Output Shift models are parts of the transition models that describe the shift of input or output modality from one device to another [23].

3.2 Transition Pathway

Transition-support design should consider all usability factors and attributes as an interconnected whole that is part of the 3 phases: pre-transition, transition and post-transition. The transition pathway can be traversed either forward (forecast) or backward (backcast) in time. In the forecast approach, recognizing the user's potential choices of device engagement (pre-transition) is the starting point to determine user efforts, potential conflicts in resources required for device shift and UI-interaction strategies (transition), and the consequences of such decision (post-transition). The backcast approach starts with the speculation of desirable outcomes (post-transition) that meet the user's goals in terms of different perspectives such as resource optimization, user satisfaction or context matching. From there, tracing back to identify the gaps/conflicts between the current and the expected/optimal UI-interaction strategies, determines the user efforts and resources utilization needed for achieving the user's goals (transition), and finally identifies the best matching device (pre-transition). Both directions share the common key steps: prioritization of user perspectives/choices, identification of appropriate UI-interaction strategy for targeted shift-to device composite, and estimation of user effort and resources required for the device composite shift. Figure 2 details building blocks of the transition pathway.

What happens after the post-transition phase? Looking back, a device composite shift starts from the pre-transition phase, goes through the transition phase before reaching the post-transition phase. With each phase's achievement comes the closeness to the user's goal–a device composite with its usability that supports the user's task or needs. The time spending at each phase varies and so does the interaction between user and device composite after the post-transition phase. The user can continue the task by interacting with the newly-shifted device composite. It could be possible that another shift in device composite (e.g. reverting back to the previous device composite, shifting to another device composite) is needed either immediately or after a short interaction with the device composite. And so, the interaction cycle of user-device composite goes on with each new instance of device composite resulted from the device composite shift. We call this *The User-Device composite Cycle*, of which the transition pathway is responsible for maintaining the continuous interactions between users and devices participating in various instances of device composites.

3.3 Informative Transition Interface

The key challenge in shifting between device composites is how to transcend differences between device composites. Transition phase plays important role in bringing together a variety of existing UIs-interaction design approaches, managing potential gaps and conflicts between device composites. As such, navigating through the transition pathway requires efficient communications of information necessary for a task to be resumed smoothly on a another device composite.

We formulate *shifting cues*, a set of independent user interfaces designed to inform users about available choices of device composite shift and to convey user's intention on device shifts. Perceived as 2-way cues between user and device, shifting cues include explicit cues in the form of UI elements (e.g. buttons), natural input modalities (e.g. voice commands) and implicit cues in the form of reading user's intention (e.g. facial recognition, emotion recognition). How shifting cues should be presented to users is critical because they could be either perceived as a disruption to the user interaction and attention, or welcomed as a stepping stone for a more efficient way to complete the task. Current design practices suggest that system alerts would be used when they convey information that will benefit users, those with high importance should be pending for user's response–unless the situation is resolved–while others with low importance can

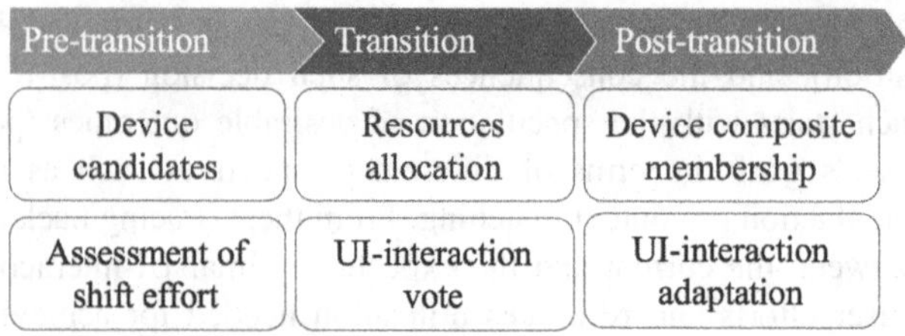

Fig. 2. Building blocks of the transition pathway.

be bypassed automatically after some time. However, the system should not send users myriad of real-time request, feedback or response for every shifting cue, considering the increasing frequency of device-shifting environment envisaged.

Table 1 details a non-exhaustive list of the shifting cues for the building blocks of the transition pathway. This way of tabulation then allows how the usability evaluation could be structured and measured by that includes a device transition as part of the task-completion interactivity.

Table 1. Shifting cues in pre-transition, transition and post-transition phases.

Phases	Shifting cues	Description
Pre-transition	Collaboration state	Choice of listening to requests from other devices: - no listening - only listen to subscribed channels - listening to all
	- Device discoverability: • available devices • device composite membership role - Value-added functionality discoverability - Recommendation of best suited device	Displaying information based on results of: - searching for devices based on spatial distance and/or social relationship - assessment of device roles: input only, output only, both input and output - searching for functionalities/capabilities–offered by other devices–that could be benefit for the task
	Initiation of device composite shift	- Explicit cues: UI elements (e.g. buttons) - Implicit cues: searching for shifting clues from user (e.g. facial recognition, emotion recognition)
	Pre-assessment of shifting efforts	- Trade-offs in engaging another device can be presented as matching score in terms of: • time • resources • privacy • compatibility • UI familiarity - Compare with transition history. Recommend best effort option

(*continued*)

Table 1. *(continued)*

Phases	Shifting cues	Description
Transition	Transition intervention	- Providing an option for transition reverse/cancellation - Providing recommendation for more suitable devices that have become available
	Transition progress	- Resources allocation: • What resources are allocated? • How much resources have been allocated? - Progression: • What is the elapse time? • How long more to complete transition? - Record transition efforts to history for future evaluations
	Pre-learn UI (if applicable)	UI-interaction voting: - Determine gaps/conflicts - How much efforts needed to learn the UI on the target device setup?
Post-transition	Transition reverse	Providing an option for user to revert back to the state before transition
	Device composite membership information	- Displaying "engaged" status for devices participating in the device composite. - Listing all device composites that a device is currently participating
	Task resume vs. restart	Providing choices for resuming and restarting the task: - Resume ensures continuity - Restart supports recall
	UI-interaction	- By default, pushing appropriate/interim UI-interaction - Providing users with alternative UI options

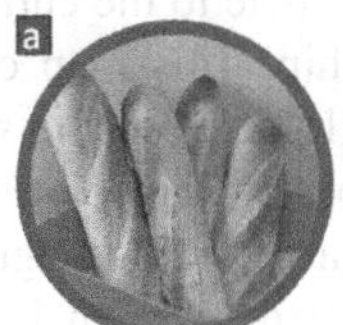

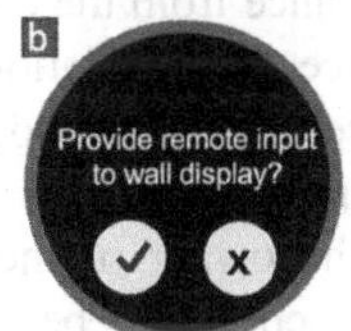

Fig. 3. Single device use: smartwatch screen displays photo (a) and prompts user to change the device role (b), co-using devices: smartwatch screen becomes input surface when the watch is used in conjunction with a simulated large display (c).

4 Prototype

To illustrate and validate the proposed transition design principles and informative transition interface, we extend our prototype developed in [19] to involve spontaneous device engagement to happen any time during a task session. Multimedia Browser is a prototyped mobile app running on Android mobile and wearable devices. When it runs on a single device, input and output modalities are self-contained on the same device (Fig. 3a). User can browse through media content using direct touch input on the device screen. However, when the content is casted to a nearby large display, user will be prompted with a message (Fig. 3b) for converting the device role (role election principle). As soon as the mobile/wearable device is turned into a remote input device for the large display (Fig. 3c), the hop-to-select traverse strategy [17] is voted to facilitate the user's visual focus on browsing media content on the distant display (UI-interaction election principle). With this interaction strategy, the user can perform motion gestures (e.g. shaking device) and coarse relative touch gestural input (e.g. tapping, swiping) on the smartwatch screen without looking at it.

In addition to content navigation and browsing, the user can invoke the device's on-screen soft keyboard to enter the search query for the content of interest. In situations when the user finds it difficult to type on the small screen of the smartwatch and wishes to seek for an available, better suited device for the task, tapping on the Input-Shift button (Fig. 4a) will bring up the information of the closest device (Fig. 5a). Alternatively, an alert message (Fig. 4b) is presented to users when certain number of repeated errors (e.g. 10 typographical errors in keyboard typing) are made. If this request happens on a device having larger screen (e.g. phone, tablet), a proximate selection map–employing the proximate selection technique [24]–visualizing surrounding device locations with respect to that of the current device (Fig. 5c) will be presented (UI-interaction election principle).

The proximate selection map shows each potential partnership device as a circle containing a device icon and information about distance, device name and social relationship between the two devices (partnership discoverability principle). The circle color denotes its social relationship to the current device. We use the 5 device-to-device social relationships identified in [23]: SocioCon-Buddies, SocioCon-Family, SocioCon-Friends, SocioCon-Friends of Friends and SocioCon-Public. The size of each circle can be determined by the distance from the candidate to the current device, or by the friendliness in device-to-device social relationship. This map can also be showed on the smartwatch when the user chooses to toggle between the single view (Fig. 5a) and full view (Fig. 5b) (partnership discoverability principle). Successful engagement of devices happens after the owner of the target device agreed to the request (Fig. 4c), after which user interaction can be shifted between both devices spontaneously.

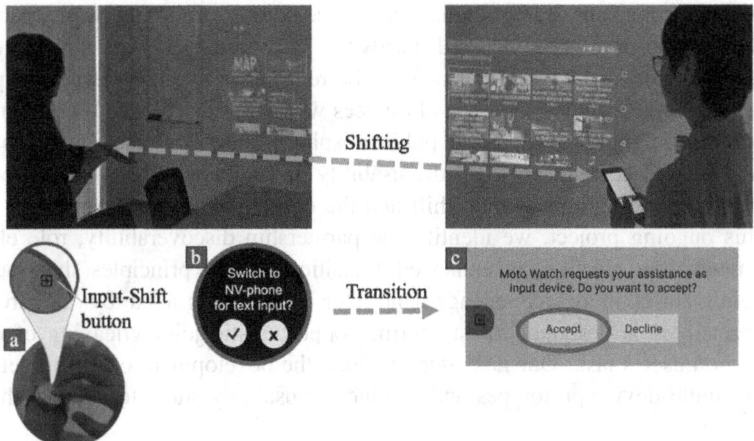

Fig. 4. Shifting cues in co-use of smartwatch, phone and simulated large display by two users.

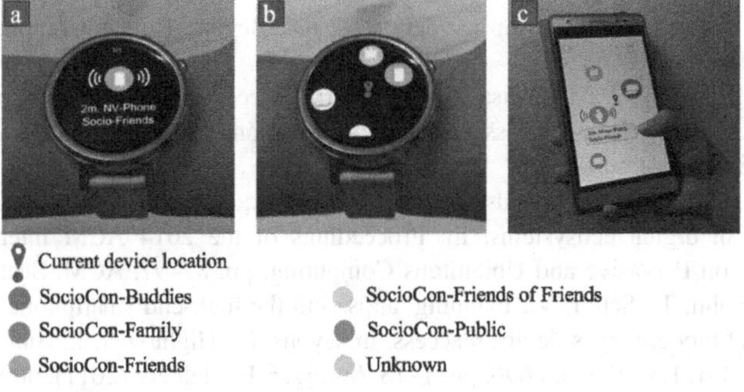

Fig. 5. Detailed view of a nearby device on the smartwatch screen (a), proximate selection map of nearby devices on the smartwatch (b) and the phone (c). This map shows each potential partnership device as a circle containing a device icon. The size of each circle is determined by the distance from the candidate to the current device. The circle color denotes its social relationship to the current device. (Color figure online)

5 Conclusion

While usability is ensured when using a single device or a pre-determined pair/ecology of devices, it might not be the case when changing to or involving another device. By considering device/device combination with its appropriate UI and interaction strategy as a basic design component–a device composite, any unexpected combination of devices can be classified to the most suitable type of device composite after which the established/interim UI-interaction strategy is activated.

Now that the co-use of multiple devices is considered, how should we see the usability issues different from conventional single-device use?: (1) optimal UI and interaction strategy for the combined use of devices needs to be studied, designed and developed; a mechanism of how unplanned device combinations can push a particular UI when it was not pre-conceived needs to be studied; (2) design principles, guidelines/heuristics we have so far need to be revised/revisited, for example, principles and guidelines for combined use of devices with large discrepancy in screen sizes and resolution (e.g. smartwatch and public display); and (3) evaluation of usability needs to take into account not only the usability of single setup, but the trade-off in usability before-during-after device shift and the consequent experience of it.

In this ongoing project, we identify the partnership discoverability, role election and UI-interaction election as enhanced transition design principles that facilitate spontaneous shifts in device engagement. Our prototype–guided by the proposed design principles–is designed for supporting opportunistic joining/leaving of device involved in a user's task. Our next steps include the development of a complete ecosystem of multi-device prototypes and conducting usability study to validate the proposed design.

References

1. Sharp, H., Rogers, Y., Preece, J.: Interaction Design: Beyond Human Computer Interaction. Wiley, Hoboken (2007)
2. Denis, C., Karsenty, L.: Inter-usability of multi-device systems–a conceptual framework. Multiple User Interfaces: Cross-Platform Applications and Context-Aware Interfaces, pp. 373–385 (2004)
3. Sørensen, H., Raptis, D., Kjeldskov, J., Skov, M.B.: The 4C framework: principles of interaction in digital ecosystems. In: Proceedings of the 2014 ACM International Joint Conference on Pervasive and Ubiquitous Computing, pp. 87–97. ACM, Seattle (2014)
4. Bales, E., Sohn, T., Setlur, V.: Planning, apps, and the high-end smartphone: exploring the landscape of modern cross-device reaccess. In: Lyons, K., Hightower, J., Huang, E.M. (eds.) Pervasive 2011. LNCS, vol. 6696, pp. 1–18. Springer, Heidelberg (2011). https://doi.org/10.1007/978-3-642-21726-5_1
5. Luyten, K., Coninx, K.: Distributed user interface elements to support smart interaction spaces. In: Proceedings of the Seventh IEEE International Symposium on Multimedia, pp. 277–286. IEEE Computer Society (2005)
6. Sousa, J.P., Garlan, D.: Aura: an architectural framework for user mobility in ubiquitous computing environments. In: Proceedings of the IFIP 17th World Computer Congress - TC2 Stream/3rd IEEE/IFIP Conference on Software Architecture: System Design, Development and Maintenance. Kluwer, B.V. pp. 29–43 (2002)
7. Wäljas, M., Segerståhl, K., Väänänen-Vainio-Mattila, K., Oinas-Kukkonen, H.: Cross-platform service user experience: a field study and an initial framework. In: Proceedings of the 12th International Conference on Human Computer Interaction with Mobile Devices and Services, pp. 219–228. ACM, Lisbon (2010)
8. Jokela, T., Ojala, J., Olsson, T.: A diary study on combining multiple information devices in everyday activities and tasks. In: Proceedings of the 33rd Annual ACM Conference on Human Factors in Computing Systems, pp. 3903–3912. ACM, Seoul (2015)
9. Lucero, A., Holopainen, J., Jokela, T.: Pass-them-around: collaborative use of mobile phones for photo sharing. In: Proceedings of the SIGCHI Conference on Human Factors in Computing Systems, pp. 1787–1796. ACM, Vancouver (2011)

10. Nielsen, H.S., Olsen, M.P., Skov, M.B., Kjeldskov, J.: JuxtaPinch: exploring multi-device interaction in collocated photo sharing. In: Proceedings of the 16th International Conference on Human-Computer Interaction with Mobile Devices & Services. ACM (2014)
11. Ohta, T., Tanaka, J.: Pinch: an interface that relates applications on multiple touch-screen by 'pinching' gesture. In: Nijholt, A., Romão, T., Reidsma, D. (eds.) ACE 2012. LNCS, vol. 7624, pp. 320–335. Springer, Heidelberg (2012). https://doi.org/10.1007/978-3-642-34292-9_23
12. Hinckley, K., Ramos, G., Guimbretiere, F., Baudisch, P., Smith, M.: Stitching: pen gestures that span multiple displays. In: Proceedings of the Working Conference on Advanced Visual Interfaces. ACM (2004)
13. De Luca, A., Frauendienst, B.: A privacy-respectful input method for public terminals. In: Proceedings of the 5th Nordic Conference on Human-Computer Interaction: Building Bridges, pp. 455–458. ACM, Lund (2008)
14. Geel, M., Huguenin, D., Norrie, M.C.: PresiShare: opportunistic sharing and presentation of content using public displays and QR codes. In: Proceedings of the 2nd ACM International Symposium on Pervasive Displays. ACM (2013)
15. Chen, X.A., Grossman, T., Wigdor, D.J., Fitzmaurice, G.: Duet: exploring joint interactions on a smart phone and a smart watch. In: Proceedings of the SIGCHI Conference on Human Factors in Computing Systems, pp. 159–168. ACM, Toronto (2014)
16. Noh, W., Lee, M., Cheon, H., Kim, J., Lee, K., Cho, J.: TakeOut: drawing application using distributed user interface for being close to real experience. In: Proceedings of the 2016 ACM International Joint Conference on Pervasive and Ubiquitous Computing: Adjunct, pp. 173–176. ACM, Heidelberg (2016)
17. Nguyen, N.T., Lee, H.: 'Hop-to-select' traverse with gestural input in an eye-off interaction. In: Proceedings of the 29th Australian Conference on Computer-Human Interaction, pp. 597–601. ACM, Brisbane (2017)
18. Horak, T., Badam, S.K., Elmqvist, N., Dachselt, R.: When David meets Goliath: combining smartwatches with a large vertical display for visual data exploration. In: Proceedings of the 2018 CHI Conference on Human Factors in Computing Systems, pp. 1–13. ACM, Montreal (2018)
19. Nguyen, N.T., Lee, H.: Understanding usability challenges in shifting between multiple devices during a task. In: 2019 IEEE International Conference on Pervasive Computing and Communications Workshops (PerCom Workshops). IEEE, Kyoto (2019)
20. Shneiderman, B., Plaisant, C., Cohen, M., Jacobs, S., Elmqvist, N., Diakopoulos, N.: Designing the User Interface: Strategies for Effective Human-Computer Interaction. Pearson, London (2016)
21. Nielsen, J.: Usability Engineering. Morgan Kaufmann Publishers Inc, Burlington (1993)
22. Gellersen, H., et al.: Supporting device discovery and spontaneous interaction with spatial references. Pers. Ubiquit. Comput. **13**(4), 255–264 (2009)
23. Nguyen, N.T., Lee, H.: SocioCon: a social circle for your interactive devices. In: Marcus, A., Wang, W. (eds.) DUXU 2018. LNCS, vol. 10919, pp. 623–639. Springer, Cham (2018). https://doi.org/10.1007/978-3-319-91803-7_47
24. Schilit, B., Adams, N., Want, R.: Context-aware computing applications. In: 1994 First Workshop on Mobile Computing Systems and Applications, WMCSA 1994. IEEE (1994)
25. Vogel, D., Balakrishnan, R.: Interactive public ambient displays: transitioning from implicit to explicit, public to personal, interaction with multiple users. In: Proceedings of the 17th Annual ACM Symposium on User Interface Software and Technology. ACM (2004)
26. Trimeche, M., et al.: Enhancing end-user experience in a multi-device ecosystem. In: Proceedings of the 4th International Conference on Mobile and Ubiquitous Multimedia, pp. 19–25. ACM, Christchurch (2005)

Head and Shoulders Gestures: Exploring User-Defined Gestures with Upper Body

Jean Vanderdonckt[1(✉)], Nathan Magrofuoco[1], Suzanne Kieffer[1], Jorge Pérez[1,2], Ysabelle Rase[1], Paolo Roselli[1,3], and Santiago Villarreal[1]

[1] Université Catholique de Louvain, 1348 Louvain-la-Neuve, Belgium
{jean.vanderdonckt,nathan.magrofuoco,suzanne.kieffer,jorge.perezmedina, ysabelle.rase,paolo.roselli,santiago.villarreal}@uclouvain.be

[2] Universidad de las Américas, Intelligent & Interactive Systems Lab (SI^2 Lab), Sede Queri, Av. De los Granados, Quito 170504, Ecuador
jorge.perez.medina@udla.edu.ec

[3] Matematica Dipartimento, Università degli Studi di Roma "Tor Vergata", Via Orazio Raimondo, 18, 00173 Rome, Italy
roselli@mat.uniroma2.it

Abstract. This paper presents empirical results about user-defined gestures for head and shoulders by analyzing 308 gestures elicited from 22 participants for 14 referents materializing 14 different types of tasks in IoT context of use. We report an overall medium consensus but with medium variance (mean: .263, min: .138, max: .390 on the unit scale) between participants gesture proposals, while their thinking time were less similar (min: 2.45 s, max: 22.50 s), which suggests that head and shoulders gestures are not all equally easy to imagine and to produce. We point to the challenges of deciding which head and shoulders gestures will become the consensus set based on four criteria: the agreement rate, their individual frequency, their associative frequency, and their unicity.

Keywords: Gesture elicitation study · Gesture interaction

1 Introduction

From the human point of view, a gesture is often defined as a communicative movement of the hands and arms which express, just as language, speakers attitudes, ideas, feelings and intentions [2,9]. This early definition focuses on gestures issued by hands and arms, which are certainly among the most mobile human limbs in terms of planes (i.e., the frontal plane along the X axis, the sagittal plane along the Y axis, and the transverse plane along the Z axis - Fig. 1), range of motion (e.g., angle with respect to a standing body), and therefore in terms of expressiveness. It also emphasizes gestures as a mean to support verbal communication (hence, the speaker). Actually, a gesture can be issued theoretically by any human limb, not just the most mobile ones [15]. And a gesture can be typically involved in any verbal or non-verbal mode of communication [18]. This is partially reflected in the

A. Marcus and W. Wang (Eds.): HCII 2019, LNCS 11584, pp. 192–213, 2019.
https://doi.org/10.1007/978-3-030-23541-3_15

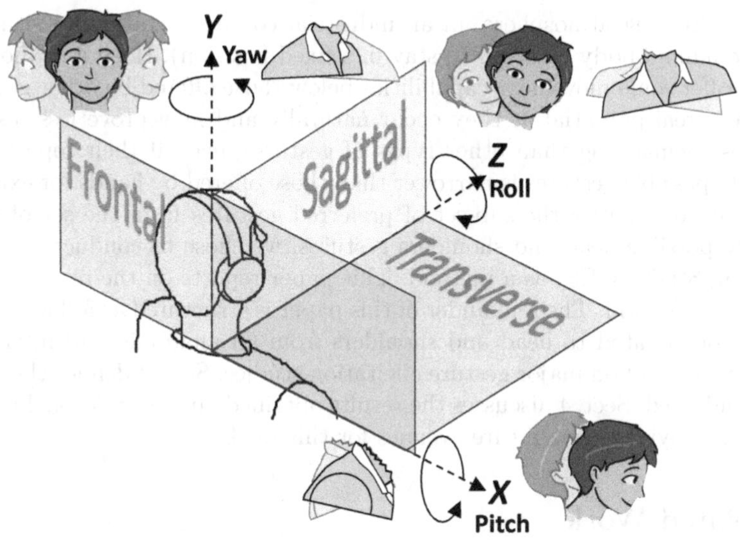

Fig. 1. Transverse, frontal, and sagittal planes for head movements (based on [8]: images by courtesy of T. Jacob, G. Bailly, and E. Lecolinet).

system point of view for gestures: a gesture is considered as any physical movement that a digital system can sense and respond to without the aid of a pointing device such as a mouse or stylus [21]. This definition does not specify what type of response should be given by the system: an object (e.g., a deictic gesture expresses a reference to an object simply by pointing to it), an action (e.g., a gesture translates a human command into an executable function like "turn a TV on"), an attribute of an object or a parameter of an action, a non-verbal information, or any combination of those (e.g., "turn this TV on my favorite channel"). By combining these definitions, we hereby refer to a *gesture* as any movement of one or many human limbs that actually convey a meaning that can be acquired, and hopefully interpreted by an agent, which can be human, software, and/or hardware.

Although our whole body can conduct gestures, they are preferably and frequently issued with our most mobile human limbs, such as fingers (especially for micro-gestures) [3], hands (especially for mid-air gestures) [1], forearms and arms (especially for body-based gestures) [15] because they belong to the most mobile limbs. Gestures issued by the human head and/or the shoulders are a particular category of mid-air gestures that are particularly appropriate in contexts of use where the other human limbs (e.g., fingers, hands, arms, legs) are already busy or cannot be used for other non-physical reasons (e.g., hygienic, social, psychological, cultural interpretations) and prevent from using them for issuing gestures. These situations include: eye-free situations [17] (e.g., driving a car, checking a machine usually require that the driver or operator does not change the locus of attention in fear of loosing control), busy-hands situations (e.g., in a freezing atmosphere, in an industrial context), stationary situations (e.g., the human body is forced to stay in a fixed position). Head and shoulders gestures offer some movement capabilities below those offered by other gestures, but have a real potential as they occur naturally and may prove less distracting or less demanding than other types of gestures, even if their repertoire of physically possible gestures is narrower than those offered by hands for example.

In order to identify the sub-set of preferred gestures from the set of physiologically possible head and shoulders gestures, we chose to conduct a Gesture Elicitation Study (GES) as a method. This paper reports on the results of conducting this method. The remainder of this paper is structured as follows: Sect. 2 reports work related to head and shoulders from an anatomic and interaction point of views and on major gesture elicitation studies, Sect. 3 defines the experiment conducted, Sect. 4 discusses the results obtained, and Sect. 5 concludes the paper and provides some future avenues for this work.

2 Related Work

This section is divided into three parts: an introduction to the anatomy of head and shoulders, a review of previous work conducted with this mode of interaction, and an overview of existing elicitation studies performed on the human body.

2.1 Anatomy of the Head and Shoulders Movements

Shoulders. According to the field of osteokinematics [4], the shoulder joints offer the following repertoire of possible movements: flexion, extension, hyperextension, abduction, adduction, medial rotation (internal rotation), lateral rotation (external rotation), horizontal abduction, horizontal adduction, and circumduction. For example, flexion occurs in the sagittal plane of motion with respect to the human body, exploits the transverse axis through the center of the humeral head, and have a range of motion between 0° and 90°. Conversely, an extension share the same plane and axis of motion than flexion, but have a more restricted range of motion, situated between 0° and 45° up to 60°. Abduction occurs in the frontal plane of motion, along the sagittal axis through the center of the humeral head, and benefits from an extraordinary range of motion: from 0° to 175° (0° to 60° in internal rotation and 0° to 90° in external rotation). Internal rotation occurs in the transverse plane, along the vertical axis, $0 - 70°$ as the arm at 90° of shoulder abduction and 90° elbow flexion. External rotation differs from internal rotation only in that it displays a range of motion of $0° - 90°$ as the arm at 90° of shoulder abduction and 90° elbow flexion. Adduction occurs in the frontal plane with respect to the human body, still along the sagittal axis, but is rapidly constrained by the trunk in its range. Circumduction combines flexion, abduction, extension, and adduction or in the reversed sequence. Consequently, movements at the shoulder joints are interesting as they can occur in every direction (flexion, extension, abduction, adduction, rotation, circumduction), they are considered as highly mobile due to the large size of head of humerus and the looseness of the capsule of the joint. But arm movements are arrested by contact of the bony surface. This repertoire reveals possible movements of the arm based on the shoulder joints, but does not identify the movements of the shoulder itself. We therefore define a *shoulder gesture* as any movement of the shoulder joint that leaves the rest of the arm unaffected (stationary). A shoulder gesture occurs in any plane of motion (sagittal, transverse, frontal) or direction (forward, backward, or circular) (Fig. 1). *Shrugging* consists in a gestural condition whereby the participant moves one or both shoulders up and/or down.

Head. Similarly, we define a *head gesture* as any movement of the head leaving the rest of the body unaffected (stationary). A head gesture could occur in any plane (sagittal, transverse, frontal) [8]. For instance, a *downhead* gesture, respectively a *uphead* gesture, occurs when a downward, resp. upward, head movement is produced. Head movements are studied in many domains, such as linguistics [18] and body language. Indeed, since our head usually turns towards a scene of interest, it indicates that some object belonging to this scene becomes the primary focus of attention for a number of reasons: we like or dislike something, we feel good or bad about something. The *nod* gesture is often considered as an approval (it means "yes", "I concur", "I agree") or a positive expression of interest for something (it means "I like it", "I am enthusiastic") while a *shaking* gesture is considered as a denial ("I disagree") or a negative expression of interest for something ("I do not like it"). We can recognize other subtle movements subconsciously because they express some feedback. A *slow shaking* gesture reveals disbelief or an expression of uncertainly about a scene being looking at. A *fast shaking* gesture reinforces the message by saying that the negative expression of interest is definitive. Non-command head gestures are different from command gestures in that they are intended to convey some idea, mood, but not an object, an action, or any combination of them. Non-command gestures are often studied in the area of body language. For example, erratic head gestures with frequent eye glances to the sides of the field of view can reveal some discomfort, some tension. A *thrust* gesture consists of a downward gesture in a fixed position expressing readiness for attacking something (like tackling a problem) or somebody (like being confronted with someone). Conversely, a *retreat* gesture consists of a head backward gesture performed in the frontal plane expressing a defense position that is opposite to the thrust. A *head tilt* is performed left or right in the transverse plane: if the head tilts to the right side of a person, the body language interprets this as a person being smart, if the head tilts to the left side, it is interpreted as a person being or willing to be more attractive.

Head and Shoulders. When combined, *head and shoulders gestures* offer the capability to produce gestures that either share the same plane of motion (for example, the head and the shoulders all move in the sagittal plane) or not (for example, the head moves in the frontal plane while the shoulders are moving in the transverse plane). Same for their directions or other parameters. Some types of gestures often occur simultaneously because the human being naturally associate them: for instance, a shrugging gesture is produced on the shoulders while a downward head gesture is simultaneously issued.

2.2 Interaction Techniques

Head gestures have been mainly employed in combination with eye gaze interaction to designate objects of reference in a scene: head gesture recognition by combining gaze and eye movement [17], head to face input [22], and gaze with head gestures [23]. The only GES dedicated to head and shoulders that we know consisted in eliciting gestures for changing the view of a 3D scene while creating objects in this scene [8]. The consensus gestures resulting from their study were ranked in decreasing order of agreement score [28]: downward and upward head and shoulders gestures for zooming in/out ($A(r) = .8$, very high agreement), downward and upward head gestures for horizontal control ($A(r) = .5$, very high), up/down head gestures for vertical control ($A(r) = .4$, high) and for horizontal orbit ($A(r) = .3$, high), head and shoulders nodding for horizontal panning ($A(r) = .3$, medium), up/down gestures for vertical orbit ($A(r) = .2$, medium) and panning ($A(r) = .19$, medium).

2.3 Overview of Gesture Elicitation Studies

Understanding users' preferences and behavior with new interactive technology right from the early stages of design empowers designers with valuable information to shape a product's characteristics for more effective and efficient use. This process is known as *Gesture Elicitation Studies* (GES) [28–30], which have been popular to understand users' preferences for gesture input for a variety of conditions studied along the three dimensions of the *context of use*:

- **On various platforms and devices**. Since their inception, GES primarily focused on some particular *platform* or *device*. For instance, Wobbrock et al. [30] reported users' preferences for multi-touch input on interactive tabletops. Vatavu [27] and Zaiţi et al. [31] addressed mid-air gesture input to control a TV set. Ruiz et al. [20] investigated users' preferences for motion gestures with smartphones.
- **In different environments**. Gestures are typically elicited in a particular physical and/or psychological *environment* in which devices are determined, such as the steering wheel in a car. Gestures can be also constrained by type, such as hand gestures [1], micro-gestures with one hand only [3] or not.
- **For diverse users**. Some studies are *user-independent* when no particular profile is involved, while some others are *user-dependent*: whole-body gestures [12] are dedicated to a particular type of *users*, e.g., children, thus underlining that the elicitation study can target any particular population of end users instead of platform or environment. Hand gestures [1] , while [6] compared freehand gestures with gestures issued on the skin, thus demonstrating that any particular human ability or physical capability or the deficiency thereof could also become the central subject of a GES.

The GES outcome consists of a characterization of users' gesture input behavior with valuable information for designers, practitioners, and end users regarding the consensus levels between participants (computed as *agreement* [28,30] or *coagreement rates* [29]), the most frequent (thus, generalizable across users) gesture proposals for a given task, and insights into users' conceptual models for performing tasks. The most recent formalization of the elicitation methodology proposed both repeated measures [28] and between-subjects [29] designs.

Virtually, any human limb capable of some mobility can theoretically be the source of a gesture. As a matter of fact, several studies have concentrated their efforts on some human limb in isolation (e.g., the legs), or combined with subsequent limbs (e.g., the legs with the feet), while others considered the human body as a whole, which is of utmost importance for full-body gesture interaction. Hence, the range of investigation starts from any limb in particular until the full body is reached. In the *human gesture continuum*, any gesture starts from any individual limb and evolves to several limbs captured together until the full-body is attained. Based on the human gesture continuum, the human body can be decomposed into one to many gesture types. For instance, the upper-body [16] gesture interaction is decomposed into several limbs that have been subject to GES: the face [22], the head [23], eye-based head gestures [17], the nose [13], the shoulders [8]. Belonging to the upper-body, the human arms are themselves subject to a gesture continuum: fingers [3], wrists [20], hands [1,6,19,30,31], arms [15], and skin-based gestures [6] in general, and from hands to other parts of the body [3]. Lower-body gesture interaction is decomposed into sub-limbs: feet [5], legs until the whole-body gesture interaction [12] is attained.

In conclusion, we motivate a GES on the head and shoulders by the following reasons: it has never been subject to any GES (apart from [8] for a 3D navigation), the gesture set explored insofar is limited to 3D movements in the 3 planes [13]), no qualitative or quantitative analysis has been carried out about the gestures preferred by end users in this case, these gestures are still in their infancy, especially in eyes-free conditions. When combined, head and shoulders gestures offer the capability to produce gestures that either share the same plane of motion (for example, the head and the shoulders all move in the sagittal plane) or not (for example, the head moves in the frontal plane while the shoulders are moving in the transverse plane). Same for their directions.

3 Design Space

Before conducting an experiment, we built a design space of all physiologically possible gestures based on the field of osteokinematics [4] and linguistics [18] (see Sect. 2.1) and the literature about head and/or shoulders gestures [7,8,17,23]. Table 1 defines these gestures based on which plane is maintained constant or left variable. For quick reference, the column 'Alias' gives a unique short name. The first row of Fig. 2 gathers the three first gestures of Table 1: for example, the 'Face left' gesture occurs when the face is maintained in the same plane, while the neck is moving left. The second, resp. third, row of Fig. 2 gathers the three possible types for tilting, resp. for rotation about each axis. The fourth row consists of the three possible shoulders gestures occurring when a translation occurs about each axis. Simple gestures appearing in the four first rows could form a compound gesture, such as rows five and six: *shrug* (raise left, right, both shoulders, then lower left, right, both shoulders quickly), *clog left, right* (raise the right, left shoulder and tilt the head to the left, right), *nod horizontally* (do a left head, then a right head quickly, possibly repeatedly, so as to express a 'no'), *nod vertically* (bend up, then down quickly, possibly repeatedly, so as to express a 'yes'), *rotate clockwise* (bend up, then right, then down, then left, then up so as to draw a circle in mid-air), *rotate counterclockwise* (bend up, then left, then down, then right, then up so as to draw a reverse circle in mid-air), *balance left* (raise left and lower right), *balance right* (raise right and lower left).

Table 1. Definition of head and shoulders gestures with their physiological movement (c=constant plane, v=variable plane).

Head	Label	Alias	Movement (frontal, trans., sagit.)
X translation	Move the head left, right	Face left, face right	Lateral translation (v,c,c)
Y translation	Move the head up, down	Face up, face down	Neck elevation, depression (c,v,c)
Z translation	Move the head forward, backward	Thrust, retreat	Protraction, retraction (c,c,v)
Frontal tilting	Tilt the head to the left, right	Bend left, right	Lateral flexion (v,v,c)
Trans. tilting	Tilt the head up, down	Bend up, down	Extension, flexion (v,c,v)
Saggital tilting	Tilt the head forward, backward	Bend forward, backward	Extension, flexion (c,v,v)
X rotation	Turn the head up, down	Uphead, downhead	Horizontal rotation (c,v,v)
Y rotation	Turn the head left, right	Lefthead, righthead	Vertical rotation (v,c,v)
Z rotation	Turn the head forward, backward	Forehead, backhead	Facial rotation (v,v,c)
Shoulders	Label	Alias	Movement
X translation	Move shoulder horiz. to left, right	Decontract, contract	Extension, flexion (v,c,c)
Y translation	Raise shoulder, lower shoulder	Raise, lower	Shoulder elevation, depression (c,v,c)
Z translation	Move shoulder forward/backward	Protract, retract	Shoulder protraction, retraction (c,c,v)

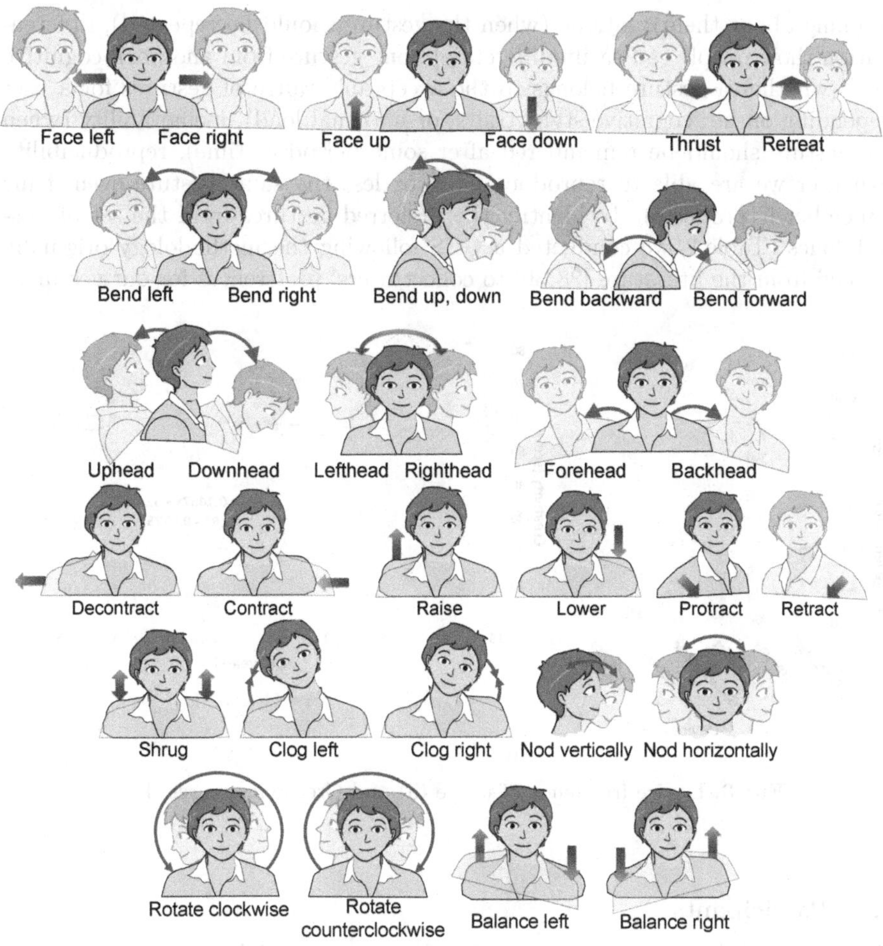

Fig. 2. Design space of head and shoulders gestures (images based on [8]).

4 Experiment

While physiologically possible gestures were identified n the previous section, we do not know which ones would be naturally suggested by people to issue gestures attached to commands or non-command interfaces. Human preference for some gestures may be fueled by various factors such as: physical difficulty of the gesture (all these gestures are submitted to constraints: e.g., the shoulder abduction is limited by different physical factors such as ligament position, elasticity, and tightness of the joint), physical ability or disability [16] (e.g., a capsulitis decrease movements of the shoulder joint), spontaneity to produce a gesture (some gestures come more naturally than others not because we are less capable of producing them, but simply because we are more akin to produce them when thinking about them), fatigue (when the gesture should be repeated), differentiation (how people can easily differentiate one gesture from another), cognitive load (whether a gesture belongs to the acceptable range of gestures for a user depending on her cognitive style, traits, or maximal load), memorability (when the gesture should be remembered after some period of time), reproducibility (whether we are able to reproduce more or less the same gesture even if me remember it properly). To identify the preferred gestures from the set of possible ones (Table 1, we conducted a GES following the methodology originally defined from the literature [28,30] to collect users' preferences for our gestures.

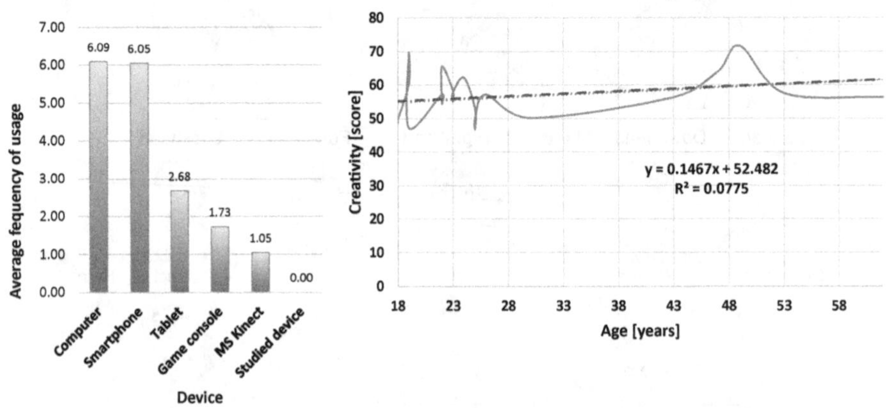

Fig. 3. Device frequency of usage (a) and Creativity scores (b).

4.1 Participants

Twenty-two voluntary participants (10 Females, 12 Males; aged from 18 to 62 years, $M = 28.95$, $SD = 12.55$) were recruited for the study via a contact lists in different organizations. Their occupations included secretary, teacher, psychologist, employee, retirees, and students in domains such as economics, nutrition, chemistry, history, and transportation. Various usage frequencies were captured: computer, smartphone, tablet, game console, and Kinect-like device. All participants reported frequent use of computers and smartphones in daily life (Fig. 3a). All participants reported that they never saw any head and shoulders interaction before and, therefore, they were not familiar with this kind of technology.

4.2 Apparatus

The experiment took place in a usability laboratory to keep the control over the experiment. A simple computer screen was used as a display for showing the referents to the participants. All the gestures were recorded by a camera placed in front of the participants to capture their head and shoulders.

4.3 Procedure

Pre-test Phase. The participants were welcomed to the setting by the researchers and were first asked to sign an informed consent form compatible with GDPR regulation. Then, they were given information about the study and the general process of the experiment. They were also asked to fill a sociodemographic questionnaire and to perform a creativity test and a motor-skill test. The researchers collected the sociodemographic data about each participant in order to use some of these parameters in the study. The questionnaire gives general information about the participants (e.g., age, gender, handedness) and asks a series of questions about their use of technologies (based on a 7-point Likert scale ranging from 1 = strongly disagree to 7 = strongly agree). We tested the participants' creativity via http://www.testmycreativity.com/: they were asked to answer a series of questions and received at the end an assessment of their level of creativity. The Motor-skill test [10] was applied to check dexterity.

Test Phase. During this phase, the experimenter explained to participants what nose interaction is all about, the following tasks that they had to perform, and the allowed types of gestures (they should be compliant with the aforementioned definition). Participants operated with the belief that no technological constraint was imposed in order to preserve the natural and intuitive character of the elicitation, such as no restriction on gesture recognition. Each session implemented the original protocol for a GES [30]: participants were presented with referents, i.e., actions to control various objects in an Internet-of-Things (IoT) environment, for which they elicited one gesture to execute those referents, i.e., gestures that fit referents well, are easy to produce and remember. Participants were instructed to remain as natural as possible. The order of the referents was globally randomized per participant based on a pseudo-random number generator (www.random.org). The thinking time between the first showing of the referent and the moment when the participant knew which gesture she would perform was timed by the experimenters. It was measured in seconds with a stopwatch. After eliciting each gesture, the experimenters asked the participant to rate it from 1 to 10 to express to what extent she thought her gesture was appropriate to the presented referent. Each session took approximately 45 min.

Post-test Phase. At the end of each session, the participants were asked to fill in the IBM CSUQ (Post-Study System Usability Questionnaire) [14], which enables participants to express their level of satisfaction with the usability of the setup and the testing process. This 16-question questionnaire is preferred because it has been empirically validated with a large number of participants on a significant set of stimuli, it is widely applicable for any system, and it benefits from a proved $\alpha = 0.89$ reliability coefficient between its results and the perceived system usability [14]. Each closed question is measured using a 7-point Likert scale (1 = strongly disagree, 2 = largely disagree, 3 = disagree, 4 = neutral, 5 = agree, 6 = largely agree, 7 = strongly agree) and summed up in: system usefulness (SysUse: Items 1-8), quality of the information (InfoQual: 9-15), quality of the interaction (InterQual: 16-18), system quality (Overall: 19).

4.4 Design

Our study was within-subjects design one independent variable: REFERENT, a nominal variable with 14 conditions, representing common tasks to execute in a home environment [27]: (1) Turn the TV On/Off, (2) Start Player, (3) Turn the Volume up, (4) Turn the volume down, (5) Go to the next channel, (6) Go to the previous channel, (7) Turn Air Conditioning On/Off, (8) Turn Lights On/Off, (9) Brighten Lights, (10) Dim Lights, (11) Turn Heating system On/Off, (12) Turn Alarm On/Off, (13) Answer a phone call, and (14) End Phone Call.

4.5 Measures

We employed the following measures to understand users' preferences and cognitive and motor performance for nose gestures:

1. We computed Agreement Scores $A(r)$ [28,30] and Agreement Rates $AR(r)$ [29] for each REFERENT r condition using the formula:

$$A(r) = \sum_{P_i \subseteq P} \left(\frac{|P_i|}{|P|}\right)^2 \geq AR(r) = \frac{|P|}{|P|-1} \sum_{P_i \subseteq P} \left(\frac{|P_i|}{|P|}\right)^2 - \frac{1}{|P|-1} \quad (1)$$

   where r denotes the referent for which a gesture will be elicited, $|P|$ denotes the number of elicited gestures, and $|P_i|$ denotes the number of gestures elicited for the ith subgroup of P.
2. Participants' CREATIVITY was evaluated using an on-line creativity test returning a score between 0 and 100 (higher scores denote more creativity) computed from answers to a set of questions which cover several factors: *abstraction* (of concepts from ideas), *connection* (between things without an apparent link), *perspective* (shift in terms of space, time, and other people), *curiosity* (to change and improve things accepted as the norm), *boldness* (to push boundaries beyond accepted conventions), *paradox* (the ability to accept and work with contradictory concepts), *complexity* (the ability to operate with a large quantity of information), and *persistence* (to derive stronger solutions).
3. Participants' fine motor skills was measured with a standard motor test of the NEPSY test batteries (a developmental NEuroPSYchological assessment) [10]. The test consists in touching each fingertip with the thumb of the same hand for eight times in a row. Higher motor skills are reflected in smaller times.
4. THINKING-TIME measures the time, in seconds, needed by participants to elicit a gesture for a given referent.
5. GOODNESS-OF-FIT represents participants' subjective assessment, as a rating between 1 and 10, of their confidence about how well the proposed gesture fits the referent.

5 Results and Discussion

A total amount of 308 gestures were elicited from 22 participants × 14 referents, which we clustered/classified into groups of similar types according to the following criteria inspired and/or adapted from various sources [19,26,27,30]:

- *Body part*: expresses which human limb is involved (head and/or dominant or non-dominant shoulders).
- *Laterality*: specifies the side(s) involved in the gesture (central, unilateral dominant, unilateral non-dominant, bilateral or a combination).
- *Range of motion*: relates the distance between the position of the human body and the location of the gesture (small, medium, or large).
- *Plane of motion*: specifies which axis/axes are concerned (transverse, frontal, and/or sagittal).
- *Composition*: expresses whether a gesture is simple (only one occurrence is produced) or compound (two or more simple gestures compose the new one).
- *Amount of strokes*: states how many strokes were involved (1, 2, 3 or more).
- *Gesture synchronization*: expresses whether a compound gesture is sequential (simple gestures are produced one after another) or concurrent (simple gestures are produced concurrently).
- *Nature*: describes the underlying meaning of a gesture (a symbolic gesture depicts commonly accepted symbols employed to convey information, such as emblems and cultural gestures; a metaphorical gesture is employed to shape an idea or concept, such as turning an invisible knob; a physical gesture is made when the gesture is produced as if it is physically acting on a real object; an abstract gesture does not convey any particular meaning).
- *Form*: specifies which form of gesture is elicited (stroke when the gesture only consists of taps and flicks, static when the gesture is performed in only one location, static with motion (when the gesture is performed with a static pose while the rest is moving, dynamic when the gesture does capture any change or motion).

Based on the aforementioned measures, the 308 elicited gestures were classified into 10 categories clustered into 3 groups (e.g., 1–4: simple gestures, 5–8: repeated simple gestures, 9–10: combined gestures) (Table 2). Instead of classifying them based on a single property, we preferred to classify them according to three levels of complexity because it enables us to quickly identify which body part is involved and to check whether combined gestures, potentially more complex than simple gestures, are viable alternatives to simple gestures, which are more intuitive in principle. For instance, a repeated gesture avoids introducing another gesture type and a combined gesture builds on previously elicited gestures, thus reducing the amount of simple gestures to remember. These results suggest that central gestures (which do not differentiate the laterality) are more frequently selected since they characterize the 4 most frequent categories covering 245/308 = 80% of gestures, the rest being considered as insignificant. It is also worth to notice that the laterality is also postponed as far as possible: dominance only appears for the fifth category, and only for one shoulder, dominance first (19/308 = 6%), non-dominance afterwards (14/308 = 5%).

Table 2. Definition of gesture categories after classification.

Cat.	Name	Body part	Laterality	Range motion	Comp.	Str.	Nature	Form
1	Single head gesture	Head	Central	Medium	Simple	1	Physical	Stroke
2	Single dominant shoul-der gesture	Shoulder	Unilateral dominant	Small	Simple	1	Symbolic	Static
3	Single non-dominant shoulder gesture	Shoulder	Unilateral non-dom	Small	Simple	1	Symbolic	Static
4	Single bilateral shoulder gesture	Shoulders	Bilateral	Small	Simple	2	Symbolic	Static
5	Repeated similar head gesture	Head	Central	Medium	Simple	≥2	Physical	Stroke
6	Repeated similar dominant shoulder gesture	Shoulder	Unilateral dominant	Small	Simple	≥2	Symbolic	Static
7	Repeated similar non-dominant shoulder gesture	Shoulder	Unilateral non-dominant	Small	Simple	≥2	Symbolic	Static
8	Repeated similar bilateral shoulder gesture	Shoulders	Bilateral	Small	Simple	≥4	Symbolic	Static
9	Concurrent compound head and shoulders movement	Head and shoulders	Combined	Medium	Com-pound	≥3	Abstract	Dynamic with motion
10	Sequential compound head and shoulders movement	Head and shoulders	Combined	Medium	Com-pound	≥3	Abstract	Dynamic with motion

Although repetition appears appealing as it reduces the amount of gestures to remember, it still concerns the least preferred gestures grouped into the "Others" pie (26/308 = 8%). Figure 4 graphically represents the distribution of elicited gestures across these 10 categories. Single head gestures are the most frequently used (102/308 = 33%), followed by compound gestures, respectively concurrent (70/308 = 23%) and sequential (44/308 = 14%). The second most frequent elicitation concerns gestures involving the head or a combination of the head with both shoulders (172/308 = 56%). Consequently, the head is reported as the principal source for eliciting head and shoulders gestures. This is confirmed by Fig. 5b,c: the

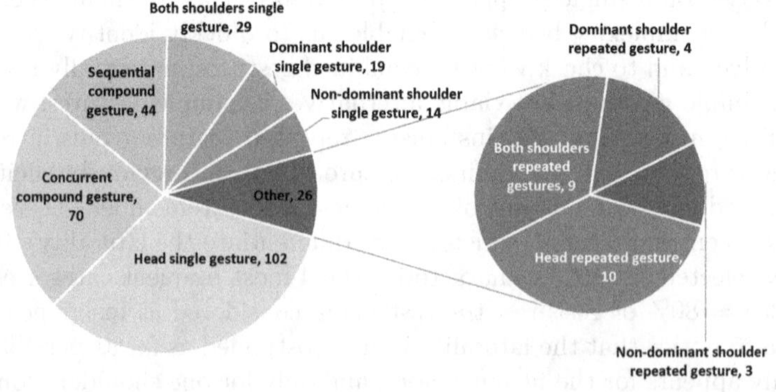

Fig. 4. Distribution of gestures per category.

head alone is involved in 51% gestures, the shoulders alone in 31%, and both in 18%; participants tend to prefer gestures minimizing the amount of strokes with one stroke in 69% of cases, two strokes for 24%, and three or more stroke in the remaining 7% of cases. The lower the physical articulation of gestures is, the more frequent it is. Figure 5a decomposes gestures based on Table 1.

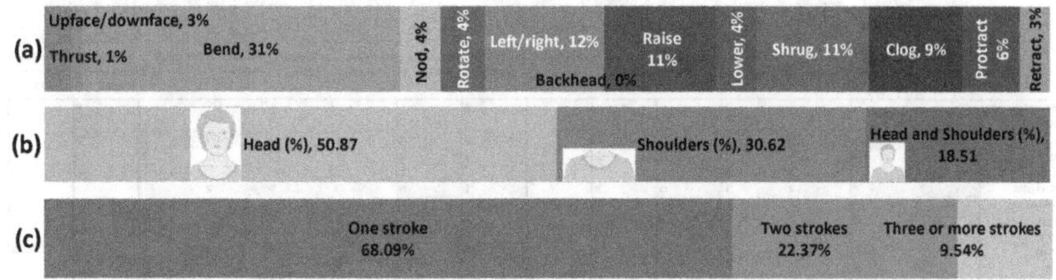

Fig. 5. Breakdown of gestures per criteria.

5.1 Agreement Scores and Rates

Figure 6 shows the agreement scores and rates (Eq. 1) obtained for each REFERENT condition sorted in decreasing order of their rates, along with the final consensus gesture. Several global observations can be made. Firstly, in both agreements, referents often appear in symmetric pairs (e.g., "Go to next and previous channel", "Answer and End Phone Call") or in semantically related ones (e.g., "Play/pause" with "Turn TV On/Off"), which suggests that participants had a higher level of familiarity with some types of referents (after all, changing a channel is a very frequent task) than with others (turning the air conditioning or heating system on/off is considered less frequent or familiar). Secondly, the least agreed referents appeared in these positions because participants were less familiar with physical commands than with popular devices like a television). Thirdly, the ordering of agreement scores and rates remains consistent from one computation to another, except for one pair of referents: "Decrease Volume" was ranked higher according to its score (#7) than for its rate (#9), which suggests that the metrics preserve the ordering apart some particular case. Overall, agreement scores and rates are medium in average magnitude, in particular for rates (which are the most demanding ones) between .104 and .368 for the global sampling ($M = .232$, $SD = .066$). Apart for the "Go to Next/Previous Channel" referents which are ranked with a *high* magnitude, agreement rates belong to the *medium* range according to Vatavu and Wobbrock's method [28] to interpret the magnitudes of agreement rates. These results are very similar to the other rates reported in the GES literature [28]. Hence, our results fall inside medium consensus ($< .3$) category with their average in the same interval (highlighted bars in Fig. 6). To decide the consensus gesture depicted for each REFERENT at the bottom of each bar in Fig. 6, four criteria were successively considered: the agreement rate (blue bars), the individual frequency of occurrence (represented

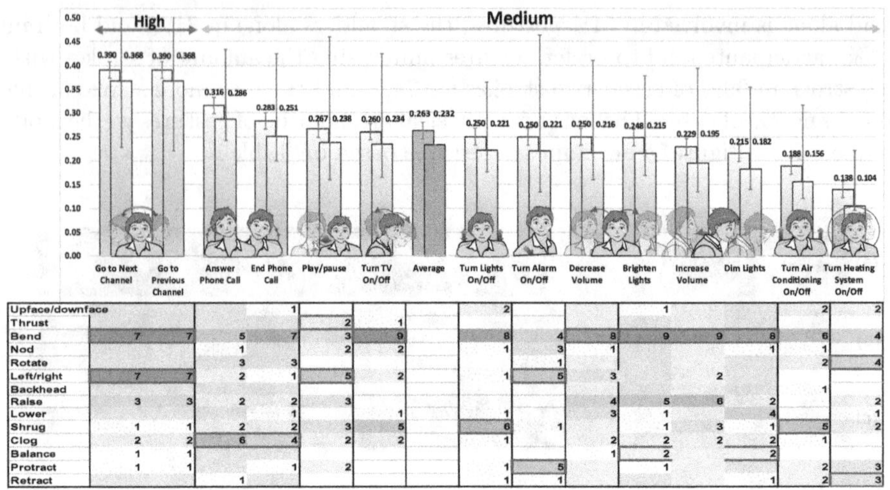

Fig. 6. Agreements Scores and Rates with error bars showing standard error (scores) and α = .95 confidence intervals (rates), the consensus gesture, and the frequency table. (color figure online)

by numbers in the bottom part of Fig. 6) for each REFERENT, the associative frequency when two referents are symmetric (e.g., "Go to next channel" and "Go to previous channel" to take into account the consensus by pair, and the unicity of each gesture (whether a gesture was elicited only for one REFERENT). By applying thee criteria, the consensus gestures for each REFERENT are (surprisingly, some common gestures have been suggested by participants, such as nod, but not in a fashion significant enough to warrant any consensus):

- "Go to next and previous channel": with the highest agreement independently from their symmetry, Bend and left/righthead were the most frequent and shared gestures between the two (both were elicited 7 times in Fig. 6). Hence, we decided to assign the **Left/righthead** gesture as symmetric gestures for this referent.
- "Answer Phone Call" and "End Phone Call": they receive the next two highest rates, above the average, and they totalize 6 + 4 = 10 **Clog** gestures, which has been the most elicited for this pair of referents.
- "Play/pause": **Thrust** has been only elicited for this mode-switching referent and has been preferred as soon as Left/righthead have been already assigned.
- "Turn TV On/Off": **Bend up/down** was by far the most frequently selected gesture for this referent (9).
- "Turn Lights On/Off": **Shrug** was the second most frequently elicited gesture (6) after bending, already assigned (8).
- "Turn Alarms On/Off": **Protract** was the most frequent (6) and uniquely assigned gesture for this referent.
- "Decrease and Increase Volume" (yellow area in Fig. 6): **Bend left/right** totalize 7 elicitations of the same type together.

- "Brighten/dim Lights" (grey area in Fig. 6): **Bend forward/backward** count 7 elicitations of the same type together.
- "Turn AC On/off": **Shrug** was also the most elicited gesture (6) but with maintaining shoulder up as opposed to the complete movement for "Turn Lights On/Off".
- "Turn Heating System On/off": **Rotate clockwise** was the first elicited gesture for this referent.

5.2 Other Measures

Goodness of Fit. Figure 7 distributes the Goodness-of-Fit into six regions depending on its respective value and current interpretation [29]. Overall, the value collected for Goodness-of-Fit for most gestures belong to the "excellent" region ($v > 7$, 12/22=55%) or the "good" region ($v \in [5.5, 7]$, $9/22 = 41\%$) between 3.36 and 8.14 for the global sampling ($M = 6.78$, $SD = 1.63$). These results are quite above the average values: participants were particularly happy with the gestures they chose and reinforces the acceptability of the elicited gestures. Participant #17 gave the maximum (8.14) and participant #21 was the most severe (3.36). All elicited gestures received an average value between 6.14 and 7.41 (good to excellent range). If we consider the order according to which referents were presented, the Goodness-of-Fit turns out to be usually more positive during the first half of the experiment than during the second part, probably revealing a progressive status of fatigue or boredom. Once could imagine that the most instinctive, spontaneous gestures bring a more important satisfaction among participants. Figure 8 compares the evolution of the Goodness-of-Fit for two randomly selected participants, one with values progressively increasing while the other progressively decreasing. The values do not

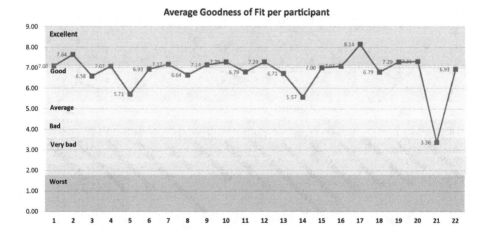

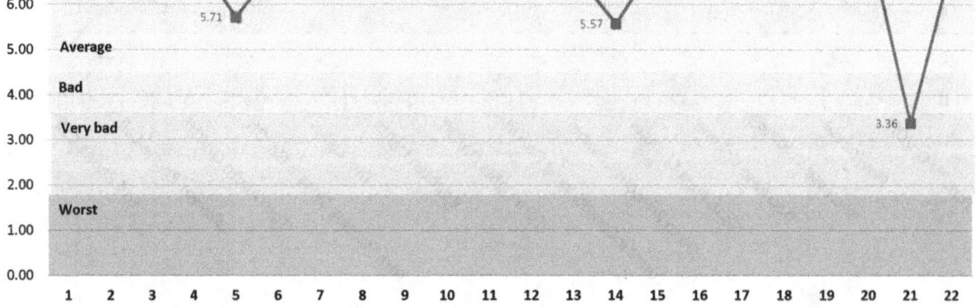

Fig. 7. Average Goodness of fit for all referents per participant.

really depend on the referent, but the order according to which they were presented. Participants were able to quickly find out a fit gesture, but when their source of inspiration was running dry, they elicited less spontaneous, adapted and satisfying gestures.

Thinking Time. Figure 9 compares the average thinking time for all referents with its corresponding agreement rate. Since referents were randomly presented, there is no particular correlation between the thinking time for pairs of related referents. For instance, "Go to previous channel" received the smallest thinking time (2.45 s) while its symmetric referent "Go to next channel" received an average time (9.64 s). Thinking times range between 2.45 s and 22.50 s for "Answer phone call". Contrarily to agreement rate which seems to be linked with the familiarity, the thinking time is apparently not correlated with the referent type. Non-familiar or non-frequent referents do not necessarily receive high times. We did not find any correlation between THINKING-TIME and GOODNESS-OF-FIT. But apparently, the agreement rate decreases when the thinking time increases: the more time a participant may need to appropriately identify a gesture, the lower the agreement rate becomes. We point out in Fig. 9 three referents for which the thinking time was significantly high than the others: "Turn AC on/off" (20.68 s), "Turn heating system on/off" (21.81 s), and "Answer Phone call" (22.50 s). While these three tasks are less frequent than others such as "Play/pause" (15.14 s), it is more their lack of physical reference that harms the time more than their familiarity. The referent "Answer Phone call" is often associated to a physical movement bringing the phone to the ears, which is impossible to achieve in this case. Figure 10 sorts referents in decreasing order of its GOODNESS-OF-FIT along with its correspond thinking time.

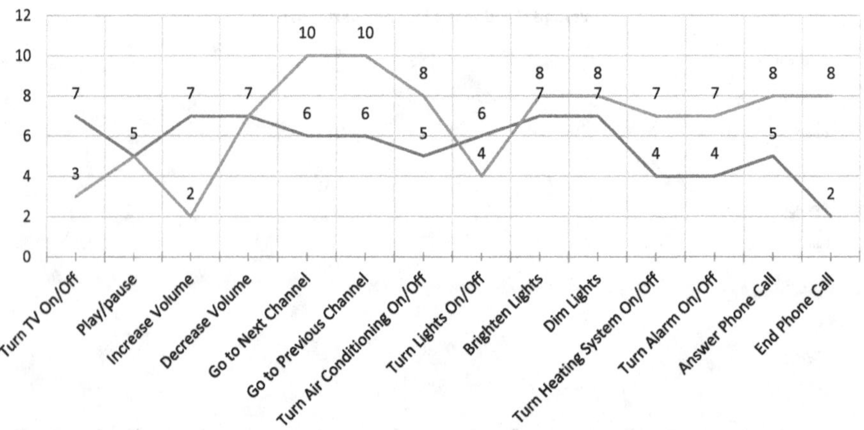

Fig. 8. Goodness of fit of referents for two participants with different evolutions.

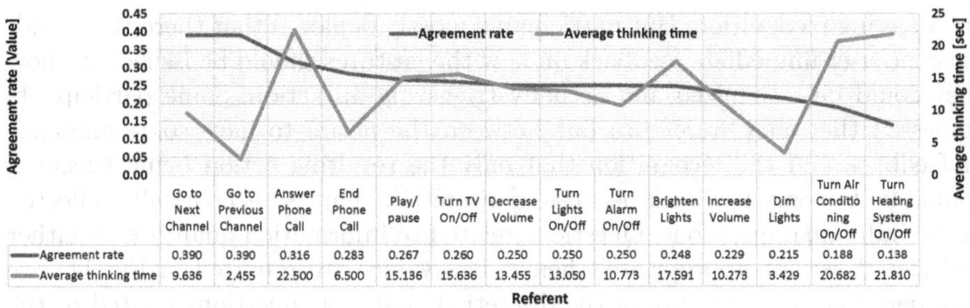

	Go to Next Channel	Go to Previous Channel	Answer Phone Call	End Phone Call	Play/ pause	Turn TV On/Off	Decrease Volume	Turn Lights On/Off	Turn Alarm On/Off	Brighten Lights	Increase Volume	Dim Lights	Turn Air Conditioning On/Off	Turn Heating System On/Off
Agreement rate	0.390	0.390	0.316	0.283	0.267	0.260	0.250	0.250	0.250	0.248	0.229	0.215	0.188	0.138
Average thinking time	9.636	2.455	22.500	6.500	15.136	15.636	13.455	13.050	10.773	17.591	10.273	3.429	20.682	21.810

Fig. 9. Agreement rates vs Average thinking time.

User Subjective Satisfaction. Figure 11 reports the results from the IBM CSUQ questionnaire expressing the subjective user satisfaction regarding nose interaction as experienced in this study (error bars show a confidence interval of 95%). First of all, the four CSUQ measures are usually considered as good enough to support the correlation with the perceived usability since their value is superior or equal to 5. Interface quality (InterQual: $M = 5.60$, $SD = 1.20$) exceeds this threshold with the widest standard deviation. System usefulness (SysUse: $M = 5.65$, $SD = 1.08$), Information quality (InfoQual: $M = 5.53$, $SD = 1.17$), and Overall satisfaction (Overall: $M = 5.61$, $SD = 1.14$) all share a value above 5, which suggests that participants were quite subjectively satisfied with head and shoulders interaction, usually more than average. Two reasons could explain this: these gestures are straightforward to imagine (the body language is quite related to some gestures), they are easy to reproduce in a consistent way without

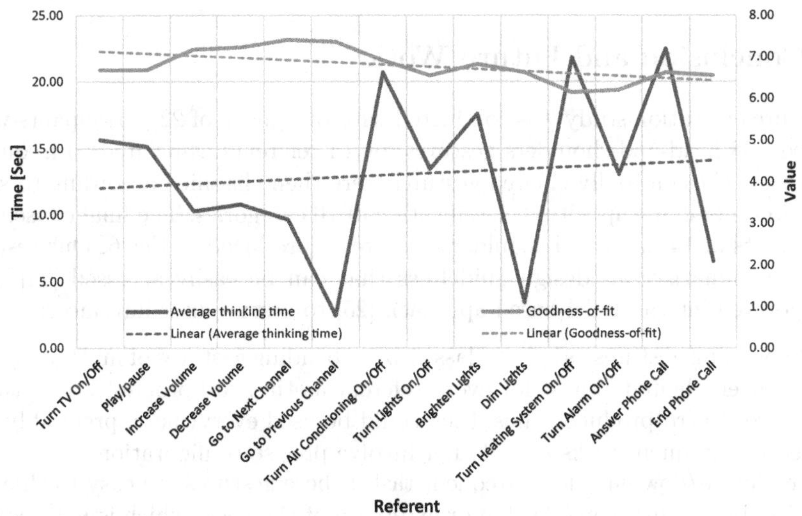

Fig. 10. Thinking time vs Goodness of fit.

endangering recognition. But participants mostly deplored that there is no guidance, no user immediate feedback on how the gestures should be issued and how they could be recognized and actually triggering an action. Some participants confessed that they were torn out between the desire to have some guidance or feedback and the recognition that only the resulting action being executed should be the only feedback because of discretion. This is also partially reflected in the individual questions. Questions related to information quality were either considered as 'not appropriate' (hence, less values are reported in Fig. 11) are considered positive because of the discretion goal. The questions related to the other measures all received some agreement. On the other hand, efficiency in achieving the tasks was recognized to be satisfying (Q3 and Q6 are the most positively answered questions).

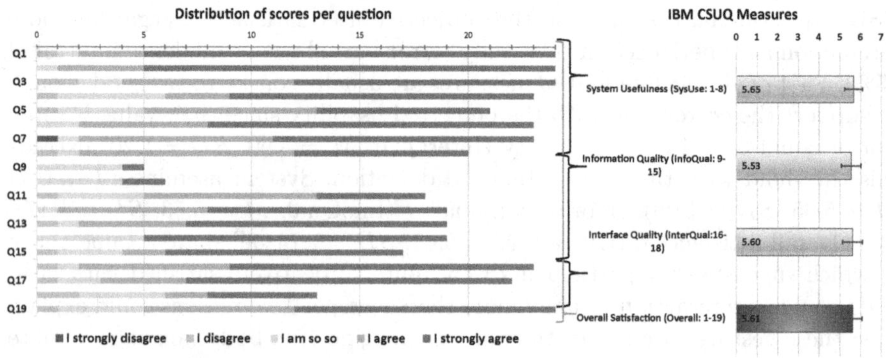

Fig. 11. Results of the IBM CSUQ questionnaire and measures.

6 Conclusion and Future Work

A gesture elicitation study was conducted with one group of 22 participants who elicited 308 head-and-shoulders gestures for 14 referents associated to frequent IoT tasks. These initially elicited gestures were then classified according to several criteria to come up with a classification of 10 categories. The final consensus set consists of 14 hand-and-shoulders gestures reproduced in Fig. 6. Our results can be summarized as design guidelines that can be easily accessed [24] and incorporated into a model-based approach [25] to gesture user interfaces:

- Use bending gestures as a first-class citizen: bending gestures of multiple types have been elicited almost for every referent as they are probably the easiest gestures to (re)produce. Thus, they could be used everywhere, preferably for the most frequent tasks that do not involve precise configuration.
- Use Upface/downface for infrequent tasks: these gestures are easy to characterize, but require some flexion or extension of the neck, which is not desired over a long period of time. For example, these gestures were accepted for turning on/off the heating and alarm systems.

- Use thrust only for play/pause: this unique gesture works for a well designated task and should not be used for other tasks.
- Forehead and backhead gestures should not be used, apart for exceptional assignation, such as turning the AC on/off, the least frequent task.

This study is limited to its particular conditions (IoT tasks) and participants (random small sampling without representativity). Hence, results are not necessarily generalizable to other contexts of used. It may be hypothesized, however, that different gestures might be elicited by varying such elements as other types of tasks and referents, overall participant posture (e.g., standing vs sitting), repetition and rhythm (several gestures were simply repeated, sometime in a rhythmic way, to augment the vocabulary), or methods of measurement. However, this particular study is not concerned with such possible variables. Rather, its purpose was to come up with a first consensus set of head-and-shoulders gestures based on a design space. This design space could serve for further experiments as it is valid everywhere. Some studies are aimed at examining the musculo-skeletal constraints and the physical fatigue induced by these movements, which is not taken in to account here. Future research may explore other variables that may contribute to elicitation of possible correlations between tasks and gestures.

Acknowledgements. The first author would like to thank Dr. Teodora Voicu for helping him with anatomy, and Thibaut Jacob, Gilles Bailly, and Eric Lecolinet for providing the images of [8] from which the design space has been drawn.

References

1. Bostan, I., et al.: Hands as a controller: user preferences for hand specific on-skin gestures. In: Proceedings of the ACM International Conference on Designing Interactive Systems (DIS 2018), pp. 1123–1134. ACM, New York (2017). https://doi.org/10.1145/3064663.3064766
2. Bressem, J., Ladewig, S.H.: Rethinking gesture phases: articulatory features of gestural movement? Semiotica **184**, 53–91 (2011). https://doi.org/10.1515/semi.2011.022
3. Chen, Z., et al.: User-defined gestures for gestural interaction: extending from hands to other body parts. Int. J. Hum. Comp. Interact. **34**(3), 238–250 (2018). https://doi.org/10.1080/10447318.2017.1342943
4. Drake, R., Vogl, W., Mitchel, A.W.M.: Gray's Anatomy for Students, 4th edn. Elsevier, Amsterdam (2019)
5. Felberbaum, Y., Lanir, J.: Step by step: investigating foot gesture interaction. In: Proceedings of the ACM International Working Conference on Advanced Visual Interfaces (AVI 2016), pp. 306–307. ACM, New York (2016)
6. Havlucu, H., Ergin, M.Y., Bostan, İ., Buruk, O.T., Göksun, T., Özcan, O.: It made more sense: comparison of user-elicited on-skin touch and freehand gesture sets. In: Streitz, N., Markopoulos, P. (eds.) DAPI 2017. LNCS, vol. 10291, pp. 159–171. Springer, Cham (2017). https://doi.org/10.1007/978-3-319-58697-7_11
7. Hirsch, M., Cheng, J., Reiss, A., Sundholm, M., Lukowicz, P., Amft, O.: Hands-free gesture control with a capacitive textile neckband. In: Proceedings of the ACM International Symposium on Wearable Computers (ISWC 2014), pp. 55–58. ACM, New York (2014). https://doi.org/10.1145/2634317.2634328

8. Jacob, T., Bailly, G., Lecolinet, E.: A study on 3D viewpoint control through head and shoulders motion. In: Proceedings of the 27th International Conference on Interaction Homme-Machine (IHM 2015), Article 25. ACM, New York (2015). https://doi.org/10.1145/2820619.2825005
9. Kendall, M.G., Smith, B.B.: The Problem of m Rankings. Ann. Math. Stat. **10**(3), 275–287 (1939). http://www.jstor.org/stable/2235668
10. Korkman, M., Kirk, U., Kemp, S.: NEPSY: A Developmental Neuropsychological Assessment. Psychological Corporation, San Antonio (1998)
11. Kühnel, C., Westermann, T., Hemmert, F., Kratz, S., Müller, A., Möller, S.: I'm home: defining and evaluating a gesture set for smart-home control. Int. J. Hum. Comput. Stud. **69**(11), 693–704 (2011). https://doi.org/10.1016/j.ijhcs.2011.04.005
12. Lee, D.Y., Oakley, I.R., Lee, Y.R.: Bodily input for wearables: an elicitation study. In: Extended Abstract of Proceedings of International Conference on Human-Computer Interaction Korea 2016 (HCI Korea 2016), pp. 283–285 (2016). https://www.dbpia.co.kr/Journal/ArticleDetail/NODE06645483
13. Lee, J., Yeo, H.-S., Starner, T., Quigley, A., Kunze, K., Woo, W.: Automated data gathering and training tool for personalized "Itchy Nose". In: Proceedings of the 9th International Conference on Augmented Human Conference (AH 2018), Article 43. ACM, New York (2018)
14. Lewis, J.R.: IBM computer usability satisfaction questionnaires: psychometric evaluation and instructions for use. Int. J. Hum. Comput. Interact. **7**(1), 57–78 (1995). https://doi.org/10.1080/10447319509526110
15. Liu, M., Nancel, M., Vogel, D.: Gunslinger: subtle armsdown mid-air interaction. In: Proceedings of the 28th Annual ACM Symposium on User Interface Software & Technology (UIST 2015), pp. 63–71. ACM, New York (2015). https://doi.org/10.1145/2807442.2807489
16. Malu, M., Chundury, P., Findlater, L.: Exploring accessible smartwatch interactions for people with upper body motor impairments. In: Proceedings of the ACM International Conference on Human Factors in Computing Systems (CHI 2018), Paper 488. ACM, New York (2018). https://doi.org/10.1145/3173574.3174062
17. Mardanbegi, D., Hansen, D.W., Pederson, T.: Eye-based head gestures. In: Proceedings of the ACM Symposium on Eye Tracking Research and Applications (ETRA 2012), pp. 139–146. ACM, New York (2012)
18. McClave, E.Z.: Linguistic functions of head movements in the context of speech. J. Pragmatics **32**(7), 855–878 (2000). https://doi.org/10.1016/S0378-2166(99)00079-X
19. Piumsomboon, T., Clark, A., Billinghurst, M., Cockburn, A.: User-defined gestures for augmented reality. In: Kotzé, P., Marsden, G., Lindgaard, G., Wesson, J., Winckler, M. (eds.) INTERACT 2013. LNCS, vol. 8118, pp. 282–299. Springer, Heidelberg (2013). https://doi.org/10.1007/978-3-642-40480-1_18
20. Ruiz, J., Li, Y., Lank, E.: User-defined motion gestures for mobile interaction. In Proceedings of the ACM International Conference on Human Factors in Computing Systems (CHI 2011), pp. 197–206. ACM, New York (2011). https://doi.org/10.1145/1978942.1978971
21. Saffer, D.: Designing Gestural Interfaces. O'Reilly Media, Sebastopol (2008)
22. Serrano, M., Ens, B.M., Irani, P.P.: Exploring the use of hand-to-face input for interacting with head-worn displays. In: Proceedings of the 32nd ACM International Conference on Human Factors in Computing Systems (CHI 2014), pp. 3181–3190. ACM, New York (2014). https://doi.org/10.1145/2556288.2556984

23. Špakov, O., Majaranta, P.: Enhanced gaze interaction using simple head gestures. In: Proceedings of the ACM International Conference on Ubiquitous Computing (UbiComp 2012), pp. 705–710. ACM, New York (2012). https://doi.org/10.1145/2370216.2370369
24. Vanderdonckt, J.: Accessing guidelines information with Sierra. In: Proceedings of IFIP International Conference on Human-Computer Interaction (Interact 1995), pp. 311–316. IFIP (1995). https://doi.org/10.1007/978-1-5041-2896-4_52
25. Vanderdonckt, J.: A MDA-compliant environment for developing user interfaces of information systems. In: Pastor, O., Falcão e Cunha, J. (eds.) CAiSE 2005. LNCS, vol. 3520, pp. 16–31. Springer, Heidelberg (2005). https://doi.org/10.1007/11431855_2
26. Vanderdonckt, J., Roselli, P., Pérez-Medina, J.L.: !FTL, an articulation-invariant stroke gesture recognizer with controllable position, scale, and rotation invariances. In: Proceedings of the ACM International Conference on Multimodal Interaction (ICMI 2018), pp. 125–134. ACM, New York (2018)
27. Vatavu, R.-D.: User-defined gestures for free-hand TV control. In: Proceedings of the 10th European Conference on Interactive TV and Video (EuroITV 2012), pp. 45–48 (2012). https://doi.org/10.1145/2325616.2325626
28. Vatavu, R.-D., Wobbrock, J.O.: Formalizing agreement analysis for elicitation studies: new measures, significance test, and toolkit. In: Proceedings of the 33rd ACM Conference on Human Factors in Computing Systems (CHI 2015), pp. 1325–1334. ACM, New York (2015)
29. Vatavu, R.-D., Wobbrock,J.O.: Between-subjects elicitation studies: formalization and tool support. In: Proceedings of the 34th ACM Conference on Human Factors in Computing Systems (CHI 2016), pp. 3390–3402. ACM, New York (2016)
30. Wobbrock, J.O., Morris, M.R., Wilson, A.D.: User-defined gestures for surface computing. In: Proceedings of the ACM International Conference on Human Factors in Computing Systems (CHI 2009), pp. 1083–1092. ACM, New York (2009)
31. Zaiţi, I.-A., Pentiuc, Ş.-G., Vatavu, R.-D.: On free-hand TV control: experimental results on user-elicited gestures with leap motion. Personal Ubiquit. Comput. **19**(5–6), 821–838 (2015). https://doi.org/10.1007/s00779-015-0863-y

The Vision of Human-Computer Interactive Game Platform for the Future of Brain Development and Interaction

Tingwei Zhao(✉)

3D Modeling and Animation Design, CDI College,
1000 Boul Saint-Jean, Pointe-Claire, QC, Canada
zhaotingwei269@sina.com

Abstract. We normally sleep for 8 h, but after wearing brain–machine interaction equipment, our perception of time in our dreams is over a week, even a month, or even more. It was only eight hours after waking up. In this way, we can do more things in our dreams. For example, we can play a game with historical themes and put it in our dreams. People only need to sleep normally for one night and then can "experience" a period of history.

Keywords: Human-computer interaction · Brain-computer interaction · Games · Lucid dreams · Brain networking

1 Introduction

What is human-computer interaction? Turn on the rice cooker, this is human-computer interaction. Well, the concept of human-computer interaction is as simple as that! But to do it well is a very difficult thing. Although it is difficult, we must still pay attention to human-computer interaction, because it is related to the difficulty and usefulness of your "rice cooker". Difficulty refers to the threshold requirements for users; Usefulness refers to whether users are comfortable with it [1] (Fig. 1).

First of all, let's elaborate on human-computer interaction—human-computer interaction refers to the communication between human and machine (computer), which may be a kind of intention; Or behavior; Or process; Or purpose.

1. Intention: You hope to complete something through machines.
2. Behavior: You start to act on the machine.
3. Process: You may communicate with the machine not only in one action, but also in a series of actions, which requires a process.
4. Purpose: You will finally get a result, which may be the purpose you want to achieve, or it may be inconsistent with the purpose you want to achieve [2].

The human-computer interaction we designed in the game revolved around the four points mentioned above. Excellent human-computer interaction system design is to make it more convenient and arbitrary for players to complete the above four steps.

The basis of game playability is the usability of man-machine interface. For game software, if its human-computer interface is not available and it has no good learnable

A. Marcus and W. Wang (Eds.): HCII 2019, LNCS 11584, pp. 214–227, 2019.
https://doi.org/10.1007/978-3-030-23541-3_16

Fig. 1. Human-computer interaction concept picture

habits, then the game players cannot get started quickly and can't play the entertainment function of the game. At this time, most players may retreat from difficulties, thus making the game completely lose its playability [8].

Immersion in human-computer interface is one of the common elements of playability in most games. Immersion of human-computer interface is to let players feel that they are in a virtual game world, such as FPS games, using a three-dimensional maze and a first angle of view (Fig. 2).

While RTS games use a top-down angle of view, making players feel in control of the overall situation (Fig. 3).

The operating efficiency of the human-machine interface is also one of the key elements of game playability. RTS usually uses one mouse to complete all operations. FPS games use keyboard to control the movement of game characters and mouse to control aiming and shooting actions. Some racing games directly use interactive devices like steering wheels. Interactive process is a process of input and output. People input instructions to the computer through the human-computer interface, and the computer presents the output results to the user after processing. The forms of input and output between people and computers are varied, so the forms of interaction are also varied. Therefore, have you ever thought about using brain control to create virtual reality content?

Brain-machine interaction [9] Interfaces (BMIs), a brand-new man-machine interaction mode, is expected to promote further research on the brain, and promote the integration and enhancement of brain intelligence and external machine intelligence (hybrid intelligence). It has great research value and application prospect, and is a rapidly rising interdisciplinary research field in the past decade. Simply put, brain–machine interaction is to transform thoughts into actions and feelings into perception.

Fig. 2. FPS game

Fig. 3. RTS game

Human beings read thoughts directly through brain wave interaction, thus more accurately and deeply interpreting the real thoughts in the hearts of "people". In the brain–machine interaction system, neural signals recorded from the brain will be transmitted to the decoder for translation, and form motion outputs including controlling computer cursor, controlling wheelchair motion or controlling robot arm. Of course, we can also apply to games. Everyone can enter a completely virtual world to do anything as long as they bring sensors connected to the brain [10] (Fig. 4).

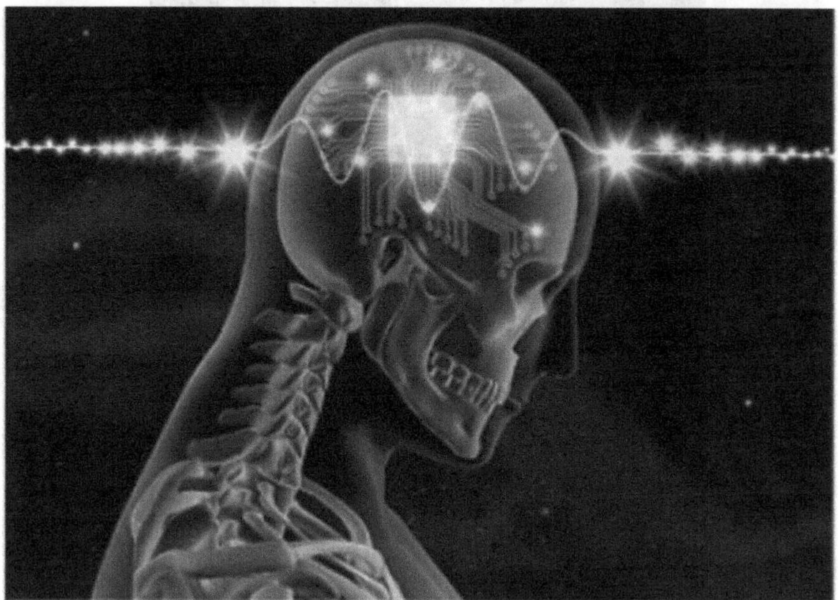

Fig. 4. Brain machine interaction concept picture

Brain–machine interface is a new technology to realize direct communication and control between brain and external environment. By collecting and analyzing bio-electric signals of human brain, it establishes a direct communication and control channel between human brain and computers or other electronic devices, so that people can express their wishes or manipulate devices through the brain without the need for language or body movements [12].

With the development of the times, I think brain–machine interaction can not only stop at manipulating machines to do something for us, but also allow machines to control our dreams and even our perception of time.

It is known that we can control our body and some objects in the dream, but the dream is vague. I hope the brain–machine interaction device can create an almost real dream, and even replace the dream with a game artificially. Our body is still resting, but we are not dreaming normally, but we are experiencing the game through the brain–machine interaction device or actually controlling our dream (Fig. 5).

Just like Animus in the game "Assassin's Creed", Animus is a machine that modern plot protagonists use to simulate ancestral experiences by analyzing ancestral memories in DNA. Simulate the living environment of users' ancestors [3] (Fig. 6).

There is also lucid dreaming that some people can dream in reality. They are also called Lucid Dreaming [4].

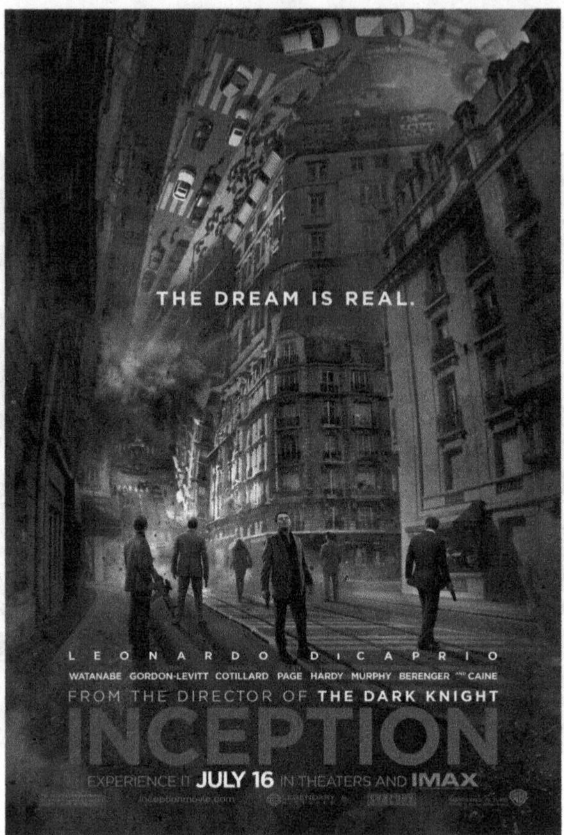

Fig. 5. Movie "Inception" poster

Lucid Dreaming is not the same as daydreams. Lucid Dreaming is the dream in which the dreamer remains conscious during sleep. Daydreaming means that the dreamer meditates or fantasizes while awake, instead of going to sleep. The word lucid dream was first proposed by Frederick Van Eeden, a Dutch doctor, in 1913. In a lucid dreaming state, the dreamer can have the ability to think and remember in a lucid dreaming. Some people can even make their dreams feel the same as the real world, but know that they are in a dream [5].

Many universities carry out continuous research on the techniques and effects of lucid dreaming. Similarly, some independent institutions such as The Lucidity Institute of Laberge carry out the same research. So far, there is no known case that Lucid Dreaming will cause physical or psychological damage to human beings [11].

The first book to recognize the unique lucid dreaming and its potential for scientific research is Celia Green's 2003 Lucid Dreaming. Looking back at the past literature and her new experimental data, Celia Green analyzed the main features of these Lucid Dreaming and concluded that they are different types from the traditional normal dreams. She predicted that they were related to REM. Celia Green was also the first

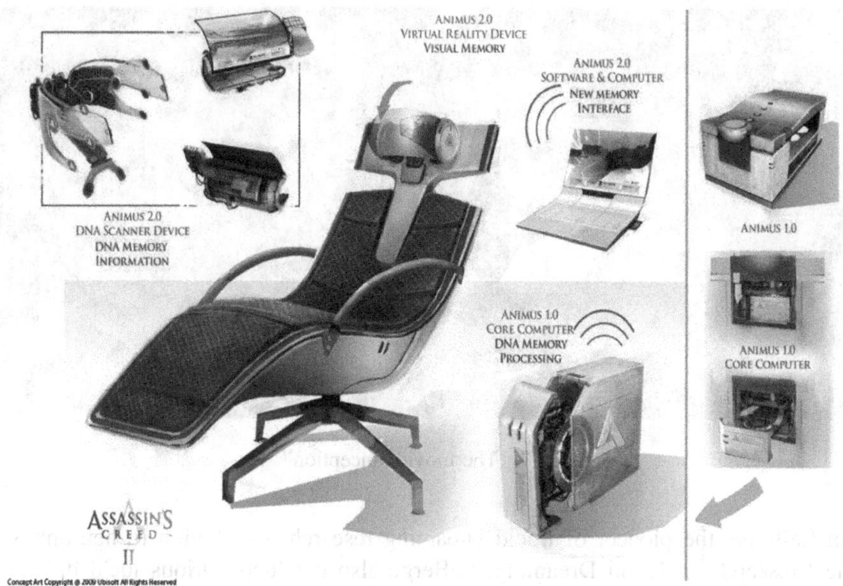

Fig. 6. Game "Assassin's Creed" Animus concept picture

person to associate Lucid Dreaming with false lucidity. The first support in lucid dreaming science was put forward by British super psychologist Keith Hearne in the late 1970s. Alan Worsley, who volunteered to participate in the experiment, marked the beginning of lucid dreaming in a multiple sleep electrogram instrument with eye movement signals. Philosopher Norman Malcolm 2012 questioned the accuracy of this method in his 2012 topic "Dream", but this experiment proves that what can be done in reality can be done in Lucid Dreaming. Stephen Laberge of Stanford University conducted a similar experiment again in his doctoral thesis. Interestingly, LaBerge is not similar to Hearne and Worley's previous similar experiments, which may be related to Hearne's failure to disclose his research results.

Although it has only received public attention in the past few decades, lucid dreaming is not a modern discovery.

1. There is controversy over whether Lucid Dreaming is mentioned in the Old Testament Song of Songs 5: 2.
2. The earliest known written record of Lucid Dreaming was in the 5th century A.D., a letter written by Saint Augustine in 415.
3. As early as the 8th century, Tibetan Buddhists practiced yoga, which believed that they could keep fully awake in their sleep.
4. According to relevant historical records, many great buildings in history were originally conceived in dreams (Fig. 7).

At present, there are many tips for guiding and training Lucid Dreaming, such as keeping a dream diary, using the characters or buildings in dreams as clues, and adopting segmented sleep. These tips may come from people's personal experience or

Fig. 7. The movie "Inception"

from LaBerge, the pioneer of Lucid Dreaming research. In addition to neurophysiological research on Lucid Dreaming, LaBerge also conducts various lucid dreaming trainings to teach people to "Dream" and enjoy the pleasure of controlling dreams. On a website called "Lucid Dreaming Research Institute" where LaBerge works, many methods are taught to improve the probability of Lucid Dreaming. In addition, he has also developed a product called NovaDreamer, which can emit a flashing red light when people enter REM sleep, prompting people to enter Lucid Dreaming.

As for the perception of time, black holes must be mentioned. Standing at the boundary of the black hole, time will slow down, in fact, it is not necessary to stand at the boundary of the black hole, just stand around. This conclusion comes from the general theory of relativity, which describes that the stronger the gravity, the slower the time passes. I believe everyone has seen "Interstellar". The strong gravity of a black hole makes the space-time around the black hole seriously distorted. As a result, time slows down. More than two hours after the hero landed on "Water Planet", 23 years have passed since the spacecraft was in orbit (Fig 8).

A black hole has no substance and does not reflect light. How do astronomers judge its existence and mass?

When a black hole inhales matter, the matter will emit radiation and other information due to high heat. In addition, the orbits of stars or interstellar clouds around the black hole will be very strange. This is due to the strong gravity of the invisible black hole, so the existence and approximate mass of the black hole can be inferred.

The center of the black hole is a strange "singularity". The space-time here has been distorted inappropriately. Curvature of spacetime is infinitely high. American astronomers have made a vivid assumption about the black hole. The sucked matter will be pulled into a "noodle shape" and then slowly gather to the center. However, the process is almost eternal in the eyes of external observers.

As you can imagine, time is also pulled into a noodle shape, becoming very long, very long, time is highly expanded, and at the singularity, there is eternity.

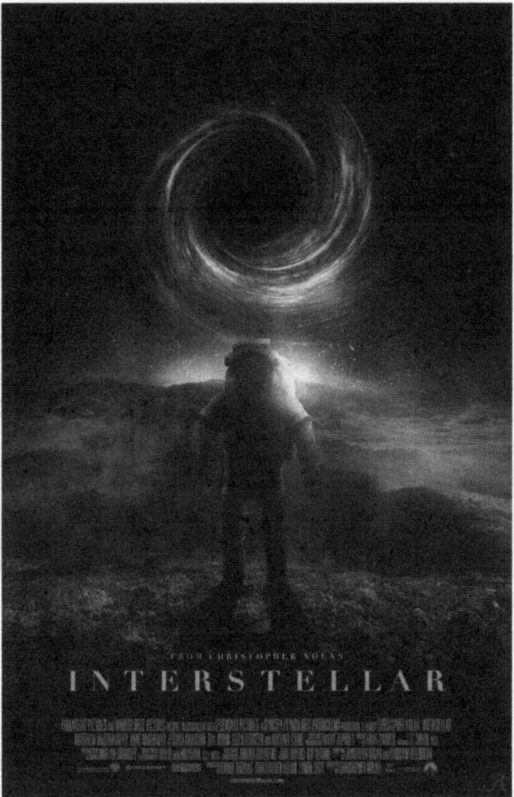

Fig. 8. Movie "Interstellar" poster (Color figure online)

The space-time curvature caused by black holes reaches its maximum at the singularity. At the horizon of the black hole, there is a boundary between the escape velocity and the speed of light.

Because time slows down, it will cause an interesting phenomenon. For example, if an object falls into the horizon of a black hole and we watch it from a distance, we will find that the object moves very slowly. The object originally fell into the horizon instantaneously, but it seems that the process of falling into the horizon will take decades or even longer. This is the result of time slowing down!

Mass matter has great gravity, which can distort space and time and expand time. For example, the velocity of time around the pyramid is slower than normal, but don't expect standing around it can prolong life, because the mass of the pyramid is simply not comparable to that of a black hole (Fig. 9).

Black holes have incomparable gravity, and even light cannot escape, so space-time around black holes will be highly distorted and time will expand extremely, so standing around black holes will slow down time.

In addition to black holes, there are time holes. Theory of Relativity from Einstein holds that gravity causes time to slow down and time can stagnate or even move

Fig. 9. Egyptian Pyramids

forward. The most well-known phenomenon of time leak is the problem of Antarctic time leak-the gate of time, which originates from some swirling gray-white smoke over Antarctica. At first scientists thought these were just ordinary sandstorms. However, the gray-white smoke did not change shape or move with time (Fig. 10).

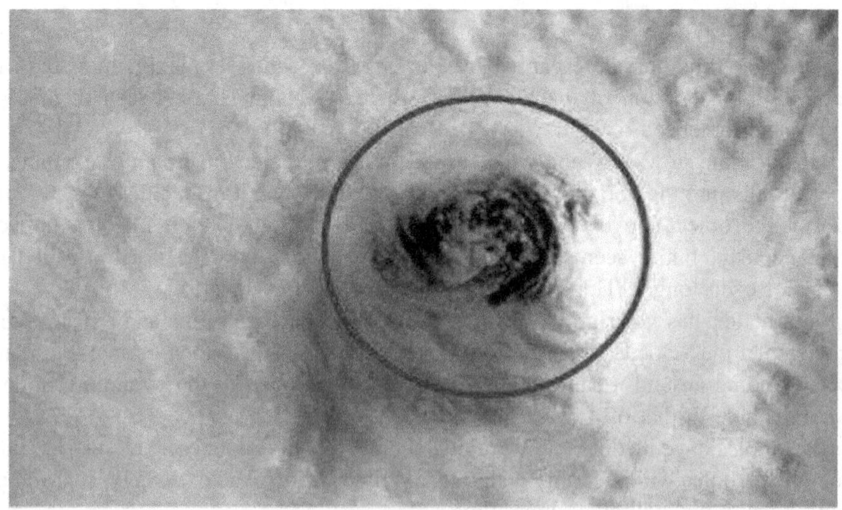

Fig. 10. Antarctic time loophole (Color figure online)

Then they launched a weather balloon equipped with instruments to measure wind speed, temperature and atmospheric humidity. Once launched, the balloon rose rapidly and disappeared soon. After a while, the researchers used a rope tied to the balloon to retrieve the balloon. However, what shocked them was that the balloon's timer showed that it was January 27th, 1965, exactly 30 years earlier!

After confirming that the instruments on the balloon were not damaged, the researchers conducted several more similar tests. But every time it shows that the time has gone backwards, and the timer shows the past time. This phenomenon is called "the gate of time".

At this point, I have to mention Animus in "Assassin's Creed" again. There is one thing that is most important in the whole game, but it is most easily ignored by the players/audience/readers. This thing makes it possible for us to go back to the past together with the descendants of ancient assassins. At the same time, it also makes the game not a costume drama, but a science fiction game. This thing is Animus [3] (Fig. 11).

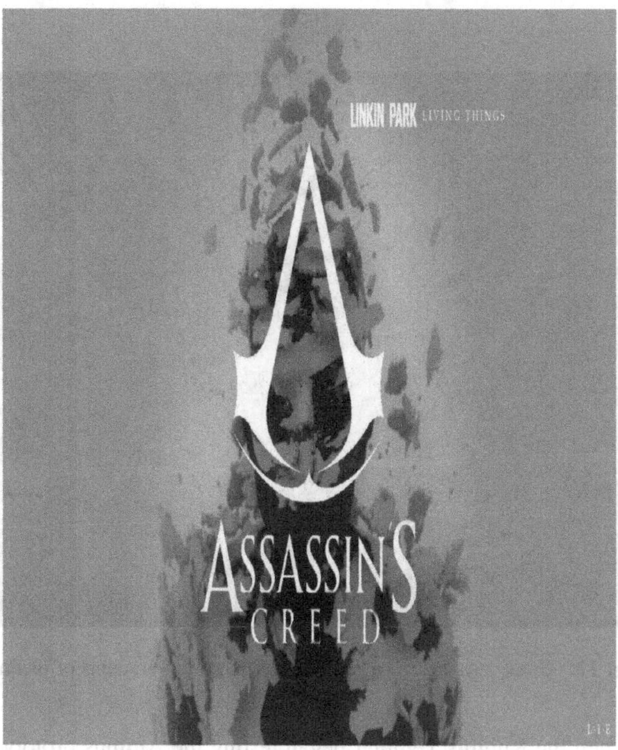

Fig. 11. Game "Assassin's Creed" poster

It is because of Animus that players are shocked by the fact that this is a science fiction play rather than a costume play when playing the first generation of "Assassin's Creed". Therefore, the game well integrates the suspense plot of the modern version with the action blockbuster of the ancient version. But also because Animus was assimilated with the game system itself from the first work of the series, it is easy to forget.

In the 1930s, the Knights Templar began to build some mysterious device in Norway under the cover of Germany's "Uranium Project" nuclear weapons program. Through the knowledge gained from Eden apples, this device is expected to realize the snooping on the memory of human ancestors. The main objective of the Knights Templar is to discover lost Eden fragments by reading the memories of the ancestors of captured assassins.

The device, called "Die Glcoke (an urban legend about Nazi time machines) was designed by Nikola Tesla and includes an anti-gravity system that can create a controllable wormhole through which to spy on the past of individuals sitting in the central chair of the device. Tesla combined his invention with the technology stolen by the Nazis from the Allies, and added knowledge from Eden Apple. The energy for startup came from the heavy water reactor. This machine is the prototype of Animus [7] (Fig. 12).

Fig. 12. Game "Assassin's Creed" Animus prototype concept picture

In 1943, when the Knights Templar began testing the Animus prototype on British assassin Eddie Gom, there was an accident. At the same time as this experiment, Eddie's grandson Maximo also (more subtle setting) entered Animus to experience his grandfather' memory, which led to time and space confusion, and the consciousness of the grandparents and grandchildren was switched to the other's body.

At that time, when I felt the series of works of "Assassin's Creed", I could feel that in the real world of the game, the protagonist entered the ancestral world after lying in Animus equipment. After doing numerous tasks in the ancestral world, I found that time had not passed for a long time. At that time, I was thinking about whether such an effect can be achieved in real life.

Perhaps people's perception of time has changed in their sleep or equipment.

Therefore, I hope that brain–machine interaction can make people's perception of time achieve that effect. For example, we normally sleep for 8 h, but after wearing brain–machine interaction equipment, our perception of time in our dreams is over a week, even a month, or even more. It was only eight hours after waking up. In this way, we can do more things in our dreams. For example, we can play a game with historical themes and put it in our dreams. People only need to sleep normally for one night and then can "experience" a period of history.

Assuming that this dream-like simulation game can really be realized as mentioned above, different individuals can even be brought online through the role of the Internet, that is, both A and B have brain–machine interaction devices, and can experience the same dream or game together through the Internet. This brings us to another concept, brain networking, which refers to a new type of computer core, that is, organic computer, which exchanges information in real time and collaboratively between the brains of multiple animals through brain interfaces.

When it comes to brain networking, here is the American TV series *Intelligence*. The protagonist Gabriel is an agent with special talents. His brain is implanted with a microchip comparable to a supercomputer, which can receive or control all electromagnetic spectrum within an effective distance. He became the first human being in the world to connect the Internet, Wifi signals, telephone communications and satellite data directly with his brain, thus obtaining the required information from the electronic grid all over the world in the shortest possible time. His brain alone can invade any data center in the world or obtain key intelligence, protecting the interests of the United States from the threat of the enemy (Fig. 13).

With the development of the times, these are no longer distant dreams. A research team in South Africa's university of the witwatersrand has made a major breakthrough in biomedical engineering. Researchers have designed a way to connect the human brain to the Internet in real time. It is called the "Brainternet project. Its essence is to transform the brain into an Internet of Things (IoT) node on the World Wide Web.

The project uses EEG signals collected by Emotiv EEG equipment connected to the user's head, and then transmits the signals to a low-cost Raspberry Pi computer, which then transmits the data to the application programming interface and displays the data on any open website that can view activities.

Adam Pantanowitz, lecturer at the University of the Witwatersrand Institute of Electronics and Information Engineering and project director, said, "Human brain networking is a frontier field of brain–machine interface systems, focusing on solving the deficiencies of human brain work and data processing. Brainternet can simplify people's understanding of their own brains and those of others, which can only be realized through continuous monitoring of brain activities and some simple interactions [6] (Fig. 14).

Fig. 13. American drama "Intelligence" poster

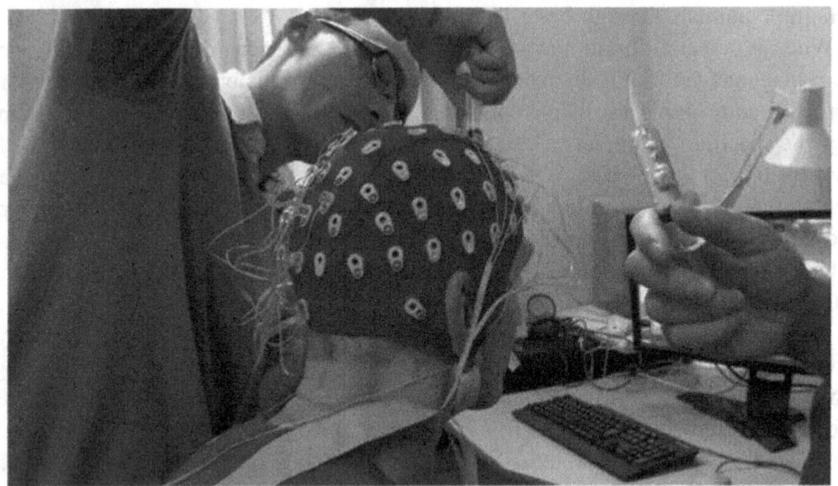

Fig. 14. Jinshan University Smart Internet Project, South Africa

The team's current goal is to create more interactive experiences between users and their brains, and some interactive ways have been built into the site, such as arm movements. Through further improvement, people will be able to classify electroencephalogram (EEG) through smartphone APP, thus providing data for machine learning algorithms. In the future, it may be possible for both parties to transmit information, i.e. input information into the brain or output information from the brain to the computer.

If these technologies can be achieved in the future, I think they can be combined and put into the game, that is, people can enter the game world by wearing brain–machine interaction equipment before going to bed, and can connect with other players in their sleep. The game time has passed for many days, but only for a few hours after waking up. I believe this can solve two major problems.

1. The problem of the number of players online is solved, and more players will be online at night, thus greatly increasing the interactivity and playability of the game.
2. It has solved many people's views on wasting time in games. Everyone can experience the entertainment and relaxation brought by the game in his sleep. Wake up will not delay anything.

I believe that if this device can be realized in the future, it will also be a major breakthrough and innovation for the game industry.

References

1. Zhou, S., Wang, W.: Human-Computer Interaction Technology, Tsinghua University Press (2016)
2. Shihai, D., Wang, H.: Human-Computer Interaction. Peking University Press (2004)
3. Tai, D.: What is Animus that makes Assassin's Creed from a costume drama into a science fiction drama? (2019). http://www.vgtime.com/topic/746336.jhtml
4. LaBerge, S., Rheingold, H.: Exploring the World of Lucid Dreaming. Ballantine, New York (1991)
5. Baidu: Lucid Dreaming (2019). https://wapbaike.baidu.com/item/%E6%B8%85%E9%86%92%E6%A2%A6/1208702?fr=aladdin&ms=1&rid=9837943143197361466
6. News: How far is "brain networking" from us? (2019). https://news.sina.cn/2017-12-22/detail-ifypwzxq5177668.d.html
7. What is the so-called game "playability"? What good games have you missed? (2019). https://baijiahao.baidu.com/s?id=1563012934129073&wfr=spider&for=pc&isFailFlag=1
8. Schell, J.: The Art of Game Design: A Book of Lenses. CRC Press, Boca Raton (2015)
9. Cairns, P., Cox, A.L.: Research Methods for Human-Computer Interaction. Cambridge University Press, Cambridge (2008)
10. Elias, G.S., Garfield, R., Gutschera, K.R.: Characteristics of Games. MIT Press, Cambridge (2012)
11. Salen, K., Zimmerman, E.: Rules of Play: Game Design Fundamentals. MIT Press, Cambridge (2004)
12. Järvinen, A.: Games Without Frontiers: Methods for Game Studies and Design. VDM, Verlag Dr. Müller, Saarbrücken (2009)

Research on Multiple Tactile Induction of Human-Computer Interaction

Yang-shuo Zheng(✉) and Shi-chao He

Wuhan University of Technology, Wuhan, China
zhengyangshuo@163.com, 2523308137@qq.com

Abstract. Objective Starting from the social scene under the background of mobile Internet, this paper explores a new information input and output scheme by connecting the human-computer interaction accompanied by the development of science and technology with the emotional needs of users. **Methods** Firstly, qualitative analysis and quantitative verification were conducted on the problems encountered by users using existing chat tools through user interviews and questionnaires. Then the interface design and interaction design were carried out based on ViP product design principles. Finally, interview, questionnaire and eye movement test were used to further improve the design scheme. **Conclusion** With the further development and improvement of science and technology, more diversified, efficient and interesting ways of information interaction will become possible.

Keywords: Human-computer interaction · Sentient input method · 3D-Touch

1 Introduction

With the development of science and technology, human-computer interaction design has already affected every aspect of people's daily life. Bill Gates, founder of Microsoft, believes that natural interface is a direct and natural interaction between human and computer. In the future, this new form may satisfy users' diversified information exchange, efficient and accurate information transmission and functional requirements, among which the multidimensional nature of the natural user interface is more prominent [1]. In today's mobile Internet context, social networking is still people's rigid demand. Interaction design is the design of human behavior. In the process of information interaction feedback design, interaction design focuses on providing a good user experience rather than only realizing a certain function [2]. "Bullet message" app (Fig. 1) compared with the previous mobile Internet social products, through improvement on previous product information architecture level, the more efficient way of interaction, meet different scenarios of information expression and interaction function: when users need to communicate with people, users don't need to enter each chat window can communicate, directly in the message list page to view messages or input. Users in meetings and other occasions is not convenient to listen to voice; inaudible speech in noisy environment or the received voice message has an accent which makes it difficult to hear clearly, the product will convert the input voice message into text and output it to the user.

A. Marcus and W. Wang (Eds.): HCII 2019, LNCS 11584, pp. 228–238, 2019.
https://doi.org/10.1007/978-3-030-23541-3_17

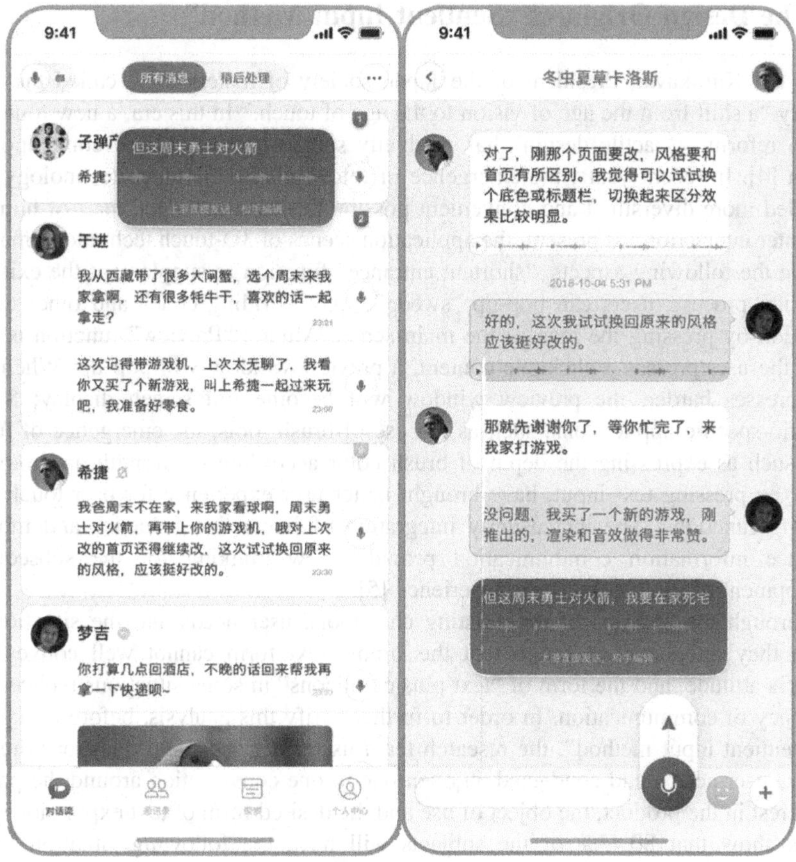

Fig. 1. "Bullet message" software interface status diagram

"Bullet message" not only improves users' chatting experience, but also improves the efficiency of communication through the analysis of users' demands in certain scenarios and the improvement of existing product structure layer in the market. Then, from the perspective of multi-dimensional perceptive design, can users have social products more suitable for the user groups in the information age in the context of mobile Internet? When users are chatting, does the designer have the space to design such an interface to increase the dimension of information in the process of input and output? Just as what Negroponte said: "there are considerable restrictions on the contact between perception and substance" [3]. Only when you design an input device that can provide tactile response can you elevate the tactile sense to a higher level [3], so as to better meet the social needs of users in the information age.

2 The Design Origin of "Sentient Input Method"

Masayuki Kurokawa, President of the Japan society of materiology, called the 21st century "a shift from the age of vision to the age of touch." In this era, a new round of design reform – "tactile design" has gradually spread to all fields of contemporary design [4]. In recent years, the emergence of touch related 3D-touch technology has provided more diversified and convenient possibilities for the "input" part of human-computer interaction. At present, the application scenes of 3D-touch technology mainly include the following aspects: "shortcut entrance" function to supplement the existing operation process, users can pop-up "sweep", "pay", "riding code" and other quick operation by pressing the icon of the main screen Alipay; "Preview" function is that when the user presses a clickable content, a preview window will pop up. When the user presses harder, the preview window will become full screen display; Some scenario-specific applications, such as the use of brush tools, the emergence of functions such as expressing the depth of brush color according to strength and moving cursor by pressing text input, have brought better user experience for user touch and pressing functions. The increasingly integration of interactive behavior and mobile interface information communication provides new thinking for the subsequent development of mobile interface experience [5].

Through the analysis of the existing chat tools, user needs and the situation in which they interact, it is found that the simple text form cannot well convey the sender's attitude, and the form of "text plus emoticons" in some situations reduces the efficiency of communication. In order to further verify this analysis, before designing the "sentient input method", the research team used interviews and questionnaires to analyze user needs, and conducted an open one-to-one conversation around the points of interest in the product, the object of use and the desired form of text expression. The results show that 80.43% of the subjects will have the following situation when chatting on social software: when they want to express a certain emotion, but only using words to express it, the other party cannot identify with them; At the same time, 67.39% of the subjects had experienced misunderstanding due to their different understanding of words (such as different sentences and literal differences). Therefore, it is very necessary to conduct research on input interaction prototype that is more related to user emotion, and the advent of 3d-touch technology brings us a new exploration dimension.

3 The Prototype Design of "Sentient Input Method"

3.1 Information Input Mode Based on Pressure Sensing

In the prototype design stage of "sentient input method", the product situation, interaction mode and user demand in the future were reflected and designed [6]. It is using 3D-Touch technology to measure real-time physical quantities such as pressure and time interval of information input by pressing the screen, combining with semantic recognition, users'real-time emotional information is obtained, which is appended to the original text information in the form of color and font, thus solving the semantic misunderstanding caused by the single expression of information in text communication, making the interaction way more diversified and communication more smoothly.

The input interface of “sentient input method” still imitates the default input method of ios system. The handwritten keyboard remains unchanged, the main changes are the English keyboard with 26 keys and the pinyin keyboard with 9 keys. To ensure that users can easily make personalized settings, both keyboards set the voice input key and the space key to the same key, and distinguish the two functions by pressing the length of time. Place the character setting key in the original voice key position. In order to reflect the user’s keystroke pressure in real time, the input method sets a pressure display bar on the right side of the selection bar. The pressure bar can display the user’s keystroke pressure in real time during the user input process. In addition, in the input process, a display preview box is set in the upper right corner outside the input bar to provide a preview of the output effect.

In the process of information input by users, the pressure display bar of “sentient input method” can display the pressure of users’ buttons in real time, and provide instant feedback through the status of the pressure display bar. In this case, three pressure bars of different shapes and colors were designed, and eye movement technology was used to test three college students, and the most suitable scheme was selected according to the results. All subjects used the same computer to test on the eye movement cloud test platform, and the eye tribe was used as The Eye tracker. Each subject was asked to browse three WeChat chat interfaces using the new input method (Fig. 2).

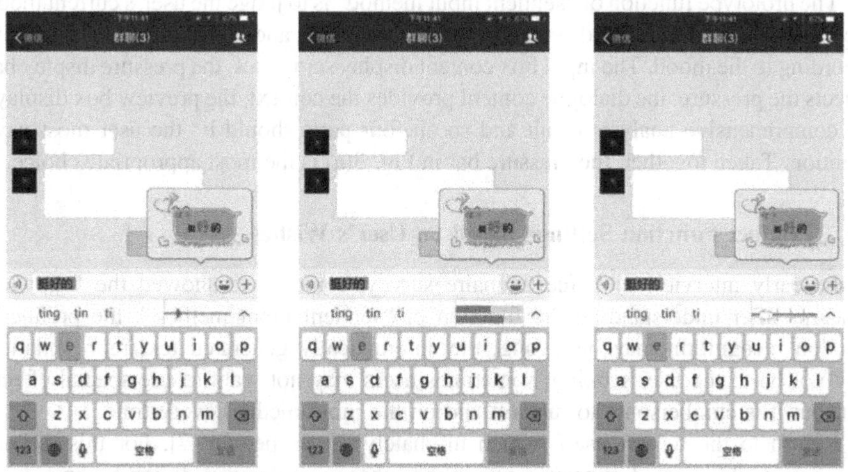

Fig. 2. Interface state of eye movement test

All images are identical except for the pressure bar on the right side of the input method. After learning the function of the new input method, the subjects imagined that they were using the product to chat, then naturally scanned each picture. No time limit was set, after browsing, subjects were presented with an equal size white screen for interference, and then the next picture was presented. The heat map of the three pictures tested is shown in Fig. 3:

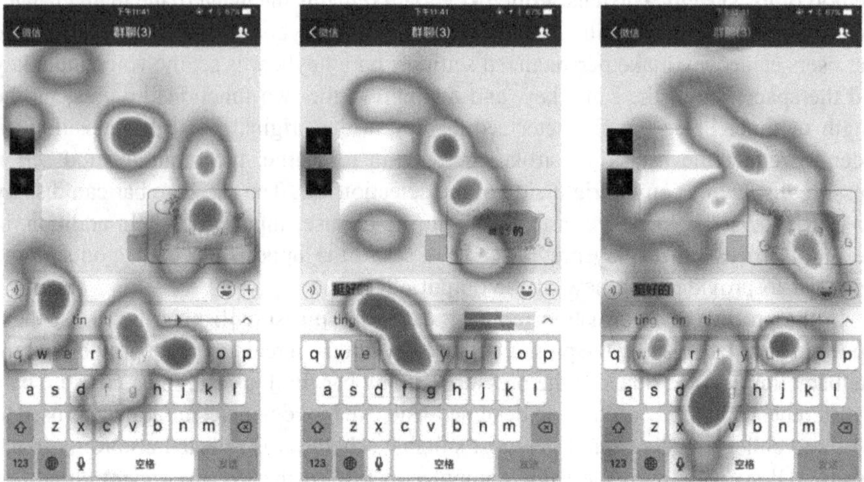

Fig. 3. Hotspots of eye movement test

The prototype function of "sentient input method" is to judge the user's current mood according to the pressure and semantics of the input text, and adjust the style of the text according to the mood. The input box content display semantics, the pressure display bar reflects the pressure, the dialogue content provides the context, the preview box displays the comprehensive analysis result and so on four parts should be the user most pays attention. Taken together, the pressure bar in Fig. 3(a) is the most appropriate choice.

3.2 Product Function Settings Based on User's Wishes

In the early interview and questionnaire survey, some users showed the following concerns after understanding the function of "sentient input method": the product's emotion recognition may be wrong; the automatically generated text representation may not be to the user's liking; sometimes users may not want to use special effects text, but it is cumbersome to turn off and on the input method every time.

Return to the design itself, which ultimately serves people [7]. For this reason, designers made targeted improvements in the subsequent iterative design scheme: first, users can customize colors and fonts to express different emotions according to their personal preferences, they can also download their favorite bubbles and decorations from the Internet. Second, users can select the text without special effects when entering each sentence, without needing to turn off the input method in the system settings. Third, the input method will provide a variety of types of text with special effects based on the analysis results of each sentence, and users can choose the one that most conforms to their emotions. Fourth, add the current pressure display bar in the user interface, users can be informed of their current input pressure, or choose to hide the pressure bar. Through the independent setting based on the user's will, users' needs in more situations can be met more intelligently and humanely.

3.3 Information Communication Standards Based on User Experience

1. **Default font setting.** In the color scheme of "sentient input method", the color expression of five emotions is determined, which is the primary goal of the product presentation layer. On the basis of questionnaire survey and user interview, the five colors of yellow, red, blue, grey and black are determined as the basis of color scheme. The determination process was as follows: 46 users were asked to evaluate which of the following colors could better convey their emotions (multiple choices) by questionnaire, and the results were shown in Table 1.

Table 1. Color preference of subjects in different emotions

	红色	黄色	蓝色	绿色	紫色	灰色	黑色
快乐	10	18	4	11	3	1	2
平静	0	3	25	14	5	2	5
愤怒	27	4	2	1	3	2	5
悲哀	0	2	7	2	6	24	5
恐惧	7	2	1	1	6	7	22

The test results in Table 1 clearly show that the subjects have different color preferences in different emotional states: yellow when happy (18 people), blue when calm (24 people), red when angry (27 people), gray when sad (24 people), and black when fearful (22 people). Therefore, this product also takes the user experience into full consideration when making improvements and satisfies the wishes of most users in the default color setting. At the same time, because the application needs to cooperate with WeChat, SMS, web page and other communication media to use, so according to the corresponding software color scheme, choose the auxiliary color system, color scheme design. Finally, the following color scheme was obtained: 1. Emotional color scheme,each mood color has 4 colors from light to deep, which can be applied to each interface according to the needs of the situation. 2. System color scheme, choose simple compatibility better color, can better with a variety of communication applications, do not advocate special changes.

2. **Control standards for various design elements of the presentation layer.** Control of important elements: logo, buttons, bars, etc. Considering the basic idea of color ring, circle is adopted as the motif of relevant color selection and logo design (Fig. 4).

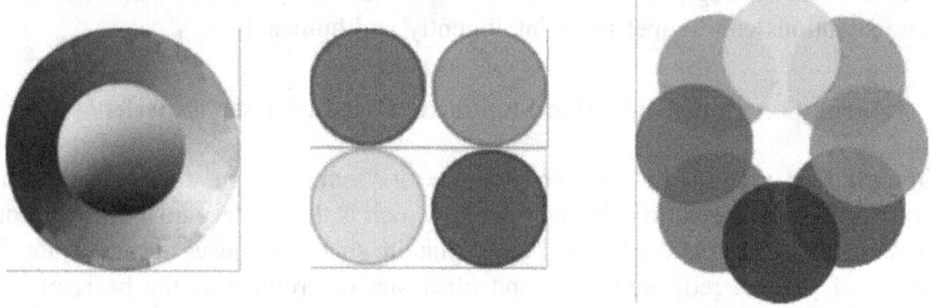

Fig. 4. Important elements

Control of font elements: it is mainly divided into three categories of positive emotion, neutral emotion and negative emotion according to different emotions. Among them, the positive emotions were selected in cute fonts, such as founder meow. Neutral mood is used wireless foot font, such as Microsoft yahei. Negative emotions were expressed in more angular fonts, such as hanyi wheat (Fig. 5).

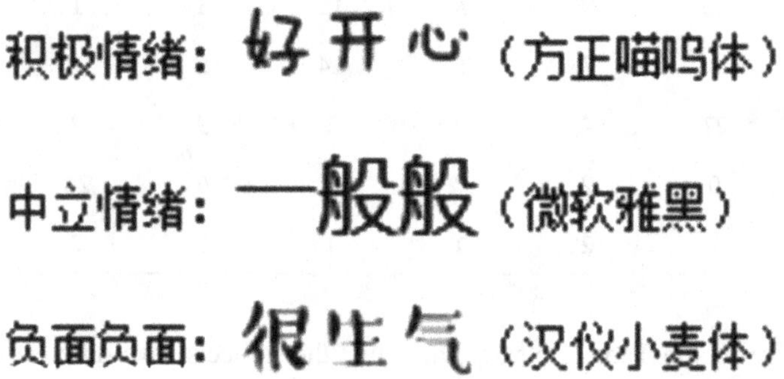

积极情绪：好开心（方正喵呜体）

中立情绪：一般般（微软雅黑）

负面负面：很生气（汉仪小麦体）

Fig. 5. Font elements

Control of emoticons: according to the questionnaire survey and interview, the main target users of this app are women. The whole expression element chooses cute style, imitation or animal image, and uses different colors to characterize and strengthen (Fig. 6).

Fig. 6. Emoticons

4 Presentation of Design Scheme of "Sentient Input Method"

4.1 A Beginner's Guide to the "Sentient Input Method"

"Sentient input method" first presents three input method introduction screens after installation. The first two pictures show the input method used in "happy" and "sad" respectively. The third screen presents the name, logo and purpose of the input method, and sets the "start using" button to guide users to start using the input method. Users can choose one of the five input methods (pinyin jiugongge, pinyin all-key, handwriting, stroke, wubi input) according to their personal input habits in the interface. After the user selects the keyboard, before the first use, the input method provides a concise input tutorial. The tutorial is divided into three pages: guide the user to input, click the preview box to send, and start using the input method. The tutorial highlights interaction and uses hand icons to guide users to click on keyboards (Fig. 7).

Fig. 7. Beginner's guide

4.2 Input Setting of "Sentient Input Method"

The "sentient input method" information architecture is shown in Fig. 8. The input interface contains the following interactive elements: when the user presses the key, the corresponding key turns gray, and the cursor of the pressure display bar moves. The distance of movement corresponds to the pressure on the keyboard. Click the word in the word selection box, the word becomes gray; The text in the input box is non-special effect text, and the preview box in the upper right corner outside the input method synchronously presents these texts according to the recognized emotion. Click the preview box to send special effect text, and click send to send no special effect text (Fig. 9).

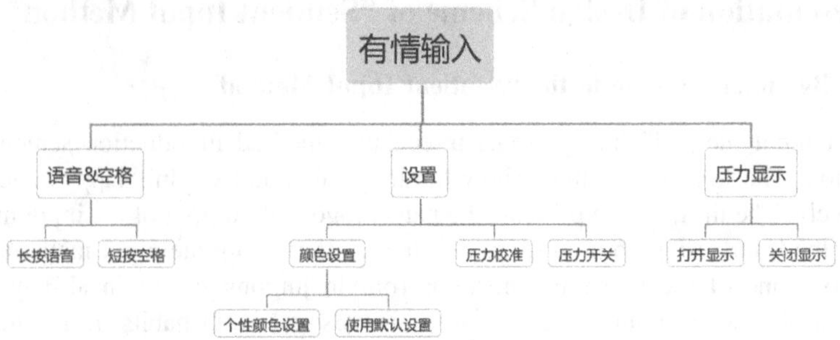

Fig. 8. The sentient input method information architecture

4.3 The Function Setting of "Sentient Input Method"

The overall interface of the setting interface is a classic vertical arrangement of buttons, with one button per line leading to a specific setting interface (Fig. 10). The prototype realizes the personalized setting interface of emotion corresponding to color, and the interface for calibrating the reference pressure at input according to the different key pressure of different users (Fig. 11).

Fig. 9. Input interface

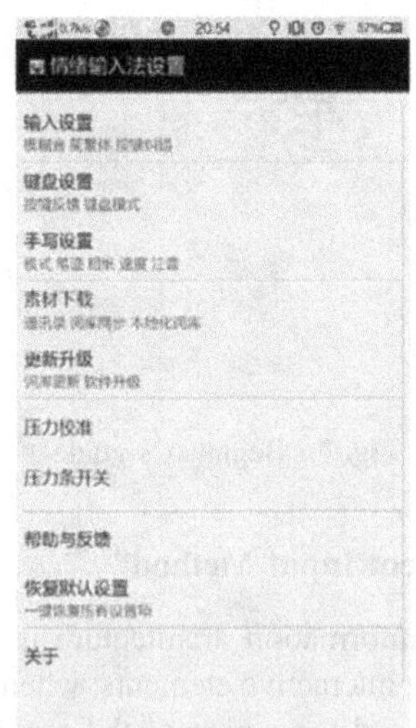

Fig. 10. Setup interface

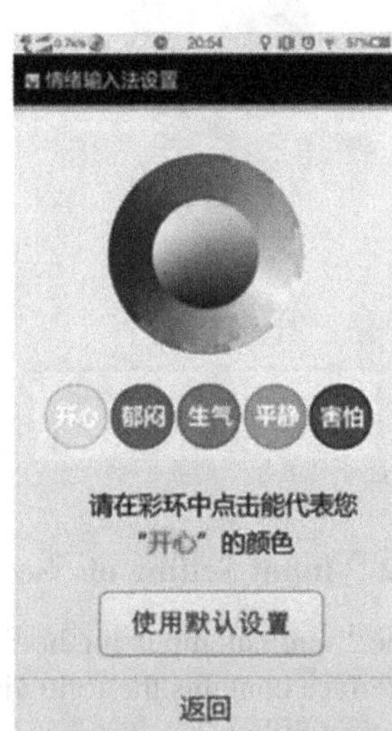

Fig. 11. Setup interface

5 Evaluation of the Four-Dimensional Design of "Sentient Input Method"

After "sentient input method" basic determine the final prototype, this study by using four dimensions of information interaction design evaluation system model [8] on the subjective evaluation experiment, for the environment characteristics, user behavior psychology, technical properties, analyzes variable factors interact and self-evaluation, and divided into four angles. This design scheme in the dimension of "environment": at present, there are a lot of input software, and people have been used to express emotions with emoticons in online communication. This trend of network social communication is becoming increasingly fierce, and simple text expression may not open the market in a short time. In "people" dimension: The input interface of "sentient input method" imitates the default input method of IOS system, and the modification on this basis basically does not change the user's original input behavior mode. In the aspect of user's psychology, it reduces the situation that users worry about the other party's incompatibility and misunderstanding when they only use words to express themselves. In the dimension of "product": based on the principle of 3D-touch, this design recognizes emotions by sensing the pressure of typing and presents them in the form of text. To some extent, it saves unnecessary time cost and makes communication more effective and convenient. In the dimension of "technology": users worry that the emotion recognition is not accurate, so it is not as convenient as sending pictures directly; In the form of text presentation, everyone's views and preferences are inconsistent, and it is currently impossible to set a complete presentation library based on big data.

In general, the prototype design of "sentient input method" has better design presentation and user evaluation in two dimensions of "product" and "person", and there is still room for continuous optimization in two dimensions of "environment" and "technology". Especially in the easy-to-use value, user value, communication value and other design point performance is more prominent, but in the value of popular science, aesthetic value should also be better to identify and match the user's emotions, using more in line with the user's expected text output form.

6 Conclusion

There was once a saying to describe human-computer interaction: the first generation relies on poke, the second on touch, the third on talk, and the fourth on wave [9]. From the way of poking and pressing to the way of realizing human-computer interaction through brainwave in the future, we can clearly see the leapfrog progress of human-computer interaction brought by the development of future technology. In fact, technology may be involved in the emergence, development and maturity of an interactive mode. The advantage of "sentient input method" lies in that it can endow users with the original written expression of the emotion they want to express, and make the communication between the two parties more close to the face-to-face communication, so as to reduce the misunderstanding caused by individual's different ways of understanding a single text information in the form of text expression. Compared with the original way of expressing emotions through text and emoticons, it greatly simplifies the user's operation process. The limitation is that everyone's opinions and preferences are inconsistent. At present, it is impossible to set up a complete repository based on big data.

In the future, with the further development and improvement of big data technology and 3D-touch technology, people are expected to go beyond the single information input mode represented by text, and more diversified, efficient and interesting information interaction mode will become possible.

Acknowledgements. This paper was supported by the research project from Chinese National social science fund "4D evaluation model research and application of information interaction design (16CG170)".

References

1. Wang, W.-C.: A brief analysis of the multidimensional nature of natural user interface design. In: Chen. Z.-G., Jiang, F. (eds.) Integration and Innovation–Teaching Research and New Business Forms of Information Interaction Design. Shanghai University Press, Shanghai (2016)
2. Liu, Y.-L., Ma, Y.-Y., Xu, B.-C., Zhi, J.-Y.: Information feedback interaction design based on process experience. Packaging Eng. **2018**(7), 95–101 (2018)
3. Bill Moggridge. Key design report – key design report that changes the past and influences the future. Citic press (2011)
4. Zhou, L.: On tactile emotionalized design in brand visual image – a case study of yuanyanzai's design. Brand Creativity **2009**(1), 31–33 (2009)
5. Ge, W., Xin, X.-Y.: Research on the design of information communication in mobile interface. Packaging Eng. **2017**(3), 81–86 (2017)
6. School of industrial design and engineering, delft university of technology. Design methods and strategies: delft design guide, p. 31. Huazhong University of Science and Technology Press (2016)
7. Sun, L., Wu, J.-T.: Research on overall user experience design based on time dimension. Packaging Eng. **2014**(1), 32–35 (2014)
8. Sun, H., Zheng, Y.-S., Wu, Y.-Q.: The design model and application of the guide system based on "human, technology and object". Packaging Eng. **2018**(8), 108–112 (2018)
9. Gao, F.: You should be obedient – human-computer interaction in the Internet era of all things. In: Chen, Z., Jiang, F. (eds.) Integration Innovation – Teaching Research and New Business Forms of Information Interaction Design. Shanghai University Press, Shanghai (2016)

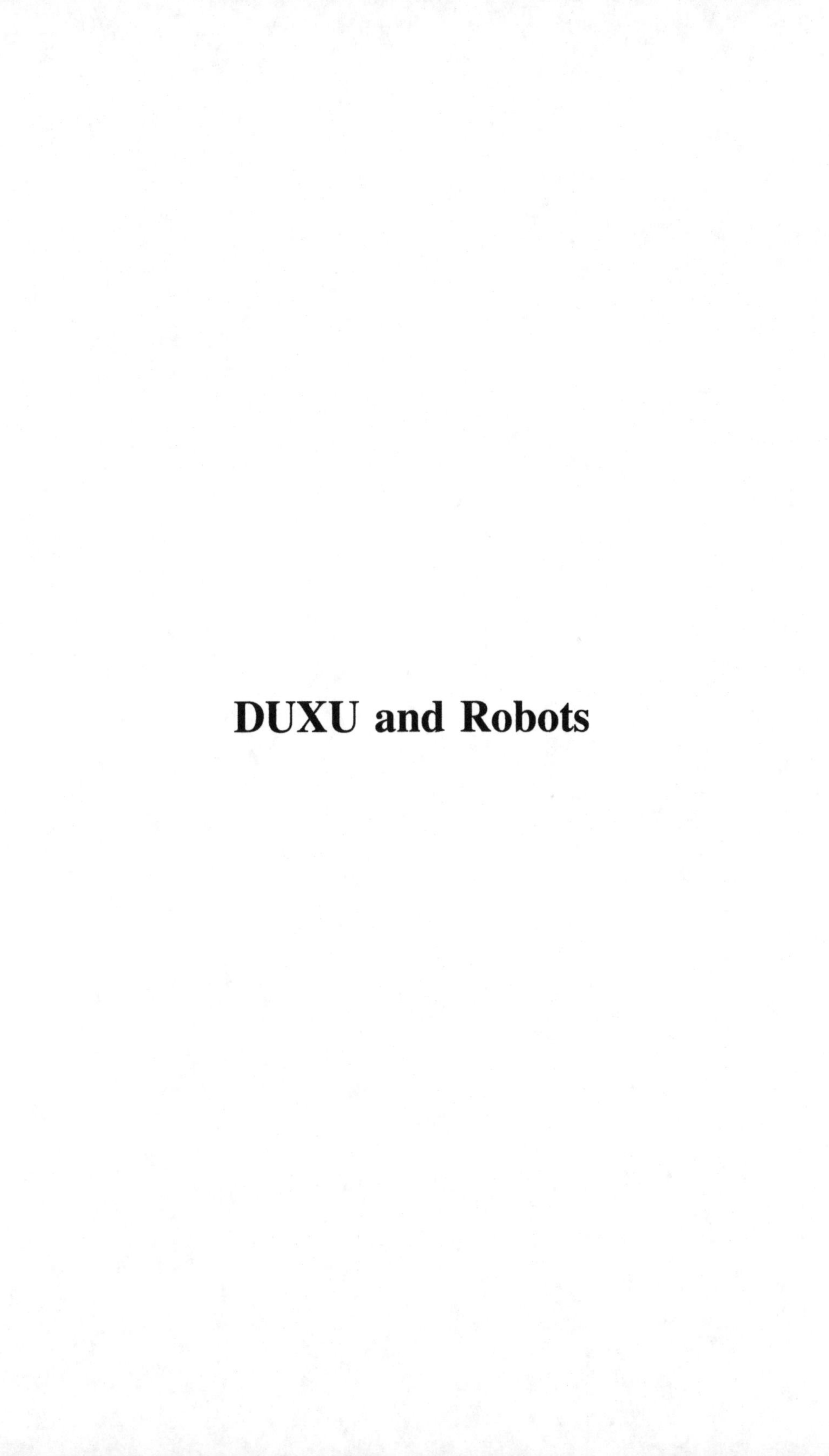

DUXU and Robots

Study on the Morphological Sensitivity of Children's Companion Robot

Xiang-yu Liu, Mei-yu Zhou(✉), Chao Li, Xian-xian Ma, and Zheng-yu Wang

School of Art Design and media, East China University of Science and Technology, Shanghai 200237, China
Zhoutc_2003@163.com

Abstract. This paper takes the children's companion robot as the research object, uses the basic principles of Kansei Engineering and the quantitative I class, explores the correspondence between the consumer's emotional image and the child's companion robot's morphological design elements, in order to facilitate the design process of children's companion robot. This paper constructs the image space of children's companion robot based on user's perceptual appeal and establishes a relationship model between design perceptual image and children's companion robot morphological design elements. A model test of the correspondence between imagery and morphological design elements.

Keywords: Children's companion robot · Morphological elements · Clustering algorithm · Quantified class I

1 Introduction

In recent years, children's companion robots have been used as a service robot. Since 2016, the industry has developed rapidly. Some traditional toy companies and technology companies have successively launched children's companion robots with different functions. In the process of social and economic transformation and development, people's consumption concepts are constantly changing. Traditional toy companies no longer only pay attention to the function and quality of products, pay more attention to whether the products are cared for by human beings, can touch the hearts of consumers, and cause emotional resonance. Therefore, the same is true for the children's companion robot industry. From the change of consumer demand, it can be seen that the core of product innovation design is also changing, and the influence of the perceptual elements of user demand on the design of the robot is gradually increasing. Therefore, it is one of the main development trends of modern product design to explore the products suitable for perceptual appeals driven by the perceptual needs of consumers.

The target users of children's companion robots are children from 0 to 12 years old, and their parents pay attention to investing in children's education. Therefore, companion robots are mainly used to accompany children to learn. However, most children's companion robots design is based on the functional design concept, and the emotional design of the children's companion robots form has not been fully

A. Marcus and W. Wang (Eds.): HCII 2019, LNCS 11584, pp. 241–252, 2019.
https://doi.org/10.1007/978-3-030-23541-3_18

developed. Based on the theory of Kansei engineering, this paper takes the morphological image as the research object and uses the quantitative method to explore the correlation between the emotional image and the consumers' morphological design elements and to design the design for subsequent research and product development. To guide the reference.

2 Morphological Image of Children Companion Robots

In the development process of children accompanying robots, the intelligent technology of products has made great progress, the product design concept integrating emotional interaction has always been valued by people. Made in China 2025 emphasizes [1] that the expression of the emotional significance of industrial design should be strengthened while product functional innovation is realized. Children's psychology is relatively simple, and they will have an instinctive curiosity and desire for experience for new things. Good design guidance is conducive to the healthy development of children's physiology and psychology, and children can acquire better learning experience [2]. Therefore, through the analysis of the modeling, color, material and other elements of the accompanied robot for children, the emotional image of children is closely combined with the product form [3], so that it has morphological characteristics in line with the aesthetic and emotional needs of children and can bring them rich memories in childhood.

2.1 Determination of Representative Samples

Please This study collects samples through shopping sites, magazines, etc. Such as commercial stores, JD, Taobao, and intelligent robot companies. After the preliminary selection of the research team, 60 product samples were collected. These product samples are then further screened according to the following principles:

1. Consider the rules of the design elements of children's companion robots. Therefore, the selected children's companion robot samples need to cover all the morphological elements and pay attention to the distribution and frequency of each morphological design elements, and the samples need to be typical.
2. Consider the actual situation of the child's companion robot form.
3. Consider the comprehensive evaluation of the research team.

Finally, 21 children's companion robots were selected as samples for research. 16 of them were selected as experimental samples to construct the relationship between sensory image and morphological design elements of children's companion robots, and the remaining 5 models were used as backup samples for test relationships.

Table 1. Representative Samples

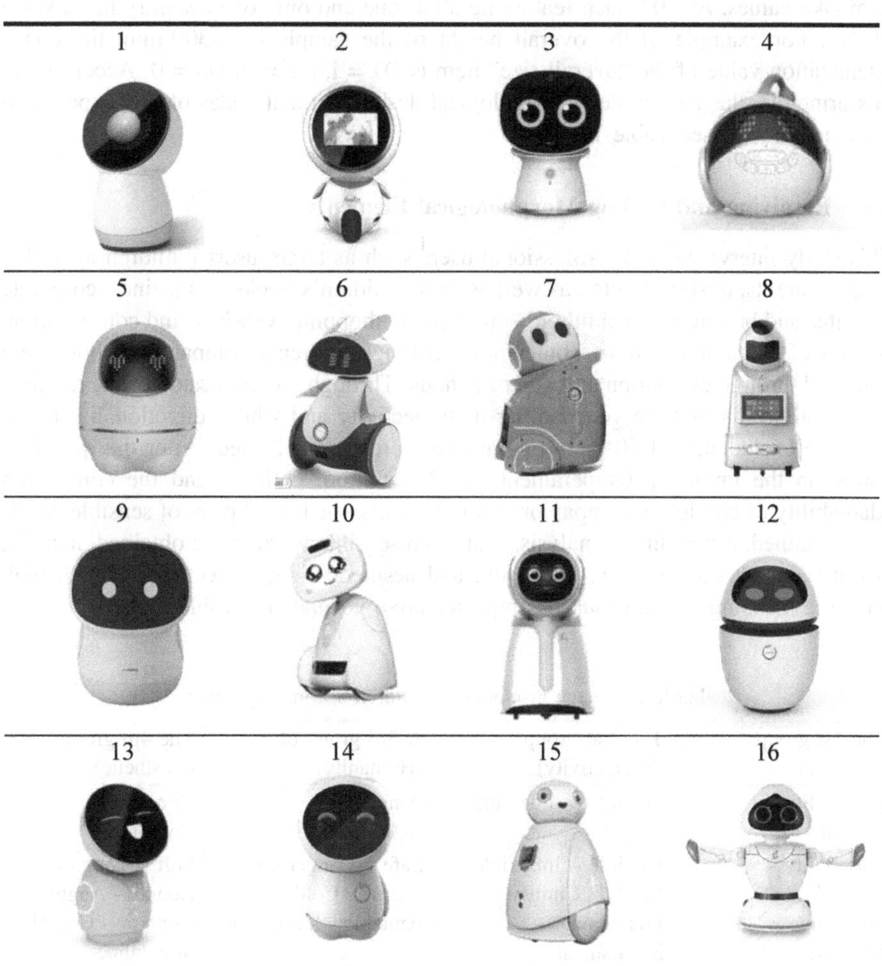

2.2 Resolving and Coding Morphological Elements

From the analysis of the components of the child companion robot, 6 elements that have a great influence on the form of the child companion robot are selected from the 9 morphological elements: body contour, display screen, head shape, size, color, and activity mode. Each featured item is further classified and a total of 20 categories are obtained.

According to the principle of the quantified class I, before performing the multiple regression analysis, it is necessary to further quantize the morphological element code values of the representative elements into a matrix containing only "0" and "1". The specific method is: for each category in each feature item, if a sample form factor item has this category, the category takes a value of "1", and other categories in the feature item take values. As "0", each feature item has one and only one category has a value of "1". For example, if the overall height of the sample is 0–300 mm, the coded quantization value of the "overall size" item is D1 = l, D2 = 0, D3 = 0. According to this principle, the 16 samples morphological design element codes of this experiment were quantified. (see Table 1).

2.3 Resolving and Coding Morphological Elements

This study interviews with professional users such as target users (children aged 3–7 years), parents, designers, etc., as well as from children's books, magazines, corporate websites and brochures on children's products, E-shopping websites, and consumption. A total of 108 emotional vocabularies describing children's companion robots were collected through evaluation and other methods. Through the discussion of the research group, 60 words that are very similar in subjectivity and whose directionality is not clear are excluded, and 60 pairs of sensible words are collected. After the questionnaires on the linguistic temperament of 22 preschool children and the companion adaptability of children's companion robot products, the top 20 pairs of sensible words were obtained. After cluster analysis, four main sensible words were obtained, namely: novelty and interaction. Sex, humanity, and aesthetics. And select words with high semantic meaning as the group has representative vocabulary (Table 2).

Table 2. Image grouping of children accompany robot

The 1st group (Novelty)	The 2nd group (Interactivity)	A 3rd group of (Humanity)	The 4th group (Aesthetic)
Personality – general	Flexible – Inflexible	Amiable - Indifferent	Concise – Complex
Personality – General Innovative - Imitative Interesting – Boring High-end – Low-end Technological – Traditional	Flexible – Inflexible Lively - Clumsy Educational – Mechanical Easy to use - Difficult to use	Safe – Dangerous Warm – Cold Amiable - Indifferent	Soft – Tough Round – Angular Concise – Complex Streamline – Geometric Fashionable – Old Textured - Not textured Light - Steady Lovely – Ugly

3 Questionnaire Survey and Data Processing

3.1 Semantic Differences Questionnaire

Sixteen children's companion robot samples and four pairs of representative vocabulary words have been selected by cluster analysis. This questionnaire survey uses the seventh-order semantic difference method questionnaire. After carefully observing the sample of the child companion robot given by the test subject, the tester gives a corresponding evaluation value for each pair of perceptual vocabulary according to his subjective feeling. Since the child companion robot of this study is a highly interactive product, the sample picture is provided in addition to the main view, including a side view and a top view, with the necessary text description.

3.2 Selection of Respondents

The questionnaires mainly include the following categories: 1. Parents (purchasing decision makers), children aged 2.3 to 7 years old. Because of the insufficient expression ability of children in this age group, the experimental methods mainly perform an emotional evaluation through vivid description and inductive questions. Only for reference. 3. Professional designers, these people have professional insights on products, they have a deeper understanding of the form of children's companion robots, and have a more professional evaluation. In this questionnaire survey, a total of 90 questionnaires were distributed and 82 were collected. After eliminating the invalid questionnaires with incomplete answers, 77 valid questionnaires were obtained.

3.3 Analysis of the Results of the Perceptual Evaluation

(1) Perceptual evaluation mean
All the valid questionnaires were input into the SPSS statistical software, and the average scores of each pair of sensory sinks were calculated. The results are shown in Table 3 below.

Table 3. Average score of perceptual words

Sample number	Personality – general	Amiable – indifferent	Flexible – inflexible	Concise – complex
1	−0.73	0.82	0.46	0.78
2	0.98	1.12	1.26	−0.76
3	0.66	−0.86	0.46	0.32
4	1.23	0.92	0.26	1.14
5	−0.13	−0.12	−0.68	1.56
6	1.78	1.87	1.12	0.67
7	0.89	0.24	0.12	0.86
8	−0.43	−1.02	−0.89	−0.65
9	−0.22	1.14	−0.57	1.98
10	0.92	−0.12	1.04	0.12
11	−0.32	0.24	0.63	−0.68
12	0.46	0.10	0.22	0.71
13	0.27	0.43	0.86	0.81
14	−0.08	0.23	1.01	−0.11
15	0.34	1.04	−0.82	0.64
16	0.73	0.64	1.06	0.23

4 Construction and Analysis of the Correlation Between Perceptual Image and Morphological Design Elements

4.1 Construction of Correlation Between Perceptual Image and Morphological Design Elements

Codes in this paper, we extracted from design elements and then get a quantitative further quantitative matrix, through a representative sample and semantic vocabulary between perceptual evaluation questionnaire data using SPSS software to calculate the average, each score and form design elements of perceptual image coded values on the basis of the theory of quantification 1 class, enter the multivariate linear regression analysis in SPSS. Among them, the independent variables in the SPSS software is the robot on section sums up the children with the sample quantization matrix form design elements, and the dependent variable is affected by the tester to evaluate each emotional vocabulary scoring average, eventually can be concluded that the children with robot under the perceptual words form design elements of the category scores, the scope of the project, etc., Table 4 is "Personality–Personality" quantification I class analysis results.

Table 4. Results of quantitative class I analysis of perceptual images

	Personality – general	Amiable – Indifferent	Flexible – Inflexible	Concise – Complex
Constant term	0.397	0.417	0.361	0.476
Goodness of fit	0.986	0.838	0.790	0.900
Multiple correlation coefficient	0.993	0.915	0.889	0.947

Generally speaking, when the goodness of fit value is greater than 0.7, the reliability of quantitative I class analysis results can be adopted. Table 5 shows that the goodness of fit value of four pairs of perceptual words is greater than 0.8, indicating that the quantitative I class analysis results have high reliability.

4.2 Construction of Correlation Between Perceptual Image and Morphological Design Elements

1. Category analysis

   The size of the category score represents the degree of correlation between the design category and the semantic meaning of each image. The higher the category score, the closer to the positive sensory image, the lower the score is closer to the negative sensory image. As above, "Personality-Personality", the higher the score, the more the category can express the "Personality" of the emotional image, and the lower the negative score, the more the category shows the opposite "popular" "This emotional image. The values of the categories relative to the vocabulary are listed in Fig. 2.

Table 5. Inductive vocabulary intention table (user rating)

	Personality - general	Amiable - Indifferent	Flexible - Inflexible	Concise - Complex
A1 trapezoid	−0.01	−0.259	−0.411	−0.272
A2 inverted trapezoid	−0.734	0.587	0.49	1.09
A3 round	1.29	0.621	0.219	−0.352
A4 bionic shape	0.229	−0.091	0.281	−0.275
B1 and the eye screen	−0.175	0.982	0.355	0.71
B2 independent display	−0.822	−1.595	−0.805	−0.625
B3 no display	0.965	−0.768	−0.105	−0.95
C1 ball type, elliptical ball type	−0.461	1.139	−0.525	1.317
C2 hemisphere	0.193	−1.037	0.643	−1.415
C3 cuboid	0.155	−0.725	0.156	0.628
C4 irregular type	0.343	0.313	−0.301	−0.255
D1 0–300 mm	−0.708	1.492	0.059	1.809
D2 300–500 mm	0.808	−0.312	0.636	−0.569
D3 500 mm or more	−0.327	−1.397	−1.028	−1.408
E1 black and white gray	0.361	−0.387	0.491	−0.657
E2 partial color	−0.743	0.658	−0.228	0.834
E3 large block color	0.396	−0.193	−0.766	0.142
F1 fixed	−0.5	−1.791	−0.396	−0.787
F2 rotary	−0.587	−0.398	−1.105	−0.031
F3 walkable	0.633	1.052	0.959	0.359

(1) "Personality – general" result analysis

As can be seen from Fig. 1, the "circle" category with the outline line of the fuselage has the highest score of 1.290 and the "Personality" emotional image. The other categories with higher positive scores were "walkable", "screen free", "300–500 mm" in overall size, and "irregular" in head shape, which was closer to the image meaning of "Personality".

Among the negative values of a category, the "independent display" score of the display screen is the lowest, which can best reflect the image of "general". The display screen used for playing video function is set on the fuselage independently and cannot be well integrated with the whole body. It is similar to the tablet computer used in flat time and has no innovation. Negative scores were also lower for "local color", "inverted trapezoid" of the fuselage contour line and "0–300 mm" of overall size, all of which tend to "public" emotional image.

(2) Analysis of the results of "Amiable – indifferent"

As can be seen from Fig. 1, the overall size of "0–300 mm" scores the highest, most able to reflect the "affinity" image. Children under 300 mm are accompanied by small and cute robots, which are in line with the age characteristics of children.

Children can hug and touch, which will give them a closer feeling. In the category negative value, the activity mode "fixed" score is at least −1.791, which best reflects the "indifferent" image. Fixed child companion robots greatly reduce interaction with children.

(3) "Flexible – inflexible" results analysis

As can be seen from Fig. 1, the activity type "walkable" has the highest score and best reflects the "flexible" image. Walkable can track children and increase the interactive experience.

The lowest score in the category negative value is the "rotational" mode of action, which best expresses the "dull" emotional image.

(4) "concise – complex" result analysis

As can be seen in Fig. 1, the overall size of "0–300 mm" scores the highest, the child's companion robot petite body shape can best reflect the "simple" image. Followed by the shape of the head "spherical and ellipsoidal", the head of this shape is more rounded and full, and the lines are smoother. The higher of the positive scores, the two categories of the body contour "inverted trapezoid", "local color" and the display "integrated with the eye screen" are more able to reflect the "simple" emotional image.'

4.3 Construction of Correlation Between Perceptual Image and Morphological Design Elements

The scope of the morphological element refers to the degree of influence of the project on a certain sensible image. The larger the scope of the project, the greater the degree of influence on the image, and vice versa.

As can be seen from Fig. 2, the emotional image of "Personality-mass" has the greatest influence: A fuselage outline (2.024); The minimum influence degree is C head shape (0.804). The "affable – indifferent" perceptual image has the greatest influence: D overall size (2.889); The minimum is A fuselage profile (0.88). The "flexible – inflexible" perceptual image has the greatest influence: Factivity mode (2.064), and the smallest: A fuselage contour line (0.901). The "concise – complex" perceptual image has the greatest influence on the overall size of D (1.809) and the least influence on the active mode of F (0.359). Under this perceptual image, the range value of each item exceeds 1, and there are three values exceeding 1.5, namely: B, display screen, C, head shape, and D, overall size. Therefore, in the design of "concise – complex" perceptual image of children accompanied by robots, the three categories should be considered in the form design.

In summary, it can be found that the main impact items under different perceptual images and the degree of influence of each item are different. According to the following table, corresponding design suggestions can be provided for different positioning products.

5 Establish a Correspondence Model Between Emotional Image and Morphological Elements and Verify

5.1 Establish a Correspondence Model Between Emotional Image and Morphological Elements

The morphological design element of the child companion robot is the independent variable, and the perceptual evaluation value is the dependent variable, and the corresponding relationship model can be established:

$$\begin{aligned} Y = & \alpha A1A1 + \alpha A2A2 + \alpha A3A3 + A4A4 + \alpha B1B1 + \alpha B2B2 + \alpha B3B3 + \alpha C1C1 \\ & + \alpha C2C2 + \alpha C3C3 + \alpha C4C4 + \alpha D1D1 + \alpha D2D2 + \alpha D3D3 + \alpha E1E1 + \alpha E2E2 + \alpha E3E3 \\ & + \alpha F1F1 + \alpha F2F2 + \alpha F3F3 + a \end{aligned} \quad (1)$$

In Eq. 1, Y is the perceptual image score value; A1, A2,…, F3 are the morphological design elements (A represents the fuselage outline, B is the display screen, C is the head shape, D is the overall size, E For color, F is the active mode), corresponding to the various categories in the class I theory; αA1, αA2….αF3 is the correlation coefficient of each design element, corresponding to various categories of points; a is a constant term value, Used to adjust the error.

According to the analysis results of the corresponding perceptual images in Fig. 1, the regression relationship model between the four images semantics and the morphological design elements can be established:

(1) The regression relationship model between "Personality-popular" and morphological elements

$$\begin{aligned} Y1 = & -0.010A1 - 0.734A2 + 1.290A3 + 0.229A4 - 0.175B1 - 0.822B2 + 0.965B3 \\ & - 0.461C1 + 0.193C2 + 0.155C3 + 0.343C4 - 0.708D1 + 0.808D2 - 0.327D3 + 0.361E1 \\ & - 0.743E2 + 0.396E3 - 0.500F1 - 0.587F2 + 0.633F3 + 0.397 \end{aligned} \quad (2)$$

(2) Regression relationship model between "affinity-indifferent" and morphological elements

$$\begin{aligned} Y2 = & -0.259A1 + 0.587A2 + 0.621A3 - 0.091A4 + 0.982B1 - 1.595B2 - 0.768B3 + 1.139C1 \\ & - 1.037C2 - 0.725C3 + 0.313C4 + 1.492D1 - 0.312D2 - 1.397D3 - 0.387E1 + 0.658E2 - 0.193E3 \\ & - 1.791F1 - 0.398F2 + 1.052F3 + 0.417 \end{aligned} \quad (3)$$

(3) Regression relationship model between "flexible-dull" and morphological elements

$$\begin{aligned} Y3 = & -0.411A1 + 0.490A2 + 0.219A3 + 0.281A4 + 0.355B1 - 0.805B2 - 0.105B3 \\ & - 0.525C1 + 0.643C2 + 0.156C3 - 0.301C4 + 0.059D1 + 0.636D2 - 1.028D3 + 0.491E1 \\ & - 0.228E2 - 0.766E3 - 0.396F1 - 1.105F2 + 0.959F3 + 0.361 \end{aligned} \quad (4)$$

(4) The regression model of “simple-complex” and morphological elements

$$\begin{aligned} Y4 = & -0.272A1 + 1.090A2 - 0.352A3 - 0.275A4 + 0.710B1 - 0.625B2 - 0.950B3 \\ & + 1.317C1 - 1.415C2 + 0.628C3 - 0.255C4 + 1.809D1 - 0.569D2 - 1.408D3 - 0.657E1 \\ & + 0.834E2 + 0.142E3 - 0.787F1 - 0.031F2 + 0.359F3 + 0.476 \end{aligned} \tag{5}$$

5.2 Verification

In order to verify whether the relationship model obtained by multiple linear regression can accurately predict the emotional image of the product, the five selected samples (as shown in Table 6) are verified, and then the verification values of the perceptual evaluation and the regression relationship model are performed. Paired sample T test to verify the credibility of the above regression relationship model.

Table 6. Verify product samples

1	2	3	4	5

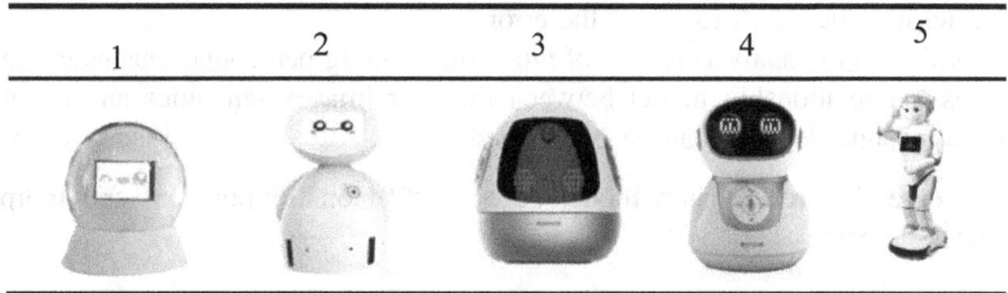

The semantic difference method questionnaire was distributed to 50 target users, and they were asked to evaluate the four pairs of perceptual vocabulary again. Then, the average of 5 samples in four pairs of perceptual vocabulary was calculated. Finally, the author will have 5 verification samples. The resulting average of the sensory image is compared with the predicted value calculated by the regression relationship model. The two sets of data were entered into the SPSS software and then paired with a sample T-test, which is the result of the final test.

As can be seen from Table 7, the significance of T-test for paired samples of the four pairs of perceptual vocabulary is greater than 0.05, indicating that there is no significant difference between the calculation results of the relationship model and the subjective evaluation of consumers, that is, the four relationship models have a high degree of credibility. In the product design and development of children’s companion robot, the emotional image of consumers can be substituted into the above relationship model to obtain the prototype design for the category purpose under the project of each element of the product.

Table 7. Paired sample T test results

Paired sentimental imagery	t	df	Sig. (bilateral)
Couple1 Y1(Personality – general)	0.338	4	0.753
Couple2 Y2(amiable – indifferent)	0.039	4	0.971
Couple3 Y3(flexible – inflexible)	−1.512	4	0.205
Couple4 Y4(concise – complicated)	1.064	4	0.347

6 Summary

Perceptual image and form design elements of the relationship between children with robot model: after the screening of children with robot sample and perceptual image spatial relation between the semantic difference method, questionnaire survey, in using the theory of quantification I kind of questionnaire on the basis of statistical analysis, obtained the related category score, range, constant term, multiple correlation coefficient and goodness of fit, established the corresponding relationship between perceptual image and form design elements of multiple regression analysis model. The specific conclusions are as follows:

"Personality – general" perceptual image: the three morphological design elements of the fuselage contour "circle", "no display screen" and the overall size "300–500 mm" have made the largest positive contribution to the "Personality" image of the child-accompanying robot; The largest contribution to the "public" image is the "independent display" of the display screen and the overall size of "0–300 mm".

"Affinity-indifferent" emotional image: the display "with the eye screen", the head shape "spherical ellipsoid" and the overall size "0–300 mm" scores three of the positive values That is, these three morphological design elements contribute the most to the "affinity" image of children's companion robots; while the "indifferent" intentions contribute the most: the display "independent display" and the activity mode "fixed" Category.

"Flexible – Inflexible" emotional image: the head shape "hemisphere type", the overall size "300–500 mm" and the activity type "walkable" three categories are positively ranked three, that is, these three forms The design elements contribute the most to the "flexible" imagery of the children's companion robots; the most important contribution to the "dull" imagery is the overall size "more than 500 mm" and the active mode "rotary".

"Concise –Complex" emotional image: the body contour "inverted trapezoid", the head shape "spherical ellipsoid" and the overall size "0–300 mm" are three of the positive values. That is to say, these three morphological design elements contribute the most to the "concise" image of the children's companion robot; the two items that contribute the most to the "complex" image are the head shape "hemisphere type" and the overall size "500 mm or more". Head.

Correspondence model test between perceptual image and morphological design elements: 50 subjects were selected again to evaluate the sensitivity of five children's companion robot verification samples, and the predicted values of subjective evaluation mean and verification sample morphological elements were substituted into the relationship model. A paired sample T-test analysis was performed, and the results showed that the relational model had a high degree.

References

1. Anonymous. "China Made 2025" planning series interpretation of the promotion of robot development. Sci. Technol. Herald, **33**(21), 76–78 (2015)
2. Aili, Z.: Research on children's product design based on emotional design theory. Popular Lit. **21**, 77–78 (2012)
3. Jianlin, N.: Analysis of children's emotional design. China Packag. Indus. **12**, 17–18 (2013)
4. Harada, A.: The parallel Design Methodology in the Kansei Engineering. Report of Modeling the evaluation structure of Kansei, pp. 309–316
5. Nagamachi, M.: Kansei engineering: the implication and applications to product development. In: IEEE International Conference on Systems, Man, and Cybernetics, vol. 6, pp. 273–278 (1999)
6. Nagamachi, M.: Kansei Engineering: a new ergonomic consumer-oriented technology for Product development. Int. J. Ind. Ergon. **15**(1), 3–11 (1995)
7. Matsubara, Y., Nagamachi, M.: Hybrid Kansei engineering system and design support. Int. J. Ind. Ergon. **19**(2), 81–92 (1997)
8. Ishihara, S., et al.: Theoretical analysis based on the design of ergonomic engineering products. Nanjing University of Aeronautics and Astronautics (2007)
9. Zhao, Q.: Perceptual Engineering and its Application in Product Design. Shandong University (2008)
10. Tang, L.: Investigation of Perceptual Engineering Methods. Nanjing University of the Arts (2008)
11. Kong, Q.: Research on the Stroller Modeling of Consumer Perception Image. Shaanxi University of Science and Technology (2015)
12. Ge, T.: Research on the Design of Sanxin 1008B Hemodialysis Machine. Southeast University (2016)
13. Ma, Y.: Research on Parent-Child Toy Design Based on Perceptual Engineering Design Method. Taiyuan University of Technology (2016)
14. Zhu, Y.: Research on shape design of family service robot based on perceptual engineering. Packag. Eng. **14**, 50–54 (2015)
15. Yuyue, Yu., Jian, Z.: Application of product semantics in family education robot design. Research **8**, 00069–00070 (2016)
16. Zhu, H., Xu, Z.Y., Xu, B.: Modeling of children's learning companion robot based on emotional design theory. Mech. Design **4**, 122–124 (2016)
17. Harada, A.: The structure of perceptual engineering: research fields and objects of perceptual engineering. In: Proceedings of 1998 Sino-Japanese Design Education Symposium, pp. 2–16. Yunlin University of Science and Technology (1998)
18. Chen, G., He, M., Deng, Y.: Integration research of composite inductive engineering applied in product development. Indus. Design **32**, 108–117 (2004)
19. Xu, Y., Chen, K., Peng, Z.: Analysis of consumer demand based on perceptual engineering. Design Art Res. **02**(3), 1–5 (2012)

Research on Active Interaction Design for Smart Speakers Agent of Home Service Robot

Jingyan Qin[1(✉)], Zhibo Chen[1], Wenhao Zhang[1], Daisong Guan[2], Zhun Wu[2], and Min Zhao[2]

[1] School of Mechanical Engineering, University of Science and Technology, Beijing, People's Republic of China
qinjingyanking@foxmail.com

[2] Baidu AI Interaction Design Lab, Beijing, People's Republic of China

Abstract. With the smart speakers agent of Home Service Robot represented by voice interaction, tangible user interface interaction and somatosensory interaction are widely present in family environment and serve multiple family members, the trustworthy AI stimulates the transition of the interaction form from passive interaction to proactive interaction, finally into active interaction. However, with the personalization of family members' needs, the improvement of emotional needs lead to user low patience and high expectations toward the home service robots, the traditional passive interaction has met the above changes of users. This paper proposes the active interaction design method to enhance the initiate of the intelligent agents to solve the user's needs, improve Interaction performance and user experience. This paper uses questionnaire analysis, user interview, expert cognitive walkthrough, field survey, and comparative research to conduct research. Through the comparative study of passive interaction, proactive interaction and active interaction, the computational analysis, context awareness, consciousness awareness and emotion analysis, combined with the actual case of Baidu smart speakers project, the author put forward active interaction model and the active interaction design form of the family agent. Apply it to the family situation and gradually improve the active interaction research of the home service robot in the family environment.

Keywords: Active interaction · Home service robot · Interaction design

1 Introduction

The Human-Agent Interaction (HAI) has experienced Command-Line Interface (CLI), Graphical User Interface (GUI), Voice User Interface (VUI) and Natural User Interface (NUI). The role of the agent transforms "no mind" machine to our family members, moves toward the interaction of human and machine integration.

Passive interaction is the main interaction form of the current home service robot which is from user to home service robot to user, but the home service robot lacks environmental awareness, mind awareness, emotion perception, knowledge graph and other factors, active interaction that predict user intent and initiate responses by

A. Marcus and W. Wang (Eds.): HCII 2019, LNCS 11584, pp. 253–263, 2019.
https://doi.org/10.1007/978-3-030-23541-3_19

intelligent systems begin to grow rapidly [1] and can effectively enhance the user experience. For the study of active interaction, DeepMind proposes to use meta-enhanced learning to achieve causal reasoning, so that the home service robot can actively interact [2]; Intel Labs China proposes to trigger active interaction through Confidence Interval(CI); Baidu proposes the NIRO system included active interaction model and put it into commercial use; Feng Yang et al. proposed an active interactive dialogue robot system and active dialogue method, and applied to the service industry. To some extent, active interaction solves technical problems such as system robustness, poor causal reasoning, and learning sample limitations.

This paper reviews and studies the passive interaction, proactive interaction and active interaction. It also conducts information classification and preliminary analysis on the main products of 50 home service robots, and the main functions, interaction forms and forms of 30 major competing products. Scientific analysis and user feedback were collected for market sales, market pricing, user feedback, etc.; data from 12 research reports were comprehensively compared; 142 valid questionnaires were collected for intelligent product demand surveys which are covering 18-71 years old, 20 The provinces and cities, the consumption level of 4 stalls, the occupation of 19 fields; the behavior observation and in-depth user interviews of three family types (three families, single-sex youth, empty nesters) are in progress.

2 Related Work

2.1 Agent in Home Service Robot

Agent refer to smart agents, artificial intelligence products, and so on. Bjorn Hermans pointed out that the basic attributes of the agent have self-control ability, social ability, reaction ability, active, temporary continuity, and goal-oriented ability [3]; Michael Wooldridge and Nicholas R. Jennings pointed out that the agent has “strong” and “weak” [4]; Daze discriminates the concept of agent and agency, and expounds the current research scope and research trends of HAI [5]; Zhao Longwen and Hou Yibin pointed out that agent is a three-tier structure consisting of mentality, internal behavior, and external behavior, it is an entity with high self-control ability that operates in a dynamic environment, and its fundamental goal is to accept and provide assistance to another entity [6]. Chen Gang et al. [7] studied the social organization method of agent and the performance of the cooperative behavior of agent in home service robot, and discussed the trustworthy relationship between agents and users.

2.2 The Needs of Users in Family Environment

With the development of Home automation, smart home systems, and pervasive computing, interaction design evolves from desktop systems to mobile devices of smart environments. In recent years, the research on agent has been more biased towards family scenarios. There have been a number of smart products with family-centric scenes such as Pepper, Luna, iRobot, Ecovacs Sweeping robot, Google Home and more. Compared with agent of typical environment such as office environment, outdoor public places and educational institutions, family agents need to consider the members privacy, individualized needs, emotional needs, appropriate interaction modes, trigger thresholds and speech design. We obtained the user's demand about family agent based on the above user interviews and questionnaires (see Fig. 1).

Fig. 1. The needs of users for home service robot smart agents in family environment

3 Three Kinds of Interaction

3.1 Passive Interaction

At present, The Human-Agent Interaction is divided into four stages: wake-up, input, calculation, and output. The user wakes up the agent through behavioral information such as languages, actions, and inputs instructions. The agent use machine vision and speech recognition to process digital and non-digitized instructions and output language, text and other feedbacks to the user. This form of interaction is passive for the user, and the author draws the passive interaction model (see Fig. 2). In family environment, users wake up the agent through the names of "XiaoDu XiaoDu" and "TmallGenie" and trigger one-way interaction with the agent. The whole process strengthens the user's initiative, and the agent lack information fusion in offline environment and online environment, lack of integration of digital and non-digital information, lack of strong correlation of knowledge graph, and lack of data migrants. Passive interaction make the whole process boring and short-lived.

Through the above questionnaires, household interviews, market research, etc., the following problems exist in the passive interaction of family agents:

- Training sample limitations, limited satisfaction with user needs
- The level of semantic understanding is not high, and the ability of continuous dialogue is poor.

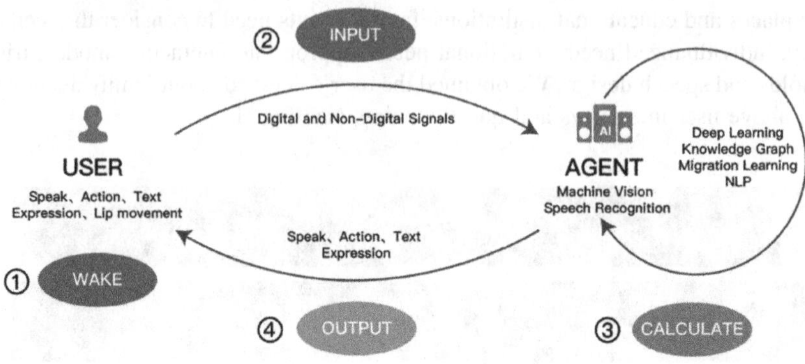

Fig. 2. Passive interaction model

- Awakening form is single, one way trigger form
- Diversity of family characteristics, lack of satisfaction with the individual needs of family members
- Low intelligence and low family integration
- The result of the answer is mechanized and predictable
- No feedback incentive
- Lack of environmental perception, emotional perception and mind awareness

3.2 Proactive Interaction

Due to the limitations of the development of artificial intelligence technology, the development of the interaction of the agent does not immediately change from passive interaction to active interaction. It needs to experience proactive interaction. At present, the distinction between proactive interaction and active interaction is not obvious at Domestic and foreign. A proactive HMI can be run on top of a context- aware system and it tries to predict next feasible action based on the context [8]. Proactive HMIs can suggest the next step from context or from the history of the user [9]. For getting the proper context proactive HMI need to monitor the world around it which requires sensors and actuators [10]. The current academic research on proactive interaction is usually to connect it to context-aware technology, emphasizing the system's calculation of the scene, ignoring knowledge graph based on entities and relationships.

The author believes that proactive interaction is an intermediate state from passive interaction to active interaction. Proactive interaction can "force" the agent to make user preference analysis results when the development of the intelligent feedforward system is not perfect. It can guide and intervene in the choice of agent solutions. The proactive interaction "forces" the agent to use the input or feedback information of the user as the data foundation for the feed-forward in the next related task. In this interaction process, the agent needs to passively collect the personalized information and preferences of the user. After passive interactive learning, the agent will actively interact according to the user's situation next time. Proactive interaction is a better way to ease technical problems. Its continuous development can make the machine reach the constant perception of the environment, consciousness and emotion, and it can form the active interaction of the agent. At present, it mainly focuses on: schedule reminder, search related information push, the active endurance charging of the sweeping robot, etc., obviously the user needs to be satisfied by the active interaction.

3.3 Active Interaction

Active interaction essentially generate intelligent information data to activate interactive scenarios through multi-modal perception, context awareness, intelligent environment technology, multi-dimensional inductive interface, cognitive science and other technologies, and the data collected can verify and correct the correlation of machine technology such as knowledge graph. Because of that, the machine continuously improves the initiative accuracy. For example, Lomo Shopping, the latest product launched by Segway Robotics, attracts many sales in the form of active communication through the technology of position sensing, NOMI with NIO ES8, Baidu Car OS, and others.

In the questionnaire survey of the agent, the choice of the agent "can't do big things" and "nothing to use eggs" accounted for 28.87% and 21.83% respectively, more than half of the doubts about the intelligence of the family agent, the user's choice and user experience have a close relationship, and the introduction of active interaction can effectively improve intelligence.

Active interaction uses Silent Interface to substitute emotional listening and Embodied cognition feedback, allowing users to self-direct into the introspective state, and actively choose to judge, the agent expresses listening and feedback after active interaction, the user choose Feedback form and recognize the results, this form can achieve the goal of human-machine to a certain extent.

Through contrast analysis with passive interaction, proactive interaction, the author divides the active interaction into five parts: knowledge graph input with entity and relationship as information source, agent feedforward, agent output, user judgment and user feedback (see Fig. 3). By continuously inputting environmental information, emotional information, and consciousness information, the agent continuously completes the accuracy of the user image under the knowledge graph, and appropriately feeds forward the opportunity when it is associated with the user, and outputs it in the form of language, text, etc., user judgment and decision intelligence. The body actively interacts with the results, and feedbacks and responses. The accumulated feedback results can form the feedforward of the active interaction, and can also improve the accuracy of the active interaction of the agent.

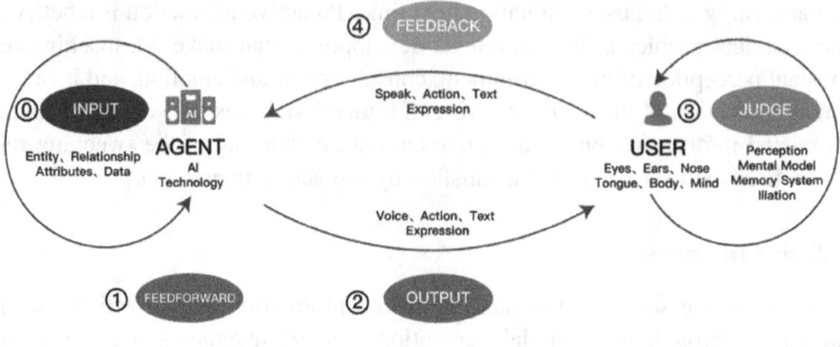

Fig. 3. Active interaction model

3.4 Comparison Study Between Active Interaction and Passive Interaction

- Different starting points
  The passive interaction process starts from the user's voice, action, text input, expression, lip movement and other user behavior such as wake-up response commands. These call points have been preset and if the user's instruction behavior is fuzzy or inaccurate, it will affect accuracy. Active interaction is not complete triggered by a specific user behavior but based on big data operations of intelligent analysis of images, scenes, behaviors, and it based on the analysis results to form a feedforward, which is speculating the user's needs and intentions. And then active provide relevant solutions to achieve the active of the interaction process.
- Different information input stages
  The information input of passive interaction occurs in the process of the task, and the user behavior as the starting point is input to the agent, but the information input of active interaction is to actively acquire the intent information, user characteristic information and space of the mobile phone before the interaction task is initiated. Environmental information serves as the basis for the formation of feedforward. The subject in passive interaction process is always the user, and the agent is the object that accepts the information and performs the task. The subject in the process of active interaction is the alternation of the user and the agent. The agent is no longer just the performer of the task, but can learn and accumulate the direction of the task, and truly realize the positive communication with the return rather than mechanical response and execution.
- Passive interaction lacks user feedback mechanism and feedforward data content
  In passive interaction, the agent's behavior for the user is a fixed input and output, which is modeled. In the active interaction, the agent continuously optimizes the feedforward mechanism of the active interaction according to the user's judgment and feedback, making it more user-friendly. Behavior and intention to form a personalized, customized service. For example, in a passive interaction, when the agent asks about the weather, the agent's answer is only to answer the local situation. In the active interaction, the agent not only answers the local weather

conditions, but also may take the initiative according to the user's schedule. Prompt for weather conditions at the destination of the trip, or proactively alert the user to the weather changes in the location of the relatives.

The author compares passive interaction, proactive interaction and active interaction (see Table 1).

Table 1. Passive interaction vs. Proactive interaction vs Active interaction

	Passive Interaction	Proactive Interaction	Active Interaction
Intelligence	High	Medium	Low
Wake-up method	Wake-up word	CM	CM, Always-on
Trigger	Single channel	Single channel	Multi-channel
Input	Single direction	Single direction	Double direction
Interactive mode	Single mode	Single mode	Multimodal
Contact	Weak	Weak	Strong
User initiative	Strong	Medium	Weak
User portrait	Coarse	Coarse	Accurate
Knowledge graph	Weak association	Weak association	Strong association
Data migration	No	No	Active migration
Info aggregation	No	Medium	Strong
Environmental perception	Weak	Medium	Strong
Emotional perception	Weak	Medium	Strong
Conscious perception	No	No	Yes
Emotional induction	No	No	Yes
Predictability	Predictable Boring	Predictable Excitement	Unpredictable Surprised

4 Active Interaction in Smart Speakers Agent of Home Service Robot

4.1 Strong Active Interaction and Weak Active Interaction

Active interaction based on the weight of the user's dominant role in the interaction process can be divided into strong active interaction and weak active interaction (see Table 2). Strong active interaction includes: notification, reminder, push and function inquiry. In this process, the user's dominance is small, the speech uses more declarative sentences, and the function inquiry is mostly judged and selected, and the options provided to the user are less, for example, "When do you need to turn on the air conditioner for you?", "Do you need to remind you tomorrow?" Weak active interaction mainly includes suggestions, content inquiries, and some careless words or actions that are not meaningful. Words use questions that have no clear options. For example, "Do you think the room temperature is right?", "Welcome home!"

Table 2. Active interaction form in family environment

Types	Interaction express
Strong active interaction	Notification, reminder, push and function inquiry
Weak active interaction	Advice, content inquiry, care

Strong active interaction and weak active interaction have no advantages and disadvantages, and fusion each other. In the design process, attention should be paid to the cooperation between strong active interaction and weak active interaction to form a coordinated and unified relationship, so as to adapt to home scenarios. Strong active interaction can effectively enhance the intelligent experience of the agent to the user, but too much makes the user feel invaded.

Weak active interaction can strengthen the user's sense of ownership, but too much will reduce the intelligence of the agent to the user. Therefore, it is especially important to find a balance between them. This requires not only the planning of functions and speech in the early design of the agent. Due to the differences between individuals and groups, the agents in the family space are more important to form a family in the process of continuous learning and accumulation. The big data of the environment provides users with personalized and active interaction solutions.

4.2 Suggestions for the Family Smart Speakers in Active Interaction Design

- Guarantee user privacy.
  Active interaction associates user information through knowledge maps, but avoids multi-member intercommunication of controversial private information, ensuring users' trust in the agent and selective sharing.
- Ensure the perceptibility of active interaction.
  Active interaction in the application process, it is necessary to let the user perceive the occurrence of active interaction through the intelligent body language and give the user the right to choose, so that the user feels the initiative of the agent, instead of feeling controlled by the agent.
- The active interaction trigger mechanism changes with the user's adaptability.
  The staged active interaction trigger mechanism is to ensure that the user does not have an "over-smart" experience for the home agent, such as the reminder of the anniversary, the push of the news.
- Provide options to give users decision-making power and initiative.
  Providing alternative results to the user, allowing the user to enhance the sense of control of the agent by selecting, can also effectively reduce concerns about over smart.
- Humanoid communication logic.
  The active interaction of the human-like communication logic needs to be output through the semantic understanding of the association, such as: Need to wear more clothes tomorrow? The agent needs to locate the weather function, answer the user's answer about the dressing, and then push the relevant weather information.

4.3 Design Case

- Design background and the target user selection
  The intervention of the active interaction of the agent can be applied in a variety of home environments to serve different groups of people. The author takes the interaction between the elderly group and the agent as a case. Through the observation of the interaction behavior of the elderly community, it is found that the elderly are full of expectations for the agent, but there are problems such as a single communication problem in the communication interaction. If you do not know the content of the conversation, you can forget the wake-up words directly. Issue instructions, talk to the agent at the same time, etc.
  The elderly do not save the artificial form. Compared with the traditional passive interface, the young people become the ashes users through learning. In the process of using the agent, the elderly group is more inclined to the rookie player forever. The operations you master will always be patient with the agent.
- User research
  The author recorded the use of smart speakers by the elderly Ren for 24 h, and excerpted the original sentence as follows (see Table 3):

Table 3. User's original words and scenes

Dimension	Time	Dialogue loop	Dialogue contents
1 Dimension	8:00	1	What is the weather like in Shenyang today?
2 Dimension	9:00	1	How is the weather today, XiaoDu?
3 Dimension	13:32	3	How many days is the eighth day of the lunar calendar? What weather is Shenyang tomorrow? Put the songs about Zhao Benshan!
4 Dimension	18:21	4	Minor, what kind of medicine do I have to eat? Minor, what kind of medicine do I have a headache? Put the songs about Zhao Benshan! XiaoDu, break, you
5 Dimension	19:48	6	What weather is tomorrow? Small, small, do I look good? Small, I have a headache? Put the songs about Zhao Benshan! Small, small, small Have a break, Du!

The author finds that the function and content of the elderly are not particularly clear to the elderly. Every time they say nothing, they don't know what questions to ask. They often forget the name of the agent, which prevents the agent from starting.

- Introducing an active interaction model
  The author made an improved design of the intelligent speaker service process based on active interaction model and active interaction form above (see Fig. 4):

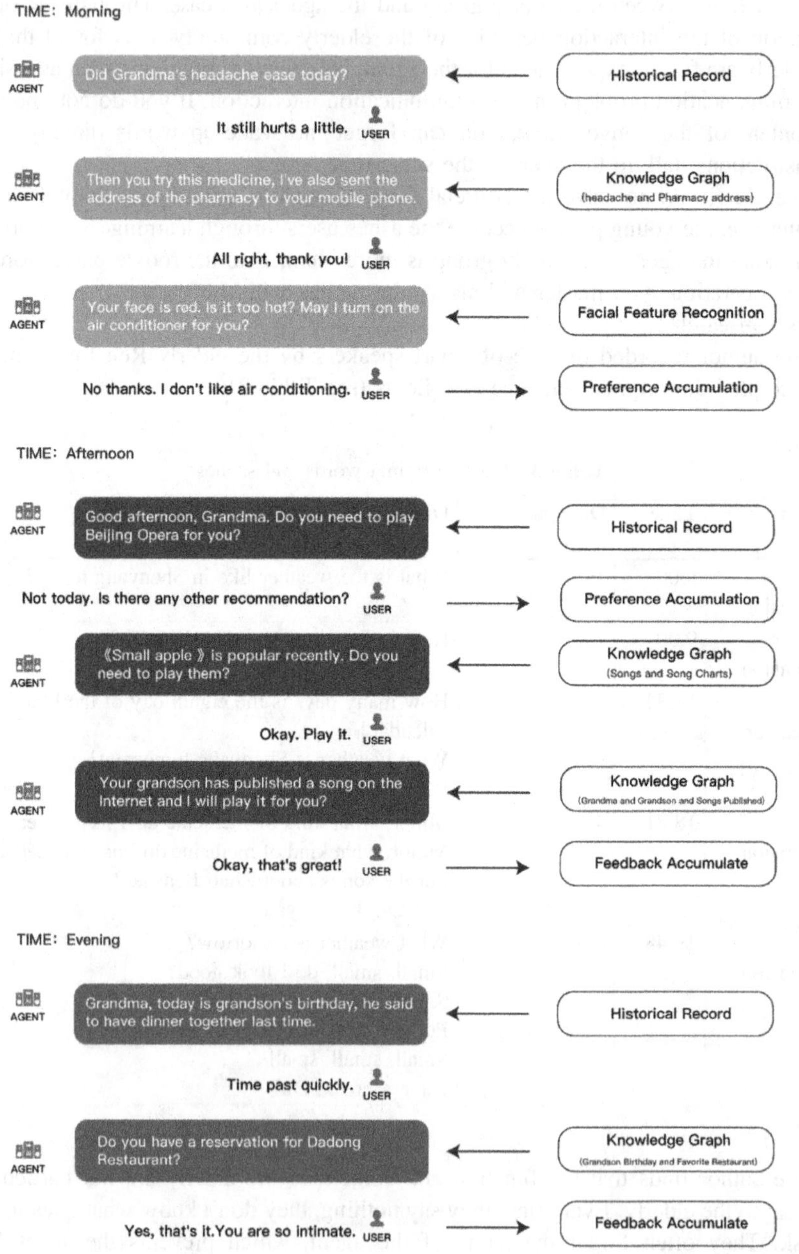

Fig. 4. Dialogue in smart speakers Human Robot Interaction for Active interaction model

5 Conclusion

The interaction from passive interaction to proactive interaction to active interaction need to accurately identify task feature information, object relationship information, spatial scene information, relationship knowledge graph, etc. in a complex environment. With the active interaction, the individual needs of the members are satisfied, and the user's trust in the intelligence of the agent is enhanced. To a certain extent, the agent do active recommendation and service through the contact of the knowledge graph which can compensate for the disadvantages of the machine semantic understanding. Active interaction also make the intelligent agent in home service robot become active which consequently enhance the user's good willing and experience to communicate with the agent.

References

1. Begole, B.: Responsive media: media experiences in the age of thinking machines. APSIPA Trans. on Signal Inf. Process., **6** (2017)
2. Dasgupta, I., Wang, J., Chiappa S., et al.: Causal Reasoning from Meta-reinforcement Learning. arXiv preprint arXiv:1901.08162 (2019)
3. Hermans B.: Intelligent Software Agents on the Internet: Chapters 6–7. First Monday, vol. 2 (3) (1997)
4. Wooldridge, M., Jennings, N.: Intelligent agents: theory and practice. Knowl. Eng. Rev. **10** (2), 115–152 (1995). https://doi.org/10.1017/s0269888900008122
5. Da, Z., Lu, C.: Interaction between human and agent: artificial intelligence system design related to people. Decoration **11**, 14–21 (2016)
6. Zhao, L., Hou, Y.: Intelligent software: from object-oriented to agent-oriented. Comput. Eng. Appl., (05), 41–43+125 (2001)
7. Chen, G., Lu, R.Q.: The relation Web model: an organizational approach to agent cooperation based on social mechanism. J. Comput. Res. Dev. **40**(1), 107–114 (2003)
8. Hämäläinen, V.P.: Usability testing methodology of proactive HMIs for virtual control room, pp. 13–14 (2014)
9. De Boeck, J., Verpoorten, K., Luyten, K., Coninx, K.: A Comparison between Decision Trees and Markov Models to Support Proactive Interfaces. In: 18th International Conference on Database and Expert Systems Applications (DEXA 2007), pp. 94–98 (2007)
10. Tennenhouse, D.: Proactive computing. Commun. ACM **43**(5), 43–50 (2000)

Research on Robot Interaction Design Based on Embodied and Disembodied Interaction Grammars

Jingyan Qin(✉), Xinghui Lu, Yanlin An, Zeyu Hao, Daisong Guan, Moli Zhou, and Shiyan Li

School of Mechanical Engineering, University of Science and Technology Beijing, Beijing, China
qinjingyanking@foxmail.com

Abstract. With the increasing complexity and variety of robotic agents in VR/AR/MR IoT and artificial intelligence and other intelligent environments, traditional interaction grammar and interaction design principles are facing more and more challenges. Based on the theory of embodied interaction and disembodied interaction in cognitive science, this paper combines field research and user in-depth interviews, usability testing, SWOT analysis, SPSS questionnaire analysis, high-fidelity prototype construction, usability testing and other research data to study the interaction grammar of embodied interaction and disembodied interaction. By designing the prototype of the robot, three typical Chinese families are selected to conduct prototype tests of embodied interaction and disembodied interaction. Then on this basis, affordance, Interactive Behavior, Interactive Feedforward of embodied interaction and Mapping Relations of Symbols, Semantics and Interactive Feedback of disembodied interaction and understanding of the construction of interactive grammar are established. This study has a certain effect on embodied interaction and disembodied interaction between human and computer interaction.

Keywords: Interactive grammar · Embodied cognition · Disembodied cognition · Robot interaction design

1 Introduction

Based on the disciplines of Phenomenology of Perception and Cognitive Science, George Lakoff, Mark Johnson, Dourish, A Clark, Edmund Gustav Albrecht Husserl, Martin Heidegger, Maurice Merleau-Ponty [1–6] and other scholars from cognition science and computer science conducted research on embodied cognition, disembodied cognition and embodied interaction. It can be seen from the above literature that the body exists in space, and participates in the visible expression form of the human subject's intention to the object as a medium for perceiving the world. The subject exchanges and interacts with the object through the sense of existence, and communicates with the traffic sympathy and so on, and constructs the concept of embodied interaction. Through tele-presence of information communication, disembodied cognition enables human consciousness to be separated from cognitive vectors, and even

A. Marcus and W. Wang (Eds.): HCII 2019, LNCS 11584, pp. 264–276, 2019.
https://doi.org/10.1007/978-3-030-23541-3_20

creates a sense of coexistence co-presence between real and virtual bodies through virtual reality and mixed reality. At the same time, AI can also concentrate group wisdom in a carrier, which produces the separation of consciousness from subject. And disembodied cognition produces disembodied interaction in the process of observing perspective of exchange consciousness, information dimension of exchange consciousness and energy of sympathetic consciousness between subjects and objects. If the interactive representation layer, the operation layer and the container layer are separated from each other, the disembodied interaction will take a leading role, and if the representation layer and the operation layer tend to be one in the entity interaction interface or the augmented reality environment, thus the embodied cognition will become dominant. Aiming at the human-computer interaction environment of robotic agents, this paper proposes the practice of interactive design using the interactive grammar of exposed interaction and disembodied interaction. By designing the prototype of the robot, three typical Chinese families were selected to perform the prototype usability test of the embodied interaction and disembodied interaction, so as to establish the mapping relationship of the embodied interaction and disembodied interaction and the understanding of the interaction grammar.

In this study, we try to use the interactive grammar constructed by embodied cognition and disembodied cognition to guide the design process of the agent and human-robot interactive user experience. In the Chinese family form, human-computer interaction content is designed for various needs of users in different scenarios, and prototype testing is carried out in a real environment. We have designed two different forms of agents. By recording the cognitive perception and interaction behavior of the user under the embodied cognition, the interactive grammar design under the embodied cognition and disembodied cognition is very important for the design of human and agent.

Considering the difference in the way in which the embodied cognition and disembodied cognition record and analyze data, we observe the user's susceptibility and functional requirements for the agent under the disembodied interaction experience of the existing agent. Through usability testing and in-depth interviews, we explore the embodied interaction and disembodied interaction of users and agents. Through the iterative tests, it proves that the function requirements and emotion experience of the agent match the interactive grammar under the embodied and disembodied cognition proposed in this study.

2 Experiment Design for Human-Robot Embodied Interaction and Disembodied Interaction

2.1 Determination of Test Content

In this study, 160 valid questionnaires were collected for the intelligent product demand survey. The questionnaires covered users' needs, product pain points and opportunity point troubleshooting, interactive form preferences, and users' trustworthy AI. The age covers 18–71 years old, 20 provinces and cities in China, 4 consumption levels, and the occupation of 19 fields, the proportion of men and women is balanced.

The survey found that users have needs in ten aspects: emotional companionship, entertainment, family interaction, social interaction, child growth and education, health management, life management, and safety monitoring. Based on the above requirements, we selected 28 scenes tasks cards, including the functions, content, and interaction of the agent.

The survey analyzes the core life claims of current families are reflected in ten aspects:

1. Accompany to get rid of loneness and ease monotony
   Accompanied by people and things, ease monotony, boring, and bring emotional comfort. Especially for solitary people and the elderly.
2. Entertainment
   Take a variety of ways to enjoy leisure and seek physical and psychological satisfaction. Especially living alone, a family of two, a family with children.
3. Family interaction
   The interaction between people and the relationship between family members. Especially between husband and wife, family and parent-child interaction.
4. Social interaction
   The interaction between people and people maintains social relationships with others. Especially living alone, the elderly.
5. Child growth and education
   Healthy growth and good education of children are one of the main demands of children's family life. Especially family and parent-child interaction.
6. Health Management
   Health is a strong concern for all families, including physical & mental health. Especially the elderly.
7. Life management
   Managing all kinds of trivial matters in life is the basic need in family life.
8. Safety monitoring
   Family security, keep home safe when not at home or sleeping.
9. Energy saving and environmental protection
   People's awareness of environmental protection has gradually increased, and all aspects of life have begun to advocate conservation to create a healthy and green living environment. (saving electricity, water, etc.)
10. Price threshold
    Due to the large and full price of the agent, for some families, the price is relatively high, and the price and function should be considered. Especially for solitary people.

The classification of needs based on four-quadrant maps of appeals is performed (Fig. 1), urgent and important ones include family interaction, companionship and ease of monotony, life management. Urgent but not important ones include child growth and education. Important but not urgent ones include health management, safety monitoring, energy saving and environmental protection. Those neither urgent nor important include entertainment, social interaction.

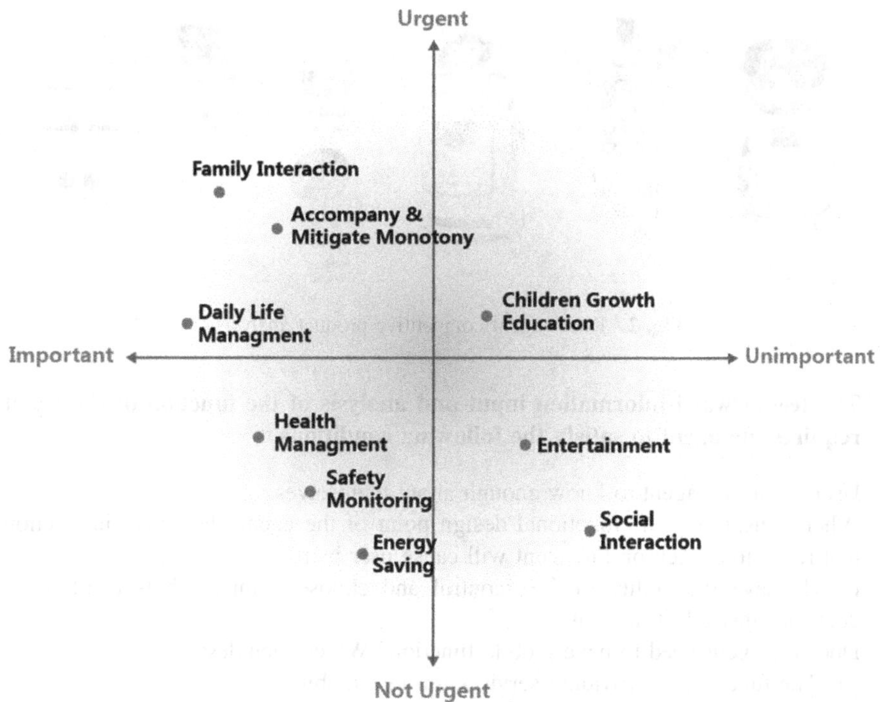

Fig. 1. Touchpoint four quadrant analysis

At present, the core pain point of home users lies in that functional operation feedforward and interactive disembodied cognition required by embodied cognition cannot be seamlessly transformed into multi-modal communication protocols by content-based speech feedback, and it is impossible to establish a mapping transformation relationship of manipulated interaction and disembodied interaction through interactive grammar.

In view of 9 field surveys, 22 in-depth user interviews, SWOT analysis results of 50 existing robot competitors and agent-related products, 9 kinds of robots and agents (including pudding Pudding Beanq, FABO, DuSmart Speaker, Xiaoduzaijia, Xiaodu robot, TmallGenie, Xiaoai Smart Speaker, Atals, Luka) (Fig. 2) are selected to perform usability test and build prototype construction and design experiment for a robotic agent that conforms to embodied interaction and disembodied interaction. Through the anthropomorphization of the agent, the roles of the six robots are designed, and 16 typical robot agent usage scenarios are designed and planned to perform the user experience test of embodied interaction and disembodied interaction.

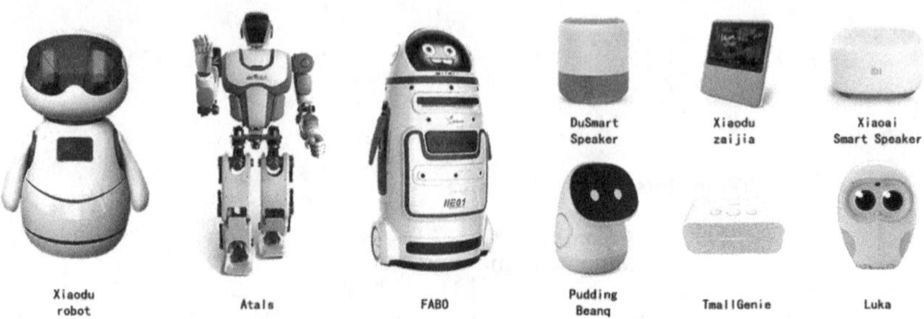

Fig. 2. Robot agent competitive product analysis

- **The feedforward information input and analysis of the function of the agent requires the agent to satisfy the following conditions**

1. Users want the agent to know enough about themselves
2. When considering the functional design point of the agent, the active interaction that relies too much on the agent will cause user inertia.
3. People have the ability to feel, control and choose, family robots can't make decisions instead of humans
4. Does the agent need to have mobile function? Which includes:
   (1) The function of providing services through mobile
   (2) Follow - emotional needs

- **Function aspects of the agent**

1. Individual
   (1) From the perspective of family space: living room, bedroom, kitchen, bathroom (information receiving object: object):
   The family has multiple spaces (functions in different spaces), different spaces, different sizes, and different task points.
   (2) From the perspective of human existence (information recipient: person):
   There are multiple scenes in the family, and scene (event) recognition is a problem.
   (3) From a personal perspective: companionship, entertainment, education – emotion:
   Different users have different function and emotion needs and launch targeted services.
2. Ecosystem
   (1) The relationship between the agent and other smart devices (smart home + mobile phone):
   The existing agent cannot handle the relationship with the mobile phone, the information did not open, and the closed loop could not be formed. The intelligent body's control of the smart home has not achieved intelligent full automation and needs to be improved.

(2) Relationship of family members:
The biggest problem with family members in communication is that the family time information is asymmetrical, and they do not understand what the other party is doing, which may lead to emotional injuries and misunderstandings. Family members have less time to communicate.

- **Content aspect of the agent**

1. The information content presented by the agent are too scattered, and the user cannot extend the data into knowledge graph, which is not convenient for information inquiry.
2. The relationship between the mobile phone and the home agent, whether the home agent can be replaced by the mobile phone, what kind of information is biased to be presented by the mobile phone, and what information tends to be presented by the smart body.

- **Performance and discovery points in terms of interaction forms include**

1. Family members have different roles and different tonality, which will result in different feedback mechanisms and content feed-forward mechanisms.
2. Users are more inclined to language input, and the choice is more inclined to touch screen selection.
3. The existing agent interaction mode is single, and the user prefers to have a physical interaction with the agent.
4. Users have more new expectations for the content output form of the agent.
5. Embodiment: Different users have different requirements for the form of the agent (appearance: color, size, material; system presentation: expression, person setting, sound, etc.) (mental model)

- **Roles of the agent**

Based on the above research and analysis, we define the family agent as the assistant, the housekeeper, the friend, the bodyguard, and the nanny at the functional level. This includes the reminder function of the assistant, the auxiliary solution to other problems in life, the management function of the housekeeping type, the function of sharing the time of the friend's entertainment, the home security of the bodyguard, the guardianship, care and help function, encyclopedia-style advisory guidance like teachers. For the interactive function, the prototype is designed for the embodied interaction and designed the disembodied interaction for the interactive content, and the prototype is designed and tested in 16 family scenarios.

The embodied interaction includes: the affordance display of functions brought about by unconscious behavior, the interaction between humans and robots, including the physical operation of touch screen control, beckoning, hugs, touching, facial expressions, etc., and interactive feedforward information for embodied interaction. The disembodied interaction specifically includes: an interaction symbol for the intelligent entity environment and digital information in the interactive interface, an interaction semantics constructed according to interactive grammar rules such as metaphor, implicit metaphor, metonymy, and the feedback function of the activated disembodied interaction based on the feedforward information of the exposed interaction.

2.2 Scene Test

For the physical test environment, we chose to test in the real home scenario (Fig. 3), which shows the relative relationship between users, agents and environment in real scenes. In this scenario, the user can be motivated by the original embodied cognition. In the prototype design of the agent, we designed two different sizes of agents to explore Cognitive Efficiency of Users on the Ability of Agents by recording the interaction behavior and distance between agent and user, the expression of agent and user's emotion, and perform mapping between the semantics of disembodied interaction and the behavior of exposed interaction in interactive grammar. Prototype testing of three typical Chinese families [one core family (second generation), one direct family (three generations), one single-person young family] is performed using the scenario of the agent, three typical family members including four office workers, 1 housewife, 1 primary school student, 1 university student, 1 old man retired at home.

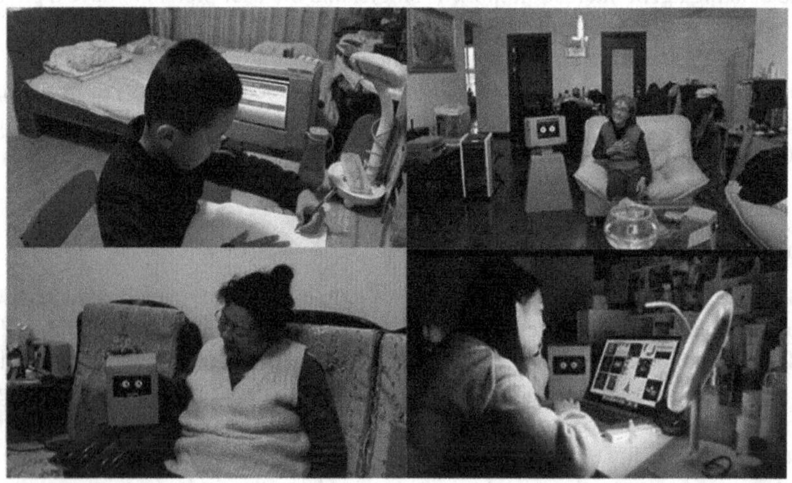

Fig. 3. People and agents in a test environment

3 Result Analysis

3.1 Analysis of the Results of the Embodied Interaction of the Agent

- **Agent appearance**

The appearance of the agent will bring about a difference in function. A large agent has a sense of presence while a small agent has a sense of family integration. The user's interaction behavior is different under the agents affordance cues. When users interact with large-scale agents, they are more of the click behavior of visual interface and the language behavior of exposed interaction under disembodied interaction. When users interact with small-sized agents, they mainly focus on exposed interaction behaviors, such as touching and tapping, hug, etc.

- **Embodied interaction behavior between human and agent**

When people interact with each other, various implicit mechanisms are used to share information about their state and interaction state. The mechanism by which the physical state of the body is changed is called a body language. Body language provides clues about personal emotions, emotions, and mental states, which can perform information communication by posture, gesture, facial expression, eye behavior, contact with body-related behavior and pronunciation behavior [7]. Studies have shown that people interact with robots in social network models [8]. When faced with complex inanimate objects, people often use social models to understand and predict their behavior [9]. As a result, such model is applied to embodied interaction between human and robot agents. In the process of interaction between humans and agents, body language behavior plays an important role in human-robot interaction. The human body language signal sends additional clues that can be observed, which characterize the user's mental and physiological state and his intentions, thus making the human-robot interaction intuitive and efficient. The signals and gestures of human body language appear in the form of clusters. The various channels of body language are semantically ambiguous and need to be understood in specific contexts. The most frequent interaction between humans and agents is the contact behavior between the two, including human touch, limb collision, greeting, hug and guidance (Fig. 4), the semantics of these interactions depend on the context, including the nature of the relationship and the way it is performed. It requires the agent to perform accurate user intention analysis and convey corresponding natural output feedback.

3.2 Analysis of the Results of the Disembodied Interaction of the Agent

- **Agent Symbols**

When designing the disembodied interaction of robotic agents, we can learn from human body language behavior and use this natural behavior to express unique personality and characteristics, which will help the strong tie between humans and robots, such as friendship and trust. By creating a symbolic system of facial expressions, body language, functional operations, and content semantics, the agent constructs human-

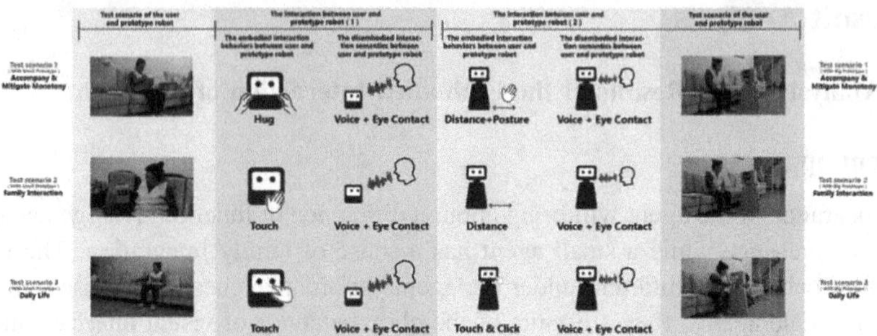

Fig. 4. The interaction between users and two different robot prototype

computer interaction in the interface performance, and correspondence with the level of interaction behavior. By symbol, signifier and sign, the language content and grammar standards of human-computer interaction are established, as show in Fig. 5.

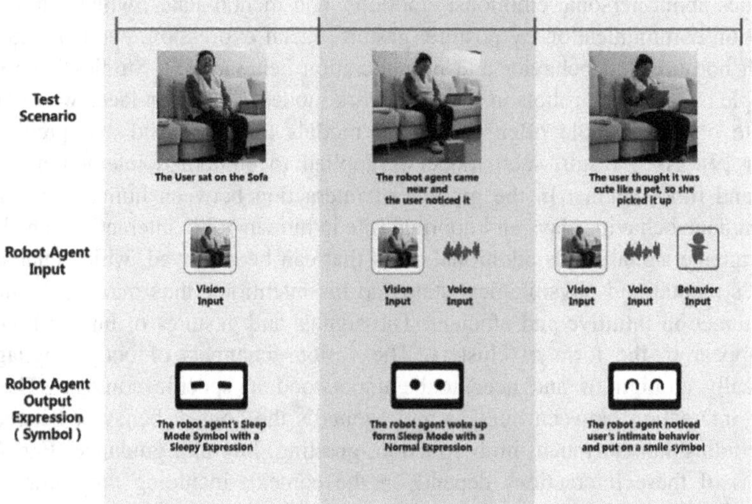

Fig. 5. The symbols of disembodied interaction between users and robot

1. Expressions
   Facial expressions are the main source of emotion. At present, most of the research focuses on six main emotions, namely, anger, sadness, surprise, happiness, fear and disgust. The expression design of the agent can be used as a reference for conveying emotions. It can be matched in view of input for user interaction, so as to express human personality characteristics to enhance the natural and real sense of human-computer interaction.

2. Postures
   The posture is used to convey information about attitudes. By designing the interactive feedback of the agent, the degree of attention paid by the user and the degree to which the agent responds to the person can be determined. The survey shows that the user prefers the agent to have a forward-looking behavior when performing interactive feedback. At the same time, the posture can also reflect the intensity of emotional state, for example, the weakness of the body is connected to the sad mood, and the nervous posture is connected to the angry emotion. Therefore, when designing the expression of the agent, it can also be combined with the body posture to increase the natural feeling of human-computer interaction.
3. Eye-contact behavior
   Eye-contact communication plays an important role in interpersonal communication. The exchange of information between people always starts with eye communication. Eye behavior plays an important role in the transmission of information. Therefore, the eye behavior design of the agent is more conducive to emotional expression. Through eye behavior, an agent can express its "emotional" state, passing on more information that languages and postures cannot accurately represent. Eye behavior is also an indicator of interest, attention or implicature. In the process of uninterrupted eye contact between the agent and the person, the user can better understand the intention of the agent and thus exchange information.

- **Semantics of agent**

Through interactive information content, the agent establishes the communication of human-computer interaction in meaning, including functional operation and language meaning. In the design of man-machine dialogue mechanism, because the mental model of human intelligence is different from the cognitive computing of artificial intelligence, and the content meaning of FBS (function behavior structure) and CMR (content model relationship) is different, then words and semantics are brought into important attention. The living data generated by the continuous source of dialogue provides an important basis for human-computer interaction data services. The design of Human-Robot Dialogue follows a semi-open dialogue structure, which can not only satisfy the openness of human dialogue and communication, but also change the functional behavior structure model that the artificial intelligence has no clear task pointing. An example analysis of the two test scenarios of the agent is performed as follows.

1. Scene 6——Child Education and Counseling
   Little brother: Hello, I don't know much about this history problem.
   Agent: I am here to help you, what is the problem?
   Brother: About XXXXX
   Agent: OK, I know, I am inquiring for you now.
   (after finding the answer)
   Agent: OK, I have found the right answer for you, come check it out!

The intelligent body-speaking design for children needs to turn children's education into heuristic education, which uses guided dialogue structure. According to the content that the user is interested in, the result of the knowledge search of the content is displayed, instead of directly giving the answer, the answer of the question is given step by step to form an interactive dialogue structure, and thus guiding the subject to actively think. The possibility of multiple answers to a question is explored using ways of encouragement and suggestion, thus allowing users to form a model of independent thinking and a unique way to explore their own answers.

2. Scene15——Reminder of sleep
   Agent: It is already 0 o'clock in the morning, you should rest.
   Youth: My work is still not finished, and I will sleep in half an hour.
   [After half an hour]
   Agent: It's been 30 min, is your work done?
   Youth: Still a little bit, but I am too sleepy, help me set a clock at 6 o'clock tomorrow, I will continue to do it tomorrow morning.
   Agent: OK, I have set an alarm clock for you at 6 o'clock tomorrow morning. Go to sleep, good night.

Verbal design of time reminder shall not apply rude tones, or sermon style, but the equal dialogue that users can accept. For example, the user should be informed of the amount of work tomorrow or the benefits of early sleep and warm heart greetings. The language content should not be too much, which may be easy to cause users to resent. In the time of sleep, it can also play related music or use low-frequency white noise to get the user into a sleepy state, and naturally remind users.

- **Interactive feedback**

The agent provides information feed-forward through the words content of the agent, and the information feed-forward provides a basis for the interactive feedback of the function symbols. Therefore, the agent should provide both the functional design of the weapon type and the content design of the container type. Integrating factors such as functions, interaction behavior, data structure, user vision and requirements, information container content, mental model and interaction model, relationship between human-machine environment, relationship between scene and story, etc., as well as the establishment of interactive grammar, a series of design meta-language and meta-translation systems of the interaction design, product design, service design and ecological design of the intelligent robot agent are constructed.

4 Mapping Relation Between Embodied Interaction and Disembodied Interaction

The disembodied interaction of the agent is extracted by the subject (human) from the object (the real environment) and the object (the real environment) to the subject (human) perception, cognition and behavior (embodied interaction). Advocates of the Embodied interaction view believe that artificial intelligence cannot completely replicate different levels of intelligence, and the biological nervous system that realizes human cognitive ability cannot be completely equivalent to computer hardware systems. Therefore, artificial intelligence does not understand the mindset and sensibility determined by the body like human intelligence. Through the knowledge graph, the cognitive experience of the human objective body (the body at the level of the biological nervous system) and the body of the phenomenon (the body experienced in the social culture) are associated with the functional requirements of the input. The embodied interaction is important for guiding the agent to do what, how, and why it interacts with people. Using the perception and cognition of the real world under the imposed interaction, the behavior feedback design of the agent is constructed to constitute the affordance demonstrativeness of the agent. In the process of human-robot interaction, the behavior of the agent stimulates the experience of the past and the new embodied interaction with the agent. The mapping relationship of the embodied and disembodied interaction is shown in Fig. 6.

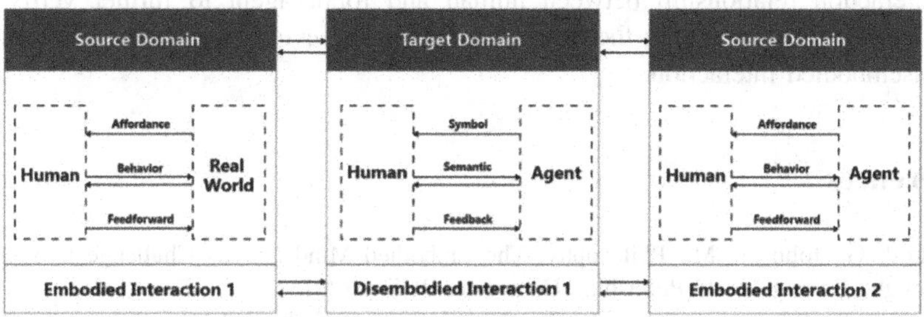

Fig. 6. The mapping relationship between embodied interaction and disembodied interaction

Since between affordance, behavior and symbols in the embodied interaction with symbols, semantics, and feedback in the disembodied interaction there is lack of mapping relationship constructed by the interaction grammar, the human-robot interaction causes insufficient interaction performance and user experience. The open learning of artificial intelligence provides feed forward information for the intelligent agents. The detection framework of the intelligent environment is more efficient. The compact and efficient depth CNN feature helps the agent to perform the identification and judgment of the outgoing interaction and the spontaneous weak supervision or unsupervised learning of the symbolic semantics, so as to form the knowledge graph of interactive semantics. Quantify-self forms the robust target representation control of the interactive object, and provides the Basis of Three-Dimensional Target Detection of Situation Reasoning in Social Network Computing of disembodied interaction, target instance segmentation of interactive disembodied interaction and embodied interaction of interaction objects to demonstration of embodied interaction, making the feedforward of the imposed interaction and the feedback of the disembodied interaction causally related to each other.

5 Conclusion

Through the questionnaire survey, in-depth interview and agent prototype usability test, this study draws the interactive content and functions mutually carried by embodied interaction and disembodied interaction. Affordance, behavior, feed-forward in embodied interaction and symbol, semantic, and feedback in disembodied interaction form a complete interactive grammar system. Then it performs Subject-Object Embodied Representation and Subject Cognition through body language, facial expressions, sentence intonation, interactive entities, and constructs systematic mapping of the origin domain between embodied cognition and disembodied cognition. The interaction grammar (interaction behavior pattern recognition; interaction model and information architecture, function and content relationship, etc.) is used to design the interaction relationship between human and robot agent to further verify the mapping relationship among the three elements in the event of embodied interaction and disembodied interaction.

References

1. Lakoff, G., Johnson, M.: Philosophy: The Embodied Mind and Its Challenge to Western Thought. Beijing World Publishing Corpotion, Beijing (2018)
2. Dourish, P.: Where the Action Is: The Foundations of Embodied Interaction. MIT Press, Cambridge (2001)
3. Clark, A.: An embodied cognitive science? Trends Cogn. Sci. **3**(9), 345 (1999)
4. Edmund, G.A.H.: Phenomenology of Intersubjectivity, p. 57. Maldinus Neihov Publishing House, Hague (1973)
5. Dreyfus, H.L.: Being-in-the-world a commentary on Heidegger's being and time, division I. Philos. Lit. **15**(2), 373–377 (1991)
6. Merleau-Ponty, M.: La Phénoménologie de la Perception. Gallimard, Paris (1945)
7. Xu, G., Tao, L., Di, H.: Body Language Understanding for Human Computer Interaction, pp. 16–18. Publishing House of Electronics Industry (2014)
8. Breazeal, C.: Emotion and sociable humanoid robots. Int. J. Hum. Comput. Stud. **59**(1–2), 119–155 (2003)
9. Reeves, B., Nass, C.: The Media Equation: How People Treat Computers, Television, and New Media Like Real People and Places. Cambridge University Press, New York (1996)

Investigating the Relationship Between Connection, Agency and Autonomy for Controlling a Robot Arm for Remote Social Physical Interaction

Ryuya Sato[1(✉)], Don Kimber[2], and Yanxia Zhang[2]

[1] Waseda University, 27 Waseda-cho, Shinjuku-ku, Tokyo 162-0042, Japan
ryuya-sato@iwata.mech.wasaeda.ac.jp

[2] FX Palo Alto Laboratory (FXPAL), 3174 Porter Drive, Palo Alto, CA 94304, USA
{kimber,yzhang}@fxpal.com

Abstract. Current telecommunication systems such as Skype cannot allow remote users to interact physically. Thus, we propose installing a robot arm and teleoperating it can realize social physical interaction. Some autonomy may be necessary to realize easy teleoperation because teleoperation requires mental workload. However, too much autonomy can decrease sense of agency, which may cause lack of connection because remote users do not feel they caused actions. Thus, in this study, we investigate the relationship between autonomy level and sense of connection of a remote person with local area and people. We focus on pushing tasks because pushing is one of the major functions in hand and arm use. Sense of agency can be categorized into the Feeling of agency (FOA) which is not conceptual and the Judgement of agency (JOA) which is conceptual. Therefore, we conducted user studies to investigate whether FOA associated with control of trajectories and joint angles affects the sense of connection. The results suggested that higher autonomy could decrease telepresence, and remote users preferred controlling joint angles for fun, but they did not need FOA for performance.

Keywords: Remote social physical interaction · Teleoperation · Sense of agency

1 Introduction

Telecommunication including virtual tours and web conferences is increasing. For example, the global web conferencing market will be around 10 billion dollars [1]. Today, many video conference systems such as Skype, appear.in and other research systems [2–4] help people communicate from remote places. One of the challenges in current telecommunication is lack of physical interaction, which can cause lack of connection for remote users. For example, those telecommunication systems cannot allow remote users to move pieces of a board game while playing with a local user. Thus, remote users can feel lack of connection because they cannot realize what they

A. Marcus and W. Wang (Eds.): HCII 2019, LNCS 11584, pp. 277–290, 2019.
https://doi.org/10.1007/978-3-030-23541-3_21

want to do [5]. We propose that installing a robot arm and teleoperating it can address the problem by enabling remote physical interaction (See Fig. 1).

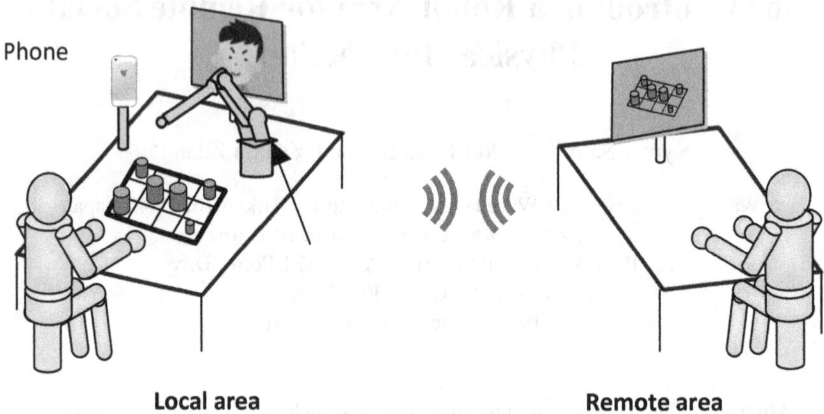

Fig. 1. Installing a robot arm to realize physical interaction

Teleoperation is found to be challenging and can induce excessive mental workload [6]. For example, teleoperation degrades work efficiency more than 50% compared with boarding operation in the construction machinery case [7]. Even for operators of construction machineries who have sophisticated skills to manipulate them, teleoperation can be challenging. Thus, some autonomy can be important because autonomy can realize easier teleoperation [8], and many researchers have achieved high efficiency teleoperation by increasing autonomy level. For example, master-slave interfaces have been proposed to allow teleoperators to input only hand position [9]. Additionally, AR based interfaces have been developed which allow teleoperators to input only the goal position [10].

However, higher levels of autonomy lead to humans feeling less sense of agency, which refers to the ownership of the actions [11]. There is a tradeoff between sense of agency and level of autonomy. Lack of sense of agency can cause lack of connection with local area and people, because a remote person does not feel they caused actions. Numerous research addresses levels of robot autonomy [12–14], and some research examines using robots to realize physical interaction [15, 16]. However, they focus on efficiency. There is limited prior work examining how sense of connection relates to agency and different autonomy levels. Therefore, we investigate the relationship between autonomy level and sense of connection of a remote person with local area and people. Figure 2 shows our hypothesis about the relationship between autonomy level and sense of connection. Lower levels of autonomy can lead to higher levels of connection as the green dotted curve in Fig. 2 because lower levels of autonomy lead to high sense of agency. The position of the green dotted curve in Fig. 2 can depend on mental workload to teleoperate because low mental workload can lead to ease teleoperation, which can lead to high levels of connection. Among many possible physical interactions, in this paper we focus on a pushing task for two reasons. First, pushing is one of the major functions in hand and arm use [17], and second, pushing something including buttons activates some exhibits in many places such as museums and theme parks.

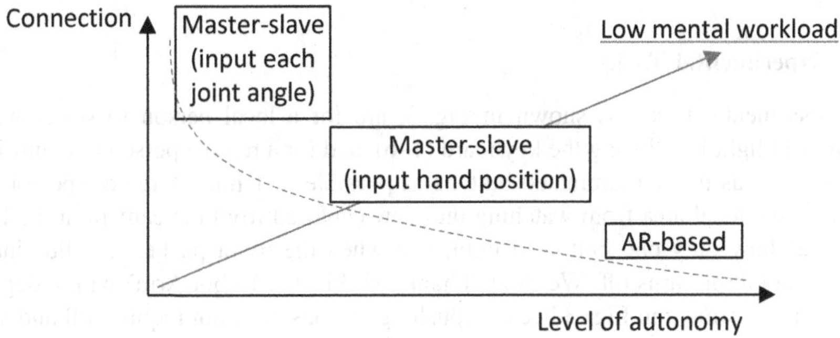

Fig. 2. Tradeoff between connection and autonomy level

2 Research Question

The purpose of this study is to investigate the relationship between autonomy level and sense of connection. Both autonomy level and sense of connection can be related to sense of agency as mentioned in the Sect. 1. Thus, in this Section, we explain sense of agency and decide autonomy levels to investigate.

2.1 Sense of Agency

Sense of agency can be categorized into the Feeling of agency (FOA) which is not conceptual and the Judgement of agency (JOA) which is conceptual [18]. For example, when people try to push buttons, they do not consciously consider all the joint angles of their upper limbs, associated with FOA, although they think about which buttons to push, which impacts JOA. In the pushing case, humans must decide which objects to push, mentally plan trajectories, calculate each joint angle for the planned trajectories [19].

2.2 Autonomy Levels to Investigate

We should investigate whether FOA associated with control of trajectories and joint angles affects the sense of connection that subjects feel with local area and people. If FOA affects the sense of connection, the interface should allow remote people to control each joint angle or trajectories. If FOA does not affect the sense of connection the robot arm control system should recognize the environment and manipulate the robot arm such as [10]. Thus, we investigate and compare the autonomy levels of three different interfaces. The first one is to input all the joint angles, the second one is to input trajectories (hand positions and pitch angles), and the last one is to input only the goal hand position.

3 Experiments

We conducted experiments to investigate the affect of FOA on the sense of connection. In this chapter, we explain the experimental tasks, the three developed interfaces, experimental procedure, results, and discussion.

3.1 Experimental Tasks

The experimental tasks, as shown in Fig. 3, are for a local person to select which buttons will light by clicking the keyboard (1–6), and for a remote person to control the robot to push as many illuminated buttons as possible in 1 min. A remote person can recognize the local area from watching the view captured from the camera in the local area. We allow only one button to light, and when the robot pushes the illuminated button, that button turns off. We used "PhantomX Pincher Robot Arm" with 4 degrees of freedom, as shown in Fig. 3 because pushing buttons does not require roll and yaw.

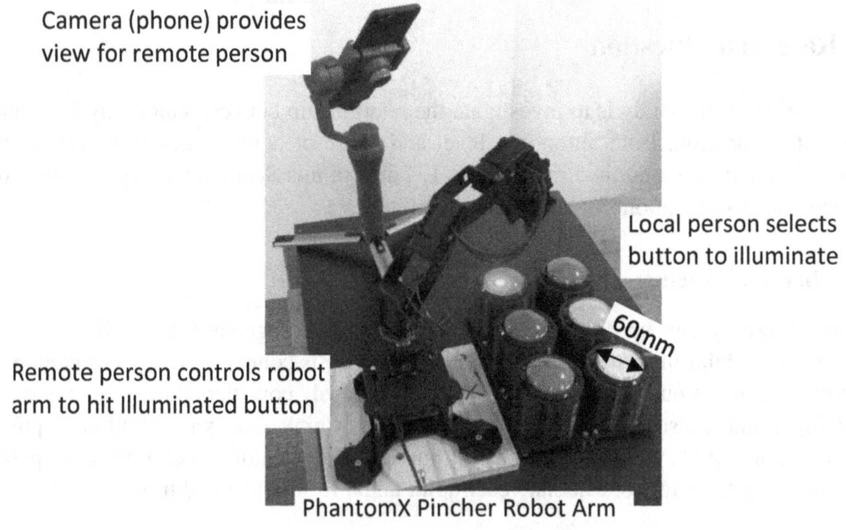

Fig. 3. Experimental setup

3.2 Development of Three Interfaces

We should investigate whether FOA affects the sense of connection as explained in Sect. 2.2. Therefore, we developed three interfaces to control the robot arm. The first one is to input all the joint angles by moving another matching robot arm (JA; Joint Angles) as shown in Fig. 4(a). The second one is to input the hand position and pitch angle tracked by using a leap motion (PP; Position and Pitch) as shown in Fig. 4(b). The last one is to input only the goal hand position of the robot by clicking the circle in the web page (GP; Goal Position) as shown in Fig. 4(c).

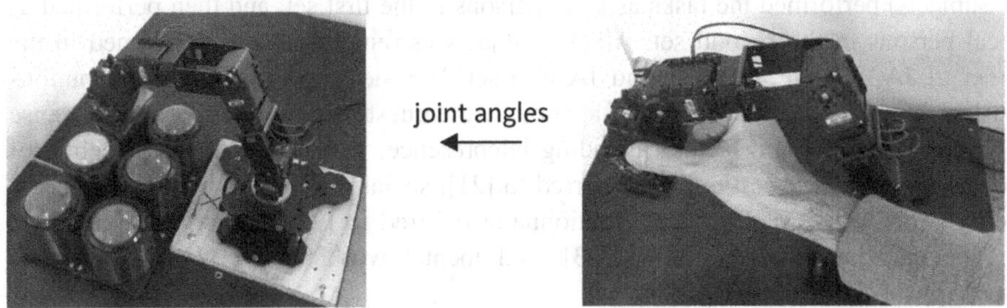

(a) Interface to input all the joint angles by moving another matching robot arm

(b) Interface to input the hand position and pitch angle tracked by a leap motion

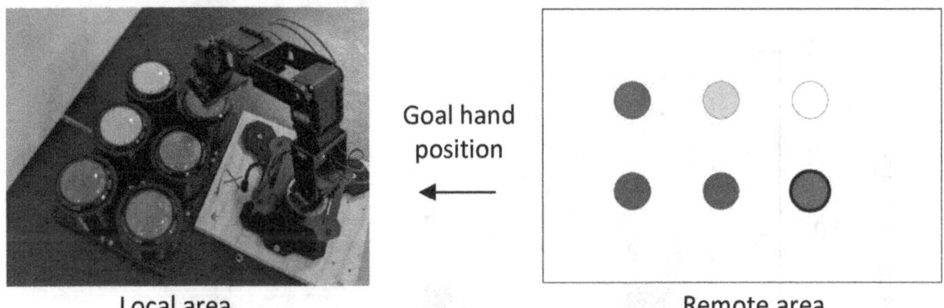

(c) Interface to input only the goal hand position of the robot by clicking the circle in the web page

Fig. 4. Experimental comparison

3.3 Experimental Procedure

14 volunteers (12 male and 2 female) were involved as subjects in this experiment. Subjects tried 2 sets, and each set includes 6 trials with the task explained in Sect. 3.1. Half of the subjects (7 subjects) performed the tasks as remote persons in the first set, and then performed as local persons in the second set, and the other half of the subjects

(7 subjects) performed the tasks as local persons in the first set, and then performed as local persons in the second set. All the subjects as remote persons performed in the order of JA, PP, GP, GP, PP, and JA in a set. We measured the number of buttons pushed as work efficiency, sense of agency by the questionnaire referred to [20], sense of connection by three factors including telepresence, which is defined as feeling of being there, by the questionnaire referred to [21], social presence, which is defined as being perceived as real, by the questionnaire referred to [22], and social connection by the questionnaire referred to [23], and mental workload by NASA-TLX [24] (see Appendix for details).

3.4 Results and Discussion

Sense of Agency. Figure 5 shows the results of sense of agency. No significant differences are observed among the three interfaces by the Bonferroni method. This result is different from the previous research which indicates that higher levels of autonomy lead to humans feeling less sense of agency [11], so we discuss below. Figure 6 shows the results of the numbers of buttons pushed correctly. The Bonferroni method indicates that GP pushed more correct (illuminated) buttons than JA and PP by a significant amount. Therefore, the results suggest that autonomy works well. Moreover, subjects can have enough JOA because they selected which buttons to push. Those can lead to high sense of agency in GP.

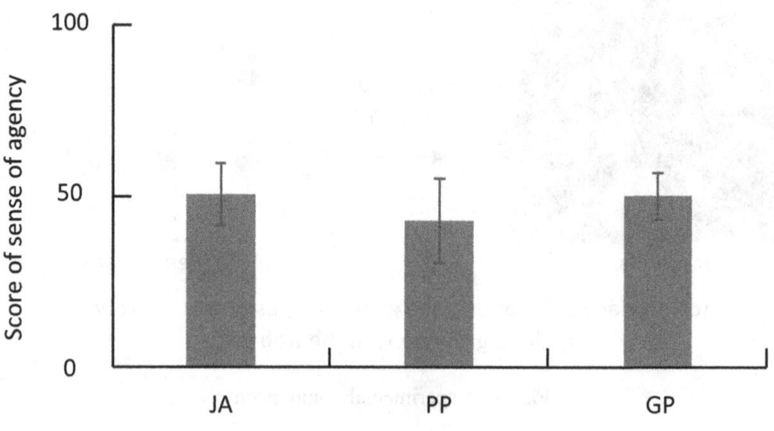

Fig. 5. Sense of agency

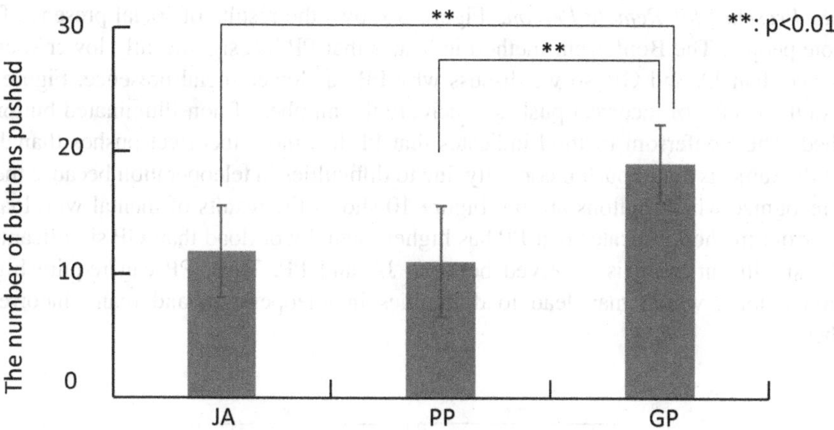

Fig. 6. The numbers of buttons pushed correctly

Sense of Connection

Telepresence. Figure 7 shows the results of telepresence. The Bonferroni method indicates that JA provides significantly higher telepresence than GP and a significant trend is observed between PP and GP. Therefore, higher level of autonomy can lead to lack of telepresence.

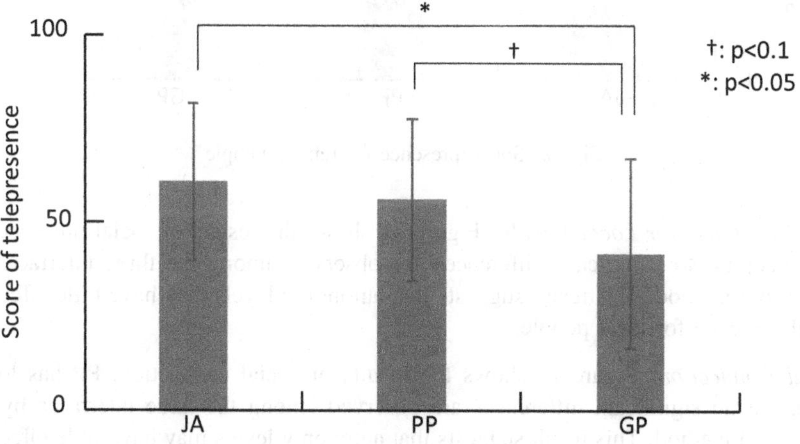

Fig. 7. Telepresence

Social Presence for Remote Person. Figure 8 shows the results of social presence for remote people. The Bonferroni method indicates that PP has significantly lower social presence than JA and GP, so we discuss why PP has lower social presence. Figure 9 shows the results of incorrect pushes which are the number of non-illuminated buttons pushed. The Bonferroni method indicates that PP has more incorrect pushes than JA and GP. Subjects could push incorrectly due to difficulties in teleoperation because they can recognize which buttons are on. Figure 10 shows the results of mental workload. Bonferroni method indicates that PP has higher mental workload than GP significantly and a significant trend is observed between JA and PP. Thus, PP can require high cognitive load, which may lead to difficulties in teleoperation and many incorrect pushes.

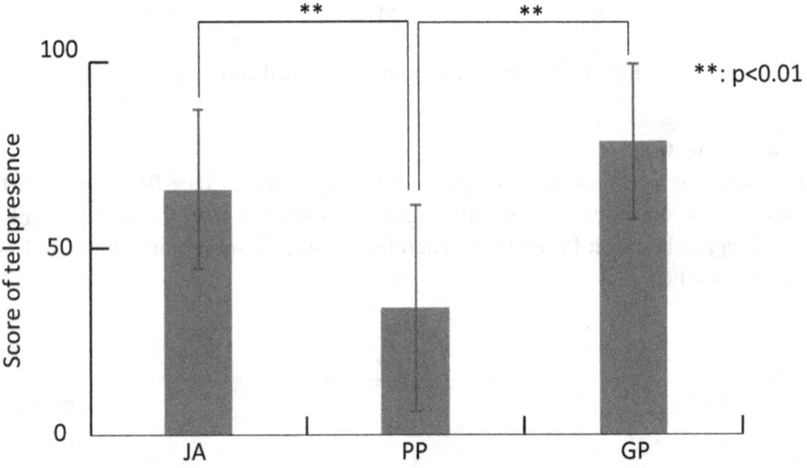

Fig. 8. Social presence for remote people

Social Presence for Local People. Figure 11 shows the results of social presence for local people. No significant differences are observed among the three interfaces by Bonferroni method. This result suggests that autonomy levels may have little effect on social presence for local people.

Social Connection. Figure 12 shows the results of social connection. PP has lower score, but no significant differences are observed among the three interfaces by the Bonferroni method. This result suggests that autonomy levels may have little effect on social connection, but we need more subjects.

Discussion. Here, we discuss the best interface. 6 subjects preferred JA, 3 subjects preferred PP, 4 subjects preferred GP, and 1 subject preferred JA for fun and GP for performance from the questionnaire. The reason given why subjects who preferred JA was for fun, and one for GP was for performance from the questionnaire. Moreover, the results suggested that JA had high telepresence and GP had high work efficiency. Therefore, people who would like to have a fun experience may prefer JA and those who would like to have high performance work may prefer GP.

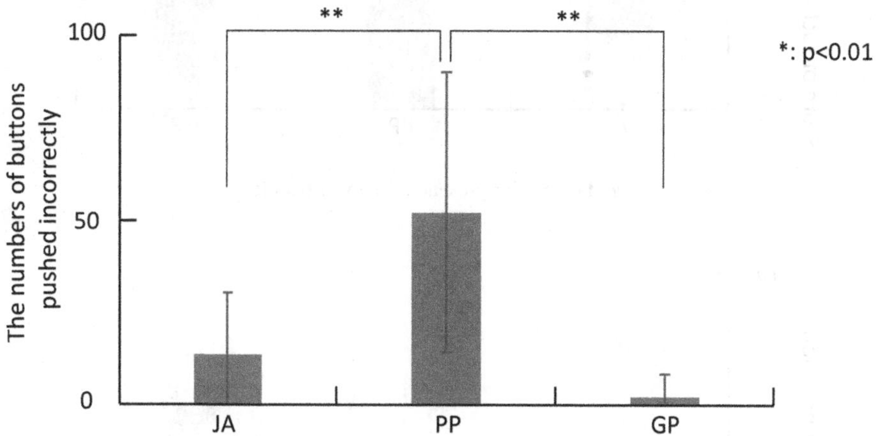

Fig. 9. The numbers of buttons pushed incorrectly

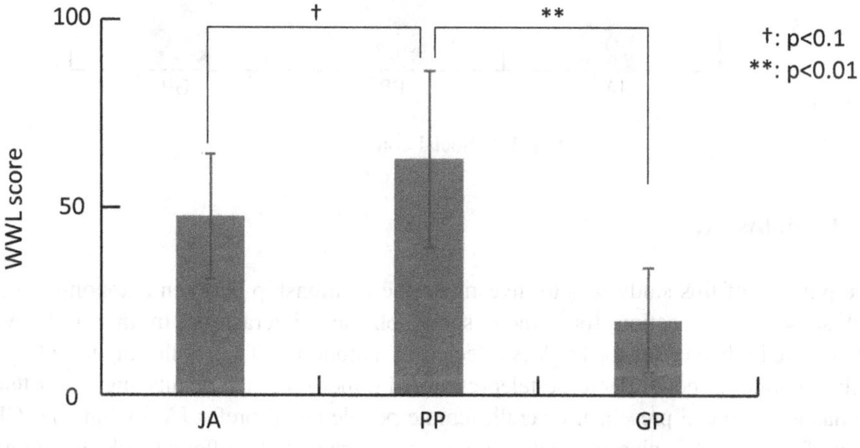

Fig. 10. Mental workload

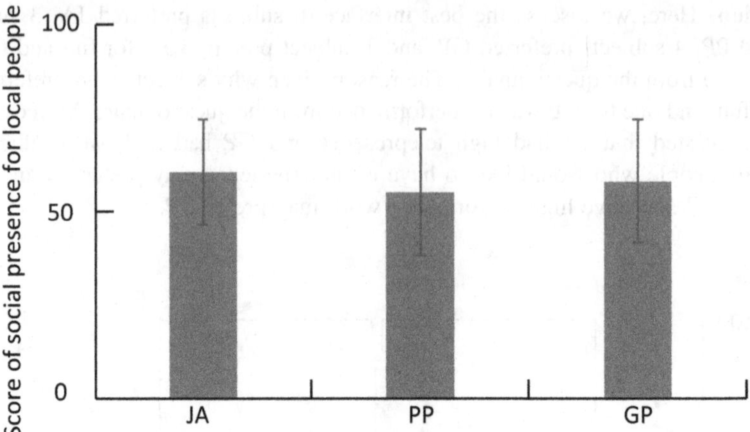

Fig. 11. Social presence for local people

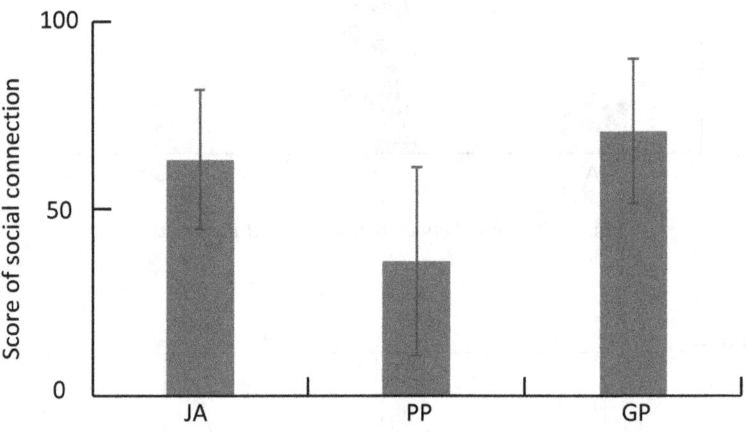

Fig. 12. Social connection

4 Conclusion

The purpose of this study was to investigate the relationship between autonomy level and sense of connection for remote social physical interaction. In the study we investigated whether or not FOA is affected by autonomy. The results suggested that higher autonomy could decrease telepresence. Furthermore, the results suggested that PP has lower social presence. Overall, remote people could prefer JA for fun, and GP for performance. We plan to conduct future experiments with different tasks including grasping and transporting.

Acknowledgement. This research was supported by FXPAL. We would also like to thank Reach and Teach.

Appendix

Followings are the questionnaire for remote people. User Research Room is the room where local people are. First three questions are for telepresence, the next five questions are for sense of agency, the next two questions are for social presence, and the last question is for social connection.

During the study, my body was in the Open area, but my mind was in the User Research Room.

Strongly disagree Strongly agree

The User Research Room seemed to me "somewhere I was" rather than "something I saw."

Strongly disagree Strongly agree

I forgot about my immediate surroundings when I was controlling a robot arm.

Strongly disagree Strongly agree

The robot responses (movements) were what I expected.

Strongly disagree Strongly agree

I was surprised by the robot responses.

Strongly disagree Strongly agree

The robot's actions felt willed by me.

Strongly disagree Strongly agree

I was responsible for the robot's movements.

Strongly disagree Strongly agree

Movements of the robot felt very similar to normal everyday movements of my arm.

Strongly disagree Strongly agree

I felt comfortable interacting by using this interface.

Strongly disagree Strongly agree

This interface enabled me to realize what I wanted to do.

Strongly disagree Strongly agree

I feel connected to the User Research Room and a local person.

Strongly disagree Strongly agree

(Only after finishing the user study)
What was the best interface?

Why was the interface the best?

Followings are the questionnaire for local people. All of the questions are for social presence.

The remote person was intensely involved in the interaction.

Strongly disagree Strongly agree

The remote person acted bored by the interaction.

Strongly disagree Strongly agree

The remote person showed enthusiasm during the interaction.

Strongly disagree Strongly agree

To what extent was this like you were in the same room with a remote person?

Not at all Very likely

To what extent did a robot arm seem "real"? (To what extent did a robot arm move like human's arm?)

Not at all Very likely

References

1. Ameri Research Inc.: Web conferencing market outlook to 2024: Key type categories (on-premise, hosted), organization size (SMEs, large enterprises), application (BFSI, retail, healthcare, education, government), regional segmentation, competitive dynamics, M&A insights, pricing analysis (IPP, OPP, RAP) and segment forecast (2017)
2. Kawasaki, H., Iizuka, H., Okamoto, S., Ando, H., Maeda, T.: Collaboration and skill transmission by first-person perspective view sharing system. In: IEEE Proceedings on International Conference on Robot and Human Interactive Communication, Viareggio, pp. 125–131 (2010)
3. Lee, G., Teo, T., Kim, S., Billinghurst, M.: Sharedsphere: MR collaboration through shared live panorama. In: Proceedings of SIGGRAPH Asia, no. 12, Thai (2017)
4. Kasahara, S., Nagai, S., Rekimoto, J.: JackIn head: immersive visual telepresence system with omnidirectional wearable camera. IEEE Trans. Vis. Comput. Graph. **23**(3), 1222–1234 (2017)
5. Russell, D., Peplau, L.A., Cutrona, C.E.: The revised UCLA Loneliness scale: concurrent and discriminant validity evidence. J. Pers. Soc. Psychol. **39**, 472–480 (1980)

6. Chen, J., Haas, E., Barnes, M.: Human performance issues and user interface design for teleoperated robots. IEEE Trans. Syst. Man Cybern. **37**(6), 1231–1245 (2007)
7. Chayama, K., et al.: Technology of unmanned construction system in Japan. J. Robot. Mechatron. **26**(4), 403–417 (2012)
8. Beer, J., Fisk, A., Rogers, W.: Toward a framework for levels of robot autonomy in human-robot interaction. J. Hum. Robot. Interact. **3**(2), 74–99 (2014)
9. Fernando, C., et al.: Design of TELESAR V for transferring bodily consciousness in telexistence. In: IEEE/RSJ International Conference on Intelligent Robots and Systems, Vilamoura, pp. 5112–5118 (2012)
10. Hashimoto, S., Ishida, A., Inami, M., Igarashi, T.: TouchMe: an augmented reality interface for remote robot control. J. Robot. Mechatron. **25**(3), 529–537 (2013)
11. Moore, J.: What is the sense of agency and why does it matter. Front. Psychol. **7**, 1272 (2016)
12. Javdani, S., Admoni, H., Pellegrinelli, S., Srinivasa, S., Bagnell, J.: Shared autonomy via hindsight optimization for teleoperation and teaming. Int. J. Robot. Res. **37**(4), 717–742 (2018)
13. Muelling, K., et al.: Autonomy infused teleoperation with application to brain computer interface controlled manipulation. Auton. Robot. **41**(6), 1401–1422 (2017)
14. Lui, K., Cho, H., Ha, C., Lee, D.: First-person view semi-autonomous teleoperation of cooperative wheeled mobile robots with visuo-haptic feedback. Int. J. Robot. Res. **36**(5–7), 840–860 (2017)
15. Saraji, M., Sasaki, T., Matsumura, R., Minamizawa, K., Inami, M.: Fusion: full body surrogacy for collaborative communication. In: Proceedings of ACM SIGGRAPH, no. 7, Vancouver (2018)
16. Sugiura, Y., et al.: Cooky: a cooperative cooking robot system. In: Proceedings of SIGGRAPH Asia, no. 17, Singapore (2011)
17. World Health Organization.: International Classification of Functioning, Disability and Health (2007)
18. Synofzik, M., Thier, P., Leube, D., Schlotterbeck, P., Lindner, A.: Misattributions of agency in schizophrenia are based on imprecise predictions about the sensory consequences of one's actions. Brain **133**(1), 262–271 (2010)
19. Bizzi, E., Accornero, N., Chapple, W., Hogan, N.: Arm trajectory formation in monkeys. Exp. Brain Res. **46**(1), 139–143 (1982)
20. Polito, V., Barnier, A., Woody, E.: Developing the sense of agency rating scale (SOARS): an empirical measure of agency disruption in hypnosis. Conscious. Cogn. **22**(3), 684–696 (2013). https://doi.org/10.1016/j.concog.2013.04.003
21. Klein, L.: Creating virtual product experiences: The role of telepresence. J. Interact. Mark. **17**(1), 41–55 (2003)
22. Gunawardena, C., Zittle, F.: Social presence as a predictor of satisfaction within a computer-mediated conferencing environment. Am. J. Distance Educ. **11**(3), 8–26 (1997)
23. Nowak, K., Biocca, F.: The effect of the agency and anthropomorphism on users' sense of telepresence, copresence, and social presence in virtual environments. Presence **12**(5), 481–494 (2003)
24. Hart, S., Staveland, L.: Development of NASA-TLX (Task Load Index): results of empirical and theoretical research. Adv. Psychol. **52**, 139–183 (1988)

ARena: Improving the Construction Process of Line-Follower Robot Arenas Through Projection Mapping

Pedro J. L. Silva, Diogo B. B. Henriques, Gustavo C. R. Lima, Júlia D. T. de Souza, João M. X. N. Teixeira(✉), and Veronica Teichrieb

Maracatronics and Voxar Labs, Federal University of Pernambuco, Av. Prof. Moraes Rego, 1235 - Cidade Universitária, Recife, PE, Brazil
{pjls2,dbbh,gcrl,jmxnt,vt}@cin.ufpe.br, juliadtsouza97@gmail.com
http://www.ufpe.br

Abstract. With the increasing number of line-follower robot championships, the problem of arenas production time arises. This study is based on a recurring problem detected by the Organization of the Brazilian Robotics Olympiad (OBR) regarding the necessity of producing arenas in a short time. Therefore, a solution was elaborated, called ARena, that uses the concept of Projection Mapping to aid in the standardized production of tracks. The result obtained from user tests was favorable to the proposal, however, improvements in the tool interface are required.

Keywords: Projection Mapping · Line-follower robots competition · Brazilian Robotics Olympiad

1 Introduction

The RoboCupJunior Rescue Robot League [20] is a competition whose primary purpose is to create robots able to cross a space that mimics inhospitable landscapes and, in the end, save balls that mimic human beings. At these competitions, the field is simulated as an arena with a white background and a black line representing the track to be followed to the area where the victims of the disaster area. Although in real life, saving people is the most import part of a rescue, at the competition, the track is as important as the rescue itself.

But, for the event organizers, building the arenas is one of the most time-consuming infrastructure parts of the event, given the number of arenas to be produced and the process involved, which is manually performed by the arena judges. Currently, the organization of the Brazilian Robotics Olympiad (OBR) [15] uses software such as the Tournamenter [2] to compute competition scores, but they do not collaborate in the process of producing the tracks themselves. From the concept of Projection Mapping, it was possible to build ARena, a web-based solution that allows projecting the track over a surface, facilitating and making the production of the tracks faster, ending the first, and most difficult and

A. Marcus and W. Wang (Eds.): HCII 2019, LNCS 11584, pp. 291–308, 2019.
https://doi.org/10.1007/978-3-030-23541-3_22

time-consuming part of the building process. Since the tool was made available on the Internet and runs inside the browser, it can be used by anyone who needs to construct tracks for line-follower robots competitions. We have validated the proposed tool with different users, of different levels of experience, and it proved to be useful, according to their feedback and time to accomplish the tasks given during tests.

The remainder of this paper is structured as follows. Section 2 lists some works related to the process of constructing line-follower tracks. Section 3 presents other software used by OBR. Section 4 explains the importance of line-follower robot competitions in the world and specifically in the Brazilian context. Section 5 details Projection Mapping, which is the main technique used by the proposed tool. Section 6 describes the ARena tool, how it was implemented and its most important functionalities. Section 7 explains how the tool was validated according to the user tests performed, while Sect. 8 provides an analysis of the data obtained. At last, Sect. 9 provides final remarks about the work and gives future directions related so that the work can be improved.

2 Related Work

Projection Mapping has been used mainly for artistic, but also for educational, health and advertisement purposes. Some examples of these cases are listed as follows.

In [11], the authors propose the use of Spatial Augmented Reality to enhance physical artistic creation. The application works by projecting an image in order to aid users to create 3D drawings without technical knowledge. The tests showed adults drawing uninterrupted for 35 to 45 min and they reported that it was the most sketching experience they have since kindergarten.

Applications of Projection Mapping have also become frequent in cultural exhibitions and advertising campaigns. In 2017, Magic Kingdom Park used Projection Mapping, a technology being employed since 2010, at one of its major attractions named *"Star Wars: A Galactic Spectacular"*. Other examples of Projection Mappings within Disney park attractions include *"Happily ever after"* show, where guests become characters in the show. Other famous examples of Projection Mapping being used in popular culture are the *"Fête des lumières"*, a yearly religious festival taking place in the French city of Lyon every December, and the cinematic movie named *Oblivion* (2013).

A Projection Mapping technique using a Kinect-Projector system focused on irregular surfaces was published in [13]. One of the first uses of Projection Mapping [22] developed an immerse virtual environment for genomics studies. Other known uses include medical sciences [14] and even face projection [23].

There are several tools for general use Projection Mapping. *Lightform* is a commercial tool offering a graphics interface to simplify Projection Mapping with an RGB camera and a projector. *Resolume Arena* is a Projection Mapping tool intended for video jockeys. *Lumo Play* is another commercial Projection Mapping tool which has been adapted for indoor games. A simple projector-camera calibration system has been written in the C++ language [12], which is also available for use. *7th sense*, *Ventuz*, and *Coolux* are all examples of commercial tools intended for both indoor and outdoor Projection Mapping applications, especially focused on architectural uses such as building fronts, museums, opera houses and stages. A Projection Mapping tool, *DynaMapper*, has also been developed specifically for mobile devices. A thorough listing of several tools is available online at [10].

3 Other Software Used by OBR

3.1 Olimpo System

The Olimpo System [8] is the site of registration of the competing teams by the responsible teachers and of the management of the teams and events by the coordination of the Olympiad.

It is also used by other robotics competitions and scientific events such as National Robotics Show (MNR) and Latin American Robotics Competition (LARC), as seen in Fig. 1.

With its database, the Olimpo System provides information for other software, the Tournament, explained below.

Fig. 1. Olimpo System webpage.

3.2 Tournamenter

The other software used in the Brazilian edition of the event is Tournamenter [2]. It is an open source software whose function is to manage time, scores and classification of the teams. since it is a general purpose software designed to help various championships, it has a specific extension for the OBR and RoboCupJunior Rescue League.

The OBR extension communicates directly with the competition information server, downloading specific competition information, such as previously allocated teams for that event. It is also possible to allocate teams at competitions tables, generate schedules, count points of each participating team and send them to the competition information server (Fig. 2).

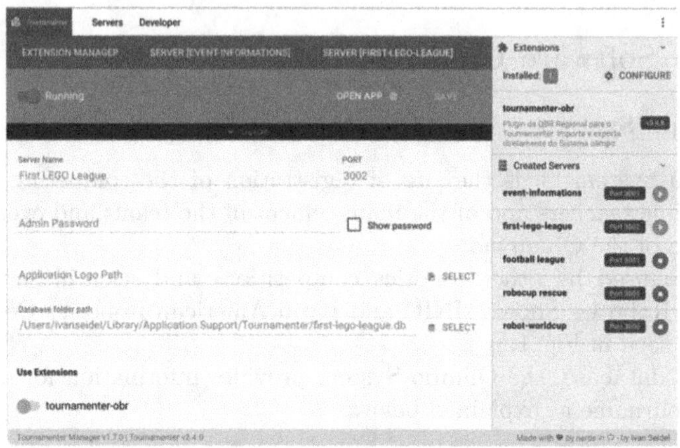

Fig. 2. Tournamenter app setup page.

Besides Olimpo System and Tournamenter, there is no official tool adopted by the Brazilian national committee of the RoboCup Junior Rescue League organization responsible for OBR nor by the International Committee for the RoboCup Junior Rescue League that is capable of supporting the construction process of line-follower arenas.

4 Line-Follower Robot Competitions

4.1 Importance at the Brazilian Context

In other countries, it is possible to observe a strong creative technological culture since childhood. In these countries, many products that have a strong market potential are patented. In Brazil, this process is still at its initial level, not having a culture that stimulates a better utilization of robotics technology in technological areas or even inside homes [18].

From the point of view of education, robotics has become an obligatory element in modern schools due to its possibility of actuation in many knowledge areas such as chemistry, mathematics, physics, history, geography, even language.

This gives rise to teaching methodologies such as the STEM, which aims to link science, technology, engineering, and mathematics in order to practice what has been taught and prepare students for life and the job market by solving real problems, present in the students' daily life. Second, [19] STEM should contribute on three main fronts:

1. Develop an attentive and capable society in Science, Technology, Engineering, and Mathematics.
2. Train students and teachers who are capable of developing the skills of the 21st century [7] within an integrated school environment.
3. Generate a research and development force in STEM-focused on innovation.

Along with the methodologies, robotic platforms emerge for educational purposes. Some are "closed" platforms, which do not allow the use of non-platform components such as SPRK+ from Spheros [5], Mindstorms EV3 [4] from LEGO Education and VEX IQ, VEX EDR and VEX Pro from Vex Robotics [21], some of them even have their own teaching plans. Other platforms such as Arduino [1], Texas Instruments Robotics System Learning Kit [9], and BBC-Microbit [6] are also tools used in methodologies, but they are "open platforms" and allow non-platform components to be used, expanding the horizons of learning.

As a promoter of robotics and automation, important areas for a country development, the Brazilian Robotics Olympiad plays a major role, since it works directly with children and young people, approximating them to technological development, robotics and automation. This way, they become direct agents of this construction and not just mere users. The OBR enters this context as a problem-providing space, where students can construct their own robotic devices with a real purpose in a space of collaborative competition. In such competitions, there is no direct confront and the search for innovation is a constant, allowing students to work on content that would only be worked on universities such as PID (Proportional–Integral–Derivative) algorithms, Fuzzy Logic, and State Machines.

4.2 The Brazilian Robotics Olympiad

The Brazilian Robotics Olympiad is the national stage in Brazil of the RoboCup Junior Rescue modality, which aims to simulate an environment hostile to humans related to rescuing in a disaster space.

Nowadays, the current challenge imposed on competitors is the construction of a robot and an efficient program capable of:

- Following the line track,
- Being robust to light variations on the lane and
- Identifying and collecting the victims.

In an analogous way, the challenge imposed on competition organizers is to build new arenas in a short time interval. There are approximately 50 regional phases, 27 state phases [16], and one national final, in which an average of 6 different arena models are produced per event using a paper blueprint as a reference with the measurements of each line and the position of each object in the arena, as shown on Fig. 3.

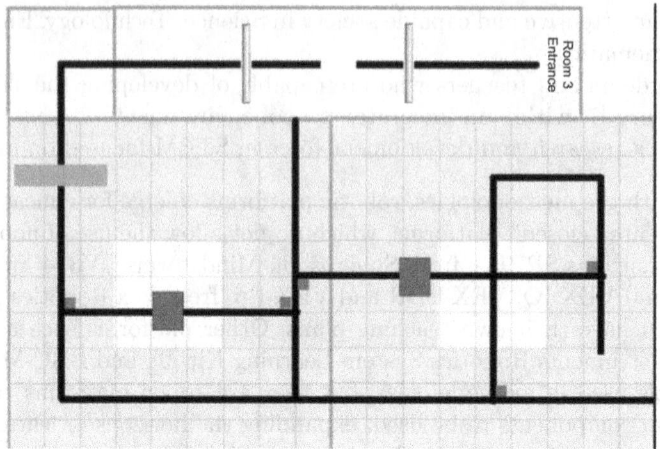

Fig. 3. Schematic sample used for arena construction. Blue rectangles represent obstacles, orange rectangle represent a portal and green squares representing turn signals. Source: OBR Database (Color figure online)

4.3 Competition Arena Contents

The main component of the scenario is the safe path, determined by a black line on a white wood substrate [17]. This line has small speed reducers up to 1 cm thick over which the robot must pass without leaving the safe path. It also has obstacles with maximum dimensions of $12 \times 10 \times 25$ cm (Length × Depth × Height), which must be bypassed by the line-follower robot after an evaluation of which path is free.

The safe path contains gaps, mimicking small holes in the way. Those should be overcome without changing the robot's direction. Also are present turn signals indicating the safe path to follow, they are marked as a green square with a 25 mm × 25 mm area. Later, in the track, there are orange portals that limit the height of the autonomous robots as at the end of the ramp leading to the victims' area. This, known as Room #3, has no track and only small balls covered with tinfoil or painted black and they are randomly positioned at the area. The final objective is to put the balls in a triangle area marked in one of the room corners. When the last victim is saved the clock stops. Competitors have about 5 min to complete all the round. Different track models can be seen in Fig. 4.

5 Projection Mapping

Projection Mapping is a well-known technique in Computer Vision and Augmented Reality sciences used to transform surfaces present in the surroundings into display surfaces for video projection. The main idea behind Projection Mapping is that any surface, be it flat or irregular, may be mapped either by an automated or user-guided procedure and used as a display. Since video output

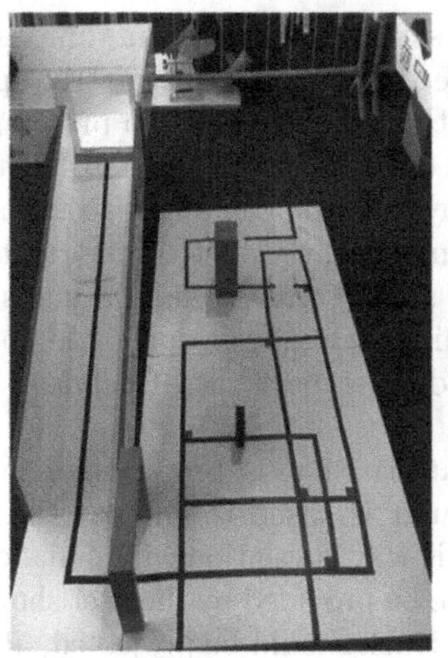
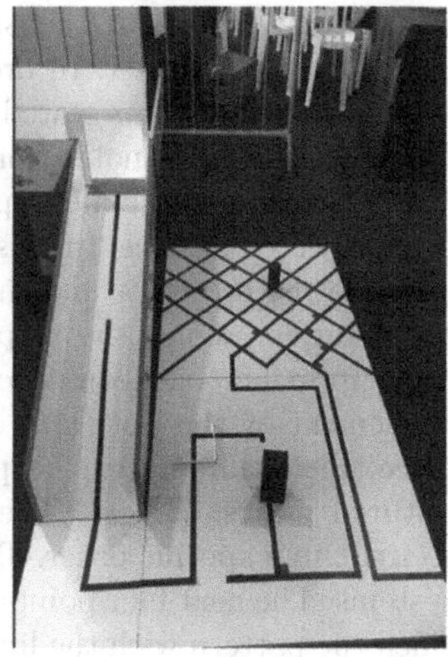

Fig. 4. Arena samples used in previous competitions. The left one has an orange portal and it is an easier level one. The right one represents a harder level.

is usually designed for flat screens, the transformation from a flat surface into the desired output surface needs to be computed and applied to the image prior to projection.

For specific purposes of this application, the desired projection surface is a flat board of unknown parallelepiped dimensions, implying a projective transformation is generally sufficient for a precise projection. Since the transformation must be computed only once, considering that the camera/projector/surface system will remain static in respect to each other, a semi-automated method was chosen.

The transformation from the screen (camera) coordinates to the surface to be projected can be calculated by multiplying two sub-transforms, one from screen to projector and the other one from a projector to surface. However, since both operations are computed by homographies, the transformation matrix can be compounded into a single operator. Let (X, Y) be the coordinate vectors of the corners of the image desired to be projected. The coordinates are transformed into a homogeneous coordinate system such that $(x, y) \rightarrow (x/w, y/w, w)$. Note that in spite of the added number of dimensions in the vector, the number of degrees of freedom remains unchanged by the transformation. This important property will guarantee that a unique inverse transformation exists.

In this method, an RBG camera is used to capture the projection surface. To find each of these transformations, the user must provide four reference points to be correlated to reference ones. The four selected points within the captured image will possess another set of coordinates (X', Y') (likely distinct from the original set of coordinates). Therefore, a projective transformation exists such that $Ma = b$, where M is a matrix operator, a is a 2D-homogeneous coordinate in the original image and b is a 2D-homogeneous coordinate in the camera captured image. This matrix operator must satisfy the constraints imposed by all four points indicated by the user. In order to solve for this matrix operator, a homography is computed [24]. As stated, this is equivalent to a projective transformation that maps the coordinates from one system (image) into another; thus projective mapping. A second homography must be computed to transform the points into the projected surface. In this manner, the first transformation maps from the camera to the projector and the second transformation maps from the projector to the surface. Once the mappings have been done, the coordinates are transformed from homogeneous coordinates back into Euclidean space by dividing each element by the last (w).

For instance, Fig. 5 illustrates the pattern that is projected in full screen and later captured by the camera. The user is asked to click at the center of each colored circle, in a specific order. This way, a relationship is made for both coordinate systems. The next four points to be provided by the user should be the corners in which the pattern with the line track should be projected, also clicked in a specific order. These points provide information that enables acquiring the projection to surface transformation. Using the final transformation, composed of the two sub ones, one can warp the original image to the projected real scenario, according to the input given by the user.

Fig. 5. The four corners of the pattern projected for screen(camera)/projector calibration. The specific color order is used: red, green, blue and yellow. (Color figure online)

6 ARena

6.1 Browser Implementation

The ARena tool runs inside a web browser and was implemented using solely HTML and Javascript. Its usage is straightforward, however, a proper equipment setup is required before using this tool and the image containing the blueprint of the track must be previously produced in a graphics editing software and exported in advance.

The use of HTML + Javascript allows the solution to be portable, with easy visual prototyping (HTML) and of fast behavioral programming (Javascript). Since Javascript is an interpreted programming language, it does not require compiling the code every time a change is made. This allows developers to almost instantaneously visualize changes made directly on the browser.

6.2 Setup and Use

Besides the computer that will run ARena (and the common materials used for the constructing line-follower arenas, such as the whiteboard and the black tape), a specific hardware setup comprising a projector and an RBG camera is required. A tripod is also recommended for positioning the projector at an adequate place. The projection surface must be placed in a position such that the projection area contains the board to be projected. A small extrapolation should be fine. The camera must be also fixed in the environment (it is usually placed on top of the projector), looking at the center of the surface to be projected (shown in Fig. 6). It is also important that the entire projection area is seen by the camera. This enables the user to click on the borders at the final stages of the process.

Fig. 6. ARena equipments' setup. While the computer is omitted from this image, the green line highlights the camera field of view while the red one highlights the projector window. (Color figure online)

After the equipment's setup, the user simply has to open ARena's website[1] and follow the step-by-step instructions provided on the screen.

In the case of multiple platforms with the same model, if a new whiteboard is placed in exactly the same place the old one was, no recalibration process is necessary. The user only has to load the new blueprint image and it will be projected following the previous calibration performed. In case the user is just replicating the whiteboard using the same reference image, this last step (loading of a new image) is not necessary.

[1] https://maracatronics.github.io/ARena/.

7 User Tests

7.1 Test Methodology

Two different blueprints of tracks were used to conduct user tests, as shown in Fig. 7. Despite different, the organizers of the competition reported that both arenas chosen were equivalent in terms of construction difficulty.

A total of ten users were separated into two groups of five users each, defined by the arena type to be constructed using ARena software and a manual scale drawing method. A uniformly random process selected whether the user would first build the path using the ARena software or the manual scale drawing. This way, it was possible to make sure that the timing of the test would not be influenced by the previous knowledge of the arena design at the second attempt.

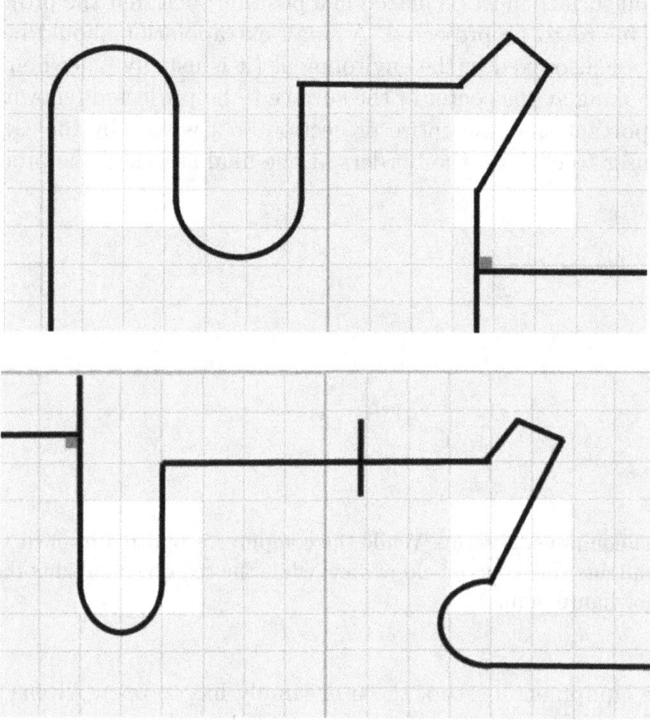

Fig. 7. Different but equivalent arena blueprints used during tests: type 1 (top), type 2 (bottom). (Color figure online)

The manual method consisted in drawing on the official whiteboard by mimicking a scaled schematics of the track and then putting adhesive black tape over it or simply by drawing control points and connecting them with black and green tapes. Instructions on how to do the manual method were passed to test users.

Using ARena software, test users were oriented as well as how to configure the software by one of the authors and, then, they were told to start the process. The steps to perform ARena configuration are shown on Figs. 8, 9, 10, 11, 12 and 13.

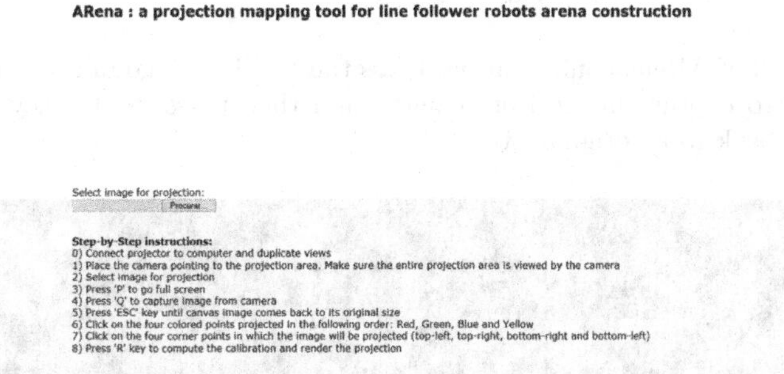

ARena : a projection mapping tool for line follower robots arena construction
Select image for projection:
Procurar...
Step-by-Step instructions:
0) Connect projector to computer and duplicate views
1) Place the camera pointing to the projection area. Make sure the entire projection area is viewed by the camera
2) Select image for projection
3) Press 'P' to go full screen
4) Press 'Q' to capture image from camera
5) Press 'ESC' key until canvas image comes back to its original size
6) Click on the four colored points projected in the following order: Red, Green, Blue and Yellow
7) Click on the four corner points in which the image will be projected (top-left, top-right, bottom-right and bottom-left)
8) Press 'R' key to compute the calibration and render the projection

Fig. 8. Step 1 of ARena configuration: Open ARena website and authorize the use of the camera.

Nome	Data de modific...	Tipo	Tamanho
track 1	13/06/2018 16:26	Arquivo PNG	12 KB

Fig. 9. Step 2 of ARena configuration: Select the image to be projected.

The construction time was measured considering both the user's preparation in the manual scaled drawing method and the ARena configuration in the ARena Software method. The time count was ended after checking that there were no missing parts and the tape was not peeling off the surface.

It is important to consider that some of the tested users had previous experience drawing arenas before. This leads to different test results when compared to other users that had no previous experience constructing line-follower arenas. Moreover, there were different ways to draw the track with the manual method, and each person chose their preferred method. The most popular technique was sketching the whole path before taping it. The second most used approach was marking the extremities of each line, based on the schematic, on the arena and then linking those marks with black tape.

Shortly after the end of each test, pictures of the board were taken so later the user could, also, compare the final result of both methods.

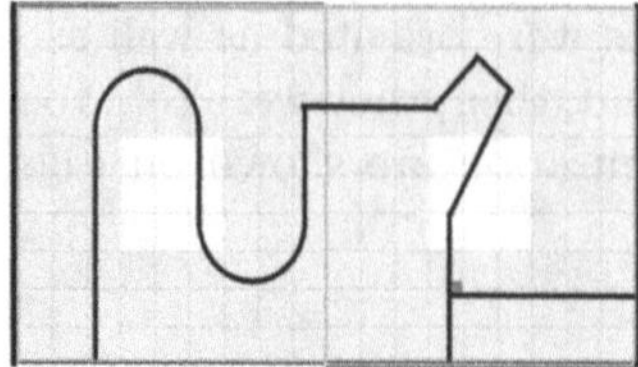
ARena : a projection mapping tool for line follower robots arena construction

Fig. 10. Step 3 of ARena configuration: Press the "P" key to go full screen, then press the "Q" key to capture image from camera and then press "ESC" key until canvas image comes back to its original size.

Fig. 11. Step 4 of ARena configuration: Click on the center of the colored dots in sequence and then click the corners of the board in the same sequence then press the "R" key to render the projection. (Color figure online)

7.2 Hypothesis Testing

Given the conducted user tests, a hypothesis test was made to infer whether the software usage had any actual advantage that could be statistically significant. Given the number of available samples, a two-tailed T-Student statistic test was performed [3]. The status quo was that the usage of the software did not incur at any advantage when compared to the traditional manual construction. This meant that a statistically significant difference between means showed that there was a clear difference between both methods. If the software-assisted meantime was lower than the manual meantime, again in using the software-assisted construction method was implied.

For arena type 1, the difference between means of both groups was of 1039.40 s (as shown on Table 1). With a 95% confidence interval, this translated into a 419.14 to 1659.66 range. The computed two-tailed P-value was of 0.0048, which meant a statistically significant difference between both groups. Since

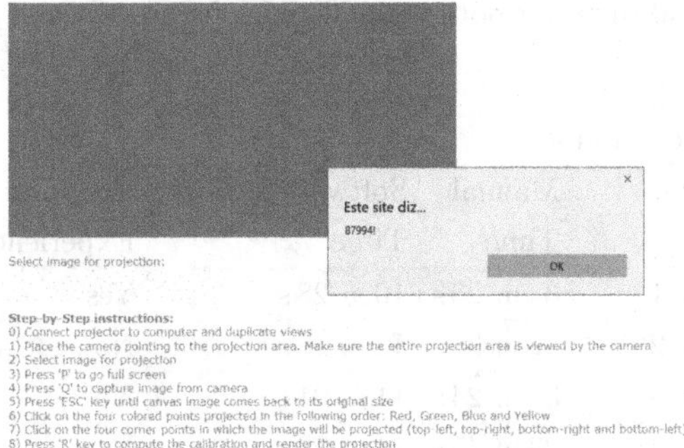

Fig. 12. Step 5 of ARena configuration: After the calibration is done, close the dialog window by clicking "Ok" and then press the "S" key on the keyboard to enter fullscreen mode.

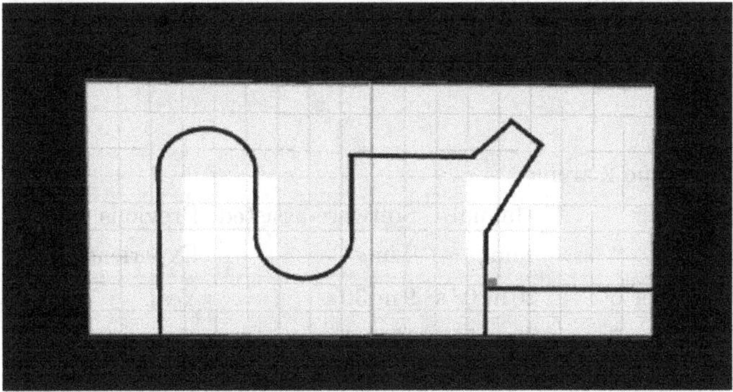

Fig. 13. Step 6 of ARena configuration: The calibration is completed and the image is projected on the board. The setup is ready to be followed by placing the adhesive black tape over the projected track.

the software-assisted time was lower than the manual construction, this meant a clear advantage in using the proposed software.

The same hypothesis testing was done for the second track (look Table 2). This time the difference between both groups was lower, 722.20 s. However, with a 95% percent confidence interval the expected range was between 201.17 s and 1243.23 s. This meant the means for the second arena type were also statistically significant with a two-tailed P-value of 0.0127. Since the mean for the software-assisted group was also lower, the tests pointed out a clear advantage in using the software-assisted technique also for the second track. Given the disparities between mean user construction times for both arena types, it is not unreasonable to expect a similar behavior for other track types that follow these same assembly principles.

Table 1. Experimental times for both manual and software-assisted arena construction (type 1).

Type 1 arena			
User	Manual Time	Software-assisted Time	Previous Experience
User 1	34 m 20 s	10 m 28 s	Yes
User 2	32 m 38 s	14 m 15 s	No
User 3	35 m 24 s	11 m 01 s	No
User 4	23 m 45 s	11 m 20 s	Yes
User 5	12 m 57 s	5 m 23 s	Yes
Mean	1668.80 s	629.40 s	–
Std. Dev.	569.79 s	192.57 s	–
P-Value	0.0048		

Table 2. Experimental times for both manual and software-assisted arena construction (type 2).

Type 2 arena			
User	Manual Time	Software-assisted Time	Previous Experience
User 6	20 m 03 s	9 m 30 s	Yes
User 7	20 m 55 s	17 m 15 s	No
User 8	21 m 50 s	10 m 30 s	No
User 9	15 m 47 s	06 m 27 s	Yes
User 10	35 m 26 s	10 m 08 s	Yes
Mean	1368.20 s	646.00 s	–
Std. Dev.	445.86 s	237.63 s	–
P-Value	0.0127		

8 Analysis

After the tests, it was possible to confirm that all users had less track production time when using ARena (as shown in Tables 1 and 2). Tests performed in type 1 arena pointed a reduction of time around 65%, while tests performed in type 2 arena pointed a reduction in total time around 55%.

By interviewing users after the tests, they pointed as main challenges of constructing the track without ARena: the correct use of the scaled drawing and keeping it uniform; the necessity of using many tools such as a square ruler, rulers, and compass. Both challenges made the manual approach demand more time in the users' opinion.

After the tests, all users agreed that the most efficient method was the one using ARena software. It has advantages such as precision on scale and simplicity to tape the most complex shapes. The biggest problems identified were curve-based paths and long diagonals. Test users claimed that without ARena software it was almost impossible to make all those shapes correctly and identical in every single one of the tables. This fact is shown on Figs. 14 and 15. They compare the same track done by a single person with and without the software. As a result of the proposed method, different people were able to stick to a pattern for the tracks better than anyone drawing two of them, as shown in Fig. 15. This pattern is important for the Brazilian Robotics Olympiad so that the championship is kept fair for every participating team and none of them will be harmed due to human error.

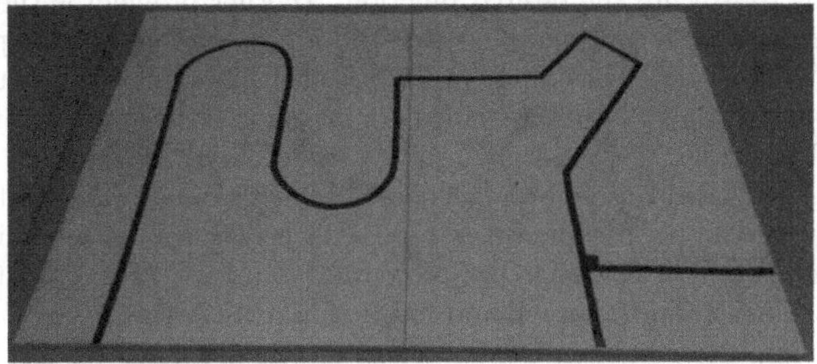

Fig. 14. Type 1 arena constructed using manual (conventional) method.

Fig. 15. Type 1 arena constructed using ARena software.

Another interesting observation is that users that completed the track using ARena software first always started complaining about the time spent drawing using the conventional method and how hard it was to do it. On the contrary, the ones that did the process backward were relieved to have this tool and impressed by their time.

Some suggestions were pointed by users, such as an upgrade on the ARena's visual interface and the reduction of the number of commands to set up the software.

Therefore, ARena reached its objective by reducing the production time of line-follower arenas, while maintaining a very similar pattern of the geometric shapes (especially curves) between them.

Users also commented about the facility of making a more precise and faithful path, due to the scale adjustment of the software, independently of the camera position and the table size/position. Some issues about ARena's included its visual interface, which was not made considering best practices on user interfaces, so it is still pretty rudimentary, leading to a less intuitive program with a series of commands to execute the desired function. Another problem is the external setup, which requires a considerable space and a base support for the projector. Definitely, the most time-consuming procedure of the method is the structure set up. The projector support can be avoided, for instance, if the arena is constructed in a vertical position.

Nonetheless, ARena users only needed to set up the software configuration once, before starting to use the black tape, which only took a few minutes for them to have the full track design projected on the surface. After that, they were free to keep working on the arena and finish it in a short time.

It is also important to mention that some testers did not draw on the white-boards before tapping them, which resulted in more imprecision, but faster procedures that must be considered at the result analysis. The Brazilian Robotics Olympiad needs that arenas be as similar as possible so that the championship remains fair for all teams.

9 Conclusion

The proposed tool showed to be effective in reducing the time needed for producing line-follower arenas, according to the tests performed.

Another important gain that comes from ARena's use was the standardization of the tracks, even when made by different people and on different surfaces, as long as the calibration is not changed. Such quality has a positive impact on competition's fairness since all participating teams compete on the same track conditions.

However, some improvements are needed as far as the user experience is concerned. From a simple click confirmation when performing the calibration steps to a more friendly interface, such improvements are planned to be performed in the course of this year, according to the feedback received when ARena is used by organizers from all country. ARena's next version should contain a track editor along with its Projection Mapping functionality. This way it will be self-contained, freeing the user from having to create the track image using a third party graphics editor application.

From the combination of Projection Mapping with line-follower robots, the idea of creating a dynamic arena emerges. Such arena would have a projector underneath it, and tracks could be easily changed, reducing the construction time to near zero. This will be further investigated in a near future.

References

1. Arduino. Arduino engineering kit (2018). https://store.arduino.cc/usa/arduino-engineering-kit. Accessed 1 July 2018
2. Ivan Seidel Tenda Digital. Tournamenter - tournament manegement made easy (2018). https://github.com/TendaDigital/Tournamenter. Accessed 29 June 2018
3. Dodge, Y.: The Concise Encyclopedia of Statistics. Springer, New York (2008)
4. Lego Education (2018). Ev3 website - about ev3. https://www.lego.com/en-us/mindstorms/about-ev3. Accessed 1 July 2018
5. Sphero Education. Sphero education website (2018). https://www.sphero.com/education. Accessed 1 July 2018
6. Micro:bit Educational Foundation. Micro:bit educational foundation - website (2018). http://microbit.org/. Accessed 1 July 2018
7. Margaret L., et al.: Hilton. Education for Life and Work Developing Transferable Knowledge and Skills in the 21st Century. The National Academies Press (2012)
8. Olimpo - Olympics management system and scientific events (2008). http://www.sistemaolimpo.org/. Accessed 2 July 2018
9. Texas Instruments. Ti robotics systems learning kit (2018). https://university.ti.com/en/faculty/ti-robotics-system-learning-kit/ti-robotics-system-learning-kit. Accessed 1 July 2018
10. Jones, B.: Software - projection mapping central (2018)
11. Hache, M., Laviole, J.: Spatial augmented reality to enhance physical artistic creation. In: Adjunct Proceedings of the 25th Annual ACM Symposium on User Interface Software and Technology, Cambridge, MA, United States, pp. 43–46 (2012)
12. Moreno, D., Taubin, G.: Simple, accurate, and robust projector-camera calibration. In: 2012 Second International Conference on 3D Imaging, Modeling, Processing, Visualization and Transmission (3DIMPVT), pp. 464–471. IEEE (2012)
13. Motta, T., Loaiza, M., Soares, L., Raposo, A.: Projection mapping for a kinect-projector system. In: 2014 XVI Symposium on Virtual and Augmented Reality (SVR), pp. 200–209. IEEE (2014)
14. Nishino, H., et al.: Real-time navigation for liver surgery using projection mapping with indocyanine green fluorescence: development of the novel medical imaging projection system. Ann. Surg. **267**(6), 1134–1140 (2018)
15. Brazilian Robotics Olympiad. Brazilian robotics olympiad - official site (2018). http://www.obr.org.br/. Accessed 29 June 2018
16. Brazilian Robotics Olympiad. Brazilian robotics olympiad - regionals (2018). http://www.obr.org.br/modalidade-pratica/etapa-regional/. Accessed 30 June 2018
17. Brazilian Robotics Olympiad. Brazilian robotics olympiad - rules (2018). http://www.obr.org.br/wp-content/uploads/2018/03/OBR2018_MP_ManualRegrasRegional_v1Mar.pdf. Accessed 30 June 2018
18. Brazilian Robotics Olympiad. Brazilian robotics olympiad - why a robotics olympiad? (2018). http://www.obr.org.br/por-que-uma-olimpiada-robotica/. Accessed 30 June 2018

19. PositivoEduc. Ebook-o que é stem? (2018). https://www.positivoteceduc.com.br/blog-robotica-e-stem/o-que-e-stem/. Accessed 1 July 2018
20. RoboCupJunior. Robocupjunior rescue robot league (2018). http://www.robocup.org/leagues/20. Accessed 29 June 2018
21. VEX Robotics. Vex robotics website (2018). https://www.vexrobotics.com/. Accessed 1 July 2018
22. Sensen, C.W.: Using cave® technology for functional genomics studies. Diabetes Technol. Ther. **4**(6), 867–871 (2002)
23. Siegl, C., Lange, V., Stamminger, M., Bauer, F., Thies, J.: Faceforge: markerless non-rigid face multi-projection mapping. IEEE Trans. Vis. Comput. Graph. **23**(11), 2440–2446 (2017)
24. Sukthankar, R., Stockton, R.G., Mullin, M.D.: Smarter presentations: exploiting homography in camera-projector systems. In: Proceedings of the Eighth IEEE International Conference on Computer Vision, ICCV 2001, vol. 1, pp. 247–253. IEEE (2001)

Stepped Warm-Up–The Progressive Interaction Approach for Human-Robot Interaction in Public

Min Zhao[1(✉)], Dan Li[1], Zhun Wu[1], Shiyan Li[1], Xiaonan Zhang[2], Lu Ye[2], Guangfu Zhou[2], and Daisong Guan[1]

[1] Baidu AI Interaction Design Lab, Beijing, China
zhaomin04@baidu.com

[2] Baidu Natural Language Processing Department, Beijing, China

Abstract. Initiating interaction is one of the most basic functions of service robots, and it has a vital impact on the subsequent interaction process. In the present study, we proposed a brand-new approach to initiate interaction—the progressive interaction approach. Specifically, robots actively send social cues to potential users in a progressively enhancing manner. Based on the concept of this approach, we modeled the behavior of a robot named Xiaodu, and further validated the practical benefits of this approach in an experimental study, in which participants were asked to rate their experience after interacting with Xiaodu with different initiating strategies. The findings suggested that compared to the reactive approach, the progressive interaction approach led to stronger positive emotions (self-reported) and was perceived to be more natural and friendly. Participants also reported higher affection and higher interaction intention towards the progressive interaction approach. The study has some implications for designing robots' behavior in the interaction initiating process.

Keywords: Human-Robot Interaction (HRI) · Initiating interaction · Progressive interaction approach · Reactive approach · Facial expression · Face recognition · Attracting attention

1 Introduction

There are increasing amount of service robots being developed and applied in various public places, such as in museums [1, 2], airports [3], train stations [4], and shopping malls [5]. These service robots are expected to interact with people and act as receptionists or information staff. Initiating interaction is one of the most basic functions of these service robots [6], and it has a vital impact on the subsequent interaction process [7].

However, there are still many remaining issues existing for robots to initiate interaction in public places. Currently, there are mainly two approaches for service robots to initiate interaction. The first is called "the reactive approach", in which a robot waits until a user to initiate interaction [8–10]. Robots who adopt this initiating strategy usually use certain behavior to exhibit their availability and recipiency [11], and to encourage users to initiate interactions [12, 13, 15]. This approach is resistant to many complex issues [14], nevertheless, it will miss out on potential users who are hesitating

A. Marcus and W. Wang (Eds.): HCII 2019, LNCS 11584, pp. 309–327, 2019.
https://doi.org/10.1007/978-3-030-23541-3_23

or uncertain about how to interact with robots. The other is "the proactive approach", in which a robot proactively seeks for people who need help [6, 8]. Compared to the reactive approach, this approach is more initiative [16] and thus more likely to help those with potential needs but do not know they can turn to robots [6]. Besides, this approach is also useful for advertisement purposes. Yet, being too proactive, it may be perceived as "rude", "disturbing", or even "annoying" [8, 15]. In summarize, neither of the two approaches are natural enough in practical applications: the reactive approach is too passive, while the proactive approach may seem intrusive and cause annoyance.

The aim of this study was to design a more natural approach for robots to initiate interaction. We expected that with this approach, even those who had never encountered robots before, could interact with them in a natural, efficient, and pleasant way. Our approach was mainly based on behavior patterns revealed in human-human interactions, as they were established through long social practices and could be accepted by the majority of people without further explanations. Specifically, we designed a range of behaviors of a robot under the guidance of the approach. Moreover, an experimental study was conducted to validate the practical benefits of the approach.

2 Related Work

2.1 Initiating Interaction Between Human-Human in Public Places

The interaction initiating process is extremely delicate, and requires cooperation [17–19]. Moreover, it is a dynamic process. In the process of initiating interaction, people will use various social cues, which are understandable to all participants of the interaction [20].

Hall [21] suggests a series of steps in the process of initiating interaction: (a) getting a person's attention; (b) assessing that person's willingness to interact; (c) creating physical proximity to enable interaction.

One key issue in initiating interaction in public places is to recognize the intention to interact. Goffman [20] points out that in public places, an "encounter" is normally initiated by one person, using specific eye contact (a brief glance) or certain body language and posture. The interaction is not considered as officially started until the cues sent by the initiator are recognized by the receiver. In return, the receiver usually sends back eye contact (e.g., gaze) or body language as recognition. Specifically, gaze, among other kinds of eye contact, is a vital social cue for initiating social contact in public places, as it is one of the most directional social cues to express the intention to interact [22, 23].

As suggested by Hall [21], once the interaction intention is recognized by mutual parties, the next step is to create physical proximity to enable interaction. Hall [24] further proposes the concept of "proxemics", which refers to the physical distance and/or closeness between people. He defines four kinds of personal spatial zones from a relatively close to far distance: "Intimate Zone", "Personal Zone", "Social Zone", "Public Zone". The widely accepted personal spatial zone was summarized by Lambert [25] in Table 1. Moreover, it appears that distance itself is not only a common social cue that can reflect and influence social relationships and attitudes [26, 27], but it can also affect one's ability to see or touch the other person, and thus play an important role in the use of other social cues. For instance, Kendon [28] suggests that friends usually exchange greetings twice, first using body language at a far distance and again by smiling at a closer distance.

Table 1. Human-human personal spatial zones (cf. Lambert)

Personal spatial zone	Range	Situation
Close intimate	0 to 0.15 m	Lover or close friend touching
Intimate zone	0.15 m to 0.45 m	Lover or close friend only
Personal zone	0.45 m to 1.2 m	Conversation between friends
Social zone	1.2 m to 3.6 m	Conversation to non-friends
Public zone	3.6 m +	Public speech making

2.2 Initiate Interaction Between Human-Robot in Public Places

In general, robots are expected to obey common social norms when they are starting and maintaining communication with humans [29]. Most people are willing to try to interact with robots if the robot showed appropriate social behavior [30].

"How to attract users' attention" is a popular research topic. Studies find that robots with humanoid bodies are more likely to attract users' attention [31], and robots with face can attract significantly more users to stop [32]. Robots can also catch users' eyes by moving their heads or blinking their eyes. However, when users are engaged in other things (e.g., watching news on television), speech turns out to be the best way to attract their attention, followed by waving gesture and eye LED blinking gesture, while attempting to build eye-contact works the worst in this kind of scenarios [33]. Gaze behavior is only valid when the robot has users' attention already [33]. Some researchers designed different possible behavior including head motions (e.g., looking at the nearest person), different facial expressions (e.g., happy, sad, and angry) and different language acts (e.g., come here, do you like robots?), After self-learning from interactions with humans, the robot developed a "positive attitude" to attract attention, that is, saying nice things, looking at people, and smiling [34].

Gaze behavior is still an effective social cue in human-robot interaction, given that the robot has attracted users' attention already. Mutlu and colleagues [35] applied key gaze mechanisms in human conversations on robots, and found that humanlike gaze mechanisms successfully helped the robot signal different participant roles, manage turn-exchanges, and shaped how participants perceive the robot and the conversation. Besides, other studies suggest that prolonged eye-contact from the robot while approaching or being approached by users can increase the user's affection towards the robot [36].

"Human-Robot Proxemics" has been another focus of research. It is suggested that when approaching robots, users are likely to keep robots at personal or social zones, same as what they will behave when they are approaching another human-being [30, 37–39]. Similarly, when being approached by robots, users will feel more comfortable when robots stopped at the personal and social zones [40, 41]. If robots were too close, users will even step back to make themselves feel more comfortable. Besides, users prefer to be approached from the front instead of from the back, and front-left or front-right is preferred than the direct front-on direction [42–44].

Although there have been abundant findings accumulating in the field of robots' social behavior, few studies have focused on the whole dynamic process of "initiating interaction". So far, studies towards initiating interaction between human-robot have been mainly concentrated on building algorithms, such as how to detect humans and track their positions, how to determine intention and interests of humans, and how to recognize humans etc., or simply on one part of the initiating process, such as how to attract users' attention. The present study focused on the whole process of "initiating interaction", and further explored how these designed behaviors based on the progressive interaction approach would be perceived by users.

3 The Progressive Interaction

3.1 The Approach of "the Progressive Interaction"

Based on analyses of human behavior and our previous investigations, we suggest that during the process of human-robot interaction in public places, robots are expected to send interaction signals more actively, and in a progressively enhancing manner. This is what we call "the progressive interaction".

Specifically, as humans and robots getting closer, humans will have different expectations towards robots. We divided the process into three stages, which are named as "far field", "mid field", and "near field", based on the order they will appear in users' mental world. Every stage is corresponding to certain distance ranges in physical world, and there are certain behaviors that will fit in users' expectations for every stage:

- **Far Field:** The aim of robots in this stage is to gain users' attention, and to make users' aware that "I'm noticed by HIM/HER". This is a critical stage, as if it failed, the following human-robot interaction would seem to be abrupt or even impossible to make. This field is corresponding to a distance ranging approximately from 2.7 to 4.2 m. Robots are expected to use facial expressions and body movements to attract attention. Such as smiling, friendly eye contact, waving, tilting head to one side, nodding, and so on;
- **Mid Field:** Robots are supposed to further express "the intention to interact", and make users clearly aware that "I'm the only one in HIS/HER eyes" and HE/SHE is intended to further interact. This will also encourage users to approach the robot spontaneously. The distance corresponding to this field is about 1.2–2.7 m. Within this distance, users expect the robot to send out interactive signals using a variety of combinations, so that the user can be certain that he/she is the target. For example, using voice to send greetings (such as good morning, hello), at the same time, smiling, or waving, etc.;
- **Near Field:** Robots need to "start a dialogue" first, and will be perceived as initiative and friendly. "HE/SHE is 'Liao' (hitting on) me", and with this impression, the dialogue between human and robot develops naturally. The distance

corresponding to the near field is within 1.2 m. Within this field, the role of language is highlighted. Users expect the robot to "initiate dialogue" first, such as introducing himself/herself and asking if any help was needed. At the same time, users expect more enthusiastic smiles and body movements (such as shaking hands, hugging, etc.).

The distance corresponding to each field was established in a previous study we carried out, in which participants (N = 32) were asked to approach a robot from certain direction and with certain pace that he/she was comfortable with. While approaching, they were asked to evaluate where were the appropriate points for the robot to attract attention (far field), express interaction intention (mid field), and start a dialogue (far field). The specific distance was measured and calculated afterwards.

3.2 Designing the Progressive Interaction

We applied the approach, the progressive interaction, on a robot called Xiaodu. The focus of the present study was listed in Table 2.

Table 2. Designing the progressive interaction

Stages	Purpose	Behavior
Far field	Attracting attention	Facial expressions
Mid field	Initiating an interactive request	Voice, facial expressions
Near filed	Starting a dialogue	Voice, facial expressions

The Robot "Xiaodu". Xiaodu is a "formal employee" in Baidu company, 160 cm tall, 110 cm width, and works as a receptionist in the company hall (see Fig. 1). Xiaodu is benefited from the AI techniques (e.g., NLP, dialogue system, speech recognition) of Baidu, and is able to communicate smoothly with users in multiple aspects, such as communicating emotions, providing information and other services.

Fig. 1. Xiaodu at work

Facial Expressions in Far Field. The aim of this stage is to attract users' attention. Facial expressions of Xiaodu need to be perceived and understood by users. In return, users will be willing to pay attention to Xiaodu, and even further interact.

Six groups of facial expressions are designed by our UX designers and researchers, based on the features of facial expressions in human-human interactions, facial expression database of Xiaodu, and popular stickers used in online chatting. Participants were invited to evaluate these expressions from far field, regarding their understanding, affection, at what degree they were attracted, and the intention to further interact. The expression of "Raised eyebrows" was selected (as shown in Table 3).

Table 3. Facial expressions of Xiaodu for different fields

The default expression: expressionless	Far field: raised eyebrows	Mid field: smiling eyes	Near field: smiling eyes with heart-shaped blush

*Face expressions were animated

Facial Expression and Voice in Mid Field. The core in mid field is to "initiate an interaction request". For this stage, users need to be able to perceive the robot's intention to interact. After the same process as in far field stage, the expression "smiling eyes" was selected for the mid field stage (see Table 3). As for voice, the classic way of "greeting" was selected—"Hi, how are you".

In addition, the dual-modality design ("smiling eyes + greeting") was favored by participants, comparing to merely smiling eyes. The former design left participants an impression that the robot was more enthusiastic, more directional, and more interactive. We further investigated whether the effect of voice was also significant after the whole interaction process in later validation experiment.

Facial Expressions, Voice and Face Recognition in Near Field. The aim for this stage is to "start a dialogue". "Smiling eyes with heart-shaped blush" was designed and selected for this stage (as shown in Table 3). As for voice, Xiaodu introduced himself/herself and then the rules for subsequent interaction–"I'm Xiaodu. If you want to chat you can just speak to me, I'm listening".

During the process of user evaluation, we found that participants paid a lot of attention to the screen in the front of Xiaodu and would spontaneously keep eyes on the screen. Xiaodu was capable of face recognition, thus, we investigated whether displaying the face of the user would improve his/her experience in later experiment (as shown in Table 4).

Table 4. The screen of Xiaodu in far field

The default display	Face recognition
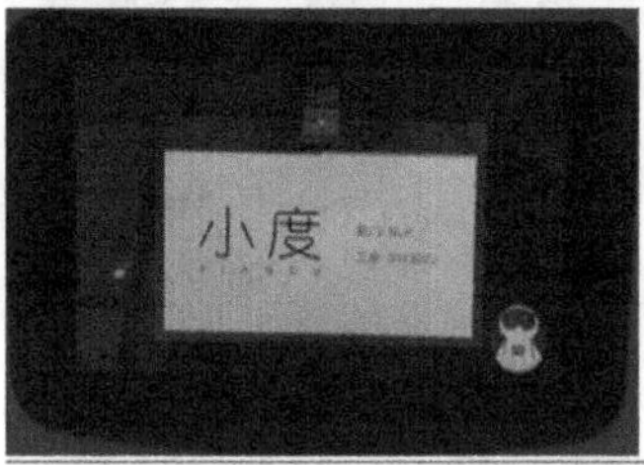	

4 Experiment Validation of the Progressive Interaction Approach

4.1 Objectives

The study aimed to investigate whether there was any difference in user experience between the progressive interaction approach and traditional initiating interaction approach (the reactive approach); and the second aim was to explore the difference in user experience among different designs in the progressive interaction approach.

4.2 Design

The experiment adopted a within-subject design, and all participants were required to experience all 5 trials. After each trial, participants were asked to fill in questionnaires regarding their emotions and attitudes.

One of the trials was the control condition, in which Xiaodu adopted the reactive approach. Specifically, Xiaodu kept the default facial expression, and participants could walk in the front of Xiaodu, touch the screen, and he/she would be reminded to pick up the microphone to start a conversation.

The other four trials were the experiment condition. They were based on the progressive interaction approach. Specifically, a 2 (*Mid field: with/without voice*) × 2 (*Near field: with/without face recognition*) design was used for the experiment condition (as shown in Fig. 2).

To minimize the influence of learning effect and fatigue effect, we randomized the order of trials for each participant.

The present study only focused on the initiating process, and later human-robot dialogue was not included in this study. Thus, to avoid the impacts of the robot's responses on participants' emotions and attitudes, all participants were required to ask the same question "How's the weather today".

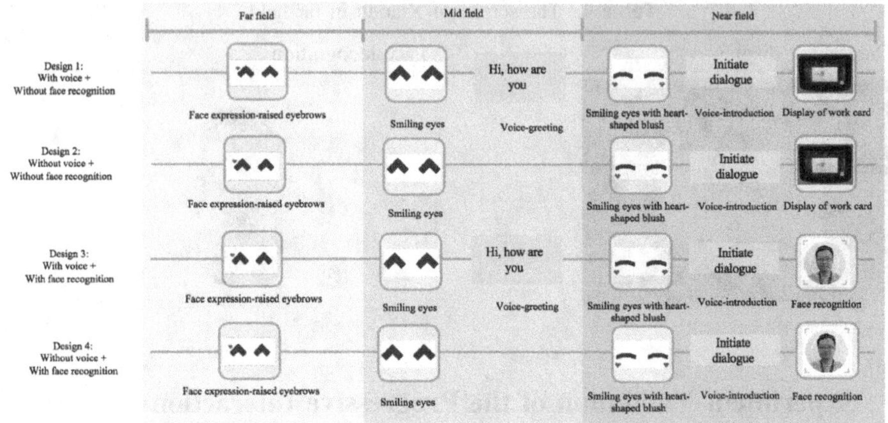

Fig. 2. Designs for the progressive interaction approach. Introduction in near field: I'm Xiaodu. If you want to chat you can just speak to me, I'm listening.

4.3 Participants

25 participants were recruited, including 12 males and 13 females. Their age ranged from 20 to 45 years old. 11 of them reported previous experience with service robots in public places. All participants reported normal or corrected to normal vision, and normal hearing.

All participants volunteered to participate in the study and agreed to make audio and video recordings of the research process. At the end of the study, all participants were given appropriate compensation.

4.4 Experiment Environment and Equipment

Experimental Set-Up. The experiment took place in the open office area of Baidu company. The whole experiment area was approximately 8 m in length, and 2.5 m in width. A white curtain was set up behind Xiaodu, and one experimenter recorded the facial expression of users' behind the curtain (as shown in Fig. 3).

The Robot Xiaodu. As mentioned before, Xiaodu is a humanoid robot in Baidu company. In different trials, it would display different kinds of behavior.

Fig. 3. The experimental set-up

To save the time and other resources needed to develop a fully autonomous robot, the experiment used the Wizard of Oz (WoZ) paradigm [45]. The facial expressions and voice of Xiaodu were actually controlled by an experimenter, who practiced multiple times to ensure consistency among different trials.

4.5 Measures

Emotions. Initiating interaction is a dynamic, subtle and transient process. In order to better evaluate user experience in this process, we included "emotion" as an important dependent variable, and it was measured with two criteria: objective face expression analysis and subjective self-report.

Objective Emotions. Noldus FaceReader [46] offers a relatively objective method to measure emotions through analyzing facial expressions, and it can automatically detect various emotions such as happiness, surprise and anger. For a given time period, face expressions in recordings will be analyzed, and different criteria will be generated, such as emotional arousal level, emotional valence.

Considering the emotions that participants might experience in the experiment, we included four kinds of emotions: happiness, surprise, neutral, and negative emotion. Specifically, negative emotion was the combination of sadness, anger, fear, and disgust. We adopted the criterion—emotional arousal level. Values for emotional arousal level range from 0–1, and higher values indicate stronger emotions.

Subjective Emotions. Participants were asked to rate their emotional intensity in an 8-point Likert questionnaire (from 0–7, higher scores indicated stronger emotional intensity), in which they were required to answer the question, "How did you feel in the process of interacting with Xiaodu just now", repeatedly for different kinds of emotions. Five kinds of emotions were rated in the questionnaire, which is, happiness, surprise, confusion, disgust, and neutral. The questionnaire was filled in after every trial.

Attitudes. Aside from emotions, we were also interested in participants' perceptions and cognitions towards Xiaodu. Thus, we also asked participants to evaluate the following attitudes, with one single question each. Participants were asked to rate in a 7-point Likert questionnaire (from 1–7, higher scores indicted stronger agreement):

- **Naturalness:** How natural do you think this interaction approach is?
- **Friendliness:** How friendly do you think this interaction approach is?
- **Affection:** How much do you like this interaction approach?
- **Interaction Intention:** If Xiaodu initiated interaction with you in this way, how much would you like to interact with him?

4.6 Procedure

Participants were first welcomed, and were informed about the aim and general process of the study. After introduction, there was a practice phase, in which participants could get familiar with the experimental set-up, the robot (those who encountered Xiaodu for the first time were usually excited), and find out the comfortable pace for him/her to approach Xiaodu. Then, the experiment began. Participants were asked to imagine that this was the first time they encountered Xiaodu, and they were intended to check the weather through Xiaodu. All participants went through all five trials (one for reactive approach and four for the progressive interaction approach). Participants' facial expressions during the experiment were recorded by one experimenter. After every trial, they filled out questionnaires about their emotions and attitudes during the trial. Finally, participants were interviewed for the reasons of their ratings after all trials.

4.7 Data Analysis

SPSS 23.0 was used for data analysis. First, we conducted descriptive analysis for all dependent variables. To evaluate the difference between the progressive interaction approach and the reactive approach, one-way repeated measures ANOVA was used. Further post hoc analysis was adopted if the ANOVA showed significant differences among the five trials.

Furthermore, we were interested in the effects of the two factors ("voice in mid field" and "face recognition in near field") in the progressive interaction designs. Thus, we conducted the two-way repeated measures ANOVA to see whether voice and face recognition were preferred by participants.

5 Results

5.1 Objective Emotions

The objective emotions of all participants in different trials are shown in Table 5. Because of technique issues, only 21 of participants were included in this analysis. In general, participants exhibited a neural or happy state in their facial expressions of all trials.

One-way repeated measures ANOVA was used to investigate the differences among different trials. Mauchly's test indicated that the assumption of sphericity had been violated except for the emotion happiness. Thus, we looked at the effects of trials after Green-house Geisser corrected (except for happiness). The findings suggested that there was no significant difference among different trials in all kinds of emotions (as shown in Table 6).

Table 5. Descriptive statistics of objective emotions

	N	Neutral		Happiness		Surprise		Negative emotion	
		M	SD	M	SD	M	SD	M	SD
Design 1	21	0.50	0.27	0.31	0.22	0.03	0.06	0.02	0.03
Design 2	21	0.48	0.28	0.30	0.23	0.05	0.07	0.03	0.02
Design 3	21	0.45	0.29	0.34	0.21	0.05	0.10	0.02	0.03
Design 4	21	0.48	0.26	0.32	0.21	0.06	0.11	0.02	0.02
The reactive approach	21	0.49	0.24	0.31	0.18	0.03	0.04	0.03	0.03

Design 1: With voice + Without face recognition; Design 2: Without voice + Without face recognition; Design 3: With voice + With face recognition; Design 4: Without voice + With face recognition

Table 6. The effects of trials on objective emotions

Emotions	Type	*df*	F	*p*
Neutral	Greece-house Geisser	2.776	0.753	0.516
Happiness	Sphericity assumed	4.000	0.483	0.748
Surprise	Greece-house Geisser	2.255	1.039	0.369
Negative emotion	Greece-house Geisser	2.336	0.595	0.581

Besides, we conducted two-way repeated measures ANOVA to investigate the different among different designs of the progressive interaction. Since both of the factors had two levels (with/without), the assumption of sphericity was considered as automatically meet. The effects of voice and face recognition, and their interaction effects are listed in Table 7. It turned out that there was no significant difference in four designs, nor is the interaction effect of the two factors significant.

Table 7. The effects of voice and face recognition on objective emotions

	Emotions	*df*	F	*p*
Voice	Neutral	1	0.049	0.827
	Happiness	1	0.596	0.449
	Surprise	1	0.937	0.345
	Negative emotion	1	0.059	0.811
Face recognition	Neutral	1	1.055	0.317
	Happiness	1	1.051	0.318
	Surprise	1	1.400	0.251
	Negative emotion	1	0.289	0.597
Voice * Face interaction	Neutral	1	1.350	0.259
	Happiness	1	0.032	0.859
	Surprise	1	0.227	0.639
	Negative emotion	1	0.700	0.413

5.2 Subjective Emotions

The ratings of different kinds of self-reported emotions in different trials are shown in Table 8. In general, participants reported more positive emotions (e.g., happiness) and less negative emotions (e.g., confusion) after the trials of the progressive interaction than after the trial of the reactive approach.

As with the objective emotions, one-way repeated measures ANOVA was used and the results are listed in Table 9. Trials had significant effects on self-reported happiness, surprise, and confusion. Thus, post hoc analysis was conducted to see the difference between any two of the five trials. Compared to the reactive approach, participants reported significantly higher scores in happiness, surprise, but lower scores in confusion for the progressive interaction approach (as shown in Table 10).

Table 8. Descriptive statistics of subjective emotions

	N	Happiness		Surprise		Confusion		Disgust		Neutral	
		M	SD	M	SD	M	SD	M	SD	M	SD
Design 1	25	4.12	2.60	2.60	2.80	0.64	1.52	0.00	0.00	0.40	1.38
Design 2	25	3.92	2.43	1.96	2.51	0.16	0.80	0.16	0.80	0.68	1.62
Design 3	25	4.32	2.38	2.48	2.80	0.88	1.17	0.16	0.80	0.00	0.00
Design 4	25	4.32	2.45	2.40	2.56	0.48	1.36	0.00	0.00	0.12	0.60
The reactive approach	25	0.36	1.32	0.76	1.93	5.00	2.14	0.44	1.58	0.72	1.72

Design 1: With voice + Without face recognition; Design 2: Without voice + Without face recognition; Design 3: With voice + With face recognition; Design 4: Without voice + With face recognition

Table 9. The effects of trials on subjective emotions

Emotions	Type	*df*	F	*p*
Happiness	Sphericity assumed	4.000	25.962***	0.000
Surprise	Greece-house Geisser	3.101	3.505*	0.018
Confusion	Sphericity assumed	4.000	50.030***	0.000
Disgust	Sphericity assumed	4.000	1.141	0.342
Neutral	Greece-house Geisser	2.424	1.668	0.192

*** Significant at the .001 level; * Significant at the .05 level.

Table 10. Post Hoc analysis. Paired comparisons between the reactive approach and other four designs respectively.

	With the reactive approach trial	Mean difference	*p*
Happiness	Design 1	−3.760***	0.000
	Design 2	−3.560***	0.000
	Design 3	−3.960***	0.000
	Design 4	−3.960***	0.000
Surprise	Design 1	−1.840**	0.006
	Design 2	−1.200	0.059
	Design 3	−1.720**	0.009
	Design 4	−1.640*	0.019
Confusion	Design 1	4.360***	0.000
	Design 2	4.840***	0.000
	Design 3	4.120***	0.000
	Design 4	4.520***	0.000

Design 1: With voice + Without face recognition; Design 2: Without voice + Without face recognition; Design 3: With voice + With face recognition; Design 4: Without voice + With face recognition
*** Significant at the .001 level; ** Significant at the .01 level;
* Significant at the .050 level.

Findings of two-way repeated measures ANOVA suggested that there was no significant difference in different designs of the progressive interaction approach (see Table 11).

Table 11. The effects of voice and face recognition on subjective emotions

	Emotions	*df*	F	*p*
Voice	Happiness	1	0.115	0.737
	Surprise	1	0.728	0.402
	Confusion	1	2.966	0.098
	Disgust	1	/	/
	Neutral	1	0.980	0.332
Face recognition	Happiness	1	0.651	0.428
	Surprise	1	0.204	0.656
	Confusion	1	1.205	0.283
	Disgust	1	/	/
	Neutral	1	3.868	0.061
Voice * Face interaction	Happiness	1	0.150	0.702
	Surprise	1	0.611	0.442
	Confusion	1	0.030	0.864
	Disgust	1	1.000	0.327
	Neutral	1	0.235	0.632

5.3 Attitudes: Naturalness, Friendliness, Affection and Interaction Intention

Descriptive statistics are listed in Table 12. Compared to the reactive approach, Xiaodu with the progressive interaction approach were generally considered as more natural and friendly, and participants also reported higher affection, higher interaction intention with.

Table 12. Descriptive statistics of attitudes

	N	Naturalness		Friendliness		Affection		Interaction intention	
		M	SD	M	SD	M	SD	M	SD
Design 1	25	4.71	1.37	5.75	1.07	5.42	0.97	5.67	1.01
Design 2	25	4.50	1.32	5.58	1.10	5.25	1.07	5.67	1.01
Design 3	25	4.79	1.18	5.63	1.06	5.46	1.02	5.63	1.06
Design 4	25	4.88	1.12	5.54	1.14	5.54	0.93	5.63	1.21
The reactive approach	25	2.76	1.33	3.24	1.59	2.84	1.21	2.92	1.66

Design 1: With voice + Without face recognition; Design 2: Without voice + Without face recognition; Design 3: With voice + With face recognition; Design 4: Without voice + With face recognition

Again, we conducted one-way repeated measures ANOVA to see if the differences of different approaches were significant, and found that there was significant difference in all four aspects of attitudes (see Table 13). Thus, post hoc analysis was conducted, and the results are listed in Table 14.

Table 13. The effects of trials on attitudes

Attitudes	Type	*df*	F	*p*
Naturalness	Sphericity Assumed	4.000	21.239***	0.000
Friendliness	Greece-house Geisser	1.590	39.338***	0.000
Affection	Greece-house Geisser	2.295	54.649***	0.000
Interaction intention	Greece-house Geisser	2.108	38.107***	0.000

*** Significant at the .001 level.

Table 14. Post Hoc analysis. Paired comparisons between the reactive condition and other four designs respectively.

	With the reactive trial	Mean difference	*p*
Naturalness	Design 1	−1.917***	0.000
	Design 2	−1.708***	0.000
	Design 3	−2.000***	0.000
	Design 4	−2.083***	0.000
Friendliness	Design 1	−2.583***	0.000
	Design 2	−2.417***	0.000
	Design 3	−2.458***	0.000
	Design 4	−2.375***	0.000
Affection	Design 1	−2.583***	0.000
	Design 2	−2.417***	0.000
	Design 3	−2.625***	0.000
	Design 4	−2.708***	0.000
Interaction intention	Design 1	−2.667***	0.000
	Design 2	−2.667***	0.000
	Design 3	−2.625***	0.000
	Design 4	−2.625***	0.000

Design 1: With voice + Without face recognition; Design 2: Without voice + Without face recognition; Design 3: With voice + With face recognition; Design 4: Without voice + With face recognition
*** Significant at the .001 level.

In addition, two-factor repeated measures ANOVA was used to see the effect of two factors (voice/face recognition) in different progressive interaction approach designs. Results showed no significant difference of the two factors in all four aspects (see Table 15).

Table 15. The effects of voice and face recognition on attitudes

	Emotions	*df*	F	*p*
Voice	Naturalness	1	0.185	0.671
	Friendliness	1	1.131	0.299
	Affection	1	0.193	0.664
	Interaction intention	1	0.000	1.000
Face recognition	Naturalness	1	1.184	0.288
	Friendliness	1	0.561	0.461
	Affection	1	1.484	0.236
	Interaction intention	1	0.058	0.811
Voice * Face interaction	Naturalness	1	0.723	0.404
	Friendliness	1	0.489	0.491
	Affection	1	1.000	0.328
	Interaction intention	1	0.000	1.000

6 Discussion

In the present study, we compared two approaches to initiate interaction: the progressive interaction approach and the reactive approach. Our main findings were that the progressive interaction approach resulted in more positive self-reported emotions, and was perceived to be more natural and friendlier. Moreover, participants reported higher affection and higher interaction intention towards the progressive interaction approach. However, no difference was found in objective emotions of the two approaches, nor in the four designs of the progressive interaction approach.

Participants reported more positive emotions and attitudes towards the progressive interaction approach than the reactive approach. The findings were also confirmed in the interview after the experiment. We found that participants successfully received the robot's intention to interact through signals the robot sent, such as facial expressions, greetings, and self-introductions. With these signals, participants started interacting with the robot naturally. On the contrary, participants were confused about "how to initiate dialogue" with the robot in the reactive approach condition.

Interestingly, no significant difference was found in the objective emotions between the progressive interaction approach and the reactive approach, and in all trials, participants mainly exhibited neutral and positive facial expressions. Culture might be one of the influencing factors of this finding. Studies suggested that compared to Westerners, Easterners were more likely to control their facial expressions, since they paid more attention to the appropriateness of expressing emotions [47]. Moreover, it was common for Chinese to use similes or laughter to cover up negative emotions, unless in front of close others [48]. Thus, it was possible that during the experiment, participants used awkward smiles to cover up their confusion and awkwardness, which were recognized as positive emotions by the Noldus FaceReader. The assumption was consistent with experimenters' observations. Moreover, participants also reported that they were confused about "how to initiate dialogue" with the robot in reactive approach condition.

There was no significant difference in four designs of the progressive interaction approach in all subjective evaluations. In general, participants had positive attitudes and emotions towards the progressive interaction designs, which suggested that these four designs were all relatively natural and friendly. However, it was worth noting that some participants expressed their concerns towards face recognition. 48% of participants reported that they did not like that their faces were shown on the screen, while only 16% of participants clearly indicated the opposite attitude. Reasons for dislikes were mainly: (1) Privacy issues, they fear that the image information might be recorded, analyzed and stored, or even be used for other purposes; (2) The image itself, the image captured by Xiaodu was not ideal because of wrong angels, looked fat or ugly etc.; (3) Interaction was not natural, as participants needed to switch between Xiaodu's face and the screen back and forth, participants could not focus on Xiaodu's face as in daily interaction. Besides, it felt awkward to communicate with his/her own image presented on the screen. On the other hand, those who liked face recognition reported that (1) High-tech feeling, face recognition made Xiaodu seemed more intelligent; (2) More directional; participants felt being seen by Xiaodu and was certain that him/herself was the target for further interaction. Thus, we suggested that face recognition should be used with caution, especially in the process of initiating interaction.

There were several limitations of this study. One was that the experiment was conducted in the constrained open office area, which was not necessarily considered as public places. A more ideal environment would be in the hall of Baidu building. Moreover, this was a very targeted study, and thus its' generalizability needs to be considered when applying the findings. Specifically, a humanoid robot was used who was often perceived to be adorable. The characters of the robot itself may have some positive impacts on users' emotions and attitudes. Moreover, our definitions of the far/mid/near fields and expectations corresponded were targeted at Chinese users. Not to mention the role Xiaodu played when we were putting the progressive interaction into concrete behavior patterns. Thus, the advantages of the progressive interaction need to be validated in other types of robots and in other cultural backgrounds. Another limitation was that we didn't include the proactive approach into comparisons in the present study, which we would be interested to investigate in the future.

There are still many interesting topics that worth investigating in the field, which we would also be dedicated to in the future. For example, how to design body language in different fields; how to make the greetings and introductions more natural and diverse.

7 Conclusions

The present study focused on service robots in public places, and proposed a brand-new approach–the progressive interaction approach, for robots to initiate interaction. Furthermore, the approach was preliminarily validated by an experimental study, in which it was compared to a relatively traditional approach, the reactive approach. Specifically, we found that: (1) compared to the reactive approach, the progressive interaction approach led to more positive emotions, and was perceived to be more natural and friendly. Participants also reported higher affection, higher interaction intention towards the progressive interaction approach; (2) There was no significant difference among the four designs of the progressive interaction approach; (3) During the process of initiating interaction, face recognition did not cause more positive experience but revealed many concerns from users. Thus, whether to use face recognition or not in application should be considered cautiously. In conclusion, our study enriched the understanding of the human-robot interaction, and made a step forward in designing a natural and friendly human-robot interaction process.

References

1. Shiomi, M., Kanda, T., Ishiguro, H., Hagita, N.: Interactive humanoid robots for a science museum. In: Proceedings of the 1st ACM SIGCHI/SIGART Conference on Human-Robot Interaction, HRI 2006, pp. 305–312. IEEE, New York (2006)
2. Thrun, S., et al.: MINERVA: a second-generation museum tour-guide robot. In: Proceedings of 1999 IEEE International Conference on Robotics and Automation, ICRA 1999, pp. 1999–2005. IEEE, New York (1999)
3. Ramírez, O., Khambhaita, H., Chatila, R., Chetouani, M., Alami, R.: Robots learning how and where to approach people. In: Proceedings of 2016 25th IEEE International Symposium on Robot and Human Interactive Communication (RO-MAN), pp. 347–353. IEEE, New York (2016)
4. Hayashi, K., et al.: Humanoid robots as a passive-social medium: a field experiment at a train station. In: Proceedings of the ACM/IEEE International Conference on Human-Robot Interaction, HRI 2007, pp. 137–144. IEEE, New York (2007)
5. Kanda, T., Glas, D.F., Shiomi, M., Ishiguro, H., Hagita, N.: Who will be the customer?: A social robot that anticipates people's behavior from their trajectories. In: Proceedings of the 10th International Conference on Ubiquitous Computing, UbiComp 2008, pp. 380–389. ACM, New York (2008)
6. Satake, S., Kanda, T., Glas, D., Imai, M., Ishiguro, H., Hagita, N.: How to approach humans? Strategies for social robots to initiate interaction. In: Proceedings of the 4th ACM/IEEE International Conference on Human-Robot Interaction, HRI 2009, pp. 109–116. IEEE, New York (2009)
7. Mead, R., Atrash, A., Matarić, M.J.: Automated proxemic feature extraction and behavior recognition: applications in human-robot interaction. Int. J. Soc. Robot. **5**(3), 367–378 (2013)
8. Kato, Y., Kanda, T., Ishiguro, H.: May I help you?: Design of human-like polite approaching behavior. In: Proceedings of the 10th ACM/IEEE International Conference on Human-Robot Interaction, HRI 2015, pp. 35–42. ACM, New York (2015)
9. Rashed, M.G.: Observing people's behaviors in public spaces for initiating proactive human-robot interaction by social robots. Ph.D. Dissertation (2016)
10. Rashed, M.G., Das, D., Kobayashi, Y., Kuno, Y.: A study on proactive methods for initiating interaction with human by social robots. Asian J. Converg. Technol. **4**(2) (2018). ISSN: 2350-1146
11. Yamazaki, K., Kawashima, M.: Prior-to-request and request behaviors within elderly day care: implications for developing service robots for use in multiparty settings. In: Bannon, L. J., Wagner, I., Gutwin, C., Harper, R.H.R., Schmidt, K. (eds.) ECSCW 2007, pp. 61–78. Springer, Heidelberg (2007). https://doi.org/10.1007/978-1-84800-031-5_4

12. Schulte, J., Rosenberg, C., Thrun, S.: Spontaneous, short-term interaction with mobile robots. In: Proceedings of 1999 IEEE International Conference on Robotics and Automation, ICRA 1999, pp. 658–663. IEEE, New York (1999)
13. Hayashi, K., et al.: Humanoid robots as a passive-social medium - a field experiment at a train station. In: Proceedings of the 2nd ACM/IEEE International Conference on Human-Robot Interaction, HRI 2007, pp. 137–144. IEEE, New York (2007)
14. Peters, C.: Evaluating perception of interaction initiation in virtual environments using humanoid agents. In: Proceedings of the 17th European Conference on Artificial Intelligence, pp. 46–50. IOS Press, Amsterdam (2006)
15. Finke, M., Koay, K., Dautenhahn, K., Nehaniv, C.: Hey, I'm over here – How can a robot attract people's attention? In: Proceedings of 2005 IEEE International Workshop on Robot and Human Interactive Communication, pp. 7–12. IEEE, New York (2005)
16. Buss, M., et al.: Towards proactive human-robot interaction in human environments. In: Proceedings of the 2nd International Conference on Cognitive Infocommunications, pp. 1–6. IEEE, New York (2011)
17. Scheflen, A.E.: Body Language and Social Order. Prentice-Hall, Englewood Cliffs (1972)
18. Kendon, A.: Conducting Interaction: Patterns of Behavior in Focused Encounters. Cambridge University Press, Cambridge (1990)
19. Clark, H.H.: Using Language. Cambridge University Press, Cambridge (1996)
20. Goffman, E.: Behavior in Public Place: Notes on the Social Organization of Gatherings. The Free Press, New York (1963)
21. Hall, E.T.: The Hidden Dimension. Anchor Books, New York (1969)
22. Argyle, M., Cook, M.: Gaze and Mutual Gaze. Cambridge University Press, Cambridge (1976)
23. Kampe, K.K.W., Frith, C.D., Frith, U.: "Hey John": signals conveying communicative intention toward the self activate brain regions associated with "mentalizing", regardless of modality. J. Neurosci. **23**(12), 5258–5263 (2003)
24. Hall, E.T.: A system for the notation of proxemic behavior. Am. Anthropol. **65**(5), 1003–1026 (1963)
25. Lambert, D.: Body Language. Harper Collins, London (2004)
26. Hall, E.T.: Proxemics. Curr. Anthropol. **9**(2–3), 83–108 (1968)
27. Sommer, R.: Personal Space: The Behavioral Basis of Design. Prentice Hall, Englewood Cliffs (1969)
28. Kendon, A.: Features of the structural analysis of human communication behavior. In: von Raffler-Engel, W. (ed.) Aspects of Nonverbal Communication, pp. 29–43 (1980)
29. Dautenhahn, K.: Socially intelligent robots: dimensions of human robot interaction. Philos. Trans. R. Soc. B Biol. Sci. **362**(1480), 679–704 (2007)
30. Breazeal, C.: Social interactions in HRI: the robot view. IEEE Trans. Syst. Man Cybern. Part C Appl. Rev. **34**(2), 181–186 (2004)
31. Imai, M., Ono T., Ishiguro, H.: Physical relation and expression: joint attention for human-robot interaction. In: Proceedings of the 10th IEEE International Workshop on Robot and Human Communication, RO-MAN 2001, pp. 512–517. IEEE, New York (2001)
32. Bruce, A., Nourbakhsh, I., Simmons, R.: The role of expressiveness and attention in human-robot interaction. In: Proceedings of the 2002 IEEE International Conference on Robotics and Automation, pp. 4138–4142. IEEE, New York (2011)
33. Torta, E., van Heumen, J., Cuijpers, Raymond H., Juola, J.F.: How can a robot attract the attention of its human partner? A comparative study over different modalities for attracting attention. In: Ge, S.S., Khatib, O., Cabibihan, J.-J., Simmons, R., Williams, M.-A. (eds.) ICSR 2012. LNCS (LNAI), vol. 7621, pp. 288–297. Springer, Heidelberg (2012). https://doi.org/10.1007/978-3-642-34103-8_29

34. Thrum, S., et al.: Probabilistic algorithms and the interactive museum tour-guide robot Minerva. Int. J. Robot. Res. **19**(11), 972–999 (2000)
35. Mutlu, B., Kanda, T., Forlizzi, J., Hodgins, J., Ishiguro, H.: Conversational gaze mechanisms for humanlike robots. J. ACM Trans. Interact. Intell. Syst. **1**(2), 12:1–12:33 (2012)
36. Mead, R., Mataric, M.J.: Robot have need too: how and why people adapt their proxemic behavior to improve robot social signal understanding. J. Hum. Robot. Interact. **5**(2), 48–68 (2016)
37. Huttenrauch, H., Eklundh, K.S., Green, A., Topp, E.: Investigating spatial relationships in human-robot Interaction. In: Proceedings of the 2006 IEEE/RSJ International Conference on Intelligent Robots and Systems, pp. 5052–5059. IEEE, New York (2006)
38. Silvera-Tawil, D., Rye, D., Velonaki, M.: Human-robot interaction with humanoid Diamandini using an open experimentation method. In: Proceedings of the IEEE International Symposium on Robot and Human Interactive Communication, pp. 425–430. IEEE, New York (2015)
39. Walters, M.L., et al.: Close encounters: spatial distances between people and a robot of mechanistic appearance. In: Proceedings of 5th IEEE-RAS International Conference on Humanoid Robots, pp. 450–455. IEEE, New York (2005)
40. Walters, M.L., Dautenhahn, K., Woods, S.N., Koay, K.L., Te Boekhorst, R., Lee, D.: Exploratory studies on social spaces between humans and a mechanical-looking robot. Connect. Sci. **18**(4), 429–439 (2006)
41. Sardar, A., Joosse, M., Weiss, A., Evers, V.: Don't stand so close to me: users' attitudinal and behavioral responses to personal space invasion by robots. In: Proceedings of the 7th ACM/IEEE International Conference on Human-Robot Interaction, HRI 2012, pp. 229–230. IEEE, New York (2012)
42. Dautenhahn, K., et al.: How may I serve you?: A robot companion approaching a seated person in a helping context. In: Proceedings of the 1st ACM SIGCHI/SIGART Conference on Human-Robot Interaction, HRI 2006, pp. 172–179. IEEE, New York (2006)
43. Walters, M.L., Dautenhahn, K., Woods, S.N., Koay, K.L.: Robotic etiquette: results from user studies involving a fetch and carry task. In: Proceedings of the 2nd ACM/IEEE International Conference on Human-Robot Interaction, HRI 2007, pp. 317–324. IEEE, New York (2007)
44. Ball, A., Rye, D., Silvera-Tawil, D., Velonaki, M.: Group vs. individual comfort when a robot approaches. In: Tapus, A., André, E., Martin, J.C., Ferland, F., Ammi, M. (eds.) ICSR 2015. LNCS (LNAI), vol. 9388, pp. 41–50. Springer, Cham (2015). https://doi.org/10.1007/978-3-319-25554-5_5
45. Steinfeld, A., Jenkins O.C., Scassellati, B.: The Oz of Wizard: simulating the human for interaction research. In: Proceedings of the 4th ACM/IEEE International Conference on Human-Robot Interaction, HRI 2009, pp. 101–107. IEEE, New York (2009)
46. Noldus Official Website. https://www.noldus.com/human-behavior-research/products/facereader
47. Hutchison, A., Gerstein, L.: Emotion recognition, emotion expression, and cultural display rules: implications for counseling. J. Asia Pac. Couns. **7**(1), 19–35 (2017)
48. Yan, W.: Facial expressions and differences between Chinese and Western cultures. Wen Shi Zi Liao **9**(1), 97–98 (2010)

DUXU for AI and AI for DUXU

Computational Evolutionary Art: Artificial Life and Effective Complexity

Tiago Barros Pontes e Silva(✉)

Brasília University, Brasília, Brazil
tiagobarros@unb.br

Abstract. On the field of Evolutionary Computational Art, artists frequently adopt a top-down process of creation, employing the algorithms only as a mean to express a previously conceived composition. In this sense, the present paper aims to discuss the use of Genetic Algorithms for the development of systems with greater level of emergence, running towards the increase of its effective complexity, understood as suggested by Gell-Mann. In this context it is presented the system Morphogenesis. It was developed as a Multi-Agent Adaptive System, built with Genetic Algorithms to generate movement, feeding, fighting and reproductive behaviors. All these behaviors are programed at the individual level, from which emerge the macro patterns of the groups, simulating the evolutionary process. The system analysis suggests that the fitness function should not be focused at the arrangements of the agents' genotype, but at the adaptation of the phenotype itself. It is expected that the use of algorithms that allow expressions closer to the evolutionary process has a greater affinity with the aesthetic notion proposed for the field of Evolutionary Computational Art. Hereupon, a qualitative exploratory study was conducted to compare the perception of the high effective complexity arrangements against random arrangements. Preliminary results show that the evolutionary process could be associated with a greater evaluation of intentionality of the compositions and could be also related with a deeper aesthetic evaluation.

Keywords: Computational Art · Artificial Life · Effective complexity

1 Introduction

Nowadays the current technology allows a variety of experimentation on the field of Computational Art. Notwithstanding the advances of the creations since its first artists like Herbert Franke, Michael Noll, Frieder Nake, Manfred Mohr or Edward Zadec, the contemporary artists and researchers are questioning their object of study and the way the poetics have been conceived. Today, the simple adoption of the computational process does not add value to the proposed works. Artists are asked how to be faithful to the chosen artifacts and materials, showing the intrinsic characteristics to the computational processes [1].

More specifically at the field of Evolutionary and Generative Art, Galanter [2, 3] presents some tangible challenges to the artists. The first one is the absence of an automatic Aesthetic Fitness Function to evolve the systems. The lack of knowledge

A. Marcus and W. Wang (Eds.): HCII 2019, LNCS 11584, pp. 331–346, 2019.
https://doi.org/10.1007/978-3-030-23541-3_24

about the human aesthetic judgement is considered an obstacle for an automated function. The human judgement is susceptible to fatigue, making the evaluation less consistent over time [4]. Besides, when this subjective judgement is directly attributed to the public by an interactive system, the processing capacity of the system is reduced, generating a limiter [5].

Moreover, another problem pointed by Galanter [3, 6] is the difference between the level of complexity existing in nature and on its genetic representation when compared to the computational systems created by artists. In this scenario, the concept of complexity is not considered simply as the amount of information of the visual representations, but a combination of organization and chaos in order to promote contextual effectiveness. Therefore, it is considered as the Effective Complexity presented by Gell-Mann [7], comprehended as the measure of the most compressed description of the regularities of a communication process or an algorithm. Nonetheless, the regularities can only be defined according to its relevance to a specific context.

The current study aims to present the Artificial Life system entitled Morphogenesis as an early answer to these questions. To seek for a greater level of emergence on its compositions, the evolutionary process will be simulated to achieve an increase on its Effective Complexity. The study begins from the premise that Effective Complexity is similar to the Organized Complexity proposed by Dawkins [8]. According to the author, the organized complexity is more than just heterogeneity. It consists of a specific type of heterogeneity that is slowly selected by nature due to a proficiency or is entirely conceived by a human top-down process to have a functionality.

2 The Features of the System Morphogenesis

2.1 Intended Aesthetics

The intended aesthetic for the system Morphogenesis is related to the composition of microscopic images. It is inspired by the first experiments of computational art, using geometric shapes as the representation of its agents. Although built as a composition of geometric agents, the system must also imply the organic feeling of a living system through its behavior. Thereby, its poetic approaches the emerging patterns of the living systems applied to the metaphoric world of microscopic images. It works as if it was possible to watch the very cells of every picture fighting to impose its shapes, colors and sounds. In other words, it is suggested to the public the experience of observing the fundamentals of visual and sound language interacting while transformed by the evolutionary process.

The main influences of the system were the Dawkins' Biomorphs [8] and the Conway's Game of Life [9]. The intention is to create a system that can navigate through the genetic space of its creatures like in Biomorphs, but with automatic rules of proximity, similar to the Game of Life. For more information about the intended levels of significance and the emergent discussions, see [10].

2.2 Development Process

The system development was considered a creative heuristic process of experimentation. The bottom-up approach was necessary to balance the agents' interactions so that life becomes probable in every performance. To achieve a self-organized arrangement a Multi-agent Complex Adaptive System [11] with Evolutionary Algorithms was built, using Genetic Algorithms [11, 12] and Swarm Intelligence [13]. The entire system was conceived using Processing 2.0.

The name Morphogenesis was chosen to represent the origin of microscopic compositions, meaning the origin of shapes. Also, it is a tribute to Alan Turing, who also wrote The Chemical Basis of Morphogenesis [14] discussing the emergence of complex structures from simple patterns. To understand the system's behavior and the meaning of the compositions, it is necessary first to comprehend its laws of creation presented below.

2.3 The Agent's Representation

Each agent has a body composed by a line that crosses 4 to 7 points randomly generated inside a square with a side between 25 and 100 pixels. It is a Catmull-Rom spline calculated to simulate a handwrite line with an assorted weight, also randomly specified. Sometimes the internal points can receive the line twice to create a loop. With this set of parameters, it is possible to simulate a scratch (Fig. 1).

Fig. 1. Two examples of the line that constitutes the agent's body. The first (left) highlights the points used to calculate the spline. The second (right) illustrates the loop of the line.

After the definition of the body's structure, three geometric shapes are inserted on the first, the second and last point. The shapes can either be a circle, a triangle or a pentagon. The first one defines the type of the agent and is also the larger shape of the body. When the agents interact to each other, shapes with a difference of sides bigger than 2 will be considered enemies, whilst agents with the same shape, or with a difference of only 1 side, will be considered friends (Fig. 2).

The agents also have 2 colors, one for the line and other for the fill, received as an RGB value. All these features are stored in the agent's DNA, retrieved later for its reproduction. With these features, it is possible to give the agent some visual identity, making it different from the others (Fig. 3).

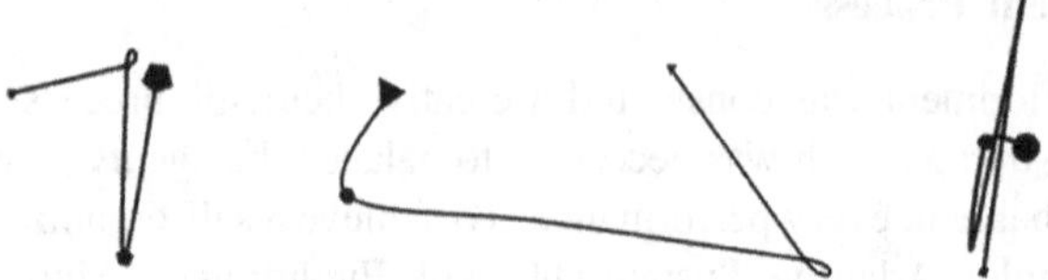

Fig. 2. Different types of agents defined by the larger shape of the body. From left to right, the pentagon, triangle and circle shape.

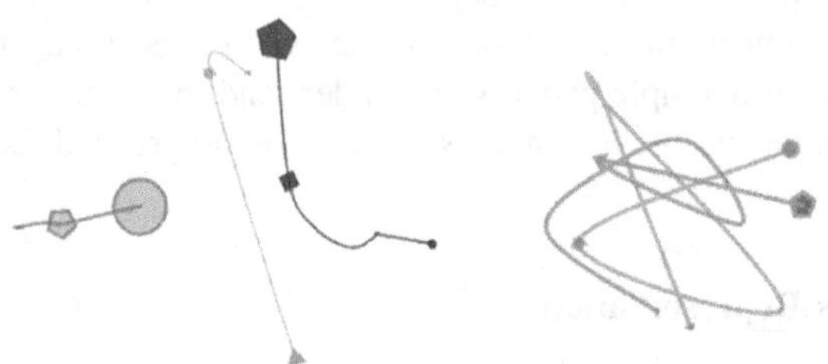

Fig. 3. Agents with its colors, one for the line and other for the fill. All the agent's information is stored in its DNA and helps to give the agent a visual identity. (Color figure online)

Also, it is possible to simulate a scrawl surface with several agents conceived with random attributes (Fig. 4). As expected, there is a homogeneous distribution of the information in this situation, implying a low effective complexity state derived from its randomness.

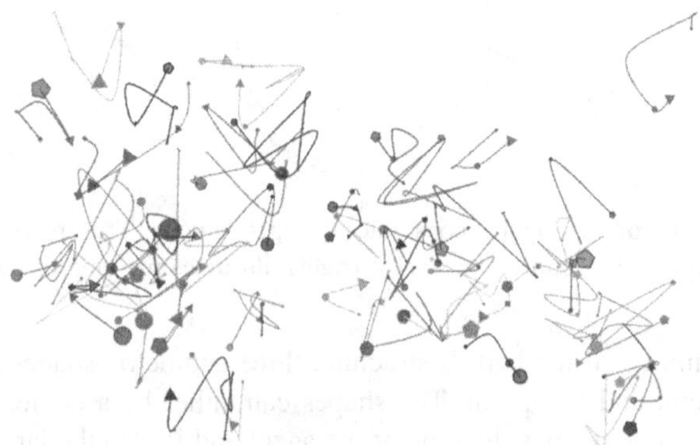

Fig. 4. Composition with 60 randomly generated agents. The variation of the agents' DNA determines the random distribution of the composition.

The agents also have a sound of their own. They are capable to reproduce a musical note from a specific instrument of the Java Sound API. Along the visual stimuli, the overlap of agents' sounds creates a symphony of random noise at the runtime's firsts stages.

There is also the representation of dead agents, where they lose their movement, colors and sounds. In this circumstance, the agent is represented in gray, always losing opacity and sound volume until completely vanished from the screen (Fig. 5).

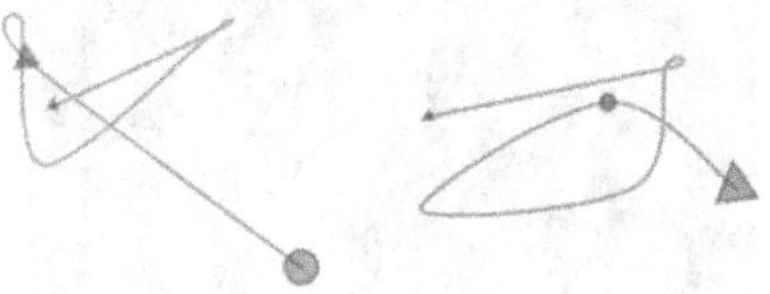

Fig. 5. Two dead agents vanishing from the screen.

2.4 The Agents' Drift

As a system inspired by Conway's Game of Life [9], the main variable to define the behavior of the agent is its position in relation to the others. Every agent has a basic random movement, a reference to the Brownian motion [15]. What determines the displacement of the agent is the resultant of all the other variables that interfere with the random probability. As an example, when an agent is influenced by another and tries to move away, the random probability of the original Brownian movement is weighted, altering the chances on each frame.

This feature prevents the agents from being perceived as bots flying on the screen. Instead, they move with an organic uncertainty that reminds the microscopic lives. When the head moves, all the other points of the body move along with an easing effect, simulating an organic elastic matter (Fig. 6).

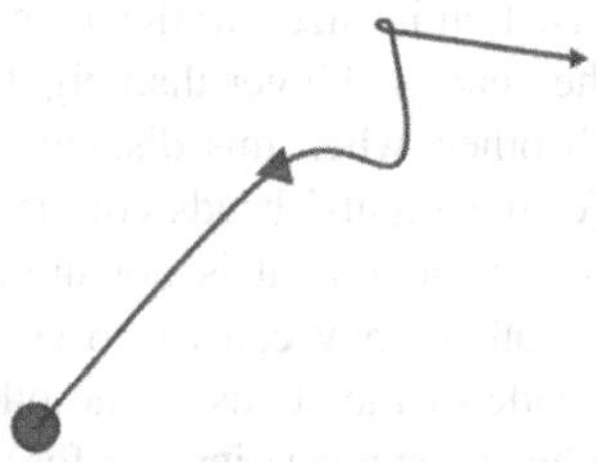

Fig. 6. Example of the easing effect that delays the movement of the points of the agent's body. With this effect the body tends to stretch during the motion and to accommodate when it stops.

2.5 The Environment

Despite the positions of the other agents, the two-dimensional space where they live has no influence on their behavior. Besides that, it is possible to choose a color to the background to improve the visual composition of the arrangement. The main choice is an automatic color calculated as the average fill colors of all agents. This allows the expression of particular compositions (Fig. 7).

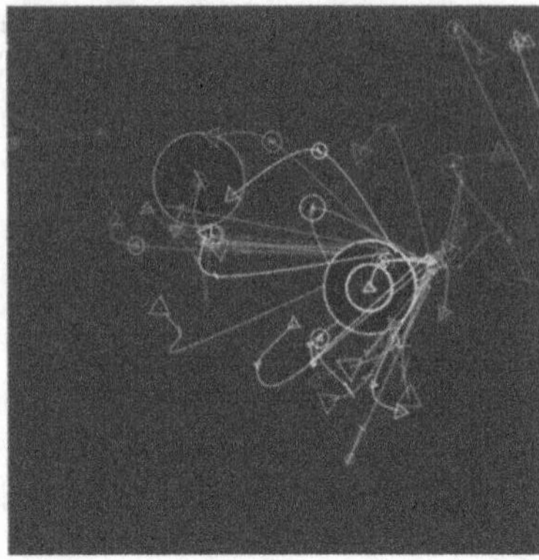

Fig. 7. Background color calculated as average fill color of all agents. (Color figure online)

2.6 Endogenous Interactions

The displacement behavior of the agents can be affected by the presence of other agents in several situations:

- a weaker foe to be chased;
- a stronger foe to flee from;
- a pair for mating;
- a friend for protection;
- a corpse of a dead friend to avoid;
- a dead foe that could serve as food.

In these cases, the collision detection occurs only on the head of the agents. There are three stages of detection based on its size: (a) the agents can't see each other, when the distance of the center of the heads is bigger than eight times the sum of the heads' radius; (b) the agents see each other, when this distance is smaller than that, but the agents are not yet colliding; (c) the agents' heads collide.

On the first stage, the agent′s movement is not influenced by another presence. When the agents can see each other, they can try to come closer or to move away, depending on the evaluation made of the status of the other agent (alive or dead), its strength, its type based on the head's shape (friend or foe) or if its ovulating and ready to mate. When the agents' heads touch each other, they can fight, reproduce, eat or do nothing at all (Fig. 8).

Also, there is a special situation when the agent's head crosses another point of the body of the other agents. In this circumstance, if the second shape of the body of that agent is the same of the agent's head, it can be trapped. While trapped, it becomes a limp of the other agent, having its life being drained. This effect happens regardless of whether they are friends or enemies (Fig. 9). Finally, there is one last possible interaction. When the agents consider themselves friends, the last shape of the body is checked. When it is the same, they can group to act like flocks, increasing the chances of staying close to each other (Fig. 9).

Fig. 8. Examples of two collision situations. The first on the left is a fight between agents, identified by a flashing square on their heads. The second on the right is a mating, identified by a circle flashing on their heads.

Fig. 9. Two examples of different interactions between agents. On the left there is a triangle agent trapped on the body of a circle agent. On the right there is a friendly group of square agents.

2.7 The Reproductive Process

After two agents ovulate, find each other and are capable of reaching their heads to a collision, the reproductive process begins. Once they can spend some time together mating, as illustrated previously, a new life is born.

Although, differently from the first generation created randomly by the system, this new life has a recombined DNA from its parents. Like other living species, the agents are constituted by a pair of variables for each feature. When they reproduce, a new recombination is generated for each pair of the agent's DNA. This allows the maintenance of the genetic variability of the system, as suggested by Dawkins [8]. Also, with that property, every agent has its own DNA composition. It can look similar to the other brothers, but not exactly the same. This effect cannot be achieved if the new DNA is composed by the mean of the parents' DNA, what would lead to a loss of genetic variability on the system (Fig. 10).

The agents' DNA is composed by 66 variables that define their color, sound, speed, amount of life, size, shape, maturity, among other properties. Also, when the reproduction occurs, there is 1% chance of mutation that can happen to each recombination, increasing or decreasing a bit the value of that feature. The mutation is another important

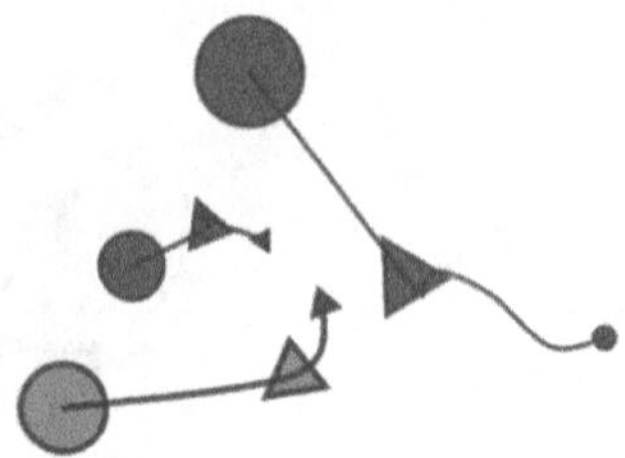

Fig. 10. A new life born near the parents with a recombined DNA.

feature for the evolutionary process. In a short-term, the persistence of the DNA is relevant for the success of the new life. However, in a long-term, mutation is necessary to shape flexible structures, making life probable on adaptable environments [8].

This effect can happen even on the shape of the head that determines the type of the agent. If this happens, the number of sides of the geometrical shape can change. If it still has a difference of only 1 side, it will be considered friend. But if the mutation continues and the difference becomes bigger than 2 sides, it will be considered an enemy. This feature is significant because it allows the navigation trough the genetic space of the agents, creating new species of geometric agents shaped by the evolutionary process, as purposed by the system Biomorphs [8].

2.8 Genetic Algorithm and Fitness Function

Nevertheless, the selection process of the most adapted agents from the system Morphogenesis differs from the Biomorphs. Due to the consistency problems of the human judgement guiding the evolutionary process [4], an automated selection was programmed. Yet, the use of the Genetic Algorithm was not directed to the ideal set of the agents' DNA as a declared Fitness Function [16]. Inspired by natural life, the selection is not calculated by a direct formal equation. Instead, all agents have an amount of life that is lost with time. The agents that are capable to live long enough and reproduce can transmit their DNA. Hence, the best properties for the agents' life are not programmed in a top-down approach. They emerge from the agents' interactions. Consequently, the properties are not selected by their genotype, but for their phenotype. The best DNA set cannot be identified at first.

The decisions taken by the agents are programmed by a state machine that relates its inputs and outcomes. The only possible outcome is a weight on the random displacement probability. With the DNA recombination and the mutation process, the agents can evolve to a complete distinct set of behaviors from the first programmed generation. If somehow a new configuration for the conditional hierarchy is established, either for proficiency or chance, it re-interprets the behavior categories presented earlier.

There are several meta-heuristics designed to optimize the search for a solution in a state space [17, 18]. Also, there are Novelty Search Algorithms [19, 20] designed to dynamically find new solutions related to previous findings. In this situation, the genetic algorithm is not used as an approximation function from a previously intendent configuration, nor considers the novelty level of previous findings. It considers the serendipity of life, it is flexible and can keep continually changing to adapt.

2.9 The Morphogenesis Compositions

When the system is launched, 60 agents are randomly created, 20 from each kind (Fig. 4). As the presented rules are applied, each frame creates a new arrangement, reorganizing the agents position and states. Due to the disorganization of the first generation, several fights occur simultaneously. With time, as the generations pass by, the selected genetic variability of the system start to emerge and dominate the scene.

The agents' colors and sounds cannot be perceived by the agents. They are indirectly selected and transmitted to the new generations. This way, they can be processed by the evolutionary process without guiding it. Therefore, the shapes, colors, sounds and arrangements represent an output of the evolutionary process of the Morphogenesis universe. The composition signifies the genetic variability of the living agents, constantly changing alongside the agents' behaviors (Figs. 11, 12, 13 and 14).

Fig. 11. Composition of a dominant red circle population. The colors represent the genetic variability of the agents. Distant groups have specific colors due to their isolation. (Color figure online)

2.10 Exogenous Interactions

The arrangements presented show the result of the endogenous interactions of the system. The interactions between the public and the system were planned to disrupt this organization as an aesthetic experience. This decision was made because it was difficult

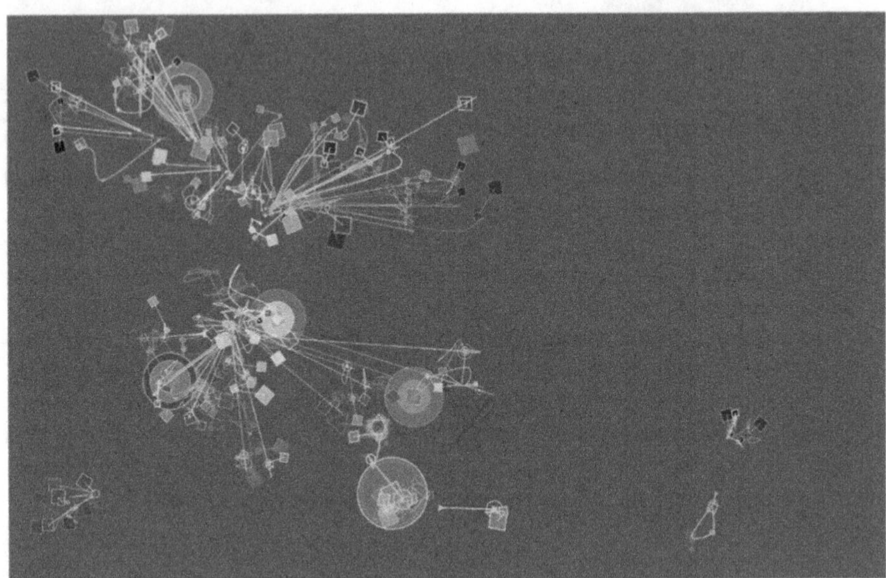

Fig. 12. Composition of a population of squares. This arrangement has a broader genetic variability than the previous one, with more colorful groups. The background becomes a more evident tertiary color. (Color figure online)

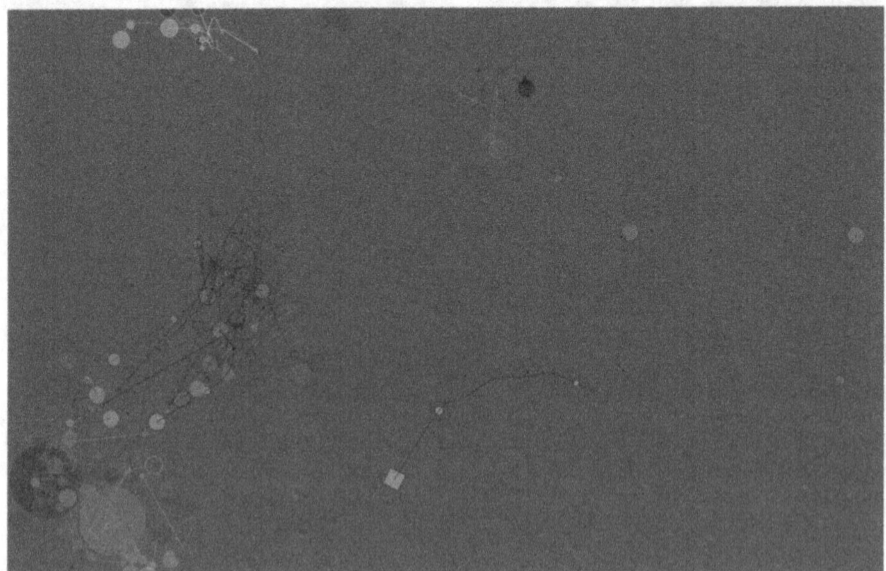

Fig. 13. Composition of a shoal of circles been predated by a stronger square. This is an emergent behavior of the system, since the conduct of the species was specialized by evolution. Circles have a short life and are weaker but succeeded as group, while the square lives alone for a longer time because it can feed from the shoal.

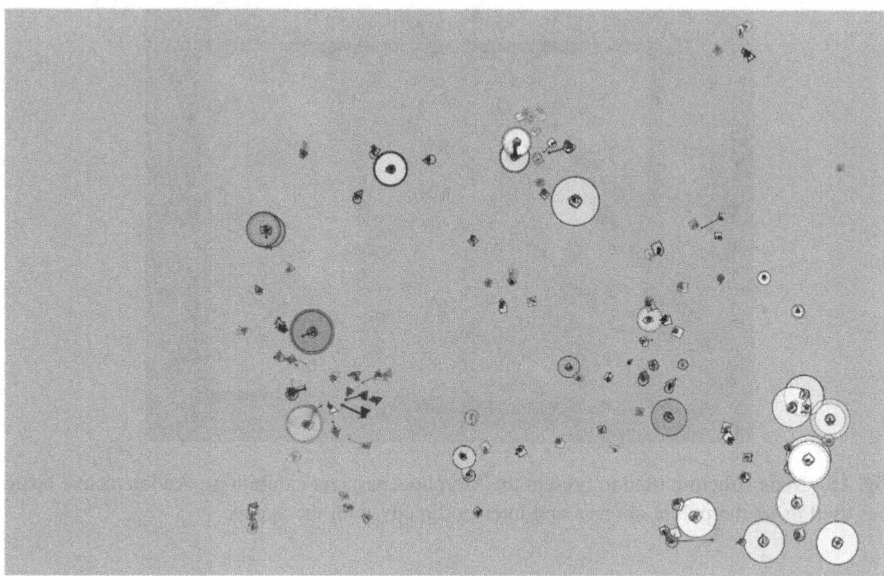

Fig. 14. Composition with a different agents' behavior, illustrating the navigation through the genetic space. This new specie only moves when there is intention of fighting, feeding, or mating with a higher speed than que first generation, specializing the use of the displacement.

to balance the behavior of the public with the evolutionary process of the species. The inconsistency and the timing of human actions tend to not contribute to the achievement of complex self-organized structures [4].

Several assemblies were tested to create means for the public to interfere on the Morphogenesis universe. The main configuration encompasses an interactive board that was used to allow touching the system's surface. The human touch bothers the agents, making they leave. Also, when directly touched, they accelerate to protect themselves. This feature alone was enough to create significant experiences, allowing the destruction of entire colonies with a single touch, leaving the public baffled (Fig. 15).

Other possibilities were tested as well, as a video game controller or cameras to capture the public actions. More information about the exogenous interactions can be found in [21].

3 Randomness and Effective Complexity

3.1 Comparison Between the Different Stages of Evolution

The first moments after launching the system creates a random composition of agents, as previously illustrated (Fig. 4). In this situation, the visual and acoustic information is chaotic, homogeneously distributed as suggested by Galanter [2, 3, 6] supported by the

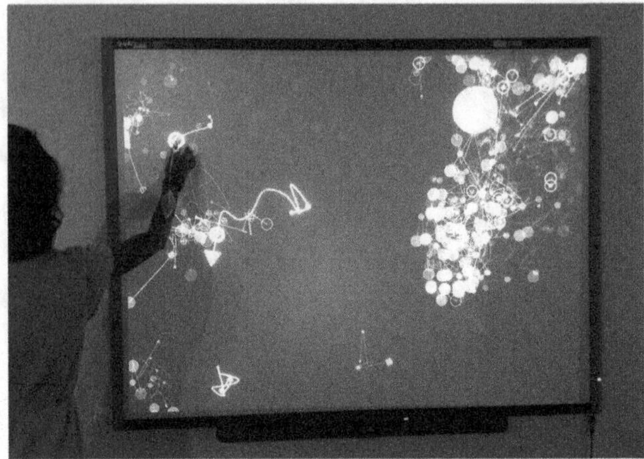

Fig. 15. Main structure used to present the Morphogenesis on exhibitions. An interactive board was used to let the public observe and interact directly with the agents.

statistical law of large numbers [22]. Considering the concept of effective complexity [7], despite the large number of agents, shapes, colors and sounds, the system in this situation is considered with a low amount of complexity. When two compositions randomly created are compared, the difference between them seems irrelevant, like noise (Fig. 16).

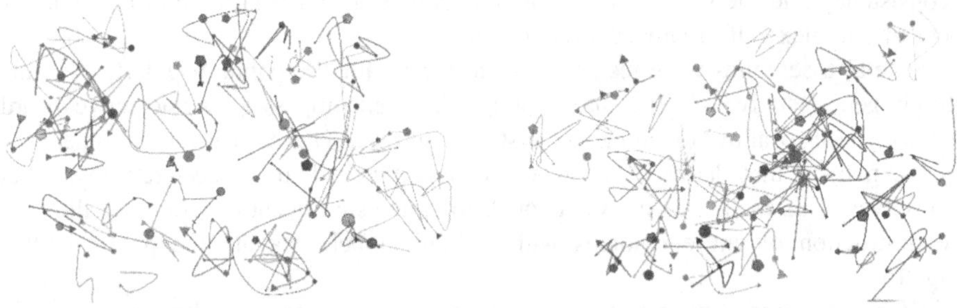

Fig. 16. Comparison between two random compositions. As predicted by Galanter and Gell-Mann, despite the large number of agents, colors and sounds, the arrangements look alike, suggesting a low amount of Effective Complexity. (Color figure online)

Otherwise, when a random composition is compared to another with agents from above 200 generations, the self-organization of the system suggests a pattern that represents the genetic variability of the population shaped by the evolutionary process (Fig. 17).

When interacting with the system in this situation in four art exhibitions performed between 2012 and 2013, the public expressed the feeling of relating with the agents' colonies that could not be completely understood but seemed intentional. This effect

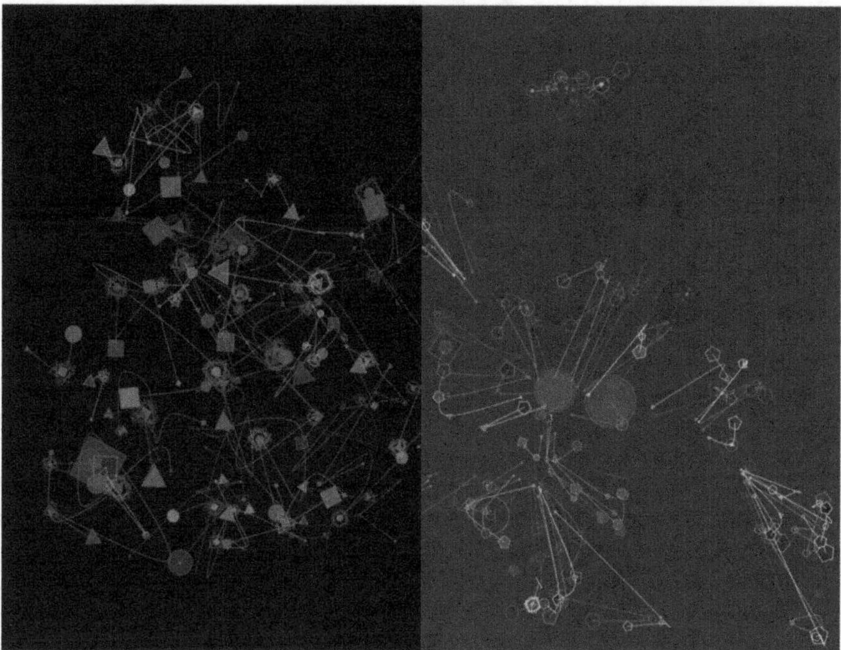

Fig. 17. Comparison between a random composition (left) and a system with agents from above the 200th generation (right). The composition self-organized has a pattern of distribution, color, sound and behavior, suggesting a greater amount of Effective Complexity than the other.

was not recurrent on early stages of development of the system. They frequently asked about the graphic and acoustic compositions of the continuously evolving system.

3.2 The System as an Instrument for an Empirical Study

Due to the public indications, a qualitative preliminary study was conducted to evaluate if the level of intentionality perceived of the arrangements, as well as the aesthetic evaluation of the participants, was related to the Effective Complexity of the composition. The empirical preliminary study is reported in [23].

A set of 30 pictures were created, 15 with random agents and 15 with agents from the 300th generation. Some configurations, as the background color or the number of agents were controlled. Two presentation orders were defined to check if it would influence the evaluation, sorting the group of 30 images in both cases. The participants were requested to answer if the picture was considered attractive and if they think it was made by a person or automatically generated by a computer. Only 10 people participate of the preliminary study to evaluate the instruments and procedures.

The preliminary results suggest that the pictures with a greater Effective Complexity were more attractive to the participants. Almost all of the participants (9 from a total of 10) expressed preference for the high complexity pictures. They expressed more interest on its colors' variations and organization, despite the difficulty to understand the meaning of the composition. It was interpreted as a more organic representation, like when they try to separate noise from a sound of a not known spoken language, suggesting intentionality.

Also, the random pictures were only interpreted as a human creation on the first occurrence. Yet, they were associated with children scrawl, while the complex pictures were perceived as more sophisticated creation. After the arbitrary pattern was recognized, the participants expressed a lack of diversification on the random images, as inferred. This effect started after the second occurrence of a random picture.

3.3 The Perceived Effective Complexity

Gell-Mann [7] defined Effective Complexity pondering its contextual relevance, excluding the noise or redundancy of the communication. However, it is not an easy approach to measure the exact Effective Complexity of some kind of systems. The present study tried to address the issue of aesthetic attractiveness of compositions considering the Effective Complexity as a possible factor. Therefore, reflecting on the Empiric Aesthetic studies of Fechner, Birkhoff [24], Eysenck [25], Berlyne [26] and Martindale [27] discussed by Nadal [28, 29], the relation between order and complexity is not yet well-defined. The recognition of a previously known stimulus is also a strong factor of influence.

Hence, the system Morphogenesis try to emulate an abstract composition with different levels of complexity. To ensure the increase of complexity of the composition without the use of figurative elements, the evolutionary process was applied to shape its visual and acoustic configuration. Consequently, the concept of Organized Complexity [8], comprehended as an output of the evolutionary process or an intentional human creation guided by a proficiency, was associated with the concept of Effective Complexity, understood as a combination of order and chaos with contextual relevance [7].

The self-organized patterns evolved from the system may have been more attractive to the public due to our specialization in recognizing natural outputs that are relevant to our survival, as food or other types of life. Therefore, our own evolutionary process may be responsible for a greater interest in such compositions, in which we are in a search for energy quality to sustain life and drive us apart from entropy, as suggested by Schrödinger [30].

Nonetheless, the role of the system Morphogenesis is to try to answer the questions purposed by Galanter about the superficiality of the current Generative Art approach. Thus, Morphogenesis tries to provide greater level of emergence than a simple algorithmic composition. A possible response learned for future works is the use of evolutionary techniques guided by an adequate proficiency for the creation of compositions with a greater level of Effective Complexity.

Also, it is a first incursion on an evolutionary poetic to provide an aesthetic experience of the evolutionary process. Due to the different manifestation scale, the evolutionary process can be comprehended, but not easily experimented with a panoramic view. The accelerated and simple universe of the Morphogenesis attempts to compress its scale to promote such experience.

4 Conclusion

The study presents the system Morphogenesis as Computer Art, more precisely at the Evolutionary and Generative field. It was conceived to discuss the superficiality of current generative compositions pointed by Galanter. He suggests that these systems should be able to perform more levels of emergence, expressed by the presence of Effective Complexity on the creations. Therefore, it was conceived as a Multi-Agent Complex Adaptive System, representing geometric shapes that should evolve when interacting with each other.

From the exhibitions and a small qualitative preliminary test, it seems that the use of evolutionary techniques was able to trigger the interest of the public in these compositions. Maybe humans tend to have an innate curiosity for this kind of complexity, that symbolize natural complex outputs or for the functioning of our own creations. When interacting with the system, with the necessary disposition to involve themselves with the suggested poetic, the aesthetic experience of the public fomented insights about our interference on another complex systems, such as the big cities or the natural environment.

But also, it provided deep reflections about how we are here and the origin of the species. Because of that, it achieved an unexpected scientific audience, used by teachers to discuss the Theory of Evolution by Natural Selection, used to help the students to understand this process by experimenting it, despite its artificial and impossible nature. This illustrates the intricated role of Art in relation to Science, corroborating Galanter's statement that Art practice includes a large body of heuristics that simulates human experiences, and each technique suggests a hypothesis worthy of scientific investigation [31].

References

1. Galanter, P.: Truth to process – evolutionary art and the aesthetics of dynamism. In: International Conference on Generative Art. Generative Design Lab, Milan Polytechnic, Milan (2009)
2. Galanter, P.: What is generative art? Complexity theory as a context for art theory. In: International Conference on Generative Art (2003)
3. Galanter, P.: The problem with evolutionary art is… In: EvoCOMNET 2010: The 7th European Event on the Application of Nature-inspired Techniques for Telecommunication Networks and other Parallel and Distributed Systems (2010)
4. Takagi, H.: Interactive evolutionary computation: fusion of the capabilities of EC optimization and human evaluation. Proc. IEEE **89**(9), 1275–1296 (2001)
5. Werner, G.M., Todd, P.M.: Frankensteinian methods for evolutionary music composition. In: Griffith, N., Todd, P.M. (eds.) Musical Networks: Parallel Distributed Perception and Performance. MIT Press/Bradford Books, Cambridge (1998)
6. Galanter, P.: Complexism and the role of evolutionary art. In: Romero, J., Machado, P. (eds.) The Art of Artificial Evolution: A Handbook on Evolutionary Art and Music, pp. 311–332. Springer, Berlin (2008). https://doi.org/10.1007/978-3-540-72877-1_15
7. Gell-Mann, M.: What is complexity? Complexity **1**, 16–19 (1995)
8. Dawkins, R.: The Blind Watchmaker. Norton & Company, New York (1986)

9. Gardner, M.: Mathematical games: the fantastic combinations of John Conway's new solitaire game "Life". Sci. Am. **223**, 120–123 (1970)
10. Silva, T.B.P.: Thoughts upon the morphogenesis. In: Fragoso, M.L.P.G., Silva, T.R.F., Nobrega, C.A.M. (eds.) Computer Art & Design for All, 1st edn., vol. 1, pp. 159–167. EBA - Escola de Belas Artes de UFRJ/RioBooks, Rio de Janeiro (2014)
11. Holland, J.H.: Hidden Order: How Adaptation Builds Complexity. Helix, Reading (1995)
12. Konar, A.: Artificial Intelligence and Soft Computing - Behavioral and Cognitive Modeling of the Human Brain. CRC Press, Boca Raton (2000)
13. Bonabeau, E., Dorigo, M., Theraulaz, G.: Swarm Intelligence: From Natural to Artificial System. Oxford University Press, New York (1999)
14. Turing, A.M.: The chemical basis of morphogenesis. Philos. Trans. R. Soc. London. Ser. B Biol. Sci. **237**(641), 37–72 (1952)
15. Einstein, A.: On the motion of small particles suspended in a stationary liquid, as required by the molecular kinetic theory of heat. Ann. Phys. **17**(8), 549–560 (1905)
16. Michalewicz, Z.: Genetic Algorithms + Data Structures = Evolution Programs. Springer, Heidelberg (1998)
17. Russel, S.J., Norvig, P., Davis, E.: Artificial Intelligence: A Modern Approach. Prentice Hall, Upper Saddle River (2010)
18. Glover, F., Kochenberger, G.A.: Handbook of Metaheuristics. Kluwer Academic Publishers, Boston (2003)
19. Lehman, J., Stanley, K.O.: Exploiting open-endedness to solve problems through the search for novelty. In: ALIFE, pp. 329–336 (2008)
20. Lehman, J., Stanley, K.O.: Abandoning objectives: evolution through the search for novelty alone. Evol. Comput. **19**(2), 189–223 (2011)
21. Silva, T.B.P.: Morfogênese: sistema autopoiético emergente de vida artificial 293, [13] p. Thesis (doctorate) - University of Brasília, Institute of Arts, Postgraduate Program in Art (2014)
22. Moore, D.S.: The Basic Practice of Statistics, 5th edn. W. H. Freeman and Company, New York (2010)
23. Silva, T.B.P.: Intentionnalité & perception esthétique dans le système de l'art computationnel. In: D'Angelo, B., Soulages, F., Venturelli, S. (eds.) Esthétique & Connectivité, 1st edn., vol. 1, pp. 105–118. L'Harmattan, Paris (2018)
24. Birkhoff, G.D.: Aesthetic Measure. Harvard University Press, Cambridge (1932)
25. Eysenck, H.J.: The empirical determination of an aesthetic formula. Psychol. Rev. **48**, 83–92 (1941)
26. Berlyne, D.E.: Aesthetics and psychobiology. New York, Appleton-Century-Crofts, Educational Division, Meredith Corporation (1971)
27. Martindale, C.: Aesthetics, psychobiology, and cognition. In: Farley, F., Neperud, R. (eds.) The Foundations of Aesthetics, Art, and Art Education, pp. 7–42. Praeger, New York (1988)
28. Nadal, M.R.: Complexity and aesthetic preference for diverse visual stimuli. Doctoral Thesis, Department de Psicologia, Universitat de les Illes Balears (2007)
29. Nadal, M.R., Munar, E., Marty, G., Cela-Conde, C.J.: Visual complexity and beauty appreciation: explaining the divergence of results. Empir. Stud. Arts **28**(2), 173–191 (2010)
30. Schrödinger, E.: What is life? The physical aspect of the living cell. Based on lectures delivered under the auspices of the Dublin Institute for Advanced Studies at Trinity College, Dublin (1943)
31. Galanter, P.: Against reductionism: complexity science, complexity art, and complexity studies. Institute for the Study of Coherence and Emergence, Complexity and Philosophy Workshop (2002)

Design and Development of a Standard Interface Component to Highlight Automated AI Recommendations in the Conta Azul Software

João Antonio de Menezes Neto(✉), Bruno Carlos Cruz, Harry Porto Schroeter, and Ludmila Rocha Ribeiro Feitosa

ContaAzul Software LTDA, Joinville, SC 89219-600, Brazil
jmenezes.n@gmail.com, viciannacruz@gmail.com, harry.porto@gmail.com, ludmilarochadf@gmail.com

Abstract. This paper reports, in a professional approach, the design and development process of a standard interface component, which highlights the information provided by two artificial intelligence engines of the Conta Azul software. This software is a cloud platform for small businesses management, developed and marketed in Brazil, in the SaaS (Software as a Service) modality, which connects to banks, the government and fintechs. As a design problem, it was necessary to stipulate, as a part of the company's Design System and as a response to the managerial challenges brought about by the accelerated growth of the R&D team, a standard interface component for the aforementioned cases, providing context to the user and scalability to team practices. These engines are used for (1) tax recommendation and (2) the categorization of bank statements. As methods stipulated, there were the analysis of support tickets, analysis of the current interfaces, benchmarking, generation of alternatives, design review, bitmap prototyping, usability tests and JavaScript coding. The result was a standard interface component. The compatibility with the schedule of the company and its objectives was considered. The project occurred in parallel with other demands, from January 2018 to December 2018. The first author of this paper is one of the design coordinators of the company, being the other authors collaborators of the Design Ops team.

Keywords: Interface · Component · Automated recommendations

1 Introduction

This paper reports, from a professional perspective, the process of designing and developing a standard interface component. This project resulted from the need to improve the user experience, decrease the learning curve and the urgency of standardization of processes and interface components experienced by the Conta Azul company, due to the rapid growth of its Research and Development (R&D) team.

The focus of the project in question refers to the use cases in which automated recommendations are made by two artificial intelligence engines of the namesake

A. Marcus and W. Wang (Eds.): HCII 2019, LNCS 11584, pp. 347–360, 2019.
https://doi.org/10.1007/978-3-030-23541-3_25

Conta Azul software, a Brazilian solution for the management of small businesses and accounting firms. These engines carry out (1) the tax recommendation and (2) the categorization of bank statements.

Thus, it was hypothesized that when standardizing the automated recommendations component from a systemic perspective, the experience of using the software in question is improved. This is achieved through the consistency of the visual representation in the use cases listed, regardless of the software screen in which the component is applied.

As a structure, this paper presents a brief theoretical review, followed by contextualization about the Conta Azul company and software, delimitation of the problematic experienced, stipulation of the project objectives and the applied methods, combined with its results. It concludes with general learning and directions for future research, in light of the convergence between user experience and artificial intelligence.

2 Context of the Investigation

This section presents a brief theoretical review, in an introductory character, for the definition of the key terms used in this report. In addition, it also presents the Conta Azul company and software, the general characteristics of the Brazilian market, organizational aspects of the company's R&D team, focusing on design, and the motivations that led to the stipulation of the project that thematizes this paper.

2.1 Theoretical Review

In order to facilitate understanding of the conceptual fields of this paper, there is the need to review different bibliographical, marketing and methodological sources about the state-of-the-art design processes in the production of software, together with the definition of artificial intelligence aspects with convergence with experience of use.

Design Ops, Design System and Atomic Design. One of the main concepts, Design Operations (Design Ops), refers to the managerial aspects of design processes in companies. For Malouf [1], the area of Design Ops allows to amplify the value of design in the products created by the companies, removing frictions present in the routine of the designers.

This managerial mentality becomes increasingly relevant as the maturity and quantity of people on the team increases. In short, Malouf [1] defines the area's responsibilities as providing fluidity to design methods, processes and solutions. Part of the inspiration for creating this concept came from Developer Ops (Dev Ops), a segment linked to software engineering.

Along with this, it is worth highlighting the relevance of the Design System concept, which is present in professional discussions. This term encapsulates the reusability mentality of graphical user interface elements, from principles and design patterns stipulated previously and derived from behavioral characteristics of their target audiences, reported in a guide format. For Suarez [2], Design System is the essential tool to provide scalability to design and design teams in the contemporary workplace.

In order to manage the elements, present in the Design System, from its documentation through implementation to evolution, it is necessary to stipulate a unique pattern of taxonomic organization.

One of the emerging means for this is Atomic Design, which suggests a metaphorical hierarchy that divides the interface layers into atoms, molecules, cells, and organisms [3]. It is worth mentioning, however, that the organization of this type of material comes from the culture of each company, being adaptable. As a recommendation, Suarez [2] emphasizes the importance of considering two fundamental pillars: to foster a standardization structure, together with a componentization structure, which must emerge from design principles.

Artificial Intelligence in the User Experience Context. Finally, it is worth to highlight the definition of artificial intelligence (AI), directly linked to its applicability in the user experience. Here, artificial intelligence is considered as computational solutions that allow the processing and obtaining of value and meaning in information, from sources with high data volume [4].

For Lee [4], the meeting of design and artificial intelligence allows designers to give meaning to the information registered by users, helping to decipher not only “the what” but also “the why” of certain actions.

Having these terms delineated, the following section details the context of the investigation from the design and organizational challenges of the Conta Azul company.

2.2 The Conta Azul Company and Software

The Technology Company Conta Azul. Having the same name as the software it develops, the company has seven years of existence and two offices, in the cities of Joinville and São Paulo, Brazil. The motivations for its foundation come from the perception of its partners about the opportunity to create simplified solutions for the complex scenario of Brazilian entrepreneurship.

Recent data highlight that the country occupies the position 72nd in the global competitiveness indicators of the World Economic Forum [5]. Even though it is the eighth largest economy in the world, the bureaucracy to have a business hinders the advancement of the Brazilian entrepreneurs.

For the Brazilian Micro and Small Business Support Service [6], the main reasons for small business mortality, which occurs at a rate of 55% in two years, are the lack of planning, the lack of training on management and the lack of control over revenues and expenses.

Given this opportunity, and with the motivation to improve this reality, the Conta Azul company sought capital in investment funds to accelerate its growth strategies, in order to offer its software to small companies and Brazilian accounting firms, with accessible monthly fees.

The company obtained investment in different rounds, both of Brazilian funds and foreign funds. The latest round of Tiger Global and Endeavor Catalyst, at the end of 2017, worth US$ 25 million, helped the company and its team to double in size [7].

The essential factor, however, is to notice that at the same time that growth allowed the expansion of the company's channels of action, it brought managerial challenges of greater complexity.

As a direct consequence of this accelerated growth, 250 new professionals were received between January and December 2018, and the complexity of process and people management was increased.

It was necessary, then, to create new models to maintain the quality and consistency of the deliveries of different departments, avoiding inconsistencies that eventually undermined the user experience.

Currently, the company has a total of 420 employees. Of these, 120 work in the R&D area, 20 of them being user experience designers. All authors of this paper are part of this team.

The designers are pulverized in multidisciplinary teams, in the likes of "tribes and squads" inspired by the Spotify model [8]. The other professionals connected to this department are back-end, front-end and data engineers, product managers and compliance consultants.

Regarding the design team, one of the main responses to mitigate the pain caused by the increase in managerial complexity highlighted above was the implementation of a Design System, in order to regularize, describe and manage the applicability of interface components, interaction patterns and software terminologies. Figure 1 shows *Magica*, the website that describes the Design System.

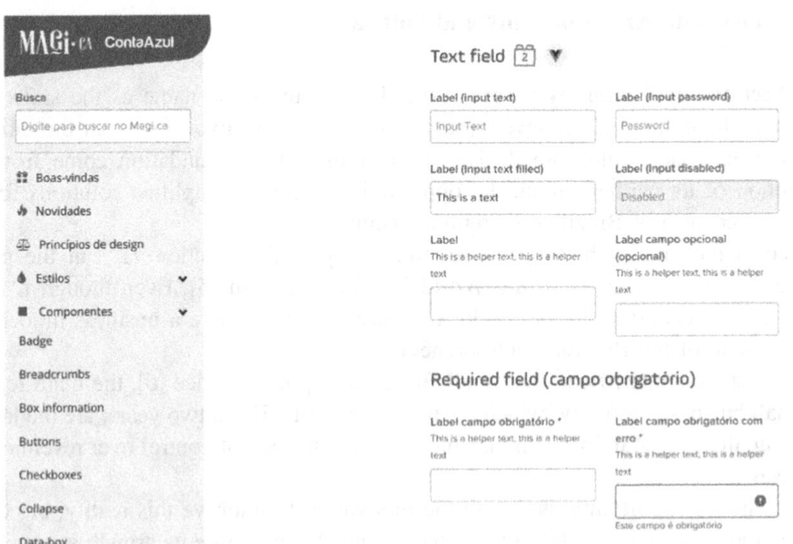

Fig. 1. Conta Azul's Design System, *Magica*

Prior to the implementation of the Design System, that occurred in 2017, the company had only one master file in the Sketch software, with bitmap elements, without specification and regularization of its application, which created risks of fragmentation in the projects.

The Conta Azul software. In relation to its software, developed and marketed exclusively in Brazil, in the SaaS (Software as a Service) modality, Conta Azul is focused on connecting owners of small companies to their accountants. The objective is to assist in the management and exchange of information about the business, through Internet browsers, in the cloud.

Similar to the concept of ERP (Enterprise Resource Planning), the platform presents modules for controlling sales, purchasing, finance, fiscal and, above all, accounting aspects.

One of the possible features is that all the actions registered in the platform by the small business generate accounting debits and credits, in real time, enabling the issuance of accounting books and tax forms automatically. The software homepage, called "Dashboard", displays the main indicators of the small business in a playful and graphical way (see Fig. 2).

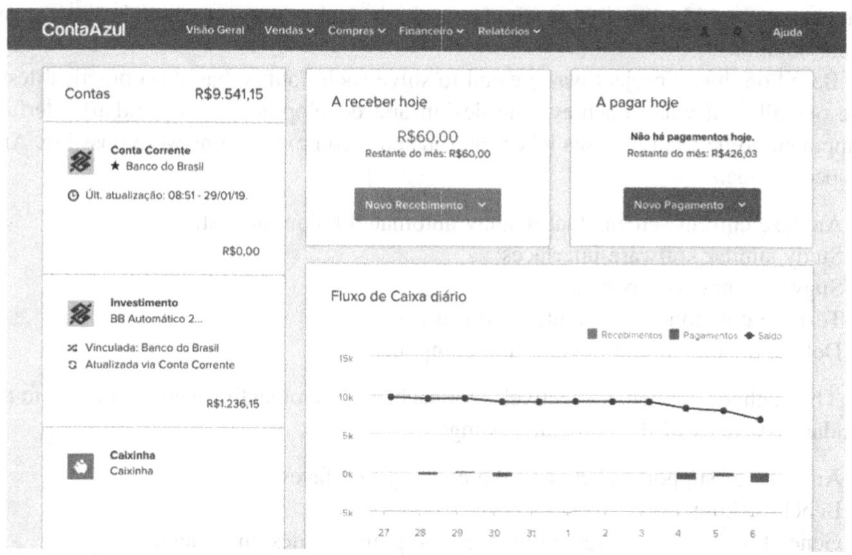

Fig. 2. Conta Azul's dashboard

Once the contextualization of the market, the company and the software has been reached, the next section shows the factors that led to the specific research focus in relation to a standard component of automated recommendations. It also presents the inquiries of the designers of the company, along with the methods planned for the design and development of the component in question.

3 Delimitation of the Problem and the Scope of the Project

Because it is a complex software, with different user flows, the designers of the company raise inquiries at their weekly meetings, called Design Reviews, in order to reach best practices to provide consistency in the interface and user interaction resources.

In one of these meetings, held in January 2018, there were discussions about the need for improvements in the display of automated tax recommendations, a resource belonging to the Fiscal module of the software.

Already considering the systemic mentality required by the Design System, the scope of the discussion was extended to evaluate all the points of contact of the platform that exhibit automated recommendations, independently of the module.

Regarding the automated recommendations, some of them are already generated by two artificial intelligence engines that learn and increase their assertiveness with the growth of the user base. These engines are (1) tax recommendations and (2) categorization of bank statements.[1]

In consensus, the group hypothesized that stipulating a standard to communicate what is being displayed on the screen as an automated recommendation, made by artificial intelligence, could contribute to the improvement of the user experience. However, it was questioned whether, even with recommendation engines and different contexts, it would be possible to stipulate a single design language, both in present and future solutions.

Based on this, a project was created to solve such doubts, based on practical tests. The overall goal was to achieve the design and development of a standard interface component to be used in cases where automated recommendations were possible. And as specific goals:

1. Analyze current screens that display automated recommendations;
2. Study similar software interfaces;
3. Suggest a new component;
4. Test the component recognition with users;
5. Define, document and develop the component.

The methods applied, respectively, for each specific objective were chosen from the standard practices of the company, being:

1. Analysis of support tickets and the existing interfaces;
2. Benchmarking;
3. Generation of alternatives, bitmap prototyping and design review;
4. Usability testing;
5. Writing of documentation and coding in JavaScript ("Vanilla").

The execution of the project occurred as a parallel activity, in conjunction with other demands of the R&D area, being conducted by Design Ops professionals and completed in December 2018.

[1] The methods used by the engines to generate information are omitted in this report due to information confidentiality.

4 Project Development

Once the problem was delimited, the team put into practice each method, based on the specific objectives listed. The following section details the methodological progression and the partial results of each step.

4.1 Study of Screens that Use Automated Recommendations

One of the factors that drove the prioritization of this demand was to test it as a possible solution to reduce tickets of usability doubts regarding the issuance of service and product invoices, that require, in Brazil, detailed taxation framings.

Conta Azul's R&D team had risen this hypothesis before, derived from previous studies of taxation doubts, carried out in the first quarter of 2018.

During the aforementioned study, it was noted that tax input was one of the features that generated the most doubts in the users of the software, corresponding to about 16% of the monthly support tickets opened[2].

Another factor that motivated the development of the project was the fact that the old version of the software, called the Classic Workflow, had a tax scenario configuration screen. In it, the user or his or her accountant could pre-register specific taxes scenarios. This ensured more agility to the issuance of invoices, since taxes were already parameterized according to that particular business needs.

In the current version of the software, however, it is still not possible to parameterize taxes or scenarios, causing the user or his accountant to manually enter the taxes for each invoice. However, after issuing his first invoice, the artificial intelligence engine learns to make recommendations by cross-referencing the product and customer data, as shown in Fig. 3, in fields with yellow outline.

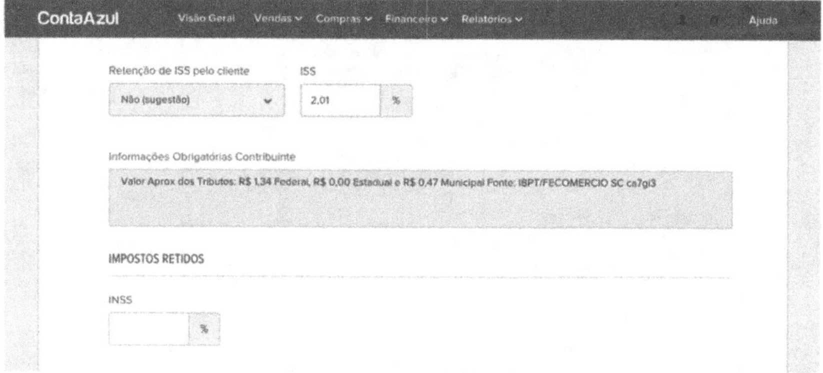

Fig. 3. Conta Azul's invoice screen highlighting the tax input form

[2] The absolute number of tickets and users is omitted due to information confidentiality.

During the study of user doubts, the methods used to verify the possible impact of an improved tax automation solution on the clients' day-to-day life were: monitoring of incoming calls in Customer Support, reading and categorization of tickets and face-to-face and telephone interviews with impacted users.

During this study, the team identified users that contacted Customer Support up to 17 times in a single month. This finding was important to the R&D team, in order to investigate potential problems of invoices and taxes information.

The data collected during this study were tabulated in a document. In it, the information extracted was separated by categories: problem report, number of occurrences, standardization of reports and – from a fiscal perspective – source of the problem.

For example, errors resulting from failure to communicate with the Brazilian government's Treasury Department were categorized as "Treasury". And then there was the description of the problem, such as "dubious error messages", "usability doubts", "Classic Workflow versus New Workflow", and others. Throughout the research phase, the design team had help from support analysts of the company. They also had proximity with the Product Analytics team, extracting quantitative data.

In the same period, the project to redesign the bank reconciliation interface, belonging to the Financial module, with a distinct team in relation to Fiscal, occurred. This other team also noticed the need to visually highlight category recommendations of bank statements, in order to facilitate user experience [9].

Figure 4 shows the reconciliation interface. To the left of the screen, the user sees the bank statement, that is obtained from Open Banking APIs. On the right, there is the entry which will be registered in the Conta Azul software, that has to be categorized.

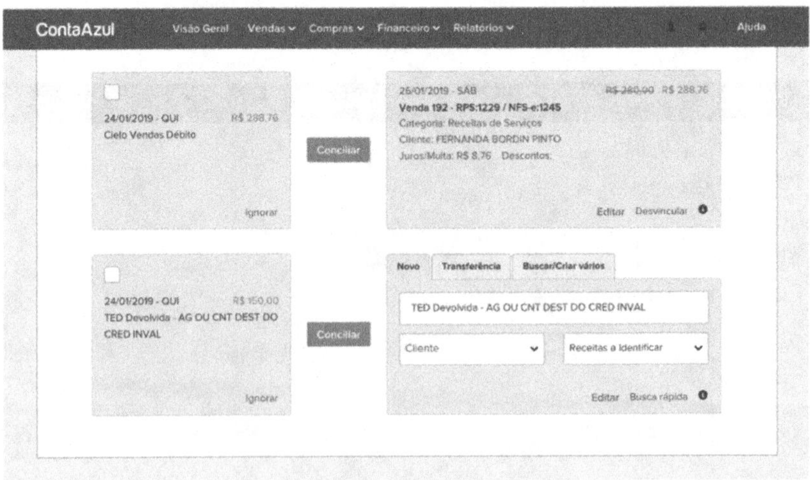

Fig. 4. Conta Azul's bank statement reconciliation interface

If the entry already exists in the software, as a provision, the Conta Azul software proposes a match between the two, learning from the user's habit. This project also took into account Customer Support input and tickets, together with other methods.

In carrying out these analyzes, it was possible to notice the importance of standardizing the recommendations component, in order to make the design language compatible with the platform as a whole.

The user's journey crosses different modules, that is, when generating a sale and issuing an invoice, soon after the user has to indicate if a parcel decurrent of that sale has been received or not. In this way, the division of teams followed by Conta Azul's R&D department is purely virtual, to facilitate the internal management of people. It should not reflect as silos in the platform, as the user journey is broader.

Based on this, it was also observed the need to evaluate similar solutions in concurrent software, of similar segments, to assist in the design of the solutions.

4.2 Similar Software Analysis

During similar interfaces studies, Conta Azul's design team realized that, in general, Brazilian competitors already suggested taxes in their software. In some cases, they even offer the parameterization of specific invoice emission scenarios. The same was true for the bank statement categorization, where categories were automatically recommended. Five competing software were analyzed.[3]

In regard of how the recommendations are displayed, competitors did not demonstrate, nor differed visually, any predefined recommendations or parameters. The fields are simply presented with the values of taxes and it is up to the user to check them.

With this, the opportunity to differentiate Conta Azul was even more latent, with the possibility of informing the user when there are recommendations on the screen. Alongside this, there was also the opportunity to evolve the user flow of registration of fiscal scenarios, also enabling accountants to perform this configuration in the New Workflow version of the Conta Azul software, since their technical knowledge may overlap or enrich the recommendations coming from the artificial intelligence engines.

It should be noticed that the possibility of setting up taxes was a request made by the accountants themselves, that is, it opens a technical reflection on the importance of the accountant's endorsement as a professional responsible for the data of their clients.

4.3 Suggestion of the New Component

From the analysis of the data obtained, five component alternatives were generated. In order to mitigate the change of existing user habits, the team chose to direct their solutions in the scope of new form inputs. The journey that the user has in the software is still the same, modifying only how he or she perceives the recommendations.

Overall, this approach was elected in order to try to reduce the number of tickets resulting from taxation doubts, but without causing considerable visual impact, focusing on highlighting accurate information to users.

[3] The names of the competitors were omitted due to information confidentiality.

The same goes for the bank statement categorization, in which the two-column visuals remained, especially due to this interface's pregnancy. Providing a complete redesign could cause increased doubt tickets, which did not meet the project aspiration, which was just the opposite.

Figure 5 illustrates the alternatives generated. Some of them took advantage of the yellow highlight already present in the software but increasing its contrast. The designers also tested markers such as a balloon icon, in different layouts – above the label of the field and also attached to the field. Another iconographic variation was a hand cursor, next to the Conta Azul logo, with the caption "recommendation". Tests were also made with green and blue color variations.

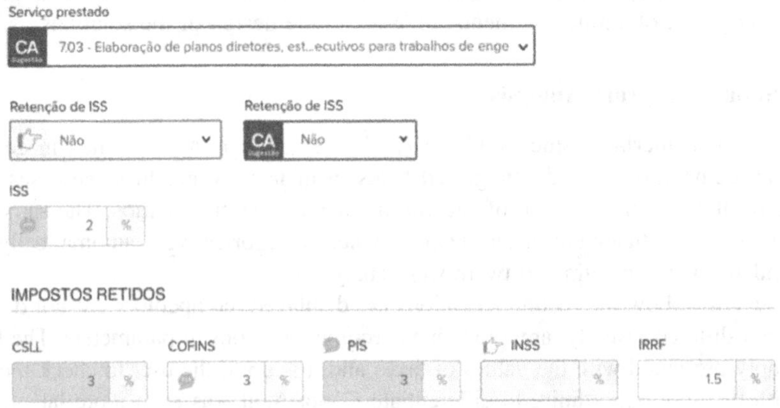

Fig. 5. Recommendation component alternatives generated

Alternatives were taken to the Design Review meeting in order to get feedback from all of the company's designers. As Design System starts from the assumption of standardization, it was essential to expose the options to all the stakeholders, to create consensus on the decisions.

The group commented that the green contouring alternatives looked like validated information, which could confuse or induce the user to accept the recommendations without weighing them and eventually causing fiscal errors.

The yellow version was criticized because of its low visual contrast. And, with this, the best evaluated alternative was the one of blue contour. Iconography, however, was not approved by the group at this time. One of the variations, for instance, suggested as a pencil icon, was assessed as a reinforcement on the need to edit the tax fields, not as a recommendation.

Based on the preliminary results, the Design Ops team returned to the drawing boards and improved the alternatives. After the internal evaluation, it was essential to test the understanding of the alternatives with real users of the platform. The following section details this step.

4.4 User Recognition Tests

In the decision process on the most adequate solution, the team considered factors such as lower user impact, truthfulness and reliability of information.

For the usability tests, the team selected the same users who participated in the interviews, as well as accountants and users with fiscal doubts, but who did not participate in previous interviews. Figure 6 shows the interface used in the tests, created as a bitmap prototype, with the iconography of a lightning and the blue outline in the fields with recommendations.

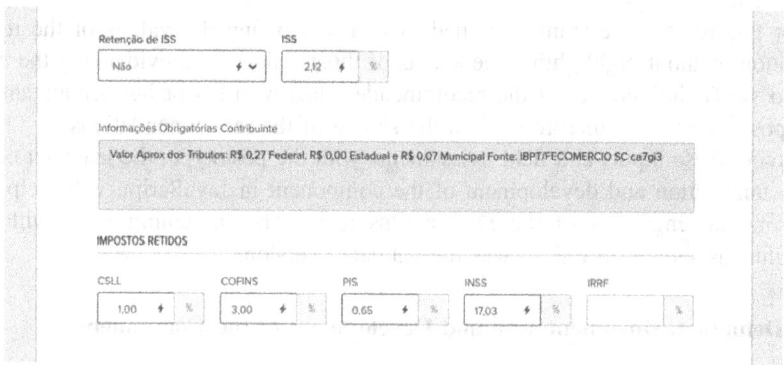

Fig. 6. Conta Azul's recommendation component used during usability tests

In the case of the bank statement categorization interface, because the inputs are inserted in a rectangle, there was also screen space to implement instructional texts. Texts have been added in the lower left corner of the card to the right of the screen, contextualizing the reason for the recommendation, such as categorization or a match of existing entries (see Fig. 7).

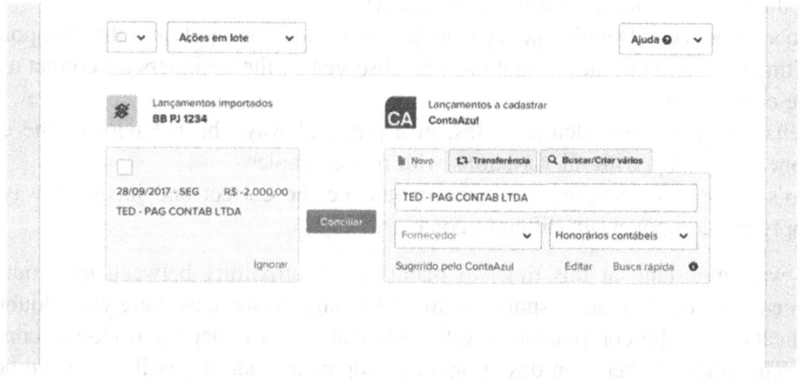

Fig. 7. Conta Azul's bank categorization interface used during usability tests

One of the hypotheses the team worked on was to explain to the user the origin of the recommendation, so that he or she understood who was responsible for presenting those values.

Thus, along with the component, it would be detailed if the recommendation had come from a previous setup by the accountant, whether it was from previously issued invoices, or an AI, automated recommendation of the platform itself. However, when testing this hypothesis, it was noticed that the users were in doubt about the reasons why certain recommendations had come from different sources.

Considering that there are scenarios where the issuer of the invoice is not necessarily the manager of the business, adding this level of complexity proved itself problematic.

For this reason, the team identified that only showing the values of the recommendation, without highlighting the agents of those values, and evidencing the user's need to verify the veracity of the recommended data with his or her accountant, had more positive answers than to explain the source of the recommendations.

Having these inputs and field assessments with the prototype, the team set out for the documentation and development of the component in JavaScript, with help from two front-end engineers of the Design Ops team. The lightening icon, with blue highlights, as shown on Fig. 6, was the validated version.

4.5 Definition, Documentation and Development of the Component

For greater consistency and alignment among the designers and front-end engineers of the Conta Azul company, a model was created to document components. This implementation was important so that the documentation was produced in a distributed manner, both by the Design Ops team and the pulverized designers. It considers the existing platform components, the usage contexts, definitions, versioning and handoff.

To propose this model, the team conducted benchmarking with different Design Systems from companies such as Atlassian, IBM, Google, Salesforce, among others. With that in mind, the standard structure for documentation proposed was:

- When to use: Cites the contexts that that component should be applied;
- Anatomy: The morphology of the component is shown, describing each of its parts in the form of a numbered list, objectively;
- Good practices: Details the appropriate practices for applying the component. Citing rules and limitations that must be observed by the designers for correct use of the component;
- Behavior: This topic demonstrates, in a practical way, the behavior of the component, together with all variations with real examples;
- Do's & Don'ts: Demonstrates what would be the correct and incorrect ways to apply the component in different contexts.

It was important, at this time, to maintain the proximity between the front-end engineers and the designer responsible for the Design System, as there were doubts or modifications to the components due to technical issues or legacy back-end connections. This trade-off between design and development made it possible to have better components, both on technical and usability perspectives, fostering scalability.

The front-end engineers opted to develop the component using regular, "Vanilla" JavaScript, which allowed better interoperability with frameworks such as AngularJS and Vue. They prioritized not only the automated recommendations component, but also all of the most-common form inputs, creating layers of abstraction that allowed the implementation of specificities with ease.

At the end of December 2018, the project was presented to the whole R&D team and executive directors of company, highlighting the rapid evolution of documentation and the productivity gained through the Design System mindset. As the next steps, beginning in January 2019, the Design Ops team will also be responsible for implementing new components to production environment, going beyond its original attributions, which were only to document them and provide the engineering frameworks.

The automated recommendation input will be one of the first components to be updated in production, allowing the team to measure in real-case scenarios if it will, effectively, help in the comprehension and reduction of doubts of Fiscal, Financial and any other information generated by automated AI recommendations.

5 Conclusion and Further Research Opportunities

The Design System mindset was evaluated as a valid solution to provide the support and scalability necessary to Conta Azul's growth, even if at first it was interpreted as a creative hold-back, in the sense of following strict rules when generating user interfaces. The design leadership committee of the company had, as a responsibility, to develop the technical skills of the designers in order for them to think systemically, instead of locally. This was an endorsement of evolution in design maturity.

Regarding the process of creating the automated AI recommendations component, it was of great value to have help from Customer Service and Product Analytics. These teams helped the Design Ops professionals to understand the context as a whole, both on the user's perspective and the manners that the AI engines operated. The downside was the long time taken to implement the components structure in production environment. As a response to this, the company invested in the growth of the Design Ops team, that in January 2019 has receive one more front-end engineer.

In the perspective of user experience, the correlation to artificial intelligence in the context of a small business management software opened discussions related to regimentation of the use and property of information, the expectations of users to understand the factors that cause a recommendation, among other reflections – especially in relation to the insecurity of accountants to trust these suggestions, as they are legally responsible for the Fiscal aspects of their clients.

As further research opportunities, the team intends to share a new paper as soon as the results of the implementation in production environment is done, and also detail some other contexts in new papers, such as date selection, population of tables and, utmost, reports generated by the real-time accounting features, in the light of AI opportunities to foster user experience, satisfaction and retention.

Acknowledgment. The authors would like to thank the Conta Azul company for supporting the development of this study, as well as Heloisa Candello and Juliana Ferreira for the opportunity of sharing our learning.

References

1. Malouf, D.: Introducing Design Ops. https://www.designbetter.co/designops-handbook/introducing-designops. Accessed 30 Jan 2019
2. Suarez, M.: Introduction Design Systems. https://www.designbetter.co/design-systems-handbook/introducing-design-systems. Accessed 30 Jan 2019
3. Frost, B.: Atomic Design. http://bradfrost.com/blog/post/atomic-web-design/. Accessed 30 Jan 2019
4. Lee, E.: You can be an AI designer. https://uxdesign.cc/you-can-be-an-ai-designer-46a0fd45f47d. Accessed 30 Jan 2019
5. Arruda, C., Burcharth, A., Rodrigues, D.: Nova metodologia de avaliação da competitividade favorece países comprometidos com a inovação e com o desenvolvimento sustentável. Brasil fica na 72ª posição. https://www.fdc.org.br/conhecimento-site/nucleos-de-pesquisa-site/Materiais/Analise_do_Relatorio_Competitividade_WEF_FDC_2018.pdf. Accessed 30 Jan 2019
6. SEBRAE: Sobrevivência das empresas. https://datasebrae.com.br/sobrevivencia-das-empresas/#causas. Accessed 30 Jan 2019
7. Grossklags, G.: ContaAzul levanta cerca de R$100 milhões em nova rodada de investimento. https://noticias.contaazul.com/contaazul-levanta-cerca-de-r-100-milh%C3%B5es-em-nova-rodada-de-investimento-eee2f424c0e9. Accessed 30 Jan 2019
8. Kniberg, H.: Spotify engineering culture (part 2). https://labs.spotify.com/2014/09/20/spotify-engineering-culture-part-2/. Accessed 30 Jan 2019
9. De Menezes Neto, J.A.: Redesign of the bank reconciliation interface of the ContaAzul software. In: Blashki, K., Xiao, Y. (eds.) IADIS International Conference on Interfaces and Human Computer Interaction 2018, pp. 3-10. IADIS, Madrid (2018)

Usability in the Development of a Project Management Software Reinforced with Machine Learning

Jorge Espinoza(✉), Pamela Loarte, Freddy Paz, and Luis Flores

Pontificia Universidad Catolica del Perú, Lima 32, Peru
{jeespinozam, ploarte, fpaz}@pucp.pe,
luis.flores@pucp.edu.pe

Abstract. Software development stages can represent a challenge due to the increase of final user demands since it must comply with standards and metrics that assure the quality of the final product, especially when related to the interface structure, considering that this could lead to the software failure or success. In the case of software oriented to project management, it is important to present them as a simple and practical tool to avoid generating a lack of interest in the final user. Therefore, in this study, we focus on the usability application process for a project management software reinforced with machine learning by analyzing requirements and integrating Nielsen usability guidelines in the design stage of the traditional methodology applied in the software development. The results show that the elements of the graphical interface were easily endorsed enabling a close up to a user-friendly software in the management of PM4r projects.

Keywords: Project management · PM4r · Software development · Design · Nielsen usability guidelines · Usability

1 Introduction

Nowadays, software is used in different branches of human activity and the demands of users to work with them has increased considerably, being necessary to meet certain standards and attributes that meet the needs of the user [9] [10]. The success or failure of software can be largely determined by the quality of its interfaces, so the latter represents one of the essential parts to be developed. Given this, usability is presented not only as the treatment of the appearance of an interface but also considers the interaction of the software with the user. The usability evaluation is in charge of proving that the software allows the user to perform tasks in a practical and intuitive way [2].

In the current competitive environment, there is a large amount of project management software that serves as tools to manage and keep track of projects. However, this kind of software, sometimes, are not presented as an easy tool to use and can generate a loss of interest in the final user. A project software must have as objective and fulfill the maximum amount of visibility and control of the project with the

A. Marcus and W. Wang (Eds.): HCII 2019, LNCS 11584, pp. 361–378, 2019.
https://doi.org/10.1007/978-3-030-23541-3_26

minimum effort [4]. This is why the application of usability during software development has become an essential requirement and so, the use of techniques or methodologies with maximum explanatory power for usability problems such as the 10 Usability Heuristics for User Interface Design developed by Jakob Nielsen, which serve more as a general rule of thumb than a set of hard rules [8].

Therefore, in this paper, the analysis and design, under traditional methodology, is studied specifically focusing on the requirements and the usability application by reviewing the Nielsen guidelines for the design of PM4R project management software reinforced with machine learning for the prediction of project time estimate. The research shows the results of the application of the aforementioned to achieve quality criteria in order to generate an appropriate interface for the end user, as well as a view to future work.

2 Background

2.1 Concepts

PM4R: It is a combination of good practices and internationally accepted standards to ensure the achievement of specifics objectives (result, product or service) of the project within the established time [11]. The methodology is based on 7 steps, which are [11]:

- Step 1. WBS: Work breakdown structure in which components, subcomponents, products, deliverables, and work packages are created and edited.
- Step 2. Schedule: Time estimation
- Step 3. S Curve: Resources use curve, called "S curve" because the costs are lower, both in the beginning and at the end.
- Step 4. Acquisitions Matrix: The contracting of goods and services, the type and way of acquisition of the same and the estimated dates are detailed.
- Step 5. Risk Matrix: Presents the risks, probability of occurrence evaluation, its impact and the answers assigned to a responsible.
- Step 6. Communication Matrix: Specifies the quantity and quality of information that must be communicated at the appropriate time to stakeholders.
- Step 7. Responsibilities assignment Matrix: connects the organization chart with the WBS and is based on RAM.

Machine Learning: Kovahi and Provost (1998) define Machine Learning as the discipline that allows the construction of algorithms to learn from data as cited in [7], also known as machine learning algorithms. These algorithms according to Bishop (2006) build models to make predictions or make decisions as cited in [7].

Usability: It is the efficiency, effectiveness and satisfaction by which specific users achieve a set of specific tasks in particular environments [5]. These three components cannot be evaluated independently; while the effectiveness is related to the accuracy and completeness, the efficiency is given by the speed by which users can complete their tasks that may cause or not the satisfaction of the user [1].

Nielsen Usability Guidelines: The 10 principles of Nielsen are considered because they are a set of rules that allow the development of user-friendly systems and are defined as heuristics because they are generalizable to evaluate non-specific designs. These are [8]:

- Visibility of system status: The system should keep users informed about what is happening, through an appropriate comment in a reasonable amount of time.
- Match between system and the real world: The system must speak the language of the users, with words, phrases and familiar concepts for this, instead of terms oriented to the system. It will follow the conventions of the real world, making the information appear in a natural and logical order.
- User control and freedom: Users often choose system functions by mistake and there must be a clearly marked "emergency exit" to exit the unwanted state without extensive dialogue. Support to undo and redo.
- Consistency and standards: Users should not have to ask themselves if different words, situations or actions mean the same thing. Follow the conventions of the platform.
- Error prevention: It must have a design that prevents the occurrence of a problem. A confirmation must be submitted to the user before performing an action.
- Recognition rather than recall: Reduce the user's memory load. This should not have to remember the information from one party to another. Instructions for use or easily recoverable must be visible.
- Flexibility and efficiency of use: Interaction accelerators for the expert user. Allow users to adapt frequent actions.
- Aesthetic and minimalist design: Dialogs should not contain information that is irrelevant or rarely necessary.
- Help users recognize, diagnose, and recover from errors: Error messages should be expressed in simple language (without codes), indicate the problem accurately, and constructively suggest a solution.
- Help and documentation: It may be necessary to provide help and documentation.

2.2 Case of Study

Because of the lack of software for PM4R project management, development projects, which include actors such as public institutions, non-governmental organizations, development agencies, among others, represent an unexplored data source [4].

This problem was addressed as an end-of-career project in [3]. This paper focuses on the analysis of requirements and usability through a review of Nielsen's guidelines at the design stage, the development of a Software for the management of PM4R development projects reinforced with machine learning for estimating the duration of projects.

3 Methodology

As mentioned in the case study, a traditional software development methodology is applied through the cascade model shown in Fig. 1 and is considered a revision of the Nielsen usability guidelines in the Design stage.

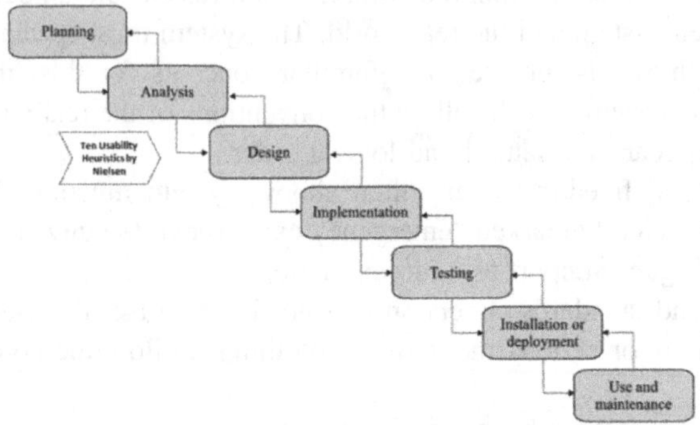

Fig. 1. Software development life cycle - Waterfall model

It is important to mention that in this study we only focus on the first and the second stage of the model previously presented based on [6]:

1. Analysis: Settle what is needed and priorities each requirement.
2. Design: Definition of the general structure, standards and, with the application of the Nielsen guidelines, the base flow software.

4 Results

4.1 Analysis

The objective of this section is to specify the functional (Table 1) and non-functional (Table 2) requirements of PM4R development project management software, as well as their prioritization (Table 3).

Table 1. Catalog of functional requirements.

Nª	Description	Priority
1.	As a manager, I want to create, edit and delete a project	1
2.	As a manager, I want to add members to the project	1
3.	As a manager, I want to filter the projects based on their characteristics	2
4.	As a manager, I want to visualize the total of projects divided by pages	2
5.	As a manager, I want to have visibility into which phase of the PM4R is a project	1

(*continued*)

Table 1. (*continued*)

Nª	Description	Priority
6.	As a manager, I want to create components, subcomponents, products, deliverables and work packages per project	1
7.	As a manager I want my selection (component, subcomponent, product, deliverable and work package) to be persistent when reloading a page	1
8.	As a manager, I want my selection of the phase I am working on to be persistent when reloading a page	1
9.	As a manager, I want to create, edit and delete activities and their dependencies	1
10.	As a manager, I want to log, for the months in which the project is in development, the estimated costs and actual costs and visualize if they follow the pattern of a curve S	1
11.	As a manager I want, for each product or deliverable, to create, edit and delete required acquisitions	1
12.	As a manager, I want to create, edit and delete existing risks for components, subcomponents, products or project deliverables	1
13.	As a manager, I want to create, edit and delete communications	1
14.	As a manager, I want to create responsibilities for the project	1
15.	As a manager, I want the system to offer me an estimation report of the project duration by classification	1
16.	As a manager I want the system to offer me the option to configure the classification parameters	1
17.	As a manager, I want the system to offer me an estimate of the project duration by regression	1
18.	As a manager, I want the system to offer me the option to configure the parameters of the regression	1

Table 2. Catalog of non-functional requirements.

Nª	Description	Priority
1.	The system must generate a report of errors generated during its use	2
2.	The system must be displayed correctly in Chrome browsers	1
3.	The system will maintain the Google Material design standard	1
4.	The system will have a graphic interface in the English language	1
5.	The front-end will be developed using the programming language Typescript and Angular 6 framework	1
6.	The system will use a PostgreSQL database engine	1
7.	The system will use an API Rest server developed in Python, using Django Rest framework	1

Priority: determines the importance of the requirement for software implementation.

Table 3. Priorities of requirements.

Value	Description
1.	High
2.	Medium
3.	Low

4.2 Design

The objective of this section is to define the structure (Table 4) and standards (Tables 5 and 6) of the graphics interfaces to be used during the development of the software, and with the application of the Nielsen usability guidelines, the base flow of the software (Figs. 2, 3, 4, 5, 6, 7, 8, 9, 10, 11, 12, 13, 14, 15, 16), through mockups related to the requirements.

Table 4. General structure

Desktop version	Mobile version
Header Menus Footer	Sidebar

Table 5. Font standards

Element	Font	Size	Style
Title	Roboto	18px	Bold
Subtitle		16px	Regular
Text		14px	Regular
Button		14px	Regular

Table 6. Color standards

Colors	Hex	Sample
Primary	3F51B5	
Secondary	EDEDED	
Link Button	E94362	

Software Base Flow: Below is a description of each view, its relationship with the previously presented requirements, the application of the Nielsen principles and the final design obtained. The complete flow between views is available in: https://marvelapp.com/7e164hb/screen/49848726.

1. Home screen

Description: The list of all projects is presented in Fig. 2, with the option to select and delete. In addition, to present the always visible buttons for the creation of projects and the estimating module. On the other hand, it has the paging component.
Requirements: 1, 3, 4
Usability guidelines:

- Principle 2. The presence of the icons to eliminate, filter, more information, paging, search, etc., are consistent in the platform and the Google Material standard is handled.
- Principle 3. Presence of the text 'Projects' represents a fixed emergency exit.
- Principle 4. There is a consistency of color and structure standards.
- Principle 5. When you delete a project, the alert of Fig. 15 is displayed.
- Principle 6. The filtering of projects by many fields allows access to the required information without needing to remember a lot of information.
- Principle 8. The table covers the maximum possible height and width without considering the header or footer and paging.

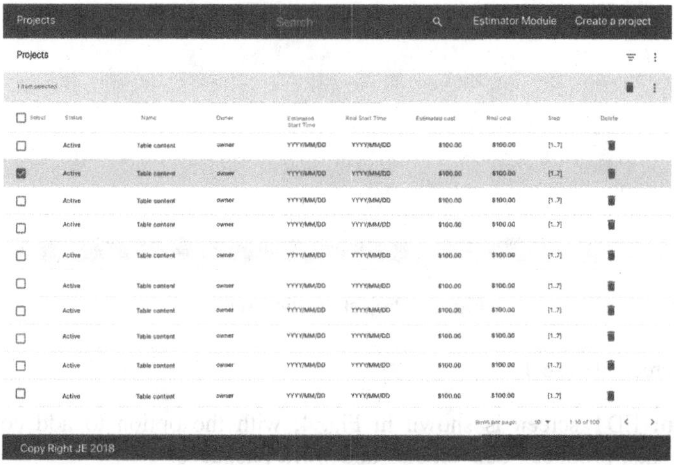

Fig. 2. Home screen

2. Project creation screen

Description: Create or edit projects screen is shown in Fig. 3, in addition to the option to add users from a total list to a selected list.
Requirements: 1,2
Usability guidelines:

- Principle 2. Use of the arrow down icon to display information in the accordion component.
- Principle 3. Presence of the text 'Projects' represents a fixed emergency exit. Additionally, the 'back' button is available if the user does not identify the first option. Ultimately this can use the 'back' icon of the browser itself to return to a previous view.
- Principle 4. There is a consistency of color and structure standards.
- Principle 6. Component of autocomplete when selecting the 'owner' of the project, immediate filtering when selecting the users and also the accordion component of 'Steps' is a permanent instructive.
- Principle 8. The required space to complete the project information is offered, the accordion has a fixed position to accompany the user when it scrolls down in the view.

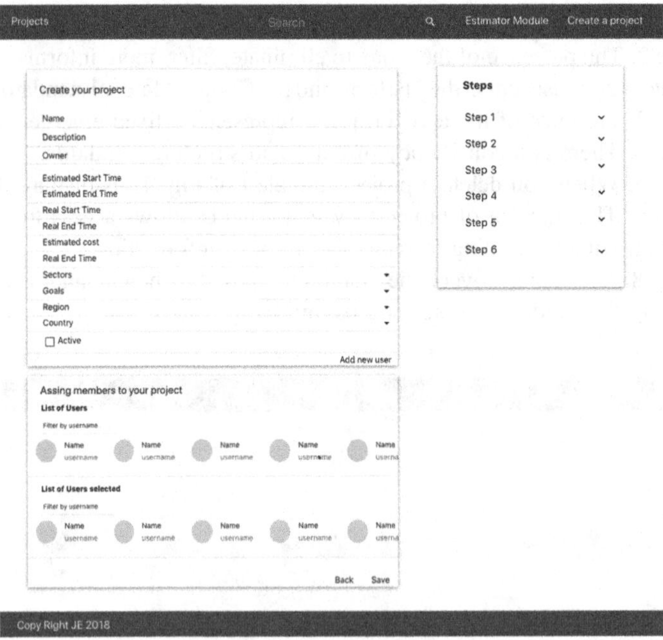

Fig. 3. Project creation screen

3. PM4R screen: Phase 1

Description: EDT screen is shown in Fig. 4, with the option to add components, subcomponents, products, deliverables and work packages.

Requirements: 5,6,7,8
Usability guidelines:

- Principle 1. Presence of the stepper for the user to identify that he is in phase 1.
- Principle 2. The arrow icon to the right and the 'plus' icon to add maintain the Google Material standards that in this case mean continuing to the next phase and adding another element of the EDT respectively.
- Principle 3. Presence of the text 'Projects' represents a fixed emergency exit.
- Principle 4. There is a consistency of color and structure standards.
- Principle 5. When removing an element from the EDT, the alert of Fig. 15 is displayed
- Principle 8. The EDT covers the entire screen and the current box that requires elements has a larger size to represent that it is selected.

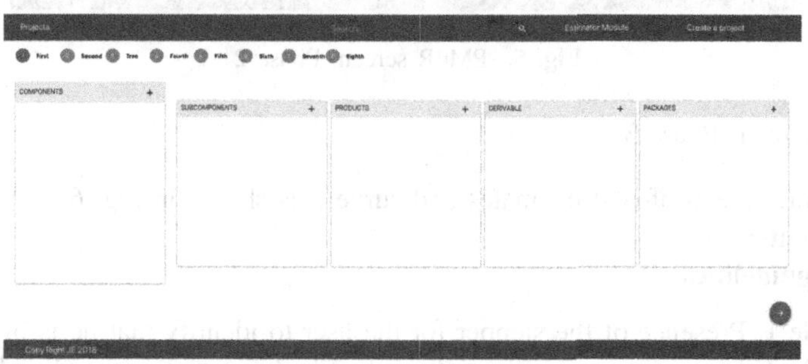

Fig. 4. PM4R screen: Phase 1

4. PM4R screen: Phase 2

Description: Activity creation screen is shown in Fig. 5.
Requirements: 9
Usability guidelines:

- Principle 1. Presence of the stepper for the user to identify that he is in phase 2.
- Principle 2. The arrow icon to the right and to the left maintain the Google Material standards that in this case mean continuing and moving back one phase respectively.
- Principle 3. Presence of the text 'Projects' represents a fixed emergency exit.
- Principle 4. There is a consistency of color and structure standards.
- Principle 5. When you delete activity and when you try to create an activity that is not in the start and end range of the project, the alert in Fig. 15 is displayed.
- Principle 6. The start and end date of the project is presented so that the user can take them as a reference in the creation of tasks.
- Principle 8. The screen is divided into two sections in such a way that the Gantt has greater visibility on the screen and the minimum space required (minimalist) to create new activities.

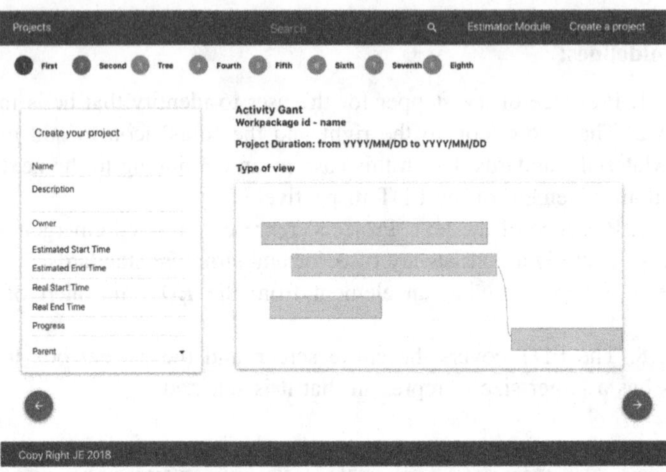

Fig. 5. PM4R screen: Phase 2

5. PM4R screen: Phase 3

Description: Screen of cost estimates and curve S is shown in Fig. 6.
Requirements: 10
Usability guidelines:

- Principle 1. Presence of the stepper for the user to identify that he is in phase 3.
- Principle 2. The arrow icon to the right and to the left maintain the Google Material standards that in this case mean continuing and moving back one phase respectively.
- Principle 3. Presence of the text 'Projects' represents a fixed emergency exit.
- Principle 4. There is a consistency of color and structure standards.
- Principle 8. The screen is divided into two proportional sections in such a way that both the table and the graphic use the minimum space required (minimalist).

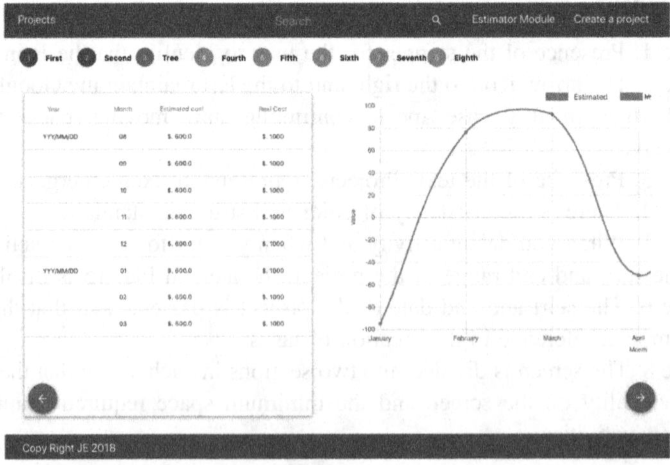

Fig. 6. PM4R screen: Phase 3

6. PM4R screen: Phase 4

Description: Acquisitions screen is shown in Fig. 7.
Requirements: 11
Usability guidelines:

- Principle 1. Presence of the stepper for the user to identify that he is in phase 4.
- Principle 2. The arrow icon to the right and to the left maintain the Google Material standards that in this case mean continuing and moving back one phase respectively.
- Principle 3. Presence of the text 'Projects' represents a fixed emergency exit.
- Principle 4. There is a consistency of color and structure standards.
- Principle 5. When you delete an acquisition, the alert shown in Fig. 15 is displayed
- Principle 7. The tables should not require a button to save the changes because this implies an additional action for the user, consequently, the inputs must automatically save the minimum change, therefore, there will be efficiency of use.

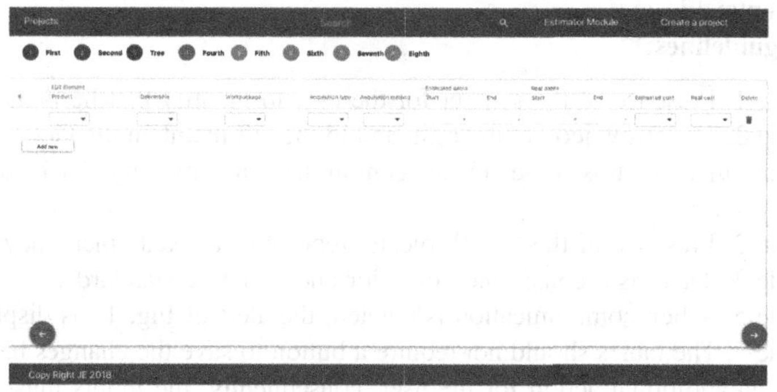

Fig. 7. PM4R screen: Phase 4

7. PM4R screen: Phase 5

Description: Risk screen is shown in Fig. 8.
Requirements: 12
Usability guidelines:

- Principle 1. Presence of the stepper for the user to identify that he is in phase 5.
- Principle 2. The arrow icon to the right and to the left maintain the Google Material standards that in this case mean continuing and moving back one phase respectively.
- Principle 3. Presence of the text 'Projects' represents a fixed emergency exit.
- Principle 4. There is a consistency of color and structure standards.
- Principle 5. When eliminating a risk, the alert of Fig. 15 is displayed
- Principle 7. The tables should not require a button to save the changes because this implies an additional action for the user, consequently, the inputs must automatically save the minimum change, therefore, there will be efficiency of use.

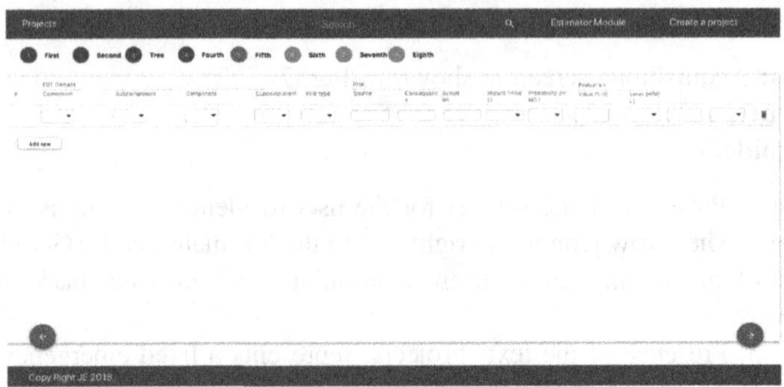

Fig. 8. PM4R screen: Phase 5

8. PM4R screen: Phase 6

Description: Communications screen is shown in Fig. 9.
Requirements: 13
Usability guidelines:

- Principle 1. Presence of the stepper for the user to identify that he is in phase 6.
- Principle 2. The arrow icon to the right and to the left maintain the Google Material standards that in this case mean continuing and moving back one phase respectively.
- Principle 3. Presence of the text 'Projects' represents a fixed emergency exit.
- Principle 4. There is a consistency of color and structure standards.
- Principle 5. When communication is deleted, the alert of Fig. 15 is displayed
- Principle 7. The tables should not require a button to save the changes because this implies an additional action for the user, consequently, the inputs must automatically save the minimum change, therefore, there will be efficiency of use.

Fig. 9. PM4R screen: Phase 6

9. PM4R screen: Phase 7

Description: Responsibilities screen is shown in Fig. 10.
Requirements: 14
Usability guidelines:

- Principle 1. Presence of the stepper for the user to identify that he is in phase 7.
- Principle 2. The arrow icon to the right and to the left maintain the Google Material standards that in this case mean continuing and moving back one phase respectively.
- Principle 3. Presence of the text 'Projects' represents a fixed emergency exit.
- Principle 4. There is a consistency of color and structure standards.
- Principle 5. When deleting a responsibility, the alert of Fig. 15 is displayed
- Principle 7. The tables should not require a button to save the changes because this implies an additional action for the user, consequently, the inputs must automatically save the minimum change, therefore, there will be efficiency of use.

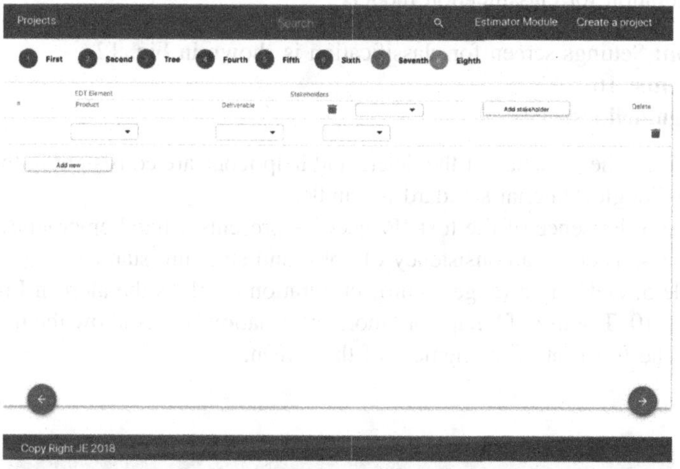

Fig. 10. PM4R screen: Phase 7

10. PM4R screen: Completed

Description: Screen at the end of all phases of the PM4R is shown in Fig. 11.
Requirements: 15
Usability guidelines:

- Principle 1. Presence of the stepper for the user to identify that he is in the final phase.
- Principle 2. The arrow icon to the left maintains the Google Material standards, which in this case means moving back one phase.
- Principle 3. Presence of the text 'Projects' represents a fixed emergency exit.
- Principle 4. There is a consistency of color and structure standards.

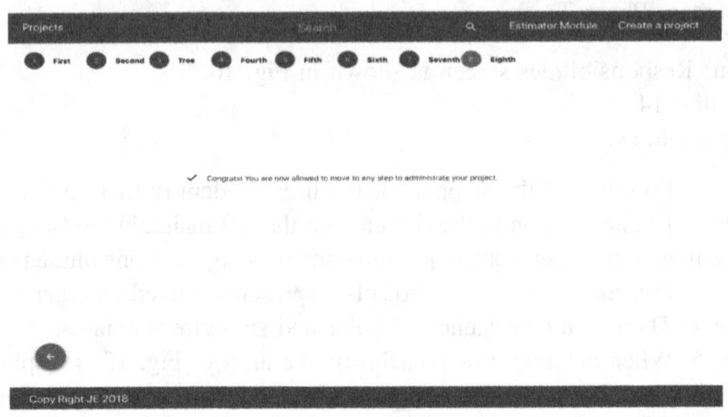

Fig. 11. PM4R screen: Completed

11. Configuration for classification models

Description: Settings screen for classification is shown in Fig. 12.
Requirements: 16
Usability guidelines:

- Principle 2. The presence of the delete and help icons are consistent in the platform and the Google Material standard is handled.
- Principle 3. Presence of the text 'Projects' represents a fixed emergency exit.
- Principle 4. There is a consistency of color and structure standards.
- Principle 5. Deleting a range of project duration displays the alert in Fig. 15
- Principle 10. The use of "help" or "more information" icons allow the user to know what is the function of an element of the screen.

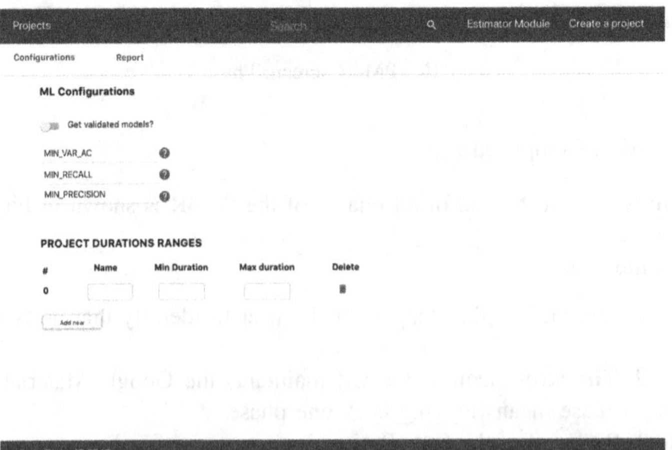

Fig. 12. Configuration for classification models

12. Configuration for regression models

Description: Settings screen for regression is shown in Fig. 13.
Requirements: 18
Usability guidelines:

- Principle 2. The presence of the help icon is consistent in the platform and the Google Material standard is handled.
- Principle 3. Presence of the text 'Projects' represents a fixed emergency exit.
- Principle 4. There is a consistency of color and structure standards.
- Principle 10. The use of "help" or "more information" icons allow the user to know what is the function of an element of the screen.

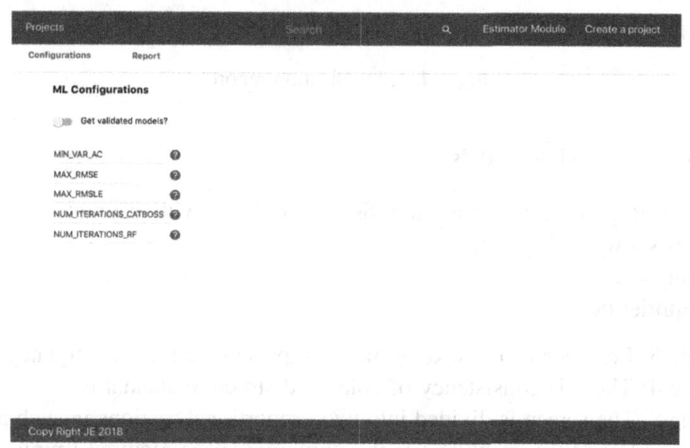

Fig. 13. Configuration for regression models

13. Classification report

Description: Report screen with the list of projects with the duration estimated by classification is shown in Fig. 14.
Requirements: 15
Usability guidelines:

- Principle 3. Presence of the text 'Projects' represents a fixed emergency exit.
- Principle 4. There is a consistency of color and structure standards.
- Principle 8. The screen is divided into two proportional sections in such a way that both the table and the graphics use the minimum space required (minimalist).

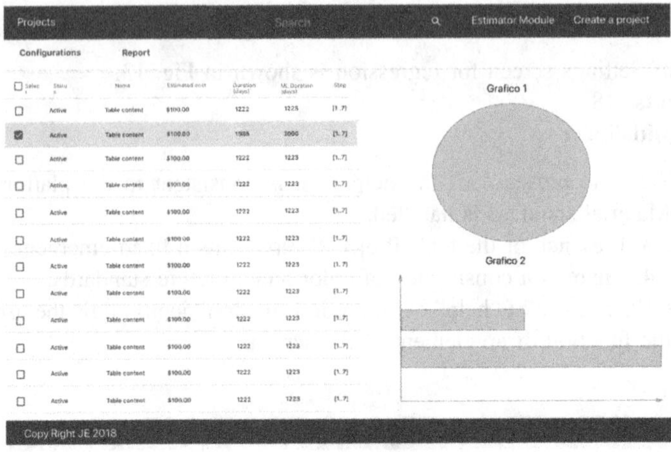

Fig. 14. Classification report

14. Report for regression models

Description: Report screen with the list of projects with estimated duration by regression is shown in Fig. 15.
Requirements: 17
Usability guidelines:

- Principle 3. Presence of the text 'Projects' represents a fixed emergency exit.
- Principle 4. There is consistency of color and structure standards.
- Principle 8. The screen is divided into two proportional sections in such a way that both the table and the graphics use the minimum space required (minimalist).

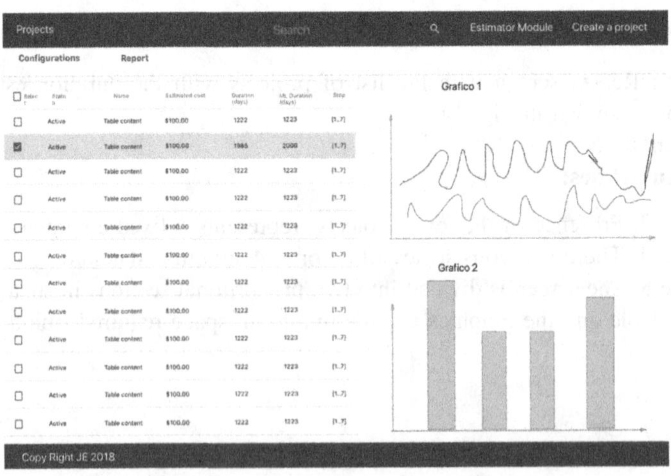

Fig. 15. Report for regression models

15. Dialog of alerts for the platform

Description: Alert dialog when deleting a project is shown in Fig. 16.
Requirements: None
Usability guidelines:

- Principle 4. There is consistency of color and structure standards.
- Principle 5. When you delete a project, the alert is displayed.
- Principle 9. Dialogs should be available to show the reason for an error (diagnosis) through a function that handles exceptions (recognition) and allow the user to take corrective actions.

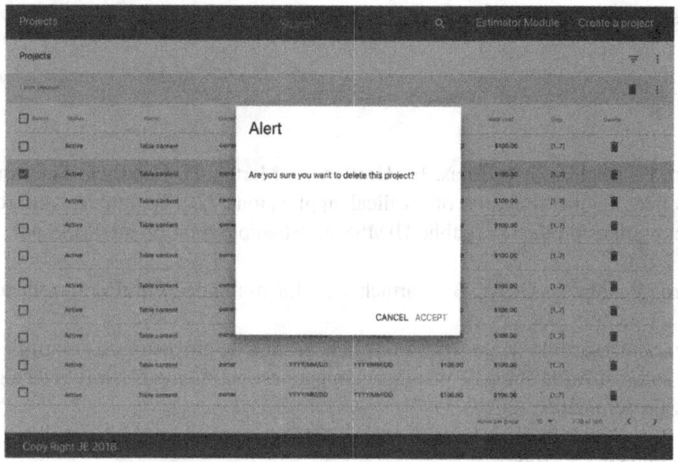

Fig. 16. Dialog of alerts for the platform

5 Conclusions

The first phase 'Analysis' allowed to transform the phases of the PM4R methodology into requirements for its subsequent implementation. In the second phase 'Design', it was possible to obtain the mockups that represent a visualization closer to the final software. Likewise, the design obtained is linked to the requirements established at the beginning to guarantee their consistency, this means that there are no contradictions.

Finally, the first two stages of the traditional methodology with a revision of the Nielsen usability guidelines allowed to establish the elements of the graphical interface easily endorsed in its 10 principles, with which a user-friendly software was obtained in the management of projects.

6 Future Works

Although this paper focuses on the first two stages of Software development and its integration with Nielsen's usability guidelines, it would be appropriate to add, as an additional step, the experts review to the traditional methodology at the end of the development stage, to evaluate possibilities of software improvement.

Additionally, it is possible to deepen in the form in which Machine Learning results are presented, since in this paper we sought to apply generalizable concepts; however, before the imminent impact that this could have, it must have a differentiated analysis.

Finally, and as previously mentioned in the case study, this paper is part of a thesis and as such, future work is related to increasing the range of algorithms, integration of more Machine Learning concepts to strengthen certain project management activities, among others. These can be reviewed in the thesis in question.

References

1. Arellano, P., Bochinski, J., Elias, B., Houser, S., Martin, T., Head, H.: Selecting a mobile app: Evaluating the usability of medical applications (2012). http://s3.amazonaws.com/rdcms-himss/files/production/public/HIMSSguidetoappusabilityv1mHIMSS.pdf. Accessed 28 Dec 2018
2. Chimarro, V., Mazon-Olivo, B., Cartuche, J.: La usabilidad en el desarrollo de software (2015)
3. Espinoza, J.: Desarrollo de un software para la gestión de proyectos de desarrollo PM4R que permita automatizar la etapa de planificación para estimar tiempos a través de algoritmos de aprendizaje automático (2018)
4. Fomin: Pequeños Proyectos Gran impacto (2015)
5. ISO: ISO 9241 – 1 (1992)
6. Letelier, P.: Proceso de Desarrollo de Software. Universidad Politécnica de Valencia, pp. 1–14 (2003). http://ldc.usb.ve/~abianc/materias/ci4712/ProcesoSW-Letelier.pdf. Accessed 01 Jan 2019
7. Monleon-Getino, A.: El impacto del Big-data en la Sociedad de la Información. Significado y utilidad. Historia y Comunicación Social **20**(2), 427–445 (2016). https://doi.org/10.5209/rev_HICS.2015.v20.n2.51392. Accessed 26 Dec 2018
8. Nielsen, J.: 10 Usability Heuristics for User Interface Design (1995)
9. Paz, F.: Método para la evaluación de usabilidad de sitios web transaccionales basado en el proceso de inspección heurística. Doctoral Thesis, Pontificia Universidad Catolica del Peru, Lima, Peru (2017)
10. Rannikko, P.: User-centered design in agile software development. M.Sc. Thesis, University of Tampere, Tampere, Finlandia (2011)
11. Siles, R., Mondelo, E.: Gestión de proyectos de desarrollo. Certificación Project Management Associate (PMA). Gestión De Proyectos De Desarrollo, 4th ed. (2015)

Modeling People-AI Interaction: A Case Discussion with Using an Interaction Design Language

Juliana Jansen Ferreira(✉), Ana Fucs, and Vinícius Segura

IBM Research, Av. Pasteur 146, 22290-240 Rio de Janeiro, Brazil
{jjansen,anafucs,vboas}@br.ibm.com

Abstract. Artificial Intelligent (AI) system development is the current challenge for all areas related to software development practice and research, including Human-Computer Interaction (HCI). Most AI systems' research has been focused on the performance and accuracy of Machine Learning (ML) algorithms. Recently, new research questions concerning people in the loop of AI systems development and behavior have been emerging such as bias, reasoning, and explainability. In this new people and AI systems scenario, humans and computers collaborate, using their unique and powerful capabilities in a kind of symbiosis. In this new setting, AI systems are now real social actors as they are active players in the interaction with people. Defining and understanding the behavior of an AI system and its motivation for suggestions and reasoning are definitely a complex endeavor. HCI and Software Engineering communities, with their designers and developers, use models to represent, discuss and explore different domain scenarios in different stages of the software development process. In this paper, we present and discuss a scenario represented in an interaction modeling representation and how it can enable the representation and discussion of the people-AI symbiosis.

Keywords: Artificial Intelligence · Interaction model · User models · Software models

1 Introduction

The development of Artificial Intelligence (AI) systems is a current challenging scenario for all people involved in the software development process. Most AI systems' research has been focused on the performance and accuracy of Machine Learning (ML) algorithms [1, 15]. Recently, new research questions concerning people in the loop of AI systems development and behavior have been emerging such as bias, reasoning, and explainability [3, 4, 12, 13]. Defining and understanding the behavior of an AI system and its motivation for suggestions and reasoning are definitely a complex endeavor.

In this new people and AI systems scenario, humans and computers collaborate, using their unique and powerful capabilities in a kind of symbiosis. On the one hand, computers bring their capability to deal (organize, relate, present, etc.), in different ways, with large sets of data, which is not possible for the human brain. On the other

A. Marcus and W. Wang (Eds.): HCII 2019, LNCS 11584, pp. 379–388, 2019.
https://doi.org/10.1007/978-3-030-23541-3_27

hand, humans provide their capability to judge, make decisions, to assess situations considering their intuition and knowledge (structured, unstructured, tacit, etc.), and their ability to innovate in a given domain. The human cognitive abilities and computer processing prowess can now be coupled very tightly, and the resulting partnership will present new ways for the human brain to think and computers to process data [9].

AI Systems are now real social actors as they are active players in the interaction with people. They can learn and change their behavior while they interact with users. This new context presents new experiences and challenges not only for users but also for technology developers [6]. As developers cannot foresee all the possible scenarios, the User eXperience (UX) design becomes even more important in the dialogue between people and AI Systems. Considering this new characteristic of having a dynamic behavior, the AI system can have different roles in the interaction with users: (a) it may behave as a traditional system – a black-box with a fixed set of inputs/outputs, or (b) it may behave as an active player in the interaction with humans in the context of their work practices – an "AI-powered user" with its own set of biases and the ability of establishing a cooperative work with end-users, generating new knowledge pieces, and adapting to the user's profile, preferences, and context (goal, environment, emotional status). That last role can have several possibilities still not explored. The possible AI system's different roles should be taken into account throughout development and use times of an AI system.

The communities of Human-Computer Interaction (HCI), with designers, and Software Engineering (SwEng), with developers, use models to represent, discuss and explore different domain scenarios in different stages of the software development process. For this human-computer symbiosis we did not identify any specific models to support the representation of this new symbiotic interaction. In the early stages of development, identify and explore AI systems interaction "what-if" scenarios, with and without users, can enable designers and developers to cover a broader space for problem solving. We believe that it can also enable both communities to identify possible undesirable outcomes and handle them very early in the development process.

In this paper, we present a case scenario with people-AI interaction modeled with an interaction design language and discuss if the notation provides the resources to represent and explore the people-AI interactions possibilities for the development of an AI system. Our discussion scenario is a knowledge-intensive domain where people and the AI system need to interact to execute a set of tasks part of a decision-making process. Our goal is to start an investigation to assess if the existing modeling approaches can be applied or adjusted to represent the people-AI symbiosis scenarios or if we need new modeling approaches for those cases.

2 Models for Understanding and Communication

Models are partial or simplified representations of reality that present a set of objects, with properties (*i.e.*, relations, functions, associated operations, etc.) accurately and consistently defined. Models are abstractions of some object or aspect of the real world. The idea of creating abstractions of the world to understand complex issues is inherent in human behavior. To investigate a complex phenomenon, we may use various models and each of them has a different approach to represent the context. [7] A model should present three main characteristics [8]:

1. **Reduction characteristic** – the model reflects only a relevant selection of properties of modeled object, so that it focuses on certain aspects of interest in the object.
2. **Mapping characteristic** – the model is based on an object in the real world and taken as a reference in relation to some property of this object.
3. **Pragmatic characteristic** – the model must replace the original object, that is, be usable, in some aspect or purpose.

Models, with their diagrammatic representations, are resources that help us solve problems. By modeling, representing the problem domain, we may have different views and consider parts or the whole, simulating different scenarios in search of the solution for a problem [5]. Through interaction with model diagrams, those who seek to solve the problem, have an object that can be manipulated during discussions and experimentation to represent different situations and proposed solutions that continue to foster discussions of possible solutions.

Regardless of the methodology of software development, models are always present as artifacts produced in several stages of the process. Their use is recognized and presented in the most traditional references of the Software Engineering [pp. 126–127, 11] and Human-Computer Interaction [10] and occurs in practically all stages of development: from requirements specification, with domain models and use case model, passing the specification of architecture, to the physical model of the final software database.

Models have different abstraction levels and visions about the software to be developed. The semantics of the model varies according to the need of the development stage. There are various notations defined as standards and used for modeling during software development. The models used for problem contextualization and understanding are powerful communication instruments between all people involved in the process. In Software Engineering [pp. 175–180, 11] and HCI [pp. 380–381, 10], we use models that represent tasks performed by users and how users may interact with the system under development. Those conceptual models help all people involved to express and discuss the scenarios that users and system may work together to achieve their goals.

There are different models and notation for modeling software and interaction aspects. To start our investigation, we chose MoLIC (Modeling Language for Interaction as Conversation) as our modeling language. MoLIC is an interaction design language [2] that perceives the interaction as a conversation between designers (represented by their proxy: the system) and users. It allows the representation of the interaction as a set of conversations that the user can have with the designer's proxy (system), expecting that the designer present the metamessage clearly. The language also serves as an epistemic tool, leading designers to improve their understanding about the problem to be solved and the artifact to be created. The described characteristics, particularly the focus on user-designer (system) interaction, made MoLIC a pertinent modeling language to explore human-AI interaction.

3 People-AI Interaction Modeling Case

We defined a case scenario for building a model to represent and discuss people-AI interactions. We aim to investigate the possible scenarios of people-AI interaction by representing it in the form of a diagram. We decided to use an existing model (MoLIC) to assess if we can use the same notation for this new necessity (represent people-AI interaction), if we can adapt the notation, or if we need to define a new notation to support the people-AI interaction representation and discussion.

3.1 Case Scenario

The people-AI interaction case scenario, inspired by CoRgI [14], is of a personal assistant (pA) used by a PhD student (Mary) while studying a paper. This pA has access to Mary's university annotated papers database, built for students to share their notes about papers. Considering the process of "studying a paper", we can list a few tasks performed to achieve the goal (*e.g.* look for other publications from the paper's authors, check the paper's references, etc.). For our scenario, we will focus on the task "annotate paper". There are some premises that need to be defined to contextualize the pA on helping Mary in achieving her goal of learning by annotating the paper. We can define a set of initial questions that may provide contextual information for the task in hand. This contextualization process is done by Mary every time she reads a paper. Therefore, the pA can help her by speeding the task and also making the relations Mary could not do (*e.g.* identify that the 2nd author of the paper works with the most prestigious researcher on a given field and he has a publication with that prestigious researcher). Other questions from this contextualization process that could be considered are:

- Which is the conference of the paper? Is this conference relevant in a specific theme area? Are there other papers in the same conference related to the same topic? Which are the most referenced papers in this conference?
- Which is the main theme of the paper? Which are the keywords of the paper? This impacts on reference suggestion, similar papers.
- Who are the authors? Are they reference author on some research area? Which are their most recent publications?

3.2 Selected Model Notation – Interaction Model with MoLIC

MoLIC (Modeling Language for Interaction as Conversation) is an interaction design language proposed by Barbosa and Paula [2]. As the theory perceives the interaction as a conversation between the designer's deputy and the user, MoLIC allows the representation of the interaction as a set of conversations that the user can have with the designer's deputy (system), expecting that the designer presents the metamessage clearly. The language also serves as an epistemic tool, leading designers to improve their understanding about the problem to be solved and the artifact to be created. The MoLIC models and their descriptions are presented in Table 1.

Table 1. Elements of the MoLIC language

Visual representation	Description
(filled circle)	**Opening point**
(rounded grey bar)	**Ubiquitous access:** the opportunity for user to change the topic of the conversation, starting from any other scene
Topic / d + u: Dialog	**Conversation scene:** stage of the conversation between user and designer's proxy about a specific subject (topic)
u: Content →	**User utterance:** exchange of turn, in which the user passes the control of the conversation to the designer's proxy (system)
(filled square)	**System processing:** hidden moment for the user, where s/he expects the system is performing the operation that the user requested from the proxy
d: Content →	**Designer utterance:** change of turn, in which the designer's proxy informs the user on the result of a processing, and can return control of the conversation to the user – if the speech destination is a scene – or proceed to other processing
d: Content ·····▸	**Breakdown utterance (designer):** change of turn, the designer tells the user about an unexpected system processing, and can return control of the conversation to the user – if the speech destination is a scene
u: Content ·····▸	**Breakdown utterance (user):** change of turn, the user tells the designer about an unexpected system processing, and can return control of the conversation to the designer's proxy
(circled dot)	**Closing point**

The core element in the MoLIC model is the scene. The scene is composed by (i) the topic of the scene, which is the subject of the conversation caught in the scene, represented by a phrase in the infinitive, which can be read as a talk from the designer and user; and (ii) conversation units that focus on different aspects of the topic of the scene.

4 Modeling People-AI Interaction for "Annotate Paper" Process

The scenario model was built by an experienced modeler and researcher in the modeling notations area. The goal was to use the elements provided by the selected modeling language (MoLIC) to represent and express people-AI interaction for the chosen scenario and report the modeling process.

After the modeler responsible to the model construction (model producer) finished the model, she presented and discussed it with other two people with experience in design and development of systems. They also have experience in developing system with AI features. These two professionals acted as model consumers and helped the model producer to assess and discuss the use of an existing model to represent people-AI interaction. The model built is shown in Fig. 1.

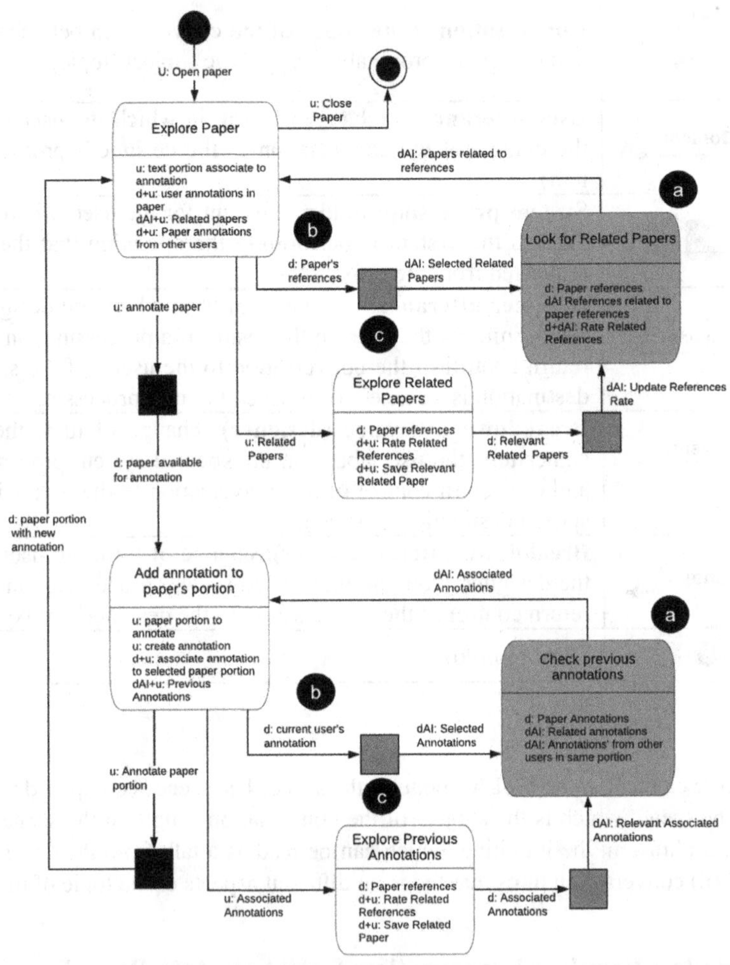

Fig. 1. "Annotate Paper" MoLIC model

To build the model with MoLIC we considered as our premise its characteristic of perceiving the interaction as a conversation between the designer's deputy (system) and the user. In that direction, we needed to represent the dialog between user and AI system. In the modeled scenario, we notice that some actions from the AI system would not be presented to or started by the user. But, considering our need to contemplate scenarios where the AI system can interact with the user, we needed to represent it, so it could be considered in the whole system construction. For that, we added three elements in the MoLIC notation. They are not new elements, but adapted ones to express the AI system participation in the communication. MoLIC already represents the system's proxy, but we felt the need to separate it from the AI portion of the system and also represent the dialog between the "traditional system" and the "AI portion" of the system. For that we created an AI Conversation scene, an AI Designer utterance and an AI System processing (Table 2). The explicit representation of the AI portion of the interaction, with user or system, expresses points of turn changing from one part and another in the dialog. According to MoLIC definition [9], the scene change can only be done through a user utterance, but in the dialog between the system and the AI portion the system, a system utterance (d) flows (Fig. 1b) to an AI system processing (Fig. 1c) so it can flow to an AI Conversation scene where there are dialog only between d (system) and dAI (AI portion of system) (Fig. 1a)

Table 2. AI related elements

Visual representation	Description
Topic d+dAI: Dialog	**AI Conversation scene:** stage of the conversation between main system designer's proxy and AI designer's proxy about a specific subject (topic). **This scene is not visible to the user.**
dAI: Content →	**AI Designer utterance:** change of turn, in which the AI designer's proxy informs the system designer's proxy on the result of a processing.
■	**AI System processing:** hidden moment for the user, where he expects that the system is performing the operation that the user requested from the proxy

In our scenario, the dialog between user and dAI led to a feedback cycle (highlighted in Fig. 2). In the AI Conversation scene, some AI-based processing was performed and then presented to user for feedback. In the feedback scene, the user provided input to be processed by dAI in the same AI Conversation scene in a posterior interaction. For example, when the user opens a paper, 'd' informs 'dAI' about that paper references. In the "Look for Related Papers", AI can locate in public datasets other papers related to the current open paper – its theme, its authors, etc. – that may be relevant for the user. After identifying relevant papers, 'dAI' informs the user about relevant papers and the user may "Explore Related Papers" to provide feedback to 'dAI' about those papers for that user.

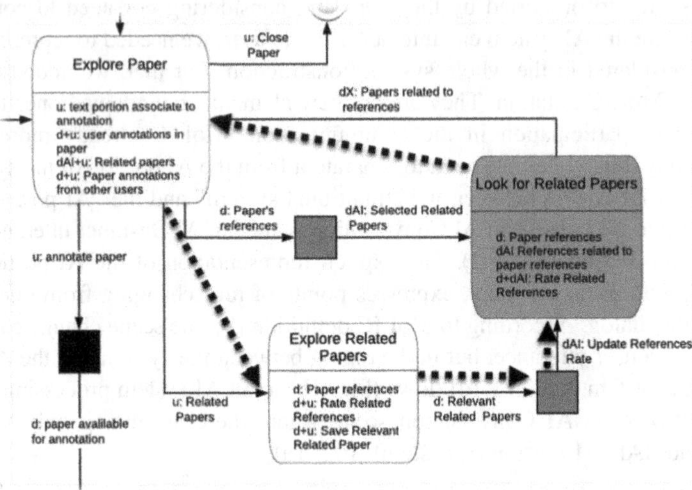

Fig. 2. dAI-User feedback cycle

An analogous feedback cycle was represented from the scene "Add annotation to paper's portion". The user can see other users' annotation while going over the paper (as illustrated in Fig. 3), but an AI scene can be designed to "Check previous annotations" and relate to users' annotations. The AI system can deal with more data and make relations that the user cannot make alone. Therefore, 'dAI' show the user the associated annotations and the user will tell which ones are relevant for him in that context.

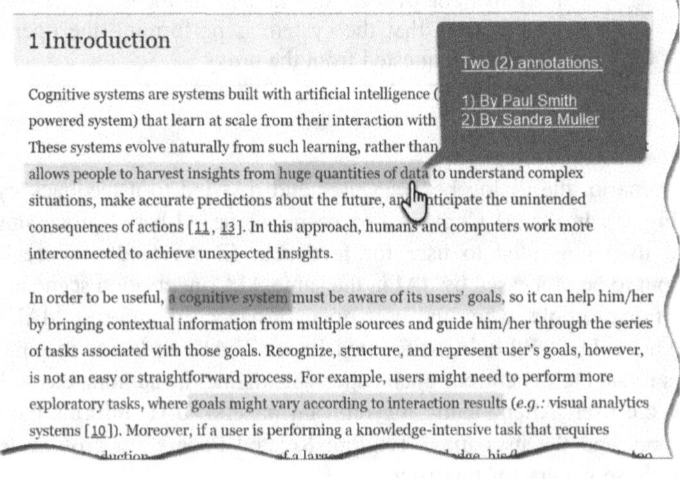

Fig. 3. Annotations from different users in the same paper

5 Final Remarks and Future Work

The people-AI interaction modeling with MoLIC pointed relevant investigation paths about on how a model can enable the representation and discussion of the people-AI symbiosis. As an initial study, we start the investigation about the application or adjustment of existing modeling approaches to comport the people-AI symbiosis scenarios and the possible need for new modeling approaches for those cases.

The model presented in this paper was a first investigation of one case with a modeling notation to represent and discuss the people-AI interaction. It presented interesting findings to be further explored with other scenarios, more discussion, with diverse people involved in the software development process.

Although the MoLIC notation offers an interesting approach to model the interaction as a dialog between user and system' proxy, it is not a well-known language. The experience with this language can be used as input for future experimentation with other languages, for example, explore UML (Unified Modeling Language) diagrams that are broadly used in the Software Engineering community.

References

1. Artificial Intelligence Journal. https://www.journals.elsevier.com/artificial-intelligence
2. Barbosa, S.D.J., de Paula, M.G.: Designing and evaluating interaction as conversation: a modeling language based on semiotic engineering. In: Jorge, J.A., Jardim Nunes, N., Falcão e Cunha, J. (eds.) DSV-IS 2003. LNCS, vol. 2844, pp. 16–33. Springer, Heidelberg (2003). https://doi.org/10.1007/978-3-540-39929-2_2
3. Biran, O., Cotton, C.: Explanation and justification in machine learning: a survey. In: Aha, D.W., et al. (eds.) IJCAI 2017 Workshop on Explainable AI (XAI), Melbourne, Australia, pp. 8–13 (2017)
4. Floridi, L., et al.: AI4People - an ethical framework for a good AI society: opportunities, risks, principles, and recommendations. Minds Mach. **28**(4), 689–707 (2018)
5. Funt, B.V.: Problem-solving with diagrammatic representations. Artif. Intell. **13**(3), 201–230 (1980)
6. Hill, C., et al.: Trials and tribulations of developers of intelligent systems: a field study. In: 2016 IEEE Symposium on Visual Languages and Human-Centric Computing (VL/HCC), pp. 162–170. IEEE (2016)
7. Lieberman, B.A.: The Art of Software Modeling. Auerbach Publications, Boca Raton (2006)
8. Muller, P.-A., et al.: Modeling. Softw. Syst. Model. **11**(3), 347–359 (2012)
9. Nass, C., et al.: Computers are social actors. In: Proceedings of the SIGCHI Conference on Human Factors in Computing Systems Celebrating Interdependence - CHI 1994, pp. 72–78. ACM Press, Boston (1994)
10. Preece, J., et al.: Interaction Design: Beyond Human-Computer Interaction. Wiley, Chichester (2015)
11. Pressman, R.S.: Software Engineering: A Practitioner's Approach. Palgrave Macmillan, Basingstoke (2005)
12. Rossi, F., Mattei, N.: Building Ethically Bounded AI (2018). arXiv preprint: arXiv:1812.03980
13. Samek, W., et al.: Explainable Artificial Intelligence: Understanding, Visualizing and Interpreting Deep Learning Models (2017). arXiv preprint: arXiv:1708.08296

14. Segura, V., Ferreira, J.J., Fucs, A., Moreno, M.F., de Paula, R., Cerqueira, R.: CoRgI: cognitive reasoning interface. In: Kurosu, M. (ed.) HCI 2018, Part II. LNCS, vol. 10902, pp. 398–409. Springer, Cham (2018). https://doi.org/10.1007/978-3-319-91244-8_32
15. The Journal of Artificial Intelligence Research (JAIR). https://www.jair.org/index.php/jair
16. Unified Modeling Language (UML). http://www.uml.org/

Towards Explainable AI Using Similarity: An Analogues Visualization System

Vinícius Segura[1(✉)], Bruna Brandão[2], Ana Fucs[1], and Emilio Vital Brazil[1]

[1] IBM Research, Rio de Janeiro, RJ, Brazil
{vboas,anafucs,evital}@br.ibm.com
[2] University of Calgary, Calgary, AB, Canada

Abstract. AI Systems are becoming ubiquitous and assuming different roles in our lives: they can act as recommendation systems in multiple contexts, they can work as personal assistants, they can tag images, etc. Whilst their contributions are clear, the reasoning behind them are not so transparent and may need explanations. This need for interpretability created new challenges for developers and designers from different communities. Visualizing multidimensional data and exploring the objects' similarities can help with the explainability of an AI system. In this work, we discuss the visual inspection of high-dimensional objects being complementary to machine learning techniques. We present RAVA (Reservoir Analogues Visual Analytics), a system that employs machine learning and visual analytics techniques to empower geoscientists in the task of finding similar reservoirs.

Keywords: Visualization · Similarity · Analogues · AI systems

1 Introduction

In the last four decades, the growing computational power and the adoption of new sensors have increased the data volume and dimensionality in many domains [5]. More recently, AI Systems are becoming ubiquitous and assuming different roles: they can act as recommendation systems in multiple contexts (*e.g.*, suggesting new things to buy, new content to watch), they can work as personal assistants (*e.g.*, answering queries, notifying time to leave for the next appointment), they can tag images (*e.g.*, organizing photos into different albums, detecting people in surveillance footage), etc. Whilst their contributions are clear and present on our daily lives, the reasoning behind them are not so transparent and may need additional explanations and interactions – (such as: why is the system recommending something? based on what dimensions of the object? based on what dimensions of the user? how can the user tweak the recommendation?). As Lipton states in his "Prototypical call to arms" [8]:

> I work with medical data. We work with doctors and they're interested in predicting risk of mortality, recognizing cancer in radiologic scans, and

A. Marcus and W. Wang (Eds.): HCII 2019, LNCS 11584, pp. 389–399, 2019.
https://doi.org/10.1007/978-3-030-23541-3_28

spotting diagnoses based on electronic health record data. We can train a model, and it can even give us the right answer. But we can't just tell the doctor "my neural network says this patient has cancer!". The doctor just won't accept that! They want to know why the neural network says what it says. They want an explanation. They need interpretable models.

This need for interpretability created new challenges for developers and designers from different communities – visual analytics, information visualization, machine learning, data science, among others. Visualizing multidimensional data and exploring the objects' similarities can help with the explainability of an AI system.

On the one hand, dimensionality is a well-known problem in visualization and statistical analyses communities, having a huge impact on data understanding. On the other hand, the identification of similar objects is not yet commonly explored in AI systems, although being useful to understand data and make relevant observations. Similarity is a main concept in psychology, playing a central role in the cognition and transfer-learning theories [9]. Many human activities hinge on similarity to construct new ideas and/or fill missing information by inference from similar objects. For instance, when doctors are studying treatments for a given patient, they try to find the most similar cases to ground their decisions.

In this work, we discuss the visual inspection of high-dimensional objects being complementary to machine learning techniques. We try to shed light on the question of how to visually compare high-dimensional objects and find similar objects.

In the following section, we present some background regarding the concept of explainable AI. In Sect. 3 we describe RAVA (Reservoir Analogues Visual Analytics), a system that employs machine learning and visual analytics techniques to empower geoscientists in the task of finding similar reservoirs. We conclude with Sect. 4 discussing some future steps in this research.

2 Background

Recommendation systems traditionally uses three kind of inputs (Fig. 1):

1. Knowledge about the **objects**: the object's properties and characteristics.
2. Knowledge about the **users**: the users' profiles, preferences, and behaviors.
3. Knowledge about the **relation** between users and objects: usually collected due to an user action, which can be:
   - Explicit: the action itself establishes the relation, generally expressed as some sort of rating (like/dislike, number of stars, etc.)
   - Implicit: the action is interpreted by the system as an indicator (*e.g.*, watched a movie, bought a product, listened to a song).

When giving a recommendation, these system usually displays a brief textual explanation with a previous user action, but not providing actual insights of the

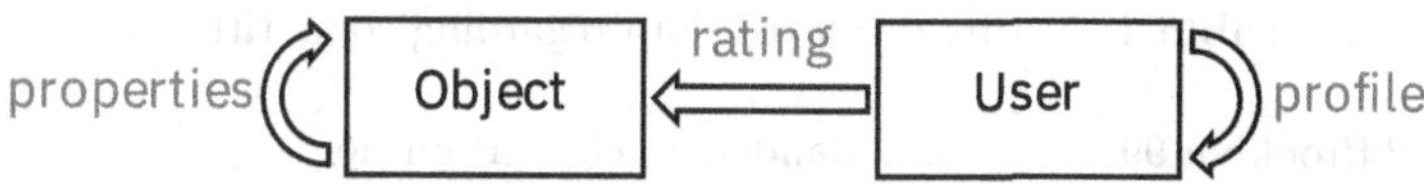

Fig. 1. A simple overview of a recommendation system.

recommendation itself. For example, when Netflix suggests a content, it provides a brief explanation "Because you have watched `something`", but it provides no clue whatsoever regarding why the items were suggested and how they are related to the previously watched content.

Fig. 2. Example of Netflix's recommendation.

Figure 2 shows an example of such recommendation. Users (may) recognize their past behavior ("watched Brooklyn Nine-Nine", a comedy TV show about a police precinct), but going through the list, the recommendations are not clear. It may suggest contents that are not the same type ("Popstar: Never Stop Never Stopping" is a movie) or even different genres ("Punisher" is a violent TV show). Users may try to build an explanation ("Popstar" has the same lead actor, the two first rows are comedies) but the system does not confirm such hypothesis.

Even if users try to drill down the available information, they may be unsuccessful. For example, Table 1 shows the provided information for the target TV show ("Brooklyn Nine-Nine") and two other recommendations, highlighting in bold the similarities. It is possible to notice that the "Black Mirror: Bandersnatch" suggestion does not have any explicit similarity with the "Brooklyn Nine-Nine" regarding the content's properties ("starring", "genres", and "labels") while the "Punisher" has a single one (both are "Crime TV Shows").

The user is left wondering if there are properties that are not being displayed (*e.g.* more of the known dimensions – "starring", "genres", and "labels" – or even other unknown dimensions – number of awards, viewership, etc.) – in which case

Table 1. Netflix displayed data regarding some titles

	Brooklyn 99	BM: Bandersnatch	Punisher
Starring	Andy Samberg Andre Braugher Stephanie Beatriz	Fionn Whitehead Will Poulter Craig Parkinson	Jon Bernthal Ben Barnes Amber Rose Revah
Genres	Crime TV Shows Sitcoms TV Comedies	British Movies British TV Shows TV Dramas	**Crime TV Shows** TV shows based on comics US TV shows
Labels	Goofy	Cerebral Mind-bending Offbeat	Gritty Violent

the system could highlight the similarities – or if it is using other data sources (*e.g.* knowledge about user's profile and previous ratings). Looking at data from different users (Table 2), the user's data seems to play a role, but it still isn't clear.

Table 2. Netflix recommendation order for different users. Lines in bold highlight the same content from Table 1.

Content	U1	U2	U3
Popstar: Never Stop Never Stopping	1	1	1
Archer	2	2	2
That 70's Show	3	3	3
Arrested Development	4	4	4
The Good Place	5	5	5
Friends	6	6	no
That's My Boy	7	7	6
Rick & Morty	no	8	7
Unbreakable Kimmy Schmidt	8	9	no
Lucifer	no	10	8
BoJack Horseman	9	11	9
Black Mirror Bandersnatch	**10**	**12**	**10**
Sherlock	no	13	11
Punisher	**11**	**14**	**12**
The Ranch	12	no	no
The Good Cop	13	15	13
Suits	14	no	14
Big Mouth	15	no	no
Marlon	no	no	15

AI systems build on recommendation systems by taking the users' context and goals into account. Users, therefore, do not only want to "watch something", but "watch something *in this context*" (*e.g.*, while in transit, in different times of the day), and the system should act accordingly (*e.g.*, giving different recommendations, adjusting video quality). As the complexity of the system increases, we must try to increase its explainability. This opens new ways to users provide more valuable input and tweak the recommendations to their likeness, improving the overall performance of AI systems.

Lipton [7] categorizes the techniques for model interpretability into two main categories: *transparency* and *post-hoc explanations* (Fig. 3). Transparency is related to the model's inner workings (as opposed to a "black box"/"opaque" component), looking at the entire model (*simulatability*), individual components (*decomposability*), and the training algorithm (*algorithmic transparency*). Dues to the focus on the model, these techniques are better suited to AI systems developers, since they rely on a knowledge of the model itself. Post-hoc explanations techniques, focusing on the results of the model, can be better understood by final users, since they do not introduce a new object (the AI model) to deal with. They have many approaches, but the most common ones are text explanations, visualizations (of learned representations or models), and explanations by example. Analogues play a crucial role in the last approach, since what drives the explanation hypothesis is the similarity between the presented examples.

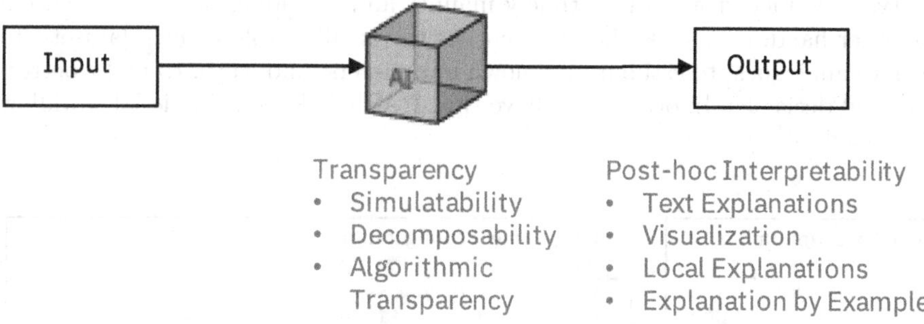

Fig. 3. Techniques to enable or comprise interpretations according to Lipton [7].

Medin *et al.* [9] observed that there is a research body that associate the concept of similarity with context and task: to define two objects as similar it is important to define in what aspects. For instance, going back to the doctor example, patient A can be considered similar to patient B in a diabetes study (they share the same age, physical conditions, and habits) but useless in a uterus disorder study (they are of different genders). AI Systems, therefore, should consider the user's current context and task when selecting the most suitable set of attributes to compare two objects from the multidimensional data.

Once the similarity is numerically established by the AI system, we now have to face new challenges: the similarity presentation (how to visualize that the objects are similar) and validation (if the user's notion of similarity matches the AI system one). They are closely intertwined, since the representation of the similarity may affect how users perceive it and the users' perception should guide the representation. Several studies tackled these problems, analyzing the notion of similarity [6,10], different visualizations [3,4], and the order and arrangement of dimensions [1,12].

3 RAVA: Reservoir Analogues Visual Analytics

Given the importance of similarity in common tasks and its usefulness in AI system explainability, we have developed RAVA – Reservoir Analogues Visual Analytics. RAVA [2,11] is a system built to empower geoscientists in the task of finding similar reservoirs given a target one with incomplete information. Geoscientists have to make business critical decisions – such as the "go/no go" of new acquisitions – with incomplete data, due to errors (*e.g.*: malfunctioning of the measurement tools) or not having available data (*e.g.*: during the bidding phase for new areas to explore). A common strategy is, therefore, make use of available known information from similar reservoirs to better estimate the unknown information, drawing a more complete picture of the target area.

RAVA integrates the knowledge of the geoscientists with AI. On the one hand, it applies machine learning algorithms to go through extensive datasets of reservoir characterization in a timely manner and providing unseen results. On the other hand, it enables the geoscientists to visually explore such datasets, to retrieve analogues, to estimate unknown parameters, and, thus, to make better-informed decisions. In other to achieve this, RAVA follows a simple UI workflow illustrated in Fig. 4.

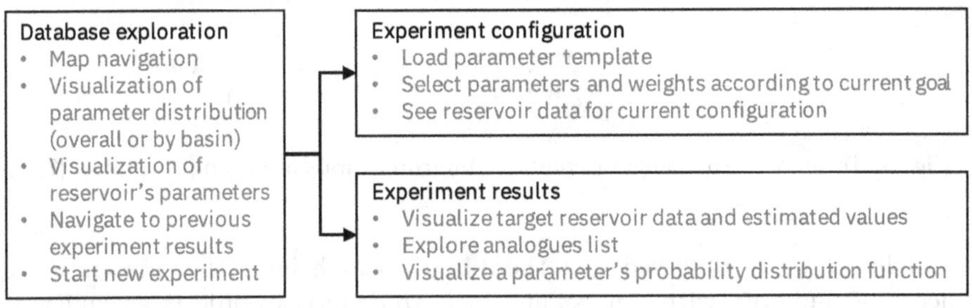

Fig. 4. RAVA main UI workflow.

Users start in the *database exploration* page (illustrated in Fig. 5). It shows the database information on a map, highlighting the geographical distribution of reservoirs (a circle in each reservoir's position) and parameters (given a selected parameter, each circle is colored according to the parameter value or gray if the reservoir does not have information for the parameter). Besides selecting a parameter to visualize on the map (Fig. 5a), the user may also select a basin (using the dropdown on the left, Fig. 5b) or a reservoir (by clicking on a circle in the map).

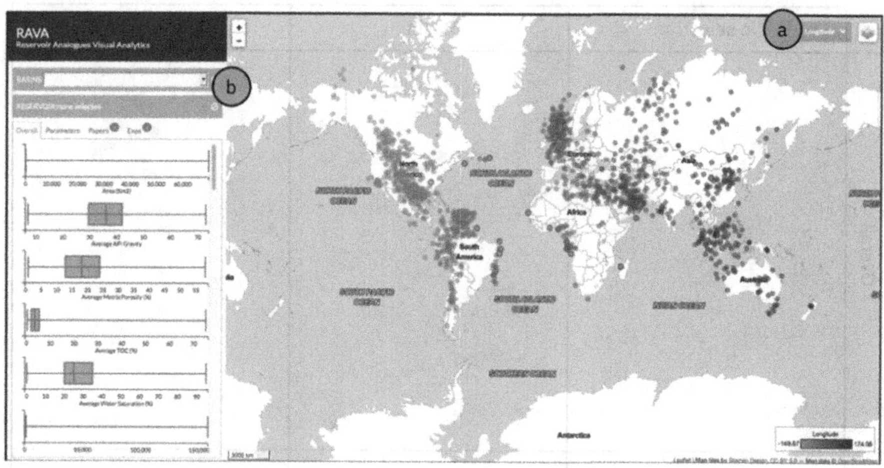

Fig. 5. RAVA database exploration page.

The left panel changes according to the current selection, offering more insights about the parameters' distribution, a list of related papers, and the previous experiments' list (Fig. 6). The "Overall" tab allows the visualization of multiple parameters, whilst the "Parameter" tab focuses on the current selected parameter. If neither a basin nor a reservoir is selected (column "No selection" in Fig. 6), the "Overall" tab offers the distribution of the whole database and the "Parameters" offers the distribution of the current selected parameter grouped by continent. If a basin is selected, the "Overall" tab compares the distribution of the reservoirs in the selected basin to the whole database and the "Parameters" shows more details (such as mean, variance, minimum, and maximum values) regarding the distribution of the current selected parameter in the selected basin. Finally, if a reservoir is selected, the "Overall" tab compares the reservoir known values (the red dot) with the whole database distribution and the "Parameters" tab changes to display the parameter information associated to the reservoir.

With a reservoir selected, users may start a new experiment to find analogues given the selected reservoir as the "target" one. In the *experiment configuration* page (Fig. 7), the user selects the parameters and their weights to be used in the experiment (the list on the left side). There are also different parameter templates that the user may choose as a starting point to the configuration, loading a preset list of parameters and weights. This configuration is closely related to the user's current goal and s/he may experiment with different configurations to see how the AI is affected, exploring different results and scenarios.

A reservoir visualization of the target reservoir occupies the central part of the page, encoding the target reservoir's parameters values. It uses colors to group the parameters into 4 main groups ("Petroleum Systems", "Fluids", "Petrophysics", and "Production"). The visualization can be split into two parts: the radial chart – encoding numeric parameters – and the list visualization – encoding categorical parameters. The radial chart shows each numerical parameter in their own "slice", displaying a mnemonic of their names in the outer circle

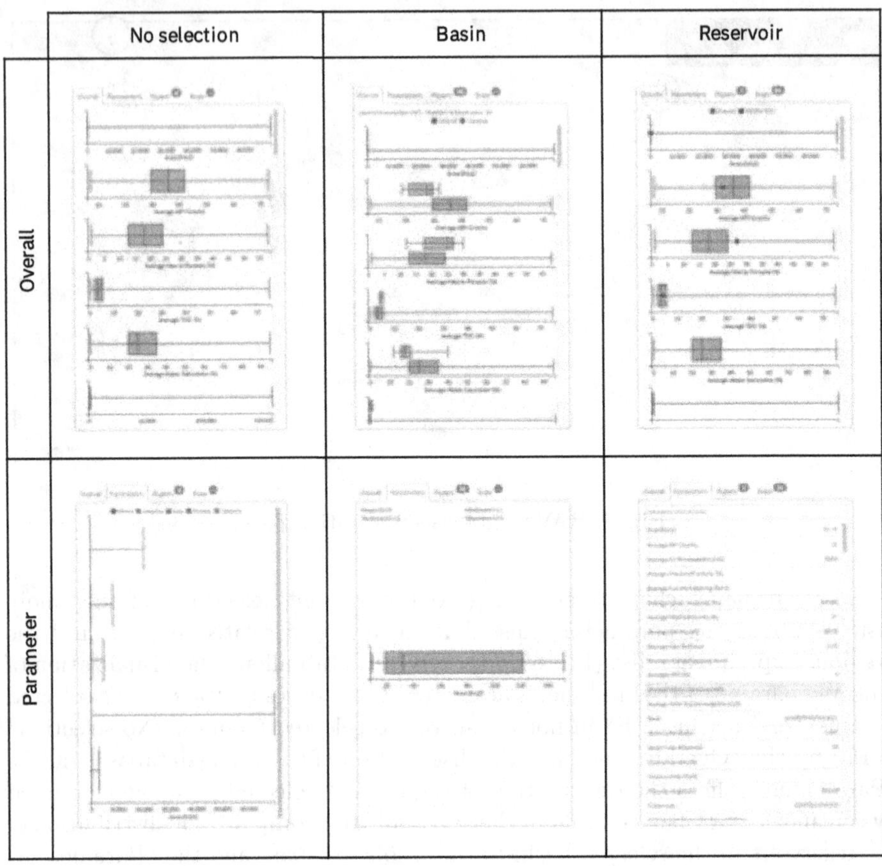

Fig. 6. Detail of RAVA's left panel depending on the current selection.

and the value in the middle of the slice. The list visualization on the right side has a row for each categorical parameter. Each row has a small square indicating if the parameter is known (colored square) or unknown (empty square), the parameter value, and the parameter mnemonic.

After an experiment runs successfully, the user may go to the *experiment results* page (Fig. 8). The left panel shows the experiment configuration parameters, displaying the target reservoir's known values and the estimated values for the missing parameters. At the bottom, a small map shows the target reservoir with a marker and the selected analogues. The right column shows the analogues list, ordered by similarity (the number in gray below each analogue reservoir name). Each analogue is displayed using the same reservoir visualization from the experiment configuration page. Finally the central part can toggle between two views. It starts with the target reservoir visualization (not shown in Fig. 8), showing both the known and estimated values. If the user selects a parameter, the user may toggle the visualization to a probability distribution graph of

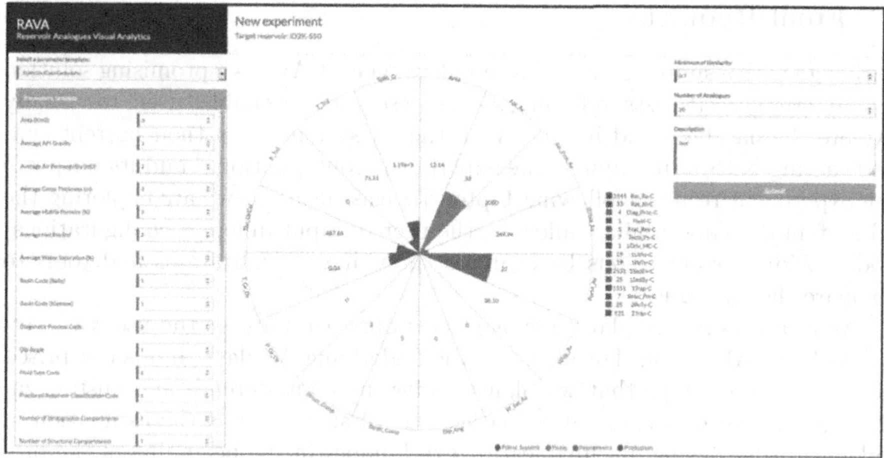

Fig. 7. RAVA experiment configuration page.

the selected parameter amongst the chosen analogues (besides the name of each analogue there is a checkbox to select the analogue).

With these tools, users can analyze the experiment results. The map allows users to evaluate the location of the target reservoir and its analogues. More than representing the distance between them, the location itself is loaded with valuable geographical information. For example, reservoirs in the west coast of Africa is traditionally similar to the ones in the east coast of Brazil due to their geological formation (they were close together at some point in time). Using the same representation for the target reservoir and analogues allow the user to visually evaluate the similarity and validate the calculated value. Finally, by allowing the selection of a subset of analogues to visualize the probability distribution function, we are empowering users to express their notion of similarity and indicate which results are actually relevant.

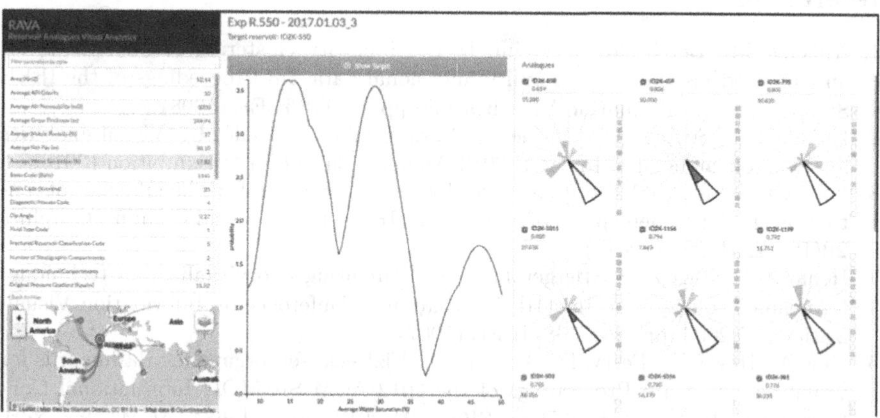

Fig. 8. RAVA experiment results page.

4 Final Remarks

Although with a simple UI workflow and few pages, RAVA is a promising solution to empower geoscientists in finding similar reservoirs. It enables users to visually explore the database and interact with the AI system given their current context, acting both in its input – the experiment configuration – and its output – the experiment results. Following Lipton [7] classification, we are exploring the AI system decomposability (allowing the user to input different configurations) and providing explanations by example (providing visualizations and tools to compare the analogues).

As future work, we plan to explore new opportunities for the user to interact with the AI system. For example, the underlying AI algorithm is comprised of a sequence of steps that we plan to allow user interference and customization, generating new exploration paths. One of such steps is the estimation of unknown values using machine learning techniques in the beginning of the process. We want to enable users to tweak these estimations, thus affecting the final analogues list. Another example is to help users selecting the experiment configuration, providing different parameter templates according to the user's goals, for example.

We also aim to study different visualizations and evaluate the perceived notion of similarity. The current visualization was chosen with a different set of requirements (to be used in a tabletop) and may not be the better suited one. We plan to compare different visualizations and interaction techniques to see which one performs better. Moreover, we will study how users perceive the similarity and find ways to integrate this user feedback into the AI system's suggestions.

Finally, RAVA was developed focused on the reservoir problem, but the underlying tools and techniques are way broader than that. We plan to apply this framework into different contexts and establish an analogues platform to be used in different scenarios.

References

1. Ankerst, M., Berchtold, S., Keim, D.A.: Similarity clustering of dimensions for an enhanced visualization of multidimensional data. In: Proceedings of the IEEE Symposium on Information Visualization, pp. 52–60. IEEE (1998)
2. Brazil, E.V., Segura, V., Cerqueira, R., de Paula, R., Mello, U.: Visual analytics for reservoir analogues. In: ACE 2018 Annual Convention & Exhibition (2018)
3. Fuchs, J., Isenberg, P., Bezerianos, A., Fischer, F., Bertini, E.: The influence of contour on similarity perception of star glyphs. IEEE Trans. Visual Comput. Graphics **20**(12), 2251–2260 (2014)
4. Henley, M., Hagen, M., Bergeron, R.D.: Evaluating two visualization techniques for genome comparison. In: 11th International Conference on Information Visualization, IV 2007, pp. 551–558. IEEE (2007)
5. Key, A., Howe, B., Perry, D., Aragon, C.: VizDeck: self-organizing dashboards for visual analytics. In: Proceedings of the 2012 ACM SIGMOD International Conference on Management of Data, SIGMOD 2012, pp. 681–684. ACM, New York (2012)

6. Latecki, L.J., Lakamper, R.: Shape similarity measure based on correspondence of visual parts. IEEE Trans. Pattern Anal. Mach. Intell. **22**(10), 1185–1190 (2000)
7. Lipton, Z.C.: The mythos of model interpretability. arXiv preprint arXiv:1606.03490 (2016)
8. Lipton, Z.C.: The doctor just won't accept that! (2017)
9. Medin, D.L., Goldstone, R.L., Gentner, D.: Respects for similarity. Psychol. Rev. **100**(2), 254–278 (1993)
10. Pandey, A.V., Krause, J., Felix, C., Boy, J., Bertini, E.: Towards understanding human similarity perception in the analysis of large sets of scatter plots. In: Proceedings of the 2016 CHI Conference on Human Factors in Computing Systems, pp. 3659–3669. ACM (2016)
11. e Silva, R.D.G., et al.: Sensitivity analysis in a machine learning methodology for reservoir analogues. In: Rio Oil & Gas 2018, vol. 1 (2018)
12. Yang, J., Peng, W., Ward, M.O., Rundensteiner, E.A.: Interactive hierarchical dimension ordering, spacing and filtering for exploration of high dimensional datasets. In: IEEE Symposium on Information Visualization, INFOVIS 2003, pp. 105–112. IEEE (2003)

Artificial Intelligence Augments Design Creativity: A Typeface Family Design Experiment

Zhen Zeng[1,2](✉), Xiaohua Sun[1], and Xiang Liao[3]

[1] College of Design and Innovation, Tongji University, Shanghai 200082, China
zz611@126.com, xsun@tongji.edu.cn
[2] Sichuan Fine Arts Institute, Chongqing 401331, China
[3] Center for Neurointelligence, Chongqing University, Chongqing 401331, China

Abstract. This paper attempts to explore a way to augment design creativity with artificial intelligence through a typeface family design experiment. At the beginning, the article briefly reviews the theory of creative generation, and based on the commonality of these theories, the design creative model of "Inspiration - Creation - Reflection - Re-Creation - Re-Reflection" is summarized. Then, the hypothesis of artificial intelligence augment design creativity based on this model was proposed. In order to prove the feasibility of this hypothesis, we have carried out an experiment of typeface design for Chinese characters. The problem to be solved in this experiment is the contradiction between traditional Chinese character design method and large-scale diversification of information needs. We propose to design a Chinese character typeface family instead of designing a typeface which provides diverse character experience based on the concept of "one character with thousands of forms". In order to obtain the typeface family, we adopt Generative Adversarial Networks and select different typical Chinese typefaces as data for model training, finally generate the diverse typefaces. This design method is completely different from the traditional typeface design method and it has produced a new typeface design form. In general, the designer initiated the button of design creativity according to the design problem. The artificial intelligence continuously gives the result of the learning while the designer continuously responds to that. The interaction between designers and the artificial intelligence brings out a new type of Human-machine collaborative relationship, that is: artificial intelligence augments design creativity.

Keywords: Design creativity · Artificial intelligence · Generative Adversarial Networks · Style Transfer · Typeface design

1 Introduction

Five years after the Dartmouth meeting, J. C. R. Licklider defined the relationship between humans and computers. He believes that Men will set the goals, formulate the hypotheses, determine the criteria, and perform the evaluations. Computing machines

A. Marcus and W. Wang (Eds.): HCII 2019, LNCS 11584, pp. 400–411, 2019.
https://doi.org/10.1007/978-3-030-23541-3_29

will do the routinizable work that must be done to prepare the way for insights and decisions in technical and scientific thinking. The symbiotic partnership will perform intellectual operations much more effectively than man alone can perform them [1]. Indeed, the AI pioneer Herbert Simon is also renowned for his work on bounded rationality: We humans must settle for solutions that "satisfice" rather than optimize because our memory and reasoning ability are limited [2]. Donald A Schön believes research should focus on computer environments that enhance the designer's capacity to capture, store, manipulate, manage and reflect on what he sees [3]. The pioneers in the field of artificial intelligence and design have clearly pointed out the inevitable trend of Human-machine collaborative development long time ago, which is the basis and direction of research on the relationship between design and artificial intelligence.

In recent years, with the re-emergence of artificial intelligence, Google and IBM have carried out in-depth research on human-machine collaboration design and artificial intelligence integration. IBM explored how to integrate the key aspects of design with the computing characteristics of intelligent system Watson from the perspective of Design Thinking [4]. Google's AI and UX departments use the concept of "human-oriented machine learning" to integrate AI into UX design [5]. It can be seen that the relationship between artificial intelligence and people in the field of design is not a substitute or being replaced. Artificial neural networks can discover invisible principles about the world and identify them. Design ideas can be considered as the result of the principles from training data and constrained by users.

However, most of the current intelligent design focuses on the use of artificial intelligence to replace the repetitive work in the design, while ignoring the subversive changes of thinking and methodology brought by artificial intelligence. Shan Carter of Google Brain and Michael Nielsen of YC Research believe that artificial intelligence will augment human intelligence at the "software level", which will change the way people think and expand the scope of human creativity [6]. In the trend of intelligent development, creativity will become the core competitiveness of human beings. AI will not only replace the creative ability of designers, but also provide new approaches to augment design cognition. Therefore, we should not worry that the work of designers will be replaced by AI. In this article, we will explore how to use artificial intelligence to augment design creativity, expand new design methods and design forms, and improve the quality of design, not just increase the quantity of designs.

2 Artificial Intelligence Augments Design Creativity

2.1 The Model of Design Creativity

Creativity is not the exclusive ability of designers and artists, but the ability that every field and industry needs. So how does this happen to the idea of creativity? Not only designers and artists are thinking, but also psychologists, philosophers, and educators are exploring their answers from their own perspectives. There is no standard answer to this question, but commonalities can be found in different studies, and these commonalities will become the theoretical basis of this paper.

From a broad perspective, creativity is the solution that people seek when they encounter confusion. The process of creation is the process of continuous interaction between relevant internal experience and external factors. We may recapitulate by saying that the origin of thinking is some perplexity, confusion, or doubt. Thinking is not a case of spontaneous combustion; it does not occur just on "general principles." There is something specific which occasions and evokes it [7]. The process of creativity is more cyclical than linear. How many iterations, how many cycles, and how many holes are needed depends on the depth and breadth of the problem being addressed. Sometimes the gestation period lasts for several years, sometimes only a few hours [8].

From a narrow perspective, creativity is the solution and expression of specific problems in the field of design. The process of creation is the mutual stimulation and reflection between the designer's creative methods and specific problems and existing creative experiences. Designing is a reflective conversation with materials whose basic structure - seeing-moving-seeing- is an interaction of designing and discovering [9]. A model of creative design as the co-evolution of problem/solution spaces …… We suggest that creativity in the design process can validly be compared to such 'bursts of development' [10].

Whether in a broad or in a narrow sense, creativity is the result of continuous interaction between creation and reflection. An external design problem will motivate the designer to create an intrinsic idea; a creation will be presented as a design by the designer's production; Designers will link and react the design works representing the internal creativity with the external design problems and past design experience. Similarly, reflection will stimulate new design ideas and start a new round of creation and reflection. The definition of this creative process is the basis of the research of this thesis, as well as the framework of the experimental development (Fig. 1).

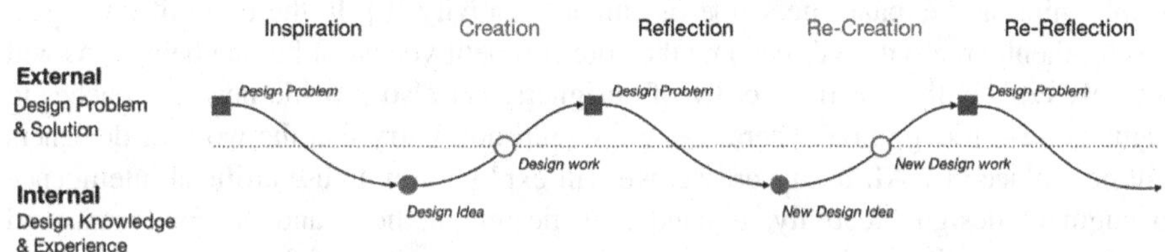

Fig. 1. The model of design creativity

2.2 Using Computational Thinking to Promote Creative Thinking

Creative thinking and computational thinking are the ways of thinking that designers and artificial intelligence use in solving problems. Creative thinking runs divergent thinking and inductive thinking, this is the charm and difficulty of creativity; Computational thinking runs abstract thinking and recursive thinking, this is the most inadequate ability of human beings. Artists and designers have unique ways to inspire creativity. For example, surrealist artists use psychoanalytic techniques to inspire their creativity [11]. In fact, we don't really know where the inspiration comes from, but we try to find the moments when things are related and the relationships that are never connected. On the one hand, artificial intelligence has the ability to learn and discover the underlying laws behind massive data, which provides a playground for establishing the correlation between design elements, providing a hotbed for inspiring designers' creativity; on the other hand, it has the ability to execute the design results quickly, which helps the designers to reflect on the creative results in time (Fig. 2).

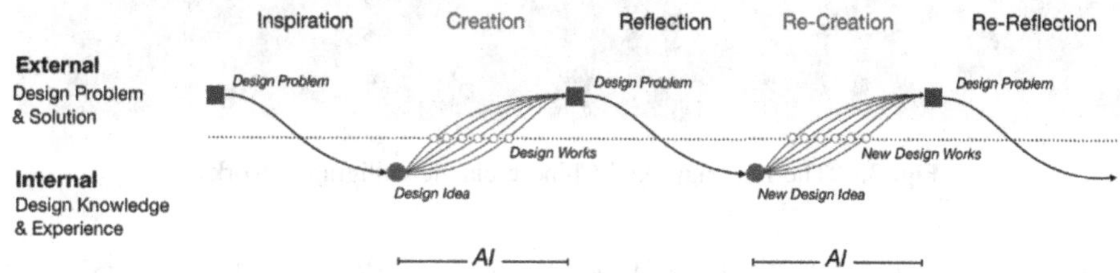

Fig. 2. Artificial intelligence augments design creativity

This paper attempts to incorporate the computational thinking of artificial intelligence into the creative thinking of designers. Based on the creative model of creation and reflection, we explore a method of using artificial intelligence to continuously and effectively promote the interaction process between creation and reflection, and to summarize the law of artificial intelligence to enhance design creativity through a design experiment with Chinese character typeface design as the object.

3 Artificial Intelligence Augments Chinese Character Typeface Design

3.1 Design Background and Design Problem

Chinese characters carry the mission of knowledge record and cultural communication. Over a long period of time, the design and production of Chinese characters has undergone a transition from pluralism to unity. In the era of Chinese character design by writing and engraving, each type of typeface exists in a group. This means that in a typeface, although the same word presents different shapes each time, they have similar shelf structure and writing style. This has become an aesthetic feature of Chinese characters that are ever-changing but not separated (Fig. 3). In the industrial age, for the demand of large-scale consumption, the same character that is designed for one time can be transmitted in any media indefinitely. The evolution process of the one-sided character reduces the cost of information dissemination, and speeds up the information dissemination, but at the same time erases the beauty of the Chinese character - one character with thousands of forms (Fig. 4). In the era of big data, more and more products and services can provide thousands of personalized experiences because they can accurately collect user data and accurately analyze user needs. Under such a trend, how should Chinese character design meet the reading and aesthetic needs of hundreds of millions of people?

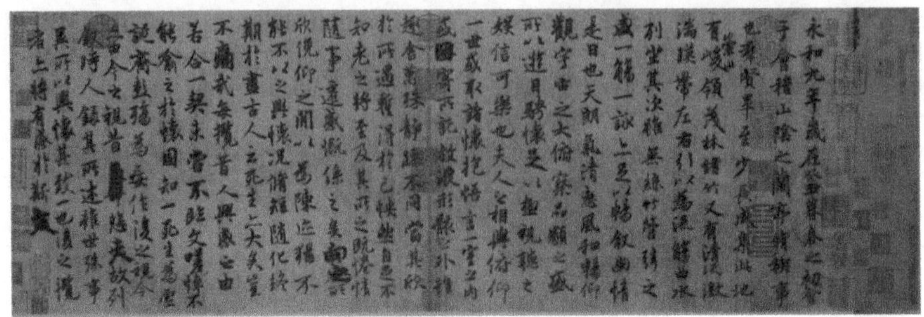

Fig. 3. "The Lantingji Xu" Chinese classic calligraphy works

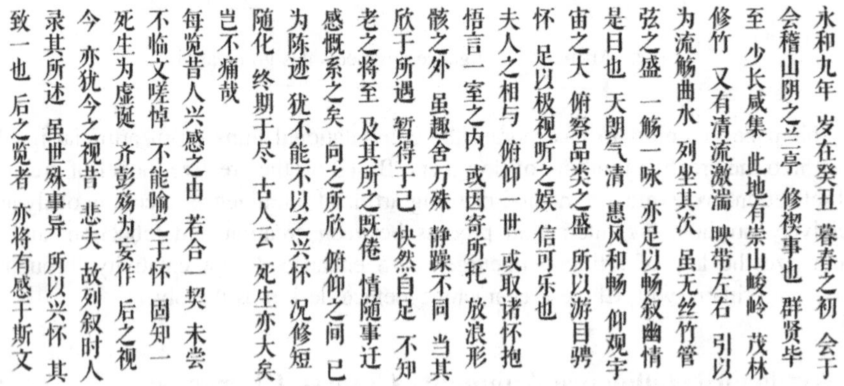

Fig. 4. "The Lantingji Xu" Printing typeface (Typesetting with FZQKBYSJW by author)

Looking back on history, perhaps the feature of "one character with thousands of forms" just coincided with the cultural experience of thousands of people in the era of big data, and provides users with dynamic and diversified text experience with relatively uniform typeface family design. However, the traditional design method of describing Chinese characters by stroke is obviously impossible to adapt to the production and dissemination of this huge amount of information. The contradiction between traditional Chinese character design method and large-scale diversified information requirements is a problem that needs to be solved.

3.2 Design Purpose

Driven by this problem, we have started an artificial intelligence augment design experiment for Chinese character design. The powerful learning and computing power of artificial intelligence will augment the designer's typeface creativity and design ability. The purpose of the research is two aspects. One purpose of this study is to design a Chinese character typeface family, rather than a typeface, that is each word corresponds to several similar typeface forms, so as to break through the stable single form that typeface design has been pursuing for a long time and present the state of "one word with thousands of forms". Another purpose is to explore how the collaborative work of designers and artificial intelligence is carried out in the design process, and try to summarize the key links and operation rules of artificial intelligence to augment design creativity.

3.3 Training Neural Network for Chinese Character Typeface Family Design

Neural Network. For the purpose of designing Chinese character typeface family, we need a neural network that can generate many similar typefaces. This neural network can learn the characteristics of different typefaces, and can establish the connection between these features. Finally, these features are integrated in different dimensions to form different but similar new typefaces, which together constitute a typeface family. This design requirement is similar to the computational principle of Image Style Transfer [12]. The purpose of image style migration is to generate A+ images according to the style, color, texture and stroke style of B image. Therefore, the design purpose of image style migration is to get A+, which is different from our design purpose. However, in the process of migrating A to A+ image, there will be many continuous changing intermediate states, which present different but similar images. The calculation process is similar as we want to generate different but similar typefaces which is our purpose. Therefore, we use the Convolutional Neural Networks (CNN) which are commonly used in Image Style Transfer as the basic neural networks in this experiment.

Training Data Selection. In the design of Chinese typefaces, the most classic design idea is to combine the structure and writing-style characteristics of the two types of typefaces. For example, Song (Typeface) and Hei (Typeface) are integrated into the Song-Hei (Typeface), Xing (Typeface) and Kai (Typeface) are integrated into Xing-Kai (Typeface). When faced with two typefaces, designers can find a subtle integration relationship between them to design new typefaces. However, when faced with more than two typefaces, people's cognitive ability becomes inadequate, which is also the reason why there is little integration of more than two typeface styles in traditional typeface design. In this experiment, in order to obtain a more diverse and dynamic typeface style, we decide to select four typefaces as training data. These four typefaces are the most representative of the four types of Chinese typefaces, one of which is the core typeface – Song, and the other three typefaces are similar or opposite to the structure and writing-style of the Song.

Training Model. The neural network used in our study is based on a 'zi2zi' modell [13], which combined from 3 GANs [14–16] for Chinese font-to-font 'translation', i.e., mapping from one type of Chinese character to another. The zi2zi model is working in an end-to-end process, extracting abstract structural information from thousands of characters and generating desired outputs.

The neural network model was implemented based on TensorFlow. Both model training and inference were performed on GTX 1080 Ti graphical processing unit (GPU), Nvidia. We trained model with 4 different fonts, 5000 examples for each font.

The batch size was simply set to 16. The training started from a learning rate of 0.001 and then reduced it by half after every 10 epochs. The other model parameters were kept as defaults. It took roughly 10 h on a single GPU to train the model over 30 epochs (Fig. 6).

4 Designers Collaborate with Artificial Intelligence

4.1 The Design Process

Looking on the entire design experiment, the process of intelligent typeface design by designers and neural networks is not a one-way process of computer-aided design, but is a collaborative design process that stimulates and reacts to each other.

The Inspiration Phase. The designer put forward the design issue based on the thinking of the traditional typeface design method, and set the assumption to solve this problem.

The Creation Phase. The designer combined the perceptual typeface aesthetics and rational calculation thinking by using GANs as the experimental neural networks, and selected four typefaces: FZQKBYSJW, HYYakuHei-45W, HYZiYanHuanLeSongW and FZZJ-XJXCJW, as the first-round training data (Fig. 5). The neural networks extract the abstract structure information of the Chinese typefaces based on the training data and generate the typeface family. There are 117 different typefaces in this group.

Fig. 5. The typefaces for the first-round training

The Reflection Phase. The designer selected the typefaces of the red circle area in 117 typefaces, compared it with the training data, and also associated it with the design purpose of "One character with thousands of forms". The designer found that the beginning of vertical strokes of HYYakuHei-45W was not obvious, which led to the low accuracy of all of the character's vertical strokes, and the structural influence of HYZiYanHuanLeSongW is too strong, which leads to the structural form of some generated fonts being too similar (Fig. 6). These problems did not meet the basic readability requirements of typeface design and the purpose of "One character with thousands of forms".

The Re-Creation Phase. According to the results of reflection, the designer decided to replace the training typeface data which did not perform well in the training, replace

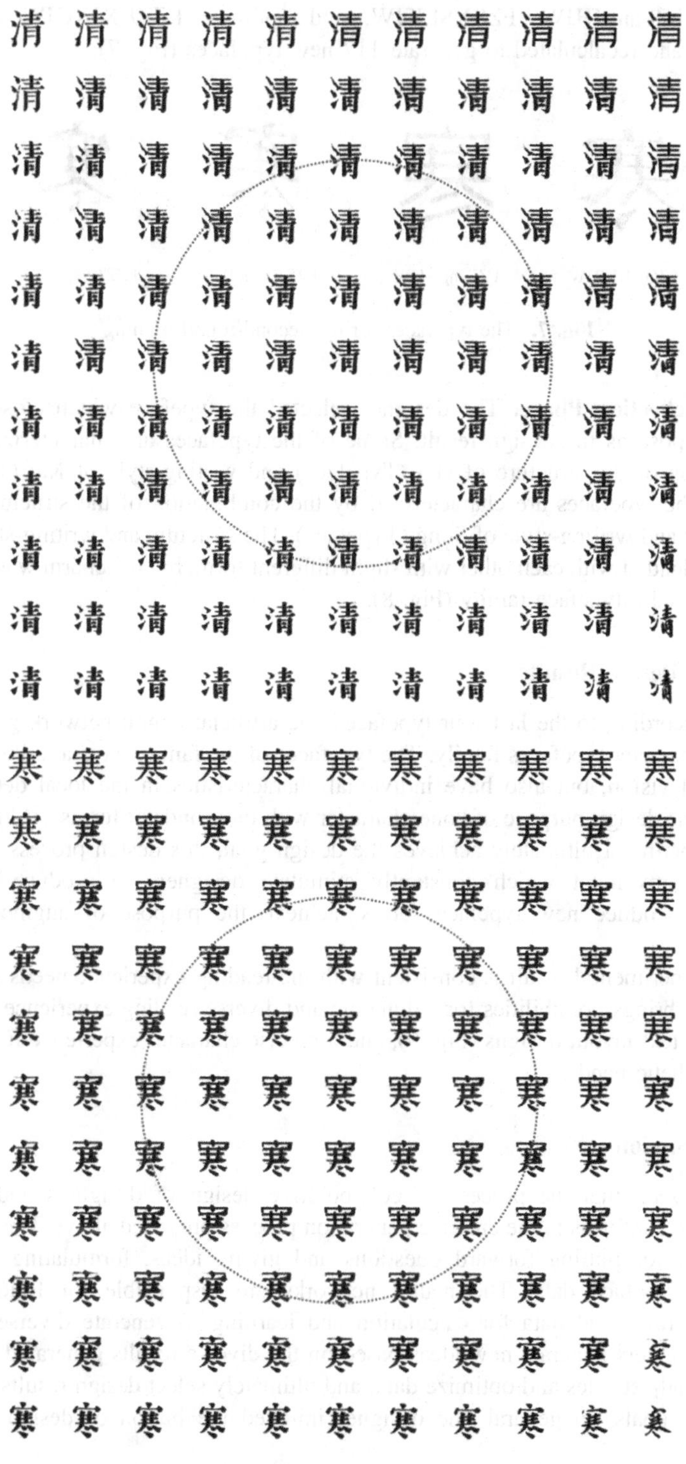

Fig. 6. The results of the first-round training (Color figure online)

them by FZFangJHJW, FZSXSLKJW, and optimize FZZJ-XJXCJW to FZZJ-SHXSJW, and recalculated to generate 117 new typefaces (Fig. 7).

Fig. 7. The typefaces for the second-round training

The Re-Reflection Phase. The designer selected the typeface which closest to the design purpose as the design result. Some of the typefaces are characterized by the combination of the structure of Hei (Typeface) and writing-style of Kai (Typeface). Some of the typefaces are characterized by the combination of the structure of Kai (Typeface) and writing-style of Song (Typeface). The structure and writing-style of the typeface blended with each other with slight different form, but the charm was the same which formed a typeface family (Fig. 8).

4.2 The Design Results

Finally, according to the last four typefaces, the artificial neural network generated a Chinese character typefaces family. The typefaces of the family have a unified style in the overall vision, but also have individual characteristics in the local details, thus realizing the design purpose of "one character with thousands of forms". Although the design experiment ultimately achieves the design goal, this design process can make further improvement which constantly stimulate designers to produce more re-reflection, produce new typeface forms, achieve the purpose of augment design creativity.

The experimental result is consistent with the reading experience needs of the big data era. It brings possibilities for a dynamic and diverse reading experience to a large number of text layout designs (Fig. 9), and a precise character experience for different users' aesthetic needs.

4.3 Discussion

It can be seen that the process of collaborative design of designers and artificial intelligence conforms to the creative generation process proposed above. Designers are responsible for putting forward questions and giving ideas, formulating rules and providing typeface data. The neural networks are responsible for following the designer's rules and data for calculation and learning to generate diverse typeface forms. Designers generate new ideas based on the diverse results generated by neural networks, adjust rules and optimize data, and ultimately select design results that meet the design goals. In general, the designer initiated the button of design creativity

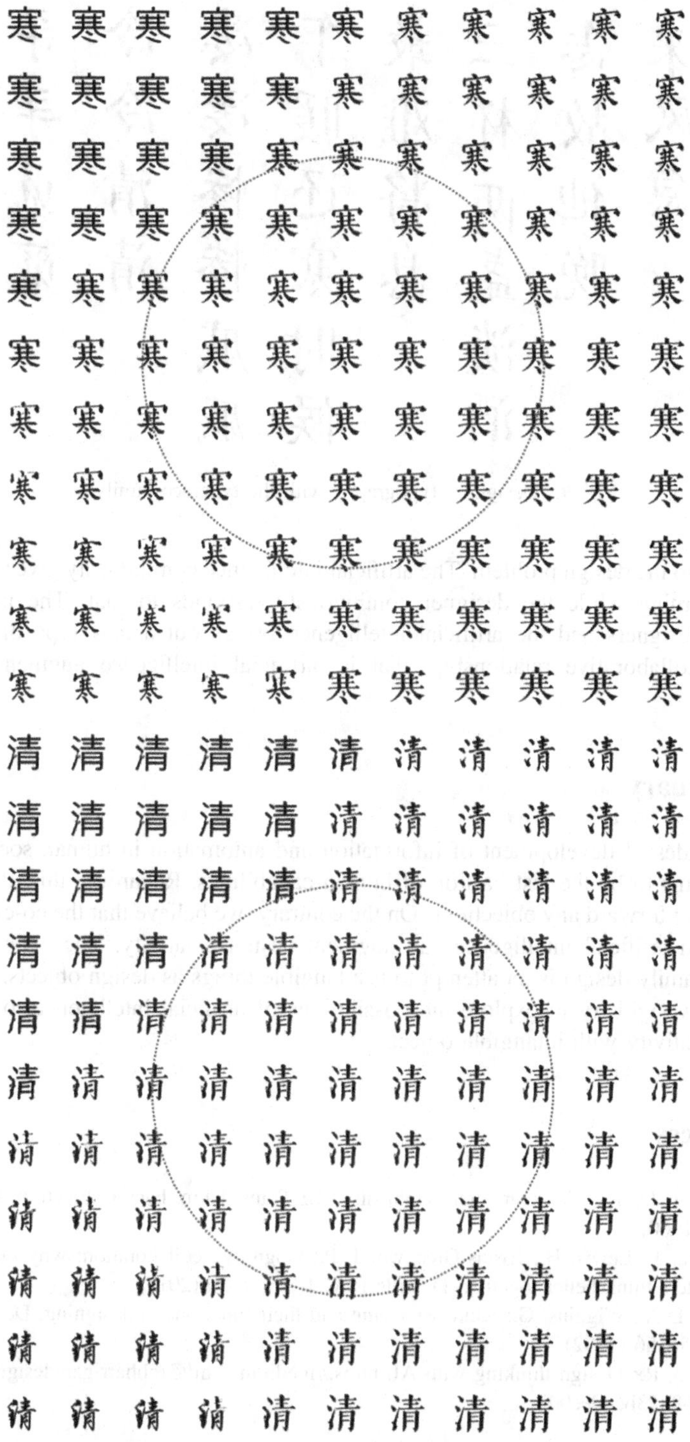

Fig. 8. The results of the second-round training

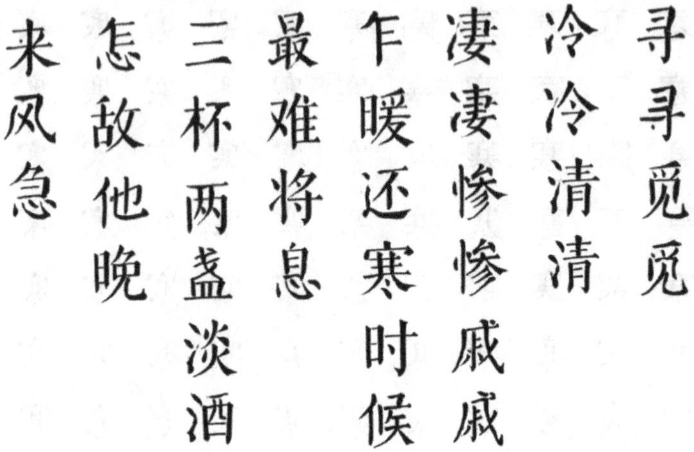

寻寻觅觅
冷冷清清
凄凄惨惨戚戚
乍暖还寒时候
最难将息
三杯两盏淡酒
怎敌他晚
来风急

Fig. 9. Designing typography with the typeface family.

according to the design problem. The artificial intelligence continuously gives the result of the learning while the designer continuously responds to that. The interaction between designers and the artificial intelligence brings out a new type of Human-machine collaborative relationship, that is: artificial intelligence augments design creativity.

5 Summary

After decades of development of information and automation in human society, creativity seems to be the last bastion of human capabilities. Regarding this, this article does not put forward any objections. On the contrary, we believe that the co-creation of human and artificial intelligence can augment design creativity. The experiment of typeface family design is an attempt to use tangible things as design objects. In future research, we will try to explore the possibilities of artificial intelligence to augment design creativity with intangible objects.

References

1. Licklider, J.C.R.: Man-computer symbiosis. IRE Trans. Hum. Factors Electron. **HFE-1**(1), 4–11 (1960)
2. Guszcza, J., Lewis, H., Evans-Greenwood, P.: Cognitive collaboration: why humans and computers think better together. Deloitte Rev. **1**(20), 7–30 (2017)
3. Schon, D.A., Wiggins, G.: Kinds of seeing and their functions in designing. Des. Stud. **13** (2), 135–156 (1992)
4. Harrigan, R.: Design thinking with AI. https://medium.com/@robharrigan/design-thinking-with-ai-8813bcd9ee00

5. Lovejoy, J., Holbrook, J.: Human-centered machine learning. https://medium.com/google-design/human-centered-machine-learning-a770d10562cd
6. Carter, S., Nielsen, M.: Using artificial intelligence to augment human intelligence. Distill (2017). https://doi.org/10.23915/distill.00009
7. Dewey, J.: How We Think. Dover Publications, Mineola (1997)
8. Csikszentmihalyi, M.: Creativity: Flow and the Psychology of Discovery and Invention. Harper Collins, New York (1996)
9. Schön, D.A.: The Reflective Practitioner: How Professionals Think in Action. Basic Books, New York (1984)
10. Dorst, K., Cross, N.: Creativity in the design process: co-evolution of problem–solution. Des. Stud. **22**, 425–437 (2001)
11. Schmitt, P.: Augmented imagination: machine learning art as automatism. http://adht.parsons.edu/designstudies/plot/augmented-imagination-machine-learning-art-as-automatism/
12. Gatys, L.A., Ecker, A.S., Bethge, M.: Image style transfer using convolutional neural networks. In: The IEEE Conference on Computer Vision and Pattern Recognition (CVPR), pp. 2414–2423 (2016)
13. Tian, Y.: Learning Chinese Character style with conditional GAN. https://github.com/kaonashi-tyc/zi2zi
14. Isola, P., Zhu, J.-Y., Zhou, T., Efros, A.A.: Image-to-image translation with conditional adversarial networks (2016). Preprint at http://arxiv.org/abs/1611.07004
15. Odena, A., Olah, C., Shlens, J.: Conditional image synthesis with auxiliary classifier GANs (2016). Preprint at https://arxiv.org/abs/1610.09585
16. Taigman, Y., Polyak, A., Wolf, L.: Unsupervised cross-domain image generation (2016). Preprint at https://arxiv.org/abs/1611.02200

Dialogue, Narrative, Storytelling

Multimedia Exhibition Design: Exploring Intersections Among Storytelling, Usability and User Experience on an Interactive Large Wall Screen

Danielle Behrens(✉), Erika Espinoza(✉), Darby Siscoe(✉), and Jennifer Palilonis(✉)

Ball State University, Muncie, IN 47306, USA
{dnbehrens, efespinoza, drsiscoe, jageorge2}@bsu.edu

Abstract. A research team engaged in a user experience and usability evaluation of a large wall screen display for multimedia exhibitions. This process included two concept tests and two task-based usability tests to understand how storytelling, usability and user experience intersect on a large wall screen presentation. This approach illuminated key requirements for designing for large wall screens that supports multimedia storytelling.

Keywords: User experience · Large wall design · Multi-touch interactions · Storytelling exhibitions · Interaction design

1 Introduction

Free choice learning environments like museums and exhibitions have struggled to become more interactive and collaborative. They have also been challenged to balance the focus of the interactive displays with the needs of the exhibition [10]. For example, adding interactive multimedia displays can monopolize the attention of visitors and the focus becomes on the technology, rather than the exhibition. As technology progresses, more options become available to create engaging digital solutions for visitors [11]. These solutions replace the standard, static displays that are common in traditional museum settings. For example, Planar, a company that provides digital technologies for museums, notes that large video displays and interactive flat screens have become a fixture in many modern-day museums [15]. Planar also notes that large video displays introduce an exhibition and set visitor expectations, encourage engagement, and create visually rich experiences. The ultimate goal of these displays is to encourage return visits, attract visitors, and create memorable experiences within an exhibition.

Although large wall screens may make learning experiences more appealing to museum visitors, without quality content, a large wall screen is an expensive piece of wall art. Contrast Creative, a company that designs for large interactive wall displays, describes them as, "the perfect vessel for imagination. Imagine content that comes alive when someone approaches and where no users have the exact same experience twice" [9]. Currently, there are limited studies that focus on the storytelling potential on large wall

A. Marcus and W. Wang (Eds.): HCII 2019, LNCS 11584, pp. 415–427, 2019.
https://doi.org/10.1007/978-3-030-23541-3_30

displays. Rather, they reference stories as the content on large wall displays and then focus on the design and interactivity associated with software and hardware. Multiple studies exist to understand how large displays function and to assess usability. As large wall screens grow in popularity, some studies have been conducted to determine possible heuristics for designing large displays. Usability experts from the Nielsen Norman Group have conducted studies to understand the user experience of large touch screens. Additionally, studies have explored how multiple users interact with one display [13]. However, fewer studies seek to understand the relationship between interaction design patterns for large touch screens, information architecture for a complex collection of artifacts, and content for a multimedia integrated exhibition. In museums, digital displays are sometimes gamified in order to tell their stories, referred to as "edutainment" [2]. However, studies that focus on edutainment often focus on understanding the gamification of learning rather than the interplay of HCI and storytelling.

Large wall displays are increasingly incorporated in museums and exhibitions, as well as public places to support social activities [4]. Also, [4] discuss different ways to design interactive displays that invite interaction and engagement. Their study indicates that social embarrassment is the leading factor preventing people from participating in public interactions. Therefore, for public interaction to become acceptable, the large display must have strong physical and social affordances, so visitors can easily become more familiar with the display. In order to promote public participation in large wall displays, the user experience must be simple and intuitive. Additionally, the interface needs to be clear so that users are reassured that the experience will be quick, enjoyable, and a low commitment activity. It is important to acknowledge the behaviors of museum visitors and other users in order to build the right experience for the space.

This paper chronicles the results of research conducted in the context of an interdisciplinary project to explore rich narrative content with cutting edge technology, specifically, a large touch screen display. To better understand the interplay of human-computer interaction and storytelling in the designs for this display, a series of design concept and usability tests were conducted. Results indicate that large displays with complex narratives should consider the height and display of icons, affordances are crucial for users to understand interactions such as scrolling, complex storytelling should be concise, and the design should encourage exploration.

2 Background

This literature review draws from three main areas of study: (1) the evolution of storytelling in museums and exhibitions, (2) interactive exhibitions in museums, and (3) usability research on large, interactive displays.

2.1 Storytelling in Museums and Exhibitions

At the heart of a great museums or exhibitions is robust storytelling that provides visitors with both depth of information and richness of experience. The best storytelling allows visitors to make personal connections with engaging exhibits because the displays support interpretation and multiple perspectives [3]. A case study on narrative in exhibitions [3] argues that "narrative allows people to imagine themselves in an unfamiliar world" (p. 31). In the first half of the 20th century, exhibit stories were usually directly related to the historical context of an artifact. However, in the latter half of the 20th century, museums began to evolve exhibition storytelling by offering thematic arrangements and presenting multiple points of view [10]. Likewise, as technology continues to improve, museums have developed new ways to communicate stories associated with exhibitions. In fact, experts have asserted that as museums work to make exhibit spaces more interactive, developing a cohesive narrative is increasingly important [11].

Edutainment experiences in museum exhibitions have increasingly made use of interactive technologies to attract and engage audiences. [7] note that "digital technologies allow more sophisticated nonlinear stories; allowing visitors to interact with the story at different points in time" (p. 106). This research evaluated the use of narrative in digital interactive storytelling and found that most audiences appreciated interactivity as a central part of the story design. They also found that users will stay engaged with an interactive exhibit as long as they perceive that the content is of high quality. In addition to quality of content, perceived ease of interaction and users' level of enjoyment also determine users' level of engagement.

However, most museums are challenged to effectively balance narrative content with technology. [10] argued that "richness and complexity of information, in combination with the availability of a variety of media (audio, visual, haptic) should not take the focus away of the initial goal which is to tell a story from a specific point of view that gains the visitor's interest" (p. 422). To achieve this balance, the authors argue that visitors should feel a sense of personal connection with stories. When museums work to personalize stories, users become less overwhelmed by the interplay between content and interactivity. Museums are still adopting more technology to encourage interactive storytelling, however, there are few best practices to guide the creation of a narrative on a large wall display [10].

2.2 Interactive Exhibitions in Museums

As interactive exhibits become popular in art, history, and cultural museums, technologies are also becoming increasingly valuable for visitor engagement and involvement. Not only does interactivity promote immersion, but also helps understand and recall exhibits and their content [1]. According to [1], interactive exhibits can be memorable, as visitors were able to describe the feelings they had at the exhibits months after their visit. Additionally, rather than interactive exhibits offering a different experience, visitors can use these as a tool to enhance their visit and appreciation of the museum [12].

There are key factors in the implementation of interactive exhibits or kiosks in museums e.g. they should be strategically positioned within the space, they should have a well-designed welcome screen, and a clear indication of interactivity as oppose to signage for non-interactive screens. In a study conducted by [14], four characteristics were examined to test the effectiveness in holding the attention of visitors in a science museum: technological novelty, user-centeredness, sensory stimulation, and open-endedness. Technological novelty and open-endedness showed positive correlations with the amount of time spent at the exhibits. Aside from these characteristics, the physical context where the digital media is experienced influences visitor interaction; as visitors consider the space and time they spend at each exhibit. If users have space to comfortably interact with kiosk or similar experiences, they will more likely engage with them.

Museums have begun to integrate multimedia storytelling exhibits beyond physical or medium-screen touch screen kiosks. [16] explore digital representations of large-scale artifacts in non-instrumental, location-based, multi-user interactions in order to enhance engaging experiences for visitors. Their computing system displays artifacts that are difficult for the public to access. Its features allow for visual and textual annotations of the artifact, as well as additional background information about the object or creators. Visitors can interact with these digital representations by walking around a location-based and motion-sensored space. For example, a wall painting from the museum was used as the digital artifact, and users had the opportunity to experience it by triggering designated hotspots located at different locations on the floor. Systems like this increase visitor engagement and provide innovative ways to access difficult museum artifacts.

2.3 Usability of Very Large Displays

One-way museums are incorporating multimedia storytelling and technology into exhibitions, is through the use of large touch screen displays. Dorothy Shamonsky, Lead UX Designer for ViewPoint and a large touch screen kiosk designer, reports that the freedom and novelty of a large screen are the two most appealing qualities. She notes that humans find it incredibly satisfying to have information presented in a large view and the option to interact with the information through the freedom to "play." Additionally, Shamonsky asserts that very large displays allow users to become an entertainer. "Obviously, others can observe what you are doing, so you become a performer of sorts with the application, which can be fun" [13]. When it comes to the usability and design of a very large touchscreen, [13] states that there are still several basic guidelines that apply to any screen size, including to allow natural gestures; minimize the interaction cost of tapping, typing, and moving between screens; offer user feedback via simple animations; make it easy to decipher which elements are tap-able; make targets easy to tap; and offer legible text and graphics. Despite this, there are important differences when designing for large touch screens compared to mobile phones. [8] used an eye tracking device and interviews with both expert and non-expert users to study usability on very large touch displays. [8] found that users adapted easily to new gestures within the large multi-touch display system based of their previous habits, users were satisfied using the large multi touch display system, eye movements of all users were around the center of the screen, the most common used gesture is tap, and users preferred to use both hands for multi touch gestures like zoom in, zoom out, and rotation.

3 Methodology

To understand the relationships among interaction design patterns for large touch screens, information architecture for a complex collection of artifacts, and content for a multimedia integrated exhibition, this study employed a mixed-methods approach that included two concept tests and two task-based usability tests.

3.1 Concept Tests

Concept tests were conducted to understand the interactions, designs, and concepts that users would most enjoy. Two sessions were conducted with five users who had some prior experience with interaction design either in school work or professionally. During the sessions, researchers walked participants through the design concepts for the large wall screen. Participants could ask questions, interact with the screen, and provide ideas. At the end of the session, participants were given a post-test questionnaire to solicit users' feedback about the design, storytelling content, navigation and overall experience. The post-test questionnaire included open-ended questions that allowed participants to provide suggestions, thoughts, and insights about the design. A medium-fidelity, interactive prototype was then developed to be used in a subsequent usability test (Fig. 2).

Fig. 1. Initial concept consisted of a carousel displaying different artifacts.

Fig. 2. Second concept displayed each artifact and narrative in a grid form.

3.2 Usability Tests

Two task-based usability tests were conducted, the first of which occurred after the design was revised based on feedback from the two concept tests. This first test included five participants with little-to-no prior experience with large wall displays. The second usability test was conducted after the designs were again revised based on feedback from the first usability test. The second usability test included five expert users, with professional experience or academic instruction on interaction design and five novice users, with no prior experience in interaction design. The goal of testing users with varying skill levels was to determine how well the large wall design was understood by both novice and expert users. This is important as the large wall screen is prototype of a public display intended for an exhibition created for all types of users.

Task-based usability sessions lasted approximately 15 to 30 min each. Five tasks were designed to explore the key interaction patterns in the design and navigation, i.e. swiping to browse through the layered narratives, identifying key icons and affordance elements, recognizing multimedia content, and understanding the interface structure. Participants were asked to think-aloud during their testing sessions to inform researchers of their thoughts while attempting to complete a task. Each test was audio recorded.

At the end of each task, participants completed a task difficulty questionnaire, and researchers completed success rating scales intended to gauge how successful each participant was in completing a task. The rating was based on the following scale: successful–users were able to fully complete the task; partial success–users completed part of the task; failure–users were unable to successfully complete the task; and quit–users abandoned the task. Each rating was assigned a value as follows: successful (3), partial (2), failure (1), and quit (0). At the end of the testing session, participants were asked their thoughts on the design and the experience. Finally, all participants completed a System Usability Scale (SUS) [5] questionnaire to assess the overall usability of the system. Finally, an open-ended post-test questionnaire was used to gauge how users felt about the narrative content and if they were able to understand it.

4 Results

4.1 Concept Tests

The concept tests yielded important qualitative data. Open-ended questions provided insights into how to further develop the wall screen design. Six key themes emerged from the users' feedback: (1) users are only be willing to go three to six clicks into a story before losing interest; (2) tap-able elements in the initial design were not easily identifiable; (3) users were open to sharing the same touch-screen space with one another; (4) sound would add to the experience, but headphones may be needed; (5) more movement and animation are desired for the design; and 6) a user's height may determine accessibility to all content.

4.2 Usability Test One

The overall ratings of the large wall screen during the first task-based usability test indicate that the experience was easy for participants to use. A perfect score for all tasks completed was 75 (Table 1). The total score from the test was 48, an overall task success a 64%. This data suggests that users completed each task with some issues. For example, task one required users to scroll and select a narrative (Fig. 1). All users selected a narrative, but three out of five did not know to scroll in order to browse. The most difficult rated tasks were task three and four. Task three tested whether users could locate the artifacts from the navigation by locating the carousel icon. Task four tested whether users could switch between themes.

Table 1. Usability test 1 - Tasks and overall task success rates.

Tasks	Expected outcome	Success rate
Task 1: Imagine you are interested in learning about Dave's legacy in Late Night television. Find a story that interests you	Scroll to browse Tap on a story	87%
Task 2: Now, imagine you want to learn more about Dave's relationship with his mother. Find that narrative and play a video	Scroll to find narrative grid. Tap on video affordance	73%
Task 3: Browse through the artifacts in the collection and find the "Beavis and Butthead" cartoon	Users navigate to the artifact screen	47%
Task 4: Now, find the second theme to learn about Dave's relationship with sports	Switch theme the user is viewing	60%
Task 5: Now, find and explore the complete story about Oprah Winfrey and Uma Thurman	Tap on underlined names or artifacts to open more layers	60%

Icon recognition was a problem many users suggested should be addressed in order to avoid confusion. For example, the icons on the side navigation were difficult to find, causing confusion as how to further explore the experience (Fig. 3). For example, users had the most trouble completing task 3, which asked them to identify certain items in the collection (Fig. 3). The artifact carousel icon did not register significance, which kept users from successfully completing the task (Fig. 3). Additionally, each narrative began with a story title and a down arrow to indicate each grid element was could be tapped (Fig. 3), but participants had difficulty identifying this feature for each narrative grid. Users were unable to identify different narratives within the grid, as they did not understand there were different narratives to explore. Another problem was the swiping affordance to differentiate where the narratives began and ended (Fig. 3). For example, users did not know how to interact with the design in order to find additional narratives. Participant 2 stated, "Oh, I didn't know that scrolled" when completing this task.

The layering system was also a problem many users encountered and should be addressed to improve navigation (Fig. 4). For example, all users were able to find the correct story within the design, but they were unaware that they could dive deeper into each story and bring up additional content through the layering system (Fig. 4). Additionally, users believed stories in the layers should be concise. User 2 stated, "I think it's really interesting and a cool way to give an overview of a topic or a person's life, but I'm not sure how often I'd come back to the same story." Other users indicated that they would be interested in using this system but would prefer shorter stories so they would not become fatigued while exploring multiple different narratives.

4.3 Usability Test Two

Overall ratings for the large wall screen during the second test indicate the experience was easier for users than the first design (Table 2). The system usability score for the first test was a 72, and the final test was a 75.25. For the second test there was an overall 85% success rate across all tasks. Users still struggled to recognize the scrolling interaction, despite the implementation of a down arrow at the bottom of the screen (Fig. 5). The addition of the menu icon at the top of the screen made it easier for users to navigate to the most difficult rated tasks (Fig. 5), like tasks three and five. Task three tested whether users could locate the artifacts from the navigation by locating menu icon and selecting artifacts from the navigation. Task five tested whether users could

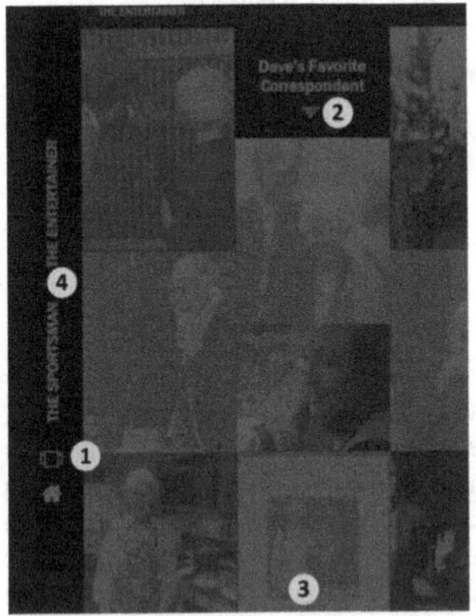

Fig. 3. (1) Icon recognition: Users struggled to find this specific icon to explore the carousel feature. (2) Users consistently tapped on this static arrow. (3) No swiping or scrolling affordance to direct users to complete action. (4) Main navigation bar difficult to interact with and not user friendly for height.

Fig. 4. (1) Each narrative grid consists of individual explanations for the selected media content. (2) Complex and longer narratives have additional ways to explore content as "pop ups." The additional content layers are identified through highlighted or underlined keywords or phrases.

switch between themes. The implementation of key words like "switch theme" or "artifacts in the collection" paired with corresponding icons helped users identify these features. Although users had an easier time doing this with the new menu icon, it was rated as a more difficult task. Users suggested moving the menu icon to the bottom of the screen for easier accessibility and repositioning the top menu from the middle to the top-right corner. Expert 5 stated, "I thought that was decoration" when referring to the location of the menu icon (Fig. 5).

Another recurring issue was the lack of understanding between the meaning of an artifact versus a story, which left users unable to navigate between the stories section and the featured artifacts. While there was a 30% success rate improvement on this task, users experienced difficulty identifying an artifact in the carousel feature (Fig. 5), as they searched in the wrong layer of the experience. Users felt that in order to understand the design and appreciate the narrative, exploration of the design was required. Novice 4 stated, "I feel like if I was just left to do it, without tasks, I would have figured it all out, just exploring and messing with it." Lastly, users were unaware that they could swipe up and down to scroll through the stories. Task 1 tested that users would scroll and choose a story, while all users were able to select a story, only two users scrolled to see additional content.

Table 2. Usability test 2 - Tasks and overall task success rates.

Tasks	Expected outcome	Success rate
Task 1: Imagine you are interested in learning about Dave's legacy in Late Night television. Find a story that interests you	Scroll to browse. Tap on a story	80%
Task 2: Now, imagine you want to learn more about Dave's relationship with his mother. Find that narrative and play a video	Scroll to find narrative grid. Tap on video affordance	93%
Task 3: Browse through the artifacts in the collection and find the "Beavis and Butthead" cartoon	Users navigate to the artifact screen	77%
Task 4: Adjust the position of the menu	Move the menu to a new location on the screen	83%
Task 5: Now, find another theme to learn about Dave's relationship with sports	Switch theme the user is viewing	87%

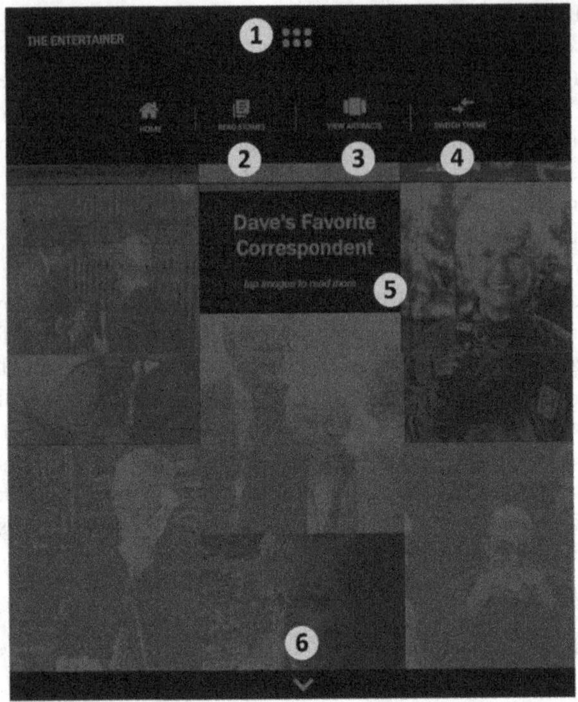

Fig. 5. (1) A Google Design icon was implemented for the navigation bar. This icon hides the navigation options and shows them when tapped. (2) The narrative grid was redefined as "stories." (3) Specific language was used to identify the artifacts in the collection. (4) An option to "switch" to a different theme was added to signify the difference of both themes. (5) The arrow was removed and replaced with key phrasing. (6) Down arrow was added to encourage swiping through the narrative grid but had no effect on the usability.

5 Discussion

This study chronicles the usability and interaction patterns of a large touch screen display. There are three key interaction design issues that were illuminated by this study, which can be characterized as follows: (1) the location and height of key icons should be within reaching distance for all users, (2) if scrolling is included in the design, it should use more visible affordances, and (3) complex storytelling should be concise and encourage exploration.

Key icons should be placed at reasonable heights and locations, because not all users are the same. When the menu icon was placed at the top in the center of the screen, users had difficulty identifying it because it was too far out of their immediate field of vision. Although the icon was moveable and could be re-positioned by the user to account for height differences, its design did not indicate that specific functionality. As a result, users were not aware the icon could be dragged to move it. Icons that are essential to navigation should be easily recognizable and be accompanied by keywords if the concept is too complex. Second, if scrolling is a key interaction for navigation, the design of scrolling content should include more visible affordances. This feature resulted in the least successful task, as users did not immediately know they could swipe the narrative grid up and down. Despite adding explicit and implicit affordances, such as arrows and cut-off content, users did not immediately understand the scrolling interaction. They needed time to explore before discovering the option to scroll. Key design indicators should be present to suggest swiping or scrolling. Using a carousel feature could work, giving the user visual cues of where they are present in the design or storyline. Finally, scrolling on a large display will also allow users to view the content at their desired height for comfortable viewing.

Complex storytelling should be concise and encourage exploration. Information must be displayed in short "chunks" instead of long-form text displays. The initial design presented challenges with in-depth storytelling and limited user attention. To solve this problem, we introduced a layering method intended to break up long narratives into shorter "chunks." The layering method easily organized the use of extensive stories and multimedia elements into smaller, easier-to-digest text blocks. However, through usability testing we discovered the layering method was not an effective way of displaying content. We found that all five users from the first usability test were not likely to go deeper and read more than the first layer of information. Rather, the users were more intrigued and entertained by multimedia elements. Additionally, due to the large amount of information, users become overwhelmed by the narrative elements. Therefore, long text paragraphs should be avoided. User 4 from the first usability test stated, "It [the large wall screen] was a lot of fun. My only thing is, if you're trying to find stuff on the spot, you get really nervous." The user went on to say she liked the interaction, found it entertaining, but that she would need lots of time to explore. While users are less likely to read long paragraphs of text, they do engage with media content. Jumping from layer to layer, or screen to screen should be smooth, intuitive, and clear to the user. If the design encourages exploration, users are more likely to engage with the content provided on the display. Additionally, if the design encourages exploration users are more likely to see how different stories are connected. Encouraging exploration on a large display will make users more comfortable with the experience. With the expansive amount of content, exploration allows users to quickly learn how to interact with the system as well as efficiently navigate between different layers of the design.

5.1 Limitations and Future Work

The software used to design and build this large wall experience was Intuiface Inspector and Intuiface Player, a multi-touch and sensor-driven tool used to build web-based platforms or kiosk experiences without coding. Although it supports different types of media such as images, videos, documents, websites, 3D models, and more, it limits the number of experiences that can occur at a single given time and location. Although many users can interact with it at once – i.e., they can touch and drag objects – multiple users do not have the ability to freely have a one-on-one experience in the space. Additionally, Intuiface also limits user interface design options, such as typography and iconography. Designers can import original designs, but these are placed as raster images, often reducing the quality of work. Furthermore, Intuiface does not support basic animations like "sliding," "appearing," "fading in and out," and "pulsing." These simple animations are crucial affordances for user understanding and facilitating key interactions with the design. Finally, a big limitation and weakness of this experience was the lagging and slow response from the large wall screen. Because the software contained multiple content layers, due to its limitation in holding two experiences at once, the experience reacted slowly, leading users to believe some interactions were not functional.

Future research opportunities include exploring how gesture-based interaction patterns affect user experience. Gesture-based technology would allow users to stand farther back and have a greater view of the large display. This would prevent the need for users to strain themselves by looking up or down, thus providing a greater opportunity for them interact with more of the content and more quickly see necessary icons. Additionally, future research could also include usability testing with multiple users interacting with the display to better understand how large touchscreen designs affect multi-user environments.

References

1. Allen, S., Gutwill, J.: Designing Science Museum Exhibits With Multiple Interactive Features: Five Common Pitfalls (2004). https://www.exploratorium.edu/vre/pdf/Interacty_article3_finweb.pdf
2. Balloffet, P., Courvoisier, F.H., Lagier, J.: From Museum to Amusement park: the opportunities and risks of edutainment. Int. J. Arts Manag. **16**(2) (2014)
3. Bedford, L.: Storytelling: the real work of museums. Curator Mus. J. **44**(1), 27–34 (2001)
4. Brignull, H., Rogers, Y. (n.d.): Human-computer Interaction, INTERACT 2003: Enticing People to Interact with Large Public Displays in Public Spaces. https://books.google.com/books?hl=en&lr=&id=PTg0fVYqgCcC&oi=fnd&pg=PA17&dq=largewalltouchscreens&ots=OaNIvGfCs-&sig=4w6T-5izGwqschGF4Yp1en4xuU4#v=onepage&q=largewalltouchscreens&f=true
5. Brooke, J.: SUS-A quick and dirty usability scale. Usability Eval. Ind. **189**(194), 4–7 (1996)
6. Burmistrov, I.: Touchscreen Kiosks in Museums, 22 September 2015. https://www.slideshare.net/IvanBurmistrov/touchscreen-kiosks-in-museums
7. Danks, M., Goodchild, M., Rodriguez-Echavarria, K., Arnold, D.B., Griffiths, R.: Interactive storytelling and gaming environments for museums: the interactive storytelling exhibition project. In: Hui, K.-C., et al. (eds.) Edutainment 2007. LNCS, vol. 4469, pp. 104–115. Springer, Heidelberg (2007). https://doi.org/10.1007/978-3-540-73011-8_13
8. Dönmez, M.: Use of large multi touch interfaces: a research on usability and design aspects, p. 155 (2015)
9. Interactive Walls Display Engaging Content, 8 January 2018. http://www.contrastcreative.com/blog/interactive-wall-displays/. Accessed 30 Oct 2018
10. Ioannidis, Y., Raheb, K.E., Toli, E., Katifori, A., Boile, M., Mazura, M.: One object many stories: Introducing ICT in museums and collections through digital storytelling. In: 2013 Digital Heritage International Congress (DigitalHeritage), vol. 1, pp. 421–424 (2013). https://doi.org/10.1109/DigitalHeritage.2013.6743772
11. Johnson, L., Becker, S.A., Estrada, V., Freeman, A.: NMC Horizon Report: 2015 Museum Edition. The New Media Consortium (2015). https://www.learntechlib.org/p/182009/

12. McIntyre, M.H.: Engaging or distracting? Visitor responses to interactives in the V&A British Galleries, June 2003. http://media.vam.ac.uk/media/documents/legacy_documents/file_upload/5877_file.pdf
13. Pernice, K.: A Few Mobile UX Design Skills Help With Very Large Touchscreen UX Design (2015). https://www.nngroup.com/articles/very-large-touchscreen-ux-design/. Accessed 29 Oct 29
14. Sandifer, C.: Technological novelty and open-endedness: two characteristics of interactive exhibits that contribute to the holding of visitor attention in a science museum. J. Res. Sci. Teach. **40**, 121–137 (2003). https://doi.org/10.1002/tea.10068
15. Trends in the use of digital displays in museum environments (2015). http://www.planar.com/blog/2015/1/13/trends-in-the-use-of-digital-displays-in-museum-environments/. Accessed 18 Oct 2018
16. Zabulis, X., Grammenos, D., Sarmis, T., Tzevanidis, K., Argyros, A.: Exploration of large-scale museum artifacts through non-instrumented, location-based, multi-user interaction (2010). https://s3.amazonaws.com/academia.edu.documents/41341862/vast_2010.pdf?AWSAccessKeyId=AKIAIWOWYYGZ2Y53UL3A&Expires=1542836925&Signature=P9/U8 He aLOGohI323N1KQefk=&response-content-disposition=inline; filename=Exploration_of_large-scale_museum_artifa.pdf. Accessed 21 Nov 2018

Interactive Storytelling in V.R.: Coming Soon?

Andy Deck(✉)

School of Visual Arts, New York, NY 10010, USA
Adeck@sva.edu

Abstract. There have been many smart people throughout history who have misidentified the potential, or lack thereof, of new technologies. Thomas Edison, for all his genius, failed to anticipate the market for cinematic entertainment. His company's early films lacked storytelling, and its film display technology, the Kinetoscope, permitted only one person to watch at a time. Perhaps there are lessons here for Virtual Reality (V.R.). Some have assumed that as entertainment becomes increasingly immersive, movies will somehow be absorbed into V.R. Even as many of the technical preconditions for this vision have fallen into place, there remain logistical and practical problems. Translating conventional forms of story authorship into the immersive, interactive context may not be sought-after. What is an interactive movie, after all? Even if strategies can be found to write and produce interactive V.R. movies, the results may be different from what people have been expecting.

Keywords: Interactive · Virtual Reality · Storytelling

1 The Confusing Evolution of V.R. Movies

1.1 A Comparative Approach

There are a number of promising applications for immersive V.R. media that don't involve storytelling. The virtual camera opens up thought-provoking new views of human anatomy and the stars. One may learn about the past by traveling in time and space to explore historical events and civilizations. Whether it's synthetic views of historical reconstructions, or the 360° video of V.R. documentaries, the user's ability simply to turn and navigate may constitute sufficient interaction within these "spaces" of discovery.

The distribution of Google's "Cardboard" (a cheap, head-mounted display system for cellphones) in editions of the New York Times in late 2015 signaled the arrival of emotionally moving documentary V.R. content for a wide audience. After donning a Cardboard and opening *The Displaced* (2015), one was transported into an immersive video recording of children displaced by war. But documentaries – whether immersive or conventional – don't generate the amount of buzz that has surrounded V.R. in recent years. The same can be said about historical reconstructions of ancient cities and monuments that can be explored through V.R. They are not the kinds of V.R. applications that genuinely excite venture capitalists.

That Facebook paid $2.3 billion for Oculus suggests how serious Mark Zuckerberg is about V.R.'s social media potential. V.R.'s head mounted display technology also

A. Marcus and W. Wang (Eds.): HCII 2019, LNCS 11584, pp. 428–439, 2019.
https://doi.org/10.1007/978-3-030-23541-3_31

has enormous potential for video games, where it offers a rich, immersive virtual presence. While immersive social media and video games are mostly beyond the scope of the present paper, there is little question that V.R. can flourish in those contexts.

But despite the existence of such promising applications for V.R., there's just something about V.R. that makes people believe that, beyond gaming, it will also become a medium for telling stories. Somehow "V.R. movies" will become a big thing, rather than a fantasy born of Hollywood science fiction. Some might object that talk of "people" believing in the inevitability of V.R. movies amounts to a straw man argument, but it's just not true. Anyone who has been to a V.R. conference or trade show knows that the popular imagination of the future of V.R. is expansive. Cinematic, interactive V.R. is a dreamy technology that is supposed to arrive before the flying car. And if you don't believe it, check out the streams of venture capital for emerging concerns like V.R. animation [1]. What follows is not simply an analysis of why this dream remains unfulfilled. It's also an attempt to imagine a realistic version of this whole V.R. movie scenario. Charting a course for the advancement of interactive V.R. storytelling is not just a technical problem: it demands a deeper look at V.R. as a storytelling medium.

1.2 Beyond the Bells and Whistles

In a sense the Netflix V.R. app does bring movies into V.R. But reviews for this very limited V.R. experience reflect considerable frustration and disillusionment. There is certainly no interactive storytelling involved in this display adaptation: streams of movie and television video are simply texture mapped onto a rectangular surface in a 3D environment. If you don't want anyone else to know what you are watching, maybe there's a reason to trade a flat screen for a head mounted display with Netflix V.R. Otherwise don't bother.

When intoxicated with technological novelty, people are often mislead by appearances. Head mounted displays, after all, seem like an advancement over the 3D glasses that appeared in 1950s movie theaters. They both make three dimensional illusions possible. Nevertheless, intriguing photos of theaters full of V.R. spectators (e.g. promotional photos of the "Samsung Galaxy Studio Gear VR Theater") can't change the fact that in true V.R. the camera's point of view is identical to the spectator's point of view, and that's just not how movies have worked since the 19th century. Letting the spectator aim the camera is a radical change in the orientation of cinematic content.

1.3 Accommodating the User's Perspective

The pioneering filmmaker, James Cameron, who has worked extensively with motion capture and the integration of photography and simulation, articulates an important distinction concerning 360° videography and "true" V.R.:

> [W]hat most people are calling V.R. right now isn't V.R.. It's really omnidirectional camera. And because you don't really have any spatial control – any spatial movement is baked in – you [only] have the ability to look around in an environment, and that's not true V.R.. [In] true V.R.,

> you can move around. And you have a lot of control over where you are spatially in the environment [2].

This critique applies to a number of contemporary V.R. movie experiments. For example, *The Limit* (2018), directed by Robert Rodriguez and billed as a Virtual Reality Film, uses a passive V.R. approach that locks the user to the position of the 180° camera throughout. Its first person style resembles *Hardcore Henry* (2015) in this respect. One reviewer said of it "The constant jumps and forced head turns quickly cause motion sickness and take you out of the film …. the whole experience was literally nauseating" [3].

There are also some exceptional works of V.R. that rise above the struggles of innovation, like Patrick Osborne's short format *Pearl* (2016), which uses music and editing effectively. The spectator's point of view in *Pearl* is fused to the passenger seat of a car throughout, providing a fairly restrained visual field. Making head rotation the user's only notable freedom allowed the director to rely more on traditional filmic problem solving.

Although V.R. production contains elements of movie production, the similarities can overshadow remarkable differences. The use of omni-directional cameras represents a significant challenge to movie making. It's no wonder that many V.R. movie directors today opt to constrain viewers to an "on the rails" point of view, or to employ devices like a shark cage. If V.R. movies trend toward "true" V.R. with spectator mobility, the disruption in how movies are made will be even more profound.

Today most mainstream movies still employ live action and traditional camera work. Yet that mode of production with its lights, dollies, hydraulic jib arms, and microphones doesn't really lend itself well to immersion. Computer generated imagery removes all that visual clutter of film production, and the focus shifts to modeling, virtual lighting, and virtual set design. Under these circumstances of virtuality, where the camera's point of view becomes the spectator's, the discipline of cinematography disappears.

This subtraction represents a loss of control for the storyteller. Consider the pre-production process. In a conventional movie, a storyboard is often used to plan for framing, composition, editing, and camera angles. But for an immersive movie in which a user controls the camera, many of the concerns of a storyboard are swept up in uncertainty. The visual language of editing and camera angles is overcome by unknowns. A user could be staring at the sky or at his own navel. Each moment of a storyboard needs to be drawn as a spherical panorama in order to encompass the user's potential visual experience. Such indeterminate conditions for aiming and framing make it very difficult for a director to anticipate a spectator's visual experience of a story.

2 Adding Interaction to V.R.

2.1 The Mobile Observer

The implications of V.R. described to this point, as radical as they are, do not encompass giving spectators much more than the ability to control the camera. Can wandering around an open world, and being visually immersed, satisfy the expectations of progress that people may bring to V.R. movies? Since 2011 an off-Broadway theater in New York City has been running an experimental production called *Sleep No More* that illustrates one approach to interactive drama. It presents Shakespeare's Macbeth in a spatially distributed way that lets spectators move from room to room, where actors enact scenes as though they were looping. There is a notable rule: spectators are not meant to affect the scenes. Visitors just circulate among actors as if they were walking past artifacts at a museum. This raises important questions about what forms of interaction belong in V.R. movies.

If viewers can skip scenes, or affect them, the resulting stories are non-linear. This means that there's no official version. The shared experience people associate with reading the same book or watching the same movie does not apply. With non-linear V. R. movies, two participants could come away from a viewing with the sense that they didn't watch the same movie. Instead they might feel that they experienced a similar genre, or that their stories took place in some of the same places. Would the Oscar for Best Picture go to the version that happened when spectators took the staircase to exit the opening scene?

2.2 Interacting with a Movie

Since adding any sort of interactivity to movies breaks with convention, it stretches the definition of a "movie" to make audiences do something other than watch (applaud, laugh, etc.). Are viewers who are accustomed to traditional movies and television primed for this empowerment? It's worth noting that the DVD already adapted movies into one interactive format. Through the DVD menu users discovered options for languages, deleted scenes, and director voice-overs. This interactive overlay did not bother many people, perhaps because it was "bonus" material – there was always a comforting and prominent button that began playback of a regionally-specific default version of the movie. Could a V.R. movie provide a similarly interaction-free default, enabling a conventional movie experience if one faced forward and watched? Such a gentle introduction of V.R. could follow the path of the 3D movie in becoming a generally accepted optical enhancement.

Limiting the spectator's control of the point of view would have the added benefit of keeping spectators in their seats and maintaining continuity with the director's traditional practices of framing the story for the viewer. Even so, it's hard to imagine that user curiosity could be bottled up by treating head mounted display systems like glorified 3D glasses.

The very nature of V.R., which reacts fluidly to a user's movements with sensors, suggests that a V.R. movie must explore interactivity more deeply. Yet, from the point of view of the filmmaker, how could one manage the unruly spectator's desire for control? The invention of a navigable virtual space in a "movie" is a radical departure from tradition. Letting wandering viewers tear down the fourth wall wreaks havoc with the visual language of cinema in so many ways. Jump cuts from locale to locale, which are normal in conventional editing, compete with spectators' sense of camera control, making them feel as though they're being teleported all over the place. And just where should people don their head gear? Which "tracking mode" is best? Should users watch a V.R. movie from inside a spherical hamster wheel so that their actual confinement doesn't spoil illusions of virtual space?

Of course anyone familiar with contemporary video games knows it's possible to feel movement in a virtual space from a seated position. But do people really want to navigate V.R. movies with a mouse or a game controller? It's certainly not intuitive for non-gamers.

2.3 Interface Innovations

While there is no universally agreed-upon mechanism for enabling a spectator's participation in an interactive story, there are a number of possible solutions, some of which are already being used in games. The exhilaration a player feels while driving a video game experience has its own intrinsic appeal, to be sure; but importing that "player" involvement into a story that feels like a movie is something of a riddle. Movies in theaters have essentially no user interface: eyes are paired with a luminous image. In V.R. there are several possible forms of feedback, including gestures. With head mounted displays there is no definite need for things like buttons, game controllers, or menus, although these are often used now. A spectator's gaze to the left or right can trigger changes in the movie. This type of activating gaze is implemented nicely in the *Land's End* (2015) puzzle game, for example. Although theaters have discouraged talking during movies, the voice is another way to interact with V.R. movies.

2.4 Identity Problems

With the appearance of more and more V.R. games, some are beginning to emphasize storytelling more. The V.R. movie short *Blade Runner 2049: Memory Lab* (2017) – which uses a game controller – can be considered a game, too. Just not a good one. The narrator often calls attention to the game controller and how it must be used in order to advance to the next chapter. Although it is a tie-in for a feature film, its distribution, reviews, and documentation belong to game ecosystems in which terms like "Game Play" and "Game Mode" frame the user's expectations. Is it a game? An interactive movie? It can be a little bit of both with immersive game-movie hybrids. But in the end it's hard to care when the story is as perfunctory as the game play is tedious.

It is tempting to apply "duck test" abductive reasoning to this ambiguity. If it walks like a duck, swims like a duck, and quacks like a duck, it's probably a duck. In other words, if the types of interaction in V.R. look and feel like game play, it's probably a game. Likewise, if a V.R. user's actions situate her imaginatively in a drama, comedy, or thriller, then the interaction belongs to a V.R. movie. But this approach is problematic because the many permutations of game and cinematic elements seem to defy rigorous taxonomy. The awkward marriage of cinema and game interaction has led some industry commentators to wonder what can be done. The V.R. reviewer Jaime Feltham cites a quote from Hideo Kojima as "a touchstone" for his reporting on V.R.:

> [Kojima] said that game developers "see VR as an extension of traditional games, but I think it is not." While I've always agreed with that sentiment, I've also longed to know what he thinks V.R. is. And maybe it's this; maybe it's not an extension but a splicing of both games and film,

> something that takes their core attributes and builds on top of them to deliver media that is genuinely new [4].

It's unsurprisingly that emergent V.R. animation and V.R. movies borrow from gaming in many ways, relying on game logic, button pushing, and other game elements to accommodate the spectator's participation. Opinions are bound to differ about how much of the gamer's toolkit belongs in a V.R. movie, but there's no denying that today it's mostly gamers who own head mounted display systems. The distribution networks and production tools for V.R. and video games are virtually the same phenomena. But borrowing doesn't always work if the goal is to make something new.

While it may seem like injecting interactivity into the story structure of movies transforms them into interactive games, there is ample evidence from the domains of Net Art and media art that interaction does not magically turn user experience into game experience. As more people who are not interested in games begin making V.R. movies, they will find ways to use interactivity that are unrelated to gaming.

2.5 Incompatible Parts

Immersive and interactive storytelling "that is genuinely new" will remain elusive until directors and developers gain a stronger grasp of what works well in V.R. As V.R. storytelling finds its identity, the influence of cinema can be as problematic as the influence of games. The embedded plot-expository video ("cutscene"), is an example of one problematic technique. It is a cinematic storytelling device that appears in both video games and V.R. experiences. Transplanting it into an immersive, interactive context may serve the storyteller. But at what cost? Cutscenes feel like canned elements that interrupt the user's sense of being in a scene. Writer Danny Bilson has called them the "last resort of game storytelling" [5]. When cutscenes stall the usual interactive dynamics of an environment with unavoidable story development, it can feel intrusive and superficial. While cutscenes, which are sometimes called "cinematics," can inject some cinematic flavor into a V.R. environment, a reliance on them to orient the spectator can feel like a collision of two creative forms. As interactivity becomes a more common cinematic element, the embrace of film language will continue to evolve.

2.6 Translations and Mis-translations

There are already countless game and movie hybrids. The struggle for the V.R. movie to emerge from the shadows of cinema and video games is taking place at a time when games are being adapted as movies, and movie elements are being integrated into games. In an interview with *Fortune* in 2015, the gaming legend Shigero Miyamoto said "Because games and movies seem like similar mediums, people's natural expectation is we want to take our games and turn them into movies…" [6]. His skepticism about this conversion is rooted in his feeling that games are interactive whereas movies are passive.

An array of poorly-rated game-inspired movie crossovers support Miyamoto's view. Movie adaptations of popular video games reveal that script writers often struggle to translate the quest and task preoccupations of game users into a conventional movie format. The variability of game play doesn't seem to map well onto the dependable sameness of the playback of linear movies.

2.7 The Non-linear "Page Turner"

By comparison, adapting novels to the silver screen is a piece of cake. It is done all the time. Even though the visually-oriented language of film differs from the textual novel, there is a direct parallel between the beginning, middle and end of stories in each medium. Movies may not excel at some of the things that a novel can do well, like internal monologue, but at the end of the day they are both linear media.

Adapting a novel to an interactive, non-linear medium is a trickier proposition. Riddles like "What happens in the race sequence if the main character hasn't yet met his adversary?" are problems that belong to authors wrestling with non-linearity. Orchestrating a complex non-linear story is not for the feint of heart.

In a 1936 letter to novelist John O'Hara, F. Scott Fitzgerald advised young novelists to start with a big outline: "put down an outline of a novel of your times enormous in scale … and work on the plan for two months. Take the central point of the file as your big climax and follow your plan backward and forward from that for another three months" [7]. For Fitzgerald, laying the foundation for a solid novel meant five months of heavy lifting.

In order to achieve a tight plot – a page turner – the author Michael Crichton committed his story ideas to note cards. Later he would anguish over the sequencing of scenes and dialogue. This deliberation was a crucial first step in crafting his best selling novels. These details about writing process just go to show what many failed authors already know: writing a linear story that dazzles readers is very difficult. Creating reconfigurable non-linear stories with alternative plots, each of which feel similarly resolved and suspenseful, is an even bigger challenge. Moreover, this arduous conceptualization process is an aspect of V.R. "authoring" that is treated as a bit of an afterthought in the curricula of many college programs where students are learning to make V.R. content.

Given this bias, it is unsurprising that a celebrated V.R. movie like the short-format *Jurassic World: Blue* (2018), which is advertised as "stunning" and "groundbreaking" by its creators, has essentially no story whatsoever. Like the earliest and most provisional films ever made in the 19th century, which also lacked conceptual savvy, it only delivers an impressive feeling of presence. In the absence of a story, the spectator just gets to look around at dinosaurs that play and fight inexplicably. It needs a genre title, so let's call it "gawker V.R."

2.8 The Illusion of Meaningful Interaction?

In the early 1990s experimental "hypermedia" interactive stories were common. They often confined users to a few forking paths. Although it was fun for a while, the market for CD-ROM-based hypermedia – always small by comparison with DVDs – was short-lived. The tendency to reduce storytelling to a series of mundane choices (clicks) probably contributed to the decline. The experiences often felt more labyrinthine than fictional. Ultimately it just wasn't a very compelling form of storytelling.

With V.R. some similar storytelling habits have emerged. Limited user control of stories is the path of least resistance for interactive V.R. production. It's easier to script V.R. that offers few plot-triggers, and that funnels users into a mostly linear story. Given the state of the art, it's understandable that developers would want to coax spectators onto a linear path: the production of multiple plot lines is time-consuming.

Before long people will become tired of the illusion of choice. Should developers then go the extra mile to invent non-linear stories for users to navigate? It's worth asking whether there's even a demand for V.R. movies that have branching stories. After all, it hasn't been an especially popular format in other media.

Netflix made a notable effort to explore the potential of user-controlled branching stories in 2017. The streaming format required viewers to control animated stories every few minutes by choosing either a left or right directional button. One title, *Puss in Boots: Trapped in an Epic Tale,* was produced by Dreamworks Animation Television. Far from earning accolades, by 2019 it had yet to earn a score from Rotten Tomatoes for lack of audience and critic ratings. Another offering, produced by American Greetings Entertainment and named *Buddy Thunderstruck: The Maybe Pile*, generated such a tepid response that by 2019 there were no reviews on either the Internet Movie Database or Rotten Tomatoes.

If there really were audience demand for movies with multiple endings, wouldn't the phenomenon have surfaced in more ways? The existence of multiple editions of movies demonstrates that at least some *directors* want different endings than their studios. But director's cut DVDs and Bluray editions – featuring new edits, deleted scenes and alternative endings – have only ever been a minor, niche market. Often a studio will opt to leave an alternative ending on the cutting room floor, after conducting focus group testing to establish which conclusion audiences like best. What's more, the audiences that watch both endings are compensated with free tickets: their contribution to the production is treated like a chore.

2.9 After the Hype Settles

At some point the limitations of branching V.R. stories and gawkers will become more apparent than they are today, when all things V.R. still feel brand new. The allure of omni-directional cameras will wear off, as will watching conventional movies with head mounted displays. What then?

Low-hanging fruit approaches to doing stories in V.R. may never generate the audience interest that venture capitalists are hoping for. Sure it's not too hard to make V.R. stories in the form of *Sleep No More* that restrict user interaction to wandering in an open world where movie scenes transpire. But it doesn't sound like the next big thing in cinema. It's also easy to ignore the demise of early 1990s hypermedia, and Netflix's interactive animation failures. V.R. movie directors can keep trying to find an audience for branching stories that offer periodic choices, or a few different endings. But that doesn't look like a recipe for a popular revolution in film arts, either. In the near term, as V.R. tie-ins for feature films, studios will probably continue to fund free-to-download gawkers that keep spectators glued to the cameraman's point of view. But these spectacles will leave people wanting more.

2.10 Dynamic Interactive V.R. Movies

A phenomenon that deserves the name "V.R. movie" needs more than just a navigable virtual space – what Cameron calls "true" V.R.: it ought to have a compelling interactive story that is impacted – even *transformed* – by user behavior. The ability to interact in profound ways with a story that's unfolding would undoubtedly feel new and different. The question is how to accomplish this, practically speaking. Producing V.R. experiences that give spectators creative control of a story is hard.

Transitioning to this form won't be a simple matter of adopting a new breed of camera. Ceding control over a story's sequence and the viewer's point of view requires a major rethink of the whole production process. Each option given to spectators could demand more work for content developers. Empowering spectator co-creators to pursue personal interests in a story framework also raises quality control issues. If spectators are allowed, somehow, to co-author a story, they will still want to feel that "their" story ends well. Who is responsible for the resulting story? Can audiences be relied upon to do the heavy lifting to resolve the narrative consequences of their (potentially haphazard) interventions? Wrestling with the user interface and user experience problems of weaving interactivity and immersion into the movie form is already a lot to ask. Should the responsibilities of the movie makers expand to include every potential story arc, too? It seems that the desires of spectators for control may overwhelm the abilities of V.R. movie makers to satisfy them.

You might think that these kinds of dilemmas would concern V.R. investors. Given that the transition to interactive V.R. movies is disruptive and difficult, it's reasonable to wonders whether the motivations to fight through logistical challenges are strong enough? For the moment, at least, the race to monopolize this new terrain continues. Disney, for one, has been pouring money into interactive animation even though the near-term results don't appear to be profitable [8].

3 Making Interactions Movie-Like

3.1 Being Present but not Passive

How can V.R. spectators become participants and co-creators of a story? How do content developers accommodate greater freedom of user interaction without generating a crazy work-load for themselves? It may help to look to the past for some answers.

Traditional live theater has always allowed actors some communication with the audience, permitting them to respond to laughter, shock, tears, or boredom with nuanced performances. This could be automated. It is possible for sensors to detect when a user laughs or cries, and then to apply this feedback to the story. But instead of automation it might be more interesting simply to bring more of the live, human element of theater into V.R.

Perhaps interactive storytelling in an immersive context is well suited to actors and writers. The actor Walter Matthau once claimed that his true talent was performing in theater rather than in films. "On the stage I could move with freedom and ease. And I had something: presence. On screen, all the power is in the hands of the director or the editor" [9]. Shifting the balance of power towards actors and letting them *ad lib* could be worth watching. If a cast of actors convened in an immersive setting, interesting movie-like experiences could be enacted. The loosely-scripted ensemble comedies directed by Christopher Guest in the 2000s (Best in Show, A Mighty Wind, etc.), demonstrate that actors are capable of ingenious improvisation. Even so, the results in this scenario would only be as good as the participants. It's hard to envision this phenomenon being very popular because most people are not talented improvisational actors.

Of course amateurs could also behave as actors in cyberspace, engaging in play that resembles live theater. Maybe this type of participative V.R. could work despite a lack of talent, like karaoke. Variations on this general idea, like historical reenactments, or a Rocky Horror Picture Show style of fan participation in V.R., could become popular, too. But in some ways these kinds of collaborative behavior seem more closely related to social media applications for V.R. After all, when people get together to screw around, it usually doesn't result in something that feels like a movie.

3.2 Movie Machines

Jonathan Swift, in his 1726 book *Gulliver's Travels,* described a mechanical device capable of generating sequences of words. He attributed the engine to ridiculous inventors; and with it, he relates,

> … the most ignorant person, at a reasonable charge, and with a little bodily labour, might write books in philosophy, poetry, politics, laws, mathematics, and theology, without the least assistance from genius or study [10].

In the spirit of Swift's Academy of Lagado, every gathering devoted to advancing V.R. includes a contingent of believers who will dismiss every deficiency in contemporary V.R. as a technical challenge. At the risk of bolstering this dubious analysis, it's worth entertaining the possibility that technical innovations will indeed reshape some of the problems of authorship and interactivity in V.R. movies. Perhaps it's wrong to ask *who* will be responsible for the work of resolving storytelling problems. It may be more a question of *what* will govern the interactive stories.

Story sequencing and plot dynamics of V.R. movies may become an interplay among conventional authors, participative spectators, and software constructs that leverage advancements in artificial intelligence. Indeed, A.I. may bring about an entirely new balance of "creative" control between authors and machines.

According to a New York Times report, many news organizations are already employing A.I. to "write" news articles.

> A.I. journalism is not as simple as a shiny robot banging out copy. A lot of work goes into the front end, with editors and writers meticulously crafting several versions of a story, complete with text for different outcomes. Once the data is in — for a weather event, a baseball game or an earnings report — the system can create an article [11].

While today's automated news articles represent a fairly basic automation of journalistic grunt work, they also demonstrate the potential of machines to encroach upon the role of the writer.

Years ago, as a graduate student focused on literature, I happened upon Dr. Wendy Lehnert's quirky A.R.P.A.-funded research entitled "Plot Units and Narrative Summarization" [12]. The ways that she abstracted and analyzed stories struck me as obtuse, and the article's hand-drawn diagrams seemed absurdly mechanistic. Yet with the passage of a generation since it was published, the approach looks more and more like groundwork for the emergence of artificial intelligence in the domain of stories.

With further developments in A.I. and natural language processing, encounters between V.R. spectators and bots could become indistinguishable from dialogue among human actors. Free-form conversations with artificially intelligent avatars could be folded into flexible plots. In addition, if the plots of a lot of existing stories could be effectively "learned" by an A.I., then it seems plausible that people could become actors within stories that are adaptively refactored according to their actions. In other words, an A.I. construct could draw upon many learned plots in order to generate a story that adapts spontaneously to user behaviors. The A.I. would introduce plot twists to drive the collaborative story toward a satisfyingly familiar conclusion. It may not sound like the kind of immersive, interactive movie that people have anticipated for V. R., but it does seem like an extension of the movie form that could generate a sizable new audience.

3.3 Limited Solutions

However, if software does begin to supplant the works of human actors, directors, and writers with artificial intelligence pastiche, the trend could be more objectionable than the V.R. mediocrity that prevails today. Whereas human writers and directors live in the historical moment and produce new work that is a reflection of feelings and analyses of the world around them, an artificially intelligent movie system that is taught to mimic existing work would not grapple with change, history, and mortality in a comparable way.

An A.I. capable of personalizing stories would also undermine the way one thinks of a movie as a discrete creative work. Choosing a V.R. movie would become like a self-centered a-la-cart configuration: after calling up "an action thriller set in Europe with a washed-up gambler as a protagonist and a comical villain," the A.I would drop you into the first scene. In some ways this resembles the dystopian future in the Wim Wenders film *Until the End of the World* (1991), in which everyone became screen-addicted to handheld devices that let them watch their own dreams.

But perhaps it's not the viewer's dreams that are most troubling. If people strap into virtual encounters with artificial intelligence on a regular basis, it matters who designed the A.I. and why. It's reasonable to question whether meaningful interaction and quality of storytelling even matter to the venture capitalists who are feeding the V.R. frenzy. At some point the question must be asked: to what limitation in existing movies does the move to interactive audiences respond? Is it that traditional audiences are not pressing BUY buttons fast enough? Does V.R. figure to improved yields from embedded advertising? Would giving moviegoers virtual guns attract more gamers? Maybe big companies are scared that they'll get left behind if they miss the next wave.

Despite the specter of cynical motivations, the future of the V.R. movie can only further "industrialize" people's minds, as Enzensberger has put it, with contributions from creative workers [13]. There are now many thousands of people involved in building, evaluating, and imagining this new V.R. art form, summoning it into existence. Despite the many half-baked provisional experiments of the present, which seem incapable of sustaining interest for long, the V.R. movie is in its infancy. There is still a viable potential for V.R. to appeal to an engaged, impactful spectator/participant – a potential that could make inventing the V.R. movie worthwhile. Will the V.R. movie become a beautiful and vibrant new art form, or a blindingly seductive distraction that envelops us ever deeper in a cocoon of virtuality and e-commerce? It's up to the people who shape its further development.

References

1. Lang, B.: Penrose Studios raises another $10 million for V.R. animation and storytelling (2018). https://www.roadtovr.com/penrose-studios-series-a-investment/. Accessed 28 Dec 2018
2. Lang, B.: James Cameron: 'If I wasn't making Avatar [sequels] I would be experimenting with VR' (2017). https://www.roadtovr.com/james-cameron-if-i-wasnt-making-avatar-sequels-experimenting-with-vr/. Accessed 12 Feb 2019
3. Chungus, B.: THE LIMIT not recommended (2019). https://store.steampowered.com/app/971350/Robert_Rodriguezs_THE_LIMIT_An_Immersive_Cinema_Experience/. Accessed 12 Feb 2019
4. Feltham, J.: Editorial: for VR to shine, film and gaming must overlap. UploadVR (2019). https://uploadvr.com/vr-film-gaming-overlap/. Accessed 12 Feb 2019
5. Devore, J.: THQ's Bilson: cutscenes the last resort for storytelling. Destructoid (2011). Accessed 11 Feb 2019
6. Morris, C.: Shigeru Miyamoto talks Nintendo's return to the movie world. Fortune Magazine (2015). http://fortune.com/2015/08/21/nintendo-movie-partnerships/. Accessed 11 Feb 2019
7. Turnbull, A.: The Letters of F. Scott Fitzgerald, p. 545. Penguin Books, New York (1963)
8. Solsman, J.: Disney greenlights 'top secret' VR short film project. CNET (2019). https://www.cnet.com/news/disney-has-green-lit-a-top-secret-vr-short-film-project-sundance-cycles/. Accessed 6 Feb 2019
9. Ansen, D.: The sourpuss we loved. Newsweek (2000). https://www.newsweek.com/sourpuss-we-loved-161659. Accessed 14 Feb 2019
10. Greenberg, R., Piper, W.B. (eds.): The Writings of Jonathan Swift: Authoritative Texts, Backgrounds, Criticism, p. 156. Norton, New York (1973)
11. Peiser, J.: The rise of the robot reporter. New York Times (2019). https://www.nytimes.com/2019/02/05/business/media/artificial-intelligence-journalism-robots.html Accessed 5 Feb 2019
12. Lehnert, W.G.: Plot units and narrative summarization. Cogn. Sci. Multi Discip. J. **43**, 293–331 (1981)
13. Enzensberger, H.M.: The Industrialization of the Mind. Critical Essays, pp. 3–14. Continuum, New York (1982)

Do Smart Speakers Respond to Their Errors Properly? A Study on Human-Computer Dialogue Strategy

Xiang Ge(✉), Dan Li, Daisong Guan, Shihui Xu, Yanyan Sun, and Moli Zhou

Baidu AI Interaction Design Lab, Beijing, China
gexiang@baidu.com

Abstract. As smart speakers with voice interaction capability permeate continuously in the world, more and more people will gradually get used to the new interaction medium–voice. Although speech recognition, natural language processing (NLP) have been greatly improved over the past few years, users still may encounter errors from time to time like "cannot understand", "no requested audio resource (such as music)", which can frustrate users. Therefore, when an error message is reported, it is vital that the smart speaker gives an effective and proper response. However, currently the response strategies adopted by leading smart speaker brands in China differed mainly on two dimensions: "apology or not" and "humor or neutral". We explored user's preference of response strategies under two error scenarios——"cannot understand" and "no requested audio resource". A 2 (apology: yes vs. no) × 2 (error message expression tone: humor vs. neutral) within-subjects experiment was conducted. Two dependent variables (satisfaction and perceived sincerity of response) were measured. The results showed that participants were more satisfied and perceived higher sincerity when smart speaker apologized in both error scenarios. In the "no requested audio resource" scenario, humor had no significant impact on the perception of satisfaction and sincerity. But in the "cannot understand" scenario, humorous expression decreased perceived sincerity.

Keywords: Voice interaction · Smart speaker · Error · Emotion · Human-computer interaction · Humor · Apology

1 Introduction

As smart speakers with voice interaction capability permeate continuously in the world *(According to statistics of IDC, global shipments were 99.8 million from Q1 to Q3 of 2018* [1]*)*, voice interaction is more widely used and becoming an important human-computer interaction method.

Although speech recognition, natural language processing (NLP) technologies have been greatly improved, users still encounter errors from "recognition", "understanding", and "fulfillment" aspects [2, 3]. By conducting a structured walkthrough on how the three key smart speaker brands in China (Xiaomi, Baidu, Alibaba) would respond to errors under task-oriented dialogue interaction, we found the strategies varied in two

A. Marcus and W. Wang (Eds.): HCII 2019, LNCS 11584, pp. 440–455, 2019.
https://doi.org/10.1007/978-3-030-23541-3_32

aspects: "apology or not" and "humor or neutral". When error occurred, some of them would make an apology, but not in all errors. Besides, when the humor will be showed in error message (e.g. self-deprecating) is unpredictable. Whether a smart speaker would make an apology or not was inconsistent under different error scenarios. Moreover, for a given error scenario, whether or not humor would be showed in the error message (e.g. self-deprecating) was unpredictable.

Coping with errors is a common research topic in HCI. Traditionally, researchers studied how to provide error message effectively to help user recover from errors [4–7], as well as how positive listening, sympathy, encouragement could eliminate the frustration caused by machine [8–12].

But previous studies on response strategies were mostly based on traditional interactions. Responses were mostly presented visually (texts or pictures) and not acoustically. Moreover, smart speakers differed from traditional machines as they are anthropomorphic, and users spontaneously show human-human communication characteristics when interacting with them [13, 14]. Thus, it is worth to explore the users' demand and experience on error response strategies adopted by smart speakers. The present study focused on two aspects, "apology or not" and "humor or neutral", which were consistent with two principles proposed by Suo [15] in human-human interaction, the "courtesy criteria" and the "humor criteria".

In the study, we used the method of "Wizard of Oz". Participants were asked to complete a series of specific tasks on a smart speaker. During the process, they experienced pre-setup conversation errors: when errors occurred, the smart speakers responded in different strategies. The goal of the experiment was to explore the participants' preference of apology and humor. The results of this experiment can provide implications for speech design in voice interaction.

2 Related Work

2.1 Error and Its Impact in HCI

In the process of human-computer interaction, errors such as program crash, delay, no requested results, unexplained problems occur due to factors such as technology, design, and environment etc. When it comes to voice interaction, errors also exist but in different types. In previous studies and our own observations, it was found that errors came from "recognition", "understanding", and "fulfillment" aspects, including "inaccurate recognition of foreign language and dialect", "recognition failure" "unable to understand multiple demands" "no requested audio resource" [2, 7, 16, 17].

Klein [4] concluded that researchers improved user experience by determining and fixing errors, or preventing them from happening in advance. But it was impossible to solve and predict all mistakes because of various environment and users. Instead error message could help user recover from error. Nielsen [5] proposed that a good error message should be polite, precise, and constructive. Starting with a simple and slightly apologetic statement would be necessary for some instances [6].

Errors can easily evoke user's frustrations. Frustration will not only damage user experience during the interaction process, but also jeopardize the long-term willingness to use and trust smart devices. Some researchers proposed that it was crucial to deal with the frustration. Combing emotional management theory, Klein et al. [4] designed an interface agent which could actively "listen" to the users' frustrations caused by computer and "show" empathy. Users' frustrations were alleviated and they were more willing to keep playing the game comparing to those who didn't get affective support. Hone et al. [9, 10] further proved that an embodied agent was more effective, and female agent was better than male agent. Some researchers [12, 18, 19] used the emotion detection module, algorithms or other means to identify user's negative emotions and give emotional support in real time, such as empathy encouragement, to reduce the user's frustration.

In summarize, when errors occur, in addition to trying to solve the problem, coping with frustrations is also important to improve user experience.

2.2 Apology in HCI

In interpersonal communication, an apology is often used to express regret, to mitigate anger caused by offender, to restore relationships, to save one's dignity, and to receive reduced punishment. "Compared to other approaches, such as making excuses, justifying the action, or denying the blame, apologies are perceived as the most trust engendering and sincere manner to resolve interpersonal conflicts and restore harmony, regardless of the severity of the circumstances" [20]. Blum-Kulka & Olshtain [21] proposed that there were five apologizing strategies: (1) an illocutionary force indicating device (IFID; such as, "I'm sorry", "I apologize", or "Excuse me", "I apologize"); (2) an explanation or account; (3) take on responsibility; (4) an offer of repair; (5) a promise of forbearance. And IFID and "take on responsibility" were more universal across different contexts and cultures [22].

Studies about the utility of apologies in human-computer interaction didn't draw any common and unified conclusion. At first, compared to plain computer messages, apologetic messages from computer could be seen as apologies by users [23]. Basing on a study on information retrieval systems, Park et al. [24] revealed that the users perceived the apologetic system as more aesthetically appealing and usable than the neutral or non-apologetic system. Tzeng [23] found that although apology did not improve the overall evaluation of the game, user's psychological experience during the game was better. Akgun [22] further found that an apology made the user feel being respected, and 60% of users thought that a machine should make an apology when it couldn't meet the user's requests. However, Park et al. [20] studied the utility of apologies in voice interaction on television and found that apologies did not significantly increase the positive evaluation on TV. Baylor et al. [25] compared "apology" and "empathy" and found that apologetic message was significantly more believable and sincere than empathetic message. Jaksic et al. [26] conducted a study with the "Wizard of Oz" methodology to evaluate the effectiveness of social agents in reducing user frustration. Participants were divided into different groups to experience different levels of frustration. The social agent apologized (by message) actively when participants showed negative facial expressions. It was found that apology increased the frustration of users with high level frustration, and reduced the frustration of users with moderate level of frustration. De Visser et al. [27] found that making an apology could help to restore trust in the machine.

Summarizing previous studies, it could be concluded that impact of apology was not uniform in improving users' evaluation on machine, but the majority of studies reported that an apology at least improved the experience of the interaction process.

2.3 Humor in HCI

Humor is an important interpersonal communication method. Humor can increase personal attraction, promote relationship, ease embarrassment and break the ice [28]. But humor cannot always bring positive impact for its utility depends on the context. At the same time, cultural diversities, individual differences and other factors have a great impact on the effectiveness of humor [29].

Although humor generally has a positive impact in interpersonal communications, attempts of applying humor in the field of human-computer interaction seem to be cautious. Efficiency is always one of the most important goals pursued by HCI designers, by minimizing task steps and reducing learning time etc. Some researchers believe that humor distracts users' attention and leads to reduction of efficiency during human-computer interaction [30]. Dolen et al. [31] found that for an e-commerce website, the impact of humor was influenced by the process experience and the outcome. In a task of reserving a vacation accommodation on the website, if participants had a good experience during the process but the result did not go well, participants had higher satisfaction and preference for the website with humorous elements, but if the process and the result were both dissatisfying, humor elements had negative impacts. Tzeng [32] found that for an error message on a website, users preferred neutral and apologetic expression, instead of a humorous expression, and humorous expressions were perceived to be unclear and unfriendly.

However, for products with more anthropomorphic and social features, such as virtual agents and robots, studies show that humor might have positive impacts. Morke et al. [30] empowered the machine with the humor character by pre-programming some task-related jokes, and found that the user showed higher affection and greater willingness to cooperate. Khooshabeh et al. [33] thought the pre-programmed conversations in Morke's study were not natural and dynamic enough. Thus, they further improved the natural dialogue capabilities of virtual agents, and found users preferred humorous virtual agents as well. Niculescu et al. [34] found users experienced more pleasure for a humorous service robot, and the findings were confirmed for virtual agents [35, 36]. However, these findings were based on scenarios that focused on conversation and cooperation. For a smart speaker, with which the interactions are strongly task-oriented, the impacts of humor still need to be studied. Niculescu et al. [37] proposed an assumption that when an error occurred in a task-dialogue scenario, a humorous expression might alleviate the stress in the dialogue and make the user be more tolerant of the error, but the assumption still needs to be tested.

3 Method

3.1 Experiment Design

The purpose of the experiment was to explore users' preference over "apology" and "humor". A 2 (*apologize: yes vs. no*) × 2 (*error message expression: humorous vs. neutral*) within-subjects experiment was conducted. Two dependent variables were measured using a 7-point Likert scale: The satisfaction and sincerity of smart speaker's responses.

"I'm sorry" was selected as the apologetic message since it is an effective apology strategy [21]. At the same time, "I'm sorry" is also the most commonly used apology in China. The humorous expressions were chosen from a pilot study.

In the experiment, two common error types were simulated, which were "cannot understand" and "no requested audio resource". "Cannot understand" included situations that voice was detected but not recognized or understood by the agent. "No requested audio resource" meant that demands were correctly recognized and understood, but couldn't be fulfilled because of no copyright of requested music or other audio contents. These two types of errors are frequent. In our previous survey, we found that users were dissatisfied most with these two scenarios, with 89% and 91% of respondents (N = 202) clearly expressing their dissatisfaction. The responses are listed as below (see Tables 1 and 2).

Table 1. The responses under "Cannot understand" error scenario

Apology	Humor	Responses
Yes	Yes	I'm sorry, my IQ is still recharging, please repeat it again
Yes	No	I'm sorry, I didn't understand, please repeat it again
No	Yes	My IQ is still recharging, please repeat it again
No	No	I didn't understand, please repeat it again

Table 2. The responses under "No requested audio resource" error scenario

Apology	Humor	Responses
Yes	Yes	I'm sorry, I haven't nailed the song yet
Yes	No	I'm sorry, I don't have the copyright of the song yet
No	Yes	I haven't nailed the song yet
No	No	I don't have the copyright of the song yet

3.2 Participants

A total of 27 participants (13 male and 14 female) were recruited. The age of these participants ranged from 20 to 45 years (M = 27, SD = 4.48). The participants' experience of smart speaker was balanced. 14 of them reported previous experience with smart speakers (i.e., they had used smart speakers at home in the past three months).

3.3 Tasks

The participants were asked to complete different tasks on a smart speaker. These tasks were selected from four kinds of functions with high usage frequency, namely "listen to music", "listen to audio resource (such as audio lessons), "check the weather" and "set an alarm".

"Cannot understand" Scenario. We generated 3 tasks from each of the functions, which ended up 12 tasks in total. The 3 tasks from same category of function differed in detail. For example, for the function of checking the weather, the 3 tasks were about weather in different places. In daily use, errors will occur now and then. To increase ecological validity, we tried to simulate the real situation. Specifically, participants were asked to complete all 12 tasks and only 4 of them would induce error messages. During the 4 experimental tasks, the smart speaker couldn't understand what the participants said at the first time and respond with an error message. Then the participants tried again and the smart speaker would succeed. Here is an example of "check tomorrow's weather in Shanghai" (wake-up stage was not included):

Participant asked: How is the weather in Shanghai tomorrow?
Smart speaker responded: I'm sorry, my IQ is still recharging, please repeat *it again.*
Participants asked: How is the weather in Shanghai tomorrow?
Smart speaker responded: It's raining tomorrow in Shanghai; the temperature is 11–15 °C.

In order to balance the effect of order, researchers controlled: (1) among the 12 tasks, the 4 failure tasks (experimental conditions) occurred randomly; (2) the 4 failure tasks occurred equally in the four functional types ("check the weather", "listen to the music", "listen to audio resource" and "set an alarm").

"No requested resource" Scenario. We generated 2 tasks from each of the 2 kinds of functions, "listen to music" and "listen to audio resource. The sequence of the 4 tasks was also randomized for each participant. Different from the former scenario, there was only one conversation round in each task. Here is an example of "ask for Mai Sheng Children's story":

Participant asked: I want to listen to Mai Sheng Children's story.
Smart speaker responded: I don't have this copyright of the audio resource yet.

Each task should be perceived by users as equally difficult for the smart speaker to avoid its impact on users' evaluations [26]. To ensure the task difficulty was effectively controlled, we asked the participants to subjectively evaluate the task difficulty (in a 7-point Likert scale) after each task. The question is "How difficult do you think the task is for the smart speaker?" The results of repeated measures ANOVA showed that the difficulty of tasks had no significant difference for both error scenarios ($F(3,63) = 0.058$, $p > 0.05$, $F(3,63) = 0.705$, $p > 0.05$). The results confirmed that the tasks were perceived to be equally difficult for the smart speaker.

3.4 Procedure

The experiment adopted the "Wizard of Oz" methodology. A computer was used to manipulate the response of smart speaker, simulating the human-machine voice interaction process.

The whole experiment process consisted of three parts: First, the participants completed the tasks under the "cannot understand" error scenario and evaluated the response after each task. Then the user completed the tasks under the "no requested audio resource" error scenario, and evaluated the response after each task. Finally, worrying that the participants might pay too much attention to finish tasks and ignore the difference of responses, we asked the participants to evaluate the responses again. In this step, all responses were printed in a paper together so participants could compare directly.

Before the experiment, researchers explained to the participants of the experimental procedure and how to interact with smart speaker with voice. Participants were requested to interact with the smart speaker to familiarize themselves with voice interaction. After that, the formal experimental began.

After each task, the participants were asked to evaluate the difficulty of the task fulfillment they had on the smart speaker. In addition, for the 4 failure tasks (experimental conditions), the participants also needed to answer the following questions: (1) spontaneously recalled the first response (error message) of the smart speaker; (2) perceived satisfaction and sincerity of the response.

After all the tasks, all error messages during the experiment were presented together in print. The participants were asked to evaluate their satisfaction and sincerity again for each error message as they could directly compare the 4 different responses strategies under each error type. Then they were interviewed for reasons of their ratings.

Besides, for the two humorous expressions used in the experiment, participants were asked to evaluate their humor level and semantic accuracy (both in 7-point Likert scale).

3.5 Data Analysis

We used the SPSS 23.0 to analyze the data. First, repeated measures ANOVA was used to check the manipulation result of difficulty. The, we conducted descriptive analysis of all dependent variables. To evaluate the impact of "apology" and "humor", repeated measures ANOVA were used. At the same time, we qualitatively analyzed the recall of error messages, and reasons collected from participants.

4 Result

As explained in part 3.4, "satisfaction" and "sincerity" were measured twice in the experiment: the first time was after each task during the experiment (Natural perception), and the second time was after all the tasks were finished (Direct comparison perception). The results were showed separately.

4.1 "Cannot understand" Error Scenario

Results of Natural Perception
The mean scores of satisfaction and sincerity of 4 different responses are showed as below (see Table 3). Response of "apologetic & neutral expression" was perceived the most satisfied and sincerest. While response of "non-apologetic & humorous expression" was perceived to be least satisfying and sincere.

Table 3. The Mean(*SE*) of responses under "cannot understand" error scenario

	Satisfaction		Sincerity	
	Humorous	Neutral	Humorous	Neutral
Apology	5.04(*1.29*)	5.30(*1.46*)	5.48(*1.58*)	6.15(*0.95*)
No apology	4.78(*1.55*)	5.07(*1.41*)	5.30(*1.71*)	5.59(*1.42*)

Satisfaction. The results of repeated measures ANOVA showed no significant interaction effect between "apology" and "humor" on perceived satisfaction (F (1,26) = 0.016, $p > 0.05$). And there were no main effects on "apology" (F (1,26) = 1.876, $p > 0.05$) and "humor" (F(1,26) = 1.457, $p > 0.05$). This indicated when smart speaker couldn't understand what user said, apologizing and being humorous had no impact on perceived satisfaction.

Sincerity. The results of repeated measures ANOVA showed significant interaction effect between "apology" and "humor" on perceived sincerity (F(1, 26) = 4.319, $p < 0.05$). Further analysis was conducted. When smart speaker made an apology, neutral message was perceived sincerer than humorous message (F(1, 26) = 5.032, $p < 0.05$). When smart speaker didn't make an apology, being humor or not had no significant impact (F(1, 26) = 0.815, $p > 0.05$). This indicated when smart speaker made an apology, neutral response could significantly improve perceived sincerity.

Results of Direct Comparison Perception
The mean scores of satisfaction and sincerity of 4 different responses are showed as below (see Table 4). Response of "apologetic & neutral expression" was perceived the most satisfied and sincerest. While response of "non-apologetic & humorous expression" was perceived the lowest satisfied and sincerest.

Table 4. The Mean(*SE*) of responses under "cannot understand" error scenario

	Satisfaction		Sincerity	
	Humorous	Neutral	Humorous	Neutral
Apology	5.04(*1.65*)	5.63(*1.21*)	5.37(*1.80*)	6.22(*0.97*)
No apology	4.56(*1.67*)	4.89(*1.28*)	4.85(*1.77*)	5.48(*1.19*)

Satisfaction. The results of repeated measures ANOVA showed no significant interaction between “apology” and “humor” on perceived satisfaction (F(1,26) = 1.874, $p > 0.05$). There was main effect of apology on perceived satisfaction (F(1,26) = 15.730, $p < 0.01$)”, but the main effect of humor didn’t exist (F(1,26) = 1.930, $p > 0.05$). This indicated when smart speaker had no requested audio resource, apologizing could improve perceived satisfaction, and being humorous had no impact.

Sincerity. The results of repeated measures ANOVA showed no significant interaction between “apology” and “humor” on perceived sincerity (F(1, 26) = 2.208, $p > 0.05$). There was main effect of “apology” and “humor” on perceived sincerity (F (1,26) = 18.809, $p < 0.001$)”, (F(1,26) = 5.955, $p < 0.05$). This indicated when smart speaker had no requested audio resource, apologizing could improve perceived sincerity, and humor had negative impact on perceived sincerity.

4.2 “No requested audio resource” Error Scenario

Results of Natural Perception

The mean scores of satisfaction and sincerity of 4 different responses are showed as below (see Table 5). Apologetic responses had higher satisfied and sincere scores.

Table 5. The Mean*(SE)* of responses under “no requested audio resource” error scenario

	Satisfaction		Sincerity	
	Humorous	Neutral	Humorous	Neutral
Apology	5.52*(1.50)*	5.52*(1.40)*	6.11*(1.01)*	6.11*(1.12)*
No apology	5.44*(1.48)*	5.41*(1.53)*	5.78*(1.48)*	5.85*(1.38)*

Satisfaction. The results of repeated measures ANOVA showed no significant interaction between “apology” and “humor” on perceived satisfaction (F(1,26) = 0.031, $p > 0.05$). And there were no main effects on apology (F(1,26) = 0.308, $p > 0.05$) and humor (F(1,26) = 0.010, $p > 0.05$). This indicated when smart speaker had no requested audio resource, apologizing and being humorous had no impact on perceived satisfaction.

Sincerity. The results of repeated measures ANOVA showed no significant interaction effect between “apology” and “humor” on perceived sincerity (F(1,26) = 0.325, $p > 0.05$). There was main effect of apology (F(1,26) = 4.522, $p < 0.05$)”, and the main effect of humor didn’t exist (F(1,26) = 0.032, $p > 0.05$). This indicated when smart speaker had no requested audio resource, apologizing could improve perceived sincerity, and humor had no impact.

Results of Direct Comparison Perception

The mean scores of satisfaction and sincerity of 4 different responses are showed as below (see Table 6). Apologetic response had higher satisfaction and sincerity scores.

Table 6. The Mean(*SE*) of responses under "no requested audio resource" error scenario

	Satisfaction		Sincerity	
	Humorous	Neutral	Humorous	Neutral
Apology	5.81(*1.04*)	5.63(*0.93*)	6.11(*0.97*)	6.11(*0.89*)
No apology	4.89(*1.28*)	4.81(*1.18*)	5.44(*1.42*)	5.48(*1.12*)

Satisfaction. The results of repeated measures ANOVA showed no significant interaction between "apology" and "humor" on perceived satisfaction (F(1,26) = 0.382, $p > 0.05$). There was main effect of "apology" on perceived satisfaction (F(1,26) = 26.202, $p < 0.001$)", but the main effect of humor didn't exist (F(1,26) = 0.554, $p > 0.05$)". This indicated when smart speaker had no requested audio resource, apologizing could improve perceived satisfaction and being humorous had no impact.

Sincerity. The results of repeated measures ANOVA showed no significant interaction between "apology" and "humor" on perceived sincerity (F(1, 26) = 0.088, $p > 0.05$). There was main effect of "apology" on perceived sincerity (F(1,26) = 20.469, $p < 0.001$), but the main effect of "humor" didn't exist (F(1,26) = 0.014, $p > 0.05$). This indicated when smart speaker had no requested audio resource, apologizing could improve perceived sincerity and being humorous had no impact.

The results indicated when smart speaker had no requested audio resource, making an apology could improve the perception of satisfaction and sincerity, but the humor had no impact on both aspects.

4.3 Results Summary

In general, descriptive statistics results of natural perception and direct comparisons showed same tendencies. However, there were more significant results in the direct comparisons (see Tables 7 and 8). The results showed that for both error scenarios, making an apology could improve perceived satisfaction and sincerity. Humor had least positive impact on perceived satisfaction and sincerity, and even had negative impact when the smart speaker could not understand users' requests.

Table 7. Summary of significance differences tests under "Cannot understand" scenario

	Natural perception		Direct comparison perception	
	Satisfaction	Sincerity	Satisfaction	Sincerity
Interaction effect	No	**Yes**	No	No
Main effect of apology	No	No	**Yes**	**Yes**
Main effect of humor	No	No	No	**Yes**

Table 8. Summary of significance difference tests under "No requested audio resource" scenario

	Natural perception		Direct comparison perception	
	Satisfaction	Sincerity	Satisfaction	Sincerity
Interaction effect	No	No	No	No
Main effect of apology	No	**Yes**	**Yes**	**Yes**
Main effect of humor	No	No	No	No

5 Discussion

5.1 Natural Perception vs. Direct Comparison Perception

In the experiment, "Satisfaction" and "Sincerity" were measured twice: the first time was after each task during the experiment (Natural perception), and the second time was after all the tasks were finished (Direct comparison perception). To do the direct comparison, all the responses were printed and presented together to the participants. It was found that users' evaluation differed greatly in perceptions. (see Tables 7 and 8).

Analysis of post-experiment interviews demonstrated our pre-experimental speculations. First, in the experiment environment, participants were more focused on whether the tasks were finished. When an error occurred, they allocated most cognition resources to comprehend what error message conveyed rather than to pay attention to how the error message was expressed. Second, the four failure tasks were given in a random sequence during the whole process, and the participants evaluated one response at a time. But during the direct comparison, all the responses were presented to users together so the participants could recognize the difference and make a rational evaluation at this time.

5.2 Attitude Toward Apology

When error occurred, an apology from the smart speaker made participants feel more satisfied and sincerer. In the post-experiment interviews, 21 participants preferred smart speaker making an apology. And 4 participants thought it didn't matter whether it apologized or not. Analysis of participants' reviews showed there were mainly four reasons.

(1) *An apology showed smart speaker's friendliness and politeness, which alleviated the perception of dissatisfaction.*
(2) *The apology attributed the responsibility to the smart speaker.* This opinion was consisted with acknowledged effect of apology [20], which, at the meantime, let participants feel less frustrated sometimes by proving they didn't do wrong [31].
(3) *Making apology attitude was educational for children.* In China, children are one of the important user groups of smart speaker. Many parents said that the smart

speaker was a playmate for their child. But they worried the smart speaker may teach the children to be rude, which seemed to be a global concern [38]. So, this is important reason why smart speak should apologize.

(4) *The apology could be seen as a signal of an error.* Participants said that "I'm sorry" prompted them to concentrate quickly and to comprehend the error message. This could improve the interaction efficiency and make the process smoother. To some extent, the finding was in line with Zillmann's study [39]. His found that humorous stimuli increased subjects' attentiveness and helped to acquit information ultimately.

Only 2 participants expressed reluctance on receiving apologies, concerning the apology made the smart speaker sound verbose, especially when the error message was long. In a task-oriented dialogue process, participants indicated that they needed to know why error happened quickly, so that they could adjust dialogue strategy to achieve the ultimate intention.

Generally, making an apology could improve user experience when a smart speaker triggers users' dissatisfaction. But an apology increased the length of error message and conveyed humble attitude. A perfect apologetic error message should be clear, simple, and modest but not humble.

5.3 Attitude Toward Humor

Our results indicated that compared with neutral response, humorous response did not get a higher score in perceived satisfaction and sincerity. And when a smart speaker couldn't understand, the humorous response reduced the its sincerity. Half of the participants (13 out of 27) clearly expressed dislikes towards the humorous expression. Analysis of participants' reviews showed there were mainly six reasons.

(1) *Individual differences in perception of humor.* Though the two humorous responses used in this experiment got higher score of humor in the pre-experimental test, there were still 29.6% and 25.9% of participants respectively perceived no humor. This consistent with other research's findings [29].

(2) *Humor required more literal comprehension which could be a barrier of understanding.* The use of humor in human-machine interaction has always been controversial. One of the main reasons is the impact on efficiency. Most humorous expressions used by smart speaker in China are from internet. Not everyone is familiar with them.

(3) *Humorous expressions were prone to be ambiguous.* Although most participants in this study accurately understood the meaning of the response, they still expressed their concerns.

(4) *Humor reduced the perceived responsibility of smart speaker.* The participants thought the smart speaker was perfunctory and prevaricated when responded wittily. In the experiment, that also the reason why humorous expression was less sincere under "cannot understand" error.

5) *Humorous expression might be hard to be understood by children.* As mentioned before, children are an important group of users in China. Some parents worried

that humors in error messages could be a barrier to understand smart devices for children because of their immature cognitive ability.

(6) *Repeated humor tended to be boring.* Although each humorous expression was repeated only once in this experiment, some participants still reported that the humorous expression lost sense of freshness the second time it appeared.

13 participants had positive comments on humorous expression, mainly because humor made the smart speaker more interesting, lovable, more emotional and vitality.

Researchers believe that when a smart speaker triggers user dissatisfaction, responding in a humorous way should be carefully considered. As discussed above, humor had certain disadvantages in terms of attitude, efficiency and enjoyment. Considering the attitude, inappropriate humor could easily lead to irresponsible, slick impressions humorous voice-feedback could easily create an assistant image quite irresponsible and flippant, especially when it couldn't achieve the users' simple request. Secondly, humorous responses might decrease the efficiency of voice interaction because of misinterpreting, culture barrier, impaired ability etc. Finally, perceptions about humor varied by age, social group and culture. Therefore, the accuracy, readability and universality of humor should be taken into account when designing humorous response.

6 Implication

Theoretical value could be found in this study. It could be verified that when a user was in a negative mood of dissatisfaction, the response with emotional mood was more preferred by the user. Indeed, the emotional response is friendly, but its content should not be too casual. Therefore, a response with an apology was more favored. And a humorous message feels no better than a neutral one.

Practical value could also be found in this study. On one hand, the results of this experiment provided a valuable VUI response strategy that the "apology & neutral" response was more preferred. On the other hand, the qualitative results in this experiment found the suggestions and guides of response wordings. For example, the length and attitudes were critical for apology phrases, and they should sound modest, instead of humble. When design humorous response, the accurate meanings, easy to understanding, and the sense of humor were universal and important principles.

7 Limitations and Future Study

The limitations and prospects for future research of this study can be concluded as below. Firstly, due to multi-tasks were assigned to each participant, task evaluation might be easily affected by the degree of achievement in previous tasks although each respondent was instructed to treat each experimental task as an independent task and dialogue. Random tasks had been assigned to reduce this impact, the mutual interference among the tasks was still not been ruled out. To improve this, the experimental designed by crossing occasions among respondents or by collecting the users daily real human-machine dialogue data (with acknowledgement and agreement) can be employed for analysis and study. Secondly, this study mainly focused on frustrations caused by smart speakers in the first round of dialogue. For future study, it is necessary to investigate repeatedly frustrations in which negative moods of users may deepen and lead to more dissatisfactions because of unresolved key needs. Thirdly, this study did not explore the impacts from different task occasion, respondents' background and characteristics and the relationships between users and device. For future studies, they can be explored more on responding theory. Finally, this study focused on smart speakers' best response strategy for users' frustrations. For future studies, we can explore on more different devices, such as smart navigation system, smart television, and smart mobile voice assistant.

8 Conclusion

The findings of this study are listed below: (1) Apology response from smart devices significantly increased users' perception of sincerity, and it prominently improved both satisfaction and sincerity under direct comparison perception. (2) The factor of humor in responses had no impact on the perception of satisfaction and sincerity, but it can observably decrease the perception of sincerity when the smart speaker could not understand users' requests. Therefore, when smart speakers trigger users' dissatisfactions, an apologetic and neutral response may be the best way to present.

References

1. IDC. Smart Home Devices by Category, 2018 and 2022. https://www.idc.com/getdoc.jsp?containerId=prUS44361618. Accessed 1 Oct 2018
2. Pyae, A., Joelsson, T.N.: Investigating the usability and user experiences of voice user interface: a case of Google home smart speaker. In: Proceedings of the 20th International Conference on Human-Computer Interaction with Mobile Devices and Services Adjunct (MobileHCI 2018), pp. 127–131. ACM, New York (2016)
3. Gao, Y., Pan, Z., Wang, H., Chen, G.: Alexa, My love: analyzing reviews of Amazon echo. In: 2018 IEEE Smart World, Ubiquitous Intelligence & Computing, Advanced & Trusted Computing, Scalable Computing & Communications, Cloud & Big Data Computing, Internet of People and Smart City Innovation, pp. 372–380. IEEE Press, New York (2018)
4. Nielsen, J.: Error message guidelines. http://www.useit.com/alertbox/20010624.html. Accessed 24 Jun 2001
5. Neilsen, J.: Improving the Dreaded 404 Error Message. https://www.nngroup.com/articles/improving-dreaded-404-error-message/. Accessed 14 Jun 1998
6. Bargas-Avila, J.A., Brenzikofer, O., Roth, S.P., Tuch, A.N., Orsini, S., Opwis, K.: Simple but crucial user interfaces in the world wide web: introducing 20 guidelines for usable web form design. In: Matrai, R. (ed.) User Interfaces. InTech (2010)
7. Bargas-Avila, J.A., Oberholzer, G., Schmutz, P., de Vito, M., Opwis, K.: Usable error message presentation in the world wide web: do not show errors right away. Interact. Comput. **19**(3), 330–341 (2007)
8. Klein, J., Moon, Y., Picard, R.W.: This computer responds to user frustration: theory, design, and results. Interact. Comput. **14**(2), 119–140 (2002)

9. Hone, K., Aktar, F., Saffu, M.: Affective agents to reduce user frustration: the role of agent embodiment. In: Proceedings of Human-Computer Interaction (HCI 2003), Bath, UK (2003)
10. Hone, K.: Empathic agents to reduce user frustration: the effects of varying agent characteristics. Interact. Comput. **18**(2), 227–245 (2006)
11. Feigenblat, G., Konopnicki, D., Shmueli-Scheuer, M., Herzig, J., Shkedi, H.: I understand your frustration. In: Proceedings of the 19th ACM Conference on Computer Supported Cooperative Work and Social Computing Companion, pp. 25–28. ACM, New York (2016)
12. Rajendran, R., Iyer, S., Murthy, S.: Personalized affective feedback to address students' frustration in ITS. IEEE Trans. Learn. Technol., 1 (2018)
13. Purington, A., Taft, J.G., Sannon, S., Bazarova, N.N., Taylor, S.H.: Alexa is my new BFF: social roles, user satisfaction, and personification of the amazon echo. In: Proceedings of the 2017 CHI Conference Extended Abstracts on Human Factors in Computing Systems, pp. 2853–2859. ACM, New York (2017)
14. Lopatovska, I., Williams, H.: Personification of the Amazon Alexa: BFF or a mindless companion. In: Proceedings of the 2018 Conference on Human Information Interaction & Retrieval, pp. 265–268. ACM, New York (2018)
15. Suo, Z.Y.: Pragmatics in Chinese: A Course Book. Beijing University Press, Beijing (2000)
16. Luger, E., Sellen, A.: "Like Having a Really Bad PA": the Gulf between user expectation and experience of conversational agents. In: Proceedings of the 2016 CHI Conference on Human Factors in Computing Systems, pp. 5286–5297. ACM, New York (2016)
17. Myers, C., Furqan, A., Nebolsky, J., Caro, K., Zhu, J.: Patterns for how users overcome obstacles in voice user interfaces. In: Proceedings of the 2018 CHI Conference on Human Factors in Computing Systems, p. 6. ACM, New York (2018)
18. Prendinger, H., Ishizuka, M.: The empathic companion: a character-based interface that addresses users' affective states. Appl. Artif. Intell. **19**(3–4), 267–285 (2005)
19. Woolf, B., Burleson, W., Arroyo, I., Dragon, T., Cooper, D., Picard, R.: Affect-aware tutors: recognizing and responding to student affect. Int. J. Learn. Technol. **4**(3–4), 129–164 (2009)
20. Park, E.K., Lee, K.M., Shin, D.H.: Social responses to conversational TV VUI: apology and voice. Int. J. Technol. Hum. Interact. **11**(1), 17–32 (2015)
21. Blum-Kulka, S., Olshtain, E.: Requests and apologies: a cross-cultural study of speech act realization patterns (CCSARP). Appl. Linguist. **5**(3), 196–213 (1984)
22. Akgun, M., Cagiltay, K., Zeyrek, D.: The effect of apologetic error messages and mood states on computer users' self-appraisal of performance. J. Pragmat. **42**(9), 2430–2448 (2010)
23. Tzeng, J.Y.: Toward a more civilized design: studying the effects of computers that apologize. Int. J. Hum. Comput. Stud. **61**(3), 319–345 (2004)
24. Park, S.J., MacDonald, C.M., Khoo, M.: Do you care if a computer says sorry? User experience design through affective messages. In: Proceedings of the Designing Interactive Systems Conference, pp. 731–740. ACM, New York (2012)
25. Baylor, A.L., Warren, D., Park, C.H., Shen, E., Perez, R.: The impact of frustration-mitigating messages delivered by an interface agent. In: Artificial Intelligence in Education: Supporting Learning through Intelligent and Socially Informed Technology, vol. 125, pp. 73–79. IOS Press, Amsterdam (2005)
26. Jaksic, N., Branco, P., Stephenson, P., Encarnaçao, L.M.: The effectiveness of social agents in reducing user frustration. In: CHI 2006 Extended Abstracts on Human Factors in Computing Systems, pp. 917–922. ACM, New York (2006)
27. de Visser, E.J., Monfort, S.S., McKendrick, R., Smith, M.A., McKnight, P.E., Krueger, F., Parasuraman, R.: Almost human: anthropomorphism increases trust resilience in cognitive agents. J. Exp. Psychol. Appl. **22**(3), 331 (2016)

28. Nijholt, A.: From word play to world play: introducing humor in human-computer interaction. In: Proceedings of the 36th European Conference on Cognitive Ergonomics, p. 1. ACM, New York (2018)
29. Nijholt, A., Niculescu, A.I., Valitutti, A., Banchs, R.E.: Humor in human computer interaction. A short survey. In: Adjunct Proceedings of INTERACT 2017, pp. 192–214. IDC, Indian Institute of Technology, Bombay, India (2017)
30. Morkes, J., Kernal, H.K., Nass, C.: Effects of humor in task-oriented human–computer interaction and computer-mediated communication: a direct test of SRCT theory. Hum. Comput. Interact. **14**, 395–435 (1999)
31. Dolen, W.M., Ruyter, K., Streukens, S.: The effect of humor in electronic service encounters. J. Econ. Psychol. **29**(2), 160–179 (2008)
32. Tzeng, J.Y.: Matching users' diverse social scripts with resonating humanized features to create a polite interface. Int. J. Hum. Comput. Stud. **64**(12), 1230–1242 (2006)
33. Khooshabeh, P., McCall, C., Gandhe, S., Gratch, J., Blascovich, J.: Does it matter if a computer jokes. In: CHI 2011 Extended Abstracts on Human Factors in Computing Systems, pp. 77–86. ACM, New York (2011)
34. Niculescu, A.I., van Dijk, B., Nijholt, A., Li, H., See, S.L.: Making social robots more attractive the effects of voice pitch, humor and empathy. Int. J. Soc. Robot. **5**(2), 171–191 (2013)
35. Niculescu, A., Banchs, R.: Humor intelligence for virtual agents. In: Ninth International Workshop on Spoken Dialogue Systems Technology (IWSDS 2018), Singapore, vol. 1 (2018)
36. Dybala, P., Ptaszynski, M., Rzepka, R., Araki, K.: Humoroids: conversational agents that induce positive emotions with humor. In: Proceedings of the 8th International Conference on Autonomous Agents and Multiagent Systems, vol. 2, pp. 1171–1172. International Foundation for Autonomous Agents and Multiagent Systems (2009)
37. Niculescu, A.I., Banchs, R.E.: Strategies to cope with errors in human-machine spoken interactions: using chatbots as back-off mechanism for task-oriented dialogues. In: Proceedings of ERRARE, Sinaia, Romania (2015)
38. BBC News. Amazon Alexa: is it friends with your kids? https://www.bbc.com/news/technology-44847184. Accessed 16 Jul 2016
39. Zillmann, D., Williams, B.R., Bryant, J., Boynton, K.R., Wolf, M.A.: Acquisition of information from educational television programs as a function of differently paced humorous inserts. J. Educ. Psychol. **72**(2), 170 (1980)

Storytelling Research of Virtual Image Based on User Experience

Jing Li[(✉)] and Ling Zou

Digital Media School, Beijing Film Academy, Beijing 100088, China
{lijinglib, zouling}@bfa.edu.cn

Abstract. The VR image not only has the watching characteristic of movie, the immersion of drama and the interaction of game, but also its unique conception. At present, a new type of narrative mode adapted to VR image features has not yet reached a consensus. The purpose of this paper is to analyze the importance of research on the user experience to VR image creation, so as to point out the urgency of using iterative thinking in creating works, at the same time, to explore the possibility of collaborative creation by utilizing the creators and users of intelligent tool. The key to construct a narrative systematic frame which accords with the VR image's characteristics of visual, audition, touch, taste and touch is put forward. This paper adopts the methods of qualitative research, which includes desktop research and network user research as well as the quantitative researches, so as to conduct the validation studies about the habit, feeling, expectation and participation of users when they experience VR image. Finally, the conception of narrative systematic framework that is suitable for VR image and the suggestions for future research direction are put forward.

Keywords: Virtual image · Storytelling research · User experience

1 Introduction

With the innovative development of narrative theory and practice in the digital age, many related terms have emerged continuously, such as Cyberspace, Database Cinema, Post-plot Cinema, Participatory Audiences, Transmedia Storytelling, Synergistic Storytelling, Textual Poacher, Participatory Culture, Convergence Culture, Interactive Narrative, Cinema 3.0, All-encompassing Interactive Digital Medium, Viewers, AI Narrative and so on. The theoretical research of virtual image narrative is to think and summarize the newly emerging problems existing in film creation practice in time. At the present stage, the research on VR image narrative mainly focuses on discussing the difference between traditional film and the VR image. The discussion about view concentrates on the condition that when all of the following aspects become insignificant, for example, the "push, pull, swing, shift, follow" of camera's movement, the "full view, distant view, middle view, close view, close-up shot, extreme close-up" of scenes, the depth of field conversion of focal length, the "out of picture" and "in the picture" of actors and the audiovisual language like "montage", how to continue to innovate new narrative methods based on the traditional movies, there is little consensus at this stage. During the past ten years, the narrative characteristic, focus and

A. Marcus and W. Wang (Eds.): HCII 2019, LNCS 11584, pp. 456–470, 2019.
https://doi.org/10.1007/978-3-030-23541-3_33

mode of VR image have changed, while the audiences of VR image have changed even more. VR image has broken through the boundary restrictions of traditional movies and constructs virtual space, so that giving the audience a strong sense of presence. Michael Heym, an American scholar, firstly proposed three features of virtual reality in his famous book From Interface to Cyberspace: Metaphysics of Virtual Reality, that is, immersion, interaction and imagination. Therefore, the focus of VR image narrative will shift from "story" and "narration" to "environment" and "interaction", and the focus of creation will shift from the design of "narration" to the interactive environment the narration happens, that is, the design of "narrative space". However, the audience in the world of VR image embodies a great degree of "autonomy". Users can walk into the scene of VR image and then looking at any angle around you, in addition, the users also can interact with person or thing in the scene and create a storyline that belongs to the specific personality, so as to recreate personal life, personal experience in the process of virtual experience.

VR image based on user experience need to establish the creative thinking that is centered by user experience. The goal of VR image creators should always be located on the position of verifying the creation process from a user's point of view, rather than from a hypothetical perspective. The creator creates a typical user model by observing the behavior of audiences and listening to the attitudes as well as the viewpoints, thus drawing PERSONA, discovering and meeting the needs of users, optimizing the interactive design, and enhancing the user experience, so as to realize the goal of creation. The narrative of VR image should always be a continuous process, and the creators should adopt the systematic and iterative thinking to create the narrative of VR image. Making use of Deliberated Narrative, firstly, creators set a "story goal", then the users participate in this frame and tell different stories by adopting different strategies at will. Simulation-based Approaches can also be used by different types of users according to their own characteristics, so that letting them participate in telling their own stories. The creation of VR image should break the traditional boundary between creator and user, which is no longer the relationship between creation and watching. Users should also be given the possibility to participate in creation. Through the expectation and experience on VR image, the users' creative passion can be stimulated, so as to realize their own creative expression on the basis of narrative content provided by the creators. Through the continuous enrichment and perfection made by creators, this kind of expression put forward by the users can form new narrative content, which is connected and intertwined with each other, thus constructing a dynamic growth of story community at last. The creators and the audiences also have established a new relationship mode of collaborative creation. There is not only the watching characteristic of movies with VR image, but also the immersion of dramas and the interaction of games, at the same time, the VR image also has their own unique conception. Therefore, based on the characteristics of VR image, user experience research, iterative creative thinking, collaborative creation mode and intelligent tool, the research goal of this paper is to construct a narrative systematic frame that in accordance with the characteristics of visual, audition, touch, taste and touch with VR image.

This paper is composed of Third parts. First of all, I adopt the method of desktop research to collect papers that are related to VR narrative, conducting interviews of creators who create VR masterpieces, at the same time, I also summarize industry reports and network data, so as to probe into the narrative method and narrative characteristics of VR image works at the present stage. Secondly, through the network questionnaire survey of VR image users, quantitative studies on the motivation, habit and expectation of users to experience VR image. Thirdly, this paper selects the Chinese VR film "The Dream Collector" as the empirical research object, adopting the usability test method to carry on the field observation and the interview to VR users' experience, qualitative studies on the motivation, habit and expectation of users to experience VR image as well as the possibility of participating in the creation. Several methods of combining analysis, investigation and usability tests are used to study the related researching points, so the reliability of the verification is ensured by verifying the same researching point through the results of different methods. At last, the frame of narrative system for VR image and suggestion for future research are put forward.

2 Research on Motivation, Habit and Expectation of VR Image Users

2.1 Experimental Design

(1) Experimental objective and significance.
The research aims to understand the key factors that affect the experience of VR image users, and to explore the motivation, demand as well as expectation of the user experience, so as to provide validation support and reference for the research of VR image narrative systematic frame.
(2) Questionnaire design and distribution.
There are 19 questions in total, of which objective questions (16) subjective questions (3). All of the questions are divided into the following eight parts in accordance with the aspect of investigation, that is, watching (3), narration (3), experience (4), interaction (3), attention (6), motivation (1), demand (1), expectation (1).
(3) Experimental conditions and procedures.
The online investigation service platform is used to create questionnaires, distribute questionnaires, retrieve questionnaires, export data, analyze data and write reports.

2.2 Data Analysis

(1) Watching.

Data are showing in Figs. 1 and 2.

The users want to experience the perspectives of first person and the third person, even the second person, so as to play different roles from different perspectives to enhance the feeling of immersion and freshness in image.

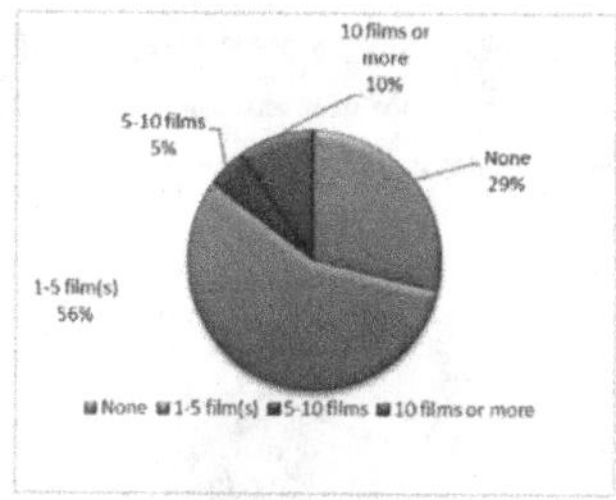

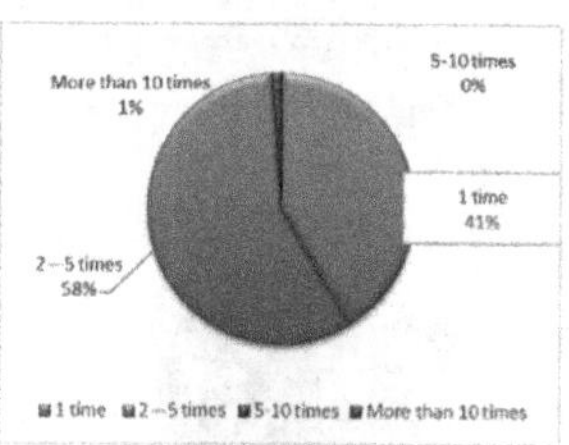

Fig. 1. How many VR films have you seen? And how many times do you watch a VR film?

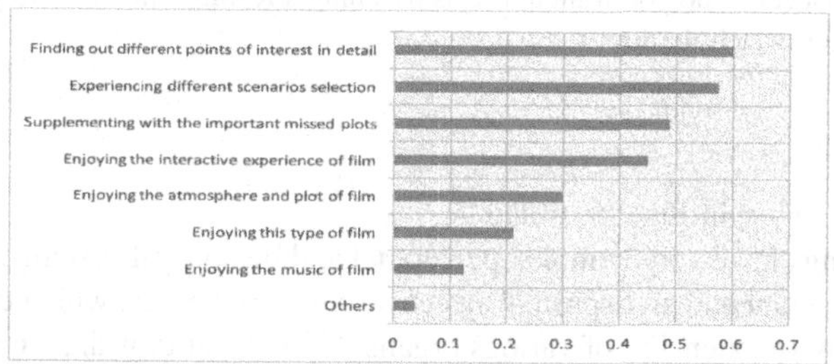

Fig. 2. What is the purpose of watching the same VR film for many times? (multiple choices)

(2) Narration.

Data are showing in Figs. 3 and 4.

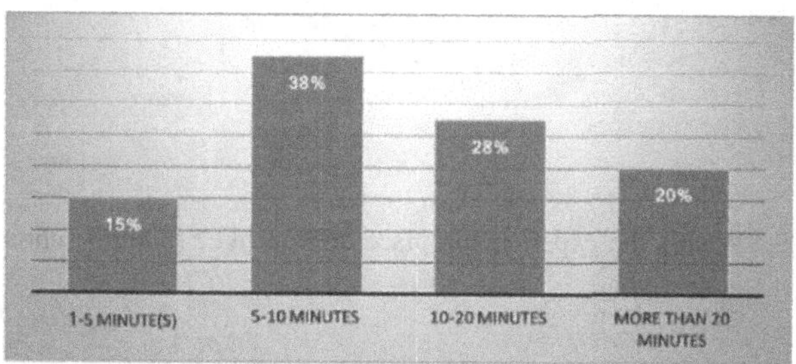

Fig. 3. How long do you think VR movies should last?

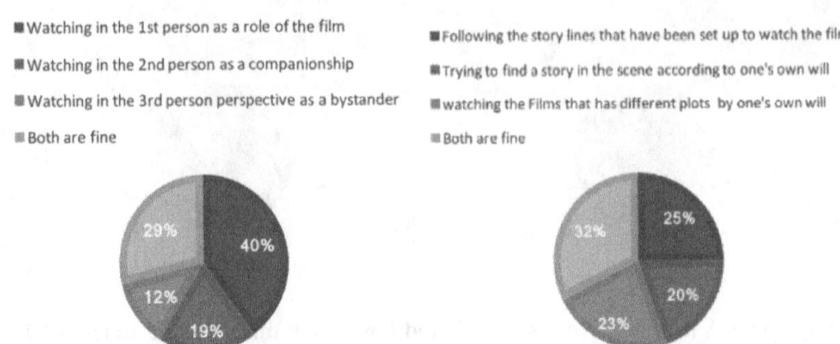

Fig. 4. What perspective do you want to use as watching VR film? And how do you want to see the story when you watch the film?

(3) Experience.

Data are showing in Figs. 5, 6 and 7.

Human beings have very complex perceptual and behavioral systems, while the VR image extends the mental and spiritual systems of human beings, which can be thought as a comprehensive extension of various organs. Users want to walk, sit, run, touch the narrative contents, they want to experience the unprecedented new feeling brought about by the integration between virtual and reality.

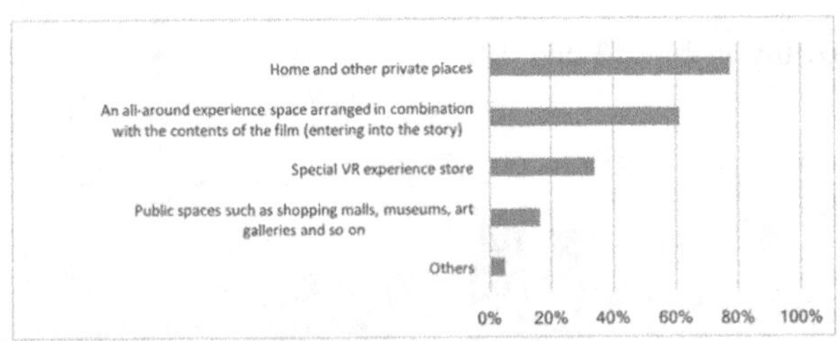

Fig. 5. What's the experiencing place do you like? (multiple choices)

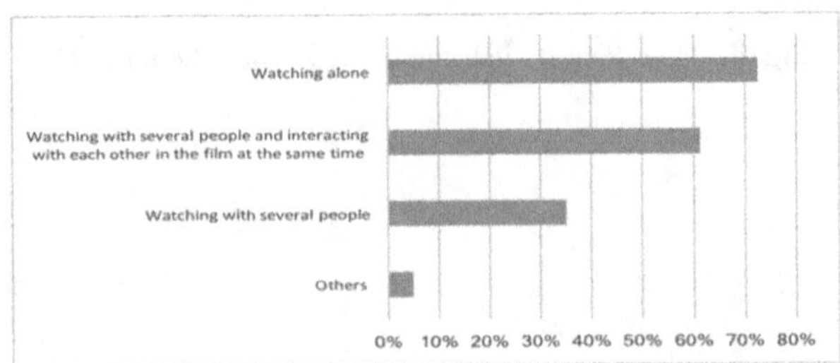

Fig. 6. What is your favorite way to watch? (multiple choices)

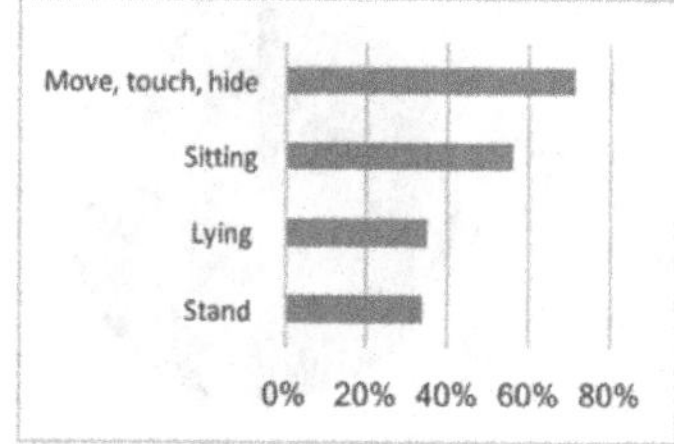

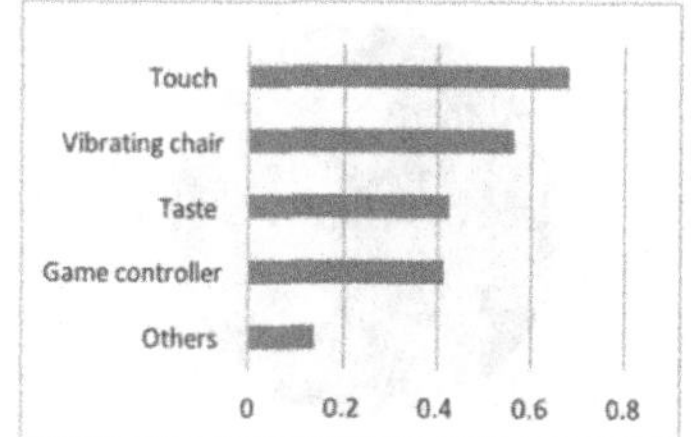

Fig. 7. Do you like the process of watching VR (multiple choices)? And what other multiple dimensions for experience do you want to add in VR film in addition to the audiovisual experience? (multiple choices)

(4) Interaction.

Data are showing in Fig. 8.

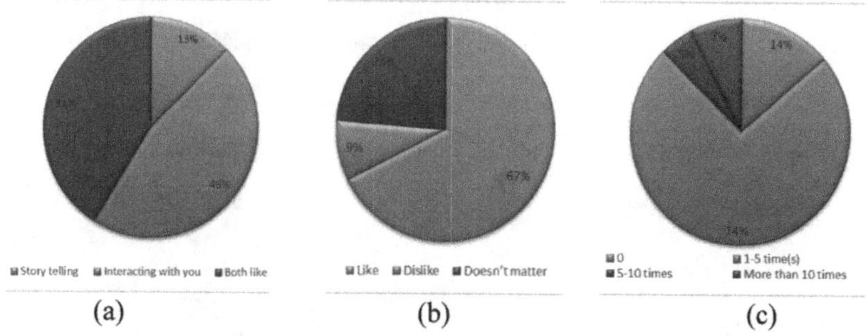

Fig. 8. (a) When you watch VR film, do you prefer the story telling or the interaction with you? (b) Do you like to be able to choose different development scenarios in the process of watching film? (c) What type of VR film do you like? (multiple choices)

(5) Attention.

Data are showing in Figs. 9, 10 and 11.

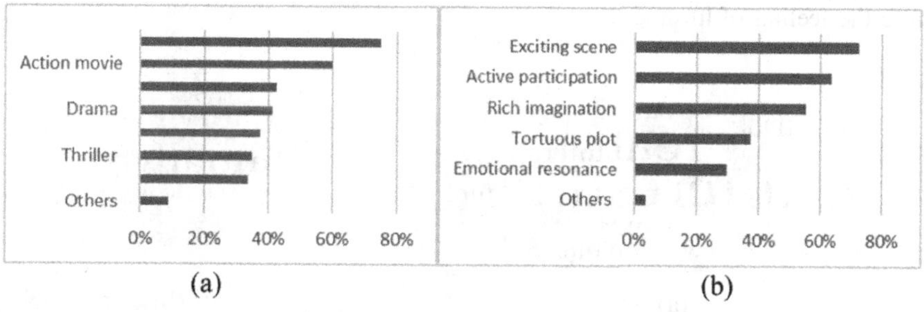

Fig. 9. (a) What type of VR film do you like? (multiple choices) (b) What are the features of VR film that appeal to you more? (multiple choices)

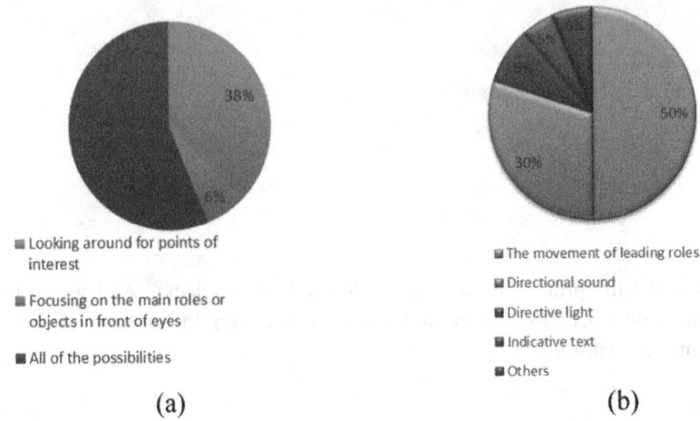

Fig. 10. (a) What do you do first when you wear the helmet into the scene of film? (b) Which is the most attractive factor during the process of watching the film?

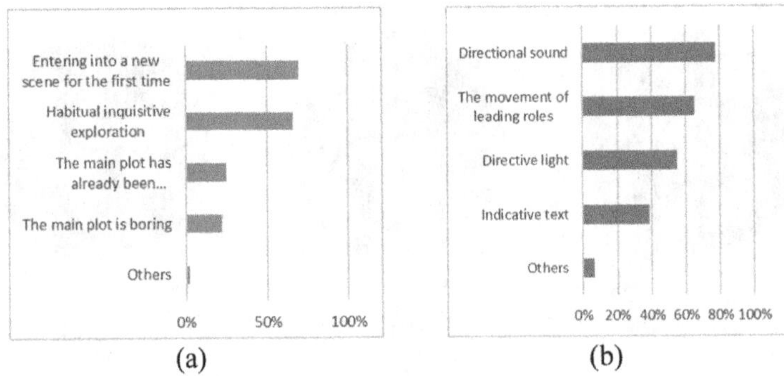

Fig. 11. (a) When you watch the VR film, under what circumstances do you take the initiative to observe the environment and discover the details? (multiple choices) (b) Which is the attractive factor during the process of watching the film? (multiple choices)

(6) Exploring the user's motivations: why do you want to experience VR film?

As shown in Fig. 12(a), these key words have been mentioned for many times: curiosity, fun, new technology, being personally on the scene, shock and surprise before the feeling of freshness.

Fig. 12. Keyword cloud map of user motivation and user's demands

(7) Exploring the user's demands: what will attract you in VR film?

As shown in Fig. 12(b), these key words have been mentioned for many times: scene, interaction, plot, creativity, immersion, lifelike, story, creativity, being concerned.

(8) Exploring the user's expectations: what do you want from the VR experience?

As shown in Fig. 13, these key words have been mentioned for many times: sense of reality, feeling of freshness, being personally on the scene, interaction, happiness, more sensory experience, excitement, cool, craziness, pleasure, experience that is different from reality.

Fig. 13. Keyword cloud map of user motivation and user's expectations

2.3 Experimental Summary

(1) The user's demand for watching more than once verifies the necessity of adopting iterative method in VR image creation.
(2) The user's attitude towards content reflects user's needs to enjoy freedom and be guided in virtual reality.
(3) The user's demand for experience expresses the user's desire for a better immersive sense through multiple sensory experience.
(4) The user's choice of factors that influence attention verifies the effectiveness of guiding attention conducted by creator.
(5) The user's choice of interaction expresses the user's desire for multiple ways of interaction, at the same time, it also shows user's willingness to actively participate in the story, which verifies the feasibility of collaboration between the creator and the user.

3 Research on the Audience Availability of "The Dream Collector"

3.1 Experimental Design

(1) Selection basis and analysis of the film

"The Dream Collector (2017)" produced by Pinta Studios and directed by Mi Li is selected as an object of empirical research. This film tells a story about chasing, giving up and regaining dream and it is shortlisted in the main competition unit of VR in the 74th Venice International Film Festival. The roles in film are designed for two leading roles and two supporting roles, what's more, 4 scenes (general environment ahead and below the viaduct, inside the house of old man, inside the house of youth and the secret space) are built. The development of the story's plot is to guide the audience to experience the four scenes in 7 times through the setting of "scene props", the fade-in and fade-out arrangement as well as the reverse use of Spotlight Scope. Before and after the conversion of each scene, the design of camera location is used to ensure that the audience can pay attention to the leading role's performance in main visual area when entering the next scene. The sound effect of this film is produced by the sound effect designer Chen Guang, who is "specially employed by Wang Jiawei". The sound effect is designed to guide the audiences' attention for many times. The soundtrack of 5 originally created films, "Dreams", "Opening Title", "Seasons Montage", "Christmas Time", "Ending Credits" are created by Guo Hao, a famous composer, so as to set off the whole atmosphere and guide the attention of audience.

(2) Experimental purpose and significance

The purpose of this experiment is to explore whether the various kinds of narrative methods used in the VR image "The Dream Collector" can bring the audience experience of immersion, interaction and conception. In order to research on the influence generated by the narrative mode of VR image on the audiences' experience, the following factors are tested: scene setting, sound, light, object movement, color, emotional guidance, transition follow and so on. The problems can be found through testing the availability, so as to enhance the satisfaction degree and the loyalty degree of audiences by improving the problems, thus reducing the cost of audiences' experience. We hope to understand the needs and expectations of VR image audiences through experimental research, and to discover the problems existing in VR image creation from the perspective of user experience. This paper also tries to put forward the frame and creation process of VR image narrative and to provide a meaningful guide scheme for Chinese VR image creation.

(3) Experimental objects and conditions

A total number of 16 users with no or less VR experience are selected to watch "The Dream Collector". One room is selected as the observation room (as shown in Fig. 14), in addition, one observer, one recorder, one pico all-in-one head display, one liquid crystal television, one camera and one voice recorder.

(4) Experimental procedures

The average duration of this experiment is 25 min, including 10 min of watching and 15 min of interview. First of all, interviewing the audiences before watching the film. Secondly, the audiences are arranged to wear the head display to watch the film and enter into the official experiencing stage (observation and record). During the process of audiences' watching, the observer obtains same picture as the audiences by watching the liquid crystal television and observes the changes in audiences' attention

Fig. 14. User observation and interview sites

during the watching process, at the same time, the recorder records key points in the audiences' experience through on-the-spot observation and video playback. Finally, after watching the film, the feedback interviews about the audiences' responses are conducted, so as to get the answers of questions in the test, focusing on the reasons behind the phenomenon and suggestions for the works. By observing what the audiences are doing and what the interviewed audiences are saying to make sure whether the audience act and think the same way. The audiences are surveyed before and after watching the film to assess their expectations and reactions to the work.

3.2 Data Analysis

According to the characteristics of user research, the creators have carried out a lot of presuppositions in the aspects of scene, role, moving object, sound, light, color design and so on. This chapter is based on the observation and interview of users after their watching, so as to verify whether the creator's presupposition matches with the user's response. Through conducting the research on users, the ability of creator in predicting and controlling the user's attention in virtual scene can be further improved.

(1) Scene design verification

The space can be divided into story space and mental space and the space is composed by the scene as well as the elements of scene (as shown in Fig. 15). According to the user's response to four scenes in the film, it can be seen that the broader the scene and the more abundant the elements in the scene, the more distracting the user's attention will be, so that the curiosity of user to explore freely is easier to be aroused. The general environment of viaduct and the interior space of the old man's home account for the largest number of users and the largest number of visits.

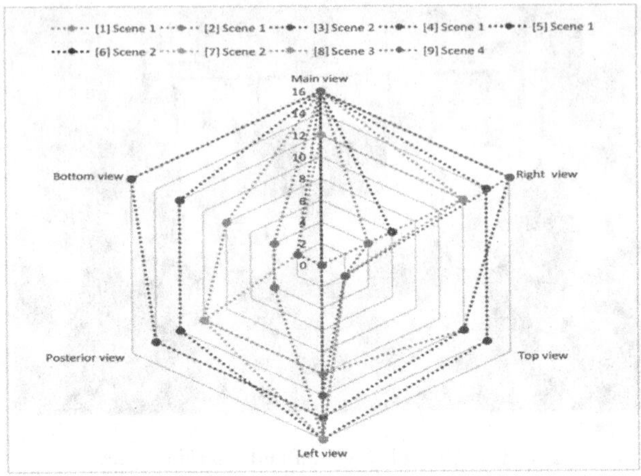

Fig. 15. Design layout of scenes

(2) Leading role movement and Moving objects design and verification.

The change of distance between the roles and the audiences is a vertical movement, which will arose and attract the attention of audiences, while the horizontal movement will lead the audiences' sight to follow the movement. Judging from the user's experience response, we can see that the guidance of leading role's movement is very effective, and the user will unconsciously follow the movement of leading role, looking at the direction where they go and the place where they look. When the leading roles disappear into the user's vision, the users will take the initiative to look for them again.

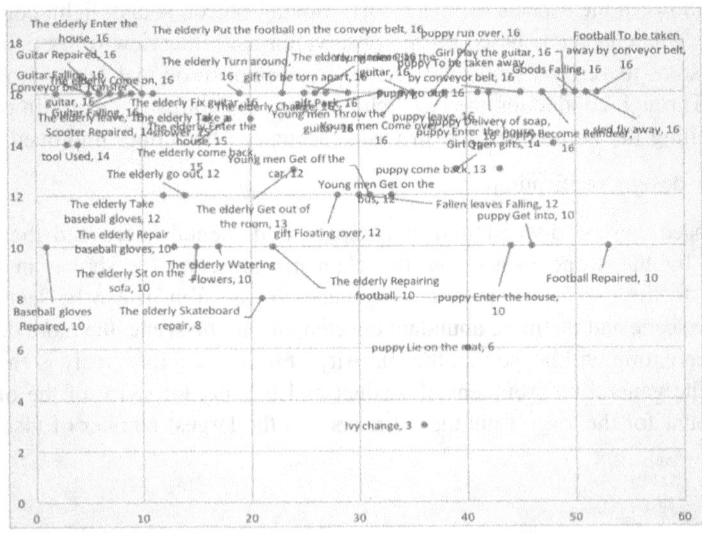

Fig. 16. Role and object movement noticed by users in nine scene

For example: the users look down following the young man Diuji, following the movement of the old man and the dog to come in and out, to enter the house and go out, following the old man to put things on the conveyor belt, thus thinking about where the things go through the conveyor belt. Following the old man and looking back, we can find more and more objects that represent dream are abandoned by others.

Through the response of audiences, we can know the moving object is very effective for guiding the audiences' attention, no matter how small or unnoticeable the object is. As shown in Fig. 16, for example: throwing guitar, changes of young man's clothes, falling leaves, dog soap, flying snowflakes and so on, all of these images have successfully attracted the attention of most users.

(3) Sound design verification

Users' reactions also demonstrate that auditory cues are particularly effective in attracting the user's attention and in preparing for some important events. A 360-degree VR picture often leaves the users unaware of the direction in which the leading role might be presented, at this point, the sound can be used to remind users. When the scene is changed, the well-timed music and sound effect can quickly pull the users back to the scene, this design also provides a short buffer time for the audiences' adaptation (as shown in Fig. 17).

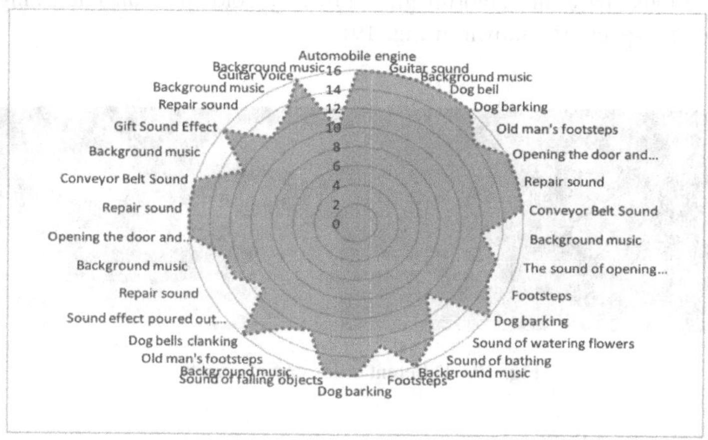

Fig. 17. Sound noticed by users in nine scene

(4) Light design verification

The light and shade contrast is mostly used in guiding users—setting light zone to highlight the places in the scene that need to be focused by audiences, and arranging the position relation between characters and light zone in accordance with the plot, so as to shape the characters. This work tries to use the Spotlight Scope, at the beginning of the film, the whole environment is completely dark, then it gradually expands into the visual range, but it's not the light, just a range of sphere (as shown in Fig. 18).

This shape can be customized and the visual range has a blurry edge, which can cooperate with the user to carry out a variety of visual expansion methods.

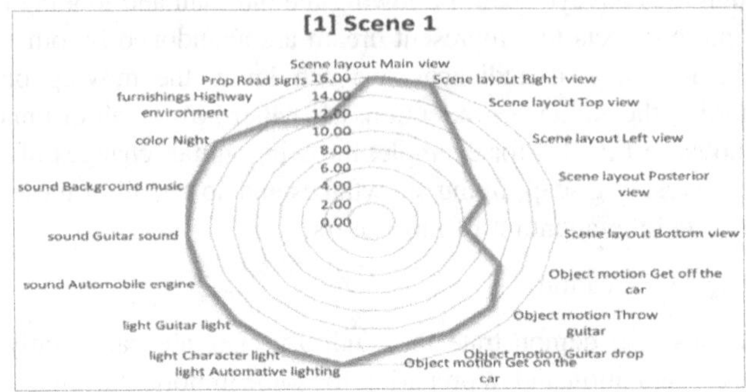

Fig. 18. Light noticed by users in nine scene

(5) Color design verification

Color can guide the mood and create atmosphere, the change of four seasons, the change of cloudy and sunny weather, the alternation of night and day, the change of black mysterious space and colorful gift shown by color play an interesting role in conveying atmosphere (as shown in Fig. 19).

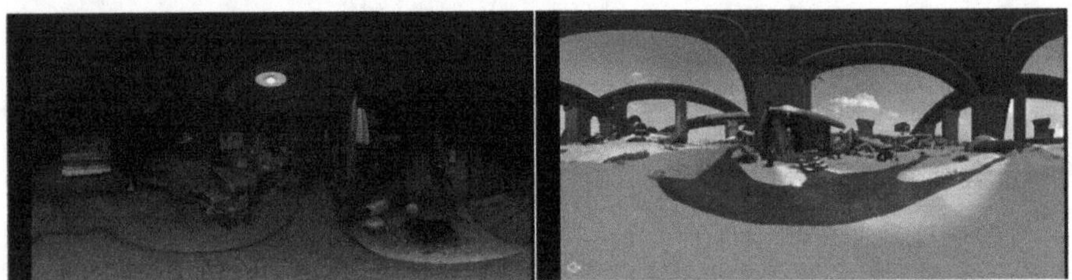

Fig. 19. Different color environments

3.3 Experimental Summary

(1) Differences play an important role in guiding the user's attention: one element in a scene is different from other elements, that is, the element can attract the attention of users. For example, the difference in grouping, in color, in proportion, in shape, in visibility, in motion and so on.
(2) The creator should fully understand the difference between users and respect the difference in creation. The elements in the scene and the changes of elements should be enriched as much as possible, and the initiative of focusing the elements in the scene should be left to users as much as possible, so that the user can find more details that are concerned by them in the story and finding their unique pleasure.

(3) The creator gives the audiences as much space as possible to move around in the story, and providing the users with the freedom degree to choose their own angle of view to discover the plot, so that each user has the opportunity to understand the story personally and deeply.
(4) From the user interview, we found that many users show an interest in continuing the story. Many users have put forward their own ideas in the role design, scene setting, plot development and other aspects. The active participation of users in the creation of VR image proves the necessity of collaborative creation and conforms to the principle of iterative thinking.
(5) From the user interview, many users hope to further expand the storyline and perfect the story of baseball gloves, skateboarding and football existed in the story. At the same time, I hope to increase the dream story related to me.
(6) From the user interview, it is found that many users want to increase more participation opportunities, such as having users to participate in story from the first or second perspective, so as to pick up something they are interested in and experience a story about what happened to this object. The users can fix things by themselves, in addition, they can give gifts to people who have the same dreams and make dreams come true again.

4 Conclusion

The framework of VR image narrative system needs three important parts: adopting the VR image creation method on the basis of user experience, at the same time, using the collaborative creation platform of intelligent tools between creator and user to establish the VR image creation mechanism of iterative thinking. Further use of intelligent tools can achieve the natural interaction mode and socialized experience mode. The user research methods can be divided into 3-dimensional framework: Attitudinal vs. Behavioral, Qualitative vs. Quantitative, Context of Use, among which there are several methods that are adaptable to VR image user research, that is, participatory design, focus groups, interviews, eyetracking, moderated remote usability studies, unmoderated remote panel studies, concept testing, customer feedback, A/B testing and so on. Deliberated Narrative or Simulation-based Approaches can be adopted, at the same time, using speech recognition, graphic and image recognition, natural language processing, deep learning, artificial intelligence and other technologies to build the collaborative creation platform, so as to realize the vision of collaborative writing among creator, user and AI three aspects. Establishing the iterative thinking mechanism, in order to allow users to truly become creators, performers, improvers, experiencers, and sharers of VR image. Sharing the experience of VR video world with people around you will perpetuate the commercial value of VR image, which has a certain degree of persistence.

References

1. Mateer, J.: Directing for Cinematic Virtual Reality: how the traditional film director's craft applies to immersive environments and notions of presence. J. Media Pract. **18**(1), 14–25 (2017). https://doi.org/10.1080/14682753.2017.1305838
2. Munt, A.: Cinematic Virtual Reality: towards the spatialized screenplay. J. Screenwriting **9** (2), 191–209 (2018). https://doi.org/10.1386/josc.9.2.191_1
3. Dooley, K.: Storytelling with virtual reality in 360-degrees: a new screen grammar. Stud. Australas. Cinema **11**(3), 161–171 (2017). https://doi.org/10.1080/17503175.2017.1387357
4. Dooley, K.: Scripting the virtual: formats and development paths for recent Australian narrative 360-degree virtual reality projects. J. Screenwriting **9**(2), 175–189 (2018). https://doi.org/10.1386/jocs.9.2.175_1
5. Ayiter, E., Dahslveen, H.: "The Tower and the Quest": a storytelling space for avatars. Technoetic Arts J. Speculative Res. **11**(1), 15–25 (2013). https://doi.org/10.1386/tear.11.1.15_1
6. Nas, K.: Virtual reality witness: exploring the ethics of mediated presence. Stud. Documentary Film **12**(2), 119–131 (2018). https://doi.org/10.1080/17503280.2017.1340796
7. Larsen, M.: Virtual sidekick: second-person POV in narrative VR. J. Screenwriting **9**(1), 73–83 (2018). https://doi.org/10.1386/jocs.9.1.73_1
8. Riedl, M.O., Bulitko, V.: Interactive narrative: an intelligent systems approach. AI Mag. **34**, 67–77 (2012)
9. Hernandez, S.P., Bulitko, V., Spetch, M.: Keeping the player on an emotional trajectory in interactive storytelling. In: Eleventh Artificial Intelligence and Interactive Digital Entertainment Conference (2015)
10. Riedl, M.O., Young, R.M.: Narrative planning: balancing plot and character. J. Artif. Intell. Res. **39**, 217–268 (2014). https://doi.org/10.1613/jair.2989
11. Riedl, M.O., Young, R.M.: Narrative planning: balancing plot and character. J. Artif. Intell. Res. **39**, 217–268 (2010)

Narrative Controllability in Visual Reality Interactive Film

Jinning Wang(✉) and Feng Ye(✉)

Beijing Film Academy, No. 4 Xitucheng Road, Haidian District, Beijing, China
357577041@qq.com, 510863715@qq.com

Abstract. Even though there is no final conclusion about if images collide "interactive" can be regarded as a film at present, designers could not stop digging the radically innovative features, modes, and structures of interactive virtual reality media. It is necessary to explore the essential innovation of digital media creation brought by the Virtual Reality since the VR tech accepted by the digital media area. The author believes there are three new directions can guide designers to develop the VR interactive digital artworks more efficiently such as non-linear story-telling based on the circular narrative structure of the interactive image, the new mode of sensory guidance in VR interactive image, the new interactive image operation and selection behavior optimization of VR interactive image.

Keywords: Visual reality · Interactive film · Circular narrative

1 Introduction

With the development of digital media technology and new interactive technology, image transmission has made revolutionary progress in terms of production efficiency, image performance, transmission and preservation, and so on. Image resolution are becoming clearer, digital colors are becoming brighter and wider, and shooting techniques are becoming increasingly convenient. However, image arts creation and public viewing methods still abide by the traditional image laws and rules, and no great changes have taken place due to the emergence of new image technology. In addition, the advent of new technology has not changed the traditional narrative modes which the core of a traditional film making. It has been more than 100 years since the development of image art, the narrative structure and methods have basically formed a fixed pattern, and it is difficult to innovate in form, while the emergence of Virtual Reality technology makes it possible for the digital image art to have a new evolution.

The arrival of Virtual Reality image era will be a major subversion of image production, which will no longer stop at a traditional image expression and immovable viewing method. The technological change of VR image will break the drama concept of French enlightenment thinker Denis Diderot's "Fourth wall". The core of this major change is not only the 360-degree immersion imaging replaced traditional planar, but also the interactive function mixed with mature digital media manifestation method. At present, the form of virtual reality interactive image is still in its initial stage, and the technology is the technology of "new media", but in terms of the artistic output or

A. Marcus and W. Wang (Eds.): HCII 2019, LNCS 11584, pp. 471–483, 2019.
https://doi.org/10.1007/978-3-030-23541-3_34

artistic work, they are still the art of "traditional media". This is precisely the bottleneck problem that digital image creators are facing at the stage of application and creation of new technologies artworks. What does Virtual Reality image creation need is a revolution in form and a change in the way of production, while this change cannot just stop at subversion or upgrading of VR image's "audio-visual" aspect, but the "interactive" function should have a new narrative form on such a new platform. As a result, in the creation of Virtual Reality interactive images, designers and creators need to deeply understand and break through the three key points within the film creation, as well as the creation form of the script, image narrative guidance and exploration of image interactive mode.

2 Non-linear Plays and Circular Narrative Structure of Interactive Image Narrative

The script creation of traditional video plays is basically based on the clue of single timeline, with a relatively closed structure, attaching much importance to the design of the basic structure of the unified ending and putting emphasis on the logical relationship of cause and effect. With the rapid development of commercial films, this kind of script creation is even more obvious. If it goes back to Aristotle's "*Three Unities*" in Poetics [1], such a narrative rule has been used for nearly 2,000 years. It has formed a complete set of drama aesthetic system, and countless movie creators have tried many times, and the audience is also delighted. In the process of image development, image media creators are constantly challenging the traditional narrative logic, proposing and trying many breakthroughs in non-linear narrative, requiring breaking the linear image mode, emphasizing the transformation of image narrative from multiple viewpoints, and using the synchronicity of space to cut off the continuity of drama time. However, such "non-linearity" is more manifested in the director's personal subjective narrative technique than in the breakthrough of the narrative at the level of the play like using inversion of storytelling and flashbacks in the form of fragments, changing perspectives and so on. Those artistic film expressions usually appear only locally and occasionally, rather than macroscopically in the structure of the film play. On the whole, the narrative of most video works still belongs to linear narrative. The non-linear narrative proposed in this paper refers to the linear narrative that is different from the traditional narrative law and the classical drama law in the whole drama structure, which does not follow the general space-time sequence or logic, but appears in a fragmented and discrete form. The specific performance characteristics can be summarized as multi-perspective, non-timing, contingency, fragmented multi-branch interactive ring narrative structure.

As shown in the figure, in the traditional non-linear script creation, the choices provided at each plot point can be more branches such as AB, ABC and ABCD. But at the same time, it should be noted that each additional plot point in this structure will multiply the workload of the creator and make it grow at the speed of geometric progression. Therefore, on the one hand, it is necessary to control the number of plot points, and on the other hand, it is vital to integrate or interrupt many branch clues in time (interrupts represent the end of the story of this clue), so that the clues in the binary tree structure are controlled within a reasonable range. This interactive narrative structure has been widely used in the British interactive film Late Shift, the film has 40 plot points to choose from, and the audience has achieved a better experience of controlling the narrative trend of the film through interactive means. However, due to the number of branches, the total complete length of this interactive film has reached more than 240 min, which is much longer than the length of a single narrative thread reached (Fig. 1).

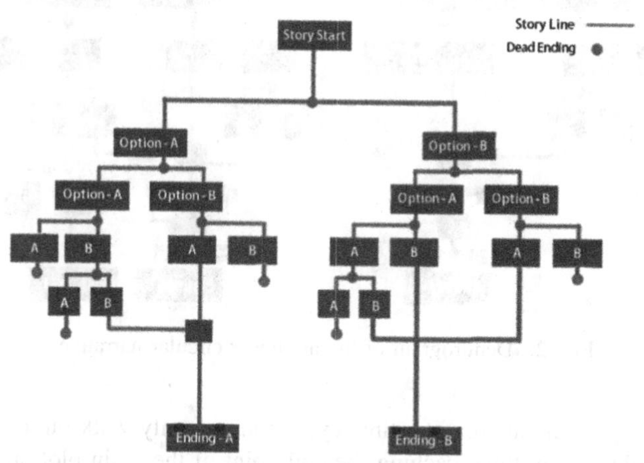

Fig. 1. Dendrogram of the nonlinear narrative

When we have understood what is the non-linear narrative of traditional images, we will ask a question whether there will be an end to every linear plot or whether there will be a possibility of restarting the film play cycle when the viewers feel the storyline they selected is not perfect. In interactive video creation, it is difficult for viewers to accept an interrupted plot development and a "dead end". As a result, on the basis of non-linear narration, it is necessary to design the plot route to return to the main plot at the end of the selection of each subplot, so that the development of each subplot can return to the main plot. As shown in the Fig. 2, each tree branch node is a choice node for audience to participate in the interaction, and only one of the branch nodes is the end point of the main plot. A complete non-linear interactive narrative drama structure and an interactive circular narrative drama structure are formed in the design of a reasonable loop of the branch plot.

In the movie Black Hollow Cage, the plot in this suspense movie is very in line with the story structure of non-linear circular narration, and viewers can make choices that affect the plot in VR interactive environment. If this choice is not leading to the main plot development direction arranged by the director, viewers will experience the plot again and again to the interactive selection point, especially in suspense plots, such circular plot development will not cause viewers' boredom, but will strengthen the suspense and drama participation of the plot. Another classic film case with a circular plot structure is the film Accro, which also has circular narrative features in the play. The plot setting and story features are similar to Black Hollow Cage. The characters in

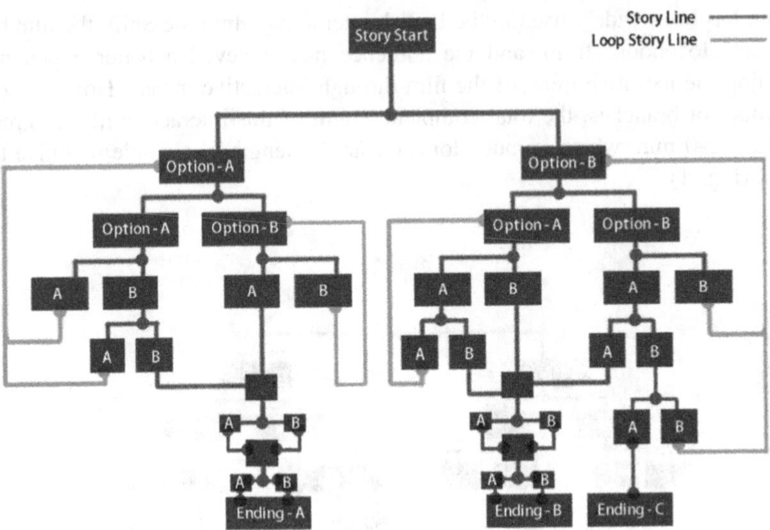

Fig. 2. Dendrogram of the nonlinear circular narrative

the story are trapped in an area of a time cycle and can only walk out of this cycle by making the right action, thus reaching the end point of the main plot arranged by the director. Based on this interactive circular narrative drama structure, in Virtual Reality interactive image creation, subplots can be different directions of traditional story development, or events experienced by different characters in different spaces in the same period of time. Thus, viewers can choose memories, dreams, parallel time, space crossing and so on at nodes, forming a multi-viewpoint narrative structure in a single interactive film. Viewers can choose to enter the story from a certain point of view and have the interactive option of jumping between several points of view. Its abstract narrative model structure can be seen in Fig. 2. This interactive narrative is similar to a parallel montage to some extent, and the audience's choice of jumping between different perspectives is a clip. Therefore, the benefit of VR interactive film is given to the audience the editing right, rather than the director to control everything in the traditional film. The advantage of which is that the audience dominates the observation right of the film-watching experience. This controlling right which belongs to directors in the traditional film switches to viewers can enhance the audience's sense of immersion and experience, which is the future direction of VR virtual reality image development.

3 Sensory Guidance and Picture Optimization of VR Virtual Reality Interactive Image Narrative

Compared with the traditional image needs to design a 16: 9 plane picture content, the visual input of VR image is a 360-degree spherical camera. Thus, the virtual reality interactive image is different from the traditional image due to the vision wideness, it needs to design a 360-degree spherical screen surrounding image. Besides, the area of the picture is more than 6 times larger than that of the traditional image. In addition to designing a 360-degree full-motion video in virtual reality interactive images, it is also necessary to design gyroscopes for lens control. And interactive triggers and trigger modes in the interactive engine. All of this assist to achieve the characteristics of immersive visual effects, free and controllable lens experience and interactive scenarios. VR images can simulate the visual experience of human eyes while emphasizing the depth of scene. Therefore, virtual reality interactive images can create a specific visual experience and display a unique visual display effect. However, it is precisely because of this completely immersive free-lens feature and special shooting technique that the controllability of the camera becomes weak. The excessive liberalization of the audience's lens control right makes it easy for the picture to deviate from the focus of the plot development or ignore the important film content which emphasized by the script and the director.

Points of interest has always been a very important design element. In the traditional image design, film artists can control the audience's interest points according to composition, character costumes, scene scheduling, and so on. However, in the 360-degree panoramic image, there are many "hidden frames" that affect the visual focus in the virtual reality environment. Besides, scenes and environments beyond the viewer's horizon or main line of sight in the VR digital film are more critical to control visual guidance and set the position of interest points when making VR films. In order to guide the audience's visual center to pay attention to the designed "points of interest" or the core picture content, the designer needs to design the narrative guidance of the image around the human visual, auditory, tactile and three sensory systems. Thus, VR designers could achieve the sensory narrative guidance of the virtual reality interactive image through the in-depth design of the core guiding point of the visual picture, the orientation guiding point of the auditory music sound effect and the tactile sensation auxiliary guiding point.

3.1 The Core Guiding Narration of Visual Images

As we all know, the shooting technique of 360-degree panoramic images is simple, and a panoramic camera can be placed. However, the lighting layout and scene scheduling of 360-degree full-motion video shooting are very difficult, the stage feeling is weak, and the core role is not prominent. Even if the lighting inspector can arrange the scene layout carefully, it is extremely difficult to avoid the lighting devices appear in the audiences' view by accident. Here we propose to use the interactive engine to optimize the artistic effect of 360-degree full-motion video. Designers can do real-time editing of the video in engine which can enhance visual guidance and enhance the visual color, purity, brightness and contrast of the core narrative points in the Interactive engine. The more important advantage of using engine is setting the real-time lighting triggers which can be activated by viewers' actions and motions. At present, the popular interactive engines on the market, Unreal4 unreal engine and Unity3D engine, both have 360-degree panoramic image input and playback functions. Also, the construction method is relatively simple and friendly, that is, attaching the photographed 360-degree full-motion video to the inner surface of a sphere in the engine, with the audience control character standing right in the middle of the sphere, and realizing the real-time turning control of the camera by the Blueprint, thus realizing the viewing of 360-degree full-motion video in the engine and completing the interactive input of VR influence, which is only the first step.

The next step is the secondary lighting of interactive scenes in the sphere image. There are three specific lighting types: static lighting adjustment, dynamic lighting guidance and real-time interactive lighting tracking. Visual creators need to arrange preset points according to the lights of the video, find out the specific coordinate positions where the lights appear on the sphere, and use the physical lights created in the engine to conduct secondary lighting and color adjustment on the image, such as designing spotlights or complementary color spotlights to guide the key items of decryption in the suspense films, arranging character spotlights for the core characters of plot development, and adjusting the color of lights on scenes, etc. These lights are all binding coordinate positions and will not be adjusted in real time according to the viewer's viewing angle changes for the secondary lighting on the screen part requiring light adjustment.

Dynamic lights guidance is a new lights layout method which is different from traditional image production. The angle between the viewer's visual center and the main subject of the scene is calculated by programming the code for lights in the interactive engine, so that the light color can be adjusted in real time according to the angle. Even though the viewer can freely control the 360-degree camera angle in VR sphere video, interactive lights can adjust the color and brightness of the light in real time in line with the field of view and focal length to simulate the real light perception of the pupil of the eye. Another unique feature of interactive engine light distribution is real-time dynamic tracking to control the position of lights. The simplest and most intuitive case is VR animation film Buggy Night. The film is a dark scene as a whole, and the clue of the whole article is a spotlight. When the spotlight moves to any position, the audience will actively follow the spotlight to focus on the set plot direction. Although this work is not interactive, it can be said to be a VR virtual reality image with interactive features (Fig. 3).

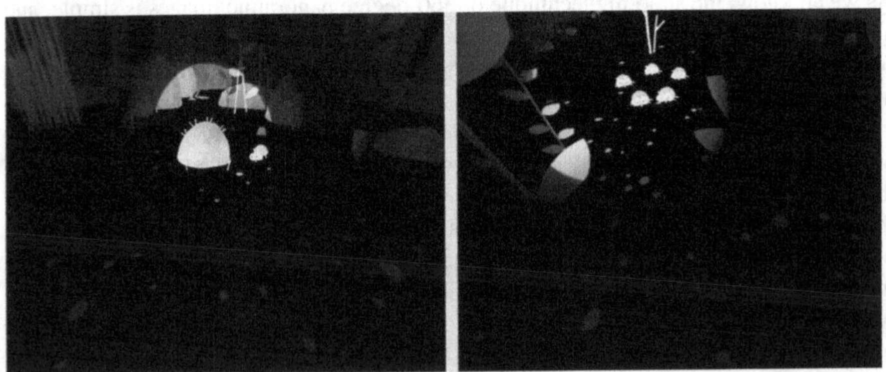

Fig. 3. Animation, Buggy Night, 2016

In addition to real-time lighting layout, real-time color adjustment is also an advantage of interactive engine editing. The visual guidance technique of VR animated image Henry is very outstanding, and the way of "contrasting" is often adopted to attract the audience's attention, which also ensures that their interest points can focus on the "main line flow" of the story. For example, a small range of colorful action elements are added to a large number of static scenes, and dynamic light-emitting objects are set in a dark environment. What's more, a function called "look at" was added to the VR animated image Henry in its early design, and the protagonist little hedgehog in the animation can change the direction of vision with the action of the experimenter and sometimes produce different expressions. This function gives the designer a new direction guidance, namely real-time AI color and light processing in accordance with the viewer's visual point, so as to achieve visual guidance.

Moreover, in addition to the real-time editing in the later stage, designers can increase visual obstacles, hide or weaken the invalid narrative information part of VR interactive images, and highlight 180-degree viewing angle videos. The horizontal visual angle of human eyes can reach 188° at most, and the visual angle of human eyes can be 124° when the human eyes coincide with each other, that is to say, the visual acceptance range of the audience is 124–180°. When designing VR panoramic images in the early stage, designers have always considered how to make the audience experience more 360-degree content, but it is because of the over-quantification of visual information (360-degree visual images) that the audience cannot follow the story development line designed by the director. Here, we propose to mix 180-degree images in full-motion video to help narrative, post-process half of the images that are irrelevant to narrative, weaken or even arrange obstructions so that viewers can focus on viewing useful information, guide the visual center of the audience to the part where drama development is needed, and block a large amount of useless narrative information from filling the audience's field of vision. In the classic VR panorama animation Henry, the research set the VR observation position in a small and closed indoor environment, and the machine position is set very close to the wall, so that the viewer will naturally face the visual angle to the main scene direction and back to the wall, thus leading the viewer to pay attention to the scene part where the plot occurred and using the wall as a visual obstruction prop.

3.2 Narrative Guidance of Auditory Feeling, Music and Sound Effects

The sound design of VR images is an extremely complex system, and the overall sound perception includes non-directional sound information and directional sound information, in which the recording and later position tracking of multi-track music, sound, dialogue, narration and other sound information need to be implemented in the interactive engine. At present, Google, Valve and Facebook all provide VR audio SDK to developers to facilitate the developers to embed 3D audio and enhance the immersive VR experience, but the production of 360-degree dynamic surround audio source files is still in the traditional technology.

The traditional method of making 360-degree dynamic surround is that it records the 3D audio through "human head recording" equipment, which relies heavily on the recording equipment and cannot be post-produced, and the price of the recording equipment is as high as 34000. The second is to use an extremely complex plug-in editor (such as Panorama 5), which requires the audio editor to use his brain to fill the 3D space scene and manually adjust the XYZ value of the audio source. Compared with the first method, the second method can bring richer 3D audio content, but the plug-in still needs extremely complicated work. Of course, the characters in the story will move, and the sound will move with it. It is also worth exploring whether to set different XYZ at each time node, moving at a constant speed or accelerating. Even if designers set it up and listen with ears, audiences will not be able to accurately recognize the XYZ of this sound source (Fig. 4).

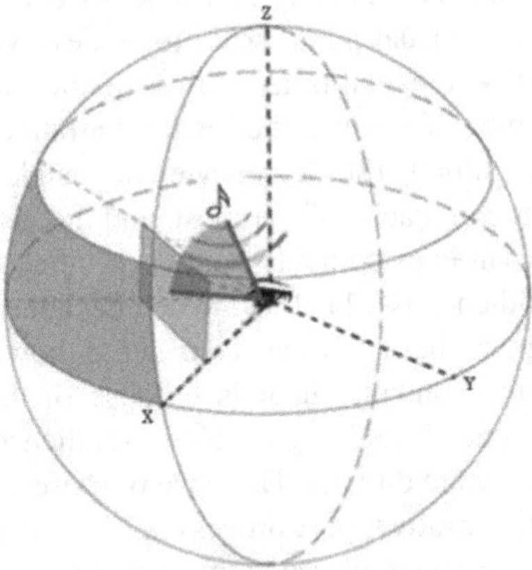

Fig. 4. Graphic of 360° Audio.

Here we recommend a paradigm of editing 360-degree dynamic surround sound in real time in VR environment, namely, Sound Flare, VR audio surround editor of Mint Muse, Sound Flare allows 3D audio content to be edited visually in VR scenes. In VR environment, content producers can wear VR headset show and drag audio files directly on the software interface they see. In addition to the basic functions of adjusting audio duration, editing and volume adjustment, the distance of sound can also be changed according to the sound path by means of dotting and dragging key frames so as to make the sound characters match the sound effect. The sound material is visualized as a sound source ball, providing an intuitive editing operation, allowing the audio editor to design the audio playing track by dragging without needing to supplement XYZ coordinate values. While editing audio, you can also run VR image content to analyze and judge the correctness of audio design in real time. Everything becomes efficient and fast, and what you see is what you get. 3D audio edited through Sound Flare can be exported and embedded into VR content to achieve spatial sound effects. Up to 7 audio clips can be loaded into the track once. These audio clips can be arranged in time by dragging forward and backward. You can position each audio clip in 3D space and immediately hear their sound from that location, you can adjust the volume, mute or solo of each clip in 3D audio software editing. Once the audio is located, you can save the mix as a WAV file for listening or further editing with other software.

Mint Muse Technology said that Sound Flare is still a very early version. At present, it has realized the production of binaural 3D audio (HRTF and directional spatialization) and only supports VR devices with HTC VIVE. Ambisonics (ambient stereo) will be added in subsequent versions to achieve full immersion space sound effect. With good technical support, the designer needs to make a new design idea on the plot guidance. In the interactive engine, the guiding sound source is bound in a fixed position of the spherical image, and the real-time adjustment of the left and right volume is made according to the clip angle between the visual square of the character and the sound source, with the smaller included angle, the larger the volume (Fig. 5).

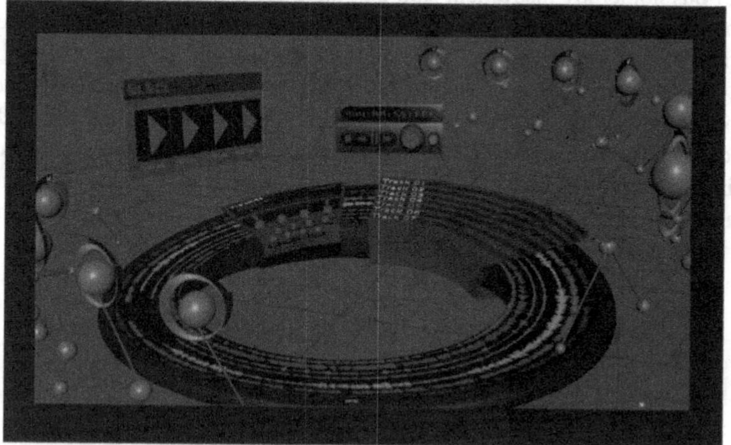

Fig. 5. Working interface of Sound Flare

3.3 The Assistance of Tactile Feelings for Guiding Narration

With the development of VR market, the technology and product pages of somatosensory recognition are constantly being innovated and updated, such as tactile handles, bracelet, tactile clothing, somatosensory seats, and so on. At present, the four VR headsets manufacturers Oculus, Sony PSVR, HTC Vive and Samsung HMD all adopt virtual reality handles as standard interaction modes: two hands separated, six degrees of freedom space tracked (three rotational degrees of freedom and three translational degrees of freedom), and handles with buttons and vibration feedback. Such a device is obviously used for some highly specialized game applications (as well as light consumption applications), which can also be regarded as a business strategy, because the early consumers of VR display should be basically game players. However, the advantage of such a highly specialized/simplified interactive device is obviously that it can be used very freely in applications such as games, but it cannot adapt to a wider range of application scenarios.

The scene that can be realized in terms of the type of touch feeling experiences simulated touch, simulated contact between wind and smoke, and temperature sensing that are roughly earthquake-sensitive. The commonly used tactile sensation realization techniques are vibration motors and can generate vibration sensation, which can be experienced in common interactive handles. The muscle electrical stimulation system simulates many contact experiences through micro-clicks. We use a VR boxing device, Impacto, to illustrate that Impacto combines tactile feedback and muscle electrical stimulation to accurately simulate the actual feeling. Stimulation of muscle contraction movement by electric current. The combination of the two can give people the illusion that they hit their opponents in the game, because the device will produce a "sense of impact" similar to real boxing at the right time. However, the insiders have some disputes about this project, and the current biotechnology level cannot use muscle electrical stimulation to highly simulate the actual feeling. A researcher working on a pain relief physiotherapy instrument said that there are many problems to overcome in simulating real feelings with electrical stimulation of muscles because the nerve channel is a delicate and complex structure and stimulation from the external skin is unlikely, but it is possible to "casually" stimulate the muscles to move as feedback. This paper believes that the development of VR virtual images and the audience's experience needs can no longer be satisfied with the use of simple vibration handle, and the continuous improvement of VR virtual image's visual reality does not match the old vibration touch, so VR image designers must continue to pay attention to the latest research and development of haptic technology (Fig. 6).

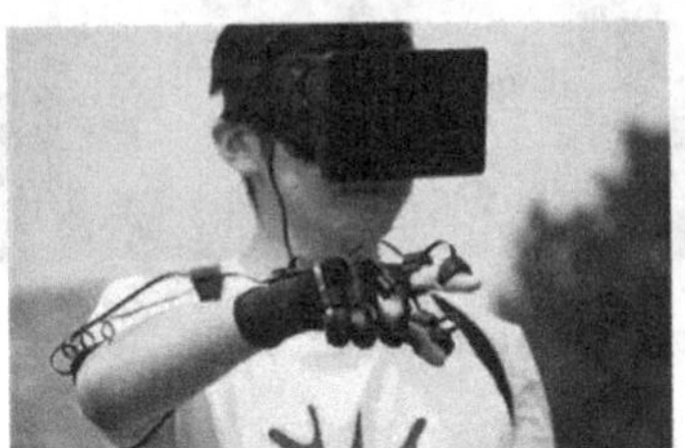
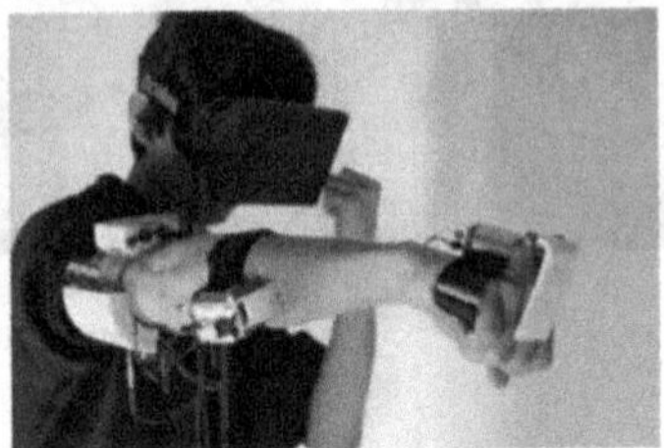

Fig. 6. VR Boxing Template, Impacto

4 Story Building, Interactive Image Operation and Selection Behavior Optimization of VR Virtual Reality Interactive Image

4.1 Level Construction of Story of VR Virtual Reality Interactive Image

Unlike the post-editing of traditional digital images, using some movies effects software to edit the images, VR interactive video is no longer a simple VR video player that plays video from the beginning to the end. Viewers simply control the camera's angle. In VR interactive images, the video material of VR 360-degree panoramic virtual reality images needs to be spherical stitched first to ensure the image integrity of each frame of images. Mistika-SGO is a relatively mature VR video stitching software in VR field. Mistika-SGO is used for 360-degree video stitching cutting edition and color adjustment, cutting the video into tree fragments and performing level management. Editors need to edit VR video into clip images rich in level relationship, and divide the plot into several progressive levels around the starting point of the main plot and the setting of the director. After the progressive level relationship, the fragmented video segments are managed hierarchically according to the plot tree logic diagram, and then the videos of different levels are structured using the blueprint function of the Unreal Engine 4 interactive engine, and are connected with the GUI system of Unreal Engine 4 to realize the interactive click input to the tree subplots, thus completing the interactive functions of video playing and clicking in the interactive engine. A simple input terminal change is a great innovation in the editing method and logic composition of the entire VR image.

VR's interactive narrative story is not like the traditional timeline narrative. VR's interactive narrative has a plot stop and a static loop of pictures on the interactive node. When the audience chooses to complete, the plot will develop with the audience's different choice branches, and the pictures will then start to enter the next level of video files from the static or short loop. The VR 360-degree Stereo Panomic Movie Capture plug-in of the Unreal Fantasy 4 interactive engine is used to acquire images, VR editing is performed using Visual Studio code editor to process the images to form left and right eye images, and an automatic combination single image at the output of VR head-mounted glasses is set to project the images onto a 360-degree sphere to form a spherical player.

4.2 The Optimization of Operation and Selective Behaviors of Interactive Images

After building the hierarchical story structure of VR virtual reality, effective and reasonable interaction methods are needed next. This article recommends using blueprint function in Unreal Engine 4 to add interactive triggers and select buttons or triggers. For VR interactive images, the most common way of interaction is to influence the selection behavior of content. The engine needs to identify and feedback the audience's selection behavior, and achieve seamless video connection and weaken the audience's selection process. At present, the most mature and common way of interaction is visual direction tracing. One of the most important technologies in VR field is to realize real-time tracking of vision through real-time sensing of gyroscope's displacement information. The further development of this field is not only eye tracking technology. Oculus founders Palmyrac once called it "the heart of VR" because its detection of human eye position can provide the best 3D effect for the current viewing angle and make the VR helmet display more natural and less delayed, which can greatly increase playability. At the same time, because the eye tracking technology can know the real gaze point of human eyes, the depth of field of the viewpoint position on the virtual object can be obtained. Therefore, eye tracking technology is considered by most VR practitioners as an important technological breakthrough to solve the problem of helmet vertigo in virtual reality.

In VR interactive image creation, a tracing point can be added to the viewer's visual center, and the direction tracking of VR helmet can be used to control the user's tracing point selection in VR virtual image and even the person's advancing direction. However, if you use direction tracking to adjust the direction, it is likely that you will not be able to turn over, because the user does not always sit on a swivel chair that can rotate 360°, and may have limited space in many cases. Many designers use other buttons on the handle to return to the starting point or adjust the direction through the rocker, but the problem still exists. Taking the direction of the user's face as the walking direction, the matching of steering and vision greatly enhances the immersion feeling, but it will increase the fatigue during interaction and weaken the comfort. However, the selection of visual tracing points is the most comfortable way of direction tracing selection in the current experience test. In the interactive image work Late Shift and using direction tracing points for plot selection.

Secondly, gesture and motion tracking is also an interactive way that conforms to the participation behavior and weakens the selection action. The use of gesture tracking as an interaction can be divided into two ways: the first is to use optical tracking, such as a depth sensor such as Leap Motion, and the second is to wear a data glove with the sensor on your hand. The advantage of optical tracking lies in its low use threshold and flexible scene. Users do not need to take off the equipment on their hands. It is a very feasible thing to integrate optical hand tracking directly on the integrated mobile VR headsets display as an interactive way of moving scenes in the future, but the disadvantage is that the sensor area is limited and the scene space is limited. The data glove, usually assembled with inertial sensors on the glove, tracks the movement of the user's finger and even the whole arm. Its advantage is that there is no field of view limitation, and it can completely integrate feedback mechanisms (such as vibration, buttons and touch) on the device. Its drawback is that the use threshold is high: the user needs to wear and tear off the device, and its use scenario as a peripheral is still limited: for example, it is unlikely to use a mouse in many mobile scenarios. However, there is no absolute technical threshold for these problems. It is completely conceivable that highly integrated and simplified data gloves like rings will appear in the VR industry in the future. Users can carry them with them and use them at any time, which can be understood as a lifting product controlled by the handle.

However, both techniques are only applicable to digital video works with individual themes, because the tracking of real viewers' gestures requires a real-time virtual gesture action to match in the virtual video picture, and adding a virtual body picture to the image will make viewers feel uncomfortable, but there is a great sense of interaction for some types of video works, such as opening door action in horror movies, event triggering in suspense decryption movies, simulated driving in science fiction movies, and so on.

The last mode of interaction in the exploration phase is voice interaction. In VR, huge amounts of information flooded the user. It pays no attention to the instructions from the visual center and looked around to find and explore. If some graphical instructions are given at this time, they will also interfere with their immersive experience in VR, so the best way is to use voice and not interfere with the world of images being watched by the audience. At this time, it would be more natural for users to have voice interaction with VR virtual reality world, and it is ubiquitous. It's not necessary for users to move their heads and look for them, and users can communicate with them anywhere in any direction.

Due to the restrictions of many languages and the tone and intonation of the speaker, the most difficult thing for the creator to do in the process of making voice interaction is to optimize the voice database and input the specific words and various waveform recognition of words needed in VR images, so as to achieve smooth and accurate recognition of voice. What is optimized for developers is that they can use an open voice recognition library, such as xunfei platform, Baidu cloud, tencent cloud, etc. all can use the SDK method and REST API, which provides the creator with a common HTTP interface through the REST API port to upload a single voice file within 60 s. Finally, the editing is triggered at the selection time through the original code C++ of Unreal, so that the speech selection scenario in the real virtual image develops.

5 Conclusion

As a mainstream art form, image can be said to be inseparable from the support of technical media when looking back its development process. It can also be drawn a conclusion that every major image change is closely related to the progress and integration of technology. So far, VR virtual reality technology has been recognized by the market, and has also attracted the attention of art creators in many fields. As a result, as a digital image creator, exploring the essential innovation points brought by VR virtual reality new technology is necessary, how to technically quantify the creative ideas and sort out the production logic. Whether image collide "interactive" can be regarded as a movie? At present, there is no final conclusion, but at least its creative exploration of image art on the new media platform has not stopped. Perhaps it is a form between the traditional film and the game, inheriting the film's audio-visual language, narrative techniques and performance techniques, and adding the audience's interactive experience so that the audience can control the progress and direction of the narrative to a certain extent. The author believes future image creators will dig out the radically innovative mode and standard of image creation in the new era.

References

1. Yu, S.: From nonlinear narrative film to interactive narrative film. Comtemporary Cinema, pp. 101–106, June 2016
2. Yang, Z., Zhang, Q., Zheng, H.: Unity speech recognition system based on Baidu speech. Chin. Softw. J. **8**, 1672–7800 (2017)
3. Wei, Z.: Dynamic image interactive design in new media art. Beauty Times J. **J0-05**, 21–22 (2012)
4. Song, Y.: The characteristics of interactive narration in the new media age. Journalism Res. J. **G206-3**, 1674–8883 (2014)
5. The VR 360 degree sound flare of Mint Muse tech. https://blog.csdn.net/qq_34113388/article/details/69389333. Accessed 06 Apr 2017

Study on Visual Guidance on Scene Art Design of Immersive Video

Songheng Wang[1(✉)] and Zhimin Wang[2]

[1] Beijing City University, Muyan Road, Yangzhen, Shunyi District, Beijing, China
214615824@qq.com

[2] Beijing Film Academy, No. 4 Xitucheng Road, Haidian District, Beijing, China

Abstract. The absence of narration language is a vital problem in immersive video creation. This paper tries to find out a way to satisfy audiences' aesthetic and visual requirement, and then realizes visual guidance of immersive video which based on scene art design, and guide them to follow the narration of immersive video and realize the effective visual narration of immersive video. The case analysis and experimental analysis method are applied as the main study method in this article. And we came to the conclusion that in the scene art design of immersive video, scenery form, position distribution, spatial relationship, color, light and shadow can help to tell the story of the video and catch the attention of the audience solely or cooperatively. With they successfully catch audiences' attention, immersive video can enhance the way to tell their idea of the story thus makes the narration more easily to convey the meaning of the work.

Keywords: Immersive video · Scene art design · Visual guidance

1 Introduction

With the increasing maturity of virtual reality shooting and projection technology, more and more immersive video works appear one after another. But how to tell the story clearly has become a problem that immersive video creators have to solve. The purpose of this paper is to explore the possibility of enhancing the narrative ability of immersive images in the field of scene art design. From the perspective of art creators, this paper explores the main elements of scene art design, such as landscape design, landscape distribution, color design, light and shadow design, dynamic design. Authors found potential of visual guidance in these scene design elements. As long as they are carefully arranged and designed, scene art can be used to achieve effective visual guidance. Thus the narrative ability of immersive images can be strengthened.

2 Immersive Video Narration Requires Visual Guidance

Deficiency of shot and scene which are essential elements of traditional video, immersive video cannot convey what director wants to convey to audience. Moving cameras and changing scene are the most common way to use in narrating a story while

A. Marcus and W. Wang (Eds.): HCII 2019, LNCS 11584, pp. 484–501, 2019.
https://doi.org/10.1007/978-3-030-23541-3_35

they are now no more suitable in making immersive video. And as a result we could only search another way to remedy its shortcoming. An obvious characteristic of immersive video is 360° view which means audience has freedom to choose any spot and matter to see in it. However such kind of the freedom for audience can be a big problem for immersive video to tell a whole story cause audience may miss details the director try to transfer to them. On that account, effective visual guidance makes a great difference when creating immersive video. Only in attracting audience's attention can they clearly comprehend the whole story.

On the audience side, visual guidance is also important. Without an immediate or secondhand visual guidance, audience may not catch the point of the immersive video and they may feel aimless when watching.

The basic rule to determine an effective visual guidance abides by the characteristic of human visual physiology. People may be easily attracted by some kinds of visual art scene, for example colorful matter, prominent proportion of shape or size, contrasty subjects and moving matter are easy to draw attention. After knowing the characteristic of human visual physiology, we can find out effective way to realize visual guidance and apply into creating.

3 Scene Art Design, the Best Way to Realize Visual Guidance in Immersive Video

Scene art design, the biggest visual area of all visual elements in immersive video, takes the responsibility to narrate the story of the visual part. And as a result, when we create the scene art, we should remind ourselves that its function includes beauty expression and visual guidance.

However, a gigantic problem in realize visual guidance is how to catch the audience attention. Cover the whole scene and remain the part in the immersive video you try to convey? No! In this way you will only destroy the artistry of immersive video and affect the audience's watching feeling, and what is worse, make them disgusted. You can successfully catch audience's attention and eyesight by scene art design under the basic rules that no destroying the artistry of the video and conveying the whole story of the video. So, to solve the problem in reasonable visual guidance is a problem demanding prompt solution in immersive video scene art design.

Scene art design includes various elements, such as spatial distribution, pattern factory, color, light. They all have the probability to realize the visual guidance in immersive video. In a narrow cave passage, we can easily be attracted to look at the front side or the back side of the passage. In an empty house, we will be sensitive to the doodle text or figure on the white wall. In a dark space capsule, we will absolutely interested in the sound made by laser sword. These simple samples show to us that if we can grab the feature of elements of scene art design, we can easily and successfully realize visual guidance. And in this way, narration of immersive video can also be fulfill.

How to realize effective visual guidance by scene art design in immersive video is the main topic we try to find out in my research. In a short word, narration language is a short slab in immersive video compered to tradition video and we try to use scene art design to be a sally port in attracting audience.

4 Study on the Elements of Scene Art Design in Immersive Video

4.1 Visual Contrast Is a Primary Condition to Achieve Visual Guidance

To achieve visual guidance is to achieve visual attraction, and that is to attract the audience's vision. After understanding the selective characteristics of visual perception of human beings, it can be known that the "strong contrast" of scene art design can achieve an effective visual guidance effect of immersive image.

The object of visual guidance is human. And human's understanding of visual object is through visual perception rather than vision. Vision only affects whether a person can see, while visual perception affects what a person can see. The human brain has an understanding of visual objects.

Not only vision, but also other sensory functions, cognitive experience, interests and hobbies will have an impact on people's visual perception. Gregory, the visual psychologist said: "Visual perception of objects includes many sources of information. These sources of information go beyond the information our eyes receive when we look at an object. It usually includes knowledge of objects resulting from past experience. This experience is not limited to vision, but may include other senses. For example, touch, taste, smell, or temperature or pain." [1] The famous biochemist Francis crick also said: "Look is a construction process. In this process, the brain responds positively to many different 'features' of the scene in parallel, and gives previous experience as a guidance to combine these features into a meaningful whole. Seeing involves some active process in the brain, which leads to a clear, multilevel symbolic interpretation of the scene." [2] These two scholars have demonstrated that in the internal meaning of the observed thing, besides the meaning itself, it also has the subjective thought and memory of the observer. People's subjective thought of the observed object is also the element that affects the visual guidance effect.

The formation of visual perception is selective, which is extremely important in immersive video. As the subject of observation and aesthetics, people have the right to independently choose the object of observation, which is an active exploratory movement. For example, when watching a figure, the observer can choose any part of it to observe carefully and pay even more attention in this part while ignore the remaining part of this figure. Such kind of active selective feature of human vision is called visual attention mechanism by Arnhem.

Visual attention mechanism, visual focus in other words, varies from person to person. The reason for diversification is that people have different interests, hobbies, behavior custom, physiology and psychological need. For example, animal lovers prefer to observe small animals in figures. People who are used to paying attention to the facial expressions of actors will pay attention to the performance of the facial expressions of the characters in the film. People who feel hungry will be attracted to the food in the video. All these difference are caused by the different characteristic of the observers.

Even though people may be attracted only by the things they are interested in, there still exist some rules that we can follow to catch their attention. For instance, people will surely find out a red flower among the green leaves, will instantly tell a crane among the chicken, and will easily find out a herd of cattle or sheep when the wind blows the grass low. These three examples are using the principle of color contrast, body comparison and dynamic-static comparison to grab people's attention. And of course, these principles can be used in creating the scene art design of immersive video to catch audience's attention to help the director telling the whole story.

In the animation Henry, an immersive video winning the 68th Emmy, the director using the way of strong contrast of light and color to tell his story, such as the lightening dog-shaped balloon, candles and colorful balloon fluttered in the sky in a dark room. All these elements try to work together to catch audience's attention and achieve the function of visual guidance. In the immersive video and animation of Clash of Clans VR, projectiles, fireballs and flying arrows, which are full of dynamic and striking feelings, continuously streak across the audience's eyes. The film tries to guide the audience's perspective with such a strong contrast design, so as to achieve the purpose of supporting the film narrative (Fig. 1).

Fig. 1. Print screen of the immersive video of Henry and Clash of Clans VR

Only can we produce a clear contrast, we could catch audience's attention immediately. We can generate a strong contrast by various methods, for example shape form, proportion size, location distribution, light and shadow, dynamic and static. In other words, to achieve successful visual guidance in immersive video, we need to make full use of the contrast in the various components of the scene art design.

Around the theme of contrast, we can conduct visual guidance exploration on five elements of the scene art design—distribution, form, color, light and shadow, dynamic and static.

4.2 Study on Visual Guidance on Distribution and Form

Distribution and form of the scene art design are the basic elements in immersive video. Location, density and the distance between every single matter in the immersive video will influence the way the audience pay in it.

Centralization Distribution Experiment

Take a blank sheet for example, if there are many balls of the same size and shape evenly distributed on the drawing paper, there will be no prominent places in the figure. But if all the balls are concentrated in one place in the figure, and the other places are left blank, then these concentrated spheres are prominent places. In this circumstance, when dealing with an entire empty scene in the immersive video, if a mess of the balls are put in one place, they will easily catch audience's attention in no time.

According to this principle, I try to build up a VR scene by the three-dimensional software MAYA. In this scene, there are a square ground, physical skylight, virtual VR camera and a centrally placed sphere. The plane expansion effect of this immersive virtual scene is shown below (Fig. 2).

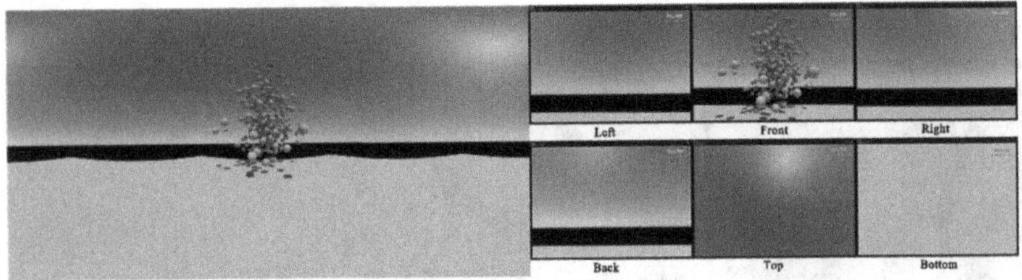

Fig. 2. The plane expansion effect and one sight in VR helmet of virtual scene in centralization distribution

As can be seen from the renderings of centralized distributed guidance, the most noticeable point of view is undoubtedly the front perspective, which is full of spheres. Eventually, the viewer will pay attention to the front perspective. That's to say such way to grab audience's attention works.

However there is an obvious disadvantage in this centralization distribution method which takes a long time for visual guidance, and viewers need to spend a certain amount of time and attention to find visual objects, which affects the viewing experience of the audience. And unclear instructions are the major taboo of film narration.

In general, the centralized distributed visual guidance method is feasible, but it has the disadvantages of unclear narration and long-time consumption.

Density Distribution Experiment

Density distribution experiment is an improvement on the previous experiment. The improvement method is to place the scene in all directions of the visual horizon, and these scenes will be concentrated in one direction from sparse to dense, forming a gradually dense visual effect.

In this experiment, we try to produce more visible objects in the immersive video to attract the audience's attention into the object that director tries to show. The specific experimental results is showed as the following Fig. 3.

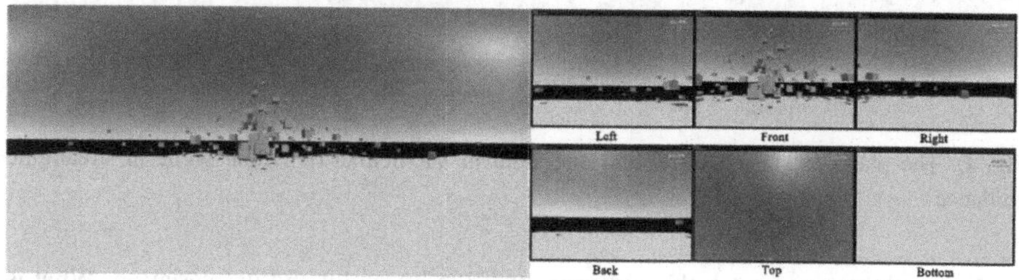

Fig. 3. The plane expansion effect and one sight in VR helmet of virtual scene in density distribution

It can be seen from the experimental renderings of the visual guidance of the density distribution that clear visual objects can be seen in the four horizontal directions of the front visual angle, the left visual angle, the right visual angle and the back visual angle. Among the four view, we will surely find out the objects in the front view are the most in quantity and prominent in effect while the objects in the back view are the less in quantity and weak in effect.

The trend the four view try to show to us is from minority to majority, from sparse to tight. As a result, audience will change their sight and follow this trend. Therefore, it can be seen that the visual guidance of density distribution is also feasible, and its visual guidance is stronger than the centralized one.

Streamline Guidance Experiment

The first two experiments take the location distribution of scenes as the main visual guidance method. Although they have certain visual guidance ability, they are still weak in the coherence of visual guidance, especially the centralized guidance. To improve this weakness we need to improve the consecutiveness of the object in the scene to better guide the viewer's perspective.

The shape of the scene has a certain degree of visual coherence. When viewing the scene, audiences tend to comprehensively observe the entire shape of the scene, which can be applied to the visual guidance of immersive images.

This experiment creates a special strip shape that runs through all directions of horizontal vision and has different thickness and density distributions depending on the primary and secondary vision. The specific sculpt and effect is showed as following (Fig. 4):

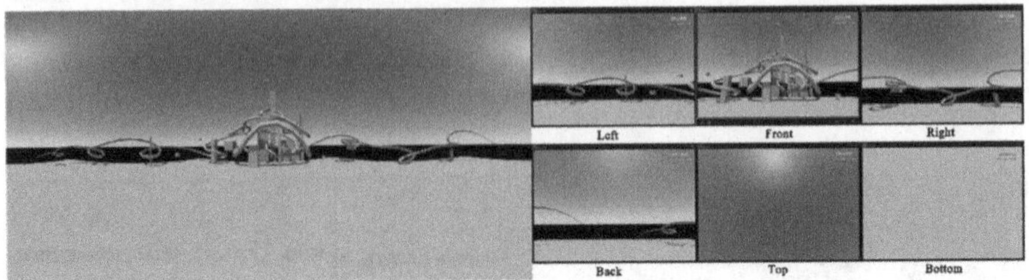

Fig. 4. The plane expansion effect and one sight in VR helmet of virtual scene in streamline guidance

Evidently, we can catch the audience attention by sculpt and its' variation. What is important, streamline guidance will be more effective compared to centralization guidance and density guidance.

For visual guidance, distribution and form of the objects in the immersive video can work together to reach the result of visual guidance.

Distribution and Form Experiment

There are many different way to achieve visual guidance by distribution of objects in the scene and form of the matter in the scene art design. The experiments mentioned above are typical case. The feasibility of these visual guidance methods can be further verified by creating cases.

In this distribution and form experiment, I am about to build up a cartoon town in an immersive video atmosphere using the unique distribution and form. As you can see, such imaginary cartoon town with various functional facility is suitable for human being to live in. The specific sculpt and effect is showed as following (Figs. 5 and 6):

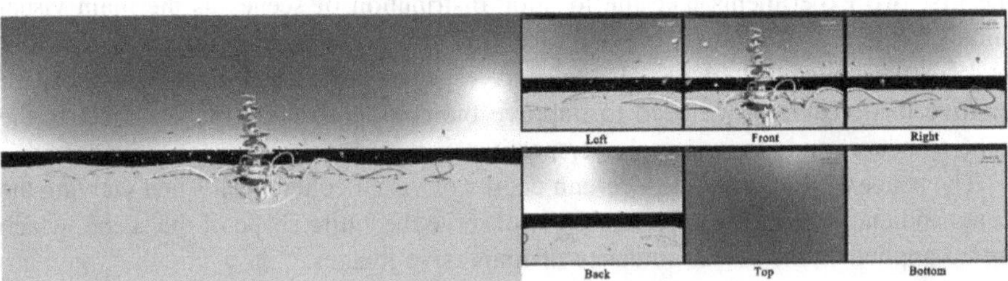

Fig. 5. The plane expansion effect and one sight in VR helmet of virtual scene in distribution and form guidance

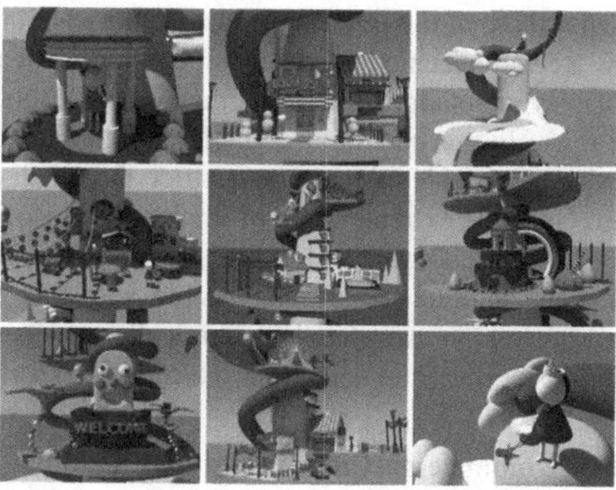

Fig. 6. Parts of the cartoon town

From the design sketch we can tell that the main cameras are surrounded by floated scenery and gigantic cirrus. The aerial town built on the basis of growing vines is in front of the camera. The overall spatial position relationship is clear, and the audience can easily understand the spatial relationship of this scene. The whole of the town is focused on the main vision, and the vines growing along the top of the cartoon town are constructed in a vertical way, so as to gradually guide the viewers' eyes to the main characters.

The overall shape of the vine town is almost a cone, with the main structure being the main rhizomes in the middle and the small rhizomes spiraling around the main rhizomes. At different heights of the rhizome, a platform is spread out, gradually becoming smaller and smaller. On the platform are various buildings and furnishings of the town, where cartoon characters live. The overall shape of the vine town is to guide the viewer's perspective upward. No matter the whole shape of the town which is big on the bottom and small on the top, or the roots of the vines which are getting thicker and thicker and spirally climbing to sky, they all indicate the audience to watch the top of this building. With the attention of the audience, the protagonist standing on the top of the main stem can start his performance and the film narrative can be carried out.

According to the content of the story, the design of the scene that limits the audience's field of vision is also an effective way of visual guidance. Design sketch as following is another experiment I want to show (Fig. 7).

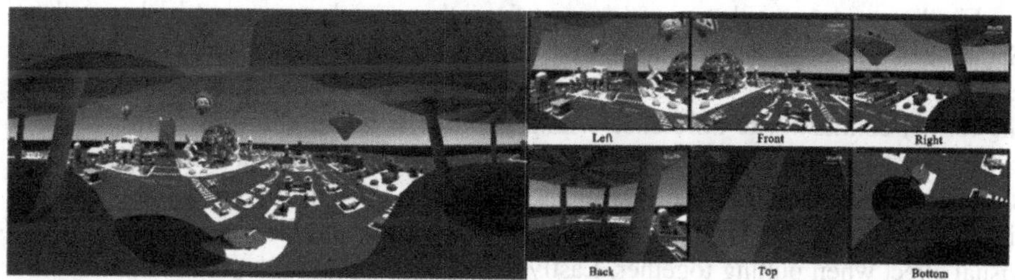

Fig. 7. The plane expansion effect in visual area restricted by hot air balloon

In this case, half visual are of the observer is restricted by hot air balloon. The top, bottom and back view are half occupied by the hot air balloon. Once the audience find it boring to watch the display in hot air balloon only, they will no doubt pay their attention to the scenery of the town. In this condition, suitable visual guidance is generated.

Making use of the reasonable scenery to restrict the flied of vision is more acceptable for human. On some extreme cases of immersive video, directors did some tough arrangements to control audience vision filed, for example, darken some part of the figure and lighten the middle part so that people will only watch the lighting part. Although such a technique can effectively limit the visual field and guide the vision, it will also seriously affect the audiences' perception experience.

4.3 Study on Visual Guidance on Color, Light and Shadow

In addition to all the elements of scene art design in immersive video, color, light and shadow can be critical to guide audience's visual line except for distribution and form of the scene. In the visual guidance method of color, light and shadow, we usually achieve a goal by different kind of contrast, such as hue contrast, saturation contrast, brightness contrast in color, form contrast, hard and soft shadow contrast, and photosynthetic efficiency comparison with special pattern with movement. Samples following are solely made to testify the visual guidance in color, light and shadow. And what's important, I try to explore the usage of them in the immersive video to effectively realize attention attraction.

Visual Guidance in Color
Color has three nature, hue, saturability and brightness included. These three attributes determine the visual effect of color. If we want to make great use of color to achieve visual guidance, we need to make experiment from every single attribute of color.

Hue Contrast Guidance Experiment
Hue is the appearance of color. If we put various hue together, we will find various visual contrast from them. The degree of hue contrast will determine the visual impact power. That is to say, if we put different color of different hue together we can get different degree of visual impact power. And such visual impact power will be a great element to achieve form visual guidance in color.

Although the different hue collocation of color has countless kinds, the collocation between them is regular. We can distinguish the difference from hue into four degree of hue. The four degrees of hue are same hue contrast, similar hue contrast, contrasting hue contrast and complementary hue contrast.

Firstly, we can see that visual impact from the same hue contrast is the weakest. Same hue contrast means the diversity of hue is in minimum, and the color in the 24 color cycle is within 10°. Secondly, effect of similar hue contrast is a bit stronger than the former contrast. The difference within two hue is within 30°–90° in the 24 color cycle. Thirdly, effect of contrasting hue contrast is stronger than same hue contrast and similar hue contrast. And the hue are within 120°–180° in the 24 color cycle. For instance, red and blue are typical contrasting hue contrast. They have a very strong visual effect when putting together. Lastly, effect of complementary hue contrast is the strongest and its' visual effect is the biggest. Complementary hue contrast means two color are beyond 180° in the 24 color cycle, for example red and green, yellow and purple, blue and orange are representative complementary color (Fig. 8).

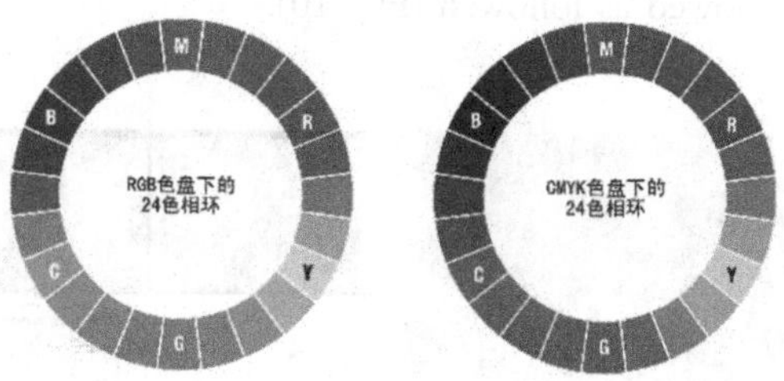

Fig. 8. Color cycle (Color figure online)

According to the characteristic of visual impact of four hue contrast, we can apply it into the scene art design in the visual guidance of immersive video. For example, we can put the hue together from weak to strong on the basis of hue contrast so that we can create visual effect forming a visual impact gradually enhancing effect. The sketch effect of hue contrast in showed as followed (Fig. 9):

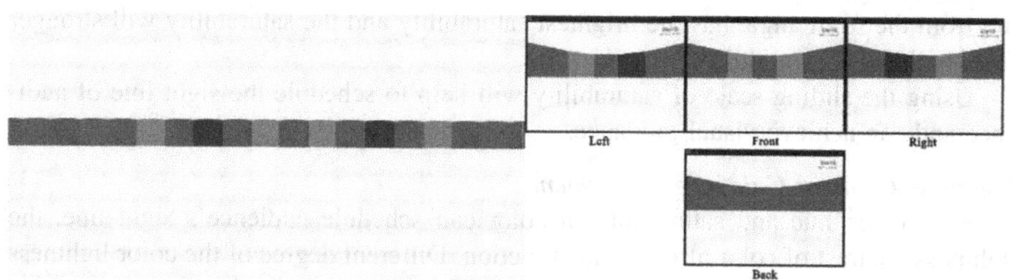

Fig. 9. The plane expansion effect and one sight in VR helmet of virtual scene in hue contrast guidance

In horizontal vision, the color contrast of the color belt is different, and the visual impact of the back perspective is the weakest, the left perspective and the right perspective are general, while the visual impact of the front perspective is the strongest, which is easier to get attention.

According to this experiment, we can design a guiding visual model in the aspect of color contrast and realize visual guidance by using the different characteristics of the contrast strength of color and hue.

Saturability Contrast Guidance Experiment

Saturability is a way to express the color brightness. The more colorful the object, the more it will attract people's attention. And this is determined by the visual physiology of human being. Hence, color saturability contrast is suitable for visual guidance.

According to the characteristics that the higher the degree of color saturation, the stronger the visual attraction, the author carried out an experiment guided by saturability contrast. In this experiment, I put the graphic with the highest saturability at the end of the line that lead the audience's visual line and put the graphic which getting weaker and weaker in saturability at the horizontal view angle to schedule their line angle. The sketch is showed as followed (Fig. 10).

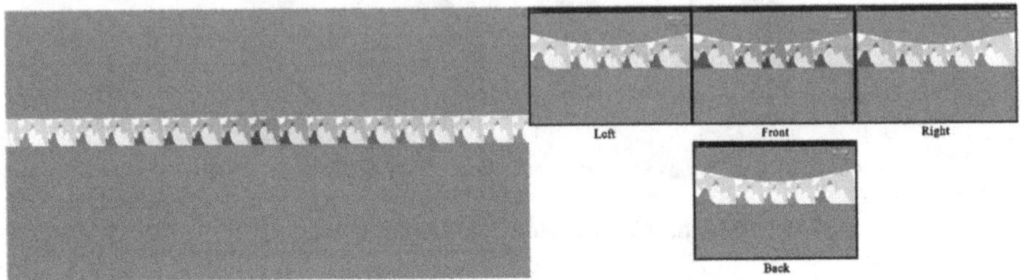

Fig. 10. The plane expansion effect and one sight in VR helmet of virtual scene in saturability contrast guidance

According to the figure above, the post-viewing angle has the lowest image saturability and the most bland visual effect. Figures from the left and right angle have gradual change in saturability and have the effect of leading people's sight line. Figure from the front angle has the brightest saturability and the saturability will stronger from both sides to middle.

Using the sliding scale of saturability will help to schedule the sight line of audience and can achieve visual guidance.

Lightness Contrast Guidance Experiment
Except for the hue and saturability in color can schedule audience's sight line, the lightness contrast of color also has this function. Different degree of the color lightness contrast can produce different result on visual effect. For instance, in the dark tree hole of Star War 8, there is only one bright white line in this pitch-dark figure. As a result, the key object in the story stands out in this scene (Fig. 11).

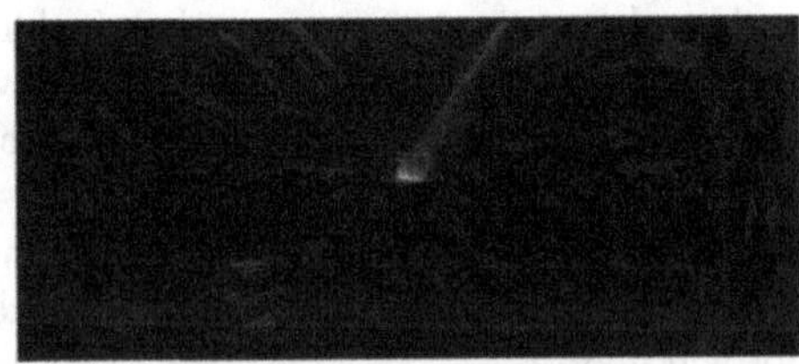

Fig. 11. A pitch-dark figure from tree hole in Star War 8

Experiment of lightness contrast guidance is similar to the one of hue or saturability contrast guidance. Finally, we can get a sketch as followed (Fig. 12).

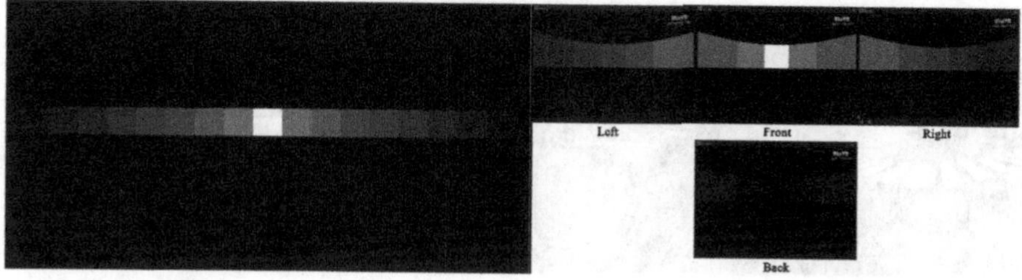

Fig. 12. The plane expansion effect and one sight in VR helmet of virtual scene in lightness contrast guidance

According to the sketch effect, we can see the biggest contrast in lightness is in the middle of front angle while the smallest contrast is in the middle of back angle. Front angle has the strongest visual effect. The results from lightness contrast are same with saturability contrast guidance experiment and they can also be applied in the visual guidance design.

Color Design Visual Guidance Comprehensive Experiment
Based on the visual guidance of color saturability, color filed ratio of optesthesia and scenery distribution, we can expand creation in immersive video scene. In this case, I build up a cartoon town. And I try to use a bright yellow car to lead people's visual line.

In this cartoon town, there are succinct and clear urban architecture. I use roads to divide the city into disparate part and cars to indicate movement area. Of course, I also use color to emphasize objects. Effect are showed as followed (Fig. 13).

Fig. 13. The plane expansion effect and one sight in VR helmet of virtual scene in color design visual guidance comprehensive experiment 1 (Color figure online)

According to the renderings, except for one or two specific buildings, the buildings and the ground in the whole scene are displayed in low saturation colors. Only trees, hot air balloon, street lamp, waste bin and some cars are in high saturability. This design not only creates the artistic style of the film, but also highlights the subject and assists the narration of the film.

The second comprehensive experiment focuses on the visual guidance effect of color contrast and brightness contrast. I try to set up a high hue contrast visual guidance. Design sketch is showed as followed (Fig. 14).

Fig. 14. The plane expansion effect and one sight in VR helmet of virtual scene in color design visual guidance comprehensive experiment 2

According to the effect diagram, although the scene color saturation is high, it seems to be more average. But in fact these scenes in the color hue and brightness of the contrast are different, there are different visual impact between the scenery. The color collocation of scenery can play a certain role in visual attraction.

Analysis on Visual Guidance by Color
Currently, some immersive video has already applied visual guidance by scene art design in color. In the Dear Angelica, for instance, director highlighted hue, saturability and lightness contrast to achieve visual guidance. On this purpose, it helps to set off emotion and mood, and provides powerful narrative (Fig. 15).

Fig. 15. Visual guidance in color of Dear Angelica

Visual Guidance in Shadow Design

In a scene, where there is light, there is shadow, which with different degree of hard and soft, and intensity. So shadow is an ingredient in scene art design. Different shapes and intensity of shadow can produce different visual effects. In special situations, shadows can also serve as visual guides.

Take the simple shadow modeling visual guidance experiment as an example to show the visual guidance effect of the shadow. Design sketch is showed as followed (Fig. 16).

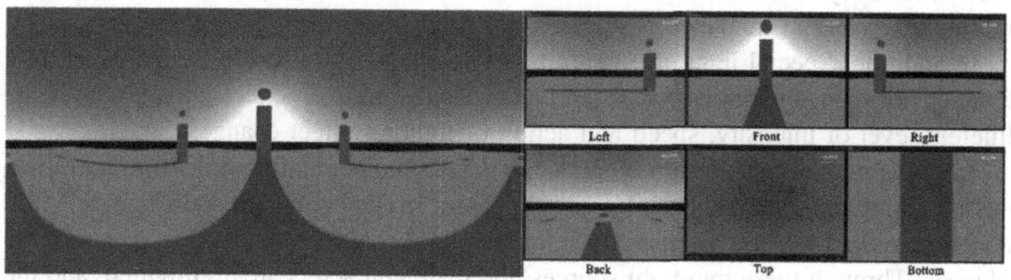

Fig. 16. The plane expansion effect and one sight in VR helmet of virtual scene in visual guidance in shadow design

According to the rendering, figure from back angle can only show the shadow of scenery. This shadow performs a long shape and extend to the other side. Audience will follow this long shadow and finally put their sight at the object from front angle. Extensibility of shadow is a key point in visual guidance of shadow.

In addition, hard or soft shadow margin can produce big contrast and has the potential to lead visual guidance.

Visual Guidance in Lighting Effect

Efficient lighting effect can play a role in setting off atmosphere, displaying artistic style, expressing environmental state or indirect narration. Lighting effect has a high degree on lightness contrast and color saturability contrast so it has a strong visual impact and attraction. It's an ideal visual guidance element.

The indirect visual guiding effect can be achieved by using the luminous effect of different intensity of object. The experimental effect is shown below (Fig. 17).

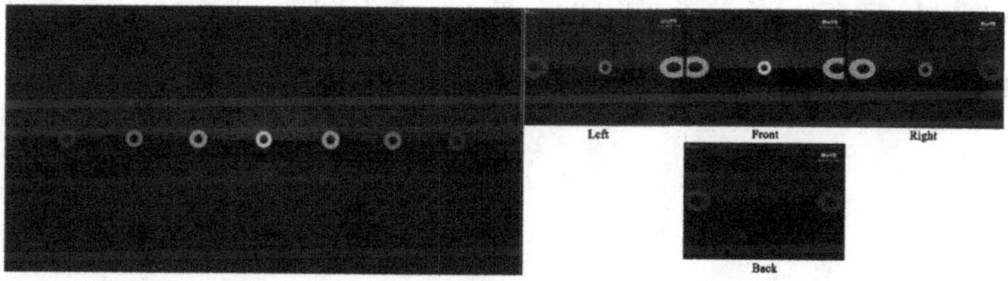

Fig. 17. The plane expansion effect and one sight in VR helmet of virtual scene visual guidance in lighting effect

As can be seen in the figure above, the visual impact of objects varies with the intensity of their light emission. If the lighting effect get strong, visual impact will get strong too; vice versa. Especially in the pitch-dark environment, the lighting effect will be even stronger. Under this situation, visual guidance put into effect.

Another common application of special lighting effect visual guidance is image symbolization design. When combining light effect and symbolic shape, it can make the visual guidance more clear and direct. For instance, the arrowhead is illuminated in the dark scene, and the audience can instantly understand the inner meaning of the arrowhead. They will naturally look in the direction indicated by the arrow. Symbolic lighting effect visual guidance is realized.

In addition, Special light effects are not only static, but also can be displayed in a dynamic form in an immersive video. The visual guidance effect changes with the different level of intensity, speed and action of lighting effect changes.

Lighting in the scene design of We Wait is both the beginning of the film narrative, and the important undertaker of film visual guidance. The main light sources in this film are the searchlight of the Marine police and the light of the mobile phone screen of the refugees. Through these two light sources, the main characters are highlighted, and the visual guidance of the film is also realized through these two light sources. It can be said that the lighting design in the scene of We Wait is extremely ingenious, which is not only a necessary stage for narration, but also a tool for visual guidance (Fig. 18).

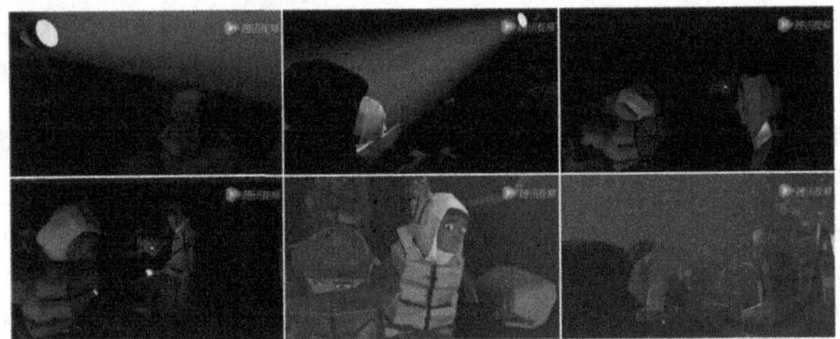

Fig. 18. Visual guidance of lighting effect in the scene of We Wait

And in Son of Jaguar, the lighting design skillfully combines narrative and visual guidance. An extension of the overhead light in the passage, the concentration of stage lights, character transformation lighting effect expansion have shown strong visual guidance and impact. It is a successful case of visual guidance of lighting and shadow design (Fig. 19).

Fig. 19. Visual guidance of lighting effect in the scene of Son of Jaguar

4.4 Study on Visual Guidance on Dynamic Scene

Visual Guidance Experiment of Scene Dynamic Design

In the scene design, the common dynamic scenes related to the plot are flames, running water, cars, wind and cloud, etc., which not only meet the needs of the plot, but also play the role of visual guidance. Cars and ferris wheels in the following creation experiments are good examples, as well as exaggerated rain and clouds in VR animation Rain or Shine (Fig. 20).

Fig. 20. The plane expansion effect and one sight in VR helmet of virtual scene visual guidance in scene dynamic design

According to the static figure of this case, three-dimensional arrowheads mark the movement of objects. The main moving objects in the scene are ferris wheel and cars on the road. Based on people's visual preferences, dynamic things get more attention. It is easy to be carried away by a moving car or drawn to a spinning ferris wheel. The audience's eye will eventually be directed to the main view of the frame.

Dynamic design visual guidance has a priority among objects. When there are multiple moving objects in the video at the same time, the object with more intense movement can get more attention. Of course, it is in the relative case.

Dynamic design visual guidance should be integrated. In coordination with color changes, luminous changes, form changes, and changes in the field of vision, it will make the guiding effect more efficient. The glowing gifts float across the full field of vision and slowly converge to the front view in The Dream Collector. This section is a typical visual guidance of integrated dynamic design (Fig. 21).

Fig. 21. Visual guidance experiment of dynamic luminescence design in The Dream Collector

In Rain of Shine, the clouds rain from the beginning to the end of the film has played an important role in visual guidance. The clouds always follow the leading role. The dark clouds won't disappear until she takes off her sunglasses. Dark clouds and rain, as the key to the narrative of the film, not only show the fun, but also always attract the attention of the audience to the main character. We can say that the rain and clouds are the key to the narrative of Rain or Shine (Fig. 22).

Fig. 22. Visual guidance experiment of dynamic dark clouds and rain design in Rain or Shine

5 Conclusions

In the creation of immersive video, scene art design can achieve a certain visual guidance. This is an important supplement to the lack of immersive video narration

In the design of immersive video scenes, the distribution and form of the scene, color and shadow and dynamic effect design can form a certain visual guidance effect. Visual guidance design in art design needs to be integrated in many aspects. This paper systematically enumerates the possibility of implementing visual guidance in a small part of scene design to attract the attention of more creators so that they can further explore and study the art design and immersive video narration.

References

1. Gregory, R.L.: Visual Psychology. Beijing Normal University Press, Beijing (1986)
2. Crick, F.: Amazing Hypothesis. Hunan Science and Technology Press, Hunan (2002)
3. Arnheim, R.: Art and Visual Perception. China Social Science Press, Beijing (1984)

The Application of Visual Image and Interactive Storytelling to Stage Performance

Zhen Wu(✉) and Ximin Zhou

The School of Creativity, Beijing Dance Academy, No. 1, Wanshousi Road, Haidian District, Beijing, China
wuzhen@bda.edu.cn

Abstract. New media technologies bring to light new techniques in representation and storytelling. Particularly, in theatre performance that is delivered live to the audience, new techniques have the capacity to create more immersive experiences to audiences. In recent years, Chinese audience are witnessing an increasing number of new representation and storytelling techniques being applied on stage productions. These technological innovations on stage are rapidly developing and inherit tremendous creative potentials. This paper focuses on the application of game engine-powered technologies such as real-time rendering used in 3D mapping, interactive, Virtual Reality, Mixed Reality etc. On the frontstage that is visible to the audience, the way of storytelling and the visual narration of the creative concept appears to be the result of these technological innovations on stage. This paper focuses on the application of technologies such as real-time rendering, virtual reality, and mixed reality on stage performances powered by game engine to realize intermixing of storytelling. Throughout the paper, we provide examples of various stage productions, such as theatre, music performances, and dance productions. These examples demonstrate the wide range of applications that are possible in enriching ways of storytelling and engaging audience. Yet, despite all of the above benefits, we also call for is a reflection upon the relationship between technology and arts. We argue that in spite of the availabilities of these technologies, it is imperative to also slow down and reassess the content we are going to create and begin a series of creative conversations between artistic expressions and technological excursions.

Keywords: Visual image · Stage performance · Montage

1 Introduction

The advent of technological innovations has given the theatre and stage performance a new facelift. New media technologies have also brought to light new techniques in representation and storytelling. In theatre performance that is delivered live to the audience, particularly, new techniques arouse different (i.e. more immersive) experiences to those who are watching the show. The intensity of physical and emotional impact upon the audience is heightened as a result. However, amidst the fast developing

A. Marcus and W. Wang (Eds.): HCII 2019, LNCS 11584, pp. 502–516, 2019.
https://doi.org/10.1007/978-3-030-23541-3_36

representation and storytelling techniques that have brought stage productions to a higher level in terms of sophistication and audience engagement, the paper calls for a moment of reflection upon the relationship between technology and creativity.

In recent years, Chinese audience have witnessed an increasing number of new representation and storytelling techniques being employed in stage production. These technological innovations on stage are rapidly developing. Particularly, in the application of game engine-powered technologies include real-time rendering in 3D mapping, realtime interactive, Augmented Reality, Virtual Reality, Mixed Reality etc. The growing use of these technologies in stage production, performance is pushing the demand for more and better integration between software and hardware in achieving smoother orchestration of content and system operation. In other words, the architecture behind the whole system into which new technologies are inserted is also changing in response. At the same time, programming language (e.g. GLSL Shader) also changes in accordance to the ever rising technical demands in realising these innovations.

On the frontstage that is visible to the audience, the way of storytelling and the visual narration of the creative concept appears to be the result of these technological innovations on stage. For example, a more immersive and visually impactful backdrop gives the audience the in-situ experience, as a result of 3D Mapping; or the use of real-time rendering in bringing immersive storytelling to life allows people to experience the past, present and the future simultaneously. The ability to transform a single object on stage, for example, through 3D mapping allows this single object to be used in multiple scenarios. Instead of seeing the physical changes of stage props in terms of their shapes, sizes and locations, the transformation of space and time is also made possible because of the new technologies. Parallel experience of space and time is no longer limited to film production but also possible on stage production. As a result of spatial and temporal manipulations with the use of new technologies, the supposed boundary between reality and dream becomes more blurred.

In this paper, discussions focus on looking into the details in the application of real time rendering, augmented reality, virtual reality, and mixed reality on stage powered by game engine to realize intermixing of storytelling. The paper begins with the use of montage in storytelling on stage as a conventional technique and the existing methods practised by producers in bringing the story to life and making the experience of time in non-linear fashion possible on stage. The intervention of game engine powered technologies mentioned above on stage innovation opens up more avenues for presenting stories, on the one hand, and emotional and physical experience on the other.

With the examples of various stage productions (e.g. theatre and music performance, dance performance, etc.), this paper demonstrates the wide range of applications that are possible in enriching ways of storytelling and engaging audience. Indeed, the opening up of game engine such as Epic, to hobbyists, artists, scientists, architects beyond their immediate benefactors – game makers, motivates the outreach of game engine in representation and storytelling on stage. Game engine also allows for a wide range of inputs that give a high level of flexibility and adaptability of game engine powered technologies. As a result, the intervention of game engine powered technologies also makes technical sense for production, visual representation and storytelling on stage. The application of technological innovations also widens by association and demand. In particular, for stage performance, what was considered technically impossible has now become the norm thanks to advanced tracking and interactive technologies.

Yet, despite all of the above benefits, what should also be called for is a reflection upon the relationship between technology and arts. Performance arts and stage production are cultural products of our society. In China, the rising popularity of performance arts demands technological innovations to catch and retain the attention of the audience. However, instead of grabbing their attention, producers and performers should shift the focus back to creative innovations powered by technological advancement. Technology is a tool that simplifies what used to be highly complex processes and still create spectacles for the audience. However, such spectacles should not be the motivation behind bringing in new technologies but the boost for more creative endeavours.

2 Montage – The Use of Conventional Visual Image on Stage Performance

Conventional visual image stems from films, animations and video arts. In this paper, we use the term to refer to visual images on stage with projection and LED screens. Video content comes from taping, 3D animation, etc., which has been applied to stage performance as early as 2007 when it began to take off. At the beginning, it was used as a substitute for stage backgrounds. After that, the use of montage also became popular.

The word 'montage' comes from an architectural root in French 'monter', meanings 'to mount'. It is a technique often used in filmmaking, of selecting, editing and piecing together separate sections of film to form a continuous whole. How to use montage on stage, with the combined application of real life video and stage performance, to bring together the whole visual elements of performance is an important aspect to consider, as far as the creative process is concerned.

Take a production called *The Story of Pujiang River* for which the author designed in 2008 for the Shanghai Circus, for example. The author designed a multimedia set on stage, not only to enrich the atmosphere for the audience, but also to compliment the narrative on stage. Take one scenario where a rainy scene emerged as an example. In this scene, a young man holding an umbrella walked from behind a mesh rising curtain onto the stage. At the same time, a photo of a shop was revealed on the screen, which evoked a distant memory of his sweetheart (see Fig. 1).

Fig. 1. Multimedia design for *The Story of Pujiang River* in 2008.

Today, years have passed. The level of image quality has also improved from 720p to high resolution of 1080P, 4K or 8K. Yet a question remains. How does the use of visual image on stage exceed the status quo?

A four-hour monologue Mo Fei – the Alcoholic (funded by the National Arts in 2016) marks the revolutionary leap towards such innovation. This production was directed by Krystian Lup who was also responsible for the visual design and adapted by Chinese writer Shi Tiesheng. The stage background is a movie screen and the actor is an alcoholic with sheer daydream. Unfolding stories through the mind of a seemingly weary alcoholic gradually unveiled the truths to which many sober souls are often oblivious. A clear reminder of the many sober people in the audience, blurring the line between dreams and realities.

Today, the kind of images we see on stage employs a more traditional technique. That is real time recording and non-linear narrative, from the same perspective. Audience witness the passage of time from a fixed spatial position. Time passed with the everyday life unfolding repeatedly in the immediate surroundings of the same spot where Mo Fei, the alcoholic sat day in and day out. From an empty plot of land to a construction site covered in snow, the same spot frequented by Mo Fei is coloured by a sense of prolonged loneliness (see Fig. 2).

Fig. 2. Photos of the production *Mo Fei – the Alcoholic.*

The use of montage is realised on stage with a tracking camera that follows the protagonist walking through the courtyard lanes on his way home, capturing the intricate details of the suspecting gaze of his neighbours. With the cameras being fixed in a position from above, the intimate acts of love, comfort and empathy take place in bed become visible to the audience (see Fig. 2). The same goes with the mother and son scene in which the two performers are having a heartfelt conversation under a tree.

During the state of delirious drunkenness, the protagonist went back to the past. He saw his own birth under the shadow of a failed marriage of his parents, a pep talk with his innocent childish self, and of him reaching out to the divorced wife who is walking away. All these scenes are brought to life by the use of visual images on stage.

Having been inspired by the approach, The designer borrowed the idea of applying real-time filming onto the stage to produce the montage effect in the production of Su Yuan Memories in 2018, in order to better convey emotions in the performance. The production was funded by the China National Arts Fund as part of the 2017 arts productions, produced by Suzhou Performing Arts Centre. The performance opened to the public in November 2018, and I was responsible for the multi-media design of the production with four divisions based on seasonal changes.

Real-time filming and animated effects are the two main ways in multimedia production. Animated images are used to express the conceptual elements, for example, the visual conversation between flowing water in film and the moving long sleeve on stage. The emphasis upon the aesthetics in landscaping Suzhou gardens is strengthened by the interaction between the 3D architectural animation and the main protagonists taking stroll in the garden through their dance. Scenes of the garden change as a result of moving with images (see Fig. 3).

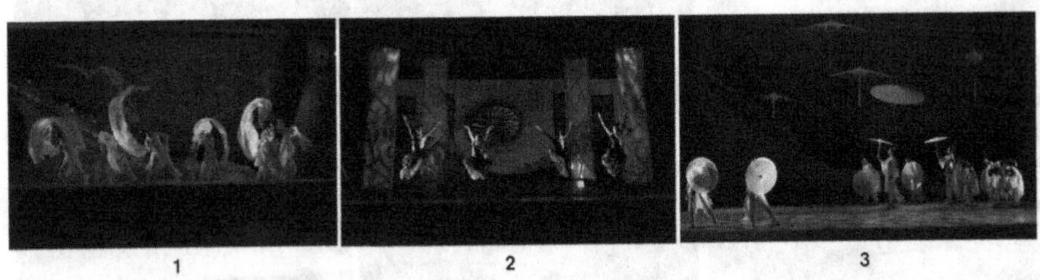

Fig. 3. Dance - Su Yuan Memories: animations in multimedia image.

Real-time filming makes it possible for the details of physical expression of intense emotions to emerge on stage. For example, the emotions of nervousness and excitement are captured and made visible to the audience when the female protagonist first stepped into the garden and peeped through the moon-shaped hole to admire the garden from afar; or those intense emotions are expressed through the encounter between the male and female protagonists in the garden; or that when the point of his brush animates the words that reflect the emotional duet between them. High speed 4K camera (120fps) was used with slow motions applied unveils more visual details of the production (see Fig. 4).

Fig. 4. Photos of *Su Yuan Memories*: multimedia and real time filming.

3 Intervention of Game Engine on Stage, with Real-Time Rendering, Virtual Reality, Augmented Reality, Mixed Reality

The gradual infiltration of game engine into film production and new media industry was inaugurated by the 1998 film *Lora Craft*. The film changed the perception of screen aesthetics for audience. The fast moving images enabled by game engine bring audience into the story. Developers of mainstream game engines (such as Unity and Unreal) and real-time rendering technology such as Notch have all begun to venture into areas beyond the realm of gaming to real-life stage performances.

However, all these advanced applications would not have made their claim to fame without the development of GPU that came to save a great amount of time from rendering, increasing the overall efficiency of the creative and operational processes. With the genius combination of the game engine, real-time rendering technology and interactive media, large-scale stage performance, improvisational and experimental performances also became the site where multimedia creatives innovate.

3D pre-visualisation, 3D projection mapping, real-time interactive effects, and playback of multimedia files together call for media servers that integrate different departments of hardware in creating a unique workflow. For example, *disguise*, a UK-born media servers producer, also partners with Notch, Noitom and BlackTrax to bring together different elements and integrate their functions into *designer*, a software that allows creatives to collaborate and communicate effectively between themselves and with clients. The creative media for stage performance become more multidimensional and come in different shapes and sizes. The video jockey form of real-time interaction is also becoming more popular. VR theatre has emerged as a result of VR and AR powered by game engine (see Fig. 5).

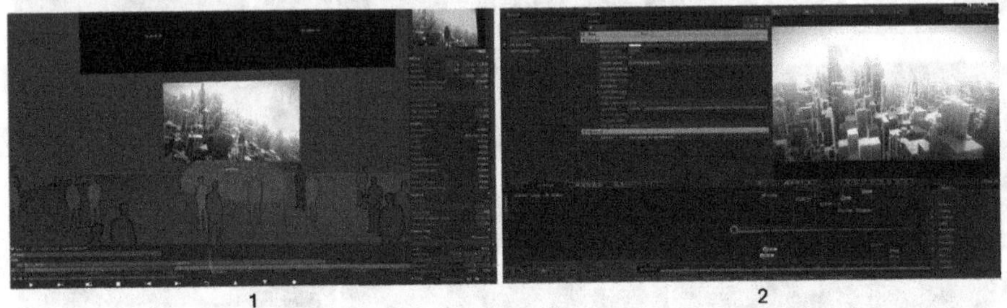

Fig. 5. Notch, BlackTrax and Noitom feature in disguise software – designer.

3.1 The Combined Use of Media Server, Capturing and Tracking in Enriching the Visual Effect on Stage

Montage effect can therefore be achieved through motion capture and real-time rendering of the actor/actress, and real-time animated effects on stage. The interaction between the performer(s) and moving images created based on their bodily movement brings the perfect blends between the reality and the virtual (see Fig. 6).

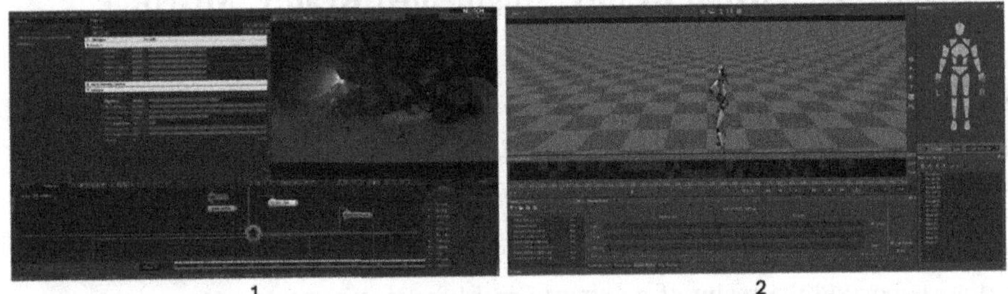

Fig. 6. Notch and Noitom.

The tracking technology afforded by BlackTrax allows the synchronisation between real-time imaging and performing, giving multiple dimensions and layers to the interactive performance.

In 2018, I was responsible for the multimedia design for a production called "The valley of Light," presented at and produced by the Wuhan Opera House. For this production, disguised designer was used with the 3D model of the stage loaded into the software. The stage is comprised of six moving cubic installations and six rolls of curtains, connected with a projection surface of 15-m long and 7-m wide. The base consists of six mechanical boxes that move according to the performance.

During the performance, the coffee shop scene in Act Two was brought about by two boxes going forward to the front of the stage, Make the stage more spacious (see Fig. 7).

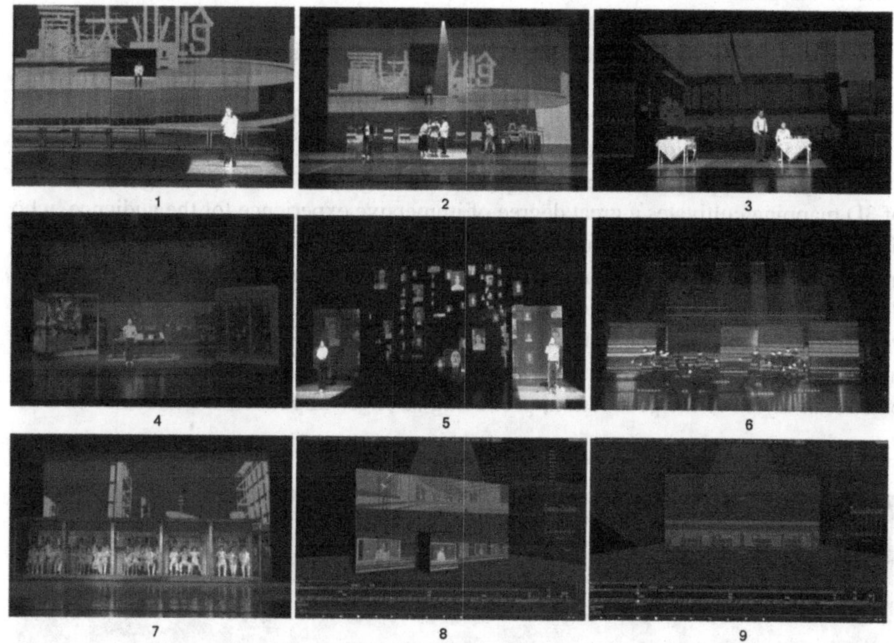

Fig. 7. *The Valley of Light* produced by Wuhan Opera House in 2018.

Two projectors were used for the production. One was used for direct projection onto the boxes in the front and the other for projection from above, onto the boxes on the back. The simulation works (including projector positions, lumin setting, integration) are all produced with the final output projected onto the stage through designer. Likewise, the motions of the boxes captured with BlackTrax are input into the servers and synchronised with performance on stage, forming an immersive experience through the visual effect.

3.2 From 2D to 3D Projection Mapping on Stage with Multimedia Methods

The intervention of game engine on stage performance further pushes the development of visual design, 3D mapping, and led to increased application of laser projector. At the same time, it also reduced the impact of stage lighting on projection mapping on stage.

Creative ideas have evolved from 2D to 3D mapping. The latter allows images to be projected onto surfaces such as building facades, car bodies and even musical instruments such as piano, human faces, etc. Visual designers can thus experiment with more creative and innovative ideas to enrich the form and the experience it evokes. However, such innovation also comes with the challenge of increasing the difficulty of narrative. More elements are added to stage production with higher complexity, which forces designers and operators to consider the intricate relationships between different parts of the production?

Indoor projection mapping has also gone from projection on a two-dimensional plane to a 3D environment consisting of multiple dimensions of flooring, ceiling as well as vertical walls. Meanwhile, visual expressions have also shifted from realism to abstraction to bring the essence of the internal activities of human beings.

The 2017 production called Nanni Bay at the Beijing Dance Academy exemplifies the use of 3D mapping in the creative process of stage production (see Fig. 8). The use of 3D mapping cultivates a great degree of immersive experience for the audience, who find the joy in seeing bountiful harvests falling from the sky, or feeling the anxiety induced by the falling rocks. For performers, their bodily movements become fused with the corresponding images projected onto the surroundings, depicting a story of perseverance in overcoming the hardship of fighting against the natural environment. The interaction between performers and the 3D mapping on stage bring more visual and emotional layers to the production, producing stronger impact on the audience in awe.

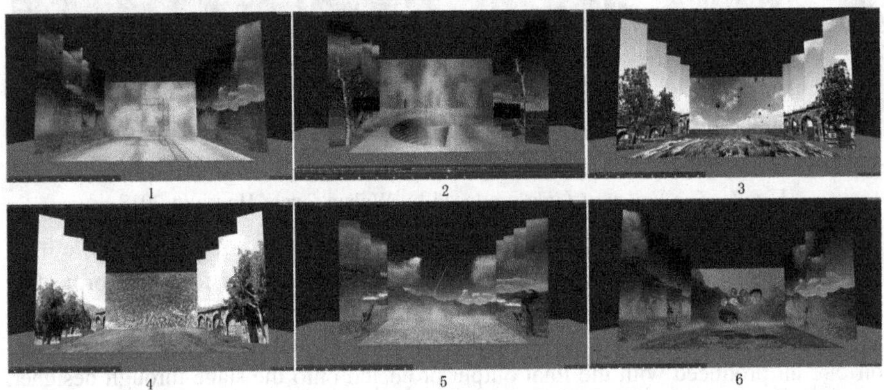

Fig. 8. Multimedia design in *Nanni Bay* - Beijing Dance Academy production December, (2017).

In realizing all of the above, the pre-visualisation stage is absolutely imperative in ensuring the success of the execution of these technologies. The concept stage in the disguise workflow demonstrates exactly this point. The pre-visualisation stage allows the creator, operator and clients to have a direct view of what the outcome would be and encourage further creative communication between different parties. The timeline on designer software also allows the sequencing to be done more efficiently and directly by moving around different block-based units of the production, allowing any large- scale production to be broken down into bite-size micro managements of its parts (see Fig. 9).

Fig. 9. Stage photos of *Nanni Bay* (2017).

3.3 The Emergence of Real Time Rendering and Programming Powered by Game Engine in VJ (Video Jockey) Mode

Some of the audio visual shows we have seen to date take the files already created by game engine (e.g. Unity 3D) and integrate with MIDI through programming software such as Touch Designer or VVVV. Visual and audio designs can come together with real-time render, allowing more room for improvisation, making it easier and more efficient in creating an immersive environment. This creative method was developed by Keijiro Takahashi who was the creator of game engine called Unity. Takahashi was also the person who brought VRDG+H that puts sound and image into fusion, which has been used by many emerging new media artists in China. At Today's Museum in Beijing, the audio visual show employed exactly this technique at the closing ceremony of ZIP Future Wild Anticipation. The visual designer "In K" brought real-time rendering into effect by real-time control of millions of particles, interacting with the music (see Fig. 10).

Fig. 10. ZIP Future Wild Anticipation at Today's Museum 2017 in Beijing, designed by InK.

Likewise, the same immersive installation was used in "Emergence" accompanied by music "HoydeA", at Yin 2019 Pop Music Launch sponsored by Tencent China. Kinect 2 was used to carry out real-time capturing of body motions and forms, digitalizing motions and converting them into images. Information is processed and reconstructed by computer calculation, feeding into the apparent organized chaos unfolding in front of the audience. It is an act of abstraction of the concrete (see Fig. 11).

Fig. 11. "Emergence" at Yin 2019 Pop Music Launch, by Tencent China, designed by InK.

This kind of VJ of real-time image control emphasizes the synchronicity between image and audio, the rhythm and visual impact of the real-time interaction with performers. It enhances emotional expressions and creates thickness in visual narrative.

Utilizing computer calculation, this kind of VJ technique is not applied in a seemingly chaotic manner but with systematic parameters that bring out the digital aesthetics of mathematics. The use of this technique for montage effect adds strength and structure to the multimedia practice. Without creative imagination and exploration, the mechanical manifestation of aesthetics would only be repeated rather than appropriated.

3.4 The Combined Use of VR Technology and Immersive Stage Performance in Affording More Real-Life Experience for Actors and Actresses

The term Virtual Reality was coined by the founder of VPL, Jaron Lanier who is currently in his early 80s. It is also known as spiritual technology or artificial environment. In recent years, more and more stage productions see the use of VR technology in their creative and production processes.

VA theatres have begun to use the power of game engine to create different kind of performances. For example, Render Ghost: XATAR produced by NAXS Taipei was one of the many examples (see Fig. 12). In 2018, this production was brought to Beijing where the author had the opportunity to see the performance. In the production, the creator attempted the mixing of light, sound, electricity and virtual reality. Being surrounded by light, sound and smoke, participants in protective suits wore VR screens

Fig. 12. Render Ghost: *XATAR* (2018).

walking the environmental debris created by game engine. The external sounds, smoke, fog, winds, particles and laser lighting further enrich the entire sensory experience of the production.

The live performers are nonetheless different from the pre-programmed characters in the virtual reality. These live performers are placed on the motion capture platform during their performance. Participants are then invited to carry on the creative process and finish the production in a way that is different from the previous and the next. Yet what that implies is the challenge for artists to become familiar with the logic and linearity of computer systems.

The advent of 5G network also brings more exciting development for the VR technology. Immersive VR theatres are on the rise in popular cultural consumption of performing arts (e.g. Sleep No More). Although it is rather cumbersome to wear VR headsets, the speeding up of mobile network and the advancement of VR technologies will bring world famous performance live to homes around the globe.

3.5 Bringing Augmented Reality Technology on Stage

In contrast to VR, Augmented Reality (AR) denotes to the augmentation of physical spaces and architectures by mapping virtual imagery onto location with specific latitudes and longitudes. It is often used on live broadcast of stage performance, allowing the real-time interaction between performers and the imagery. The core of AR technology is tracking which is enabled by active and passive infra-red tracking.

Active tracking means the performer is captured by tracking cameras positioned within the physical space of performance. After calibration, a signaling equipment will then track the position information within the space. Any movements on stage will send information back to the server to produce references for real-time rendering software such as Notch. Passive tracking means that within the range of camera, markers are placed on the floor, and after calibration, the movements of camera will send signals back to media servers. Passive tracking is used mainly in an indoor environment where the lighting level is stable and under control. Life Stage Mixed Reality is the manifestation of these two tracking methods, combined with the use of real-time rendering.

The use of AR can be found in the 2018 Einfach Himmlisch Christian Music Festival in Cologne, Germany. After setting up the tracking camera, the visual designer began to work on the AR environment in order to expand the visual experience. The combination of C4d and Notch, animation artist used C4D for the 3D model building, which will be loaded into Notch. Real time integration sends out signal for AR content to become RGB rendering with key/matte/alpha output (see Fig. 13).

The use of Notch provides the benefits of real-time correcting of the parameters of the AR effects on screen. The Notch blocks in disguise designer converts these output into signal and carries out real time mixing with the imagery. Online audience can thus witness the effect on screen (either on the Internet or TV).

Similar technique was also used on Yin 2019 Popular Music Launch held in Nanjing by Tencent. "Red Spy Stype" was used as the tracking system, in combination with rendering engine, Notch in gx2 by disguise for the visual effect.

Chinese singer Wang Yuan performed in the visual effect enabled by AR technology. During his performance, a geometrically shaped glass box encased the singer,

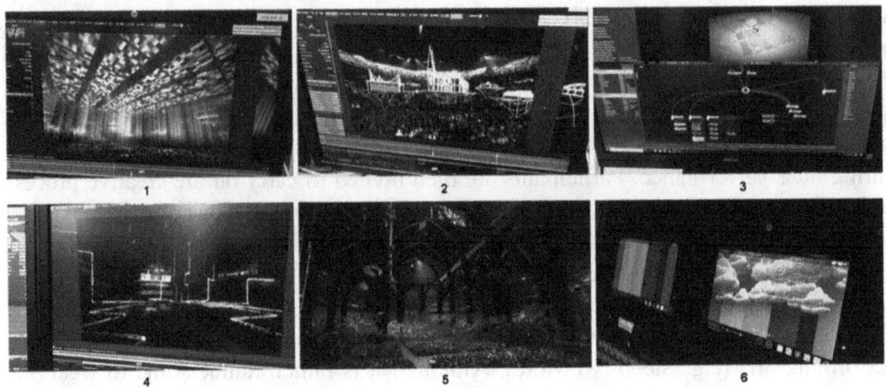

Fig. 13. 2018 Einfach Himmlisch Christian Music Festival, Cologne, German.

evoking a sense of loneliness and suffocation, which eventually became dismantled as the emotions heightened. A sense of break-through was thus activated by the visual effect. The shards would then be reconstructed into the form of a beast and a human (see Fig. 14).

Fig. 14. Chinese singer Wang Yuan performing in the visual effect enabled by AR technology.

Yin 2019 Popular Music Launch was broadcasted only online and would be taken down after 100 h of broadcasting. As a result, the end of the show came to an end by fire flame engulfing the whole stage, announcing the death of the physical. This effect was again powered by AR technology to galvanize one reality into another The online broadcasting of the AR effect could not be experienced by live audience, and that the visual effects had to be designed prior to the rehearsal as an extension of the stage effect (see Fig. 15).

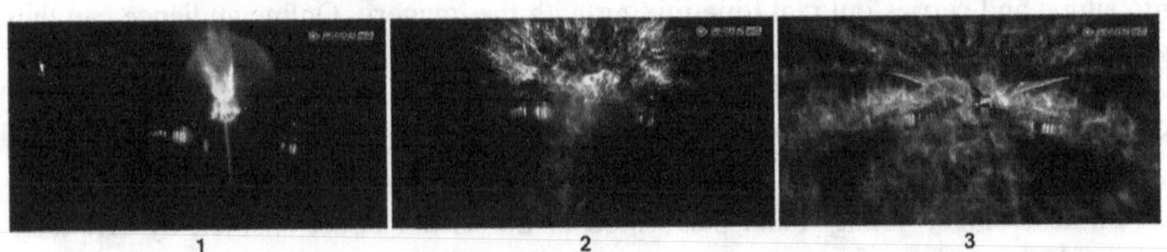

Fig. 15. The ending of Yin 2019 Popular Music Launch (online broadcast only).

4 Conclusion

AR technology afforded the magic visual effect on stage, making it more imperative to collaborate with visual artists from abroad. That is mostly due to the small number of Chinese trained visual designers and artists. Various reasons contribute to the low number of Chinese creatives that are in comparison with the number abroad (mostly based in EU and the US). The creative innovation of AR amongst Chinese designers/artists is yet to surface.

In recent years, the increased use of multimedia on stage has been accompanied by a decrease in narrative, a lack of artistic sensibility and a reduction of thematic relevance. This issue thus reminds us of the need to reassess the relationship between art and technology. Advanced production and presentation technologies have allowed producers to go beyond the physical presence of the bodies and helped audience to imagine beyond the concrete reality. Yet the blind embrace of advanced technologies such as AR and VR on stage often comes with a slight disrespect for the conventional technique in storytelling on stage. Game engine (for real-time rendering), programming software and various other tracking equipments and software, combined with performers' bodily movements, audio production and real-time interactive animation, becomes increasingly favored by producers for non-linear narratives delivered through montage. Yet what results is the replication of the same thing over and over again, applied to one production after another.

Employing advanced technologies do not necessarily imply a total disregard of conventional techniques. In some cases, the use of advanced technologies returns them to their original nature – that is the tool for enhancing its foundational content rather than replacing it. In the case of The Last Warrior Elephant, 59 Production team chose their techniques based on the content and the context. Instead of embracing all that is new and exciting, they resolved to the use of 2D animation, with the help of disguise media server Solo to enhance the montage effect, rather than undermining it (see Fig. 16).

Fig. 16. The Last Warrior Elephant, produced by SMG, designed by 59 Production.

We are now at the crucial moment to reflect upon the use of new media on stage production and our intentions in using them in the first place. Advanced technologies do not provide the answer for all creative innovations, which require years of experience and practice. While we will see multimedia being used in various and innovative ways on stage (dance performance or theatre, etc.), we should also slow down and reassess the content we are going to create and begin a series of creative conversations between artistic expressions and technological excursions. One of the ways we may consider in this balancing act is to build a model of workflow that takes into account of the artistic consideration and technological enhancement. With all being said, we should first and foremost reposition the respective roles of art and technology, with the former taking the lead, while the latter taking the supportive role in the creative process.

References

1. Paul, C.: Digital Art, 3rd edn. Thame & Hudson Ltd., London (2015)
2. Notch Homepage. https://www.notch.one/portfolio/einfach-himmlisch-simply-divine-ar/. Accessed 31 Jan 2019

Exploration of the Interactive Narrative Modes and Application Form of AR Animations

Shen Yongliang[1(✉)] and Niu Bosi[2(✉)]

[1] Beijing Union University, No. 97 Beisihuan East Road, Chao Yang District, Beijing, People's Republic of China
740642432@qq.com

[2] Beijing Film Academy, Haidian District West TuCheng Road 4, Beijing, People's Republic of China

Abstract. The purpose of this paper is to explore the interactive narratives and applications of VR animations. Comparative study, literature survey, case study and other methods are adopted. It is demonstrated in the research that, in addition to the improved immersion, VR technology will surely cultivate an artistic experience of animation arts totally different from traditional ones. The paper thus concludes that the strong interactive capability of game engines provides unlimited possibilities for the future interactive design of VR animations while the technical innovation will promote the reform of interactive narration, which will embrace a great many approaches in forms, pushing itself to a deeper level. For example, the control of perspectives, the adjustment of story volume, the manipulation of narrative rhythms and the selection of endings will all help form a vigorous and personalized interactive narration and really hand over the story to the audience.

Keywords: VR technology · Animation · Interactive mode · Application form

1 Introduction

The history of film is essentially one of the parallel development of film technology and art. Every leap in film art is inseparable from the breakthrough of technology, i.e. high-resolution images and sounds, as well as the research and development of modern digital technology. Based on such continuous evolvement and innovation of film technology, this form of art has grown from the black-and-white and silent one to the color and sound one. What change will happen to films in the upcoming years? Filmmakers have raised varied opinions based on current audio-visual technologies. The concept of the third-generation films proposed by Beijing Film Academy seems to herald the future model of films.

Among the three keywords of the third-generation films, interactivity, along with digitalization and stereoscopy, is the nucleus. Interactivity is also the focus of VR films that we are mainly studying. The third-generation films, a byproduct of the development of computer digital technology in the new era, have three prominent features, that is, digitalization, interactivity and stereoscopy. Digitalization means that the films involve digital photography, production, editing and effects; interactivity indicates the

A. Marcus and W. Wang (Eds.): HCII 2019, LNCS 11584, pp. 517–528, 2019.
https://doi.org/10.1007/978-3-030-23541-3_37

viewers' participation and controllability i.e. views can control the plots and take part in the group interactive games during the film; stereoscopy means to focus on the development of stereoscopic video content and the stereoscopic projection where crystal-clear stereoscopic films are presented to the audience through the stereoscopic technology which is at the cutting edge globally.

Interaction is the uniqueness of third-generation films and has given rise to more features. The interactive control technology has brought about subversive changes to film viewing and aesthetics. They mainly involve three respects – narrative modes, story development and film viewing experience. Specifically, the linear narration where audience are in a passive position has been transformed into a proactive interactive mode; the single storyline has developed into a multidimensional one while the predictable ending has been extended to a number of unpredictable ones; in terms of film viewing experience, the individual passive viewing has been escalated to group interaction by which the audience lead the story. From the perspective of film creation and aesthetics, the most prominent breakthrough of third-generation films is that the free creation space of directors is completely opened for the audience's free choices. This liberates the audience's mind and vision and allows them to have unprecedentedly free experience and perception of the dream world.

2 History of VR Technology

VR is the word most talked about in media, entertainment, culture and other industries. This technology surged with Facebook's acquisition of Oculus in 2017 followed by the presence of HTC and SONY. A number of industries, including game, film, education, tourism and healthcare, expect to seek new opportunities through VR technology. All those phenomena occur in the context of the functional expansion of VR in recent years. New manufacturing processes and display modes have appeared with the support of computer science and the Internet and are likely to be commercialized. Particularly, the design and release of the wearable device for panoramic viewing, i.e. VR glasses, have given rise to a new media channel different from film, television and smartphone. The combination of VR technology and the panoramic display will stimulate people's unlimited imagination of artistic creation with VR.

Utilizing computer technology, VR can generate a digital space highly similar to the real environment, the objects in which can be felt by users in real time without limitation. In spite of the debates on the specific approaches to and time of its actualization, the augmented experience brought about by such space is represented by the viewing experience that is completely immersive and interactive. Thanks to wearable devices and mobile terminals, the audience can be immersed or even involved in the stories as a role therein, trying different stories and endings. The audience is empowered with more proactive control and more realistic experience of the film's progress. The linguistic form and thinking of film creation are thus reformed. Such a film where the audience can interact and influence the progress is essentially a game with a cinematic structure and dramatic property, a "game film". From this point of view, developing animation films into VR ones can exert unique advantages, as animations and post-production can end up with the best effect with the most fluent and strongest sense of immersion. The reason for this is that they are not produced in a live-action manner but a computer-aided one, allowing producers not to bother camera movement, lighting and other technical issues. However, just as any other milestone revolution in the film history, the story contents, film languages, narrative methods and the styles of presentation necessitate a great adjustment. Change in any element can distinguish an animation film from others, giving rise to a typical film genre – genre animation films. Films with clear styles are better memorized by the audience with an enhanced charm of expression.

After the continuous development and popularization, the term VR technology has penetrated into military, medicine, education, media, games and other various industries and fields. Its application in the field of film, television and animation is no exception, as reflected by the constant emergence of animated films produced based on VR technology. The massive sales of VR head-mounted devices and the promotion of offline experience stores have impelled VR animation to become a new type of film familiar to the public.

As the audience have extreme freedom to choose, the film must take into account every angle that the audience can reach. Only in this way can the audience have the most realistic experience. VR specifically requires the director to adjust the overall style based on a game-designing way of thinking, so as to ensure the story is interpreted in line with the modern aesthetics, hi-tech sound and image design, scene transfer and realism. Two points should be paid attention to – the sense of impact and recollection. As to the first point, the perceptive impact is mainly achieved via audio-visual elements while the spiritual one via the story and progress. Recollection, on the other hand, arises from the integration of the thoughts of the character and the audience realized by driving the audience to enter and be integrated into the spiritual status of the character. Whereas entering is a gradual process of environment building, suspense and foreshadowing, as well as story development, integrating means to integrate the audience with the character and his thoughts via narrative methods and character building.

As the animation technology progresses, animation creation has gradually separated the performance of the animated characters from the audience, who could only enjoy the animations recorded on films without taking part in the creation. Thus they could not experience the excitement of participation. In contrast, VR technology focuses on immersion and interactivity, two crucial features for the combination of the VR technology and animated films. Nevertheless, many creators are restricted to the immersive feature while ignoring or avoiding interactivity. In a certain sense, the birth of VR films, for the first time in history, pushes down the fourth wall of films and brings the audience directly into the scene so that the audience may enter the film with the identity and perspective of a character. In other words, the viewing experience of VR animated films will be greatly impacted if the audience can only be immersed through watching and experiencing, totally unable to make a difference or participate in the interaction and thus deprived of the sense of presence. Centering on storytelling, creators should design carefully, starting with all elements of the film and properly conveying the story-based interactive design to the audience, so as to enable them to interact with the story happening in the virtual world with a real sense of presence and participation. Only in this way can VR animation really drive the audience into a new dimension of film viewing. Animated films based on the VR technology have emerged constantly in large. The massive sales of VR head-mounted devices and the promotion of offline experience stores have impelled VR animations to become a new type of film familiar to the public.

The animation technology so far has gradually separated the performance of characters and audience in creation. The audience may only watch the images recorded on films and are deprived of the right to participate in the creation and the joy of participation. Immersion and interaction, on the other hand, happen to be the two most prominent features of VR technology and will exert great importance in the combination of VR and animated films. However, many filmmakers tend to focus on immersion while ignoring or avoiding interaction. To a certain extent, VR films, for the first time, have torn down the fourth wall and push the audience right into the scene, make them enter the film with the identity and perspective of a character. What VR animations present to the audience are a point of view without limitation and an observation angle that can be randomly moved. By such means, viewing is granted with a new connotation – narration. The narration has become a process where the audience are no longer bystanders but participants. Progressing the story and set up guiding information thus are the most important part of VR audio-visual language. The guidance is usually completed via sounds, light, movement of objects, or key characters to tell the story or express the emotions. However, limiting to viewing and immersive experience without influencing and interacting with the story avoids the sense of presence and compromises the experience of VR animations. Filmmakers need to elaborate their creations by appropriately focusing on all elements of the film and delivering to the audience the interactive design reasonably based on the story. On the basis of sound storytelling, the audience need to interact with the story happening in the virtual world. Only with the real sense of presence and participation acquired therefrom can VR animations drive the audience to a new dimension of film viewing. There have been abundant animated films based on VR technology and these VR animations, as a new genre, have been popular to the public thanks to the massive sales of VR headsets and the promotion of experience stores. Traditional filmmaking process actually leaves limited space for the interactive design of VR videos and animations. In an era of advanced real-time rendering, optimal options of VR animation production lie in the combination of game engines and traditional film making processes. Companies such as Unity and Unreal have produced real-time rendered VR films. Despite the fact that the quality is still far from line rendering, low costs and timeliness are what help game engines prevail (see Fig. 1). These two advantages are even greater in terms of VR animations. In the works of Oculus Story, for instance, the audience may experience the stories from every angle thanks to the utilization of game engines. They directly go through the fourth wall and enter the world of the characters. The conventional offline rendering is three degree of freedom behind this approach. Plus, the production of panoramic animations is known for its difficulty and the hairball theorem strongly impacts the immersion effect. Compared to this, the real-time rendering of game engines perform much better for it completely adopts the real-time computing of GPU and the rendering quality is getting closer to that of CPU. Attracted by this, a number of companies are researching how to apply game engine computing to the visual effect of animations. In addition, the powerful interaction of game engines exerts unmeasurable possibility for the interactive design of future VR animations.

VR interactive animations, which were born from the step-by-step integration of traditional films and animations, are produced in close connection with the development of the film industry. Since its birth, animation art has been in an exploratory period in terms of the theme connotation, the means of expression, the form of art and the medium of communication, in particular, the creative medium of animations. An early form of animations is a pottery bowl found in Shahr-i-Sokhta, Iran, which was painted with five frames of images, allowing people to see a goat jumping to a pear tree when rotating the bowl. This dynamic scene formed by the interaction between men and a carrier can be deemed as the origin of interaction-driven animations. Digital technology has been integrated into animation creation along with the development of computer science, driving animations to evolve from a paperless flat stage through digital stereoscopy and VR animation.

Fig. 1. Experience schematic of VR game "The Lab" (Source: www.soomal.com)

3 Exploration of the Interactive Modes in the Combination of VR and Animations

Immersion and interactivity, the two most prominent features of VR technology, are still important for judging the quality of a VR animation that combines VR technology with traditional animation techniques. However, given the uneven level of studios on the market that produce VR animated films and the lack of detailed and standardized specification requirements for films and television as in the traditional film industry, the quality of VR animations currently viewed and experienced by the public varies greatly, and so do the immersive and interactive experience, giving rise to countless problems, such as screen-door effect, feeling of vertigo, confusion and solitude, which greatly compromise the audience's experience in watching. Some of the problems result from hardware problems, yet most of them are attributed to the defects in interactive design.

Some VR animations, which are essentially a spherical panoramic video, where the only thing the audience can do is to passively follow the already-designed animation. By rigidly copying the traditional film and television production process, these animations do not take into account users' need to experience the differences between VR images and traditional plain ones, let alone the interactive design. The audiences tend to be dizzy watching these animations, not knowing what they are about, which is really a torment. Some other ones make the audience confused, as they often miss a lot of plots due to their attention is far from sufficient to catch everything. The reason is that wearing the VR glasses, the audience's attention is distracted to a 360° panoramic environment, where they cannot concentrate on the story, for the instinct of human beings as animals decide that they need to first figure out where they are and what is around them by looking around. If the story is presented before the audience get used to the environment, the audience will probably miss a lot, and fail to keep up with the story development even though they finally are focused. To avoid these elementary mistakes, we must scientifically observe the feedback and needs of the audience watching VR videos, from physiology to psychology. This indicates the necessity of studying the interactive design of VR animation, only by which can we avoid mistakes and bring excellent interactive experience, better serving the audience and telling stories.

Without a doubt, the interactive design of VR animations is more than simply slowing down the pace to give the audience a longer reaction time. A series of issues should be considered, such as the role and the perspective of the audience during the viewing process, the elements of the films with which the audience can interact, whether the audience should interact with such elements, when such interactions should take place, and the appropriate frequency of interaction. If these issues are well handled, the VR animated film will not only tell the story well but also make the audience experience the charm of immersion and interaction. Otherwise, the film may even hardly convey the story. Thus the significance of interactive design for VR animations is seen.

The reform of film viewing conceived in third-generation films is specifically about the transformation from individual passive viewing to group interactive games where the audience determine the story development. In this concept, the audience experience group interactive games in cinemas as a group entertainment distinguished from the conventional films. At the entrance of cinemas, each viewer receives a terminal device of interactive control. The audience are divided into three or more groups and voluntarily become interactive controllers of the group game at the gaming points of the film, each group unites to interact or compete with the others. Such a fun approach will form a lively, happy and united atmosphere and help the audience get closer to each other. The group with the strongest cohesion will be entitled to choose the story direction as wished, directly impact the ending. Game modes are also applied – the selections in RPG games. The interactive feature of RPG, i.e. players control the hero to lead the plots and change the story, is experienced by the viewer and thus become another characteristic of interactive VR films with game playing.

The combination of VR and animation through game technology can provide the audience with a more realistic experience. However, this idea just focuses on experience, while the deeper interaction with the missions in the film is the key to the success of VR animation. It is believed that the following aspects of VR interaction are worth exploring:

3.1 Multi-line Development of the Story

Just like men doing multiple choice questions in their lives where each choice will have an impact on the final outcomes, various endings in games may be introduced to the story organization as an analogy of the butterfly effect. In the story development of interactive animation, the audience can act as an external force to drive the story to the ending as they wish. That is to say, the audience are prompted to make several rounds of selections in order to see the ending they expect. Instead of creating the story in a linear order, different nodes of the story can be set in the animation script, leading to distinguished endings. Currently, the "mind map" is used in creating the script of an animated story as a conceiving approach (see Fig. 2), i.e. the characters, events and other elements of a certain story are taken as the starting point of creativity to trigger different storylines. The steps in developing a map generally include establishing a

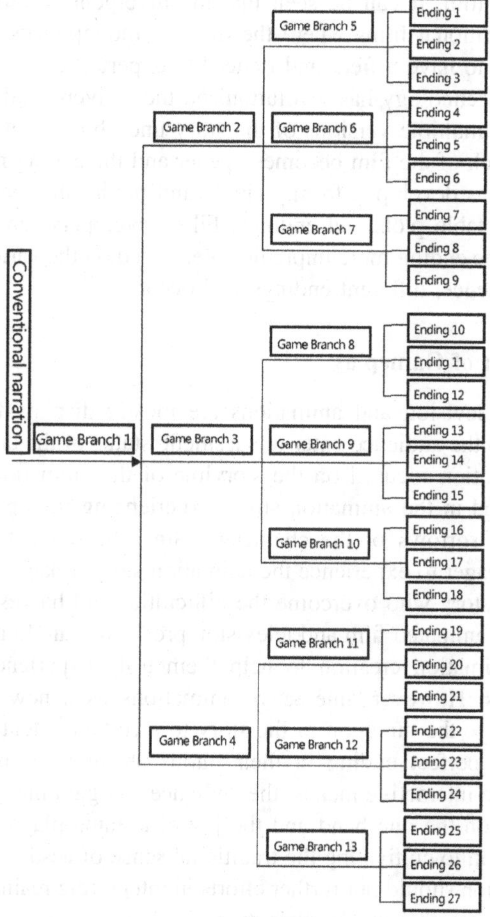

Fig. 2. The sketching approach using "mind map" (starting from elements such as characters and events of a story, varied storylines will be triggered).

central idea, initiating a structural map, integrating and concatenating the materials, and clarifying the narrative streams and sequence. This creative way of mapping emphasizes a professional training of divergent thinking, stitching together irrelevant characters, scenes and story elements in the animated story to form the storylines of different fractals before creating an animation with interactive narration.

In the past, the narration of films was usually dominated by the director's thoughts and followed a certain fixed and linear narrative approach, allowing the audience only to passively accept the contents of the film. To a large extent, the audience watched completely passively and learned the events and the ending that the director had organized. The audience may either agree or disagree with some of the contents, yet they could only quietly watch the contents of the film already planned by the director. This film narrative mode is typically linear and fixed, with the ending even completely predictable. Now, however, the audience can experience completely different interactive contents and savor different lives through the lifestyles they choose during multiple views of one same film. It can be seen that the divergent narrative method, which differs from the traditional films where the director monopolizes the narrative style, allows the audience to have a freer and richer life experience.

The interactive technology has revolutionized the conventional narrative model of films. Owing to the multiple versions of the story underlying in the viewing process, the narrative approach of the film becomes opener and the ending more unpredictable. The storyline also has developed from a single and predictable one into a number of completely unpredictable plots and endings. Film developers can set a few different storylines to make the ending more unpredictable. Based on the various story directions selected by the audience, different endings will occur.

3.2 Enhancement of Gameplay

Traditional films, television and animations are mostly displayed in a dark cinema environment to help the audience enter the aesthetic status of the animation from daily life. With their attention focused on the storyline of the animation, the audience are completely immersed in the animation story, experiencing the ups and downs of the story, the joys and sorrows of the characters. Since the advent of animations, the audience has been eager to experience the animation story, imagining that they are the protagonists of the story who overcome the difficulties and harvest successes. Unfortunately, traditional animated film and television programs can do nothing in engaging the audience in animation creation to help them truly experience the emotions of animated characters. However, interactive animations as a new medium allow the audience to determine the direction of the story to a certain extent via interaction and thereby realize the perfect ending in their minds as much as possible. Under the intervention of these interactive means, the audience can gain the aesthetic pleasure of the animated story on the one hand and the joy of a game player on the other hand. Therefore, in addition to cultivating the traditional sense of aesthetics, professionals of VR animation creation should put further efforts in integrating reality and virtual world, sensory experience, creation and participation.

In the wake of the emergence of smartphones and other mobile smart terminals, and the integration of human somatosensory devices, the medium of animation creation has spanned from traditional to interactive practical dimensions. Today, VR technology is broadly used in both films and games, more abundantly in games. VR games such as *Fancy Skiing*, *Mercenary* and *Furballs* have been very popular among players. Steam recently unveiled the Top Selling VR Games of the year. Five games, which are either VR monopoly and or VR support, were nominated, namely *The Elder Scrolls V: Skyrim VR, VRChat, Beat Saber, Fallout4 VR* and *SUPERHOT VR*. It is reported that the authority of Dubai has launched its first VR training center that is equipped with high-end equipment and tools for VR technology. With its software developed by the GIS Center team in Dubai, the training center offers training courses in a wide range of areas such as urban planning, land surveying, and construction supervision. In the future, more projects are expected to be added to cover other relevant professional fields. The training center will be accessible for various departments and agencies.

The innovation of VR contents and their industry application have brought new ideas to the development of the cultural industry, for they enhance people's preference of the industry while enhancing the entertainment feature. In the field of games, most VR games are currently stuck in the DEMO phase as limited by hardware, venue, technology and other conditions. To highlight the advantages of VR, the development idea is to emphasize the experience. Most contents are developed in clips, ranging from car racing, mountain climbing to natural exploration. Though not mature enough, these clips give users a strong sense of impact. The latest trend is to make real complete VR games. EVE Valkyrie, a space combat shooting game developed by the Icelandic developer CCP, has attracted much attention thanks to its high quality and complete game mode and map. What the game does is to ensure the 100% participation by players by allowing them to talk, fight and kill, and even choose to change the direction of the story.

In the field of VR animated films, VR technology also reinforces the entertainment of the story. For instance, when there is a battle scene, the audience can control the game character to fire an arm, which makes the original animation story more entertaining. Oculus Story Studio has produced several animated shorts including *Henry*, a story of a hedgehog. Great breakthroughs have also been made in immersive documentaries, such as *Waves of Grace*, which describes the cruel reality in Liberia. When the volunteers in protective suits are putting the corpses of Ebola patients into the graves, the audience will feel they are next to the grave, surrounded by more graves. Such an immersive feeling is more touching than any news report to the audience. Discovery, BBC and so forth have also attempted virtual natural documentaries in the first-person perspective. In China, Caixin Media has launched its latest VR documentary *Kindergarten in the Mountain Village*; while Sightpano produced *Blind Circle*.

In addition, VR technology has penetrated into the news service industry as well. It has been found in thorough researches and explorations that VR technology is suitable for producing news in the form of a panoramic video for such form and its unique point of view can bring about strong immersion. New York Times, BBC, ABC News, Associated Press and Chinese media like Xinhua News, People's Daily, Caixin Media and Sina have all made their attempts and achieved satisfactory results.

When appreciating a VR animation, the audience is eager to participate in the creation and to seek a realistic experience in the virtual story. This requires the animation works to give feedback in time after the interaction, that is, the interactive effect, which can be a cool visual animation, a voice comment, and a tactile experience such as shakes or vibrations. This kind of interactive effect is more applied in new media animation games. For instance, the birds in *Angry Birds* use the huge inertia of the slingshot to strike the castle and express their rage at the King Pig's stealing of eggs in an interactive effect triggered by the finger drawing the slingshot. Such effect gives the audience a pleasant feeling of interaction. In another game *Talking Tom Cat,* the player can interact with Tom Cat by directly touching the screen. The cat may meow, or break wind and make other sounds with the corresponding button pressed. These interactions will interest the audience with a realistic feeling of playing with a cat.

4 Exploration of the Communication Models of VR Interactive Animations

Despite the rapid development of VR technology, it is usually costly to produce an interactive animation. In view of the need of multiple story versions for the audience to freely choose in interaction, greater input of manpower, material and financial resources is demanded than traditional animations. What's more, in addition to directors, key animators and post-production staff required in traditional animations, experts in interactive design and technology are required in the production team. This implies that talents of interdisciplinary creative applications are called for in animation creation, the function division in the creation mode should break through that in traditional animations which include character design, scene design and key animation, and more emphasis should be laid on the learning and innovation of interactive technology and forms. In the meantime, unlike the previous animations whose interactions are designed based on tactile sensings such as multi-touch and gravity-induced tilt, interactive designs in the future will apply more motion sensing and limb motion techniques.

Hence it can be seen that interactive animations undoubtedly have much higher production costs and at the same time a wider coverage of technologies compared with traditional animations. Given the fact that many excellent interactive animation projects have been suspended due to fund insufficiency, it is necessary for film designer to consider the communication model that the film can rely on. For example, cloud transmission and other Internet viewing modes provide convenience for the audience to download the resources from the cloud at a high rate; costumes and props available for the characters can be designed in the films as in games; advertising may also be placed appropriately in the films. When watching the film, the audience can click and buy their favorite props or costumes. Surely there are other communication models worth exploring. Such a combination of contents and communication models is a prerequisite for the sustainability of the costly VR interactions, and represents a sound exploration.

The emergence and development of every new medium constantly create the conditions and opportunities for the progression of animation art, while the animation art itself is also constantly creating miracles in the era of high-tech new media. In the future, new media animations will create dynamic images in an artificial manner based on digital technology and Internet technology, embodying the fusion of science and art. New media animation as a major involves art and industry and other disciplines, inclusive of the intersection and integration of drama and film science, art, design, computer graphics, interactive technology and media communication. It is the special professional background that makes possible the diversified new media animation works, such as game animations, interactive films, interactive displays and interactive picture books.

The interactive design of some children's books provides a good experience for the readers. For example, the electronic picture book *The Fantastic Flying Books* allows the reader to use gravity sensing to control Mr. Morris' flying direction in the sea of books by tilting the iPad; *Dandelion* allows the reader to simulate the physical characteristics in the natural life utilizing the gravity sensing system of the smart mobile terminal, such as blowing against the microphone to scatter the dandelion on the screen. Such an interactive experience can effectively spur children's interest and enhance the realism of the experience. The "Arts Future Lab" launched in January 2016 is a novel art platform built by the "Art Plus" innovative model. The laboratory is aimed to explore the future forms of art with big data and cloud computing as the core, and intelligent computing, intelligent interaction, smart devices and smart applications as the means. This is also the direction of new media animations in the future – to introduce more interactive devices and forms that trigger more sensual experience to create a kind of new media animation where the audience can immerse themselves, control the story development and go through a variety of experiences and feelings of the characters.

In the future, the production of VR interactive animation films should not only address the audience experience but also handle commercial advertising, in a bid to solve the problem of high production costs and limited channels of capital recovery. Only by doing so will more outstanding, groundbreaking and revolutionary interactive films emerge.

5 Prospects of VR Interactive Animations

Apart from the escalated immersion via hardware approaches, VR technology is destined to cultivate the artistic experience of animations that is completely different from traditional ones. VR images are capable of carrying complete and meaty narrations. Only those bearing deep artistic meanings are qualified for video arts, otherwise, they are only "special effect films". In this sense, production devices, software and film players are among the aspects to be improved. Given the multiple storylines of VR films, a video database for HD films which has storage over 10T and enables videos not lower than 1080P is needed. In the meantime, a Next Generation video interaction engine will be introduced and developed based on the latest research achievements of digital image processing and an interactive control system of video stories on an interaction engine platform for high-resolution and high-detail Next Generation game videos. This engine requires the close collaboration of a CPU with a high rate, a GPU with an image coprocessor and the HD video interaction engine system. The audience will experience the high-resolution VR films based on the advanced automatic separation and display system of stereo images from nVidia.

The technical evolvement promotes the transformation of interactive narration, to which there are a lot of approaches. Multiple storylines are one of them and have been mentioned a lot. This approach itself, however, is essentially the same with traditional narrative modes of films. In addition, multiple storylines are less feasible in the case of live action production. On the other hand, if the digital virtual production and real-time rendering by digital engines are applied, there will be abundant possibilities of interactive narration. The design experience of game interaction can be transplanted to VR films, helping realize deeper interactive narration. For example, the choice of story volume, the control of narration rhythm and the selection of ending all establish a personalized 3-dimensional interactive narration and the story is truly handed over to the audience. The audience will be granted with free choices and the right to think independently, which are the real charm of VR films.

6 Conclusion

In addition to representing innovations in technology, the innovative development of VR also provides the cultural industry with a new form of media and a new way of development thinking. In the future, VR will further evolve from 3Is (immersion, interaction, imagination) to 4Is (the 3Is plus "intelligence"). It is conceivable that the cultural industry will develop following such a trend, leading to a future worth looking forward to.

References

1. Kristin, T., David, B.: Film History: An Introduction. McGraw-Hill Education (Taiwan) (1998). Translated by Liao Jinfeng
2. Committee for the Research Report on Chinese Film Industry: The Research Report on Chinese Film Industry 2010. China Film Press, Beijing (2011)
3. Li, J.: The narrative style and cultural awareness of animation films. Movie Lit. **19**, 65–68 (2015)
4. Zhao, Y.: A new innovation of VR technology – immersive VR films. Guang Ming Daily, p. 4, 29 Feb 2016
5. Tang, Z.: Art Theory of Animated Films. China Book Publishing House, p. 32 (2013)
6. Chen, Y.: A unique visual language of animation – the comparative analysis of the visual languages of animated and live-action films. Art Des. (Theory) **2**, 249–251 (2012)
7. Mark, R.: Art in real-time: theatre and virtual reality. University of Kansas
8. Gao, E.: The virtual reality technology brings reforms to visual arts. Art Res. (2016)
9. Gao, H.: The status quo, challenges and trends of China's Virtual Reality (VR) Industry. Mod. Commun. (J. Commun. Univ. China) (02) (2017)
10. Cong, G.: A brief discussion on realizing the styles of VR animated films. Adv. Motion Picture Technol. (2017)

Author Index

Printed in the United States
By Bookmasters